T0379780

The Routledge Handbook of English Language Studies

The Routledge Handbook of English Language Studies provides a comprehensive overview of English Language Studies. The book takes a three-pronged approach to examine what constitutes the phenomenon of the English language; why and in what contexts it is an important subject to study; and what the chief methodologies are that are used to study it. In 30 chapters written by leading scholars from around the world, this *Handbook* covers and critically examines:

- English Language Studies as a discipline that is changing and evolving in response to local and global pressures;
- definitions of English, including world Englishes, contact Englishes and historical and colonial perspectives;
- the relevance of English in areas such as teaching, politics and the media;
- analysis of English situated in wider linguistics contexts, including psycholinguistics, sociolinguistics and linguistic ethnography.

The Routledge Handbook of English Language Studies is essential reading for researchers and students working in fields related to the teaching and study of the English language in any context.

Philip Seargeant is Senior Lecturer in Applied Linguistics at the Open University, UK.

Ann Hewings is Director of Applied Linguistics and English Language at the Open University, UK.

Stephen Pihlaja is Reader in Stylistics at Newman University, Birmingham, UK.

Routledge Handbooks in English Language Studies

Routledge Handbooks in English Language Studies provide comprehensive surveys of the key topics in English language studies. Each Handbook focuses in detail on one area, explaining why the issue is important and then critically discussing the leading views in the field. All the chapters are specially commissioned and written by prominent scholars. Coherent, accessible and carefully compiled, *Routledge Handbooks in English Language Studies* are the perfect resource for both advanced undergraduate and postgraduate students.

The Routledge Handbook of Stylistics
Edited by Michael Burke

The Routledge Handbook of Language and Creativity
Edited by Rodney H. Jones

The Routledge Handbook of Contemporary English Pronunciation
Edited by Okim Kang, Ron Thomson and John M. Murphy

The Routledge Handbook of English Language Studies
Edited by Philip Seargeant, Ann Hewings and Stephen Pihlaja

The Routledge Handbook of English Language Studies

Edited by Philip Seargeant, Ann Hewings and Stephen Pihlaja

LONDON AND NEW YORK

First published 2018
by Routledge
2 Park Square, Milton Park, Abingdon, Oxon OX14 4RN

and by Routledge
711 Third Avenue, New York, NY 10017

Routledge is an imprint of the Taylor & Francis Group, an informa business

British Library Cataloguing-in-Publication Data
A catalogue record for this book is available from the British Library

Library of Congress Cataloging-in-Publication Data
A catalog record has been requested for this book

ISBN: 978-1-138-91345-5 (hbk)
ISBN: 978-1-351-00172-4 (ebk)

Typeset in Times New Roman
by Sunrise Setting Ltd., Brixham, UK

Contents

Figures

Tables

Contributors

Esther Asprey is a Research Fellow in the School of English at Birmingham City University. Her current research is on identity creation through dialect use in the Black Country region of the West Midlands of England.

Kingsley Bolton is Professor of English Linguistics at Nanyang Technological University, Singapore, and Professor Emeritus at Stockholm University, Sweden. He is co-editor of the journal *World Englishes*, and a member of the editorial boards of *Applied Linguistics Review*, *English Today*, *English World-Wide*, and the *Journal of World Languages*. He has published widely on English in the Asian region, language and globalization, sociolinguistics, and world Englishes.

Zsófia Demjén is Senior Lecturer in Applied Linguistics at the UCL Institute of Education, University College London, specialising in the discourses of ill/wellness. She is author of *Sylvia Plath and the Language of Affective States: Written Discourse and the Experience of Depression* (2015, Bloomsbury) and co-editor of *The Routledge Handbook of Metaphor and Language* (2017).

Ana Deumert is Professor of Linguistics at the University of Cape Town. Her overall research program is located within the broad field of African sociolinguistics and has a strong trans-disciplinary focus. Currently she focuses on questions of sociolinguistic theory from a southern perspective.

Robert Fuchs is an Assistant Professor in English Linguistics at the University of Hamburg. His work focuses on the phonology, syntax and sociolinguistics of English as a first, second and foreign language.

Gavin Furukawa currently works at the University of Tokyo as a Project Assistant Professor with the Center for Global Communication Strategies. His research interests include L2 writing and spoken fluency, sociocultural linguistics, gender studies, and media discourse.

Ofelia García is a professor in the Ph.D. programmes in Urban Education and Hispanic and Luso-Brazilian Literatures and Languages at the Graduate Center of The City University of New York. She is the editor of *The International Journal of the Sociology of Language* and co-editor of *Language Policy*.

Christopher J. Hall is Professor of Applied Linguistics in the School of Languages and Linguistics at York St John University, where he conducts research on non-native speaker Englishes and leads the Language and Identities in InterAction (LIdIA) Research Unit.

Geoff Hall is Professor of English and Dean of Humanities and Social Sciences at University of Nottingham Ningbo China. He was editor of *Language and Literature* from 2005 to 2016, and is the author of *Literature in Language Education* (2nd edition, 2015). His research interests are in world Englishes, including world literatures in English.

David Hann is a lecturer in English language and Applied Linguistics at the Open University. His current research focus is on humour in the classroom as a means of both asserting individual identity and creating group cohesion.

Ann Hewings is Director of Applied Linguistics and English language at the Open University, UK. She teaches and researches on disciplinary variation and academic writing. She is series editor for *Worlds of English* (Routledge) and co-editor of *Futures for English Studies* (Palgrave).

Christina Higgins is a professor in the Department of Second Language Studies and Co-director of the Charlene Junko Sato Center for Pidgin, Creole, and Dialect Studies at the University of Hawai'i. at Mānoa, USA. She is a sociolinguist who researches multilingual practices and identities.

Simon Horobin is Professor of English Language and Literature at the University of Oxford. His research focuses on the History of English, with particular reference to the development of a standard variety.

Sara Laviosa is Associate Professor at the University of Bari Aldo Moro. She is the author of *Corpus-based Translation Studies* (2002) and *Translation and Language Education* (2014). She is founder and editor of the journal *Translation and Translanguaging in Multilingual Contexts*.

Robert Lawson is Senior Lecturer in Sociolinguistics at Birmingham City University. His research focuses on language and masculinities, the application of language research beyond academia, and language in the public eye.

Constant Leung is Professor of Educational Linguistics in the School of Education, Communication and Society, King's College London. His current research includes additional/ second language pedagogy and assessment in multilingual contexts with particular reference to school-aged and university students.

Angel M. Y. Lin is Professor and Head of English Language Education Division at the Faculty of Education, University of Hong Kong. She is well-respected for her interdisciplinary research in classroom discourse analysis, plurilingual education, academic literacies, Content and Language Integrated Learning (CLIL) and language policy and practice in postcolonial contexts.

Lian Malai Madsen is Associate Professor in the Psychology of Language at the University of Copenhagen, Denmark. Her research includes the interactional-sociolinguistic and ethnographic analysis of multilingual practices among adolescents in school and leisure contexts, with specific attention to issues of social categorisation and societal inequalities.

Geraldine Mark is a freelance researcher and writer. Her principal research interests are in corpus linguistics and its pedagogical applications, particularly in relation to spoken language, pragmatics, discourse analysis, grammar and lexis, in both first and second language users of English.

Dan McIntyre is Professor of English Language and Linguistics at the University of Huddersfield, where he teaches stylistics, history of English, corpus linguistics and audiovisual translation. His major publications include *Stylistics* (Cambridge University Press, 2010; with Lesley Jeffries) and he is editor of the journal *Language and Literature*.

Carolyn McKinney is Associate Professor in Language Education in the School of Education, University of Cape Town, South Africa. Her current research focuses on how language ideologies shape language and literacy practices and pedagogies in multilinguals contexts. She is author of *Language and Power in Post-Colonial Schooling: Ideologies in Practice* (Routledge).

Clara Neary is Senior Lecturer in English Language at the University of Chester. Specialising in literary and cognitive stylistics, she is particularly interested in metaphor analysis, narrative point of view, narrative empathy and reader immersion, cognitive grammar and the expansion of stylistic enquiry into genres such as autobiography.

Anne O'Keeffe is Senior Lecturer in Applied Linguistics at Mary Immaculate College, University of Limerick, Ireland. She is author of several books and papers on Corpus Linguistics and its applications to English Language Teaching, among other areas.

Diane Pecorari is Professor of English at City University of Hong Kong. Her research has investigated aspects of English for academic purposes and second-language writing, including source use and plagiarism, as well as the widespread and growing phenomenon of English medium instruction.

Gill Philip is a senior lecturer at the University of Macerata (Italy), where she teaches English corpus linguistics, translation, and cognitive linguistics. Her research is centred on the interaction of cognition and communication, particularly in figurative language and phraseology.

Stephen Pihlaja is Reader in Stylistics at Newman University, Birmingham. His research focuses on the dynamics of discourse, particularly in interaction around religious issues.

Hazel Price is Research Information and Communications Officer in the Department of Linguistics and Modern Languages at the University of Huddersfield, where she teaches stylistics and descriptive linguistics. She is Editorial Assistant for *Babel: The Language Magazine*.

Louise J. Ravelli is Associate Professor in the School of the Arts and Media at the University of New South Wales, Australia. She researches communication in professional contexts using social-semiotic approaches, including systemic-functional linguistics and multimodal discourse analysis. Books include *Museum Texts: Communication Frameworks* (Routledge, 2006) and *Multimodality in the Built Environment: Spatial Discourse Analysis* (Routledge, 2016, with Robert McMurtrie).

Helen Ringrow is Senior Lecturer in Communication Studies and Applied Linguistics at the University of Portsmouth, UK. Her current research explores discursive representations of femininity in blogs about motherhood and modest fashion.

Edgar W. Schneider is Chair Professor of English Linguistics at the University of Regensburg, Germany. He has written and edited about 20 books, including *Postcolonial*

English (Cambridge University Press, 2007) and *English Around the World* (Cambridge University Press, 2011), and many articles, recently mostly on World Englishes.

Jeremy Scott works at the border between literary and language studies at the University of Kent. He is interested in fictional technique, literary representations of dialect and stylistics-based approaches to creative writing and creativity in general. As well as his own fiction, he has published on contemporary British and Irish writing and literary stylistics.

Philip Seargeant is a senior lecturer at the Open University, where he specialises in language and communication. He has published several books on topics ranging from social media to linguistic creativity and English around the world. His most recent titles include *Creativity in Language* (2016) and *Taking Offence on Social Media* (2017). He is a regular contributor to publications such as *The New European*, *The Huffington Post*, *The Washington Post*, *Times Higher Education* and *The Independent*.

Joe Spencer-Bennett is a Lecturer in Applied Linguistics at the University of Birmingham. His research focuses on the political and ethical life of language.

Tereza Spilioti is Senior Lecturer in Language and Communication in the Centre for Language and Communication Research, Cardiff University. Her current research focuses on areas of digital language and communication, particularly multilingualism, language ideologies, and research ethics.

Paula Tatianne Carréra Szundy is Professor of English and Applied Linguistics at the Federal University of Rio de Janeiro (UFRJ), Brazil. She was the president of the Association of Applied Linguistics of Brazil (ALAB) from 2009 to 2011 and once again from 2016/17. Her research interests include English as an Additional Language teaching and learning processes, teacher education, speech genres and teaching, literacy practices at school and university and language ideologies.

Lionel Wee is a Provost's Chair Professor in the Department of English Language and Literature at the National University of Singapore. His latest book is *The Singlish Controversy: Language, Culture and Identity in a Globalizing World* (Cambridge University Press, 2018).

Melissa Yoong is Assistant Professor of Sociolinguistics at the University of Nottingham Malaysia Campus. Her research focuses on sexist, postfeminist, and neoliberal discourses in the mass media.

Acknowledgements

The authors and publishers would like to thank the following copyright holders for permission to reproduce the following material:

Extract from *Un abito qualunque: Poesie*, a collection of poems authored by Elena Malta with a preface by Vito Moretti, Edizioni Tracce, Pescara © Copyright 2011. Used with permission.

Extract from Ngũgĩ wa Thiong'o. 1986. *Decolonising the Mind: The Politics of Language of African Literature*. London: James Currey. Used with permission of Boydell & Brewer Ltd.

An introduction to English language studies

Philip Seargeant, Ann Hewings and Stephen Pihlaja

Aims and objectives of the book

There is a strong argument that the study of language is crucial to the study of almost anything. As the most flexible and extensive means of communication that humans possess, language mediates all our social relationships, plays a part in all our social interactions, and is the foundational element of our civilisation as a species. The cognitive revolution that took place 100,000 years ago, and which marked the evolution of language in homo sapiens, set humankind on a path to intellectual pre-eminence among the rest of the animal kingdom. The invention of writing five millennia ago gave our ancestors a reliable means of recording and accruing knowledge, of passing it from generation to generation, and of creating complex and expansive societies. Language, as has often been remarked, is an essential part of what makes us human.

Language is also an endlessly complicated phenomenon. The processes that allow a child, with no formal education and with limited input, to learn to speak within two to three years of being born, are still not fully understood and remain an area of intense academic controversy. Yet despite this complexity, communicative competence is something we nearly all master in the first few years of our life, and which we mostly take for granted throughout adulthood. And it is this paradox of language's complexity and importance versus its familiarity and the instinctive mastery we have over it, that leads to something of an identity complex for Language Studies as a subject. Add to this the fact that because everyone has a practical expertise in it, they also feel they have some sort of theoretical expertise in it – at least as far as making pronouncements about its nature and status goes – and the necessity of studying it is considered far less than its importance in all aspects of our life would seem to merit.

As a wide-ranging overview of English Language Studies (ELS), this book aims to argue for the essential importance of a dedicated understanding of how language works, the roles it plays in society and the ways it influences all aspects of our lives. As the title indicates, the focus is specifically on the English language, rather than language in general. There are a number of reasons for this, ranging from the practical to the political to the ontological. The practical reasons relate to the fact that the book is written in English and produced by an English language publisher. The political relate to the position that English now occupies in the world, and the particular issues this produces. And the ontological reason is that, as social individuals, we all first experience (or are socialised into the idea of) different languages rather than language as a general or abstract concept. As such, the immediate point of reference for people is a specific language – e.g. English – and thus this is a useful place to start any analysis into language studies generally. Having said this, as many of the chapters in the book discuss, the distinction between language and languages, and the way that discrete, named languages are conceptualised, is a complex and in some cases controversial one. Thus, although it is a useful starting point, it is far from being an axiomatic one – and a great deal of the book concentrates on exploring what exactly it is we mean by 'English'.

To offer a few upfront pointers on this issue, the book gives a comprehensive overview of the subject of ELS by taking a three-pronged approach to the topic: examining what constitutes the phenomenon of the English language; why and in what contexts it is an important subject to study; and what the chief methodologies are that are used to study it. In doing this the book offers both a survey and critique of the subject, mapping out its shape and also providing arguments for its relevance and usefulness as an important area of academic study in present-day society.

Given the fundamental position the English language has in the daily existence of millions (if not billions) of people around the world, along with the part it plays in social organisation and the construction and expression of individual and group identities, ELS can play a crucial role in a range of social and cultural issues. The book therefore not only provides an in-depth overview of the different components involved in the study of the subject, but also makes a strong case for the relevance of ELS as an area of study in today's world. It adopts a purposely global coverage of what constitutes the discipline of ELS: how particular approaches to the discipline have developed and how it is changing and evolving in response to local and global pressures, as well as evolving scholarship within the subject. In this introduction we first consider what constitutes ELS as an area of study, before considering a number of important and emerging issues that are structuring it. We conclude with an overview of the shape and content of the book.

What is English Language Studies?

Despite ELS being an academic field with a long history, what it delineates is understood differently in different places and educational institutions. It often forms part of what is referred to as 'English' or 'English Studies' at university level, where it combines with the study of literature, creative writing and allied sub-disciplinary areas. For the purposes of this introduction we can distinguish between three different understandings of ELS. First, as English has developed into the pre-eminent global lingua franca, the terms 'English language' or just 'English' are used to indicate its study as an additional language. The teaching of this takes place in schools, universities and private institutions in both Anglophone and non-Anglophone settings. It has given rise to a significant industry around teaching English as a second or additional language (TESOL) and for academic purposes (EAP). Those teaching English as a second or additional language have need of an understanding of how the language works, and for some this is fulfilled by a curriculum designated under the general umbrella of ELS.

This theoretical knowledge about the language is what constitutes the second understanding of ELS as a subject, and this conception of it is closely allied to linguistics, applied linguistics, TESOL and in some cases philology. The shared content in these curricula are most likely to be related to language description and possibly language teaching pedagogy at undergraduate and postgraduate levels.

The final understanding of ELS draws on research and scholarship on the description of English, but importantly also on how English is used in context and the nature and implications of its history and worldwide spread. This combines an understanding of how language – and English specifically – is used as a resource for communication across the variety of human social and cultural engagements, from the local and individual to the international and political. This is the academic discipline of ELS as experienced in many UK universities and schools, and the one that most closely approximates to the focus of this handbook.

Historically, the study of the English language in universities is grounded in understanding the origins and evolution of the language through close textual analysis. Gupta (2015) has charted approaches to English Studies generally, the separate developments in English linguistic and literary study, and the variability within institutional and geographical contexts. In doing so, he highlights the significant degree to which 'English linguistics . . . engages directly with the extraordinary global reach of the language' (p. 203), an engagement which unites the three strands of ELS discussed above. Conceiving of the English language as pluralistic, i.e. no longer centred predominantly on particular national centres, moves the discipline away from a focus on norms and standards arbitrated by an Anglophone heartland. It recognises the different Englishes used by both those for whom it is a first language and those for whom it is an additional language.

The breadth of coverage described above enables ELS to contribute to debates within the broad fields of education, humanities and social sciences, and, indeed, to provide a bridge between them. The methodological pluralism that links creative, qualitative, empirical and quantitative approaches provides a variety of lenses with which to examine language. It allows for the complexity and interconnectedness of communication to emerge from spoken, written, multimodal, intercultural, synchronous, asynchronous, face-to-face, online, one-to-one and one-to-many uses of English (to name just a few of the communicative permutations related to the language!). It recognises the importance of linguistic building blocks – from phonemes to discourses – alongside the value systems in which English is implicated. Carter (2016) refers to complexity, criticality, context and creativity in relation to English Studies as a whole, but these areas are all relevant to ELS more specifically and to the different strands of ELS in different degrees. They are all also relevant to current concerns within society. For example, the English language is implicated in social justice at an individual and a global level where access to the language or to particular varieties of English influence people's life chances. Then there is the way that literacy in English is a gatekeeper both for those for whom it is a birth language and for those acquiring it later. And foundational to all education are skills such as the ability to critically examine texts and to understand how they are constructed to instruct, persuade or entertain; and to perceive the rhetorical nature of language and learn to evaluate it. Some of these key issues are explored more fully below and in the individual chapters of the book.

Key issues and debates

Given the variety of conceptualisations of ELS and its global scope, researchers have opportunities to contribute to numerous contemporary debates and challenges. Educators, similarly, have a diverse set of methodological lenses and issues with which to engage students and promote new and deeper understandings of the world. Below we use four broad headings to structure a brief overview of current areas of interest and relevance within ELS.

Criticality

The basic methodological tools used within ELS rest on description of the English language: its history, structure and use. In addition, much research now focuses on using these tools to critically interrogate how English is used and taught in both Anglophone and non-Anglophone contexts and how it is implicated in the exercise of economic and political power. In higher education in the UK, this type of criticality is specifically embedded in the subject benchmark statements for English, where 'high-order critical, analytic and research skills' (Quality Assurance Agency 2015: 5) are part of the expected broader skills graduates will develop.

Critical approaches to the analysis of a variety of texts, both spoken and written, has focused on the exercise of power through language (Fairclough 1989; Gee 1999). In the US context, for example, Gee highlights the interconnectedness of various social practices with the ability to use different registers, or what he refers to as 'Discourses (with a capital D)'. Put simply, because of the way in which society values certain Discourses over others, access to these prestigious ways of communicating (which are often acquired as a result of family circumstances) provides some people with educational and social advantages and ultimately greater access to wealth and power, while excluding or disenfranchising others. The focus on language not as a transparent medium but as part of the social practices of everyday life with the capacity to constrain or promote people's life chances has led to a profound change in the ways in which language is researched, and subsequently the ways in which students are taught. The emphasis on seeing language not (just) as a system but as a set of oral and literacy practices (Street 2012) emphasises the contextual nature of communication. Critical perspectives based on this conceptualisation of language use then aim to deepen understandings of and influence pedagogical approaches to powerful genres, and thereby to widen access to and influence over what constitutes these genres.

Critical approaches have also been influential in examining the role of the English language internationally, and particularly in relation to processes of globalisation. Phillipson's (1992) critique of the way that English language teaching (and the ELT 'industry') is implicated in the domination of much of the world by Anglo-American economic and political interests has significantly altered debate about the factors that have shaped the status of English as the world's current pre-eminent lingua franca. While parts of his thesis remain controversial, it has challenged the idea of language teaching as a non-ideological undertaking; an issue which has also been the focus of challenges to the importance attached to, and therefore the greater influence of, native-speaker English teachers (Widdowson 1994). In terms of the use – or indeed need – of English for migrants and refugees, a critical lens has focused on government policies as they relate English language learning to ideological conceptions of integration, multiculturalism and multilingualism. Leung (2016), for example, traces policy decisions on English as a second or additional language (ESL/EAL) in English schools since the 1970s. A move away from initially separating out pupils to give them specific English language skills was motivated by a concern to avoid segregation along racial lines, and to create greater equality of opportunity for all. This resulted in provision for ESL/EAL pupils becoming part of the mainstream curriculum provision. Leung concludes his discussion of this issue by questioning whether the ideology of greater equality which initially promoted the move to a more inclusive approach has withstood the current neoliberal discourse which strongly favours competition and individual differentiation. Critical reflection of this sort on all aspects of ELS is a common thread throughout much of the discussion in the chapters below.

Social relevance

Closely related to critical approaches, ELS has also focused on social relevance in research and teaching. This trend can be partially linked to the significance now given in UK funding to the 'impact' of research, although in ELS the focus on social relevance predates this government agenda to some extent, particularly in health, education and the law. In the 1980s, applied linguists were contributing to the training of doctors through the application of discourse and conversation analysis, and more recently what has become known as medical humanities draws on ELS analytical techniques of narrative, discourse analysis and corpus analysis to understand the experiences of those with illnesses and those treating and supporting them. For example, Demjén (this volume, and 2015) examines the journals of Sylvia Plath using corpus and metaphor analysis to discover ways in which depression is represented and may be recognised through particular language choices. Others have applied narrative analysis to ways of dealing with grief (Giaxoglou 2015), and discourse analysis to understanding and support for carers of those with dementia (Wray n.d.). The focus in these cases is on using linguistic analyses to understand a phenomenon and then to disseminate the findings to those for whom it has value and who may usefully be able to apply it in their own situations.

The importance of literacy in society, and thus the significance of learning to read and write, also give educational applications within ELS particular social relevance. Learning to speak and read both a first and subsequent language have been the subject of much research, both in terms of understanding the processes involved, and looking at ways to improve teaching. The concepts of languaging and translanguaging, which have attracted a great deal of research attention recently, challenge the notion of discrete languages (as discussed above), as well as the role of languages generally in the classroom. Translanguaging involves the use of any available language resources in order to communicate. In classroom situations, this questions the orthodoxy of monolingualism and prioritises *communication* over *language* learning. In countries such as the UK, USA and Australia, with significant numbers of children with multiple different languages in schools, it recognises and builds upon contexts in which English is only one among many languages (NALDIC 2016). Alongside this the theoretical concept of a language such as English being 'a mental code mastered by an individual . . . [is] being complemented by views of language as a continually emerging, socially mediated, and self-organizing resource for identity construction and interaction' (TESOL International Association 2014: 8). 'Languaging' is the verb used to capture this emergence and social mediation. It emphasises the process of communication *through* language rather than language as a fixed entity that can be mastered. Both languaging and translanguaging arise in a period where globalisation and migration are influencing the intellectual landscape of the 'global north'. Making use of multiple linguistic resources is not new, but acknowledging the social reality of superdiverse and plurilingual contexts, particularly in large cities where variety in linguistic, cultural, religious and ethnic backgrounds is the norm, challenges the monolingual, national language focus of the past and in which ELS has evolved.

Applications of language analysis are also increasingly being applied to legal contexts, often in situations where socially marginalised people or groups are involved. Under the banner of forensic linguistics, or language and the law, analysts critically examine spoken and written texts such as police interviews and emergency calls in order to consider how language may be interpreted or misinterpreted within the legal process. For example, analysis of courtroom talk by Eades (2012) in Australia demonstrated particular bias in the treatment of Aboriginal people by the justice system. She argues that courtroom talk operates as a form of neo-colonial control by the state over Aboriginal people. Her claims are based on analysis of the implicit understandings contained in language that may be harnessed to maintain and explain away unjust social structures (see Seargeant, this volume, for a discussion of ideologies in language). Forensic linguistics then, like medical humanities or literacy research, illustrates the trend towards applying research and pedagogy within ELS towards the goals of greater social justice.

Creativity

Within the broader concept of English Studies as a discrete subject or discipline area, ELS lines up alongside Literary Studies and Creative Writing. Although often studied – and thus conceptualised – as distinct disciplines (and spread across different departments and faculties in universities), their focus on the use and functions of language mean they share many concerns, and also have several elements which overlap in significant ways (for further discussion see Hewings et al. 2016). To define Literary Studies and Creative Writing in rather reductive terms, both have a particular focus on the *artful* use of language, whereas ELS considers language in broader terms, from the natural and extempore use of it to highly reflective and self-consciously creative manipulation. One key area of overlap between the three (sub)disciplines, however, is the examination of what it is that counts as creativity – that is, how the concept should be understood when associated with language. In ELS, a relatively recent line of research (e.g. Carter 2004; Demjén and Seargeant 2016; Maybin and Swann 2006) has been tracking and illuminating the ways in which everyday language use is creative – and indeed, displays many of the same features that would traditionally be understood as 'literary' uses. A counterpart to this is a focus on the different ways in which linguistic creativity can be analysed, with approaches ranging from those which concentrate predominantly on textual features, to those which highlight the importance of (social) context, to those which consider the critical or political environment in which concepts of creativity exist (Hann and Lillis 2016; Maybin 2016).

A complementary approach links theory with practice through the analysis of linguistic data combined with composition. This 'critical-creative' approach (Pope 1995) involves engaging directly with creative processes rather than simply theorising them. For example, by creatively rewriting a text (for example, transferring it from one genre to another) one can consider the stylistic choices that are involved in composition, the generic constraints and conventions within which the writer is working and so forth. By then combining this practice-based approach with reflective analysis, it is possible to gain a different perspective on the nature and purposes of linguistic creativity within society and culture.

Methodological pluralism

As can be seen from this last example, ELS draws upon a wide variety of methodologies, often in an interdisciplinary way. Another notable recent example of this is the increasing use of ethnographic methods to examine language use – an approach which underpins linguistic anthropology in the US and linguistic ethnography in the UK. Close analysis of situated language use is able to provide insights into how language and the social world mutually influence and shape each other. This brings a highly contextualised dimension to understanding language which complements more traditional linguistic approaches that are founded on regularities within language structures and use (Rampton et al. 2004).

Ethnographic enquiry has permeated linguistics to a greater or lesser degree over many decades; from early work by linguists with Native American oral narratives (e.g Hymes 1981) to Blackledge et al.'s (2016) observations of communication by Chinese stallholders in a Birmingham market. A commitment to trying to understand the culture and communication context of those being researched requires data collected over weeks, months or even years in order to understand what Maybin (1994) describes as the 'long conversation' (see also Madsen, this volume). Work by Lillis and Curry (2010) for example, on academic text production by non-Anglophone scholars, has so far stretched over 15 years.

While linguistic ethnography is reliant on close observation over time in order to understand the context and significance of texts, ELS has also been following a more technologically focused route to researching and understanding language. The use of computers to store and help analyse data has continued to provide new insights into communication since the early corpus studies of the 1960s and 1970s. Textbooks and reference guides for those learning English have been greatly influenced by the insights into collocation and word frequency that are enabled by corpus work such as that of the COBUILD dictionary project (Sinclair 1987), and more recently by Carter and McCarthy's (2017) work on the grammar of speech. Corpora based on different registers have enabled comparisons of lexical and grammatical choices and contributed to English language pedagogy for a variety of learners and users of English (Biber et al. 2002; Nesi and Gardener 2012; O'Keeffe and Mark, this volume). Corpora are also used in the analysis of social issues particularly with the application of semantic tagging. Paterson et al.'s (2017) work analysing conversations on the topic of welfare claimants and class, or Turner et al.'s (2018) work on linguistic constructions relating to same-sex marriage and homophobia are recent examples.

Analysis of speech is another area which has been facilitated in recent years through the use of computational means. Analytical software can consistently differentiate sounds and, together with computer models of vocal organs, contribute to an understanding of how we produce and make sense of connected speech. This type of knowledge is relevant to pedagogy for those with speech and learning difficulties, as well as for English language teaching (see Fuchs, this volume). Changes in accent in different varieties of English, which have been the subject of intensive small-scale research, are also now amenable to investigation using computational means. The ability to distinguish subtle variations through acoustic measurements is supplemented by the ability to collect larger data samples and analyse these using a variety of software. For example, Setter et al. (2014) analyse production and reception of boundaries between ambiguous word pairs where there are no phonemic differences (e.g. nitrate and night-rate). They compare English usage in Hong Kong English, Singapore English and British English with the aim of increasing understanding around mutual intelligibility of different English varieties.

The four key issues identified – criticality, social relevance, creativity and methodological pluralism – combine to define ELS as a discipline engaged with the challenges of the twenty-first century. It has a core of robust analytical techniques but is also flexible and works creatively alongside other disciplines. The questions and problems addressed are both practical and also inspirational. Pedagogically, ELS offers students multiple ways to reflect on their own lives and language and the historical, political and social context in which English operates globally.

The structure of the book

Given the aims outlined above, and the context in which ELS sits, the book is divided into three sections, each focusing on a different theme. The first part, 'Defining English', examines the development of English through history, its nature in terms of phonology and grammar, and its influence in terms of hybrid languages and the spread of loanwords. The book begins with a chapter on ideologies of English, and the important role these play in the relationship people have with the language, which opens up some of the questions about what counts as English and why it is a topic of such social and cultural (as well as linguistic) interest. This, in combination with the other chapters in Part One, aims to provide a comprehensive picture of the state and status of English as it is positioned within history and understood as both resource and concept in present-day global society.

Part Two, 'The Relevance of English', then moves to an examination of the rationale for ELS in terms of the important issues and social phenomena the subject area relates to. This section includes a focus on socio-political issues (identity, class, gender); as well as aesthetic and creative issues (stylistics, literature, creative writing); developmental issues (schooling and higher education); and communication-related issues (persuasive language, the use of English in broadcast and social media). For each of these domains, the chapters explain why the study of English language can offer vital resources and an important perspective on a range of aspects to do with our social and cultural lives.

The final part, 'Analysing English', turns to issues of how the subject is studied. It examines the methodologies used in the study of English and its (sub)disciplines, and how different frameworks offer ways for analysing the issues covered in Part Two. The section covers approaches from stylistics to linguistic ethnography, and corpus linguistics to psycholinguistics, and ends with a look at the relationship between English and translations studies. For each of the different approaches, the overarching question is how they contribute to the broader discipline of ELS, thus providing a comprehensive overview of the subject as it is currently conceptualised. In the following subsections we look in more detail at how the various chapters contribute to this overall aim.

Part One

'Defining English' begins with Seargeant's chapter (1) on the 'idea of English', in which he examines how English has been historically, and is currently, conceptualised as a language, and the implications these conceptualisations have for both social scientific and socio-cultural issues. This tension around what English is perceived to be and how English experientially exists in the world remains a central topic of discussion throughout the book. The next four chapters explore the history of the development the English language, along with how that history has been constructed. First, Horobin (2) introduces the topic by describing the development of English Studies from the earliest beginnings to the modern period and the consequences that previous approaches have had for how English has been studied, particularly in terms of a reliance on written data. The chapter maps a shift towards methodologies that attempt to explain *why* and *how* changes in English have occurred over the years, mostly moving beyond description of English as a system to a focus on the impact of larger social and ideological issues. Following on from this, Schneider (3) examines the central role of colonialism in the spread and current identity of English, while discussing how this history can inform an understanding of English as it is used today, in terms of its forms, functions and politics. This leads into Bolton's (4) discussion of World Englishes paradigms, which dissects the ways in which 'English' as a named language now encompasses a wide range of different varieties and functions across the globe, with multiplex identities. García and Lin's chapter (5) broadens this discussion of linguistic diversity by looking at the place of English in the study of multilingualism, with a particular focus on translanguaging and seeing English as part of an ecology of linguistic resources. They argue strongly for the way that historical and political forces have shaped the lens through which both English and multilingualism are conceptualised, and suggest instead a far more fluid approach to the study of the way people actually draw on linguistic resources in the way they communicate.

The next two chapters continue this focus on the problematisation of what 'English' is, and how speakers understand and interact with its development, especially as it relates to other languages. Wee (6) addresses these issues with reference to the notion of standard English, and the distinction between viewing language as product and process. This is a recurring theme throughout the book, as scholars describe the tension between English as a system of language owned and taught by native speakers and English as an evolving part of a complex social system incorporating a variety of different actors, all of whom contribute to its diverse identity. This is followed by Higgins and Furukawa's chapter (7), which describes this process of evolution by looking specifically at contact between English and other languages, with a particular focus on the structure and status of pidgins, creoles and hybrid languages, along with the social implications of code-switching and translanguaging, another theme which recurs at several points throughout the book.

Moving on from this cultural-historical focus, the final two chapters in this section look at the different levels of language investigation as these are applied to English. Fuchs (8) begins by examining how phonology is used to describe the production and reception of the sound system of English, including descriptions of World Englishes and the presentation of the language in teaching contexts. Political issues introduced in earlier chapters also form part of the debate here in that Fuchs argues that the phonetic realisations of English and the teaching of its pronunciation often have ideological implications in the way that 'Inner Circle' countries and 'native speakers' are favoured over others. O'Keeffe and Mark (9) then describe a similar effect in the evolution of approaches to grammar in ELS, and how perennial debates around prescriptivism and descriptivism, and written and spoken texts, are being played out in contemporary global contexts. They too argue that the teaching of grammar, like pronunciation, is also a tool for spreading particular ideologies when certain constructions are favoured over others.

Part Two

Part Two covers the relevance of English, touching on the different ways in which the diversity of approaches to ELS can be applied to the study of identity and the means by which language and, with it, ideology are spread. The section begins with Hewings's chapter (10) addressing the topic of English in higher education in both Anglophone and non-Anglophone national contexts – and through this, how it operates as a discipline and subject area. She distinguishes studying *about* the English language – its history, structure, and social relevance – from learning to *use* the language, as well as the role it plays as a medium of instruction in several countries. In doing this she considers the educational values that are inscribed in ELS around the world, and based on this argues for the wide-ranging relevance of the subject in twenty-first century education.

This is followed by three further chapters focusing on pedagogic issues relating to English. The first of these, McKinney's chapter (11) on literacy in English, investigates pedagogies for developing literacy – or rather, multiple literacies – in global contexts. And here again, the issues of colonialism and the privileging of 'native' voices is confronted and problematised. Leung and Szundy (12) then consider the role of English as an 'additional language' both in England and Brazil, discussing the practical curriculum implications of national policies about English and tying conceptualisations of English to their practical outworking in real teaching contexts. This is followed by Pecorari's (13) discussion of TESOL, in which she addresses debates about how 'native' English-speakers are privileged within the teaching profession, and how the industry of ELT relates to the hegemonic position that English occupies globally as a result of the politics and history that were discussed in Part One of the book.

Moving beyond teaching, the next few chapters look at how English language in a global context relates to speakers' and communities' cultural identities. Asprey and Lawson (14) begin by describing how the study of English has been used to contribute to an understanding of the social construction of identity; how it relates to different markers of social class, and the role it plays in the production and reproduction of social (and cultural) distinctions among people. These differences in language use are often, as Asprey and Lawson show, essential to how speakers view themselves in relation to others, and to how they construct group identities. Yoong (15) then considers how language relates to sexuality and gender, and how specific discourses around gender are produced and received. In this discussion again, the ideologies that have animated and resulted from the spread of English are of key relevance; for example in the way that perceived differences between how men and women speak and act are deeply embedded in broader cultural understandings and stereotypes relating to gender.

Following on from this, the section then turns to the use of English in media, politics and other forms of cultural production. These various chapters map both the possibilities and constraints that new technologies and approaches afford in the contemporary world, where access to the voices of others does not automatically result in these voices being heard. First, Spencer-Bennett's chapter (16) on English politics considers ideology in language use, and the dynamics by which power is constructed in political contexts. He illustrates the extent to which language is tied to the maintenance of political power, and how it serves as a kind of political actor in its own right, construing the social world and positioning us as subjects within that world. Hann's chapter (17) then considers the ways in which language is used as a powerful tool for persuasion in a huge variety of different domains, including advertising, rhetoric and political speeches, and the role it can play as a medium for persuasion in online and digital contexts. The next two chapters focus on more explicitly 'literary' uses of English: Geoff Hall's chapter (18) discussing the relationship between literary studies and ELS, and how (the study of) literature has influenced understandings and valuations of English throughout the years. Scott (19) then looks as the comparatively underexplored relationship between Creative Writing and ELS, arguing that this can be a site for self-conscious engagement with the mechanics of English language, and with it, the expression of one's own identity and position in the social world.

The section concludes with two chapters on English and media: the first of these, by Neary and Ringrow (20), offering a survey of the ways that English is studied in different media contexts and how these may affect linguistic issues, including both traditional media and new and emerging media online. Spilioti's chapter (21) takes up this latter context in further detail, examining the way that online technologies influence the way we communicate in English and the potential effects of the use of internet technology on the development of English over time.

Part Three

The final section of the book focuses on approaches to analysing English, identifying different ways in which language can be studied in a variety of different contexts, and with a variety of different methods. The focus here is on the tools that can be used within ELS to describe and analyse the different issues introduced and expanded on in the first two parts. The section begins with McIntyre and Price's chapter (22) on the empirical study of language in literature, what the study of 'style' can illuminate about the nature of language in both literary and non-literary contexts, and how choices in style have consequences for the production of identity beyond literary contexts. Deumert's chapter (23) then examines the methods and theories for analysing the relationship between language and society, particularly in terms of issues of variation, ideology and inequality. Together, these two chapters show how linguistic variation can be the consequence of both explicit choices made by speakers and implicit patterns of speaking, often without clear demarcations between the two.

The next few chapters look more specifically at the practical tools that can be employed in ELS to describe and analyse language use. Philip (24) introduces corpus linguistics, showing how large bodies of texts can be analysed with computer software in order to look for significant patterns in usage. As a method, this can be used to look at variation among the whole of the language, using large general corpora, or to describe specific registers and varieties through analysis of specialist corpora. Philip discusses the possibilities and limitations of corpus methodologies in the different areas of linguistics, suggesting that it has potential to offer insights into a great range of different forms of linguistic analysis. Pihlaja (25) then discusses different approaches to the analysis of discourse, focusing both on the turn-by-turn interaction of speakers in language-in-interaction, and the political ideologies which influence or structure language use. This is then followed by Madsen's chapter (26) on the relationship between language and culture and linguistic-ethnographic methodologies for studying this. These three chapters represent different scales of analysis, but they also suggest ways in which the methods can be mixed to show connections between individual interactions and larger trends in language use and variation.

The relationship between individual choice and the 'system' of English language is further explored in Chris Hall's chapter (27) on the psycholinguistics of English. He discusses the place of language in internal thought, and how language is mentally represented and processed, before moving to consider how this can affect the ways in which language is learned and understood. As a complement to this, Demjén (28) then looks at Metaphor Studies as they relate to ELS, mapping the growth of this field of study from conceptual metaphor theory in the early 1980s to the diverse collection of approaches used today, and discussing how its study can lead to important insights into the relationship between language and thought.

The final two chapters move not only back beyond the mind, but also beyond English itself, reflecting a broad trend within the book of the importance of seeing the language within a wider context of linguistic and semiotic resources. Ravelli's chapter (29) discusses approaches to the analysis of multimodal English, looking at communication in which language is one mode among many. Laviosa (30) then addresses the topic of translation, considering how the relationship between translation studies and ELS can be particularly illuminating for an understanding of the role that English plays in the world today. In this way the chapter returns to many of the main themes of the book: thinking about the possibilities afforded by English as a medium for interaction across cultures, one that both expands and constrains individuals as they express themselves and their identity in an increasingly interconnected global context.

References

Biber, D., S. Conrad and G. Leech (2002) *The Longman Student Grammar of Spoken and Written English*. London: Longman.

Blackledge, A., A. Creese and K. Trehan (2016) Enterprising Communities: How Everyday Entrepreneurs Create Better Communities. Working Papers in Translanguaging and Translation (WP. 11).

Carter, R. (2004) *Language and Creativity: The Art of Common Talk*. London: Routledge.

Carter, R. (2016) 'English pasts, English futures', in A. Hewings, L. Prescott and P. Seargeant (eds), *Futures for English Studies: Teaching Language, Literature and Creative Writing in Higher Education*. Basingstoke: Palgrave, 11–18.

Carter, R. A. and M. J. McCarthy (2017) 'Spoken grammar: Where are we and where are we going?' *Applied Linguistics* 38 (1): 1–20.

Demjén, Z. (2015) *Sylvia Plath and the Language of Affective States: Written Discourse and the Experience of Depression*. London: Bloomsbury.

Demjén, Z. and P. Seargeant (2016) *Creativity in Language: From Everyday Style to Verbal Art*. Milton Keynes: The Open University.

Eades, D. (2012) 'The social consequences of language ideologies in courtroom cross-examination', *Language in Society* 41 (4): 471–497.

Fairclough, N. (1989) *Language and Power*. London: Longman.

Gee, J. P. (1999) *An Introduction to Discourse Analysis: Theory and Method*. London and New York: Routledge.

Giaxoglou, K. (2015) 'Entextualising mourning on Facebook: Stories of grief as acts of sharing', *New Review of Hypermedia and Multimedia* 21 (1–2): 87–105.

Gupta, S. (2015) *Philology and Global English Studies*. Basingstoke: Palgrave Macmillan.

Hann, D. and T. Lillis (eds) (2016) *The Politics of Language and Creativity in a Globalised World*. Milton Keynes: The Open University.

Hewings, A., L. Prescott and P. Seargeant (eds) (2016) *Futures for English Studies: Teaching Language, Literature and Creative Writing in Higher Education*. Basingstoke: Palgrave.

Hymes, D. (1981) *'In Vain I Tried to Tell You': Essays in Native American Ethnopoetics*. Philadelphia: University of Pennsylvania Press.

Leung, C. (2016) 'English as an additional language—a genealogy of language-in-education policies and reflections on research trajectories', *Languages and Education* 30 (2): 158–174.

Lillis, T. and M. J. Curry (2010) *Academic Writing in a Global Context: The Politics and Practices of Publishing in English*. Abingdon: Routledge.

Maybin, Janet, ed. (1994) *Language and Literacy in Social Practice*. Clevedon: Multilingual Matters.

Maybin, J. (ed.) (2016) *Narrative, Language and Creativity: Contemporary Approaches*. Milton Keynes: The Open University.

Maybin, J. and J. Swann (eds) (2006) *The Art of English: Everyday Creativity*. Basingstoke, UK: Palgrave Macmillan.

NALDIC (National Association for Language Development in the Classroom) (2016) '*What is translanguaging?*' Available at www.ealjournal.org/2016/07/26/what-is-translanguaging/, accessed 23 August 2017.

Nesi, H. and S. Gardner (2012) *Genres Across the Disciplines: Student Writing in Higher Education*. Cambridge: Cambridge University Press.

Paterson, L. L., D. Peplow and K. Grainger (2017) 'Does money talk equate to class talk? Audience responses to poverty porn in relation to money and debt', in A. Mooney and E. Sifaki (eds), *The Language of Money and Debt: A Multidisciplinary Approach*. Basingstoke: Palgrave, 205–231.

Phillipson, R. (1992) *Linguistic Imperialism*. Oxford: Oxford University Press.

Pope, R. (1995) *Textual Intervention: Critical and Creative Strategies for Literary Studies*. London: Routledge.

Quality Assurance Agency (2015) '*Subject benchmark statement: English*', Available at www.qaa.ac.uk/en/Publications/Documents/SBS-English-15.pdf, accessed 28 September 2016.

Rampton, B., K. Tusting, J. Maybin, R. Barwell, A. Creese and V. Lytra (2004) '*UK linguistic ethnography: A discussion paper*', Paper published at www.ling-ethnog.org.uk, accessed 23 August 2017.

Setter, J., P. Mok, E. L. Low, D. Zuo and A. Ran (2014) 'Word juncture characteristics in world Englishes: A research report', *World Englishes* 33 (2): 278–291.

Sinclair, J. M. (1987) *Looking Up: An Account of the COBUILD Project in Lexical Computing*. Glasgow: Collins ELT.

Street, B. (2012) 'New literacy studies', in M. Grenfell, D. Bloome, C. Hardy, K. Pahl, J. Rowsell and B. Street (eds), *Language, Ethnography, and Education: Bridging New Literacy Studies and Bourdieu*. Abingdon: Routledge, 27–49.

TESOL International Association (2014) '*Research agenda 2014*', Available at www.tesol.org/docs/default-source/pdf/2014_tesol-research-agenda.pdf?sfvrsn=2, accessed 23 August 2017.

Turner, G., S. Mills, I. van der Bom, L. Coffey-Glover, L. L. Paterson and L. Jones (2018) 'Opposition as victimhood in newspaper debates about same-sex marriage', *Discourse and Society* 29 (2).

Widdowson, H. G. (1994) 'The ownership of English', *TESOL Quarterly* 28 (2): 377–389.

Wray, A. (n.d.) '*Understanding the challenges of dementia communication*', Available at www.cardiff.ac.uk/news/view/856229-helping-dementia-carers-make-sense-of-their-experiences, accessed 24 August 2017.

Part 1
Defining English

1
The idea of English

Philip Seargeant

Introduction: studying something which doesn't exist

In a famous gesture intended to prove a realist understanding of the world, the philosopher G. E. Moore held up first one hand and then another to indicate that there are external objects in the world. As everyone present could see, here were his hands, and thus it followed that an external world must exist generally (Moore 1939). We can perhaps do something similar with the English language and say that, as I'm now writing this sentence in English, it stands to reason that the English language exists. This seems obvious enough – basic common sense, in much the same way that Moore's proof was (to his mind at least).

The reason for beginning the discussion of English language studies in this way – i.e. by pointing to seemingly simple truths about the existence of the entity which the book as a whole is about – is that over the past few years there has been a strain in some scholarship which questions whether we *can* really say that an entity called 'English' exists. Or at least, can we take it as self-evident that it is simple common sense that we know what this entity is, and that this belief should thus be accepted as an uncritical starting point for all discussions of the language?

Characterising the argument as being that certain scholars are saying English doesn't really exist is perhaps slightly over-exaggerating. A more accurate way of putting it would be that for some, viewing languages as discrete entities is starting to be seen as sociolinguistically problematic. Alastair Pennycook, for example, wonders if

> [p]erhaps it is time to question the very notions that underpin our assumptions about languages [and] ask whether the ways we name and describe [them] as separate entities . . . are based on 20th century epistemologies that can no longer be used to describe the use of languages in a globalizing world.
>
> (Pennycook 2010: 121)

The argument here is that categories such as 'languages' (as well as 'varieties', 'dialects' and so on) are not scientifically real so much as products of a particular set of events in Western intellectual history. If we fail to take this into account when discussing or analysing English, we risk simply reinforcing the beliefs that produced the concept of the language in the first place, and this can constrain our investigation into the workings, functions and implications of language use.

Specifically, this argument is centred around the premise that the concept of discrete languages as we understand them in Western thought is a consequence of the promotion of the nation state as the principal politico-cultural unit in eighteenth-century European political philosophy (Anderson 1983). As part of this worldview, the language practices of a community were valorised as an essential element of that community's cultural-political identity. And with the principal unit of community being understood as the nation state, so the ideology of idealised 'national languages' was created. These national languages were identified with a particular high-prestige standard, which was codified in grammar books and dictionaries, thus cementing its status as the 'correct' form of the language (Milroy and Milroy 1985). The ideology then worked in consort with the theories that developed into the modern discipline of linguistics. Although research into sociolinguistics does regularly acknowledge the idealised nature of categories such as discrete languages and varieties (Swann 2007), these nevertheless still have deep roots in the ontological presuppositions of much academic research in the subject (Seargeant 2010), and are even more central in popular perceptions of a language such as English.

The main reason that recent scholarship has drawn attention to the ideological foundations of some of these underlying presuppositions is because the eighteenth-, nineteenth- and twentieth- century frameworks of social organisation which gave rise to them are arguably no longer valid for the world we now live in (Blommaert 2009). The impact of globalisation particularly has altered the social, cultural and political landscape, and with it the sociolinguistic practices of millions of people around the world. Yet there is a disjunction between the practices people manifest in their everyday language use, and the way language is conceptualised, be it in public discourse, policy initiatives, or even in different disciplines of scholarship. Or to put it another way, there is a division between the language practices and resources that speakers of English use, and the idea of English as a particular cultural, political or (social) scientific entity. And an understanding of the latter – the concept of English – is of vital importance because the way people think about a language influences the attitudes they take towards it, as well as towards broader social issues in which language is involved. This chapter, therefore, will examine the 'idea' of English as it is constructed in society. It will begin with an overview of the theoretical concerns which shape this approach to English, before moving to analyse examples of the ways in which concepts of English are constructed in various different domains, and the implications these have for English language studies more generally.

Current issues and topics

Linguistic ideologies

In his essay on 'Oratio imago animi', the seventeenth-century dramatist Ben Jonson writes of the way that language acts as a marker of a person's character (Jonson 1947 [1641]: 625):

> Language most shewes a man: speake that I may see thee. It springs out of the most retired, and inmost parts of us, and is the Image of the Parent of it, the mind. No glasse renders a mans forme, or likenesse, so true as his speech.

The belief expressed here is that the way a person uses language is an index, or indictor, of his or her character. Jonson is talking of articulate thought ('speech is the image of the mind', as the title of the essay has it), but in expressing one's mind the material form this takes – in terms of accent, style, prosody and so forth – is something upon which we make judgments about the social status, moral character and cultural background of the speaker. These judgements are a product of the shared beliefs that circulate within communities, and which interpret linguistic traits as metonymic for statistically co-occurring social attributes and stereotypical social features (related to class, gender, ethnicity and so forth).

These shared beliefs are what are commonly referred to as language ideologies. In his foundational paper on this topic, Silverstein (1979: 193) describes language ideologies as 'any sets of beliefs about language articulated by users as a rationalization or justification of perceived language structure or use'. In other words, they are the embedded beliefs that a group shares about language and language use which structures the way in which language is perceived by a particular group and in which it operates as social practice within that group. These beliefs are occasionally articulated as explicit conceptualisations of language, but they can also implicitly shape the way language is used, or the attitudes and stances people take towards it. It is this structuring that Silverstein calls the 'indexical' layer of language – the way certain elements of language use point towards embedded beliefs concerning the social, political or cultural nature of acts of speech.

A key point within this theorisation of language and social practice is that language ideologies are never about language alone. Instead, they incorporate the ties between language and other social dynamics such as gender, class and nationality (Woolard 1998). Use of a particular syntactical form, for example, can index a complex of ideological beliefs about class or cultural background, and these then provide a frame in which interaction between participants takes place. Furthermore, syntactical features or particular accents always exist within a wider ecology of linguistic practices wherein diversity is marked differentially, so that a particular feature is given symbolic significance in relation to the other features with which it is contrasted (and particularly 'standard' concepts of the language).

Another conceptual distinction introduced by Silverstein (1998) is that of the 'language community' as opposed to the more common sociolinguistic notion of the 'speech community'. Whereas a speech community is the grouping who have broadly similar patterns of language use in terms of accent, dialect, pragmatics and so forth, a language community is one which has a shared conception of the language as a named entity, and thus consider the *idea* of the language as part of their collective identity. An example would be groupings who view English (or a particular variety of it) as in a sense 'their' language, and promote this shared commitment as a central part of their communal identity. In other words, beliefs such as the idea that language homogeneity across a nation is a natural state of the world are particular, albeit very deeply embedded, language ideologies about the relationship between societies and linguistic practices (Kroskrity 2000).

Structuring language conceptualisation

As noted above, ideologies are manifest in both discourse and practice – in how people speak about a language, as well as in how they use and relate to it. As such it is a potentially very broad area for investigation, and in this chapter I will therefore narrow the focus to concentrate specifically on the ways in which the concept of English is constructed in discourse.

So how does language conceptualisation take place? There are five key elements to the process, which can offer a useful structure for its analysis. These are the mode, the domain, the function, the context and the means – all of which I will explain in further detail below (and then provide extended examples of in the next section).

First, there are the different modes in which conceptualisation takes place. By this I mean the different semiotic resources – verbal discourse, image, movement – which can be used to communicate ideas. Clearly the most prominent in this respect is verbal discourse – using language itself to talk or write about the nature of language – as this allows for the most flexible and richest way of generating and expressing conceptual meaning. Yet representations can also take place in other modes. There are examples, for instance, of ideas of language being represented visually – either diagrammatically (e.g. family trees of historical language development) or pictorially. In the Middle Ages, for example, there was an established iconography for ideas about grammar (Seargeant 2016), and throughout the history of art the visual trope of the Tower of Babel has been a popular subject.

The second point of note is that conceptualisation occurs in different domains. That is to say, language is the object of study for a wide range of different scientific disciplines, while at the same time featuring as an idea in non-scientific domains such as the arts, humanities and social sciences. While linguistics is, of course, the principal site of study, concepts of language are also commonly constructed in the cognitive sciences and psychology, in politics and educational contexts, and in philosophy, as well as literature and everyday contexts.

Each of these have a different set of concerns and aims, a point which stands as the third element of conceptualisation. A broad division can be made here between those conceptualisations which have as their aim the representation of language as it actually is (in so far as we can determine this), and those which present language as it could or should be (in their opinion). Scientific representations, for example, aim to flesh out a concept of language which fits as closely as possible with the observed phenomena of how language exists and works in the world. This is not necessarily the case in other domains.

A useful way of looking at this divide is by means of the distinction put forward by Searle (1995), building on the work of J. L. Austin and G. E. M. Anscombe, between two 'directions of fit'. This maps the relationship that a conceptual term has with the phenomenon it is representing. There can be a 'word-to-world' direction of fit, whereby the term represents the reality of the observed phenomenon, i.e. an utterance is used to describe the way things in the world already are. For example, when I say 'I have been to Tokyo' I am describing an event that has actually occurred in the world. The opposite of this is a 'world-to-word' direction of fit, whereby the utterance is used as a declaration of something that is meant to come to pass, and thus provides a structuring device for an action or phenomenon. An example of this would be saying 'I'll meet you at half past seven', and in doing so discursively projecting a version of a future reality which then acts as a structure for my upcoming plans.

In scientific discourse, representations are aiming for a 'word-to-world' direction of fit, whereby the term 'language' or 'English' equates as closely as possible to the actuality of these phenomena, and can function as an accurate conceptual category for analytic purposes. In this context the function of conceptualisation is, on the whole, straightforward, in that it is meant to provide an accurate representation which contributes to linguistic science. As we have seen, however, there are conflicting views of precisely what language or English can mean even in this context, and indeed much of the business of linguistics is concerned with refining this conceptualisation.

The opposite direction of fit also occurs for language conceptualisation in certain domains. Language policy, for example, promotes ideas of language which are then used as a template for regulating actual language use. This is found in particular in education, where choices about which variety or register should act as the standard become a set of norms to which students are then socialised. Similarly, language planning and policy initiatives project ideas about forms of language to which communities are urged or forced to conform. In this case the functions of conceptualisation will be related to purposes of social cohesion or identity, or to other cultural and political ends. When, for example, a national standard is prescribed in the curriculum, and other (local) languages or varieties are discouraged or banned, the political aim is likely to be a means of fostering and enacting an ideology of national unity. In the pure sense, a standard national language is an ideal. There is no direct correspondence between the representation of, say, English that it puts forward, and the real-life diversity and variety in English that is found in even the most homogeneous of communities. Yet within society this concept of the language often underpins policy and pronouncements due to the role that it plays in the belief systems of those with regulatory power.

An even more salient example of the 'world-to-word' direction of fit is the case of the inventors of artificial and reduced languages, such as Esperanto or Basic English. In these cases, the aim was to make actual language practice (the 'world') adapt to the tenets of their invented or contrived systems (the 'word'). For those advocating these projects, the concept 'language' was used to refer to a phenomenon which did not actually exist in the world but which they felt could be engineered into existence and become a reality of social practice for the population through promotion and education.

The fourth consideration of language conceptualisation is that it always happens within a particular historical context, which frames the nature of the knowledge about it. In other words, an act of conceptualisation occurs in a particular place and at a particular time, and the resources available at that time and place determine (or at the very least influence) its nature. Furthermore, the aims it is pursuing will be of relevance (and often be responding) to beliefs circulating within the culture at that time.

Historical context is of particular relevance for scientific explanations of language. Despite, in certain discourses, science being presented as ahistorical, and pursuing external truths which are removed from the influence of culture, scientific theories are always themselves cultural tools, which are shaped by the disciplinary and technological resources available at the time of their formulation, and are in dialogue with the epistemic and political beliefs of their time.

The final element in the system of analysis is the means by which language is conceptualised. These means consist of various discursive strategies, including the use of narrative, or the highlighting and downplaying of certain attributes. One of the key means is the use of metaphor, for which English can be both tenor and vehicle. In other words, one can describe English with reference to other entities and phenomena, or one can use English as a metaphor for other social issues. As Bailey writes,

> English is asserted to mirror whatever the speaker or writer believes to be most distinctive of Anglophone culture – whether the best or the worst. English at once liberates and enslaves, enlightens and thwarts, affirms and denies those who use it.
>
> (Bailey 2009: 2)

We will look at a number of examples of these means of conceptualisation in the next section.

Examples and implications

Naming the language

To examine all this I will look at two case studies, one from political discourse and policy, the other from fiction and popular culture. The study of linguistic ideologies is mostly studied as part of particular disciplines or sub-disciplines, examining specific domains. Looking across different domains, however, and seeing how similar processes of conceptualisation take place there, is useful not only in highlighting the generic structural properties of conceptualisation, but also in understanding how ideas circulate throughout and across society and culture. Before moving to the two case studies, though, let us consider briefly the naming of the language, and the role this plays in its conceptualisation, as this, in recent years in particular, has become an important first step in the analysis of the nature of English around the world.

In its very earliest incarnation in the linguistic ecology of the people of Britain, English was just one language among many. It had no particular status over the other languages spoken on the island – the *Anglo-Saxon Chronicle* lists also Brito-Welsh, Scottish, Pictish and Latin (Freeborn 1992: 13) – was very much a local language, and was without a strongly defined identity. While it had first emerged sometime during the fifth century AD when Germanic tribes from the north of Europe arrived in Britain, bringing with them their various indigenous dialects, it was not until at least four centuries into its existence, sometime during the ninth century, that the term 'English' began to be regularly used to refer to it (Crystal 2005: 27).

Today, of course, its identity – and with it the discourses around it – are vastly different from these very modest beginnings. While English today may still be only one among many languages spoken across the British Isles, it is very much the dominant one. It is also the principal language in several other countries, and over the last century has emerged as the dominant international language of the present era. So much so, in fact, that there have been various suggestions about the need to rename it. Toolan, for example, just prior to the turn of the millennium, proposed that the language as it is spoken in international contexts – and especially where it functions as a lingua franca – is so far removed both culturally and politically from the traditional national language of England that the term 'English' is simply no longer appropriate. The identity of the language today is far, far broader than this name suggests, and thus instead he suggests changing it to 'Global' (Toolan 1997).

While this particular renaming strategy never gained much traction, there are others which have. Braj Kachru, for example, arguing that due to the fact that 'English now has multicultural identities' and thus its traditional name does not capture the 'sociolinguistic reality' of the way it is now used (Kachru 1992: 357), instigated use of the plural form 'Englishes'. His contention that it is no longer possible to speak of a single English language is now an accepted precept across a great deal of the subject area, and this fairly small grammatical refinement has led to a number of fundamental reconceptualisations of the language. Following on from this, and with the continued expansion in the use of English around the globe (as well as the associated growth in scholarship examining this expansion), there have been several proposals for new technical names to refer to the language and its varieties – from Global Englishes and Postcolonial Englishes to English as a lingua franca (see Bolton, this volume, for further discussion of this issue) – each of which represents a distinct theoretical stance. Naming strategies, in other words, can act as the first step in a discursive re-examination of the ontological assumptions which underpin research into the nature and usage of the language.

National identity and English only policies

Despite the reappraisal within academia of many of the longstanding 'common sense' assumptions about the concept of English, there are still mainstream societal discourses which remain focused on the ideological relationship between language and national identity. While Noah Webster may have attempted to establish the notion of an 'American tongue' all the way back in 1828 with his creation of a national dictionary (along with selective spelling reform) (Webster 1991 [1789]: 93), for many the concept of English is still married to the identity of what it means to be American – and this idea acts as a powerful identification feature for certain factions in political circles. In 2014, for example, local media reported that a senator in Arizona, John Huppenthal, had pseudonymously written a succession of inflammatory comments on online forums, including some calling for the banning of all Spanish-language media, with the exception of menus at Mexican restaurants (Planas 2017). The unorthodox means of communicating his message notwithstanding, the agenda he was pursuing was part of a long-running dispute in Arizonan politics over the primacy of English in society, which in turn is part of a broader pattern of 'English only' advocacy campaigns in the United States.

The 'English only' ideology gained renewed national impetus in the United States in 2016 and 2017 with the election of Donald Trump to the presidency. During the election campaign, Trump took a position which bucked recent trends by presidential candidates by explicitly asserting, as part of a critique of one of his Republican rivals, that 'This is a country where we speak English, not Spanish' (Goldmacher 2016). Despite the fact that over 37 million US citizens now speak Spanish (Lopez and Gonzalez-Barrera 2013), he continued to press this line once in office by, for example, removing the Spanish-language pages from the White House website (Sharman 2017).

Trump's position is symbolically pointed, but without policy implications. At federal level there is no official language policy, and thus it is left to the states to determine this themselves. In Arizona, where Senator Huppenthal was campaigning for the linguistic purification of everything except restaurant menus, a law was passed in 2006 known as the English as the Official Language Act, which required state and local government representatives to 'preserve, protect and enhance the role of English as the official language' (Ballotpedia 2006). The state has a long history of supporting 'English only' policies (Terry 1998), and three decades earlier, a similar law was passed calling for *all* government business to be conducted solely in English, yet this was subsequently overturned by the state's Supreme Court on the grounds that it interfered with citizens' access to government (*Washington Times* 2006). The 2006 bill included a number of situations in which 'a language other than English' could be used by state or local government, such as petitioning the government, teaching other languages and preserving Native American linguistic heritage, issues related to public health and safety, tourism and international trade contexts, and informal communications between officials. Beyond these exceptions, though, English was to be the default and promoted language for all governmental business.

The ideologies that shape the concept of English in this case are discursively articulated in a very explicit way, drawing on the standard national language ideology, and using tropes such as metaphor and analogy to persuade of the naturalness of this. The sponsor of the bill, for example, argued that 'A common language promotes unity and understanding and is as vital to the health of a nation as having a common currency' (Ballotpedia 2006). The stated purpose of the conceptualisation here is social cohesion, though many media outlets also noted that it had a specific exclusionary function, and was 'viewed by many as a backlash against illegal immigration' (*Washington Times* 2006), if not against migrants in general. The demographic context is important here in that, according to census data from 2000, nearly 30 per cent of the population of Arizona speak a language other than English at home, and thus many of these will be effectively disenfranchised by the legislation. And subsequent rulings have further discriminated against this section of the population, building on the precedent of this law. For example, another bill, passed in 2017 by the Arizona House of Representatives, stated that should there be any differences between the English-language version of an insurance contract and a foreign language version (where the agent issues both, for the ease of the customer), it is the English version which takes precedent. Representative Mark Finchem argued this was natural given that English is the official language under state law, and that 'We spent hundreds of millions of dollars in our public education system on something called "English-language learning" ... Yet we are making excuses for people to not learn the English language' (Fischer 2017).

This same economic discourse was also voiced in the 2006 bill, which in part justified making English the official language on the basis that this would eliminate 'the wasteful spending used to translate millions of state documents into hundreds of languages', which, it argues, 'is not the responsibility of the taxpayer'. Here, two separate conservative discourses are brought together: the one advocating cultural homogeneity, the other a 'small government' agenda. At the heart of the conceptualisation however is the conviction that cultural integration is the natural state for an effective society: 'By making English the official state language we provide an even greater incentive for all immigrants to learn English, become empowered and productive citizens, and participate in society as full Americans' (Ballotpedia 2006).

The function of conceptualisation in this case, then, is clearly political. It can straddle two forms of political purpose, having both a campaigning function, where it is used as part of a repertoire of talking points aimed at appealing to and persuading the electorate (as in the Trump statements), while also having practical policy implications where it is related to beliefs about social organisation (as in the Arizona law). In terms of the domain, it is thus both political discourse and public policy. With respect to this latter context we can suggest that there is a blurring between the two 'directions of fit'. Depending on the perspective you take, an English-only agenda is either a natural state of affairs, or it is historical contingency. That is to say, from the perspective of those advocating the policy it is likely to be considered a word-to-world fit, and they are simply reflecting in their discourse the way they see English naturally existing in the world. From a social linguistic perspective, on the other hand, it is a world-to-word direction of fit, as the discourse and policy is aimed at enacting an ideology which, as discussed above, arose at a particular point of time in eighteenth-century Europe, and now, within the context of the politics and demographics of the United States, has a divisive, if not racist, element to it. Yet context is also key to understanding the renewed impetus behind the idea, where it is often part of populist movements which are riding on a backlash against globalisation.

Fictional representations: Star Wars

For the second case study I will move from the world of populist politics to popular culture. While language use in fiction is not an authentic example of extempore communication, but rather an artistic representation of such communication, it is, nevertheless, a reproduction of ideologies current in society. For a work of fiction to have cultural purchase it needs to resonate within the cultural values in which it is consumed. Works of fiction can therefore be seen as part of the wider framework by which ideologies are circulated, drawing from and feeding back into the language practices and beliefs that exist throughout society. Furthermore, given the influential role that literary and popular culture can play in shaping narratives in social life (Giglio 2007), there is an interesting relationship to be explored between the means and content of conceptualisations in these different domains.

For this second example, therefore, I will look at the representation of languages within the *Star Wars* franchise, and at how ideologies of English inform the way that language is used as part of the narrative world in this series. Depictions of language in science fiction adhere to the same paradox that exists for all types of fantasy world-building. The language spoken by an alien race needs to be significantly different from human languages to illustrate the otherness of the species, yet at the same time still be recognisable as language. It is also often used as a key ingredient in representing the alien race's culture and identity, and thus decisions made about the way it sounds or operates assist with the process of characterisation. In some cases, the nature of the language also acts as a plot complication or even as one of the major speculative premises underpinning the science fiction. A film such as Denis Villeneuve's *Arrival*, for example, is based on the conundrum of how humans might communicate with an alien race, and the philosophical complications this might entail.

Star Wars is not in this tradition, however. In terms of characterisation, whereas a number of high-profile science fiction projects (*Star Trek*, *Avatar* etc.) have employed specialist linguists to construct their fictional languages, alien communication in the *Star Wars* films was initially approached mostly as sound design rather than linguistics. The sound designer, Ben Burtt, has written that the intention was 'to use human-produced sound and the mimicry of actual languages' in order to come up with something that was 'entertaining, alien, and full of appropriate character' (Burtt 2001). In order to do this he chose languages which sounded markedly different from English, and then distorted them until he produced a sound which, to his ear, was 'alien'. For the Ewoks in the third film, for example, he started with a BBC documentary recording of an old woman speaking Tibetan which was then tampered with in post-production, while Jawaese is based very distantly on Zulu (Conley and Cain 2006), and Lando Calrissian's co-pilot Nien Nunb, who helps blow up the second Death Star, speaks something resembling the Tanzanian language Haya (Zimmer 2016). In all these cases there is no attempt to create from these sounds anything that structurally recreates the properties of an actual language (no regular phonology, lexis or grammar), but simply strings of sound.

A similar abstract process was used in *Episode VII: The Force Awakens*. For the language spoken by the Kanjiklub, one of the gangs encountered by Han Solo and Chewbacca aboard their shipping freighter, the producers enlisted a YouTube star from Finland, Sara Maria Forsberg, whose video 'What Languages Sound Like to Foreigners' had been hugely popular in 2014. For her work on *Star Wars* she used a mixture of the sounds of Indonesian and Sundanese to come up with something she described as 'suitably exotic-sounding' (Zimmer 2016).

Although none of these are conceptualisations of English, the thinking behind their design is based very much on a contrastive principle, with English being the unmarked, 'non-exotic' language. Something akin to this underpinning ideology was, in fact, written into the original film script, with directives such as 'The Sand People . . . speak in a coarse *barbaric* language' (Lucas 1977; italics added). As such it plays into a very standard tradition of science fiction, which has roots in an Orientalist mind-set. As Rieder (2008: 1) notes, colonialism has always been a significant historical context for science fiction. The genre first arises in 'those countries most heavily involved in imperialist projects – France and England – and then gains popularity in the United States, Germany, and Russia as those countries also enter into more and more serious imperial competition'. And one of the ways in which this is encoded, as the science fiction writer Ursula K. Le Guin comments, is by enacting 'the permanent hegemony of manly, English-speaking men [versus] the risible grotesqueness of non-English languages' (Le Guin 2006: xvii).

This approach to linguistic representation in *Star Wars* has resulted in some notable issues and controversies over appropriation and stereotyping. With the first film, in 1977, for example, a number of linguistic anthropologists from Berkeley were asked to record dialogue in Quechua for the film, which the filmmakers then planned to play backwards in order to create one of the alien languages. Due to ethical concerns, particularly around the idea that this might indirectly imply that 'primitives' were aliens rather than humans, the linguists in question refused (Speech Events 2015; Wilce 1999).

In contrast to these impressionistic 'languages', all the humans within the franchise speak what is known as Intergalactic Basic and which is, to all intents and purposes, English. As Stockwell (2000) notes, the use of English as a lingua franca in science fiction is in many ways a simple way of side-stepping the logistics of intergalactic communication problems. And this is very much the rationale here. But it also reinforces the hegemony of English – and of a particular type of English – as here again the same Anglophone equation applies. For the most part, a standard US accent is the unmarked code, and the more 'foreign' the sound of the accent, the more alien it is meant to be. In the first film the director George Lucas reports carefully trying 'to balance the British and American voices' so that there wasn't a regional divide between heroes and villains (Scanlon 1977). But to many the impression is still that the villainous Imperial characters speak in Received Pronunciation, while the heroic Rebels have American accents.

In the second trilogy of the franchise this standard versus non-standard divide was even more marked, leading to criticism that the symbolism behind some of the linguistic and cultural representation bordered on the racist. The Neimoidian race, for example, many of whom conspire with the main villains of the films, spoke in what sounded, to many, like a rather crude mock-Japanese accent, while their clothing had a faux Chinese aspect to it. This led critics such as John Sutherland to write that the depiction came 'straight out of the Yellow Peril propaganda of the world war two' (Sutherland 1999).

In contrast to something like the English-only policy discourse, English is here being conceptualised indirectly, and drawing mostly on deeply embedded ideologies which the makers of the film were not, at least in the early days, reflecting on in any particular critical way in their character depiction. The mode in this instance is multifaceted, and not confined to verbal discourse. It includes the use of sound engineering, meant to imitate alien language without actually being articulate speech, and which often draws on non-European language sounds to facilitate this. Then there is visual imagery, such as the iconography around the costumes of the Neimoidian people, which acts as a complement to the symbolism of the sound and speech. Plus there is the use of narrative as a means of conceptualisation, in that associations between accent and character are given a particular meaning due to the part that characters play in the plot.

Finally, the purpose behind conceptualisation is part of the broader purpose of the film as entertainment in relatively pure and simple terms. And yet as has been noted, Hollywood, even when not being purposefully political, plays a strong role in shaping normative cultural values, even if this is not an explicit intention of those involved in projects of this sort.

Future directions

Conceptualisation of English lies predominantly across three important areas for English language studies: (social) scientific investigation, political intervention, and literary representations of social life. For the first two of these it is a key element in how we study language, and one that can affect the direction of research and the structure of social practice. The third area – how language is conceptualised in the arts and humanities – is a field which has received less focus to date, but can be an important complement to the others, not least in that it often becomes a useful touchstone or analogy for discussion of political discourse (references to George Orwell's Newspeak when discussing the political manipulation of language are a recurrent example).

Within social and applied linguistics, prevailing ideologies at the present moment are that English needs to be seen from a global perspective, from a social perspective, from a political perspective and from a critical perspective. As many of the chapters in this handbook discuss, a recent turn has been towards a position which deconstructs and fragments what is meant by English. The sceptical re-evaluation of what 'English' is, and whether it exists as a singular coherent entity (an issue discussed in the introduction to this chapter), has expanded into approaches which not only pluralise English, but also highlight the way that, in a globalised world, the actual practices people use, especially in multiculturally-inflected contexts, are to draw on a variety of different linguistic – and semiotic – resources that are available to them, and engage in what is commonly referred to as translanguaging as part of their real-world communication practices (an issue taken up in other chapters in the book).

Conceptualisations of the language such as these, which occur in parts of the discipline, are not orthodox across English language studies as a whole. For example, corpus approaches to English rarely acknowledge the translanguaging paradigm. They are also in stark contrast to the way that English is conceptualised in many public policy contexts, especially those where language-related issues are co-opted as part of a broader nationalist politics, or as part of education policy. Given this discrepancy, a critically-engaged language studies may wish to address why this discrepancy exists, and how those responsible for policy might be made more aware, and take more account, of social-scientific conceptualisations, so as to confront the exclusionary politics which prescriptive attitudes, centred around particular concepts of language, often promote. As this chapter has outlined, across this and many different domains, analysis of situated acts of conceptualisation can examine how and why we have the idea of English that we do in these various different contexts – and thus provide clear foundations for all other avenues of investigation into the language.

Further reading

Richard W. Bailey's *Images of English: a cultural history of the language* (2009, Cambridge University Press) presents a history of English from the perspective of how the language has been perceived over the centuries. Drawing upon folk beliefs about English, and on debates over deterioration and change, it examines the way ideas of English have shaped its history.

Language ideologies: practice and theory, edited by Bambi Schieffelin, Kathryn Woolard and Paul Kroskrity (1998, Oxford University Press), includes a series of essays on the way concepts of language are used and function in a range of social settings.

Regimes of language: ideologies, polities, and identities, edited by Paul Kroskrity (2000, School of American Research Press), is another collection of essays looking at the role of language ideologies in contexts such as national and ethnic identities, state formation and political discourse.

Related topics

- Standards in English
- Sociolinguistics: studying English and its social relations
- World Englishes: disciplinary debates and future directions
- English and multilingualism: a contested history.

References

Anderson, B. (1983) *Imagined Communities: Reflections on the Origin and Spread of Nationalism*. London: Verso.

Bailey, R. W. (2009) *Images of English: A Cultural History of the Language*. Cambridge: Cambridge University Press.

Ballotpedia (2006) '*Arizona English as the official language, proposition 103*'. Available at www.ballotpedia.org/Arizona_English_as_the_Official_Language,_Proposition_103_(2006).
Blommaert, J. (2009) 'Language, asylum, and the national order', *Current Anthropology* 50: 415–442.
Burtt, B. (2001) *Star Wars: Galactic Phrase Book and Travel Guide*. New York: Del Rey.
Conley, T. and S. Cain. (2006) *Encyclopedia of Fictional and Fantastic Languages*. Westport, CT: Greenwood Press.
Crystal, D. (2005) *The Stories of English*. London, England.
Fischer, H. (2017) Under Arizona Bill, Contracts in Spanish Would Have Less Legal Force, *Tuscon.com*, 10 February. Available at www.tucson.com/business/tucson/under-arizona-bill-contracts-in-spanish-would-have-less-legal/article_dadac4f6-8d87-5a25-a2b1-77d1291c7fee.html.
Freeborn, D. (1992) *From Old English to Standard English*. Basingstoke: Macmillan.
Giglio, E. (2007) *Here's Looking at You: Hollywood, Film and Politics*. New York: Peter Lang.
Goldmacher, S. (2016) Trump's English-only Campaign, *Politico*, 23 September. Available at www.politico.com/story/2016/09/donald-trumps-english-only-campaign-228559.
Jonson, B. (1947 [1641]) 'Timber: Or, discoveries', in C. H. Herford and P. Simpson (eds), *The Works of Ben Jonson*, Vol. 8. Oxford: Clarendon Press.
Kachru, B. B. (1992) 'Teaching world Englishes', in B. B. Kachru (ed.), *The Other Tongue: English Across Cultures*. 2nd edn. Urbana and Chicago: University of Illinois Press, 355–365.
Kroskrity, P. (2000) 'Regimenting languages: language ideological perspectives', in P. Kroskrity (ed.), *Regimes of Language: Ideologies, Polities and Identities*. Santa Fe, NM: School of American Research Press, 1–34.
Le Guin, U. K. (2006) 'Foreword', in T. Conley and S. Cain (eds), *Encyclopedia of Fictional and Fantastic Languages*. Westport, CT: Greenwood Press, xvii–xx.
Lopez, M. H. and A. Gonzalez-Barrera, (2013) '*What is the future of Spanish in the United States?*' Rew Research Center. Available at www.pewresearch.org/fact-tank/2013/09/05/what-is-the-future-of-spanish-in-the-united-states/.
Lucas, G. (1977) *Star Wars*, original script. Available at www.scripts.com/script.php?id=87&p=24.
Milroy, J. and L. Milroy (1985) *Authority in Language: Investigating Standard English*. London: Routledge.
Moore, G. E. (1939) 'Proof of an external world', *Proceedings of the British Academy* 25 (5): 273–300.
Pennycook, A. (2010) 'English and globalization', in J. Maybin and J. Swann (eds), *The Routledge Companion to English Language Studies*. Abingdon: Routledge, 113–121.
Planas, R. (2017) Arizona's Mexican-American Studies Ban Goes to Trial, *HuffPost*, 27 June. Available at www.huffingtonpost.com/entry/arizona-mexican-american-studies_us_59510a8be4b0da2c731ce325.
Rieder, J. (2008) *Colonialism and the Emergence of Science Fiction*. Middletown, CT: Wesleyan University Press.
Scanlon, P. (1977) George Lucas: The Wizard of Star Wars. *Rolling Stone*, 25 August. Available at www.rollingstone.com/movies/news/the-wizard-of-star-wars-20120504.
Seargeant, P. (2010) 'The historical ontology of language', *Language Sciences* 32 (1): 1–13.
Seargeant, P. (2016) 'Language and art', in Z. Demjén and P. Seargeant (eds), *Creativity in Language: From Everyday Style to Verbal Art*. Milton Keynes: Open University, 277–328.
Searle, J. (1995) *The Construction of Social Reality*. New York: Penguin.
Sharman, J. (2017) Donald Trump's Administration Takes Down Spanish-Language White House Website, *The Independent*, 24 January. Available at www.independent.co.uk/news/world/americas/donald-trump-administration-takes-down-white-house-spanish-language-website-civil-rights-history-a7543121.html.
Silverstein, M. (1979) 'Language structure and linguistic ideology', in P. Clyne, W. Hanks and C. Hofbauer (eds), *The Elements of a Parasession on Linguistic Units and Levels*. Chicago: Chicago University Press, 193–247.
Silverstein, M. (1998) 'Contemporary transformations of local linguistic communities', *Annual Review of Anthropology* 27: 401–426.
Speech Events (2015) *The languages of Star Wars (Part 2): a sociolinguistic investigation*. Available at www.speechevents.wordpress.com/2016/01/24/the-languages-of-star-wars-part-2-human-languages-used-in-the-films/.
Stockwell, P. (2000) *The Poetics of Science Fiction*. London: Routledge.
Sutherland, J. (1999) Phantom Menace or Post-Modernist? *The Guardian*, 31 May. Available at www.theguardian.com/film/1999/may/31/features.starwars.

Swann, J. (2007) 'English voices', in D. Graddol, D. Leith, J. Swann, M. Rhys and J. Gillen (eds), *Changing English*. Abingdon: Routledge/Milton Keynes Open University, 5–38.

Terry, D. (1998) Arizona Court Strikes Down Law Requiring English Use, *New York Times*, 29 April. Available at www.nytimes.com/1998/04/29/us/arizona-court-strikes-down-law-requiring-english-use.html.

Toolan, M. (1997) 'Recentering English: New English and global', *English Today* 52: 3–10.

Washington Times (2006) 'Arizona makes English official', 8 November. Available at www.washingtontimes.com/news/2006/nov/8/20061108-115125-7910r/.

Webster, N. 1991 [1789]. 'An essay on the necessity, advantages and practicability of reforming the mode of spelling, and of rendering the orthography of words correspondent to the pronunciation', in T. Crowley (ed.), *Proper English? Readings in Language, History, and Cultural Identity*. London: Routledge, 81–93.

Wilce, J. (1999) 'Linguists in Hollywood', *Anthropology News* 40 (7): 9–10.

Woolard, K. (1998) 'Introduction: Language ideology as a field of inquiry', in B. Schieffelin, K. Woolard and P. Kroskrity (eds), *Language Ideologies*. Oxford: Oxford University Press, 3–47.

Zimmer, B. (2016) The Languages of 'Star Wars: The Force Awakens', *The Wall Street Journal*, 15 January. Available at www.wsj.com/articles/the-languages-of-star-wars-the-force-awakens-1452892741.

2

The historical study of English

Simon Horobin

Introduction

This chapter begins with a brief summary of what we know about the origins of the English language and then turns to how this history has been pieced together. The principal researchers and projects, the methods used and the debates that have arisen illustrate the development of historical linguistic approaches over the last 200 years. Recent cross-fertilisation from other branches of language study, including pragmatics, sociolinguistics and corpus studies, exemplify contemporary approaches to understanding the forces that have shaped and continue to shape English. From the early stages in the historical study of English, in which linguistic changes were identified and described, we witness a shift towards a methodology that attempts to explain *why* and *how* these changes occurred.

The history of English: origins

The origins of the English language can be traced back to the Germanic dialects brought to England by the Angles, Saxons and Jutes in the fifth century AD. The earliest written documents, dating from the sixth and seventh centuries, show many connections with other members of the Germanic language family, which are the origin of German, Dutch, Norwegian, Swedish, Icelandic and Danish. The Germanic language family forms part of the much larger Indo-European group, but is distinguished from other branches in several important ways. One major difference concerns a shift in the pronunciation of certain consonants, by which voiceless stops became voiceless fricatives, voiced stops became voiceless stops, and voiced aspirated stops became voiced stops (for further discussion see the account in McMahon 1994: 22–24; for a more detailed account and an attempt to explain the causes behind the change see Smith 2007: 75–87). The results of this change can be observed by comparing equivalent words, such as the following: Latin *pes*, *tres*, *collis*, *quod* and Old English *fot* 'foot', *þreo* 'three', *hyll* 'hill', *hwæt* 'what'.

Since this shift was first formulated by the German philologist and folklorist Jakob Grimm, it has come to be known as 'Grimm's law' (Grimm 1819). Although he was working on the German language, Grimm's findings had considerable importance for the historical study of the English language. Grimm was working within a continental philological tradition that could trace its roots back to a lecture delivered by Sir William Jones to the Asiatic Society of Bengal in 1786, in which he noted similarities between the Sanskrit, Latin and Greek languages, prompting him to propose that these languages had their origins in a common source. Although he observed that Gothic, Celtic and old Persian differed in important ways owing to subsequent influences, he noted that the origins of these languages could also be traced to this common ancestor:

> The Sanskrit language, whatever be its antiquity, is of a wonderful structure; more perfect than the Greek, more copious than the Latin, and more exquisitely refined than either, yet bearing to both of them a stronger affinity, both in the roots of verbs and in the forms of grammar, than could possibly have been produced by accident; so strong indeed, that no philologer could examine them all three, without believing them to have sprung from some common source, which, perhaps no longer exists.
>
> (Quoted in McMahon 1994: 4)

The Angles, Saxons and Jutes settled in different parts of the British Isles, leading to certain marked dialectal differences attested in the written records. There is evidence of four dialects of Old English: Northumbrian (in the North), Mercian (the Midlands), West Saxon (in the South-West) and Kentish (in Kent). Despite these differences, it is clear that these groups came to consider themselves part of a single country, speaking a single language known as *Englisc*.

Old English shows a number of developments that set it apart from the other members of the Germanic language family. Where other languages preserved the Proto-Germanic *ai* diphthong, Old English adopted the monophthong *a*; the results of this can be seen if we compare the Old English word *stan* with the Gothic (an East Germanic language) *stains*. Old English also shows the effects of a sound change known as i-mutation, in which back vowels were fronted when there was an *i* or *j* in the following syllable. This shift is the reason why the plural of the Old English noun *fot* 'foot' is *fet* 'feet'; a distinction preserved in Modern English. Like other Germanic languages, Old English made use of inflexional endings to carry grammatical information. However, compared to Proto-Germanic, Old English noun declensions show considerable simplification. There are fewer distinctive inflexional endings – the result of the weakening of unstressed syllables in speech. Old English resembled other Germanic languages in its reliance upon internal methods of word formation rather than on borrowing from other languages for the coining of new words. These methods include the addition of prefixes, such as the intensifying for- prefix, and suffixes, such as the -had suffix that created abstract nouns like *cildhad* 'childhood'. Another method, known as compounding, involved the joining of two distinct words, as in the compound *sciprap* (*scip* 'ship' + *rap* 'rope') 'cable'. However, the process of Christianisation of the Anglo-Saxons – which brought with it the Latin alphabet used for writing Old English – also resulted in the adoption of a number of Latin words, such as *munuc* 'monk' and *mynster* 'monastery'.

A history of the history of English

A key methodological development associated with the continental philologists who made these discoveries about the early history of the Germanic languages was the adoption of a comparative approach: by comparing forms recorded in the earliest surviving written remains, it became possible to reconstruct forms of the language that pre-date historical records. These methodological developments represented a major scientific advancement from the approaches to the historical study of English of the eighteenth century. Although Dr Samuel Johnson's *Dictionary of the English Language* (1755) included an essay on the history of the English language, it was little more than a collection of representative texts from different chronological periods. Johnson made little attempt to analyse the texts themselves, or to offer any overview of the linguistic developments to which they attest; the little discussion he did include focuses more on literary and stylistic qualities than linguistic features. A large proportion of the etymologies he included in the dictionary itself were taken from earlier authorities, or based upon his own intuitions – many of which turned out to be mistaken. His approach is well summarised by his conclusion:

> Thus have I deduced the *English* language from the age of *Alfred* to that of *Elizabeth*; in some parts imperfectly for want of materials; but I hope, at least, in such a manner that its progress may be easily traced, and the gradations observed, by which it advanced from its first rudeness to its present elegance.
>
> (Hitchings 2005: 88–93)

The study of philology and the comparative method were formally institutionalised in Britain with the foundation of the Philological Society in 1842. The most significant outcome of the establishment of this society was its role in the instigation of a project to produce a new dictionary of the English language on historical principles, adopting a method established by Jakob Grimm and his brother Wilhelm for their work on their historical dictionary of German, *Deutsches Wörterbuch* (Grimm and Grimm 1854–1961), begun in 1838. It was a lecture by Richard Chenevix Trench, presented to the Philological Society in November 1857, and entitled 'On some Deficiencies in our English Dictionaries' that sparked the beginning of the project. While drawing out some of the defects he found in earlier dictionaries of English, Trench also drew direct comparisons with the 'new German Dictionary' under preparation by the Grimm brothers, and its 'frequent and laborious discussion on synonymous words, with illustrative quotations separating them off and discerning them from one another' (Trench 1857: 47). This lecture inspired the establishment of a project to produce a new dictionary of English based upon historical principles; the resulting work was published in instalments or fascicles from 1884 to 1928 as the *New English Dictionary* (later *Oxford English Dictionary*).

Another important development in the historical study of English associated with the Victorian period was the decision to divide the English language into sub-periods; the divisions they instituted remain today in the traditional period boundaries observed by nearly all histories of English. Today these periods are known as: Old English (650–1100); Middle English (1100–1500); Early Modern English (1500–1800); and Late Modern English (1800-present day). However, in the earliest accounts of English, both the subdivisions and the names they were given vary in ways that reflect different attitudes towards the English language's ancestry. Lounsbury (1879) divided the early periods of the language into: Anglo-Saxon (450–1150); Early English (1150–1350); and Middle English (1350–1550). The term 'Anglo-Saxon' was used by Lounsbury to emphasise the extent to which the pre-Conquest period was perceived to mark the language's close connection with its ancestral Germanic cognates. The English language proper was considered to begin after the Conquest; the period from 1550 to the present day was termed Modern English. Lounsbury subdivided his Early English period further – postulating Semi-Saxon (1150–1250) and Old English (1250–1350) sub-periods. Emerson (1894) differed from Lounsbury in referring to the pre-Conquest language as Old English – a term that was deliberately intended to emphasise the continuity between pre- and post-Conquest usages, and that sought to foreground the native over the foreign components of the language. Although both Old English and Anglo-Saxon have survived into modern usage, it was the latter term that dominated the late nineteenth and early twentieth centuries, thanks to the huge popularity of two textbooks, *Anglo-Saxon Reader* (1876) and *Anglo-Saxon Primer* (Sweet 1882), edited by Henry Sweet; both of these works remain in print today in revised editions.

Research into the history of English continued to be influenced by German scholarship in the late nineteenth and early twentieth centuries. Henry Sweet, best known today as a phonetician – he is often identified as the model for Henry Higgins in George Bernard Shaw's play *Pygmalion* – began his career editing Old English texts. His connection with German philologists was a link with the Neogrammarian school, which was making important advances in the comparative method and the historical study of sound change. Another important link between the German Neogrammarian school and English philology was Joseph Wright (1855–1930). Although born into an impoverished weaving family in Yorkshire, Wright taught himself to read and studied foreign languages. He later went on to read mathematics at the University of Heidelberg, transferring to the study of comparative philology at Leipzig University. In 1901, the same year in which Sweet was appointed to a readership in Phonetics at Oxford University, Wright succeeded to the chair of Comparative Philology at Oxford.

Despite his grounding in Germanic scholarship, Wright focused his academic energies largely on the study of the English dialects; his *English Dialect Dictionary* (Wright 1898–1905) and *English Dialect Grammar* (Wright 1905) remain invaluable resources for the study of English dialects. Wright's Neogrammarian credentials meant that these works are organised on historical principles, drawing heavily upon the evidence of the earliest forms of the English, Scandinavian and French languages. This diachronic approach, also evident in Wright's *Old English Grammar* (Wright and Wright 1908), co-edited with his wife Elizabeth, differed from the synchronic approach found in other works, such as Sweet's *Anglo-Saxon Primer*, which discusses the Old English language without any reference to its earlier history. Although implicit from these differing methodologies, the distinction between synchronic and diachronic approaches was not made explicit until the work of Ferdinand de Saussure (1857–1913), whose lectures setting out this distinction were posthumously published – based on notes taken by students during his lectures – as *Cours de linguistique générale* (1916), published in English as *Course in General Linguistics* (see Harris 2013).

Sweet's influence can be seen in the later work of one of the twentieth century's most important practitioners of the historical study of English: Henry Cecil Wyld (1870–1945). Wyld read philology at Oxford, where he was taught by Sweet. On his graduation in 1899, Wyld was appointed lecturer and subsequently professor in English Language and Philology at University College, Liverpool; eventually he was elected to the Merton chair of English Language at Oxford. Wyld's most important book was *A History of Modern Colloquial English*, published in 1920; further editions appeared in 1921 and 1936 and continued to be reprinted into the 1950s. As the standard textbook, Wyld's work defined the historical study of English throughout much of the first half of the twentieth century.

But where Wright had set out to describe the English dialects, including – in his *Grammar of the Dialect of Windhill, in the West Riding of Yorkshire* (Wright 1892) – that of his native county, Wyld's account of the history of English focused exclusively on the development of the standard form of the language. Although he devoted considerable attention to his treatment of the dialects of the Middle English period, Wyld was dismissive of later dialects, frequently characterising regional forms as errors and corruptions. Although Wyld set out as a disinterested observer, for whom one variety of English was just as valuable as another – a key axiom of modern descriptive linguistics – this stance of scientific objectivity came under pressure when it came to describing the distinction between regional dialect and Standard English. Wyld began by refusing to recognise standards of usage: 'We approach the subject merely as students and observers of linguistic facts, which happen to be closely related to social phenomena. We neither blame nor praise; we are indifferent to what this or that authority may censure or approve.' Yet, despite this, Wyld proceeded to define Standard English in unambiguously approbatory terms: 'It may be called Good English, Well-bred English, Upper-class English.' Dialect use, by contrast, is characterised by grammatical and lexical 'mistakes', uttered by 'uncouth' speakers, and lacking the expressive subtlety of standard forms (Wyld 1920: 2–3). Rather than recognising that Standard English was simply one among the many dialects of English, albeit one that has been accorded an enhanced role as the variety employed for a range of prestigious functions, Wyld considered Standard English to be linguistically superior. Regional dialects that have not been granted such a role were judged to be inferior varieties. Rather than viewing dialect usages, such as 'I was sat' or 'them people', as alternatives to Standard English 'I was sitting' and 'those people', these were categorised as mistakes. Although couched as linguistic arguments, such judgements were based more on the association of Standard English with the elite classes than on the acceptability of such alternative constructions.

The historical approach characterised by Wyld's work continued to influence the work of later philologists, such as E.J. Dobson's *English Pronunciation 1500–1700* (Dobson 1957; 2nd edition 1968) and Alistair Campbell's *Old English Grammar* (Campbell 1959). Wyld's tendency to view the standard as the ideal form of the language was similarly influential; Dobson's (1955) article on the emergence of a standard form of spoken English is heavily indebted to the account and the associated assumptions set out by Wyld. Wyld's focus on spellings and sounds, at the expense of grammar, syntax and lexis, also guided the interests of later scholars. A tendency to focus on a single linguistic level characterises much of the early work on the history of English; Bradley (1904), for instance, takes a very different approach, choosing to exclude phonology and to focus mostly on the lexicon. Early attempts to write the history of English also struggled to find the appropriate distribution between extra-linguistic and intra-linguistic details; a happy balance was struck by Baugh (1935) and a subsequent co-edited volume with Cable (Baugh and Cable 1978–2012) now in a sixth edition, has served as one of the most important university textbooks, especially in American universities, throughout the last quarter of the twentieth century and into the twenty-first.

Baugh and Cable (1978–2012) adopted a chronological approach, starting with Indo-European and devoting chapters to each of the linguistic periods up to the present day, with a final chapter focusing on the English language in America. This format has been extremely durable and has been adopted by most single-volume histories. It is only recently that we have seen attempts to provide histories of English that take greater account of regional varieties, and of the English language used in the various parts of the globe where it is spoken. An important step in this direction was the single-volume account of the history of Englishes provided by Crystal (2004); a major reference work is now available in the multi-volume *Cambridge History of the English Language* (Hogg 1992–2001), with separate volumes covering English in North America and English in Britain and overseas – covering British varieties as well as English in Australia, the Caribbean, New Zealand, South Africa, and South Asia.

Contemporary approaches and debates

Having sketched out the origins of the study of the earlier history of English, this section introduces six of the most important approaches and methodologies that have characterised the modern period: socio-historical (also known as historical sociolinguistics), dialectology, corpora, historical lexicology, correspondence studies and pragma-philology. In each of these approaches we witness major advances in the transition from a methodology that traces historical changes to ones that enable researchers to better understand why such changes occurred, and to trace the process by which these changes were implemented and adopted by the wider community of English speakers. The introduction of the socio-historical approach was a major development in the historical study of English. Where Neogrammarians sought to emphasise the regularity of the sound changes they described (terming them *laws*: 'Lautgesetz'), insights derived from modern sociolinguistic methods focused on the gradual processes by which changes were disseminated, seeking to understand why they were adopted, and why, in certain cases, they were not. This new approach argued that socio-linguistic methods of studying contemporary linguistic change could be applied to the investigation of historical change – using the present to explain the past, as well as using the past to inform the present (Weinreich et al. 1968). This development also marks a decisive shift from the earlier Saussurean model that sought to make a strict distinction between the synchronic and diachronic methods. The socio-historical model further breaks with the past in its rejection of the earlier view that dismissed variation as random and inexplicable. Earlier scholars had sought only to chart and describe linguistic changes; they made no attempt to account for the differences they observed. By contrast, modern historical sociolinguists set out to explain why the language had changed, and why such changes had taken place at particular points in history. Where earlier scholars saw linguistic variation as random, modern historical sociolinguists, drawing upon the insights generated by sociolinguistic studies of contemporary usage, adopted the principle that linguistic variation is orderly and structured, according to a series of internal and external dimensions of language.

Sociolinguistic studies focusing on contemporary urban varieties, for instance, had discovered that variation patterned according to a number of factors, including the age, sex, education and social class of the speaker. Applying the Uniformitarian principle (for a discussion see Machan 2003, 2009), socio-historical linguists assume that those factors that condition language variation today will similarly apply in the past. Another important difference heralded by the socio-historical approach was the greater importance it placed on different linguistic varieties. Where previous approaches had focused their enquiries on the development of a standard form of the language, the socio-historical method gave greater prominence to the non-standard forms of English.

A good example of the possibilities opened up by such approaches is Smith's (1996) explanation of the causes of the Great Vowel Shift – the major change in the lexical distribution of the English long vowels that took place between 1400 and 1660 – by focusing on the interaction of key extra- and intra-linguistic factors. Drawing upon insights derived from social network theory, developed by the sociolinguists James and Lesley Milroy (see for instance Milroy 1992), Smith argues that the large number of immigrants who moved to London in the fifteenth and sixteenth centuries consciously emulated more prestigious modes of speech. These mobile speakers, who, in the terms employed by the Milroys, are 'weakly-tied' to their social and geographical origins, are likely to be early adopters of linguistic changes. In the case of the fifteenth- and sixteenth-century London immigrants, when confronted by the spoken systems of the more socially-elevated native Londoners, they responded by attempting to adopt these more prestigious spoken systems. A consequence of this is that the incomers were prone to hypercorrection – a term that describes the way that non-standard speakers over-generalise a linguistic rule that they perceive to be prestigious. Smith's account differed further from previous treatments of the Great Vowel Shift in its inclusion of regional variants of the shift. Where most previous studies tackled the problem purely from the perspective of its impact upon the standard language, Smith considered regional variants as separate phenomena. When considering the set of changes that Northern dialects underwent, Smith suggested that their cause and implementation may be due to different factors to those triggering the Southern shift. The Northern dialect situation is especially important for an understanding of the Southern shift since the diphthongisation of /u:/ did not take place in some of these accents. Smith's explanation of the distinct pattern taken by the Northern shift has implications for an understanding of the triggering of the Southern shift, demonstrating the importance of taking account of all the evidence, not just that pertaining to the standard variety.

But there are, of course, a number of limitations in the extent to which this kind of methodology can be applied to the historical study of English. For instance, where modern sociolinguists seek to map variation onto its social context, such contexts can be less confidently reconstructed for past periods in the history of English. Where modern sociolinguists seek to explain variation in terms of a speaker's age, sex, education, social class and so on, historical linguists have much less access to contextual information of this kind. Smith's explanation of the Great Vowel Shift, for instance, must deal in larger generalisations about age and class, and has little to say about distinctions between education and sex.

These are not the only problems that beset the socio-historical method. In their analysis of contemporary variation, modern sociolinguists focus their analysis upon the most naturally occurring linguistic forms – preferring spoken over written forms for their greater spontaneity, and preferring everyday informal speech, since that is likely to reveal language use in its most natural form. By contrast, the materials that form the basis of historical sociolinguistics are restricted to written forms of the language, much of which represents carefully crafted linguistic domains – literary writings, historical documents and official records, rather than the spontaneous and unstudied usage favoured by modern sociolinguists. Where sociolinguists can select their informants in sociologically- and statistically-informed ways, socio-historical linguists are restricted to the corpus as it survives – the result of the workings of chance and the hazards of history, rather than a process of principled selection. To some extent, the response to this situation has been to make the best of 'bad data' (Labov 1972), although in other cases certain adjustments in methodology – such as the introduction of corpus approaches (discussed below) – have enabled more structured analysis of historical data.

Another way in which the application of modern linguistic methods has revolutionised the historical study of English is in the field of dialectology. As we saw above, the historical study of English had previously focused heavily on the evolution of the standard language, ignoring the rich evidence for the history of English dialects. This evidence is particularly plentiful in the Middle English period, since there was no standard variety of the written language. For this reason, changes in the methods of historical dialectology in the light of modern approaches are best illustrated by a consideration of the work of the Middle English Dialect Project. This project was instigated by M.L. Samuels and A.I. McIntosh of the universities of Glasgow and Edinburgh respectively, in the 1950s. Drawing on methodological insights from the linguistic survey of the Modern Scots dialects, they set out to produce an atlas of the dialects represented by the Middle English written record. Despite being restricted to exclusively written materials, the Middle English Dialect project proceeded on the assumption that written variation could be subject to dialect mapping in precisely the same manner as had been achieved with spoken differences in the Modern Scots dialect survey. In seeking to apply modern dialectological techniques to the Middle English dialects, the project encountered a number of challenges. An obvious limitation imposed by the sources concerned the lack of access to the spoken language: a problem that affects all historical studies that predate the invention of audio recording technology. As well as lacking direct access to the spoken language, the Middle English dialect survey was limited by the lack of localised documents – most Middle English manuscripts were written by anonymous scribes and do not preserve important information about the date or location of their copying. The survey overcame this limitation by developing the 'fit-technique'; manuscripts were 'fitted' on the dialect map by comparing their linguistic forms with those recorded in manuscripts where the location of copying was known ('localised' or 'anchor' texts) (Benskin 1991). The result of this was the localisation of around 1,000 manuscripts copied in the period between 1350 and 1450, accompanied by extensive linguistic profiles of representative data and schematic maps indicating the distribution of representative linguistic items (McIntosh et al. 1986).

This project resulted in the publication of the four-volume *A Linguistic Atlas of Late Mediaeval English* (1986) [*LALME*]. The data assembled by *LALME*, although based mostly on written variables such as orthographic variants (e.g. the difference between *shal*, *schal*, *sal* and *xal*), has been used to attempt to recover changes in the spoken language. For example, James Milroy has shown how the survey's findings can be used to reconstruct the history of h-dropping – that is, the deletion of initial /h/ before vowels. By tracing the spellings of words where initial <h> has been omitted, as well as those instances where an unhistorical <h> has been added, Milroy is able to trace the beginnings of this change to the East Anglian dialects of the fifteenth century, where it may have functioned as a marker of prestigious speech (Milroy 1983). While the later account of the stigmatisation of h-dropping in the extensive literature of prescriptivism produced in the eighteenth century has been extensively scrutinised (Mugglestone 2003), its earlier origins and subsequent developments were much less well-known.

The publication of *LALME* represented a major breakthrough in historical dialectology; before its publication the study of Middle English dialects had relied upon the handful of manuscripts that contained internal localisations – that is, explicit statements in the manuscript as to where it was copied. The localisations offered by *LALME* enabled scholars to draw upon a vastly increased pool of regional data in order to construct a much more nuanced account of the Middle English dialects. It laid the foundation for significant advances in a range of related areas. One example is the field of Middle English Word geography. Prior to the publication of *LALME*, little was known about the regional distribution of Middle English lexis beyond early attempts to distinguish between words found predominantly in the North and those more commonly found in the South.

LALME covered the period 1350–1500 and focused on the dialects of England; its publication in 1986 marked the inauguration of two daughter projects, the *Linguistic Atlas of Early Middle English* [*LAEME*] (edited by Margaret Laing) and the *Linguistic Atlas of Older Scots* [*LAOS*] (Williamson 2008), which were designed to extend the *LALME* approach to the early Middle English and Older Scots varieties. Both the daughter projects faced similar problems to those faced by the *LALME* project in dealing with written materials, the majority of which were similarly unlocalised. For the early Middle English atlas these problems were exacerbated by the fact that many of the legal documents that had formed the bulk of the localised documents used for *LALME* were written in French or Latin during this period. Another limitation was the relative paucity of material written in English during this period, combined with the tendency for surviving texts to cluster in particular dialect areas (such as the south-west Midlands), leaving large swathes of the country unrepresented (Laing 2000). The lack of data was, however, in some ways an advantage, since it meant that it became possible to analyse the entirety of the textual record in a way that would have been impossible for the *LALME* project, which instead relied upon sampling. The complete textual coverage was further aided by advances in computer technology; where the *LALME* survey was carried out by noting down relevant forms using paper questionnaires, *LAEME* was able to dispense with the questionnaire method entirely by transcribing the complete text into electronic form. A major advantage of this approach was that it no longer required researchers to prejudge which forms were likely to be important for localisation; electronic publication of the complete corpus of texts – with lexico-grammatical tagging – means that it is now possible for researchers to carry out their own analysis of the early Middle English materials in a way that was not possible with *LALME* (Laing 2013). A subsequent project has made the *LALME* materials available online, albeit with more limited functionality than for *LAEME* and without the complete corpus of texts (Benskin et al. 2013).

Another related project, based at the universities of Glasgow and Stavanger, is drawing upon the *LALME* localisations in order to assemble a corpus of later Middle English dialect texts. The Middle English Scribal Texts project set out in 1998 to produce a reference grammar of Middle English based upon the materials assembled by *LALME*. However, it has subsequently modified both its methods and its aims; its objective is now to analyse texts according to their 'textual communities', drawing upon a greater range of defining criteria – genre, text type, domain – as well as geography, to explain a text's linguistic forms. The Middle English Scribal Texts programme [*MEST*], therefore, draws upon recent developments in sociolinguistics, literacy studies and pragmatics, as well as historical dialectology.

The Early Middle English Atlas and Scribal Texts Project exemplify a further important development in the historical study of English in the past twenty-five years: the use of an electronic corpus. Where previous studies had to rely upon the manual analysis of sources, historical corpus studies were able to draw upon large quantities of data. A leading centre for studies of this kind is the Research Unit for the Study of Variation, Contacts and Change in English, based at the University of Helsinki. The Helsinki research unit has pioneered the production of corpora whose constituent texts have been carefully selected in order to represent particular linguistic varieties. The earliest corpus to be produced in this way is the Helsinki Corpus of English Texts: Diachronic and Dialectal, a multi-genre corpus which included samples of texts across the Old, Middle and Early Modern English periods, first issued in 1991. As with the *LAEME* and *MEST* projects, the Helsinki corpus enables searching across dialects, but unlike these synchronic corpora, it also allows researchers to carry out longitudinal surveys. Since it was based upon edited texts rather than original manuscripts, however, the Helsinki corpus is less useful for studying features such as spelling, punctuation and morphology, since these are aspects of a text that may be normalised or modernised by modern editors. However, given that it includes more than one and a half million words, the Helsinki corpus is a useful means of gleaning general information about occurrences of forms, structures and lexemes across the history of English, which may then be supplemented with recourse to other more specialised corpora.

Electronic corpora have transformed our ability to correlate linguistic variation with a range of conditioning factors – such as geography, register, gender, age, social network and so on. Studies of this kind may be carried out using specialised corpora based upon Old English, Middle English and Older Scots; more recent corpora have focused on particular genres and text types: the Corpus of Early English Correspondence and the Corpus of Early English Medical Writing, both parts of the Helsinki corpus.

Other developments in historical English corpora have been associated with developments in historical lexicography. In the 1950s work began on the production of a dictionary of Middle English: a synchronic account of Middle English vocabulary that would draw upon the methods and publication of the *Oxford English Dictionary [OED]*, but which would offer a much more detailed account of the lexis of the period from 1100–1500. The *Middle English Dictionary [MED]* (Kurath et al. 1952–2001) began life as a Chaucer dictionary, but was subsequently extended to encompass the entirety of the Middle English corpus (for an account of the history of the *MED* see Blake 2002). The completed dictionary comprises some 15,000 pages of detailed lexical information, published in 115 print fascicles, based upon the analysis of more than three million citation slips.

The *MED* was completed in 2001; at the same time, an electronic version was mounted on the World Wide Web, accompanied by a suite of resources and known by the collective term *Middle English Compendium* (for an account of the production of this resource see McSparran 2002). The electronic version of the dictionary differs from its paper equivalent in a number of important ways, enabling searching of the *MED* entries not just by headword, but also by etymology, definition, cited work or author and so on. In addition to the electronic version of the dictionary, the *Middle English Compendium* includes a hyperbibliography: a comprehensive listing of bibliographical references relating to all of the sources cited in the dictionary.

A further feature incorporated within the *Middle English Compendium* is the Corpus of Middle English Prose and Verse. This corpus differs from that compiled for the related project to produce a *Dictionary of Old English* (*DOE*) in that it is a post-hoc assembly of relevant materials, rather than a resource assembled specifically for the purpose of producing the dictionary like that assembled for *DOE*. It also differs from other Middle English corpora discussed so far in its lack of explicit design. Rather than being constructed upon a set of explicit principles intended to represent a particular group of text types, dialects or genres, the Corpus of Middle English Prose and Verse is an assembly of almost 150 texts that are represented within the pages of the dictionary. Since many of the major Middle English authors and texts are represented, this corpus is most useful for carrying out linguistic analysis of major works, such as Layamon's *Brut* – both of the surviving manuscripts of this work are included in the corpus – or of canonical writers such as Chaucer, Langland and Gower. Since the texts are mostly based upon out-of-print editions, such as editions produced in the nineteenth and early twentieth centuries, there is often a degree of editorial intervention that makes them unreliable for analysis of spelling, morphology and punctuation.

The modern period has also witnessed major developments in the content and accessibility of the *OED*. Following the publication of the final fascicle of the dictionary, quotations began to be collected for an updated supplement of the work – including new instances of words included, as well as words that were omitted from the original edition. This process resulted in the publication of a Supplementary volume in 1933; alongside this, the complete dictionary was reissued in twelve volumes with the modern title *The Oxford English Dictionary*. A subsequent programme to keep the dictionary up to date was established in 1957, with the appointment of R.W. Burchfield as its editor. This project aimed to ensure better coverage of twentieth-century usage, and to spread the dictionary's net wider to include words associated with global varieties of English: US, Australian, South African and South Asian Englishes. The final version of this additional supplement was issued in four volumes published between 1972 and 1986. A further revision of this version of the dictionary appeared in 1989, under the editorship of J.A. Simpson and E. Weiner. As well as integrating the supplements into the main dictionary, the 1989 edition added some 5000 new words and numerous additional senses to existing words. But perhaps the most significant change to come with this edition was the transfer of the complete dictionary to electronic form, making it searchable in whole new ways, and laying the foundation for the dictionary's next incarnation.

The appearance of the *OED* in electronic form marked the beginning of a new lease of life for the historical study of English vocabulary, as well as for analysis of the dictionary itself. The CD-ROM format was subsequently replaced by release of the dictionary over the World Wide Web, a move that was accompanied by the instigation of a new phase in the dictionary's life: a complete revision of the entire dictionary. As well as making available the fruits of its extensive researches into the history and documentation of English words, the online dictionary enables researchers to carry out research upon the dictionary itself. Recent work by scholars such as Mugglestone (2012) and Brewer (2012) has drawn upon the search facilities of the online version to assess the dictionary's representation of particular periods or specific authors.

In the examples discussed above, we have seen how electronic databases have enabled researchers to interrogate linguistic data according to a wider variety of social parameters. Central to the socio-historical approach has been the study of texts that represent more spontaneous forms of writing. An important body of evidence for such studies are collections of correspondence, since letters are generally written more spontaneously than other types of text, such as literary, historical or scientific writing. Furthermore, where manuscripts were copied by scribes whose names and biographies are mostly unknown, personal letters are usually signed by their authors. An important exception to this are letters authored by women, which were often written by amanuenses (especially in the Middle English period). But even in cases such as these, scholars have found ways to distinguish between the contributions of author and scribe, enabling discussion of grammatical constructions and lexical choices (Davis 1972). Important attempts to apply the insights of social network theory to historical collections of correspondence can be found in Nevalainen and Raumolin-Brunberg (2000) and Bergs (2005). Studies of correspondence collections have been central in applying sociolinguistic factors such as age, gender and occupation to the analysis of linguistic variation. As well as letters, historical sociolinguists have turned to other kinds of informal texts – plays and court depositions – for evidence of written texts that more closely resemble the spoken language.

Texts like these have been central to the emergence of the field of historical pragmatics – another approach in which insights from modern linguistics are applied to texts written in earlier periods. Early interventions in this field were focused on the application of speech act and politeness theories to historical texts; classic instances include applications of Brown and Levinson (1987) to Shakespearean play texts (Brown and Gilman 1989). This approach has been important for analysing the changing uses of the second person pronouns in the Middle and Early Modern English periods. Where Middle English inherited a system in which the distinction between *thou* and *ye* was based purely on number (singular or plural), contact with French introduced a pragmatic contrast similar to the T/V distinctions found in modern languages like French. But in the early modern period this distinction began to break down, so that *you* became the default or unmarked pronoun, while *thou* became marked – used to indicate intimacy or contempt. Eventually this distinction was also lost, so that by the eighteenth century *thou* was preserved only in certain dialects and in deliberately archaic usage, such as religious language or poetry. The process by which these changes occurred has been tracked by drawing upon the pronoun usage employed in literary texts (Burnley 1983; Calvo 1992), as well as in more authentic usage, such as court depositions (Hope 1993).

The development of this field led to the establishment of a *Journal of Historical Pragmatics* in 2000; its inaugural issue included articles on the application of speech act theory to early modern spells, and a typology of 'first moves' in courtly amorous interactions (Jucker and Taavitsainen 2000). Attempts to bring historical pragmatics into dialogue with more traditional philological approaches has led to the introduction of a new field of study, termed pragma-philology. As this field develops scholars are seeking to integrate developments in pragmatics with research into the material text – considering how the visual layout of a text might influence the way its linguistic codes are interpreted. An example of this approach is found in Moore's (2011) study of the pragmatic and discourse strategies used to demarcate speech in pre-modern English – before the introduction of speech marks. In the field of book history, Wakelin's (2014) study of scribal corrections has drawn attention to the importance placed upon the visual appearance of the manuscript page in the Middle Ages, and the ways in which aesthetic factors may have influenced linguistic forms. This developing field, then, seeks to bring together these overlapping interests of book historians and historical pragmaticians in order to develop tools for analysing what has been termed 'pragmatics on the page' (Carroll et al. 2013).

With this latest development the historical study of English has returned to its roots in the philological analysis of texts and their material contexts. However, the methods with which these texts are being analysed have been revolutionised by developments in modern linguistic theory, and transformed by developments in digital technology. We have seen how, from its beginnings in the comparative approach, the historical study of English began with the study of texts, from which individual words were extracted in order to account for their phonological developments over time. But little attempt was made to study the contexts of such forms – the texts and manuscripts within which they survived – nor was there any effort to explain the processes by which phonological changes took place. The historical study of English today has returned to the texts and contexts armed with methodological insights drawn from modern linguistics, in order to ask questions about the mechanisms by which variants arose, and why certain variants were adopted by the wider speech community.

Further reading

Aitchison, J. (2013) *Language Change: Progress or Decay?* 4th edn. Cambridge: Cambridge University Press. A general discussion about how and why languages change, drawing on examples from a wide range of languages.

Horobin, S. (2016) *How English Became English: A Short History of a Global Language.* Oxford: Oxford University Press. A short history of English which also engages with questions of correctness, authority and standardisation.

Millar, R. M. (2012) *English Historical Linguistics.* Edinburgh: Edinburgh. A history of English informed by socio-historical insights.

Smith, J. (1996) An *Historical Study of English: Function, Form and Change.* London: Routledge. A methodological survey that discusses a selection of changes in writing system, pronunciation, grammar and lexis.

Related topics

- The grammars of English
- The phonology of English
- Standards in English
- Contact Englishes.

References

Baugh, A. C. (1935, 1957) *A History of the English Language.* New York: Appleton-Century-Crofts.

Baugh, A. C. and T. Cable (1978–2012) *A History of the English Language.* 6th edn. London: Routledge.

Benskin, M. (1991) 'The "fit" – technique explained', in F. Riddy (ed.), *Regionalism in Late Medieval English Manuscripts and Texts*. Cambridge: Brewer, 9–26.

Benskin, M., M. Laing, V. Karaiskos and K. Williamson (eds) (2013), *An Electronic Version of a Linguistic Atlas of Late Mediaeval English*. Edinburgh: The University of Edinburgh. Available at www.lel.ed.ac.uk/ihd/elalme/elalme.html.

Bergs, A. (2005) *Social Networks and Historical Sociolinguistics: Studies in Morphosyntactic Variation in the Paston Letters (1421–1503)*. Berlin: Mouton De Gruyter.

Blake, N. F. (2002) 'On the completion of the Middle English Dictionary', *Dictionaries: The Journal of the Dictionary Society of North America* 23: 48–75.

Bradley, H. (1904, repr. 1967) *The Making of English*. New York: Walker.

Brewer, C. (2012) 'Happy copiousness? *OED*'s recording of female authors of the eighteenth century', *Review of English Studies* 63: 86–117.

Brown, R. and A. Gilman (1989) 'Politeness theory and Shakespeare's four major tragedies', *Language in Society* 18: 159–212.

Brown, P. and S. C. Levinson (1987) *Politeness: Some Universals in Language Usage*. Cambridge: Cambridge University Press.

Burnley, J. D. (1983) *A Guide to Chaucer's Language*. Basingstoke: Macmillan.

Calvo, C. (1992) 'Pronouns of address and social negotiation in *As You Like It*', *Language and Literature* 1: 5–27.

Campbell, A. (1959) *Old English Grammar*. Oxford: Clarendon Press.

Carroll, R., M. Peikola, H. Salmi, M.-L. Varila, J. Skaffari and R. Hiltunenm (2013) 'Pragmatics on the page: Visual text in late medieval English books', *European Journal of English Studies* 17: 54–71.

Crystal, D. (2004) *The Stories of English*. London: Allen Lane.

Davis, N. (1972) 'Margaret Paston's use of "do"', *Neuphilologische Mitteilungen* 73: 55–62.

Dobson, E. J. (1955) 'Early modern Standard English', *Transactions of the Philological Society* 54: 25–54.

Dobson, E. J. (1957; 2nd edition 1968) *English Pronunciation, 1500–1700*. Oxford: Clarendon Press.

Emerson, O. F. (1894) *The History of the English Language*. London: Macmillan.

Grimm, J. (1819) *Deutsche Grammatik*. 4 vols. Göttingen: Dieterichsche.

Grimm, J. and W. Grimm (1854–1961) *Deutsches Wörterbuch*. Vol. 32. Leipzig: S. Hirzel Verlag.

Harris, R. (ed. and trans.) (2013) *Ferdinand de Saussure: Course in General Linguistics*. London: Bloomsbury Academic.

Hitchings, H. (2005) *Dr Johnson's Dictionary: The Extraordinary Story of the Book that Defined the World*. London: John Murray.

Hogg, R. (ed.) (1992–2001) *Cambridge History of the English Language*. Vol. 6. Cambridge: Cambridge University Press.

Hope, J. (1993) 'Second person singular pronouns in records of early modern "Spoken" English', *Neuphilologische Mitteilungen* 94: 83–100.

Jucker, A. and I. Taavitsainenen (eds) (2000), *Journal of Historical Pragmatics* 1.

Kurath, H., S. M. Kuhn and R. E. Lewis (eds) (1952–2001) *Middle English Dictionary*. Ann Arbor: University of Michigan.

Labov, W. (1972) *Sociolinguistic Patterns*. Philadelphia: University of Pennsylvania Press.

Laing, M. (2000) '"Never the twain shall meet" early Middle English – the east west divide', in I. Taavitsainen et al. (eds), *Placing Middle English in Context. Topics in English Linguistics*. Vol. 35. Berlin: Mouton de Gruyter, 97–124.

Laing, M. (2013) *A Linguistic Atlas of Early Middle English, 1150–1325, Version 3.2*. Edinburgh: The University of Edinburgh. Available at www.lel.ed.ac.uk/ihd/laeme2/laeme2.html.

Lounsbury, T. R. (1879) *A History of the English Language*. New York: Holt.

Machan, T. W. (2003) *English in the Middle Ages*. Oxford: Oxford University Press.

Machan, T. W. (2009) *Language Anxiety: Conflict and Change in the History of English*. Oxford: Oxford University Press.

McIntosh, A. I., M. L. Samuels and M. Benskin (eds) (1986), *A Linguistic Atlas of Late Mediaeval English*. 4 vols. Aberdeen: Aberdeen University Press.

McMahon, A. (1994) *Understanding Language Change*. Cambridge: Cambridge University Press.

McSparran, F. (2002) 'The Middle English Compendium: past, present, future', *Dictionaries: The Journal of the Dictionary Society of North America* 23: 126–141.

Milroy, J. (1983) 'On the sociolinguistic history of /h/-dropping in English', in M. Davenport, E. Hansen and H. F. Nielsen (eds), *Current Topics in English Historical Linguistics*. Odense: Odense University Press, 37–51.

Milroy, J. (1992) *Language Variation and Change*. Oxford: Blackwell.

Moore, C. (2011) *Quoting Speech in Early English*. Cambridge: Cambridge University Press.

Mugglestone, L. (1995; 2nd edition 2003) *Talking Proper: The Rise of Accent as Social Symbol*. Oxford: Oxford University Press.

Mugglestone, L. (2012) 'Patriotism, empire, and cultural prescriptivism: Images of anglicity in the *OED*', in C. Percy and M. C. Davidson (eds), *The Languages of Nation. Attitudes and Norms*. Bristol and Buffalo: Multilingual Matters, 175–191.

Nevalainen, T. and H. Raumolin-Brunberg (2000) *Historical Sociolinguistics: Language Change in Tudor and Stuart England*. London: Longman.

Smith, J. J. (1996) *An Historical Study of English: Function, Form and Change*. London: Routledge.

Smith, J. J. (2007) *Sound Change and the History of English*. Oxford: Oxford University Press.

Sweet, H. (1876) *Anglo-Saxon Reader*. Oxford: Clarendon Press.

Sweet, H. (1882) *Anglo-Saxon Primer*. Oxford: Clarendon Press.

Trench, R. C. (1857) *On Some Deficiencies in Our English Dictionaries*. London: John W. Parker and Son.

Wakelin, D. (2014) *Scribal Correction and Literary Craft: English Manuscripts 1375–1510*. Cambridge: Cambridge University Press.

Weinreich, U., W. Labov and M. Herzog (1968) *Empirical Foundations for a Theory of Language Change*. Austin: University of Texas Press.

Williamson, K. (2008) *A Linguistic Atlas of Older Scots, Phase 1: 1380–1500*. Edinburgh: The University of Edinburgh. Available at www.lel.ed.ac.uk/ihd/laos1/laos1.html.

Wright, J. (1892) *A Grammar of the Dialect of Windhill, in the West Riding of Yorkshire*. London: English Dialect Society.

Wright, J. (1898–1905) *The English Dialect Dictionary*. 6 vols. Oxford: Henry Frowde.

Wright, J. (1905) *The English Dialect Grammar*. Oxford: Henry Frowde.

Wright, J. and E. Wright (1908) *Old English Grammar*. Oxford: Henry Frowde.

Wyld, H. C. (1920) *A History of Modern Colloquial English*. London: Murray.

Websites

Middle English Scribal Texts Programme
www.uis.no/research/history-languages-and-literature/the-mest-programme/the-middle-english-scribal-texts-programme/

Helsinki corpora
www.helsinki.fi/varieng/CoRD/corpora/

Middle English Compendium: Corpus of Middle English Prose and Verse:
https://quod.lib.umich.edu/c/cme/

3

English and colonialism

Edgar W. Schneider

Introduction

Between the sixteenth and twentieth centuries European powers established colonies, exerting political power and control over foreign territories, driven by economic or other motives and often accompanied by large-scale settlement movements. Colonialism has shaped the modern world in significant and irreversible ways, having produced young, often ethnically heterogeneous nations in Africa, Asia and the Americas after decolonization. Its traces are political and economic but also cultural and, not least, linguistic. European languages have been diffused, relocated and transformed in contact situations around the globe. British colonial expansion has disseminated English to all continents, and has paved the way for its current status as the world's leading language and, ultimately, for a new conceptualization of what 'English' means: modern English cannot be viewed any longer as a single monolithic 'Standard English' but is commonly understood as a set of more or less interrelated national or regional varieties. Consequently, the notion of 'Englishes' in the plural has come to be established and accepted.

This chapter describes British colonialism, as well as the contexts of its European background, and surveys the substantial consequences it has had, both sociopolitically and structurally, for the English language and our conception of it. Clearly, this is of utmost importance for English Language Studies as a whole, since, as was just stated, the plurality of varieties of English constitutes an essential component of today's reality and needs to replace overly simple concepts of a single, uniform type of English. This issue will be touched upon again later.

Following the Introduction, the second section focuses upon colonization as a historical process, including the fact that European colonial powers practiced different strategies of imposing their own cultures and languages in their respective colonies, and the main types of colonization and their typical ecologies. In the British Empire, English was established as the language of power in all colonies, and as such it began to be adopted by indigenous populations in their respective countries. It is a controversial issue, however, whether or to what extent the British colonizers intended to pass their language on to indigenous populations, especially in 'exploitation colonies' (see below). Contrary to claims attributing to English the role of 'killer language' (cf. Skutnabb-Kangas 2000), originally the 'indirect rule' policy practiced in the Empire (and described by Lord Lugard, who early in the twentieth century was Governor of Hong Kong and then Nigeria and published a notable doctrine, which he called the 'dual mandate', in 1922) gave access to English mainly to indigenous elites. Due to its economic and political value, however, the language increasingly got disseminated and diffused down the social scale as well, a process which was, perhaps surprisingly, even accelerated during and after the period of decolonization in the mid-twentieth century.

An essential determinant of the changes which have affected English in colonial transmission is language contact. Wherever English was transported, there were indigenous peoples who spoke local languages, so speakers of both languages interacted with each other, as did their respective linguistic systems. Contact thus produced new varieties, marked strongly by local lexical borrowings as well as phonological and grammatical transfer phenomena. The third section is devoted to these processes and their characteristic linguistic outcomes. In line with a cline of transfer effects which is familiar in contact linguistics, three major types, characterized by increasingly intense contact-induced restructuring, are described: settler dialects as products of light interlingual contact and new dialect formation; so-called 'New Englishes', typically strong second languages with strong internal functions in former colonies; and English-based pidgins and creoles, products of heavy contact and restructuring. Interestingly, despite all the major differences between locations and historical settings, constant social similarities between colonizers and the colonized and the predictable patterns of their changing social relationships have led to linguistically similar developmental processes and results, which the 'Dynamic Model' of the emergence of Postcolonial Englishes (Schneider 2007) seeks to account for.

Not surprisingly, the analysis of all these processes has generated controversies, and the fourth section presents some of the key issues under discussion: both linguistic (such as to how to best account for the new types of varieties ultimately produced by colonialism) and sociopolitical (considering consequences of these processes for language attitudes, language policies, or teaching strategies).

The final section looks to the future, showing that processes initiated and shaped in colonial times did not terminate but have continued evolving to the present day. Globalization has replaced colonization as the driving force, and some media and contexts of transmission have been transformed, but the basic process of English expanding into new spheres and contexts has continued and gained strong momentum.

The historical basis: European and British colonialism

Some earlier precursors (like the Vikings) notwithstanding, European colonialism started in the late Middle Ages, with Portuguese and Spanish explorers navigating around Africa or crossing the Atlantic in search of a sea route to the Far East. Colonial activity seemed promising and profitable to European powers, and their deeply-rooted and unquestioned sense of moral (and partly religious) superiority dismissed any considerations of inflicting harm on indigenous populations, so all the major nations soon partook in the race for wealth through expansion and conquest. The Portuguese and the Spanish, who established the first Empire 'on which the sun never sets', paved the way, followed by the Dutch, the French, the British and others, like the Germans and Belgians. Interestingly enough, the main European powers practiced rather different colonization styles, and left permanent traces, both cultural and linguistic, to varying extents (cf. Belich 2009: 27–40). The Dutch and Portuguese each sent more than one million people overseas, though most were not permanent settlers but male sojourners, intending to return. The Spanish, mainly in their Mexican and South American colonies, were mostly interested in the exploitation of silver, gold and wealth and the dissemination of the Catholic faith to pagan peoples, and pursued both goals by brute force. French colonization was shaped by the same centralization directed around Paris and the Court that characterized France itself, and consequently led to gallicized colonies extensively, rooting the French language, culture and institutions to a remarkably high extent there (a policy which in the long run extends to today's 'Départements et régions d'outre-mer' of the Caribbean and Indian Ocean, which are legally fully integrated into France). British colonization, presumably continuing the important role of class distinctions characteristic of the motherland, implicitly perceived indigenous populations, and Africans in particular, as inferior (BBC World Service 2001–2002). The British Empire practiced a policy which Lord Lugard later labelled 'indirect rule', admitting local rulers and their offspring to English educational institutions and inviting them to exert and share power in the interest of the colonizers (Louis 2007: 21–22). This had important consequences for the dissemination of languages as well: while French was deliberately taught and disseminated, access to English was granted only to an elite stratum of prospective co-administrators and withheld from the masses (Brutt-Griffler 2002: 39–57, 86–105).

In fact, the British were latecomers in the colonial race, but they turned out to be considerably more successful than all others, a fact which clearly is one of the main reasons, together with America's economic dominance, for today's globally leading role of English (Belich 2009: 27). Cabot's voyages of the late fifteenth century constituted a prelude (Winks 2007: 50), but the British displayed a 'relative tardiness ... in making the switch from exploration to exploitation' (Canny 2001: 3). Serious expansionist activity started no earlier than 1600. A 'First Empire', consisting of the large-scale North American settlement colonies and commercially driven activities and possessions in the Caribbean, gave way to a 'Second Empire' in Asia, Australasia and Africa after 1783, and the ultimate loss of the North American colonies (Winks 2007: 43–72).

In its early phase, British imperialism was largely driven by economic impulses and commercial interests (Cain and Hopkins 2001: 34, 61), and its agents were entrepreneurial private trading companies like the East India Company, which received its Royal Charter on the last day of 1600. However, the level of state involvement was remarkably low until at least the late seventeenth century (Canny 2001: xi–xii). This situation remained effective for almost two centuries, during which time the Empire was 'not a structure of global hegemony' but rather a 'far-flung conglomerate' of colonies, protectorates, condominia, mandates, treaty-ports, etc. (Darwin 2009: 1). It was comparatively late, around the 1840s, that the state and Crown took over colonial authority. Consequently historians have argued that the British impact on many African and Asian colonies remained rather superficial, since the actual periods of full colonial dominance were comparatively short:

> in much of Asia and Africa substantive European empire arrived very late and did not last very long. The British did not comprehensively dominate India until the suppression of the 'Mutiny' in 1859, and they were gone 90 years later. ... For many Asians and Africans, real European empire lasted about 50 years.
>
> (Belich 2009: 22–23)

This plainly political assessment overstates the case; it is counterbalanced by the much longer period of cultural influence and contact, but clearly there is a need to carefully weigh the intensity of British impact in any given context.

Large-scale settler movements, beginning in the seventeenth century and with another strong wave mainly throughout the nineteenth century, relocated English as the main first language to as many as three continents (North America and the Caribbean, Australasia and small parts of Africa). A 'large surplus of manpower (the product of birth-rate and prevailing social conditions) fuelled Britain's "demographic imperialism", the human capacity to stock the settlement colonies and maintain their British complexion' (Darwin 2009: 9). Belich (2009), in a very thorough historical study, actually talks of a 'Settler Explosion', caused by a multitude of factors including the growth of mercantile capitalism, the impact of Protestantism enhancing literacy, improved maritime technology and transportation networks, a desire for new consumer goods such as tea and sugar, population growth (and a decline of mortality rates), the role of financial institutions such as banking and insurance, and the consequences of the scientific and industrial revolutions (cf. 10–11, 51–52, 107).

Degrees of infiltration and intensity varied, but ultimately British colonial impact and the British Empire effectively spanned the globe, as can be seen in Figure 3.1, which shows the regions which were affected by it at one time or another.

Early in the twentieth century, various processes began to trigger a desire for independence in many colonies, and a process of decolonization set in with India's release into independence in 1947. Military defeats during World War Two such as the fall of Singapore and the conquest of Burma in 1942 essentially caused what amounted to almost a collapse of an imperial system which was possibly overstretched, and which never fully recovered: 'The post-war empire was a pale shadow of its former self' (Darwin 2009: 476). There are competing interpretations as to why Britain gave in to demands for independence so quickly and ceded authority to young independent states. One explanation sees this as an altruistic move, viewing the voluntary and peaceful transition as a recognition of the competence of local institutions to manage their own affairs. Another is critical, and perhaps more realistic, regarding old-style colonialism as superfluous in times of big business growth: 'Empire had become an irrelevant burden, an obstacle to the rational allocation of Britain's resources' (Darwin 2007: 547). However, this did not entail a complete release. To the contrary, post-war British governments (first Labour and then Conservative) pursued a relatively liberal and pragmatic policy which recognized the potential future importance of the 'tropical' colonies, to be tied to the centre by the construct of the 'Commonwealth' for good (Darwin 2009: 558–579). Hence, after the colonial years of 'shoe-string budgets and skeletal government' (558) the goal of maintaining influence and generating allegiance in former colonies resulted in an increased support for the dissemination of British institutions and traces: 'to survive as a world power at all, the British were forced into much heavier intervention in their tropical empire, with its skeletal states' (654). This included the spread of the English language. Hence, unlike in the colonial days proper, in the mid-twentieth century decolonization period mass schooling of English for local populations came to be considered a worthwhile goal and gained support, and English became more accessible, and clearly also more desirable, to many less affluent Asians and Africans.

The process of decolonization mostly did not weaken English, perhaps surprisingly. Rather than removing English from the local linguistic scene, as a sign of former oppression and foreign dominance, in very many young postcolonial nations its role even became strengthened – very often because the newly independent states tended to be ethnically and linguistically heterogeneous, with borders once drawn by European politicians ignorant of local distinctions. Establishing English as an ethnically neutral tool for internal political and social functions avoided the dangerous strategy of promoting and privileging only one or some of the indigenous languages at the expense of others, which would have created serious

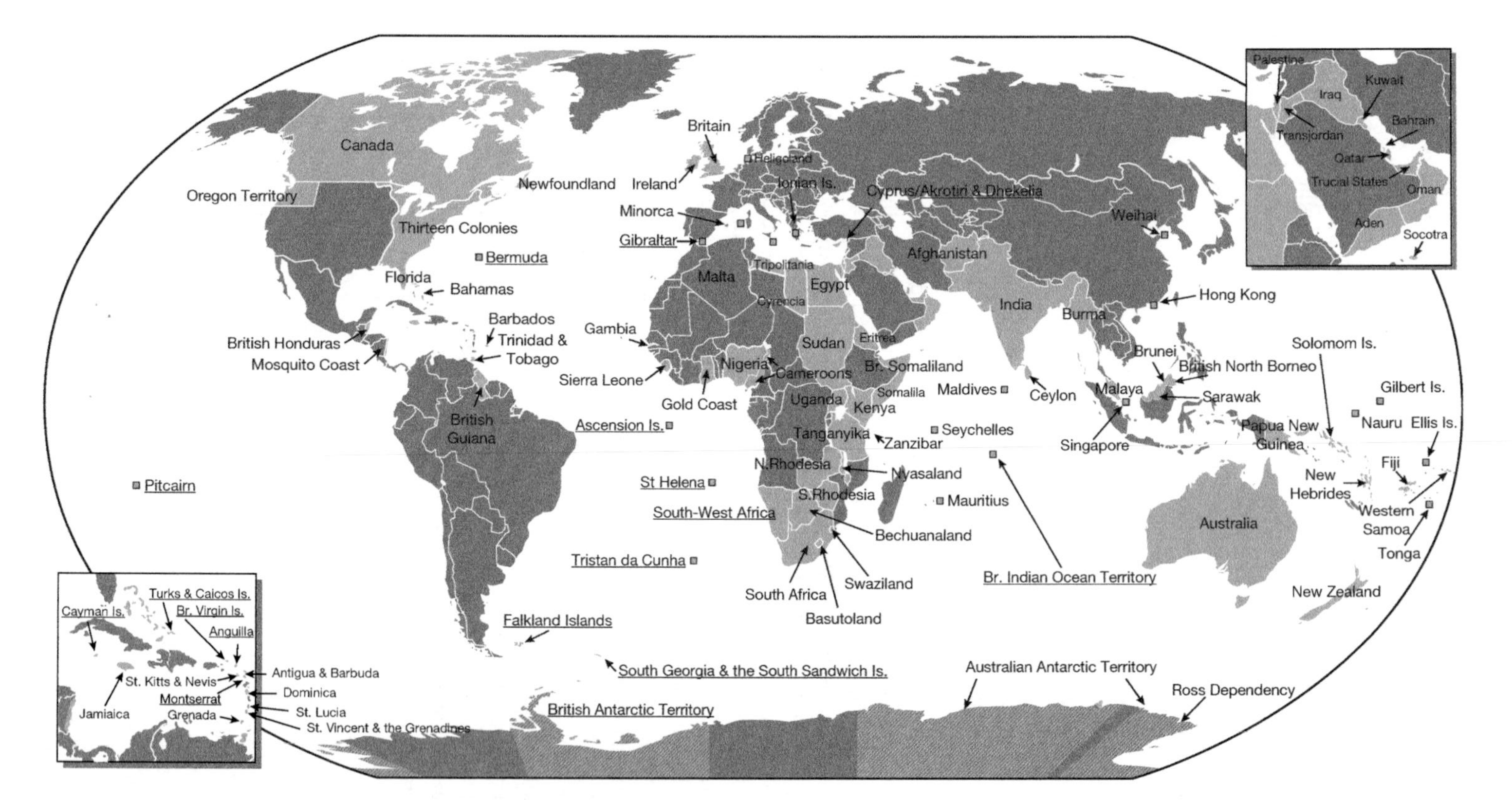

Figure 3.1 The British Empire: territories that were at one time or another part of it

Source: https://commons.wikimedia.org/wiki/File:The_British_Empire.png (The Red Hat of Pat Ferrick [public domain] via Wikimedia Commons), accessed 28 January 2016.

social tensions – and so in very many countries English has remained in a very prominent role, often as the main language of formal nationwide proceedings, politics, higher education and jurisdiction, etc. Strong cases in point are India, whose 'Three-Language Formula' failed, or Nigeria, where any steps towards elevating Yoruba, Igbo or Hausa to the status of national languages would be likely to result in ethnic riots (cf. Schneider 2007: 166–167, 206–269).

The impact on English(es): linguistic diffusion and transformation in colonization

English transported: extraterritorial diffusion

Colonists of course took their language with them, and so around the globe we now find European languages (and English especially) in use, relocated and typically transformed. Postcolonial varieties of English can be native tongues of the majority of a population and the main language of a country (as in the United States, Australia, etc.); strong second languages used widely for internal purposes, as in many parts of Africa (e.g. Kenya, Ghana) and Asia (e.g. The Philippines, India); or a foreign language still perceived as important and used often (e.g. Tanzania, Zimbabwe); or a mixture of practically all of these (as in, for example, South Africa). The diffusion patterns and the ensuing results strongly depend on sociopolitical and sociolinguistic background conditions, such as the time, place and linguistic ecology of the dissemination process in any given case, and the social status, roles and linguistic competences of the agents involved in various functions. While this can be seen as a bewildering set of varying conditions, there are also substantial similarities, and many contexts have been identified as belonging to similar types or sharing developmental processes and resulting properties.

Mufwene (2001:8–9, 204–209) suggests a typology of three main colonization contexts which focuses on linguistic consequences and has thus become influential in World Englishes research, even if his descriptions remain rather brief and fuzzy in some respects. Mufwene's colonization types correspond to what historians have identified as the major forms of European expansion: '*networks*, the establishment of ongoing systems of long-range interaction, usually for trade; *empire*, the control of other peoples, usually through conquest; and *settlement*, the reproduction of one's own society through long–range migration' (Belich 2009: 21; original emphasis). Firstly, around trading forts and along commercial and navigational routes 'trade colonies' were established (e.g. in West Africa), serving the exchange of goods. Language contact in these contexts remained thematically limited and sporadic, so as a result the emergence of trade jargons and pidgins or highly restricted forms of bilingualism were often found. Secondly, 'exploitation colonies', e.g. in India, typically constituted a later stage which grew out of trading activities, when the colonizing nation attained some sort of political authority, and her representatives stayed there for extended periods of time (some for good). In line with Britain's distanced attitudes and 'indirect rule' policy, their lifestyles often remained fairly segregated from the indigenous populations, and power structures were stratified. It is noteworthy that not only standard English was transported to the colonies, since many of the agents coming from the mother country were speakers of nonstandard dialects, so informal speech contributed significantly to local linguistic ecologies. Local elites and leaders participated in the exertion of political power in the interests of the colonizers, and were granted access to English, predominantly in scholastic contexts. The adoption and appropriation of English by these locals, and the further dissemination of second-language acquisition in the course of time, have ultimately produced the nativized varieties of 'New Englishes' which we find today, e.g. in Singapore, Malaysia, Kenya and

Ghana. Thirdly, there are the 'settlement colonies' to which larger numbers of British emigrants moved, taking their language and dialects along. In these colonies, in North America, Australasia, parts of South Africa, and elsewhere, European settlers soon constituted a majority and interacted primarily amongst themselves, so language contact with indigenous speakers and its effects remained restricted largely to lexical borrowings, constrained by the demographic disproportions. Finally, some colonies saw an extensive need for manual agricultural labour, for example for sugar production in the Caribbean, and met this need by the importation of immigrant labourers, as slaves or indentured servants. These 'plantation colonies', considered a subtype of settlement colonies by Mufwene (2001), frequently produced intensive language contact and ultimately newly-born languages, creoles, on large and segregated plantations.

The most significant quantitative expansion occurred in settler colonies around the nineteenth century; as Belich (2009: 4) puts it, 'English-speakers grew over sixteenfold in 1790–1930, from around 12 million to around 200 million ... it was the remarkable explosion of the nineteenth century that put the Anglophones on top of the world'. In contrast, in Britain's 'tropical' colonies, mainly in Asia and, later, in Africa, the presence of British native speakers was lighter, always constituting a minority. Still, for a long time it was substantial and influential even in those areas. Striking numbers of Britons migrated overseas to support and enact colonial rule (Bickers 2010a) – many of them as 'service sojourners' intending to return home after having done their duty, but many others also for long periods of time or for good. It is important to note that not only high-ranking colonial and military officers moved to the colonies, transplanting educated standard language forms, but also huge numbers of lower-class people, 'non-officials and unofficials, traders, planters, men and women in the professions, and in service trades, state functionaries at all levels – police, public works and health, customs, merchant marine, railways' (Bickers 2010b: 1), who brought all kinds of nonstandard dialects with them.

From a linguistic perspective, the decisive point is that in all types of colonies language contact took place, and the products of these processes constitute today's new varieties of English around the globe. While conditions and their outcomes vary to some extent from one type and context to another, it has also been argued, notably in the Dynamic Model of Postcolonial Englishes (Schneider 2007), that fundamental similarities and shared processes and products can also be identified (see below). One fundamental principle of language contact theory (Thomason 2001; Winford 2003) is that there is a direct correlation between the intensity of contact between peoples speaking different languages (defined by demographic proportions, power hierarchies, and the regularity of interactions) and the amount and kind of linguistic effects produced. Light, only occasional (but persistent) contact typically produces little more than lexical borrowing. Intermediate contact levels, including wide-ranging second-language acquisition, result in stronger transfer effects, also on the levels of phonology and, less commonly, morphology and syntax. And finally, very intense contact (e.g. when a group of people is forced to switch to a foreign language completely) produces new and mixed languages, such as creoles.

Settlers varieties: light contact and new dialect formation

Beginning with the seventeenth-century movements to North America, and continuing with late-eighteenth and early-nineteenth century migration strands to Australia, New Zealand and Africa (and also to smaller locations), British emigrants, often called 'settlers', moved to faraway lands in large numbers, to populate the colonies and mostly to stay for good.

They came in large numbers, so that in their new homelands they soon constituted by far the majority population, with indigenous peoples who had been there before suffering badly from being displaced, often after warfare, or decimated by diseases (Belich 2009: 180–181). Native tribes in North America were seriously reduced in numbers or eradicated completely, and only some of them have retained their ethnic vitality. Aboriginals in Australia were marginalized as a consequence of the legal 'terra nullius' fiction, which assumed the land to have been uninhabited before the settlers' arrival (Pennycook 1998: 10). The Maoris of New Zealand, while formally ceding their lands in the Treaty of Waitangi of 1840, lost their power and positions in wars of the 1860s (even if today they and their language are granted official recognition and respect to a greater extent than elsewhere). In all these cases, the quantitative and social disproportion of a minority of indigenous peoples as against huge settler numbers who were also dominant militarily produced rather distanced, light contact and caused mostly loan words from local languages to be taken over into local dialects of English. The varieties found in these former colonies today are not only distinct because of these words, however – they are products of unique mixtures of input varieties from various regions and walks of life in Britain itself, outcomes of processes known as koinéization (the emergence of a compromise dialect) and 'new dialect formation' in linguistics.

In World Englishes research, these young settler first-language varieties and their settings have been called 'English as a Native Language' (ENL) or, following the model established by Kachru (1992), 'Inner Circle' varieties. The focus of World Englishes as a research area has been more strongly on the 'ESL' or 'Outer Circle' varieties discussed in the next section, because of their innovative character, status and properties, but historically the role of the settler nations in producing today's dominance of English globally cannot be underestimated, as the historian Belich argues (2009). 'It was settlement, not empire, that had the spread and staying power in the history of European expansion' (p. 23). Emigrant numbers were significant: 'in the 18th century, about half a million people emigrated from the British Isles. In the long nineteenth century, 1815–1924, the number rocketed to 25 million. Around 18 or 19 million of these British and Irish left permanently' (p. 126). Possible causes included population growth, poverty and a reduced need for an agricultural workforce, but also the attractions of economic opportunities overseas, as well as a significant change of attitude after about 1815, when emigration was no longer viewed as 'compulsory and disreputable, the fate of convicts and [hopeless] people' (p. 145) but rather also as an attractive opportunity, 'an act of hope' (p. 556). Belich (2009) claims that the ultimate success of the settlement colonies rested on a later stage of 'recolonization', the strong retention of an economic and cultural connection of the new expansionist areas with the erstwhile homeland, strengthening both in this mutual integration.

The most important outcome of these processes is the establishment of the United States as the late-twentieth century world's superpower, and of American English as the globally predominant reference variety of English, spoken by more people than all the other native varieties put together. Australian English is following suit in adopting the role of a regional epicentre, having moved toward cultural and linguistic norms of their own roughly since the 1970s (Schneider 2007: 122–125; cf. Darwin 2009: 502–521; Belich 2009: 261–278, 356–368, 462).[1] Similarly, New Zealand, after a 'staunch' period of 'Britonism, intensifying from the 1880s and persisting until the 1960s' (Belich 2009: 464), has now come to emphasize her cultural and linguistic independence, including the recognition of Maori as a co-official language and an adoption of many more Maori words than indigenous words in the other ENL varieties.

The dialects of these settler nations are all products of new dialect formation (cf. Trudgill 1986, 2004), with mainstream American English having been strongly influenced by seventeenth-to-nineteenth century northern and Irish input and the southern hemisphere varieties sharing a largely nineteenth-century southern British base. 'Koinéization', the process typical of dialect contact, means that a compromise variety emerges which strengthens widely shared (and hence communicatively useful) linguistic forms and tends to lose rarely used, strongly regionalized dialect forms (which are typically not understood by speakers from other regions). Obviously the demographic proportions and relative strengths of speakers from diverse regions and the linguistic similarities and relationships between their respective input forms are decisive for the outcome of these processes. Trudgill (2004) voiced the strong (and controversial) thesis that the product of such a mixing process is 'deterministic': fully dependent on these input factors and hence mechanically predictable, at least in theory. The database for these claims and discussions derives strongly from evidence for the emergence of New Zealand English, which, owing to the existence of recordings with speakers born as far back as the late nineteenth century, is exceptionally well documented and researched (Gordon et al. 2004). White South African English, going back to two distinct waves of nineteenth-century settlers from Britain, in contrast, has evolved in a much more complex contact setting, and is a minority dialect (if a highly respected one) today (cf. Schneider 2007: 173–188).

In addition to these well-known and large settler varieties, British colonial expansion has also produced and (with one exception) left a few postcolonial L1 (first language) varieties which are of sociolinguistic interest because of their special, sometimes laboratory-like dialect contact settings, even if speaker numbers are comparatively small or even dwindling. These include the dialects of English found on the South Atlantic islands of Tristan da Cunha (studied by Schreier 2003) and the Falklands (Britain and Sudbury 2010), on St. Helena (Schreier 2008), in Kenya (with a British-derived settler group of a few tens of thousands of whites since the 1910s; Hoffmann 2010) and, now extinct, former Rhodesia (now Zimbabwe; Fitzmaurice 2010). Further documentation of such small-scale, mostly settler-derived 'lesser-known' varieties of English is available in Schreier et al. (2010) and Williams et al. (2015).

New Englishes: intermediate contact and structural nativization

In so-called 'exploitation colonies', motivations for colonial activity and consequently demographic proportions between British representatives and the indigenous population were different. As noted above, it was originally trading companies and their agents that gained and expanded footholds across Asia, beginning with India and followed by Malaysia and others, and established trading posts and, much later, inland expansions and, mainly in Africa, plantations. They were interested in extracting goods desirable to the homeland from the colonies, for commercial profit. Only much later did the agency of colonial activity turn to state representatives and the goal come to include political authority and cultural impact for its own sake. The number of British representatives in foreign lands, in different functions and representing the whole range of social strata, varied from one period or location to another. Usually it kept growing in the course of time, and in many cases it turned out to be a substantial, if, obviously always strong minority. It consisted of both temporary sojourners and long-term residents; many British were born in the colonies and identified with colonial service and adventurous experiences there much more than with a quiet residence in Britain. Some locations, like Singapore's Cricket or Recreation Clubs or Malaysia's 'Hill Stations', offered close-to-perfect copies of English architecture and institutions, to make the expatriates feel 'at home'.

Language contact in these settings was quite different from that in settler colonies, with English supplementing indigenous languages as an add-on tool associated with economic and political power, and also increasingly rooted in administrative structures such as jurisdiction or education. A few Englishmen studied local languages. Predominantly, however, it was the indigenous population who became bilingual and acquired (some) English (particularly those of higher social status, who were admitted to English schools). The level of contact between English and local languages was thus much more intense, and learners tended to transfer words, sounds and patterns from their native tongues into their way of using English. There was a good chance for these transfer phenomena to become regular linguistic habits of the second-language speakers, and some of these features, notably loan words, were also picked up by long-term British residents. In a process of 'structural nativization', new and increasingly firm dialects of English evolved, as products of this intermediate level of language contact, often (though somewhat controversially) called 'New Englishes'. With English playing strong internal roles, the countries in question have come to be classified as ESL or 'Outer Circle' (Kachru 1992), emphasizing their increasingly independent, norm-developing status.

These frameworks, while useful, have been found to be partly too simplistic (considering South Africa, for instance, where English is both second and native language for many) and too static given complex and rapidly changing realities (as in Singapore, where English is moving from ESL to ENL status, or Tanzania, which used to be ESL but attempted to do away with English for internal functions). Consequently, a more complex, flexible and realistic framework, the 'Dynamic Model' of the evolution of Postcolonial Englishes described and applied most elaborately in Schneider (2007), has come to be widely accepted, discussed and used. This model argues that there are enough similarities across all colonial contexts, including the ENL ones, to posit a fundamentally uniform underlying developmental process, both socially and linguistically. Its basic idea is that in the course of time (i.e. across generations and even centuries) the forces of coexistence in the same territory have caused the relationship between colonizers and colonized to change in a predictable direction. While in the beginning both groups were distanced and largely independent of each other, long-term coexistence caused increasing amounts of interaction and mutual accommodation. Ultimately a new sense of spatially-based homogeneity in a process of nation-building emerged before and after independence, because speakers came to recognize that with the erstwhile mother country no longer serving as a reference point a new common identity and basis for life and coexistence needed to be forged. The model suggests that five consecutive, if partially overlapping stages, each with their characteristic social and linguistic properties, can be identified, namely 'foundation', 'exonormative stabilization', 'nativization', 'endonormative stabilization' and 'differentiation'. At each of these stages, specific historical and political background conditions determine the interactants' identity definitions (i.e. who is perceived as belonging to the same or a different group). These, in turn, are decisive for the sociolinguistic conditions of contact, use and attitudes (who talks to whom, how regularly and with which attitudes), which then translate into characteristic structural effects (such as koinéization, the borrowing of place names and sometimes pidginization first, later followed by cultural lexical borrowing, phonological innovations and, later still, grammatical transfer). This framework allows for a certain degree of fuzziness, variability and adaptability, but still, it is remarkable that the basic pattern has been found to be stable and applicable to very many different countries and contexts.

The emergence of Postcolonial Englishes, both ENL and ESL, has thus been a direct consequence of British imperialism: language contact began to affect English as used locally immediately after all moves of colonial expansion, and the systematic emergence and increasing stabilization of linguistic innovations and new varieties then trailed the historically causative steps by a few years or decades. The seventeenth century saw the intense colonization of the eastern parts of North America and parts of the Caribbean as well as the beginnings of trade with and expansion into India, and also early stopover points set up in West Africa. Moves into what is now known as Malaysia, Cook's exploration of the Pacific, and the beginnings of the settlement of Australia followed in the later eighteenth century. In the nineteenth century, settlers moved to parts of South Africa and New Zealand, Singapore was founded, and British authority was strengthened or initiated in Malaysia, Hong Kong, India, and parts of West and East Africa, followed by early-twentieth century settlements in Kenya and Rhodesia (cf. Schneider 2011: 48–51, 58). In all these countries we find distinctive new varieties of English today, with their seeds in colonization (even if affected by substantial modifications and expansions thereafter).

English-based pidgins and creoles: heavy contact and restructuring

Situations of 'heavy contact' include those in which speakers are forced to continuously use and adopt a language which is not their own originally (and of which they often have insufficient input and knowledge). In practice, this has happened most regularly in plantation colonies, where a large number of labourers or field hands were brought together from a wide range of cultural, regional and linguistic backgrounds and had to interact with each other, while there were only comparatively few speakers of the region's target variety, in this case English, around. In the majority of instances such situations were caused by slavery; as Belich (2009: 26) explains it, 'African slaves comprised about three quarters of the eight million migrants to the Americas before 1800, though high death rates and low birth rates meant that they did not generate a proportionate number of descendants.' The number of Europeans around on plantations tended to be comparatively low, so newly arrived slaves received limited, mostly lexical input from the target language, and kept employing grammatical patterns and principles entrenched in them from their native tongues. The result typically was creolization, widely considered the birth of new languages. Creole languages are commonly described as being lexically based upon the target ('superstrate' or 'lexifier') language but grammatically characterized by heavy restructuring and pattern transfer from 'substrate' languages which otherwise could not be used in the new speech community any longer (for a comprehensive survey of the discipline and descriptions of creoles, see Velupillai 2015). The growth of creoles proceeds through stages of incomplete, natural second-language acquisition, possibly involving pidginization in between, with innovations and restructured features being continuously strengthened because new arrivals, mostly slaves, to a plantation or community picked up their new speech skills and approximated linguistically to older residents, whose speech in turn was also only an approximation and contact-induced restructuring of the superstrate. Early creolist theory assumed that creolization occurs only when children acquire their parent generation's pidgin as a mother tongue, but more recently it has been understood that in such extreme contexts adults also restructure their performance patterns substantially, thus producing creoles.

English-based creole languages are thus also products of British colonial expansion, though under much more constrained circumstances. Regionally, such languages are found almost exclusively in tropical zones: in many parts of the Caribbean, between Jamaica and Suriname; across West Africa (most importantly in Nigeria), and in many states of the South-West Pacific region, where some of these languages, conventionally called pidgins there, have attained the status of official state languages (such as Tok Pisin in Papua New Guinea, Bislama in Vanuatu, and Pijin in the Solomon Islands). Traditionally, pidgins and creoles have been dealt with as a language type of their own, independently from other contact varieties, but it is becoming increasingly clear that they come in various degrees of 'depth' and as products of extended language contact, just as do the ESL Englishes in Asia and Africa. Basic processes are the same; differences are a matter of degree, of contact intensity, and of the nature and amount of mutual influences, transfer and restructuring (cf. Schneider 2007: 60–64, 219–238; Siegel 2008).

Key areas of discussion

Linguistic outcomes: processes and structures

Traditionally, historical linguistics, rooted in nineteenth-century nationalism, has tended to emphasize the 'purity' of English and to downplay the 'contaminating' effect of other languages. For example, any possible Celtic influence on early English was considered 'almost negligible' (Baugh and Cable 1951: 76), a view no longer held in modern scholarship (cf. Filppula et al. 2008). In contrast, the importance, and even ubiquity, of language contact has been recognized generally and studied intensively for the last few decades. The basic cline of contact effects, from lexical loans in occasional encounters via some phonological and structural transfer in second-language acquisition (SLA) to massive restructuring in intense contact settings, is largely uncontroversial. The status of the outcomes of strong contact, and of creoles as independent languages or not, is disputed, however. Early creolist theory claimed creoles to be new, independent languages; Thomason and Kaufman (1988), in a classic book, even argued that they are genetically totally unrelated to their lexifier languages. This is counterintuitive, however, given the high amount of similarities – for example, Schneider (2011: 102–106) shows how a Jamaican Creole text, despite many distinct features, remains basically comprehensible to English speakers. Mufwene (2001) holds that creoles are dialects of their lexifier languages and not independent languages, though many creolists are not ready to accept this position.

ESL 'New Englishes' stand in between, being also products of language contact – more so than ENL settler varieties amongst the 'World Englishes', less so than creoles; and one question is where to draw a line. Clearly they share properties with creoles (and consequently, Schneider (2007) also includes Jamaican and Barbadian speech forms in a book on Postcolonial Englishes). At the lower end of the cline, it has been questioned (e.g. by Mesthrie and Bhatt 2008) whether it is justified to lump L1 settler dialects together with ESL Outer Circle varieties under a single overarching framework, as the Dynamic Model explicitly does (Schneider 2007). I am convinced it is: these are important sub-types, and there are differences between both (as to the demographic proportion of British-descendant native speakers of English, the amount and nature of the indigenous-language input into the new dialect, etc.), but there are also overarching shared features; this is a question of granularity, of whether a researcher wishes to highlight the shared or the dividing properties. Ultimately, this argument is important for defining the scope of English Language Studies – which, it is argued here, has to encompass all the contact varieties referred to here as well.

In general, the 'Dynamic Model' has been a focal point of many discussions in World Englishes for the last decade. It has been applied to new contexts (e.g. Cyprus, Buschfeld 2013; Japan, Ike 2012; Sri Lanka, Bernaisch 2015; the Netherlands, Edwards 2016; and many others), widely discussed, mostly accepted, but also modified and questioned with respect to some details and postulates (cf. Buschfeld et al. 2014). Schneider (2014) surveys many reactions and applications, and further contributions to the assessment process have been brought forward, both supportive and more sceptical ones. For example, Evans (2014) purports to test the model's claims concerning Hong Kong English by comparing them to historical and sociodemographic data. While his overall conclusion sounds rather critical, a closer look at his data reveals that in fact many of the basic predictions of the model are largely confirmed; it is only details of the dating of phases that appear to be in need of modification.

A controversial point concerns the role of identity in variety formation. It features prominently in the Dynamic Model (Schneider 2007: 26–28 and *passim*): as was stated above, identity-based delimitations between social groups are considered decisive for the patterns of communicative interactions and thus ultimately for the growth of group-specific dialect distinctions. In contrast, Trudgill's (2004) 'deterministic' view of new dialect formation denies that identity plays any role and suggests that the outcome of a dialect contact process can ideally be mechanically predicted, based on the nature and relative strengths of the input components. The issue was explicitly debated by several contributors in a journal issue (Trudgill et al. 2008). In my view, both claims do not really contradict each other (though I believe a fully 'deterministic' process to be too strong an assumption) because they highlight different processual stages: the mechanistic strength of input factor weights is strongest in early dialect contact, i.e. in the foundation and exonormative stabilization phases in settler contexts, while the role of identity kicks in effectively much later, notably during endonormative stabilization in ESL settings. Van Rooy (2010), weighing both alternatives, also suggests that the variability of the input deserves greater attention.

Another interface under debate is the relationship between World Englishes and 'English as a Lingua Franca' (ELF), the use of English as a link language by (mostly) non-native speakers from different cultural and linguistic backgrounds. ELF usage constitutes a popular and fairly new branch of English Language Studies these days (cf. Seidlhofer 2011; Schneider 2012; Pitzl and Osimk-Teasdale 2016). World Englishes and ELF usage show structural similarities, since both are indirectly products of SLA, and of intercultural interactions and often globalization. However, while World Englishes are usually conceptualized as reasonably stable varieties, ELF is not, and is viewed as an interaction type instead.

Social outcomes: attitudes and policies

Not surprisingly, conflicting attitudes towards English prevail in postcolonial societies. Some linguists (e.g. Skutnabb-Kangas 2000) see it as a 'killer language', one which eradicates indigenous tongues and cultures in many countries – a position which in my view overstates the role of a language and disregards internal ethnic tensions and the impact of regional languages (such as KiSwahili in East Africa). In a similar vein, Pennycook (1998) argues that colonialism has permeated the cultures and discourses of colonial and colonized nations, with effects still visible, so that in such countries English can never be seen as a neutral vehicle of communication. These are minority views held by some academics, however. In contrast, many speakers in many countries view English as a tool promising prosperity and economic opportunities, so a process of 'transnational attraction' (Schneider 2014) keeps disseminating it even further, far beyond the social spheres with which it used to be associated (Blommaert 2010; Schneider 2016). For example, an attempt of the post-handover Hong Kong government to reduce the number of English-medium schools met with serious resistance (Schneider 2007: 139).

Quite naturally, attitudes towards 'New Englishes' vary greatly. Politicians, gatekeepers and authorities tend to view them critically, as imperfect, bastardized approximations of a 'good' or 'standard' English which speakers should strive to produce. Many speakers view that differently, however: for many of them these young and also mixed varieties have a positive indexicality value, signalling new, intercultural orientations. The best-known and most indicative case in point is the ongoing debate about Singapore's 'Singlish' – vigorously opposed by the government in their 'Speak Good English Movement', but enthusiastically defended and used as an expression of regional identity by many Singaporeans.

In practice, nations need to decide on their language policies, and for many young nations in Asia and Africa (postcolonial or not) this implies the need to define the internal status of English. Many options and alternatives are available. The model case of fully embracing English is Singapore – a country basically run in English, moving towards first-language status for the majority of the population, and certainly with English being the uniting band for all. In a similar vein, English was selected as the 'sole working language' of the Association of Southeast Asian Nations (ASEAN), with only some member states having a British colonial background, and it was chosen as a national language even in the complete absence of such a postcolonial reason and motivation, as in Namibia. In India's 'Three-Language Formula' of the 1960s the intention was to remove English, the former colonial power's language – and this has turned out to be impracticable. Some former colonies, like Tanzania and Malaysia, have decided to replace English with new national languages – and have been struggling to implement this policy since then, with the pendulum swinging back and forth between promoting and curtailing English.

And finally, of course all of this has consequences for strategies of teaching English in many countries. Should English be implemented as early as possible, in elementary education? Many parents and politicians advocate this, but Kirkpatrick (2007) fights for elementary education in the children's native tongue. Should secondary or higher education be conducted in English? Should native speakers be hired as teachers? A growing consensus, though still a minority position, is 'no': teachers who have learned the language themselves are more aware of students' pitfalls and problems.

Future directions: colonial processes going postcolonial

Today, we are confronted with a range of different 'World Englishes': new varieties in their different regional and sociopolitical contexts, with structural properties of their own, and with attitudes towards them and their roles in multilingual nations varying substantially. Globalization continues to feed this process, but it was colonialism that caused the fundamental and multiplying transformation of 'English' to 'Englishes'. The reality and presence of 'Word Englishes', and Postcolonial Englishes as a major segment, constitutes an important development and topic not only for linguists, but also for social contexts around the globe. It has been argued many times that English is no longer 'owned' by the British (e.g. Kachru 1992; Widdowson 1994); it is the world language today; it comes in a multitude of varieties, and it is used in an enormously wide range of countries and contexts. Given that the English language, in any of its facets and usage conditions, is now heard and used on all continents and in so many different forms and realizations, English Language Studies as a discipline is no longer conceivable without a perspective on World Englishes. Hence, colonialism and postcolonial developments have transformed the nature of the language in fundamental ways, and for good.

Colonialism laid the foundations for this state of affairs, transmitted English to all corners of the earth and caused it to be transformed in this process. After decolonization it seamlessly found successors – forces which have continued to push, strengthen and disseminate English (see Buschfeld and Kautzsch 2017), notably globalization and cyberspace. Colonialism as a historical process is over, but its effects have been transformed and are here to stay.

Note

1 While writing this I notice with interest that the Melbourne tennis tournament is advertising itself as 'The Grand Slam of Asia/Pacific' – in my view a remarkable turn, indicative of the country's changing self-perception and reorientation.

Further reading

Belich, J. (2009). *Replenishing the Earth: The Settler Revolution and the Rise of the Anglo-World, 1783–1939*. Oxford, New York: Oxford University Press. This is a very informative historical book on colonialism, focusing on settler colonies and offering a convincing explanation for today's dominance of the 'Anglo world' and English.

Darwin, J. (2009) *The Empire Project. The Rise and Fall of the British World–System 1830–1970*. Cambridge: Cambridge University Project. Similar to Belich (2009), this is an engaging historical discussion of the development of the British Empire.

Schneider, E. W. (2007) *Postcolonial English: Varieties around the World*. Cambridge: Cambridge University Press. This is the classic scholarly study on Postcolonial Englishes, with an extensive theoretical section and practical applications of the Dynamic Model to many countries.

Schneider, E. W. (2011) *English around the World. An Introduction*. Cambridge: Cambridge University Press. A textbook which offers an accessible, non-technical introduction to the globalization of English. It contains a large number of sample texts and explains their distinctive structural properties.

Velupillai, V. (2015). *Pidgins, Creoles, and Mixed Languages: An Introduction*. Amsterdam, Philadelphia: Benjamins. This is the most recent, comprehensive and authoritative textbook on, and survey of, pidgins and creoles.

Related topics

- World Englishes: disciplinary debates and future directions
- Standards in English
- Contact Englishes.

References

Baugh, A. C. and T. Cable (1951) *A History of the English Language*. 5th edn. 2002. London: Routledge.

BBC World Service. (2001–2002[?]) *The Story of Africa*. Broadcast series. Available at www.bbc.co.uk/worldservice/africa/features/storyofafrica/, accessed 11 January 2016.

Belich, J. (2009) *Replenishing the Earth: The Settler Revolution and the Rise of the Anglo-World, 1783–1939*. Oxford, NY: Oxford University Press.

Bernaisch, T. (2015) *The Lexis and Lexicogrammar of Sri Lankan English*. Amsterdam, Philadelphia: Benjamins.

Bickers, R. (2010a) 'Introduction: Britains and Britons over the seas', in R. Bickers (ed.), *Settlers and Expatriates: Britons over the Seas*. Oxford: Oxford University Press, 1–17.

Bickers, R. (ed) (2010b) *Settlers and Expatriates: Britons over the Seas*. Oxford: Oxford University Press.

Blommaert, J. (2010) *The Sociolinguistics of Globalization*. Cambridge: Cambridge University Press.

Britain, D. and A. Sudbury (2010) '"Falklands Islands English"' in D. Schreier, P. Trudgill, E. W. Schneider and J. P. Williams (eds), *The Lesser-Known Varieties of English*. Cambridge: Cambridge University Press, 209–223.

Brutt-Griffler, J. (2002) *World English. A Study of its Development*. Clevedon: Multilingual Matters.

Buschfeld, S. (2013) *English in Cyprus or Cyprus English? An Empirical Investigation of Variety Status*. Amsterdam: Benjamins.

Buschfeld, S., T. Hoffmann, M. Huber and A. Kautzsch (eds) (2014) *The Evolution of Englishes. The Dynamic Model and Beyond*. Amsterdam, Philadelphia: Benjamins.

Buschfeld, S. and A. Kautzsch (2017) 'Towards an integrated approach to postcolonial and non-postcolonial Englishes', *World Englishes* 36(1): 104–126.

Cain, P. J. and A. G. Hopkins (2001) *British Imperialism, 1688–2000*. 2nd edn. Harlow: Pearson Education.
Canny, N. P. (ed) (2001) *The Oxford History of the British Empire Vol. 1. The Origins of Empire. British Overseas Enterprise to the Close of the Seventeenth Century*. Oxford, NY: Oxford University Press.
Darwin, J. (2007) 'Decolonization and the end of Empire', in Winks 2007: 34–557.
Darwin, J. (2009) *The Empire Project. The Rise and Fall of the British World–System 1830–1970*. Cambridge: Cambridge University Project.
Edwards, A. (2016) *English in the Netherlands. Functions, Forms and Attitudes*. Amsterdam, Philadelphia: Benjamins.
Evans, S. (2014) 'The evolutionary dynamics of postcolonial Englishes: A Hong Kong case study', *Journal of Sociolinguistics* 18: 571–603.
Filppula, M., J. Klemola and H. Paulasto (2008) *English and Celtic in Contact*. London: Routledge.
Fitzmaurice, S. (2010) 'L1 Rhodesian English', in D. Schreier, P. Trudgill, E. W. Schneider and J. P. Williams (eds), *The Lesser-Known Varieties of English*. Cambridge: Cambridge University Press, 263–285.
Gordon, E., L. Campbell, J. Hay, M. Maclagan, A. Sudbury and P. Trudgill (2004) *New Zealand English: Its Origins and Evolution*. Cambridge: Cambridge University Press.
Hoffmann, T. (2010). 'White Kenyan English', in D. Schreier, P. Trudgill, E. W. Schneider and J. P. Williams (eds), *The Lesser-Known Varieties of English*. Cambridge: Cambridge University Press, 286–310.
Ike, S. (2012) Japanese English as a variety: Features and intelligibility of an emerging variety of English. Ph.D. dissertation, The University of Melbourne.
Kachru, B. B. (ed) (1992) *The Other Tongue: English across Cultures*. 2nd edn. Urbana, Chicago: University of Illinois Press.
Kirkpatrick, A. (2007) *World Englishes: Implications for International Communication and English Language Teaching*. Cambridge: Cambridge University Press.
Louis, W. R. (2007) 'Introduction', in Winks, ed. 2007: 1–42.
Mesthrie, R. and R. Bhatt (2008) *World Englishes*. Cambridge: Cambridge University Press.
Mufwene, S. S. (2001) *The Ecology of Language Evolution*. Cambridge: Cambridge University Press.
Pennycook, A. (1998) *English and the Discourses of Colonialism*. London, New York: Routledge.
Pitzl, M.-L. and T. Osimk-Teasdale (eds) (2016) *English as a Lingua Franca: Perspectives and Prospects*. Berlin, Boston: de Gruyter Mouton.
Schneider, E. W. (2007) *Postcolonial English. Varieties around the World*. Cambridge: Cambridge University Press.
Schneider, E. W. (2011) *English Around the World. An Introduction*. Cambridge: Cambridge University Press.
Schneider, E. W. (2012) 'Exploring the interface between World Englishes and Second Language Acquisition – and implications for English as a Lingua Franca', *Journal of English as a Lingua Franca* 1. 57–91.
Schneider, E. W. (2014) 'New reflections on the evolutionary dynamics of world Englishes', *World Englishes* 33: 9–32.
Schneider, E. W. (2016) 'Grassroots Englishes in tourism interactions'. *English Today* 32(3): 2–10.
Schreier, D. (2003) *Isolation and Language Change. Contemporary and Sociolinguistic Evidence from Tristan da Cunha English*. Houndmills, NewYork: Palgrave Macmillan.
Schreier, D. (2008). *St Helenian English. Origins, Evolution and Variation*. Amsterdam, Philadelphia: Benjamins.
Schreier, D., P. Trudgill, E. W. Schneider and J. P. Williams (eds) (2010) *The Lesser-Known Varieties of English*. Cambridge: Cambridge University Press.
Seidlhofer, B. (2011) *Understanding English as a Lingua Franca*. Oxford: Oxford University Press.
Siegel, J. (2008) *The Emergence of Pidgin and Creole Languages*. Oxford: Oxford University Press.
Skutnabb-Kangas, T. (2000) *Linguistic Genocide in Education – Or Worldwide Diversity and Human Rights?* Mahwah, NJ & London, UK: Lawrence Erlbaum Associates.
Thomason, S. G. (2001). *Language Contact: An Introduction*. Washington, DC: Georgetown University Press.
Thomason, S. G. and T. Kaufman (1988) *Language Contact, Creolization and Genetic Linguistics*. Berkeley, LA: University of California Press.
Trudgill, P. (1986) *Dialects in Contact*. Oxford, New York: Blackwell.

Trudgill, P. (2004) *New-Dialect Formation. The Inevitability of Colonial Englishes*. Edinburgh: Edinburgh University Press.
Trudgill, P., S. S. Mufwene, D. N. Tuten, E. W. Schneider, N. Coupland, L. Bauer, J. Holmes and P. Kerswill. (2008) 'Discussion', *Language in Society* 37: 241–280.
Van Rooy, B. (2010) 'Societal and linguistic perspectives on variability in world Englishes', *World Englishes* 29: 3–20.
Velupillai, V. (2015). *Pidgins, Creoles, and Mixed Languages: An Introduction*. Amsterdam, Philadelphia: Benjamins.
Widdowson, H. G. (1994) 'The ownership of English', *TESOL Quarterly* 28(2): 377–389.
Williams, J. P., E. W. Schneider, P. Trudgill and D. Schreier (eds) (2015) *Further Studies in the Lesser-Known Varieties of English*. Cambridge: Cambridge University Press.
Winford, D. (2003) *An Introduction to Contact Linguistics*. Malden, MA, Oxford: Blackwell.
Winks, R. W. (ed) (2007) *The Oxford History of the British Empire Vol. 5. Historiogaphy*. Oxford, NY: Oxford University Press.

4

World Englishes

Disciplinary debates and future directions

Kingsley Bolton

Introduction

Over the last three decades, the phrase 'world Englishes' (WE) has become an established term to refer to many varieties of English found throughout the world, particularly in the Caribbean, former Anglophone colonies in Africa, and many societies in Asia. Before the 1980s, discussions of English worldwide typically employed a normative vocabulary that utilized a distinction between 'native' and 'non-native' speakers, employing such terms as 'English as a Native Language' (ENL), 'English as a Second Language' (ESL), and 'English as a Foreign Language' (EFL). Over the last thirty years, however, 'world Englishes', with its inclusive plural, has increasingly become the standard term to refer to varieties of English worldwide. Debates about the status, functions, and features of varieties of English may be traced back to the mid-1960s, and the work of Halliday, McIntosh and Strevens, who asserted that 'English is no longer the possession of the British, or even the British and the Americans, but an international language which [. . .] exists in an increasingly large number of different varieties' (Halliday et al. 1964: 293). Twelve years later, the US educator Larry Smith described English as 'an international auxiliary language', and asserted that it was 'time to stop calling it a foreign language or second language', suggesting instead the term 'EIAL' (English as an International Auxiliary Language) which, he asserted, 'more accurately reflects the present state of English language usage around the globe' (Smith 1976: 39). Since then, the work of Braj Kachru, Larry Smith and many other scholars has contributed to a major paradigm shift in English studies. Over this period, there has been a growing recognition of 'Englishes' in the plural, as in 'varieties of English', 'international Englishes', 'new Englishes', 'English languages' and 'world Englishes'.[1] Of all these designations, arguably the most popular term currently in the literature is 'world Englishes', and the last three decades have seen the rise of this discipline (or sub-discipline) in linguistics as a site for scholarly research and publication. There are now a number of academic journals, including *English Today*, *English World-Wide*, *World Englishes*, and *Asian Englishes*, devoted to the field, numerous book-length studies dealing with research in this area, and the very active International Association for World Englishes (IAWE), which regularly organizes international conferences in the US and across the globe (Seargeant 2012a).

The scope of 'world Englishes' studies

The term 'world Englishes' may be understood as having both a narrower and wider application. The narrow application of the term refers to schools of thought closely associated with the approach to the study of English worldwide pioneered by Braj B. Kachru and a group of closely-related scholars. The wider application of the concept also includes many other approaches to the study of English worldwide ranging from the regional Englishes of Britain to varieties of English in the US, Australia, New Zealand, and to the Englishes of East and West Africa and many Asian societies, as well as the study of discourse and genre in those contexts where English is regarded as a second or foreign language. Research on WE in the widest sense includes at least a dozen distinct approaches including those of English studies, corpus linguistics, features-based approaches, the sociology of language, 'Kachruvian' studies, pidgin and creole research, applied linguistics, lexicography, popularized studies, critical linguistics, and futurological approaches (Bolton 2004, 2006, 2012). To this list, we might now add current work on 'English as a Lingua Franca' (ELF), a recently emergent approach to English as an international language, which is now proving a highly productive area of study, particularly in the European context (Bolton 2011). These approaches are summarized in Table 4.1 below.

From the 1960s onwards, the English studies approach was associated with such scholars as Randolph Quirk and others active at the Survey of English Usage at University College London, including David Crystal and Sidney Greenbaum. The work of these UK-based scholars was complemented by the research and publications of a number of German scholars including Görlach (1995) and Schneider (2007), as well as that of work in corpus linguistics, which again is closely associated with an English studies approach, as in the work of Greenbaum (1996), Nelson et al. (2002) and others on the International Corpus of English (ICE) project (ICE 2016). In addition to the ICE corpora worldwide, research teams have also begun to compile their own regional corpora of Englishes, including the important SAVE corpus of South Asian Varieties of English (Mukherjee 2012).

The English studies approach and the work of corpus linguists overlap considerably with the 'features-based approach', which typically involves the linguist in identifying and making statements about the distinctive features of varieties in terms of pronunciation or 'accent' (phonology), vocabulary (lexis), or grammar (morphology and syntax). Leading examples of this approach include Trudgill and Hannah ([1982] 2013), Schneider et al. (2004), and Kortmann et al. (2004). Schneider has made an important contribution to the field through the formulation of the Dynamic Model of postcolonial Englishes (Schneider 2003, 2007). Sociolinguistic approaches to WE have included (i) 'the sociology of language' (Fishman et al. 1996); (ii) the 'linguistic features' (and dialectological) approach (Trudgill and Hannah 1982, etc.); (iii) pidgin and creole studies; and (iv) 'socially-realistic' studies of WE (Kachru 1992).

The use of the term 'world Englishes' to refer to a distinct approach to this subject is most closely associated with the work of Braj Kachru. The origin of the term 'world Englishes' can be located in the two conferences on English as a world language that took place in 1978, one in April at the East–West Center in Hawaii and the second in June–July at the University of Illinois at Urbana-Champaign, and Braj Kachru and Larry Smith played a major role in both conferences. A key theoretical and methodological tenet of the Kachruvian perspective was that the earlier three-fold distinction between ENL, ESL, and EFL was ideologically loaded and intellectually flawed, and instead an approach was adopted that categorized varieties of English in terms of a three-fold distinction between the Inner Circle (including the UK, US, Canada, Australia, and New Zealand), the Outer Circle (postcolonial societies such as

Table 4.1 Approaches to world Englishes

Approach	*Focus*	*Timeline*
English studies	The analysis of varieties of English from a synchronic and historical perspectives, against a tradition of English studies (*Anglistik*) dating from the late nineteenth century, e.g. the work of Otto Jespersen, Daniel Jones, and Henry Sweet.	1960s–present
English corpus linguistics	The accurate and detailed linguistic descriptions of world Englishes from a features perspective.	1990s–present
'Features-based' approaches	The description of English through dialectological and variationist methodologies. Situated against the long tradition of British and European dialectology.	1980s–present
The sociology of language	Research on English in relation to such issues as language maintenance/shift, and ethnolinguistic identity.	1960s–present
Kachruvian studies	The promotion of a pluricentric approach to world Englishes, highlighting both the 'sociolinguistic realities' and 'bilingual creativity' of Outer Circle (and Expanding Circle) societies.	1980s–present
Pidgin and creole studies	The description and analysis of 'mixed' languages and the dynamics of linguistic hybridization in language contact settings.	1930s–present
Applied linguistics	The exploration of the implications of world Englishes for language learning and teaching.	1960s–present
Lexicography	The codification of vocabularies of English worldwide, linked to particular postcolonial societies and issues of linguistic autonomy.	1980s–present
Popularisers	The publication of books on English worldwide aimed at a mass reading public.	1980s–1990s
Critical linguistics	The expression of resistance to the linguistic imperialism and cultural hegemony of English, in tandem with resistance to Anglo-American political power.	1990s–present
Linguistic futurology	The discussion of future scenarios for the spread of English and English language teaching worldwide.	1997–present
English as a Lingua Franca	An approach to international English focusing on those contexts, e.g. universities and international businesses, where English is used as a common language by speakers of different nationalities and linguistic backgrounds.	Late 1990s–present

Nigeria, Kenya, India, Philippines, and Singapore), and the Expanding Circle (for instance, Brazil, China, Germany, and Japan).

By the mid-1980s, a number of popular works intended for a general reading audience began to appear, including publications by Crystal (1997, 2004) and Bragg (2003). Challenging the perceived 'triumphalism' of such popular works, Phillipson's landmark *Linguistic Imperialism*

(1992), encouraged a strong interest in the politics of English, and has also informed the work of a generation of other critical scholars. The futurology perspective is best represented in research reports from Graddol (1997, 2006). From the late 1990s, linguists began to look at the increasing use of English within the Expanding Circle (or 'EFL') context of Europe, where English was quickly spreading as the common language of international university education and international business. It is in this context that English as an international language began to be redefined as ELF, with foundational work in this area including Seidlhofer (2001), Jenkins (2007), and Mauranen and Ranta (2009).[2]

World Englishes as a discipline

Within linguistics generally, and English linguistics in particular, there can be little doubt that the WE approach to English worldwide has succeeded in creating a major paradigm shift in academic English studies within the UK, and North America as well as the international academic community. Whereas English studies in the 1960s in the metropolitan academy in, for example, the US and UK, were tied almost exclusively to national literatures (especially English and American literatures), supplemented by historical approaches to language studies, today it is an almost unchallenged orthodoxy that academic English studies are regarded as global phenomena, from both literary and linguistic perspectives. Against this changing academic background, it is perhaps unsurprising that WE has emerged and been recognized as a distinct branch of linguistics at many universities worldwide. Some have even suggested that the WE approach to English studies now constitutes a distinct 'discipline' within the academy, an issue that Seargeant's (2012a) article examines at some length, highlighting at first the socio-historical and political underpinning of the field:

> [T]he discipline of world Englishes studies [. . .] did not arise out of nowhere [and] the development of the discipline is the result of a number of different social, historical and political pressures which frame the ways in which the subject is presently studied in academic circles. In other words, it is these various social, historical and political processes which have produced a mostly coherent field of study which now goes by the title of world Englishes studies, and which provide the meaning-matrix in which work executed within this tradition exists. And any subsequent work in this field will, in some sense, be a response to this general framework.
>
> (Seargeant 2012a: 114)

Seargeant then goes on to identify the various components of a 'discipline' within academia (with reference to previous theorizations), which include an academic community of practice, a shared domain of academic interest, a tradition of scholarship, a network of communications, and conceptual structures, noting that the two most important factors in the formation of a discipline are 'how knowledge is organized' and 'how organization comes about as a result of the social practices of those involved in the production or reproduction of that knowledge' (Seargeant 2012a: 115). In this context, a major influence is the adoption of teaching materials in education systems, which help 'establish a central canon of key theories and empirical studies which constitute the academic content of the discipline' and in turn lead to 'the appearance of the named subject with a relatively standardized content across different universities which marks the status of discipline within this educational context', accompanied in turn by the emergence and institutionalization of research funding and research publications in the designated field (Seargeant 2012a: 116).

More specifically, in the case of WE, Seargeant identifies a number of key factors that have led to the emergence of WE as a disciplinary field, namely (i) teaching resources and educational programmes; (ii) history; (iii) methodology and objectives; and (iv) discourse patterns (Seargeant 2012a: 121–126). Teaching resources and educational programmes include all those programmes and courses at undergraduate and postgraduate level on 'world Englishes' or closely allied topics in North America, Europe, the UK, Asia, and elsewhere, often using such textbooks as Jenkins (2003), Melchers and Shaw (2003), Kirkpatrick (2007), Mesthrie and Bhatt (2008), Seargeant (2012b) and Seargeant and Swann (2012). Research publications include the three key journals (mentioned above) in the field, as well as increasing numbers of book publications from such major international publishers as Bloomsbury, Cambridge University Press, John Wiley, Oxford University Press, Routledge (Taylor and Francis), and Springer. History here refers to the history of WE as a discipline, a topic that I have earlier attempted to tackle in some detail (Bolton 2003: 1–49). At the levels of methodology and objectives, Seargeant notes a good deal of variation, with a range of approaches, from the linguistic to the sociological/political in play, as well as a range of related discourses, all of which (reassuringly perhaps) in 'broad-based' fashion, 'allows for diverse and competing approaches to the analysis of the subject [. . .] within the wider institutional disciplinary framework' (Seargeant 2012a: 124). In this context, 'discourse patterns' refers to the multiple ways in which WE has developed varying yet distinctive 'discursive norms' in terms of a specialized vocabulary, as well as diverse norms of approach, methodologies and scholarship, while ultimately preserving coherence 'in terms of shared fundamental concerns and a focus on globally-contextualized enquiry into the spread of the English language' (Seargeant 2012a: 126). In conclusion, Seargeant summarizes the case for WE as a discipline, asserting that

> [T]here is now a stable body of knowledge that constitutes a subject entitled world Englishes studies, and the status of this is such that it is beginning to be projected onto curricula and, occasionally, departmental structures. The pedagogic implications are that there has been a paradigm shift in the way that the academic mainstream now focuses on the teaching and research of diverse varieties of English [which] affects not only sociolinguistic studies of English around the world, but also applied linguistics scholarship, and in this way feeds into the training of language professionals, specifically TESOL practitioners and those involved in language planning.
>
> (Seargeant 2012a: 126–127)

Indeed, as the above discussion suggests, at present the pluricentric and pluralistic approach of WE has become so well-established as to constitute something of an orthodoxy in contemporary English language studies and sociolinguistics. So much so, perhaps, that various linguists have begun to question this new orthodoxy, and to problematize various aspects of the WE approach, including the work of Professor Braj B. Kachru and associated scholars.

Debating world Englishes

One important challenge to the WE paradigm in recent years has been from scholars who have highlighted the 'linguistic imperialism' associated with the spread of English. The foundation document on this topic, Phillipson's (1992) *Linguistic Imperialism* was a landmark publication, which subsequently politicized the debate on WE and related issues. At the centre of Phillipson's theoretical approach to 'linguistic imperialism' are a series of arguments about the political relations between the 'core English-speaking countries' (Britain, the USA, Canada, Australia, and New Zealand) and the 'periphery-English countries', where English either has the status of a second language (for example, Nigeria, India, and Singapore) or is a foreign and 'international link language' (including Scandinavia and Japan) (1992: 17). The nature of this relationship, Phillipson argues, is one of structural and systemic inequality, in which the political and economic hegemony of western Anglophone powers is established or maintained over scores of developing nations, particularly those formerly colonies of European powers, contributing to a form of 'English linguistic imperialism', where '*the dominance of English is asserted and maintained by the establishment and continuous reconstitution of structural and cultural inequalities between English and other languages*' (1992: 47, original emphasis). Phillipson's voice in the early 1990s was original and persuasive and has subsequently influenced the work of many others, including, to some extent, such applied linguists as Canagarajah (1999), Pennycook (1994, 2001). While Phillipson's perspective was uncritical of the WE approach at first, his attitude seems to have changed somewhat in recent years. By 2009, Phillipson was maintaining that 'global English' was a 'capitalist neoimperial language that serves the interests of the corporate world and the governments that it influences', and was asserting that, in this context, '[t]here are serious theoretical and empirical weaknesses in the way world Englishes are classified and analyzed' (Phillipson 2009: 132, 164–165). In the same year, in an interview, Phillipson further commented that '[m]ost work on World Englishes in the Kachruvian sense is purely descriptive, and an over-simplification of the complexity of the sociolinguistics of English in multilingual settings' (Phillipson 2010).

Other critiques of the WE approach have included the commentaries of Bruthiaux (2003) and Jenkins (2003). The criticisms of both these authors have largely focused on the 'Three Circles' model of the Kachruvian approach, with Bruthiaux publishing a lengthy critique of this strand of the approach. The core of Bruthiaux's critique is that the Three Circles model 'has little explanatory power' and 'has left us with a primarily nation-based model which draws on specific historical events and which correlates poorly with current sociolinguistic data' (Bruthiaux 2003: 161). Similarly, Jenkins' (2003) textbook *World Englishes: A Resource Book for Students*, also contained a number of criticisms of the Three Circles model including (i) the assertion that this was 'a model based on geography and genetics'; (ii) that there were 'grey areas' between the Inner and Outer Circle countries, and Outer and Expanding Circles; and that (iii) 'the model implies that the situation is uniform for all countries within a particular circle'. Kachru's (2005) response to these criticisms emphasized that, for him, the notion of the Circles was primarily historical, which also involved a geographical (though not, in his formulation, a genetic) dimension (Kachru 2005: 213). With reference to the 'grey areas' issue, Kachru responded by quoting an earlier paper, where he had specifically argued that

> The Outer and Expanding Circles cannot be viewed as clearly demarcated from each other; they have several shared characteristics, and the status of English in the language policies of such countries changes from time to time. What is an ESL region at one time may become an EFL region at another time or vice versa.
>
> (Kachru 1985: 13–14)

On the third issue of supposed uniformity of countries, Kachru's response was that he had always argued that there was 'significant variation' within varieties, and indeed if we look back at one of Kachru's earlier articles on 'Models of English for the Third World', he reports on no less than ten distinct varieties of Indian English identified by survey respondents at that time (Kachru 1976: 234). In his (2005) commentary on criticisms of the Three Circles model he went on to emphasize that it is important to consider the spread of English from a historical perspective for a range of rather basic reasons:

> That historical reality [of the Inner Circle] and the source of English need not be negated but has to be confronted in contextualizing the process of the spread of English and its implications. The earlier colonial designs and the resultant Imperial Raj directly impacted the Outer Circle countries (e.g. Nigeria, Kenya, India, Sri Lanka) with their distinct earlier linguistic and cultural histories, which are not necessarily the same as those of the Expanding Circle countries. The post-1950s period has created a specific dynamic and energy in the Outer Circle in terms of its identities, attitudes and creativity in the language.
> (Kachru 2005: 219)

At the same time, however, Kachru was fully aware of the dynamic nature of WE, commenting that, within his model, 'each Circle, including the Inner Circle, is reshaping itself within fast-changing sociolinguistic ecologies in which the English language has become a vital partner and a linguistic icon with a variety of avataras' (Kachru 2005: 219). Ultimately, however, perhaps this model is best appreciated when compared to the prejudices against 'non-native' speakers of English that preceded it, as noted by McArthur (1993), who recognized its virtues in terms of 'the democratization of attitudes to English everywhere in the globe':

> [T]his is a more dynamic model than the standard version, and allows for all manners of shadings and overlaps among the Circles. Although 'Inner' and 'Outer' still suggest, inevitably, a historical priority and the attitudes that go with it, the metaphor of ripples in a pond suggests mobility and flux and implies that a history is in the making.
> (McArthur 1993, cited in Kachru 2005: 219)

McArthur's point here, I would argue, is well taken. The discourses that had preceded the emergence of the WE paradigm emphasized the importance and supremacy of 'native-speaker' norms, largely of the UK or US, with localized versions of English across the globe discussed in terms of 'varieties' of a notionally singular 'English'. In addition, however, I would also argue that it is misleading and simplistic to conflate WE (or the Kachruvian approach to WE) with the Three Circles model alone; not least given the much wider disciplinary underpinning of the WE enterprise, in both the Kachruvian approach, and as a wider academic enterprise.

The essence of much such criticism has been that the Kachruvian approach to WE has been too simplistic (or even too 'nationalistic') in focusing on geographically-defined varieties of English. However, this in itself may be a simplification, as the analysis of the content of the *World Englishes* journal in the twenty years from 1985 to 2005 has shown that only a minority of articles focused predominantly on linguistic features (9.4%) or areal studies (11.4%). In fact, most space in the journal in this formative period was given over to such topics as applied linguistics, contact linguistics (including code-switching and code-mixing), discourse analysis, sociolinguistics and a diverse range of other subjects (Bolton and Davis 2006). More recently, substantial space in the journal has been accorded to topics related to creativity, cultural linguistics, linguistic landscapes, media, popular culture, and a slew of issues intellectually distinct from the sole focus on geographically-defined 'varieties' in the classic sense. In my view, the WE approach as it has developed has been intrinsically dynamic and remains open both to debate and to new perspectives in research, scholarship, and theorization. Indeed I would see this flexibility, diversity, and openness as a crucial element of the 'ethos' of WE (Bolton 2005).

Saraceni's (2015) review of WE scholarship, entitled *World Englishes: A critical analysis* identifies at least two new challenges to the WE enterprise. He argues that, despite the obvious strengths of the Kachruvian approach and the success of the WE paradigm shift, WE research has recently been outpaced by the effects of globalization, and the impact of these on linguistic ecologies worldwide. Thus he suggests:

> [T]he World Englishes framework has been feeling 'pressure', as it were, from two separate fronts of scholars: on the one hand those who have been engaged with research aimed at providing insights into the forms and functions of English as a lingua franca (ELF) [. . .] on the other hand those who have concentrated their attention on phenomena related to globalization, such as 'super-diversity', language 'hybridity', 'translanguaging', 'metrolingualism' [. . .] In some ways, it could be said that both ELF and the sociolinguistics of globalization have 'eroded' some of the scope of World Englishes.
>
> (Saraceni 2015: 4)

Saraceni's views are constructive in highlighting the impact of globalization, and I would agree that what is new here (compared with WE in its earlier years of theorization) are the palpable impacts of economic, political, and cultural globalization over the past fifty years (Martell 2017).

One major example of this has been the impact of increased migration and the movements of peoples. In the case of Europe, in the last three decades in particular, the effects of multiculturalism and multilingualism have been felt everywhere, as a result of the expansion of the European Union (EU), and the movement of Europeans across national boundaries, but also as the result of large-scale immigration into Europe from outside the EU (seen most dramatically in the recent waves of immigration from the war-torn Middle East). Given the relative openness of European higher education, this has also had a major effect on academia, across the EU and even the UK. Whereas four decades ago the vast majority of students in European university classrooms would have been domestic students 'native' to particular European nations, today French, German, Scandinavian and British universities are populated by substantial numbers of foreign students, and continental European universities have experienced increasing pressure to provide curricula for such students through English. It is hardly surprising therefore that early attempts to provide theorizations and descriptions of 'European English' soon gave way to a more considered attempt to describe the lingua franca English of multicultural students in European classrooms (Seidlhofer 2011; Jenkins 2013). It was these educational and sociological conditions, I have suggested elsewhere, that have provided the direct impetus for the emergence of ELF as a distinct field of inquiry, and it may be further helpful here to understand ELF studies as (in the first instance) a European phenomenon, or, at least, as a European response to the shifting demographics of the EU as well as European universities (Bolton 2011).

With reference to the second challenge identified by Saraceni, that of 'super-diversity' studies, there can be little doubt that recent work by Blommaert (2010) on the sociolinguistics of globalization has the strong potential to expand our understanding of language contact and multilingualism in the contemporary world. Here again I would suggest that a major stimulus for such studies has again been the European response to the changing demographics of

European cities and societies, as a direct result of immigration. To take one example from Scandinavia, until the 1970s Sweden was very largely racially and linguistically homogeneous, but by the early 2000s, as a result of the country generously accepting large numbers of international refugees, over 150 different languages were recorded as 'home languages' for Stockholm schoolchildren (Bolton and Meierkord 2013).

Blommaert has persuasively argued that 'globalization forces sociolinguistics to unthink its classic distinctions and biases and to rethink itself as a sociolinguistics of mobile resources', while further arguing that '[w]e need to replace it [traditional sociolinguistics] with a view of language as something intrinsically and perpetually mobile, through space as well as time, and made for mobility' (Blommaert 2010: 1, xiv). Thus, whereas traditional sociolinguistics is concerned with the use of 'languages' or 'varieties' within or between stable 'speech communities', or with 'code-switching' or 'code-mixing', super-diversity studies have a focus on multilingualism in a globalizing world, where individuals engage in 'polylanguaging' and 'translanguaging'. In Europe, this has now resulted in rethinking sociolinguistics in at least three areas of research: (i) face-to-face communication, as in recent studies of multicultural urban dialects in the UK; (ii) Internet-based communication, including blogging, gaming, social media, and Youtube; and (iii) linguistic landscape studies, concerned with displayed public languages, commercial signage, street signs, posters, and shop names (Parkin and Arnaut 2010).

The specific linguistic effects of globalization in Europe are not necessarily duplicated elsewhere, as the linguistic realities in this context have been (re-)shaped by the transnationalism of the EU, high levels of immigration and the increasing awareness of multilingualism. In Asia, the sociolinguistics of many societies have been determined by rather different influences, not least the tension between ongoing national projects and the demands of globalization, resulting in a shift away from traditional linguistic diversity associated with regional and local varieties of languages towards a restricted combination of the standard national language, very often in combination with English. In the US, it might be argued that such dynamics are again different from those in Europe, for a number of reasons.

First, as many discussions of 'globalization' concede, the driving force of many of those cultural, economic and social phenomena associated with globalization have had their wellspring in the US, particularly since the Second World War, after which America's 'irresistible Empire' of consumer goods, global media, mass production, popular entertainment, and contemporary modernity was spread worldwide (de Grazia 2005). Second, it may be argued that, whereas many European societies appear to have enjoyed only limited success in integrating large numbers of recent immigrants into their societies, the power of the American dream seems as strong today as ever, at a time in the US when 'ethnic' minorities such as Asians and Hispanics are gaining ever more economic and political clout in society. However speculative such comments may be, such factors may at least help explain why ELF studies have emerged and gained wide popularity in the European context, but have largely failed to gain major traction in the US (although see Matsumoto 2011). Despite the huge influx of overseas students into US universities and colleges in recent years, the expectation is still strong that the vast majority of such students wish to acquire a command of a standardized (or standard-like) variety of US English as part of their educational experience, and to meet such demands, most universities have relatively well-established ESL and academic writing programs in place to meet such needs (Liou 2012). In this context, as in others, it may also be argued that the power of the US variety of English continues to parallel the continuing economic, cultural, military and political power of the US in many other spheres worldwide (Demont-Heinrich 2010). To this, one may also add the powerful effects of Internet technology, and its related 'mediating' impact on our reception and use of languages, a technology perceived as global, and yet one whose origins and key stakeholders have (often) been strategically and compactly located in California's Silicon Valley (*The Economist* 2015).

Naming and defining world Englishes

The criticisms of the WE approach of Bruthiaux (2003) and Jenkins (2003), however partial, have been repeated by a number of other commentators over the last decade or so, perhaps most recently in Galloway and Rose (2015) who propose that the field of world Englishes should be renamed 'global Englishes'. One major reason for this they argue is that the WE approach is essentially (and almost exclusively) concerned with 'national varieties' of English. Consequently, they avow, a better name for the study of English studies worldwide is 'global Englishes' as this (unlike 'world Englishes') incorporates such issues as 'globalization, linguistic imperialism, education, and language policy and planning' (Galloway and Rose 2015: xii). However, the accusation that WE has been mainly concerned with 'national varieties of English' and has not engaged with such questions ignores the pioneering research and publications of numerous WE scholars, as well as that of Kachru himself.

A number of issues are raised by Galloway and Rose's (2015) critique of the Kachruvian approach to WE. At the core of their critique is the claim that 'world Englishes' should subordinate itself to the newly-emergent 'global Englishes' paradigm, as if this were an innovative conceptualization that was entirely original and fit for purpose. Although some might regard the issue of whether the field is referred to as 'world Englishes' or 'global Englishes' as a trivial question, in many respects this is a matter of no small concern, as Seargeant's (2010) discussion of 'Naming and defining in world Englishes' explains. In this study of the nomenclature of the field, Seargeant draws our attention to the complexities of the ways in which 'Englishes' or 'varieties of English' are categorized. For example, they may be categorized according to *function* ('English as a foreign language' etc.); in terms of *community* ('native/non-native varieties'); *history* ('colonial Englishes'); *structure* ('pidgin Englishes'); *ecology* ('Inner Circle variety'); and *multiplexity* ('World English', 'English language complex'). What is significant here, Seargeant argues, is that although the creation of such nomenclature is avowedly descriptive in intention, the act of naming has performative consequences, and has an important influence on the discourses associated with particular academic activities (Seargeant 2010: 109).

There are many reasons for rejecting the re-scripting of 'world Englishes' as 'global Englishes', which might be better left to a much longer discussion elsewhere, but two important (and interconnected) reasons might be mentioned here. First and foremost, to baldly assert (as Galloway and Rose do) that 'Global Englishes *includes* the concepts of World Englishes' (emphasis added) seems at best an attempt at the (mis)appropriation of pre-existing discourses, and at worst a crude takeover bid of an existing academic discipline that, as Seargeant (2012a) has eloquently pointed out, has its own specific history, associated with diverse and open-ended approaches to the field, that have all contributed to a newly-emergent discipline bearing the name of 'world Englishes'. Second, this attempt at renaming the field, for which Galloway and Rose provide only slight scholarly justification, evidently attempts to marginalize or misrepresent at least fifty years of scholarship in the WE field, not least that of Braj B. Kachru (1932–2016). More specifically, such a rhetorical move (conscious or otherwise) represents, I would argue, a misguided assault on decades of ground-breaking and innovative empirical research by numerous distinguished scholars.

Interestingly, one important starting point for the WE enterprise was the completion of Kachru's PhD thesis on Indian English in 1962, under the supervision of Michael A. K. Halliday at Edinburgh University. While at Edinburgh, Kachru (in the company of fellow graduate students Ayo Bamgbose, Ruqaiya Hasan, and Rodney Huddleston) also took classes with such other major linguists as David Abercrombie, J. C. Catford, M. A. K. Halliday, Peter Ladefoged, Angus McIntosh, and Peter Strevens, as well as J. R. Firth, who was Visiting Professor during that time (Nelson 2012). In 1963 Kachru took up a post at the University of Illinois at Urbana-Champaign and served in the Department of Linguistics full-time, until becoming Professor Emeritus in 2002. At Illinois, Kachru played a major role in promoting linguistics through a wide range of research and publications covering such diverse fields as multilingualism and sociolinguistics, Kashmiri language and literature, Indian linguistics, and WE, as well through his academic leadership as the Jubilee Professor of Liberal Arts and Sciences and Director of the Center for Advanced Study. It is no exaggeration to state that Braj B. Kachru changed the history of English studies through his theorization of the WE paradigm in the 1980s and 1990s (Sridhar 2016). In his endeavours at the University of Illinois, from 1965 onwards, Professor Braj B. Kachru was encouraged and supported by Yamuna Kachru (1933–2013), who herself was an eminent linguist whose publications spanned such areas as Hindi linguistics, Indian languages (including Bengali, Marathi, Urdu, Kashmiri), applied linguistics, discourse analysis, literary analysis, Asian Englishes and world Englishes. Her contribution to research on WE went far beyond research and publications, and at Urbana-Champaign she was an influential and inspirational educator who supervised more than forty PhD students. In 2006, she was also the recipient of India's Presidential Award for her research and publications on Hindi language studies (Bolton and Davis 2015: 3–4).

A third foundational figure in the history of WE is Larry E. Smith (1941–2014), whose academic career at the East–West Center at the University of Hawaii ran parallel to and complemented that of the Kachrus at Urbana-Champaign. Their early collaboration at two 1978 conferences is often seen as the beginning of their collaboration and another milestone in the creation and promotion of the WE paradigm, which also involved the renaming of the *World Englishes* journal in 1985 (previously titled *World Language English*) and the establishment of the IAWE in 1992. Any history of the discipline of WE needs to acknowledge that Braj B. Kachru and Larry Smith played a decisive role in the early foundation and development of the field, not least through their insistence that their approach to the subject was pluralistic; this was deliberately and iconically captured in the title of their journal, as they explained in the editorial for the first issue:

> The term 'Englishes' is significant in many ways. 'Englishes' symbolizes the functional and formal variation in the language, and its international acculturation, for example, in West Africa, in Southern Africa, in East Africa, in South Asia, in Southeast Asia, in the West Indies, in the Philippines, and in the traditional English-using countries: the USA, the UK, Australia, Canada, and New Zealand. The language now belongs to those who use it as their first language, and to those who use it as an additional language, whether in its standard form or in its localized forms.
>
> (Kachru and Smith 1985: 210)

Arguing for a 'new international perspective' in English studies, the editorial added that '[t]his new perspective entails questioning the prevalent dichotomies and reevaluating the 'sacred cows' in literature, language, and language teaching methodology' (210–211). At the time, the Kachruvian approach to WE was nothing less than revolutionary, not least through the pluralization of *Englishes*, a designation now taken for granted, which was hotly disputed at the time. The field of 'world Englishes' can be seen in both wider and narrower perspective. In wider perspective, the boundaries of the field of inquiry may be drawn large to include all those approaches listed in Table 1 at the beginning of this article. In a narrower perspective, 'world Englishes' was originally associated most closely with the theorizations and publications of Braj B. Kachru, Yamuna Kachru, Larry Smith and associated scholars, but over the last twenty years, given the large number of textbooks and monographs devoted to the subject, the reach and inclusivity of the name has expanded to include a large range of researchers approaching the field with diverse perspectives and methodologies, and yet, as Seargeant (2012a) has noted, nevertheless sharing 'fundamental concerns' and 'a focus on globally-contextualized enquiry into the spread of the English language' (126, also cited above). Indeed, one reason why this diverse field has developed in such a rich fashion may be linked to the founding vision of Kachru and Smith, and the inclusive and pluralistic ethos of the intellectual movement that they founded (Bolton 2005: 78–79). The founding fathers and founding mother of the Kachruvian approach to WE have now sadly and rather suddenly passed on, but whatever else, the firm wish of many of their colleagues and students is that their legacy should not be forgotten, and the cooperative and humanistic vision of the founders of this field should endure into the future.

Conclusion: future directions for world Englishes

It may indeed be the case that, as Saraceni (2015) suggests, WE is facing a number of challenges, including the emergence of the 'sociolinguistics of globalization' and 'English as a lingua franca' as important new areas of academic research and publication. My own view is that the intellectual enrichment that such fields offer through synergies with WE research is both potentially challenging and exciting, but here I would again argue that the WE paradigm is sufficiently robust and dynamic to meet such challenges. One major thread of continuity throughout the development of WE has been its inclusivity and pluricentricity, its inclusivity of subject matter, and the pluricentricity of languages and views on language that a global perspective allows.

Much of the criticism of the WE approach focuses narrowly on the geographical approaches to varieties of English adopted by some researchers in the field. Actually, if one goes back to look at Braj B. Kachru's own theorization of the field, very little space, relatively speaking, was given over to the discussion of regional varieties as such. One work currently in progress sets out to compile Kachru's writings from the 1970s to the present, and so far three volumes of collected articles have been published (Webster 2015). A reading (or re-reading) of such essays reminds one at once of the breadth of vision that helped shape Kachruvian linguistics as it developed in the 1980s and 1990s. For example, Volume 1 of the collection includes essays on 'Models of English for the Third World', 'The pragmatics of non-native varieties of English', 'The power and politics of English', and 'The spread of English and sacred linguistic cows'. Volume 2 covers such issues as 'Transcultural creativity in world Englishes', 'The paradigms of marginality', and 'World Englishes and culture wars', while Volume 3 includes chapters on 'Code-mixing as a communicative strategy', 'Bilingualism', and 'Multilingualism and multiculturalism'. A common thread that runs through almost all these essays is the strong awareness of the multilingual contexts of Englishes worldwide, and the acute need to situate WE research within a sociolinguistic approach to issues within the field. For example, nearly twenty years ago, Kachru and Nelson wrote:

> It is imperative that teachers and students be aware of the sort of presence that English has in the world today [. . .] The concept of a monolithic English as an exponent of culture

> and communication in all English-using countries has been a convenient working fiction that is now becoming harder and harder to maintain. What we have now in reality is English languages and English literatures [. . .] To understand the pluralism of English, it is therefore vital to see its spread, uses, and users in sociolinguistic contexts.
>
> (Kachru and Nelson 1996, in Webster 2015, Vol. 2: 81, emphasis added)

The emphasis here on the 'sociolinguistic contexts' of English(es) was a major strand of WE theorization for Kachru, and also helps explain the major and enduring impact his work has had on the field, and on the later work of other scholars whose work has focused on issues related to code-mixing, critical linguistics, linguistic imperialism, multilingualism, the politics of language and much else. It is also salutary to consider that Kachru himself published an article entitled 'English as a lingua franca' as early as 1996, some years before the recent interest in 'ELF' studies began to gather momentum (Kachru 1996, in Webster 2015, Vol. 2). Elsewhere, I have suggested that theoretical challenges in relation to globalization may find some resolution with the recognition of the role of WE in an expanded understanding of the changing and dynamic 'language worlds' of people in diverse communities around the world, where the 'worlds of Englishes' are ineluctably linked to the multilingual realities of language use (Bolton 2013). This again resonates with Kachru's pioneering theorizations of the WE field, and the maxim that the description and analysis of WE should be centrally concerned with the 'sociolinguistic realities' of language use in multilingual societies worldwide (Kachru 1992: 11).

As WE develops in the future, it is likely that the diversity of the wider field will continue, with scholars working on a wide range of linguistic and sociolinguistic issues. In Bolton (2005), I argued that three broad approaches to WE studies exist, at least if one considers the approaches of scholars working in the field in terms of their objectives. These were: (i) WE approaches largely linguistic in orientation (for instance, English studies and corpus linguistics); (ii) approaches that share both linguistic and sociopolitical concerns (many sociolinguistic studies and the WE approach); and (iii) those approaches that are largely sociopolitical and political in orientation (for example, critical discourse analysis and linguistic imperialism studies). The latter two strands of WE scholarship have been broadly concerned with various aspects of the sociolinguistics of English worldwide, and it is perhaps from sociolinguistics that we might expect WE to draw its theoretical inspiration. Sociolinguistics continues to motivate much of the current research in the *World Englishes* journal, where important topics in recent years have included contact linguistics (including code-switching and mixing), critical linguistics, language and religion, linguistic landscapes, multilingualism, popular culture, and ELF. While the journal still publishes articles of areal interest, many of the articles in the journal also resonate with key issues linked to the sociolinguistics of globalization, with special issues on such topics as 'The Englishes of Europe', 'Perspectives on English as a lingua franca', 'Creativity and world Englishes', 'World Englishes and linguistic landscapes', 'World Englishes and international call centres', 'English in Southeast Asia', 'English in China', and 'World Englishes and language contact'. One important challenge here is the extent to which the sociolinguistic methodology and analysis of WE is informed by recent trends in sociolinguistic research, where there has been a major paradigm shift in recent years. The essential thrust of this recent paradigm shift in sociolinguistics has been to question many of the foundational tenets that were established in the decades between the 1960s and 1990s, and were tied to a 'static' view of language and society, a view now challenged by newer iterations of a 'mobile' sociolinguistics, distinguished by 'a view of language as something intrinsically and perpetually mobile, through space as well as time, and made for mobility' (Blommaert 2010: 1, xiv). This new sociolinguistics has also brought with it new terminology to describe a range of processes associated with a mobile sociolinguistics, including such notions as 'superdiversity', 'translanguaging', 'translingual practice', 'trans-glossia', 'polylingual languaging', and 'metrolingualism', the use of which has been recently critiqued by Pennycook (2016). In his review of these 'post-Fishmanian' reconceptualizations of sociolinguistic constructs, he queries 'whether a new paradigm is likely to be ushered in by such a plethora of new terms' but nevertheless argues that 'we need at the same time to understand that terms such as "diversity", "bilingualism", and "multilingualism" have become burdened by their history of use both within academic texts and across social life more broadly'. Finally, Pennycook argues that the paradigm shift in sociolinguistics appears to mark 'a moment of disciplinary upheaval', signaling that 'communication occurs across what have been thought of as languages, that speakers draw on repertoires of semiotic resources, and that language is best understood in terms of social practices' (Pennycook 2016: 212).

The relevance of sociolinguistic theory to WE is centrally important. In the 1980s and 1990s, the WE paradigm represented a fresh, innovative and pluralistic vision of English studies, at a time when the English language was spreading rapidly, particularly throughout the education systems of former Anglophone colonies. As WE studies developed, however, they were never merely focused on English alone, but were more broadly concerned with describing and analysing how the spread of English impacted multilingual societies and cultures around the world, as well as the related processes of language contact, hybridization and cultural negotiation. For Braj B. Kachru, the Englishization of African and Asian languages was as much a concern as the nativization of the English language worldwide. Kachru's work on such issues preceded and anticipated recent conceptualizations of 'trans-languaging' and 'translingual practice', and it is difficult to imagine that such theorizations would have been formed without his innovative analysis of the sociolinguistic dynamics of multilingual societies. The point here is that the relationship between WE and sociolinguistics has never been one-way. Sociolinguistics may have provided the initial inspiration for the WE turn but, over the last three decades, WE perspectives have directly influenced sociolinguistic perspective on language change, contact, and variation.

As sociolinguistic theory adapts itself to the current era of globalization, it is to be expected that WE research will follow a similar trajectory of development. The WE approach has always been intrinsically dynamic and open to debate and new perspectives in research, scholarship, and theorization, and this flexibility, diversity, and openness has been a crucial element of the 'ethos' of WE as it (Bolton 2005). One key and enduring feature of WE research has been this openness to new ideas and innovation, and this, one trusts, will continue. Earlier, I have suggested that, in coming to terms with globalization, scholars might also recognize the key role of WE research in an expanded understanding of the 'language worlds' of young people across the planet, where the 'worlds of Englishes' are ineluctably linked to the multilingual matrices of diverse and varied global communities (Bolton 2013). In this context, we might be well advised to remind ourselves of Kachru's oft-repeated axiom that WE always maintains a focus on the 'sociolinguistic realities' of language use in multilingual societies worldwide (Kachru 1992: 11).

From the 1980s to the present the WE project has contributed to a major theoretical shift in English studies worldwide, in large part through the pioneering foundational work of Braj B. Kachru, which from the outset argued for a paradigm shift of two types: (i) 'a paradigm shift in research, teaching, and the application of sociolinguistic realities to the functions of English', and (ii) 'a shift from frameworks and theories which are essentially appropriate only to monolingual countries', involving a pluralism which is 'reflected in the approaches, both theoretical and applied, we adopt for understanding this unprecedented linguistic phenomenon' (Kachru 1997, in Webster 2015: 175, Vol. 2). At this point in its development, the WE enterprise may be regarded as having reached a point of maturity or even orthodoxy within English studies and linguistics, but this remains a diverse and pluralistic field, and, as its ethos suggests, WE remains open for new directions, new insights, and new energies.

Notes

1 Interest in the diverse forms and functions of so-called 'new Englishes' throughout the world has been paralleled by a related interest in new literatures in English, particularly from writers originally from former British colonies, such as V. S. Naipaul, Michael Ondaatje, Timothy Mo, Ben Okri, Wole Soyinka, Arundhati Roy, Salman Rushdie, and Derek Walcott (King 2005).
2 To some extent, studies using an English as a Lingua Franca (ELF) approach may be seen as a contemporary updating of an earlier approach to research, which highlighted the role of English as an International Language (EIL). This approach was associated with linguists such as Smith (1976, 1981), Strevens (1980), McKay (2002) and Sharifian (2009). Theorists of ELF have stated that early EIL researchers may be seen as 'precursors' in the field of English as a Lingua Franca (Ehrenreich and Pitzl 2015).

Further reading

Bolton, K. and B. B. Kachru (eds) (2006) *World Englishes: Critical Concepts in Linguistics*. Vol. 6. Abingdon: Routledge. This provides a definitive collection of articles on WE from a range of perspectives, including theoretical approaches, regional profiles, paradigms of description, codification, intelligibility, language contact, discourse studies, corpus linguistics, the politics of language, and globalization.

Melchers, G. and P. Shaw (2009) *World Englishes: An Introduction*. 2nd edn. London: Arnold. A carefully-researched and well-designed textbook on English worldwide, which provides a detailed description of the linguistic features of varieties in many regions of the world.

Seargeant, P. (2012) *Exploring World Englishes: Language in a Global Context*. Abingdon: Routledge. A comprehensive survey of many of the contemporary debates on WE from an academic perspective, with a clear explanation of many of the central theoretical concerns in this area.

Webster, J. J. (ed.) (2015) *Collected Works of Braj B. Kachru*. Vols. 1–3. London: Bloomsbury. An extremely valuable collection of key articles by Braj B. Kachru, whose work has provided a foundational and inspirational basis for a number of important approaches in the field of WE.

Related topics

- The historical study of English
- English and colonialism
- Standards in English
- Contact Englishes
- English and multilingualism: a contested history.

References

Blommaert, J. (2010) *The Sociolinguistics of Globalization*. Cambridge: Cambridge University Press.

Bolton, K. (2003) *Chinese Englishes: A Sociolinguistic History*. Cambridge: Cambridge University Press.

Bolton, K. (2004) 'World Englishes', in A. Davies and C. Elder (eds), *The Handbook of Applied Linguistics*. Oxford: Blackwell, 367–420.

Bolton, K. (2005) 'Where WE stands: Approaches, issues and debate in world Englishes', *World Englishes* 24 (1): 69–83.

Bolton, K. (2006) 'World Englishes today', in B. B. Kachru, Y. Kachru and C. L. Nelson (eds), *The Handbook of World Englishes*. Oxford: Blackwell, 240–269.
Bolton, K. (2011) 'World Englishes, Asian Englishes, and English as a Lingua Franca'. Invited opening keynote at the Fourth International Conference of English as a Lingua Franca. Hong Kong Institute of Education, 26 May 2011.
Bolton, K. (2012) 'World Englishes and Asian Englishes: A survey of the field', in A. Kirkpatrick (ed.), *English as an International Language in Asia: Implications for Language Education*. Dordrecht: Springer, 13–26.
Bolton, K. (2013) 'World Englishes, globalization, and language worlds', in N.-L. Johannesson, G. Melchers and B. Björkman (eds), *Of Butterflies and Birds, of Dialects and Genres: Essays in Honour of Philip Shaw*. Stockholm: Acta Universitatis Stockholmiensis, 227–251.
Bolton, K. and D. Davis (2006) 'A content analysis of world Englishes', *World Englishes* 25 (1): 5–6.
Bolton, K. and D. Davis (2015) 'With admiration, gratitude, and deep respect: In honor of Professor Yamuna Kachru (1933–2013)', *World Englishes* 34 (1): 3–5.
Bolton, K. and C. Meierkord (2013) 'English in contemporary Sweden: Perceptions, policies, and narrated practices', *Journal of Sociolinguistics* 17 (1): 93–117.
Bragg, M. (2003) *The Adventure of English*. London: Hodder and Stoughton.
Bruthiaux, P. (2003) 'Squaring the circles: Issues in modeling English worldwide', *International Journal of Applied Linguistics* 13 (2): 159–178.
Canagarajah, S. A. (1999) *Resisting Linguistic Imperialism in English Teaching*. Oxford: Oxford University Press.
Crystal, D. (1997) *English as a Global Language*. Cambridge: Cambridge University Press.
Crystal, D. (2004) Subcontinent Raises Its Voice, *Guardian Weekly*, 19 November, Available at www.theguardian.com/education/2004/nov/19/tefl, accessed 23 November 2015.
de Grazia, V. (2005) *America's Irresistible Empire: America's Advance through 20th Century Europe*. Cambridge: Harvard University Press.
Demont-Heinrich, C. (2010) 'Linguistically privileged and cursed? American university students and the global hegemony of English', *World Englishes* 29 (2): 281–298.
Ehrenreich, S. and M.-L. Pitzl (2015) 'Precursors: Introductory remarks on Smith (1976, 1983[1981]) and Knapp (1987)', *Journal of English as a Lingua Franca* 4 (1): 157–158.
Fishman, J. A., A. W. Conrad and A. Rubal-Lopez (eds) (1996) *Post-Imperial English*. Berlin: Mouton de Gruyter.
Galloway, N. and H. Rose (2015) *Introducing Global Englishes*. Abingdon: Routledge.
Görlach, M. (ed.) (1995) 'Dictionaries of transplanted Englishes', in M. Görlach (ed.), *More Englishes: New Studies in Varieties of English 1988–1994*. Amsterdam: John Benjamins, 124–163.
Graddol, D. (1997) *The Future of English?* London: The British Council.
Graddol, D. (2006) *English Next*. London: The British Council.
Greenbaum, S. (ed.) (1996) *Comparing English Worldwide*. Oxford: Clarendon Press.
Halliday, M. A. K., A. McIntosh and P. Strevens (1964) *The Linguistic Sciences and Language Teaching*. London: Longman.
ICE (2016) '*International corpus of English*'. Available at www.ice-corpora.net/ICE/INDEX.HTM, accessed 11 November 2016.
Jenkins, J. (2003) *World Englishes: A Resource Book for Students*. London: Routledge.
Jenkins, J. (2007) *English as a Lingua Franca: Attitude and Identity*. Oxford: Oxford University Press.
Jenkins, J. (2013) *English as a Lingua Franca in the International University: The Politics of Academic English Policy*. Oxford: Oxford University Press.
Kachru, B. B. (1976) 'Models of English for the Third World: White man's linguistic burden or language pragmatics?', *TESOL Quarterly* 10 (2): 221–239.
Kachru, B. B. (1985) 'Standards, codification and sociolinguistic realism: The English language in the outer circle', in R. Quirk (ed.), *English in the World: Teaching and Learning the Language and Literatures*. Cambridge: Cambridge University Press, 11–30.
Kachru, B. B. (1992) 'World Englishes: Approaches, issues and resources', *Language Teaching* 25: 1–14.
Kachru, B. B. (1996) 'English as a lingua franca', in H. Goebl, P. H. Nelde, I. Stary and W. Wolck (eds), *Contact Linguistics: An International Handbook of Contemporary Research*. Berlin: Walter de Gruyter, 906–913.
Kachru, B. B. (1997) 'World Englishes 2000: Resources for research and teaching', in L. E. Smith and M. L. Forman (eds), *World Englishes 2000*. Honolulu: University of Hawaii Press, 209–251.

Kachru, B. B. (2005) *Asian Englishes beyond the Canon*. Hong Kong: Hong Kong University Press.
Kachru, B. B. and L. E. Smith (1985) 'Editorial', *World Englishes* 4 (2): 209–212.
Kachru, B. B. and C. L. Nelson (1996) 'World Englishes', in S. L. McKay and N. H. Hornberger (eds), *Sociolinguistics and Language Teaching*. Vol. 1. Cambridge: Cambridge University Press, 71–102.
King, B. (2005) *The Internationalization of English Literature: The Oxford English Literary History, Vol 13: 1948–2000*. Oxford: Oxford University Press.
Kirkpatrick, A. (2007) *World Englishes: Implications for International Communication and English Language Teaching*. Cambridge: Cambridge University Press.
Kortmann, B., K. Burridge, R. Mesthrie, E. W. Schneider and C. Upton (2004) *A Handbook of Varieties of English. Volume 2: Morphology and Syntax*. Berlin: Mouton de Gruyter.
Liou, T.-J. (2012) *Chinese-Speaking International Students' Experiences and Perspectives of ESL University Writing Programs* (Unpublished Ph.D. dissertation, New Mexico State University).
Martell, Luke (2017) *The Sociology of Globalization*. Second edn. Cambridge: Polity Press.
Matsumoto, Y. (2011) 'Successful ELF communication and implications for ELT: Sequential analysis of ELF pronunciation negotiation strategies', *The Modern Language Journal* 95 (1): 97–114.
Mauranen, A. and E. Ranta (eds) (2009) *English as a Lingua Franca: Studies and Findings*. Newcastle upon Tyne: Cambridge Scholars.
McArthur, T. (1993) 'The English language or the English languages?', in W. F. Bolton and D. Crystal (eds), *The English Language*. London: Penguin Books, 323–341.
McKay, S. (2002) *Teaching English as an International Language*. Oxford: Oxford University Press.
Melchers, G. and Shaw, P. (2003) *World Englishes: An Introduction*. London: Arnold.
Mesthrie, R. and R. M. Bhatt (2008) *World Englishes: The Study of New Linguistic Varieties*. Cambridge: Cambridge University Press.
Mukherjee, J. (2012) 'English in South Asia: Ambinormative orientations and the role of corpora: The state of the debate in Sri Lanka', in A. Kirkpatrick and R. Sussex (eds), *English as an International Language in Asia: Implications for Language Education*. Dordrecht: Springer, 191–208.
Nelson, C. L. (2012) 'Braj B. Kachru', in C. A. Chapelle (ed.), *The Encyclopedia of Applied Linguistics*, Available at www.onlinelibrary.wiley.com.ezlibproxy1.ntu.edu.sg/doi/10.1002/9781405198431.wbeal1330/pdf, accessed 11 November 2016.
Nelson, G., S. Wallis and B. Aarts (2002) *Exploring Natural Language: Working with the British Component of the International Corpus of English*. Amsterdam: John Benjamins.
Parkin, D. and K. Arnaut (2010) 'Super-diversity & sociolinguistics—A digest', *Tilburg Papers in Cultural Studies* 95: 1–6.
Pennycook, A. (1994) *The Cultural Politics of English as an International Language*. London: Longman.
Pennycook, A. (2001) *Critical Applied Linguistics*. Mahwah: Lawrence Erlbaum.
Pennycook, A. (2016) 'Mobile times, mobile terms: The trans-super-poly-metro movement', in N. Coupland (ed.), *Sociolinguistics: Theoretical Debates*. Cambridge: Cambridge University Press, 201–216.
Phillipson, R. (1992) *Linguistic Imperialism*. Oxford: Oxford University Press.
Phillipson, R. (2009) *Linguistic Imperialism Continued*. Hyderabad: Orient Blackswan.
Phillipson, R. (2010) '*Interview*' Available at www.nnesintesol.blogspot.com/2009/07/robert-phillipson.html, accessed 23 November 2015.
Saraceni, M. (2015) *World Englishes: A Critical Analysis*. London: Bloomsbury Academic.
Schneider, E. (2003) 'The dynamics of New Englishes: From identity construction to dialect birth', *Language* 79 (2): 233–281.
Schneider, E. (2007) *Postcolonial English: Varieties around the World*. Cambridge: Cambridge University Press.
Schneider, E. W., K. Burridge, B. Kortmann, R. Mesthrie and C. Upton (2004) *A Handbook of Varieties of English. Volume 1: Phonology*. Berlin: Mouton de Gruyter.
Seargeant, P. (2010) 'Naming and defining in world Englishes', *World Englishes* 29 (1): 97–113.
Seargeant, P. (2012a) 'Disciplinarity and the study of world Englishes', *World Englishes* 31 (1): 113–129.
Seargeant, P. (2012b) *Exploring World Englishes: Language in a Global Context*. London: Routledge.
Seargeant, P. and J. Swann (eds) (2012) *English in the World: History, Diversity, Change*. London: Routledge.
Seidlhofer, B. (2001) 'Closing a conceptual gap: The case for a description of English as a lingua franca', *Journal of Applied Linguistics* 11 (2): 133–158.

Seidlhofer, B. (2011) *Understanding English as a Lingua Franca*. Oxford: Oxford University.
Sharifian, F. (ed.) (2009) *English as an International Language: Perspectives and Pedagogical Issues*. Bristol: Multilingual Matters.
Smith, L. E. (1976) 'English as an international auxiliary language', *RELC Journal* 7 (2): 38–42.
Smith, L. E. (1981) 'English as an international language: No room for linguistic chauvinism', *Nagoya Gakuin Daigaku, Gaikokugo, Kyoiku Kiyo* [Nagoya Gakuin University Round Table on Languages, Linguistics and Literature] 3: 27–32.
Sridhar, S. N. (2016) 'A cultural warrior rests his case', *World Englishes* 35 (4): 489–491.
Strevens, P. (1980) *English as an International Language*. Oxford: Pergamon.
Trudgill, P. and J. Hannah ([1982] 2013) *International English: A Guide to Varieties of Standard English*. London: Arnold.
Webster, J. J. (ed.) (2015) *Collected Works of Braj B. Kachru*. Vols. 1–3. London: Bloomsbury.

5

English and multilingualism

A contested history

Ofelia García and Angel M. Y. Lin

Introduction

Although people of various origins have always had different ways of using language, it is the ways of speaking of powerful citizens that have been constructed into what are recognized as named languages, and which act as instruments of control over the rest of the population. Acts of naming languages contribute to the ideology that languages are discrete and monolithic, ignoring the complex linguistic practices of all speakers and establishing hierarchies of power and privilege among speakers.

This chapter tells the contested history of what we today name English, as well as what we today call multilingualism. The chapter makes the point that both English and multilingualism are constructed concepts that need to be interrogated. And it proposes that these constructions have served the English-speaking elite well in the past, and continue to do so in the present.

We first tell the story of how English was consolidated into the language of the greatest empire in the world. Our brief history takes the point of view not of 'English,' but of its construction. We explore how bilingualism and multilingualism have been constructed in relationship to English; first in the imperial stage, as a reason for the minoritization of non-white colonized speakers, and today, as ways of ensuring that English keeps its dominance. What has been called in the present the multilingual turn (Conteh and Meier 2014; May 2013) would not exist if it were not for the imperial origins of English, as well as the interest that it continues to hold in the imagination of many. We argue here that it is the economically-driven pursuit of English in today's global and neoliberal economy which has created the interest in multilingualism. And yet, this multilingualism continues to leave out precisely those who are multilingual, minoritized speakers whose language practices differ from those legitimized in dominant societies and schools. We show here that the construction of the English language and multilingualism have been mutually constitutive and have served a purpose of domination and control.

The chapter starts by providing an account of the evolution of this long-standing relationship between English and linguistic diversity. We then focus on the role that colonization has had in the construction of English as the most powerful language in the world, and of the understandings of multilingualism. We also identify the issues that the position of English and multilingualism raise today, as well as the debates that it has engendered.

In order to localize the arguments we make, we describe the multilingual realities of some Asian regions, focusing on how their multilingualism was erased (or occasionally used) during the colonial period, as English was promoted for domination. By focusing on the Asian context, we propose ways in which our conceptions of language, including English and what we consider multilingualism, would have to change in order to destroy the linguistic hierarchies that continue to operate in the world today.

Historical perspectives

Origins and constructions

The history of the English language as told in textbooks and historical research has always included the acknowledgement that English was shaped through contact with people who spoke differently. What we have named 'Old English' was shaped through interactions between the three Germanic tribes who invaded the British Isles around 450 AD, the Celts who were pushed north and west by the Germanic invaders, and the later invasion, in the 10th century, of Vikings from Scandinavia. When the Norman William the Conqueror defeated King Harold at Hastings in 1066, the Court, the Church and the upper classes started imitating their Norman king's ways of speaking. But merchants and people other than nobles continued speaking differently, and what we today call 'Middle English' was a result of contact between the ways of speaking of nobles and others. Middle English is the name we attach to the language Chaucer used in *The Canterbury Tales* in the late 14th century, reflecting the vernacular of the people, and containing words brought to England by the Anglo-Saxons and words brought by the Normans (Baugh and Cable 2002).

It was the homogenizing effect of the printing press introduced into England in 1476 by William Caxton that started shaping what developed into what we have learned to call Modern English (Blake 1991). Slowly, the many different ways people had of speaking became standardized, as publishers made decisions about preferred style and dialects. As the Kingdom of England, which conquered and included Wales after 1535, started to project itself as a powerful state firstly within the British Isles and then beyond its borders, the construction of English as an entity (Park and Wee 2012) became paramount. Publishers started preferring the dialect spoken by the dominant class in London, where the king resided. Borrowings from Latin and Greek, as well as Italian and German, expanded the English lexicon during the Renaissance. William Shakespeare wrote most of his works between 1590 and 1614, contributing many words. In 1604 Robert Cawdrey published the first simple monolingual dictionary of what is considered Early Modern English. And in 1611 the King James Bible was published, a major text in establishing the important status of the English language.

In 1588 England defeated the Spanish armada, consolidating the might of British maritime power. English was not simply to be used within the original island territory. The plan of the growing power was to acquire the many people and their riches in a complex of territories over which the sun never set. To do so, English as constituted by the ruling class was often seen as the only legitimate way of speaking. In contrast to other European states of the time that established language academies and published prescriptive grammars, it was London booksellers who contacted Samuel Johnson to produce a dictionary. As Johnson (1747) himself wrote in the plan, his purpose was to write a dictionary 'by which the pronunciation of our language may be fixed, and its attainment facilitated; by which its purity may be preserved, its use ascertained, and its duration lengthened.' In Johnson's mind, the fixing and purity of the English language was important if it were to be used in the growing Empire. The English language was to be, as Johnson said in his plan, 'varied and compounded, yet not destroyed.'

What we today call 'English' is thus a product of the complex historical and political contexts in which it was shaped, containing the voices and accents of diverse speakers. But for English to assume its role in the domination of people who spoke differently in the British Empire, it was necessary not only to standardize it (Algeo and Pyles 2010; Baugh and Cable 2002), but also to construct categories of people who would have access to it. In its imperial role, the language named English became celebrated, whereas the multilingual practices of indigenous colonized populations were stigmatized. To consolidate the power of white English speakers, more was needed than simply attention to the construction of English – a different authoritative form of multilingualism also had to be created which excluded the fluid language practices of many of the indigenous populations with which the English speakers came into contact.

English and multilingualism in Empire

The categorization of populations based on language became one way of producing 'governable subjects' (Foucault 2008; Flores 2013) during the growth of the British Empire between the 16th and the 19th century. Linguistically, speakers in the Empire were differently categorized as:

1. **English native speakers**, born in the territory of England, white, generally monolingual and with resources. They were valued for speaking 'standard English' and were generally school-educated.
2. **English dialect speakers**, white English speakers of poor means, born in the territory of England, and generally monolingual. They were stigmatized for speaking 'dialects of English' that were perceived as substandard and received poor schooling, if any.
3. **Indigenous bilingual populations,** indigenous whites born in Wales, Scotland, or Ireland. They were said to be bilingual or have traces of bilingualism and were minoritized because of this. If educated, they attended only English-medium schools where they mostly experienced failure.
4. **Silent populations,** enslaved black and Native American people in the New World who were excluded from learning English and from schooling.
5. **Immigrant foreign language-speakers**, white immigrants to the United States. English was imposed and their bilingualism not recognized.
6. **Bilingual/multilingual intermediaries,** brown people in the Asian, African, and Pacific colonies who served the white English-speaking masters. They were given access to learning English and English-language schooling to serve as intermediaries between the British state and the people.
7. **Indigenous multilingual populations,** brown people in the Asian, African, and Pacific colonies who were not given access to English or schooling during the colonization era.

We describe below how language served to differentiate speakers and provide (or not) access to economic rewards.

The creation of the *English native-speaker*, that is, someone who was white, born in the territory of England, and with economic resources, became an important means of domination and hierarchization; this was so whether in Wales, Ireland or Scotland, in the North American colonies, or in the Asian, African, and Pacific colonies (Holborow 1999; Pennycook 1995, 1998; Phillipson 1992). These powerful white speakers were the only ones granted the privilege of being perceived as English native speakers, with others who had not been socialized in these prosperous echelons of society branded as *speakers of English 'dialects,'* that were deemed substandard and inferior.

From the 16th through to the 18th century, the Kingdom of England gained control of Wales, Scotland, and Ireland to become the United Kingdom of Great Britain and Ireland (in 1922 the Irish Free State came into being). In the British Isles, bilingualism was not to be tolerated (Kandler et al. 2010), and *English monolingualism* became the only way to truly participate in the dominant society, as many were forced to shift to English.

In contrast to the harsh imposition of the standardized English language on the white indigenous peoples of the British Isles, the indigenous peoples of North America, as well as the enslaved people brought to the British colonies by British salve traders, were excluded from English and were not given access to the English language or to schooling. Enslaved Africans, with rich linguistic repertoires, were mixed by origin so that they would not be able to communicate. Native Americans were simply progressively exterminated or pushed into Indian territories (García 2009; Wiley 1996). The English language became not just standardized, but also racialized. For the white conquered populations of the British Isles, what was constructed as standard English became the only authoritative way to communicate. For black enslaved populations and brown conquered populations, neither their ways of speaking nor their use of the ways of speaking of white Englishmen were legitimized. These black and brown bodies were simply rendered silent in the western sociocultural and sociolinguistic paradigm that considered the English language as constitutive of Empire.

The United States inherited the linguistic practices of the British colonies. Besides the enslavement of Africans, and the conquest of Native Americans, immigration to what became the United States was paramount to its formation as an independent nation state. But as in the British Isles, the imposition of English among white immigrants who spoke other languages became an important national mission after independence. The US founding fathers debated the issue of declaring English as the official language for the new country, but decided that the economic attraction of English was strong enough that no other incentive was needed (Heath 1976). Between 1890 and 1930 sixteen million immigrants (mostly from Germany, Sweden, Ukraine, Finland, Lithuania, Poland, Slovakia, Greece, Russia, and especially Italy) entered the United States. The ways of speaking of these immigrants were constituted as 'foreign languages' and were, in the words of Theodore Roosevelt, not only 'a misfortune but a crime.' Languages other than English were not to be tolerated, and schools played an important role in the imposition of English.

As the British Empire grew in Asia, Africa, and the Pacific over the 19th century, the British came into contact with people with whom they had to maintain a colonial relationship of trade, not simply conquer. The English were constructed as white, powerful, young (Said 1978, for example, tells us that British colonizers were forced to retire at the age of 55 so that they would conserve the myth of powerful young white men), and monolingual speakers of a standardized language; the Others were mostly non-whites, powerless, weak, and speakers of what were not even considered languages. In these Asian, African, and Pacific colonies, speakers were of two types. First, there were those who were at the top of the colonial social class and served their British masters, and who benefited from the British presence. They spoke English to different degrees of ability and with their own accents and also the dominant language(s) in the society in which they lived. The English language gave them access to participate as second-class citizens in the life of the colony. This more powerful class of colonized people were permitted an *expedient bilingualism or multilingualism* to serve as intermediaries between the English monolinguals and the others. The second type of colonized people did not in any way interact with their British masters, but with the bilingual/multilingual English-speaking more powerful class of the colony. English, for them, remained inaccessible, and they remained speakers of their *own local ways of speaking*, what we might call *indigenous multilingualism*. Without schooling, and without any political or economic power, these speakers did not develop a linguistic consciousness that they spoke any named language; they simply used language to communicate locally. In the colonies, this indigenous multilingualism was constructed as a linguistic jumble associated with confused colonized people, whereas monolingualism was the mark of being the real thing: an intelligent native English speaker; a white powerful colonizer.

Native English speakers did not have to either speak or listen to subjects that were then rendered silent. Instead, the colonized were forced to understand orders in the only language authorized and legitimized. And as this one-way interactional process became socially established, only the speech of those considered native to the British Isles was to be understood and validated. This construction of an entity considered English-only in the mouths of native speakers slowly became one of the most powerful tools of the British Empire (Canagarajah 1999; Holborow 1999; Pennycook 1995, 1998; Phillipson 1992).

The multilingual origins of English were now well out of sight, substituted by a monolingual ethos. At the same time, learned multilingualism had been established as the ability to especially read (not just speak) European languages from different nation states, and, of course, Latin and Greek. This *authoritative literate multilingualism* was perceived as being very different from the *indigenous multilingualism* of the brown and black populations. An authoritative literate multilingualism was thus reserved for white elite Europeans to have access to western cultural capital, its literature and histories. But the 'indigenous multilingualism' of the colonized others did not disappear and became even more visible as the Empire crumbled.

Key issues and new construction: multilingualism and English in a new world order

During the 20th century the colonial structure started to give way to other forms of domination in which the legacy of the British Empire, the language named English, and the construction of an authoritative literate multilingualism have continued to play a major role. The Empire lost its geographical center (see Pietikäinen and Kelly-Holmes 2013), but English continued to be used in building hegemonic power relations and as a mechanism of control in local social and political relations. After 700 years of contact with speakers who spoke differently and who had a more extensive linguistic repertoire than that of white English native speakers, the ways of speaking of others started to be 'heard,' as former colonies were granted political independence.

The indigenous multilingualism of the periphery started to be recognized. For a short time, mostly during the period of what became known as the Ethnic Revival of the 1960s (Fishman 1985), multilingualism took on another dimension, as it became understood not just as a way to access another elite European culture by elites (as it had been in the past), but also to give voice to those who, as Spivak (1988) says, had not been previously allowed to speak. As the subaltern and oppressed minoritized groups in the world voiced their different belief systems, they also started speaking their indigenous multilingualism. The concept of multilingualism itself became contested. Now multilingualism was not just in the hands of white elites for whom only the major European languages were valid and important as a mark of high culture, but also in the hands of indigenous groups and regional minorities in nation states, even European ones. Multilingualism thus also needed to be controlled.

The scholarly literature around bilingualism and multilingualism started to expand around this time. Weinreich (1953/1974) and Haugen (1956) published their now famous treatises on bilingualism. And the nascent study of sociolinguistics turned its attention to language planning and language policy issues having to do with how to 'control' the multilingualism of the newly independent nations (Fishman 1974; Rubin and Jernudd 1971). It was proposed that languages, as entities, could be shaped through corpus planning, and their standing changed through status planning.

As the multilingualism of indigenous colonial people started to be heard, western scholars started to restrict understandings of bilingualism and multilingualism to fit a linguistic regime that kept indigenous multilingual speakers out of economic opportunities. Much of the now conventional wisdom about bilingualism was produced around this time. Bilingual people were said to use their languages in a diglossic relationship, that is, for different functions or in different spaces (Fishman 1964). And only diglossia was said to 'save' bilingualism, that is, maintain two languages intergenerationally.

Lambert (1974), speaking about bilingualism in education, also tried to regiment the use of languages. True bilingualism was 'additive,' with the 'second' language (L2) added separately to the 'first' one (L1). True bilingual education had to keep the two languages isolated. Immersion education was developed during this time, a way to teach students an L2 in ways that would ensure the students' bilingualism. And if the two languages were not separated in education, bilingualism was said to be 'subtractive,' leading to monolingualism. Instances of bilingual performances were interpreted as possible cases of linguistic 'interference.' The speech of multilinguals was examined through the lens of monolinguals, identifying borrowings, loan shifts, code-switching (Weinreich 1953/1974), always different from the ways in which monolinguals used language.

Sociolinguistic scholarship had good intentions, but it was constructed with western understandings of language, and as a product of North American and British scholars, it was especially attentive to conserving the power of the English of Empire. Although indigenous multilingual populations had gained political independence, economic dependence had to be assured, and here too language played a part. Language scholars, especially English-speaking ones, developed a canon of understandings about bilingualism (interestingly enough, not multilingualism) that reflected the construction of authoritative literate bilingualism, leaving out the indigenous multilingual practices that were prevalent throughout.

Taking a page from the construction of English and other named languages, conquered, colonized, and oppressed groups all over the world that now enjoyed a measure of independence claimed that they spoke 'languages,' not just corrupted dialects, as the colonizers had previously positioned their ways of speaking. They claimed that they spoke two or more languages, languages that were whole, autonomous, and legitimate, and that they used them for different functions, that is, in a diglossic relationship (see Fishman 1964). These minoritized groups contributed to the development of bilingual education programs, where their own fluid language practices were delegitimized, as if what were now recognized as different languages never touched their lips. The concept of additive bilingualism was now deeply established, not only among elite majority speakers, but also among minoritized speakers. Bilingualism and multilingualism was now conceptualized as a series of autonomous languages that conformed to certain prescriptive norms, a 'parallel monolingualism,' in the words of Heller (1999). Cummins (2005) refers to the construction of English/French bilingualism in Canada as 'the two solitudes.' Multilingualism had become recognized within institutional education, but not the language practices of indigenous multilingual speakers.

In this new trend toward multilingualism, English could have been the loser. But powerful English speakers slipped in an additional construction. English did not lose its grip on other languages. Instead, it morphed into the primary way to be recognized as bilingual and participate in the global economy. Now multilingualism was not just restricted to the powerful elite to acquire 'culture,' or just to minoritized people; it became the essential characteristic of those who needed to work or trade in the global market in a new neoliberal order that supported the free flow of capitalism in ways that benefited transnational corporations and economic elites (Flores 2013). English, as well as the commodification of multilingualism, became the fundamental ingredient for this neoliberal economy.

The new linguistic social order was not solely based on the linguistic imperialism of the British Council and other agents so well described by Phillipson (1992). The new linguistic regime now demanded that the ruling class of the world would *also* need English in order to participate in a neoliberal economy and thus obtain economic, political, and social favors. Multilingualism, understood as another language or languages plus English, became the new regime.

Other European languages, especially German and French, continued to compete in the world market, although with diminished importance. And of course, Asian languages, most importantly Chinese, have taken on great importance in these global markets. But English is still the motor behind the world's growing multilingualism.

The efforts in the European Union to promote plurilingualism can be interpreted as trying to reserve a space at the table for European languages other than English. The Council of Europe (2000) defines plurilingualism as 'the ability to use several languages to varying degrees and for distinct purposes.' This concept promotes the idea that bi/multilingualism is more than additive and that bilingual speakers are more than two monolinguals in one (Grosjean 1982). Plurilingualism indeed liberates bilingual speakers from the monolingual/monoglossic constructions of bilingualism of the 20th century. But the concept of plurilingualism has been constructed with an epistemology that responds to western dominant constructions of named languages, and thus leaves the hierarchies of languages intact. The speaker's 'first' or 'native' language is dominant and full, whereas the other linguistic practices are viewed as being the result of partial competence in a second or third named language. In moving toward this more flexible definition of multilingualism, the concept of plurilingualism also opened the floodgates for the triumph of English, for now everyone was encouraged to use it, even if they had 'partial competence.'

The construction of a new order for multilingualism in which English, as an autonomous powerful language, was the key instrument was now in full swing. Interestingly enough, the co-construction of English and multilingualism has enabled new understandings of multilingualism, understandings that in some small way open up possibilities to view the language practices of multilinguals from their own indigenous perspective. And yet, the contestation between different understandings of both language and multilingualism is today even fiercer than it has been in the past. The next section discusses how the discourse and study around English and multilingualism have changed, as well as the difficulties involved in transferring these recent theoretical understandings to practice, especially in schools.

Future directions: changing conceptions of English and multilingualism

As multilingual speakers appropriate English resources, we have started to relinquish the idea that there is but one standardized English. In the 1990s, the work of Kachru (1990, 1992) advanced the idea that English was indeed capable of 'alchemy', as he termed it in the title of one of his books. Kachru's model recognized that English was spoken in three circles – an 'inner circle,' that included the United Kingdom and the United States, an 'outer circle' that included former colonies and where English was used as a second language, and an 'expanding circle' that included nation states with no colonial connection to English, but where English was increasingly spoken as a lingua franca. Kachru's focus was on indigenized Englishes; thus his work did not focus on multilingualism. Although most important, Kachru's work and most of the work that followed on World Englishes never faced the fact that the growing multilingualism was a result of a different way in which the power of English was exercised in a neoliberal economy. In the outer and expanding circles the increased contact with English created the conditions for a growing multilingualism, whereas in the inner circle, contact with users of languages other than English constituted a transformed multilingual context. Even as they were first described, the circles no longer held their geographical and historical boundaries for English, for multilingualism was in their midst.

The work on World Englishes was extended by what became the work of proponents of English as a Lingua Franca (ELF). ELF continued the work of highlighting the renewed interest in the diversity of English, and questioned the native English norms. Instead of focusing on the code itself, especially in postcolonial contexts, as the early work on World Englishes had done, ELF now looked at how English was used as a social practice in diverse communities (Seidlhofer 2009, 2011; Jenkins 2015). Seidlhofer (2009) was perhaps the first to point out the fluidity of the ELF data, motivated, she said, by the 'situated negotiation of meaning' (p. 242). And, paying more attention to what concerns us in this chapter, Jenkins (2015) called for a repositioning of English and multilingualism in ELF; that is, as Jenkins argued, the fact that ELF cannot be treated in isolation since it is a multilingual practice.

There is, however, much tension between those who see themselves as scholars of 'English,' and those who see themselves as 'multilingual' scholars. The tension emerges from the fact that minority critical multilingual scholars, especially from the former Asian colonies, have increasingly questioned the concept of named language in an effort to give scholarly credence to their own fluid language practices (see, for example, Khubchandani 1997). In a highly critical book, Makoni and Pennycook (2007) call for the 'disinvention' of named languages which, they claim, have been instruments of colonial oppression. Taking up the old idea proposed by Bakhtin (1981) that linguistic practices are heteroglossic, the concept of additive bilingualism is also increasingly giving way to that of dynamic bilingualism (García 2009). Languages are not simply piled up as wholes in speakers' consciousness, but their repertoires are recognized as mobile (Blommaert 2010).

Speakers' fluid linguistic practices, what we previously called *indigenous multilingualism*, have always been historically present (Canagarajah and Liyanage 2012). This use of language is not new; rather what is new is the critical sociolinguistic scholarship that has called attention to the imperialistic reasons for preserving the focus on a named language like English and the authoritative literate multilingualism of the past, instead of acknowledging multilingual speakers' fluid language practices.

These fluid multilingual practices have been identified by many different names with slightly different meanings – polylanguaging/polylingual languaging (Jørgensen 2008), metrolingualism (Otsuji and Pennycook 2010), translingual practices (Canagarajah 2013), and translanguaging (Blackledge and Creese 2010; García 2009; García and Wei 2014; Otheguy et al. 2015).

Interestingly enough, translanguaging had its origin in the British Isles, in Wales, where Cen Williams (1994) first introduced *trawsiethu* as a bilingual approach to the teaching of Welsh-English bilinguals where both languages were used simultaneously, one for input and another for output. Over time, translanguaging was extended to refer to both the fluid language practices of multilingual people, as well as the leveraging of those practices for education purposes around this more inclusive vision of multilingualism (see, for example, Blackledge and Creese 2010; García 2009; García and Wei 2014; Hornberger and Link 2012). Rather than reify named languages, translanguaging makes the point that multilingual speakers have a unitary language repertoire in which their linguistic knowledge is not partitioned along the understandings of named languages in society.

Taking up the translanguaging of US Latinx English-Spanish bilinguals, Otheguy et al. (2015) argue that the language repertoire of these US Latinx is not simply made up of separate and partioned English language and Spanish language, although this might be the societal understanding. Instead, their linguistic repertoire is made up of features that they actively select from a unitary repertoire to serve them well in the communicative situation at hand. That is, speakers, and especially multilingual speakers, are constantly activating certain features, while suppressing others, in an effort to choose the best 'hints' to interact with the appropriate audience. That is to say, for multilinguals linguistic knowledge is not partitioned internally along the understandings of named languages in society. Translanguaging moves the linguistic agency and power from the nation state that starts with imposing a standardized way of speaking two or more languages to the multilingual speaker who becomes the agent of their linguistic repertoire.

Translanguaging classrooms disrupt the hierarchization that often exists in language education programs, where named languages, and especially English in today's many English-medium programmes, are given greater value than local language practices. And yet, translanguaging pedagogical practices have not been able to free themselves from the goals of monolingualism or authoritative literate multilingualism that are demanded in schools. For example, the translanguaging pedagogy developed in the United States through the work of CUNY-NYSIEB (Celic and Seltzer 2012; García and Kleyn 2016) and in García et al. (2017) also focuses on the acquisition of whole named languages, and especially English, in order to leverage the translanguaging of multilingual students. It is indeed a struggle to get schools to construct spaces where a transformative translanguaging pedagogy can free up speakers' tongues, so as to focus not on linguistic conventions, but on their power over language. Whether translanguaging pedagogy can break the cycle of promoting English, even in the midst of a multilingual turn, remains to be seen.

It is possible that translanguaging could become simply an instrument of power to ensure that there are appropriate interactions of trade and business between people who speak differently, giving English the advantage. This would generate even more interest in multilingualism with English, rather than that of minoritized people from the periphery. Flores (2013) has cautioned that if not monitored closely, this new flexibility surrounding English could become a way of having more adaptable workers, able to adjust to the changing economic conditions of today. It is important to realize that our new and positive construction of multilingualism could not have occurred without the rise of a deterritorialized English, that is an English that is spoken everywhere, in deregulated markets that need able and multilingual bodies to carry out the work of a neoliberal economy.

In the recent past, language education programmes have been transformed. For example, viewing foreign language programmes as insufficient, Content and Language Integrated Learning programmes have been developed, where the language is used as the medium of instruction for one to a couple of periods of day. Bilingual education (BE) and multilingual education (MLE) programmes have also proliferated. But despite efforts to include languages other than English, educational programmes that include English are the ones that are popular and that people desire (Piller and Takahashi 2006). In fact, in many nation states where minority groups first used BE to gain more political and economic control (for example, in the Basque Country after the death of Franco and the new constitution of the Spanish state), it is English that is promoting the transformation of bilingual programmes into multilingual programmes, now adding English to Euskara (Basque) and Spanish (see especially Cenoz 2009). And multilingual education, especially in Asia, continues to proliferate, with English always included. This is the case, for example, in Kazakhstan, which has fully embraced a trilingual model for their citizens in Kazakh, Russian and English.

In the field of English-language composition, translingualism, analogous to translanguaging but reserved for writing in English, has gained much ground since the 2011 College English manifesto (Horner et al. 2011). The 2011 manifesto encouraged the field of writing and composition studies to leverage the different ways in which people use language in writing English. The greater recognition of language diversity and difference has meant that concepts of standard English and correctness have started to be debunked. In this way, English composition and rhetoric scholars are working against the hegemonic ideals of language and the assumptions held against those who are not 'native English' speakers, while at the same time they are supporting multilingualism as an important resource.

The greater interest in multilingualism today has altered the ways in which we view it, and yet, the new study of multilingualism has also been created in and through English, ensuring that English and its speakers reserve an important role in shaping understandings of language and multilingualism that will benefit them. The number of journals in English dedicated to the study of multilingualism, in all its aspects, is significant and growing. The most respected journals in the field are all in English, issued by top UK or US global publishers, and seldom have articles in languages other than English. The major conferences on multilingual issues all over the world take place in English, with very few papers delivered in languages other than English, despite international locations. The great growth of multilingual universities throughout the globe has to do precisely with English and the transmission of western knowledge to all (see, for example, van der Walt 2011).

The move in society and education toward more bilingual or multilingual education programmes is important, for it is a way to give different people and their belief systems and cultural practices the attention they deserve. But it is essential to also point out, as we did before, that many bilingual and multilingual programmes throughout the world have been fueled solely by the interest in English, and advance notions of multilingualism that benefit only elites. This has resulted in more social and economic inequities. Often, only those who are capable of paying private tuition fees for well-resourced school programmes have access to an adequate education that includes not only English, but also the histories, mindsets and cultures of the English-speaking world. Thus, many bilingual and multilingual education programmes are instruments of western propaganda, working against the local conditions in which education takes place (García 2009).

As our assumptions about multilingualism are transformed, the imperial role of English needs to be continually questioned, as well as its role in shaping this new multilingual turn. As Foucault (1971) said, we must take up the real political task in a society, which is

> to criticize the workings of institutions which appear to be both neutral and independent; to criticize them in such manner that the political violence which has always exercised itself obscurely through them will be unmasked, so that one can fight them.
>
> (n.p.)

To highlight how the constitution of English and multilingualism has happened, we conclude by focusing on the case of Asia.

A case study: English and multilingualism in Asia

South Asia, Southeast Asia and East Asia have been described as having the greatest concentration of 'outer-circle' English using societies, where English is at least a second or official language with important intranational uses (Kachru 1990). These consist of mainly the former British colonies (e.g. India, Pakistan, Bangladesh, Nepal, Bhutan, Sri Lanka, Malaysia, Singapore, Brunei, Myanmar, and Hong Kong). The impact of Anglo colonization by the British Empire on the use of English in these regions has been significant and is well documented, but until recently the rich multilingual practices of the region had not been recognized.

Fluid multilingualism in pre-colonial times

Canagarajah and Liyanage (2012) have uncovered historical evidence of the vibrant, fluid multilingual practices in pre-colonial South Asian communities before constraining language ideologies and policies were introduced by the British colonizers. They say:

> Diversity, in all its multifaceted forms meshed in with thousands of years of sociopolitical history, is at the heart of the Indian subcontinent ... People who grew up in multilinguistic societies in this part of the world developed multiple memberships, both linguistic and otherwise, and their memberships overlapped and interlocked in amicable and productive ways to create fluid and hybrid identities.
>
> (Canagarajah and Liyanage, p. 52)

Indian scholars have pointed out that Anglo-European colonizers brought with them modernist constructs such as essentialist linguistic identity and the homogeneous speech community and used them in lands such as India to categorize people for purposes of taxation, administrative convenience, and political control, with damaging, divisive results for postcolonial peoples (Khubchandani 1997). A key impact of colonization was the introduction of linguistic hierarchies with English often placed at the top. This dominant position of English lingers on in the postcolonial era.

English and hierarchical multilingualism in postcolonial Asian societies

Colonization has had the damaging effect of essentializing multilingual language practices and identities, forcing what are fuzzy, dynamic, and fluid practices into separate language and identity categories with tight, discrete boundaries. In postcolonial societies in Asia, the sociopolitical elite were often the bilingual elite in former colonies and they often also followed in the footsteps of their former colonial masters in creating solid identity and language boundaries in their desire for modernist nation-building and management of internal diversity. For example, Rubdy (2005) calls the language policy that has evolved in post-independence Singapore one of 'pragmatic multilingualism', which is actually dominated by English:

> Singapore's multilingual model, neatly fits the nation's population into four major ethnic blocs, comprising the Chinese, Malay, Indian and 'Others', with Mandarin, Malay, Tamil and English as the respective official languages representing them. However, in effect, English has clearly been the dominant language ever since Singapore's independence in 1965, followed closely by Mandarin among the Chinese community, as a consequence of the success of the pro-Mandarin campaigns launched annually.
>
> (p. 56)

Note that this kind of multilingualism is state-defined and state-governed. The designated 'heritage language' of a schoolchild is often not a familiar home language but an official standardized language (e.g. standard Mandarin Chinese rather than a Chinese 'dialect'). The local variety of English ('Singlish') is also frowned upon by the official and educational authorities even though it is likely to be the most familiar kind of English to many Singaporeans. Commenting on the change in the sociolinguistic ecology of Singapore in the past six decades since independence, Cavallaro and Ng (2014: 33) write:

> While Singapore's language policy approach can be associated with positive outcomes, such as Singapore's economic success, there are also negative consequences, including an increasingly reduced multilingualism, official rejection of local creativity in English and communicative dislocation within families and across generations.

Likewise, in postcolonial Hong Kong, due to the dominant discourses of the global importance of English coupled with the continued colonial practice of having English as the medium of higher education, hierarchical multilingualism was firmly installed in both the institutions and subjectivities of people. Since the early colonial days, vernacular or Chinese-medium (CMI) education, which is usually practiced as Cantonese for speaking and Modern Standard Chinese for writing, received little government support. By 1911, the government was providing an English-medium (EMI) education up to university level for children largely from well-to-do families, and a CMI primary education for children from less well-to-do families (Irving 1914). In 1935, a British education inspector, Edmund Burney, visited Hong Kong and completed the famous Burney (1935) Report, in which he criticized the Hong Kong government for neglecting vernacular education. However, government resources continued to be channeled mainly into English-medium schools, cultivating a Westernized, English-conversant elite among the local Chinese population (Lin and Man 2009).

After the 1997 handover of sovereignty to China, Hong Kong installed a linguistic streaming policy in 1998, allowing only 114 secondary schools (about 25% of the total) to offer EMI while maintaining an EMI policy in most of the universities. This led to huge parental pressure demanding the reversal of the policy. In 2010 the government implemented the fine-tuned medium of instruction (MOI) policy, allowing secondary schools some flexibility in choosing their MOI (e.g. schools can choose to teach up to 25% of their curriculum in EMI). In recent years, there has been rising parental preference for English-medium education not only in former Anglo colonies such as Hong Kong or

Singapore, but also in other 'expanding-circle' societies such as mainland China, Japan, and South Korea, where English has traditionally been taught as a foreign language.

Rising popularity of International Schools and English-medium education in Asian societies: Self-imposed linguistic colonialism

The past decade has seen the rising aspirations of parents in many Asian societies for their children to acquire international education as a marker of global citizenship. For example, many mainland Chinese students leave their familiar sociocultural environments to pursue English-medium higher education in Hong Kong, Japan, Australia, or New Zealand (Ma and Li 2018). English is part and parcel of this dream of internationalization. Interestingly, international education in the form of English-medium international schools in one's home country has created the 'migrant experience' for otherwise local students. For example, local students in Hong Kong experience the marginalization of Chinese in the English-dominant culture of international schools, where speaking any language other than English is frowned upon by teachers and administrators. While becoming native-like in English, they have lost out on the opportunity to develop high levels of Chinese literacy (Li 2017). This strange 'bubble'– international schools in one's hometown – is paradoxically pursued by parents who can afford these expensive international schools in their own homeland. White native-speakerism is also rampant as can be witnessed in the advertising strategies of many international schools and English-language teaching institutes in Asia, where white teachers are advertised as superior teachers of English.

English as a Lingua Franca in Asia and recognition of multilingualism

There is, however, room for optimism as researchers begin to document the actual interactions among Asians. This closer look has meant that Asian multilingual varieties of English are emerging and gaining currency in everyday working life, even though they might not be officially recognized by the national authorities. For example, there is the building of the Asian Corpus of English, which is a corpus of naturally occurring spoken English used as a lingua franca among Asians, primarily from East and Southeast Asian societies (Kirkpatrick 2014). This work allows researchers to advocate for more ecologically sound principles for the teaching of English in Asia, and a more egalitarian kind of multilingualism. Kirkpatrick (2014) advocates against upholding the concept of native speaker or native culture in English teaching, and argues for using local multilingual teachers with teaching and assessment that is relevant to the Asian contexts. It is those who are well-versed in the multilingual context of Asia who make the most appropriate teachers of English for Asian contexts. They can provide both role and linguistic models for the students (Kirkpatrick 2014; Oda 2014).

Conclusion

This chapter privileges the diverse linguistic practices of people in interactions of power and domination, rather than the standardized language of empires and powerful nation states that is named English. We have described how, throughout the history of English/British and then American world rule, English was constructed as being spoken by monolingual white native speakers who were superior to multilingual subjects. We have also discussed how in today's neoliberal economy of global competition, it is now English that promotes the multilingualism of many. But the struggles over the power and legitimacy of English and its speakers, whether monolingual or multilingual, continue, as highlighted in the history of the Asian context. Focusing on speakers' linguistic practices, and not named languages, disrupts the hegemony of English-language studies. It is hoped that this chapter starts to replace the hierarchical multilingualism in which English is always paramount with a more egalitarian one.

Further reading

Alcón, E. and M. P. Safont Jordá (2012) *Multilingualism and English. The Encyclopedia of Applied Linguistics*. Malden: John Wiley and Sons. This book argues that the spread of English has given rise to new English varieties, but also multilingualism.

Jenkins, J. (2015) 'Repositioning English and multilingualism in English as Lingua Franca', *Englishes in Practice* 2 (3): 49–85. This article foregrounds multilingualism in ELF studies.

Khubchandani, L. M. (1997) *Revisualizing Boundaries: A Plurilingual Ethos*. Thousand Oaks: Sage. This book reveals the fluidity in multilingual interactions, especially in the Indian subcontinent.

Kachru, B. B. (1990) *The Alchemy of English. The Spread, Functions, and Models of Non-Native Englishes*. Champaign: University of Illinois Press. This book proposed the legitimation of new varieties of English.

Pennycook, A. (2006) *Global Englishes and Transcultural Flows*. Abingdon: Routledge. This book explores the relationship between the spread of English in globalization and the reuses of cultural forms in disparate contexts.

Related topics

- English and colonialism
- World Englishes: disciplinary debates and future directions
- Literacy in English: literacies in Englishes.

References

Algeo, J. and T. Pyles (2010) *The Origins and Development of the English Language*. London: Wadsworth Cengage Learning.

Bakhtin, M. (1981). *Dialogic Imagination: Four Essays*. Austin: University of Texas Press.

Baugh, A. and T. Cable (2002) *The History of the English Language*. Upper Saddle River: Prentice-Hall.

Blackledge, A. and A. Creese (2010) *Multilingualism: A Critical Perspective*. London: Continuum.

Blake, N. F. (1991) *Wiliam Caxton and English Literary Culture*. London: The Hambledon Press.

Blommaert, J. (2010) *The Sociolinguistics of Globalization*. Cambridge: Cambridge University Press.

Burney, E. (1935) *Report on Education in Hong Kong*. Hong Kong: Government Printer.

Canagarajah, S. (1999) *Resisting Linguistic Imperialism in English Teaching*. Oxford: Oxford University Press.

Canagarajah, S. (2013) *Translingual Practice: Global Englishes and Cosmopolitan Relations*. London: Routledge.

Canagarajah, S. and I. Liyanage (2012) 'Lessons from pre-colonial multilingualism' in M. Martin-Jones, A. Blackledge and A. Creese (eds), *The Routledge Handbook of Multilingualism*. London: Routledge. 49–65.

Cavallaro, F. and B. C. Ng (2014) 'Language in Singapore: From multilingualism to English plus' in J. Hajek and Y. Slaughter (eds) *Challenging the Monolingual Mindset. A Book in Memory of Michael Clyne*. Bristol: Multilingual Matters, 33–48.

Celic, C. and K. Seltzer (2012) '*Translanguaging: A CUNY-NYSIEB Guide for Educators*' Available at www.cuny-nysieb.org.

Cenoz, J. (2009) *Towards Multilingual Education. Basque Educational Research from an International Perspective*. Bristol: Multilingual Matters.

Conteh, J. and G. Meier (eds) (2014) *The Multilingual Turn in Language Education: Opportunities and Challenges*. Bristol: Multilingual Matters.

Council of Europe (2000) *Common European Framework of Reference for Languages: Learning, Teaching, Assessment*. Strasbourg: Language Policy Division. Retrieved from www.coe.int/t/dg4/linguistic/source/framework_en.pdf.

Cummins, J. (2005) 'A proposal for action: strategies for recognizing heritage language competence as a learning resource within the mainstream classroom', *Modern Language Journal* 89: 585–592.

Fishman, J. A. (1964) *Language Loyalty in the United States*. The Hague: Mouton.

Fishman, J. (1974) *Advances in Language Planning*. The Hague: Mouton.

Fishman, J. A. (1985) *The Rise and Fall of the Ethnic Revival*. Berlin: Walter de Gruyter.

Flores, N. (2013) 'The unexamined relationship between neoliberalism and plurilingualism: A cautionary tale', *TESOL Quarterly* 47 (3): 500–520.

Foucault, M. (1971) '*Human nature: Justice versus Power. Noam Chomsky debates with Michel Foucault*' Available at www.chomsky.info/1971xxxx/, accessed 11 November 2016.

Foucault, M. (2008) *The Birth of Biopolitics: Lectures at the Coll_ege de France, 1978–1979*. New York: Picador.

García, O. (2009) *Bilingual Education in the 21st Century: A Global Perspective*. Malden: Wiley.

García, O. and L. Wei (2014) *Translanguaging: Language, Bilingualism and Education*. London: Palgrave Macmillan Pivot.

García, O., S. Johnson and K. Seltzer (2017) *The Translanguaging Classroom. Leveraging Student Bilingualism for Learning*. Philadelphia: Caslon.

García, O. and T. Kleyn (eds) (2016) *Translanguaging with Multilingual Students: Learning from Classroom Moments*. New York: Routledge.

Grosjean, F. (1982) *Life with Two Languages*. Cambridge: Harvard University Press.

Haugen, E. (1956) *Bilingualism in the Americas: A Bibliography and Research Guide*. New York: American Dialect Society.

Heath, S. B. (1976) 'A national language academy? Debate in the new nation', *International Journal of the Sociology of Language* 11: 9–43.

Heller, M. (1999) *Linguistic Minorities and Modernity: A Sociolinguistic Ethnography*. London: Longman.

Holborow, M. (1999) *Politics of English: A Marxist View of Language*. London: Sage.

Hornberger, N. H. and H. Link (2012) 'Translanguaging and transnational literacies in multilingual classrooms: A bilingual lens', *International Journal of Bilingual Education and Bilingualism* 15 (3): 261–278.

Horner, B., L. Min-Zhan, J. Royster, J. Trimbur (2011) 'Language difference in writing: Toward a translingual approach', *College English* 73 (3): 303–321.

Irving, E. A. (1914) *The Educational System of Hong Kong*. Hong Kong: Government Printer.

Johnson, S. (1747) '*The Plan of an English Dictionary (1747). Ed. By J. Lynch from Johnson's 1825 Works (Oxford)*' Available at www.andromeda.rutgers.edu/~ jlynch/Texts/plan.html, accessed 24 October 2016.

Jørgensen, J.N. (2008). Polylingual languaging around and among children and adolescents. *International Journal of Multilingualism* 5(3), 161–176.

Kachru, B. B. (1990) *The Alchemy of English. The Spread, Functions, and Models of Non-Native Englishes*. Champaign: University of Illinois Press.

Kachru, B. B. (1992) *The Other Tongue: English across Cultures*. Champaign: University of Illinois Press.

Kandler, A., R. Unger and J. Steele. (2010) 'Language shift, bilingualism and the future of Britain's Celtic languages', *Philosophical Transactions B* 365 (1559): 3855–3864. Available at www.ncbi.nlm.nih.gov/pmc/articles/PMC2981914/, accessed 8 January 2017.

Khubchandani, L. M. (1997) *Revisualizing Boundaries: A Plurilingual Ethos*. Thousand Oaks: Sage.

Kirkpatrick, A. (2014) 'Redesigning the linguistic ecology of Southeast Asia: English and/or local languages?', *Journal of English Studies* 9, 1–11.

Lambert, W. E. (1974) 'Culture and language as factors in learning and education', in F. E. Aboud and R. D. Meade (eds), *Cultural Factors in Learning and Education*. Bellingham: 5th Western Washington Symposium on Learning, 91–122.

Li, Z. (2017) *Identity of University Chinese Heritage Language Learners in Hong Kong* (Unpublished doctoral dissertation, University of Hong Kong).

Lin, A. M. Y. and E. Y. F. Man (2009) *Bilingual Education: Southeast Asian Perspectives*. Hong Kong: Hong Kong University Press.

Ma, W. and G. Li (eds) (2018) *Educating Chinese-Heritage Students in the Global-Local Nexus: Achievement, Challenges, and Opportunities*. London: Routledge.

Makoni, S. and A. Pennycook (2007) *Disinventing and Reconstituting Languages*. Clevedon: Multilingual Matters.
May, S. (ed.) (2013) *The Multilingual Turn: Implications for SLA, TESOL and Bilingual Education*. New York: Routledge.
Oda, M. (2014) '*English, English Everywhere, but Whose Agenda? Public Lecture on Youtube*' Available at www.youtube.com/watch?v=aF0eTBfLnac
Otheguy, R., O. García and W. Reid (2015) 'Clarifying translanguaging and deconstructing named languages: A perspective from linguistics', *Applied Linguistics Review* 6 (3): 281–307. doi: 10.1515/applirev-2015-0014
Otsuji, E. and A. Pennycook (2010) 'Metrolingualism: Fixity, fluidity and language in flux', *International Journal of Multilingualism* 7 (3): 240–254.
Park, J. S.-Y. and L. Wee (2012) *Markets of English: Linguistic Capital and Language Policy in a Globalizing World*. New York: Routledge.
Pennycook, A. (1995) *The Cultural Politics of English as an International Language*. London: Longman.
Pennycook, A. (1998) *English and the Discourses of Colonialism*. London: Routledge.
Phillipson, R. (1992) *Linguistic Imperialism*. Oxford: Oxford University Press.
Pietikäinen, S. and H. Kelly-Holmes (eds) (2013) *Multilingualism and the Periphery*. Oxford: Oxford University Press.
Piller, I. and K. Takahashi (2006) 'A passion for English: Desire and the language market', *Bilingual Education and Bilingualism* 56: 59.
Rubdy, R. (2005) 'Remaking Singapore for the new age: Official ideologies and the realities of practice in language-in-education', in A. M. Y. Lin and P. W. Martin (eds), *Decolonization, Globalization: Language-in-Education Policy and Practice*. Clevedon: Multilingual Matters, 55–73.
Rubin, J. and B. Jernudd (eds) (1971) *Can Language be Planned? Sociolinguistic Theory and Practice for Developing Nations*. Honolulu: University of Hawaii Press.
Said, E. (1978) *Orientalism*. New York: Pantheon Books, Random House.
Seidlhofer, B. (2009) 'Common ground and different realities: World Englishes and English as a lingua franca', *World Englishes* 28 (2): 236–245.
Seidlhofer, B. (2011) *Understanding ELF*. Oxford: Oxford University Press.
Spivak, G. (1988) 'Can the subaltern speak?', in C. Nelson and L. Grossberg (eds), *Marxism and the Interpretation of Culture*. Basingstoke: Macmillan Education, 66–111.
van der Walt, C. (2011) *Multilingual Higher Education*. Bristol: Multilingual Matters.
Weinreich, U. (1953/1974) *Languages in Contact, Findings and Problems*. The Hague: Mouton.
Wiley, T. G. (1996) *Literacy and Language Diversity in the United States*. Washington, DC: Center for Applied Linguistics.
Williams, C. (1994) Arfarniad o Ddulliau Dysgu ac Addysgu yng Nghyd-destun Addysg Uwchyradd Ddwyieithog, [An evaluation of teaching and learning methods in the context of bilingual secondary education]. Unpublished Doctoral Thesis. University of Wales, Bangor.

6

Standards in English

Lionel Wee

Introduction

In this chapter I discuss the notion of standards in English by beginning with the questions 'What is Standard English?' and 'Why does it matter?' Taken together, these two questions cover the critical issues and topics that pertain to discussions about standards in English.

Regarding the first question, I briefly review a number of answers that have been proposed, including assertions that Standard English is the variety spoken by educated speakers, that there are multiple (national) Standard Englishes, and that it might even be possible to envisage a World Standard Spoken English. Regarding the second question, I try to make clear the ideological links between Standard English and the neoliberal emphasis on upward educational mobility and the development of human capital.

Following on from this discussion I suggest that the key dispute boils down to the issue of ontology. Here, I introduce a conceptual distinction between an ontologically naïve approach to Standard English and one that is ontologically curious. Whereas the former tends to treat Standard English as a product, the latter focuses on the social and political processes that stabilize specific language practices as indexical of a certain kind of personhood. From this it becomes clear that Standard English is one dialect among many, albeit one that has been elevated in terms of prestige and one where variation has been reduced. The role of actors in shaping, contesting and negotiating what ought to be considered relevant standards in English is thus emphasized.

I then close the chapter by offering, as an important direction for future investigation, a possible way of theorizing the issues raised from an ontologically curious perspective: the Deleuzian notion of assemblage. I explain what it might mean to treat Standard English as a linguistic assemblage, and why this might be especially relevant to the study of standards.

Current critical issues and topics

It is important to appreciate the difference between standardization as a process of trying to establish uniformity in language use, on the one hand, and the ideological notion of standards as markers of proper usage, on the other. The two are not unrelated, since already we have to ask who decides on which linguistic conventions are to be treated as the benchmarks from which variation should be discouraged. Nevertheless, the former process has been going on for many centuries, whereas the latter can be more directly traced to the 'history of linguistic *complaint* from the Middle Ages onward' (Milroy and Milroy 1999: 26).

Early manifestations of such complaints came from the English printer William Caxton (1490) and the writer Jonathan Swift (1712), so that by the eighteenth century there was a strong emphasis on authoritarianism and prescriptivism (Milroy and Milroy 1999: 27–28). Milroy and Milroy (1999: 30) summarize the matter thus:

> The standard ideology is promoted through public channels: in the past, standardization has first affected the writing system, and literacy has subsequently become the main influence in promoting the consciousness of the standard ideology. The norms of written and formal English have then been codified in dictionaries, grammars and handbooks of usage and inculcated by prescription through the educational system. Standardization through prescription has clearly been most successful in the written channel: in the daily conversation of ordinary speakers, however, it has been less effective. Indeed, the norms of colloquial, as against formal, English have not been codified to any extent.

Precisely because of the fact that what counts as standard is deeply ideological, it is therefore not surprising to note that there is 'no general consensus' as to what Standard English is (Bex and Watts 1999: 1). That being said, possibly the best place to start appreciating the contemporary controversies and, indeed, anxieties surrounding standards in English is to consider the assertion made, for example, by Honey (1997, see also the discussion in Cameron 1995) that Standard English is the variety spoken and written by educated speakers.

This is a highly controversial attempt to answer the question 'What is Standard English?' because it relies on a number of assumptions that appear to be problematic (see Crowley 1999). For one, since there are significant differences between the grammar of spoken and written English, characterizing both as Standard English simply evades the important question of how such differences do not undermine the claim of unity, that is, whether there is a need to distinguish between Standard Written English and Standard Spoken English. This is not a trivial issue because grammatical differences are also the kinds of things that presumably distinguish Standard English from its non-standard counterparts. This issue, if left unaddressed, means that we are left with the further and arguably even more perplexing question of how much variation (and of what kind) is tolerated before the differences in linguistic practices that distinguish Standard Written and Standard Spoken English become characterized as non-standard.

A second point is that the group, 'educated speakers', that Honey relies on to ground his definition of Standard English is not at all homogeneous, since there are different levels of education and, of course, different educational institutions that enjoy varying degrees of prestige and credibility. All these considerations bring up the question of just what kind of education is needed before a speaker is deemed to be a speaker of Standard English. This in turn raises the highly contentious question of who decides that a speaker has been sufficiently educated to be considered a speaker of Standard English. Simply asserting that other speakers of Standard English are the best judges will not do because of the vicious circularity involved in this line of argument. Claiming that there is an ineffable nature to Standard English that is clearly recognized even by those who may not be competent in it is equally problematic because it shifts the grounds of argument from scholarly debate to matters of taste and faith, and raises the contentious issue of who specifically ought to be the arbiters of such taste and faith. This shift needs to be avoided as far as possible because, as we will see shortly, what counts as Standard English can significantly impact on the social and economic fortunes of individuals. The intersection between Standard English and matters of social justice is too important to be left to the tastes and faith of a (self-)selected few.

In addition to his controversial definition of Standard English, Honey (1997, quoted in Milroy and Milroy 1999: 135) also seems to subscribe to a kind of conspiracy theory, given his argument that

> cognitive and rhetorical development is arrested when persons speak non-standard English, and that linguists as diverse as Noam Chomsky, Sir John Lyons, Stephen Pinker and Peter Trudgill (amongst others) have united to persuade such persons that there is no need to learn Standard English, thus keeping them in a disadvantaged position. This is not only implausible, but demonstrably false.

Thus, Honey is not only making the problematic assertion that speaking non-standard English leads to cognitive problems; he is also suggesting, rather incredibly, that there is a political attempt by 'enemies of Standard English' to subjugate specific segments of society by actively ensuring that they learn non-standard English.

A more reasoned and moderate position against non-standard English is offered by Quirk (1990). While generally sympathetic to the idea that non-standard English is just as linguistically legitimate as Standard English, Quirk is nonetheless concerned that the lack of institutional support for the former means that learners would be penalized socio-economically (as opposed to cognitively) if encouraged to learn non-standard English (1990: 9):

> It is neither liberal, nor liberating to permit learners to settle for lower standards than the best, and it is a travesty of liberalism to tolerate low standards which will lock the least fortunate into the least rewarding careers.

Quirk is correct that even in those countries where a non-standard English might be considered indigenous and mainstream, there tends to be a sense of stigmatization attached to both the variety and its speakers. This is despite the fact that there is no evidence to suggest that acquisition of a non-standard variety in any way impedes the acquisition of Standard English (Siegel 1999). However, as Kachru (1991) points out, by focusing on what is institutionally accepted, Quirk is limiting his concerns to a status quo that unjustly discriminates against non-standard varieties of English and, by extension, their speakers. Moreover, Quirk's position risks legitimizing and perpetuating the status quo rather than calling it into question. For Kachru, Quirk fails to acknowledge the vibrancy and reality of 'invisible language planning' (Kachru 1991: 8), where informal usage amongst non-elites in unofficial contexts (including creative works) reflects an acceptance of the growing legitimacy of non-standard varieties.

Kachru's own response is to argue that there should be '*pluralistic* centers of reference for norms and standards' (Kachru and Nelson, 1996: 84, italics in original) and as such, there is no reason to look only to traditional native speakers for directions and models. This notion of pluralistic centers is captured in his highly influential Three Circles Model (Kachru 1985, 1986). The model distinguishes between inner, outer, and expanding circles of countries, where each circle represents specific 'types of spread, patterns of acquisition and the functional domains in which English is used across cultures and languages' (Kachru 1985: 12). The Inner Circle countries (e.g. the USA, the UK) are primarily places where the traditional monolingual native speakers of English are located. The Outer Circle comprises countries with a history of colonization by English-speaking countries (Singapore, Malaysia, and

India), and where the language has continued to serve various institutionalized functions. The Expanding Circle countries (e.g. South Korea, Japan, and China) are where English has no or restricted official status and is a foreign language. This means that in addition to broadly distinguished classes of varieties according to which circle they inhabit, individual varieties associated with different nation states are also distinguished, such as British English, American English, Malaysian English and Singlish.

Kachru's model has been criticized for its assumption that it is possible to identify and demarcate varieties of English, especially along national lines (e.g. Pennycook 2003: 518, 521). Bruthiaux (2003: 168) makes a similar though more general point when he suggests that the model encourages an unhealthy tendency among scholars to contribute to the proliferation of new Englishes, suggesting that this eagerness to identify distinct varieties lacks validity. Bruthiaux's criticism is well taken, since an informal and brief Internet survey will throw up references to Chinglish in China, Manglish in Malaysia, Konglish in South Korea, Japlish in Japan and Spanglish in Puerto Rico, to mention just a few putative Englishes whose status as established varieties vary widely.

The proliferation of multiple varieties of English – notwithstanding the fact that they all manifest different levels of influence from indigenous languages and enjoy different amounts of public support as to their social legitimacy – has led to anxieties that having too many dialects will undermine the value of English as a language for global communication. To this, Crystal (1997: 137) has suggested that 'a new form of English – let us think of it as "World Standard Spoken English" (WSSE) – would almost certainly arise'. According to Crystal (1997: 137–138),

> People would still have their dialects for use within their own country, but when the need came to communicate with people from other countries they would slip into WSSE ... People who attend international conferences, or who write scripts for an international audience, or who are 'talking' on the Internet have probably already felt the full of this new variety. It takes the form, for example, of consciously avoiding a word or phrase which you know is not going to be understood outside your own country, and of finding an alternative form of expression. It can also affect pronunciation and grammar. But it is too early to be definite about the way this variety will develop. WSSE is still in its infancy. Indeed, it has hardly yet been born.

It is debatable whether Crystal's assertion about the emergence of WSSE is at all justified. Almost twenty years after this assertion, it is not clear that there is any empirical evidence pointing to the existence of this 'new form of English'. Conceptually, the basis for Crystal's assertion seems to be that intelligibility is assured only when speakers use the same variety. But this line of argument ignores the fact that multilingual competence, rather than involving multiple competences in monolingual bounded systems, actually involves partial or truncated competences in multiple languages as well as the ability to combine resources from these languages so as to creatively produce hybrid constructions (Blommaert et al. 2005; Otsuji and Pennycook 2010). In other words, there is no reason to assume that the only way that communication can be assured is via the use of a single variety. Canagarajah (2010: 19) has made this point in his own discussion of language, communication and community in the period prior to Western colonization:

> Since South Asians live in a heterogeneous community where they expect to interact with others from different languages and cultures on a daily basis, South Asians are always

> open to negotiation. Negotiation of language differences is the norm rather than the exception. Furthermore, there is no expectation of a common language as the basis for these interactions. Sometimes, there is no common language available, and even to expect one would be to impose one's own language as the vehicle for communication.

This skepticism about distinct systems is further driven home in more recent work arising from investigating language use in the workplace where speakers mix resources from Japanese and English with no resulting communicative problems (Otsuji and Pennycook 2010: 241):

> At the very least, then, we can note that such instances of English/Japanese mixed code use derive not so much from the use of different first and second languages but rather as the result of a mixed Japanese/English code becoming the lingua franca of the workplace.

From this brief survey, we can identify three major questions regarding standards in English:

(i) How do we distinguish between Standard English and non-standard English? Related to this is the role of the native speaker, whose language practices and intuitions are usually held up as reliable indicators of Standard English despite the fact that invocations of native speakerhood tend to confuse linguistic expertise with racial or ethnic affiliations (Rampton 1990).
(ii) What are the consequences for speakers of non-standard Englishes? Are they penalized in any way? Conversely, are any of the privileges that might be accorded to speakers of Standard English unfair?
(iii) Following on from (i) and (ii) are questions that relate to redress and remedy. That is, what are the changes to language policies or general attitudes that might be needed to overcome linguistic discrimination or ensure a more equitable distribution of educational opportunities?

These questions matter because, rightly or otherwise, there are strong perceptions that speakers of non-standard Englishes will be penalized. Job interviews and various language assessments in educational situations can be quite intolerant of perceived departures from what is taken to be Standard English, even if the speech community itself is characterized by widespread variation in language practices. For example, in a discussion of Singapore, a former British colony, Milroy and Milroy (1999: 89, italics in original) point out that even though 'a very distinctive *non-British* acrolectal variety of English is gradually emerging' to the point where it can be observed 'in the speech of radio announcers, university staff and business executives', there is a strong sense of prescriptivism that is reluctant to acknowledge the changing and highly variable nature of English language usage. Thus, Milroy and Milroy (1999: 90) observe,

> the educationally damaging and generally inadequate character of the prescriptions is revealed rather clearly when attempts are made to enforce them in a multilingual community like Singapore ... overprescriptivism forms an inadequate approach to reconciling the need for good standard language teaching with due recognition of speakers' existing language patterns.

And Park (2013) notes that even in the workplace, where the corporation might be committed to 'diversity management', traditionally non-native speakers such as Koreans, for example, were characterized as having English that was good enough for routine tasks but 'inadequate for more serious and fast-paced discussions and debates in strategic meetings' (Park 2013: 8–9, italics added). Thus,

> diversity management attributes any inequality that is experienced by such groups to their cultural essence – such as Koreans' 'reluctance' to speak out their views – rather than to social conditions. It thus becomes the responsibility of the group members to overcome such essential characteristics – even though they are simultaneously trapped within those characteristics by the very discourses that define them as essential to the group. *This also explains why older discourses of identity that reify national difference do not disappear in the age of commodification of language and identity*; they serve as important resources for explaining, rationalizing, and reframing issues of inequality as something innocent, something that can be transformed into a justification for the dominant social order of the workplace.

Opting out of learning English is not a realistic option either. As Block (2010: 300) has pointed out, the English language has now been commodified as 'a necessary skill' and speakers who are seen as competent in the language enjoy the concomitant cultural capital of being positioned as 'global citizens/cosmopolitan consumers'.

But the difficulty that is involved in moving away from overprescriptivism and towards greater tolerance and, indeed, appreciation of linguistic variation cannot be overestimated. Kachru (1992: 60; quoted in Mesthrie and Bhatt 2008: 205) has drawn attention to the sense of ambivalence or 'linguistic schizophrenia' that accompanies any decision about which variety of English to favor, whether it be a 'new variety' or one that has historically enjoyed comparatively greater institutional acceptance:

> The non-native speakers themselves have not been able to accept what may be termed the 'ecological validity' of their nativised or local Englishes. One would have expected such acceptance, given the acculturation and linguistic nativisation of the new varieties. On the other hand, the non-native models of English (such as RP or General American) are not accepted without reservation. There is thus a case of linguistic schizophrenia ...

And Cameron (1995: ix–x., italics in original) has emphasized how the whole issue of evaluating language practices can actually constitute a major preoccupation for many people:

> What is clear, however, is that a great many people care deeply about linguistic matters; they do not merely speak their language, they also speak copiously and passionately *about* it . . .The linguistic questions laypeople care most about are questions of right and wrong, good and bad, 'the use and abuse of language'. In fact, it would not be overstating the case to say that most everyday discourse on language is above all evaluative discourse.

These concerns and controversies revolving around the relationship between Standard English and non-standard varieties are nicely illustrated in the 'Ebonics debate' (Wheeler 1999). In December 1996, the Oakland school board in California, USA, decided to recognize Ebonics (also known as African American Vernacular English or AAVE) as the primary language of African American children. The board was concerned that many of the school children came from homes where Ebonics was spoken, and that Ebonics is significantly different from Standard English. The linguistic differences between Ebonics and Standard English were sufficiently major that these children experienced huge language learning obstacles. The school board's intention was that explicit acknowledgement of these differences would allow the school to formally implement pedagogical measures that took into specific account the differences. For example, teachers could address the use of Ebonics in the language classroom, and perhaps even treat knowledge of Ebonics as a resource for helping students acquire Standard English. Unfortunately, this decision was undermined by public fear that teachers would actually attempt to teach Ebonics in the classroom or allow students to use it in essays and tests, even though this was never the intention.

Thus, arguments about what is Standard English, and, by implication, what is non-standard, are not merely linguistic in nature. Precisely because English is considered a major language where competence in the standard variety is seen as being useful, if not actually necessary, for socio-economic advancement, any attempt to legitimize non-standard Englishes, however well intentioned, can run into serious opposition, even from those who might benefit from such a move.

Key areas of dispute and debate

The key area of dispute, particularly among language scholars, involves the nature of Standard English – which is a specific instantiation of a more general question concerning the nature of standards in language. This is not to say that such disputes do not take place in policy contexts or in society in general. But when such disputes occur in these latter domains, there is usually a presumption that language experts can provide a clear resolution to the matter; hence, there can be impatience and frustration when these experts do not agree among themselves or when they try to explain why the issue is actually a matter of some complexity.

Basically, the main question relates to how seriously to take the notion of language change and therefore whether to conceive of Standard English as primarily a product or a process. This relates to another area of dispute, which is whether to understand the nature of Standard English in primarily linguistic or non-linguistic terms, where adopting the latter means giving serious recognition to the influences of social and political factors.

No one would deny that the English language has undergone changes in grammar, lexis, and pronunciation. The issue therefore is to what extent such changes are considered negligible, such that the language can be said to be fundamentally the same. Once we acknowledge that what counts as standard inevitably changes because of the variation that inheres in the language practices of different speakers, and moreover, that there are ideological influences at work in deciding just what kind of variation to accept as being standard and what to reject as being non-standard, then we have to also acknowledge the inescapable relevance of non-linguistic factors in defining Standard English and, more generally, standards in English. In this regard, recall that Honey insists on 'educatedness' (1997: 235) as the hallmark of Standard English speakers, though he also allows for other, sufficiently 'high-status' individuals or circumstances (1997: 161–162):

> graduation from (often famous) universities, or literary reputation, or the ability in all other respects to use the language in highly acceptable ways – or [people] who are in some way other high-status figures (like royalty).

This immediately makes clear how the notion of standards in English is dependent on social and political factors, and there is no reason at all why Honey's specific choice of 'high-status figures' should prevail over the choices of other 'language mavens' (Pinker 1994). More generally and enduringly, although no less problematic, is the assumption that standards can be guaranteed by looking to the practices and intuitions of traditional native speakers of English. This reliance on the traditional native speaker persists and is extremely difficult to dislodge. Thus, Braine (1999) documents the various problems faced by non-native teachers of English, and Chelliah (2001) notes that study guides to the English language in India still rely on the traditional native speaker. The problem with this position, as Rampton (1990) observes, is that it confuses linguistic competence (an acquired property) with racial characteristics (an inherited trait). As a result, Tupas and Rubdy (2015: 3) make reference to the notion of unequal Englishes where 'The spotlight is on the unequal ways and situations in which Englishes are arranged, configured, and contested.'

Tupas and Rubdy's reference to how Englishes are 'arranged, configured, and contested' highlights the importance of attending to issues of language ontology.

Here, it is worth keeping in mind Bell's (2013) observation that sociolinguists do not often enough ask the question 'What is language?' even though such a question is not merely one of abstract metaphysical interest but in fact carries major implications for our understanding of the relationship between language and society, including implications for language policy. This is all the more so in the case of standards in English. At bottom, these areas of dispute – product versus process, linguistic versus non-linguistic factors – are about matters of ontology. That is, our understanding of what constitutes Standard English as well as our general acceptance of standards depends on just how much variation in language practices we are prepared to countenance or reject, and on what bases – where such bases will often involve language ideologies that are in themselves influenced by social and political considerations. In this regard, Widdowson (1994: 379) observes that

> the authority to maintain the standard language is not consequent on a natural native-speaker endowment. It is claimed by a minority of people who have the power to impose it. The custodians of standard English are self-elected members of a rather exclusive club.

But Widdowson (1994: 382) also points out that the global spread of Standard English has led to it being used by various communities for multiple purposes and 'these transcend traditional communal and cultural boundaries . . . develop their own conventions [and] standards [so that] you do not need native speakers to tell you what [the standard] is' (1994: 382).

It is therefore useful to distinguish between approaches that are ontologically naïve and approaches that are ontologically curious. As regards the former, consider the following statement from Honey (1997: 81):

> The study of school text books for spelling, reading, writing, and speaking make it abundantly clear that between the sixteenth and the beginning of the nineteenth centuries there was an ever more widely held notion of a standard form of English, all the elements of which were realistically accessible through book-learning.

Despite his acknowledgement of social and historical change (i.e. the references to time periods), the statement carries the suggestion that once the notion of 'a standard form of English' emerged, questions about the social, historical and political factors that played a role in its emergence, continued legitimacy, and possible dismantling no longer carry any import. This is not to say that Honey is not aware that the legitimacy of the notion of a standard might be challenged. His reference to 'enemies' of Standard English bears testament to this awareness. Rather, the point here is that he considers any serious academic questioning about the nature of Standard English as evidence of the 'enemies' at work. This is why it is not inaccurate to consider his approach ontologically naïve. Thus, Crowley (1999: 272, italics added), in commenting on this very statement of Honey's, makes the following cogent observation:

> Its danger lies in the *presupposition* that there is in some sense standard (written) English and standard (spoken) English and that they share a common structure. It is as though standard English were an ideal form of the language which is realised in practice by 'the best' users of English in the forms of standard written and spoken English.

This presupposition that the structure of Standard English is common to both written and spoken forms and that it can be found in the language practices of the 'best users' is such an article of faith that those who dare subject this presupposition to scrutiny are, as mentioned earlier, accused of attempting to engage in a conspiracy to impede the cognitive and social progress of certain segments of society.

In contrast, an ontologically curious position takes seriously the question of just how languages, including Standard English and its non-standard counterparts, are constituted, and avoids in particular taking the name of a variety at face value. This latter point is important to keep in mind because, as Park and Wee (2012: chapter 1) observe, there is a tendency to use a language name such as 'Standard English' as though it unproblematically refers to a set of language practices whilst ignoring the ideological work (sometimes explicitly, sometimes implicitly) that goes into linking the name to the practices. By ignoring the ideological assumptions that link the name to the practices, there is a serious danger of treating Standard English as a stable product, that is, the uncritical use of the name gives the impression that the name refers to a bounded and stable set of languages practices. The problem here is that the variation and changeability in language practices, as well as the ideological influences that lead some speakers and institutions to accept certain practices as 'Standard English' while rejecting others then go un-interrogated. This is a point that Schneider (2011: 155) makes in his discussion of English in Asia, where he notes that a label like 'Chinese English', 'unless understood very loosely and non-technically, implies more homogeneity than is warranted'.

The ramifications of a failure to be ontologically curious can be significant for our scholarly attempts to better understand the nature of standards in English. As Park and Wee (2013: 352) point out,

> Our research habitus that presumes language as bounded, enumerable, discrete varieties leads us to consider names as mere labels for pre-existing entities. Under this view, the linguist's assigning of names to certain sets of linguistic practices is no more than a neutral act of reference; the linguist is in no way interfering into the reality being studied, which makes this research activity completely objective and scientific. But as we have seen above, this obscures issues of descriptive adequacy and commensurability of labels, and more importantly, the fact that names are socially constituted.

Future directions

We know that a language is not simply reducible to its lexical inventory since this would only capture a listing of lexical items without giving due recognition to the degrees of regularities ('rules') that govern how these items can be used or combined. At the same time, we also know that both the words and combinatorial patterns change. New words and phrases come into existence and get accepted as conventional or grammatical.

In the case of English, as it spreads globally and comes into contact with other languages, new social and cultural environments (including new speakers, new literacy events, new technologies of communication), new varieties of English start to emerge as a result of what is both a sociolinguistically natural as well as an inevitable process. This means that it is necessary to recognize the material and symbolic dimensions of language without necessarily giving priority to one over the other. This is a point that is entirely consistent with thinking of language as an assemblage.

Deleuze and Guattari (1987: 406) tell us that an assemblage is a contingent mix of practices and things, where this contingent ensemble of physical and non-physical objects – broadly characterizable as 'semiotic' – is distinguished from yet other contingent ensembles in being 'selected, organized, stratified' and hence demarcated from an otherwise endless flow of circulating signs. So, even though assemblages are always in the process of 'coming together and moving apart' (Wise 2005: 77), this patently does not mean that at a given point in time, there is neither structure nor order to them.

It therefore needs to be emphasized that assemblages are organized and ordered; but also that this organization and order is contingent and changeable. The significant advantage of thinking in terms of an assemblage, then, is that it recognizes the role that boundedness plays in ontology, even as it at the very same time insists that we acknowledge that the boundaries can be multiple, contested, and shifting.

The concept of an assemblage therefore encourages us to further examine prevailing assumptions about the ontology of language. Why, for example, should we limit the material dimension to words (whether spoken or written)? On what grounds do we exclude the speakers/writers or the mode of communication (phone, book, blog)? Consider what we understand by graffiti. It is 'outlawed literacy' or 'criminalized' (Conquergood 1997: 354–355) precisely because its appearance on public surfaces is 'deemed a threat to property, propriety and pristine walls' (Pennycook 2008: 137). Once abstracted away from the public surface on which words and pictures may have been illegally painted, the language used no longer constitutes graffiti.

This way of understanding the ontology of objects – including the ontology of language – is actually quite radical, as Haggerty and Ericson (2000: 608, italics added) observe:

> 'Assemblages' consist of a 'multiplicity of heterogeneous objects, whose unity comes solely from the fact that these items function together, that they "work" together as a functional entity' (Patton 1994: 158). They comprise discrete flows of an essentially limitless range of other phenomena such as people, signs, chemicals, knowledge and institutions. *To dig beneath the surface stability of any entity is to encounter a host of different phenomena and processes working in concert.* The radical nature of this vision becomes more apparent when one realizes how any particular assemblage is itself composed of different discrete assemblages which are themselves multiple.

Thus, once we accept the idea of ontology in terms of assemblages, then, purely as a matter of conceptual consistency and coherence, we have to recognize that the constituent parts of assemblages are themselves further assemblages, and so on.

This brings us to two possible directions for future research worth exploring. The first has to do with how specific understandings of standards in English are assembled. From an assemblage perspective, we should no longer focus simply on the assembling of linguistic elements (although this is certainly part of the picture). Rather, we need to also consider how non-linguistic elements are actually parts of the assemblage, even if these are not usually recognized as such. In addition, we need to keep in mind that the parts of any assemblage are themselves also assemblages and are therefore also capable of continual transformation. As an illustration, let us return to Honey's definition of Standard English. Honey is keen to treat Standard English as a purely or primarily linguistic entity, one that has a common structure across its written and spoken forms. But the difficulties involved in abstracting out this common structure in any comprehensive or meaningful manner while at the same time excluding non-standard varieties make it clear that the assemblage that he wants to identify as 'Standard English' is one that is ultimately of his own making. And his reliance on educated speakers makes it clear that the assemblage he has in mind in fact extends beyond the linguistic to the social and political. Moreover, his inability to provide a clear definition of educatedness reminds us how the notion of educatedness itself is yet another assemblage. The point in critiquing Honey's notion of Standard English as an assemblage is not to suggest that it is somehow problematic qua assemblage. All other attempts to propose alternative ways of understanding standards in English are themselves also assemblages. Any talk of standards in English is, inescapably, reference to a composite entity. It therefore behooves those of us who are intent on offering or critiquing alternative assemblages of standards to be sensitive to the kinds of elements that are being included or omitted, and why.

The second line of research follows from the first, although taking on a more applied orientation. Since linguistics assemblages can (and in fact do) involve non-linguistic elements, how might developments such as the use of digital technologies and the emergence of the phenomenon often referred to as superdiversity (Vertovec 2006) affect standards in English? For example, it is well known (and perhaps all too often lamented) that social media is changing the ways in which English manifests itself. But to dismiss the English found in social media as 'informal' or 'colloquial' and thus not really standard is to already pre-judge the issue of how standards arise and are constructed. It also ignores the fact that social media is increasingly used for professional purposes and the construction of professional personae.

Likewise, the phenomenon known as superdiversity emphasizes that there have been changes to social and demographic patterns that no longer fall along the traditional lines of ethnic boundaries or even social class. In his discussion of British society, Vertovec (2006: 1) describes superdiversity as a 'dynamic interplay of variables among an increased number of new, small and scattered, multiple-origin, transnationally connected, socio-economically differentiated and legally stratified immigrants' and suggests that its implications for language mixing and multilingualism have yet to be fully understood (2006: 26). In this regard, Blommaert (2012: 3) has pointed out that

> Language, as we have seen, is no longer a fixed thing; it is also no longer a unified thing, and globalization processes again prompt us to take this seriously. Standard English is distributed in the world in fundamentally different ways than, say, HipHop English ... So statements about 'the spread of English' to place X or Y instantly beg the question: which English? Which specific resources we associate with English are effectively being spread to X and Y? And what do people in X or Y effectively do with these resources? What are their precise functions in the multilingual contexts in which they enter, and in the multilingual repertoires of users?

The increased diversity of English language speakers together with newer technologies of communication cannot help but affect the ways in which the language is spoken. Thus, it is a highly relevant and indeed pertinent question to ask about the impact of these developments on standards in English, since they also carry significant implications for language education policy including language pedagogical initiatives and assessments of language competence. Indeed, it may even be the case that such developments lead to greater appreciation of just how ideologized the notion of a standard is, so that a more reflexive even playful attitude towards standards will emerge. If so, while the idea of a standard may not necessarily disappear, it might at least become less important or treated with less seriousness – which might not be such a bad thing altogether.

Further reading

Ives, P. (2015) 'Global English and inequality: The contested ground of linguistic power', in R. Tupas (ed.), *Unequal Englishes: The Politics of Englishes Today*. London: Palgrave Macmillan, 74–91. Ives provides a macro-political perspective on the notion of inequality and how this intersects with the issue of linguistic differentiation. His starting point is that too many linguists have focused on inequality as resulting from differences between speakers, and not given enough consideration to broader structural relationships that between linguistic varieties.

Lippi-Green, R. (2011) *English with an Accent: Language, Ideology and Discrimination in the United States*. Abingdon: Routledge. In this important book, Lippi-Green looks at American attitudes towards language. She makes use of examples from the classroom, the court, as well as the media to demonstrate how linguistic discrimination, in this case, discrimination based on accent, serves to perpetuate unequal social structures.

Henry, E. S. (2010) Interpretations of "Chinglish": Native speakers, language learners and the enregisterment of a stigmatized code. *Language in Society* 39: 669–688. Henry examines Chinglish, which he points out tends to be seen as a 'deformed' version of Standard English. His goal is to show how discourses about Chinglish in China are in fact also discourses about China's anxieties over whether it is possible to be both Asian and modern at the same time. By examining how particular speech forms are metadiscursively labeled 'Chinglish' and how such acts of labeling are related to the politics of language learning, his analysis helps to demonstrate how different key actors in China's English language education industry hold different understandings of what Chinglish is.

Related topics

- English and colonialism
- World Englishes: disciplinary debates and future directions
- Contact Englishes.

References

Bell, A. (2013) *The Guidebook to Sociolinguistics*. Oxford: Wiley-Blackwell.

Bex, T. and R. J. Watts (1999) 'Introduction', in T. Bex and R. J. Watts (eds), *Standard English. The Widening Debate*. London: Routledge, 1–12.

Block, D. (2010) 'Globalization and language teaching', in N. Coupland (ed.), *The Handbook of Language and Globalization*. Oxford: Blackwell, 287–304.

Blommaert, Jan, James Collins & Stef Slembrouck. 2005. 'Spaces of multilingualism'. *Language and Communication* 25: 197–216.

Blommaert, J. (2012) 'Sociolinguistics and English language studies'. *Working Papers in Urban Language & Literacies*, Paper 85.

Braine, G (ed.) (1999) *Non-Native Educators in English Language Teaching*. London: Routledge.

Bruthiaux, Paul (2003) 'Squaring the circles: Issues in modeling English worldwide'. *International Journal of Applied Linguistics* 13(2): 159–78.
Cameron, D. (1995) *Verbal Hygiene*. London: Routledge.
Canagarajah, S. (2010) 'The possibility of a community of difference', *The Cresset* LXXIII (4): 18–30.
Chelliah, S. (2001) 'Constructs of Indian English in language "guidebooks"', *World Englishes* 20: 161–178.
Conquergood, D. (1997) 'Street literacy', in J. Flood, S. B. Heath, and D. Lapp (eds.), *Handbook of Research on Teaching Literacy through the Communicative and Visual Arts*, 354–75. New York: Simon and Schuster.
Crowley, T. (1999) 'Curiouser and curiouser: Falling standards in the standard English debate', in T. Bex and R. J. Watts (eds), *Standard English. The Widening Debate*. London: Routledge, 271–282.
Crystal, D. (1997) *English as a Global Language*. Cambridge: Cambridge University Press.
Deleuze, G. and F. Guattari (1987) *A Thousand Plateaus: Capitalism and Schizophrenia*. Minneapolis: University of Minnesota Press.
Haggerty, K. D. and R. V. Ericson (2000) 'The surveillant assemblage'. *British Journal of Sociology* 51 (4): 605–22.
Honey, J. (1997) *Language Is Power: The Story of Standard English and its Enemies*. London: Faber and Faber.
Kachru, B. B. (1985) 'Standards, codification, and sociolinguistic realism: the English language in the Outer Circle', in R. Quirk and H. G. Widdowson (eds), *English in the World: Teaching and Learning the Language and Literatures*. Cambridge: Cambridge University Press, 11–30.
Kachru, B. B. (1986) *The Alchemy of English*. Oxford: Pergamon Institute Press.
Kachru, B. B. (1991) 'Liberation linguistics and the Quirk concern', *English Today* 7: 3–13.
Kachru, B. B. (1992) 'Models for non-native Englishes', in Kachru, B. B. (ed.), *The Other Tongue: English across Cultures*, 48–74. 2nd edn. Urbana: University of Illinois Press.
Kachru, B. B. and C. Nelson (1996) 'World Englishes', in S. McKay and N. Hornberger (eds), *Sociolinguistics in Language Teaching*. Cambridge: Cambridge University Press, 71–102.
Mesthrie, R. and R. M. Bhatt (2008) *World Englishes: The Study of New Linguistic Varieties*. Cambridge: Cambridge University Press.
Milroy, J. and L. Milroy (1999) *Authority in Language*. 3rd edn. London: Routledge.
Otsuji, E. and A. Pennycook (2010) 'Metrolingualism: Fixity, fluidity and language in flux', *International Journal of Multilingualism* 7 (3): 240–254.
Park, J. (2013) 'Metadiscursive regimes of diversity in a multinational corporation', *Language in Society* 42: 1–21.
Park, J. and L. Wee (2012) *Markets of English*. London: Routledge.
Park, J. and L. Wee (2013) 'Linguistic baptism and the disintegration of ELF', *Applied Linguistics Review* 4 (2): 339–359.
Patton, P. (1994) 'MetamorphoLogic: Bodies and powers in a thousand plateaus'. *Journal of the British Society for Phenomenology* 25(2): 157–69.
Pennycook, A. (2003) 'Global Englishes, Rip Slyme and performativity', *Journal of Sociolinguistics* 7 (4): 513–533.
Pennycook, A. (2008) Linguistic landscape and the transgressive semiotics of graffiti. In E. Shohamy & D. Gorter (eds), *Linguistic Landscapes: Expanding the Scenery*, 302–312. New York: Routledge.
Pinker, S. (1994) *The Language Instinct*. New York: Harper.
Quirk, R. (1990) 'Language varieties and standard language', *English Today* 21: 3–10.
Rampton, B. (1990) 'Displacing the "native speaker": Expertise, affiliation and inheritance', *ELT Journal* 44 (2): 97–101.
Schneider, E. (2011) 'English into Asia: From Singaporean ubiquity to Chinese learners' features', in M. Adams and A. Curzan (eds), *Contours of English and English Language Studies*. Ann Arbor: University of Michigan Press, 135–156.
Siegel, J. (1999) 'Stigmatised and standardised varieties in the classroom: interference or separation', *TESOL Quarterly* 33(4): 701–728.
Tupas, R. and R. Rubdy (2015) 'Introduction', In R. Rupas (ed.), *Unequal Englishes: The Politics of Englishes Today*. London: Palgrave, 1–17.

Vertovec, S. (2006) The emergence of super-diversity in Britain. Working Paper 25. Centre on Migration, Policy and Society. Oxford University.

Wheeler, R. S. (1999) 'Home speech as springboard to school speech: Oakland's commendable work on Ebonics', in R. S. Wheeler (ed.), *The Workings of Language*. London: Praeger, 59–66.

Widdowson, H. (1994) 'The ownership of English', *TESOL Quarterly* 28 (2): 377–389.

Wise, J. M. (2005) 'Assemblage', in *Gilles Deleuze: Key Concepts*, ed. C. J. Stivale, 77–87. Montreal and Kingston: McGill and Queen's University Press.

7

Contact Englishes

Christina Higgins and Gavin Furukawa

Introduction: from language contact to linguistic heteroglossia

Language contact is a sub-field of sociolinguistics which conventionally refers to what happens when new languages are introduced into speech communities. Researchers typically focus on linguistic outcomes of language change, including lexical borrowings and codeswitching, as well as broader effects such as language shift and language death. English is arguably the consummate contact language as it has affected nearly every language around the world in some manner. Moreover, present-day English is very much the result of a great deal of contact with other languages and their speakers. The word *English* is itself the result of contact with the Romans and the widespread utility of Latin as a written language. It apparently takes an outsider perspective to name a people and a language, and the language used to name the English language was Latin. The Englishman Saint Bede the Venerable is usually the person identified as popularizing the term *Englisc* in his *Historia ecclesiastica gentis Anglorum.* As a result of contact between Romans and the people living at the angular intersection of Denmark and Germany, that land became known as *Anglaland* (literally, 'land forming a large angle'), and the people living there became known as speakers of *Anglish.* While *ish* is indeed a Germanic suffix, the first part of *English* originates from Latin, and from the Romans. Over the centuries, English has continually been influenced by other languages at the phonological, lexical, and grammatical levels, and in turn, English has changed other languages, particularly with regard to vocabulary.

All languages undergo change as a result of language contact, but English provides a special case since it has produced a number of novel linguistic forms, including Englishized languages, localized Englishes, pidgins, creoles, and lingua franca Englishes. In this chapter, we describe various types of Contact Englishes while drawing attention to the way that English is adapted for local contexts. Contact Englishes raise interesting questions regarding the linguistic boundaries between languages and the social meanings that result when speakers use a little or a lot of English. Through using an English word or a variety of English associated with a particular place or group of speakers, people style themselves as certain kinds of people. To illustrate these ideas, we first survey several areas that have historically formed the focus of scholarship on linguistic aspects of language contact involving English, which include borrowing, codeswitching, and codemixing. A common ground shared by these conventional aspects is that they treat languages as separate and compartmentalizable entities that undergo change as a result of contact with other separate and compartmentalizable languages. We then turn our focus to illustrating how language contact involving English has shifted in the past several decades in a way that we describe as *heteroglossic Englishes*, a Bakhtinian term that refers to the range of linguistic practices that make use of English to exploit its global and local meanings, including stylizations of English that produce both clever double meanings and linguistic mockery. Heteroglossia refers to the disunity of speech and to the multiplicity of meanings produced in and through language. As Bakhtin writes, 'For any individual consciousness living in it, language is not an abstract system of normative forms but rather a concrete heteroglot conception of the world' (Bakhtin 1981: 293). Often, these Englishes are *transglossic language practices* (Sultana et al. 2015) since they offer transgressive points of view and rely on transtextuality, transmodality, and translation for their full effect. By virtue of their multi-voiced nature, these heteroglossic Englishes challenge the borders around languages and show how speakers come into contact with English, often using it consciously in order to construct and contest social identities and social meanings.

An important distinction between conventional forms of language contact and heteroglossic Englishes is to be made with regard to how English is encountered. While language contact conventionally focuses on the linguistic consequences of face-to-face contact with native speakers of English who do not have linguistic proficiency in the languages in contact, heteroglossic Englishes are often born in global contact zones, where linguistic forms from English and other languages intermingle to produce new kinds of communication. In many cases, heteroglossic Englishes are produced with no face-to-face human interaction at all, as media, advertising, and technology play key roles in producing the 'input' that yields these new forms.

Thus, our use of the term heteroglossic Englishes signifies a paradigmatic shift in regard to the nature of language boundaries and the means by which English comes into contact with language users.

Current critical issues and topics

Conventionally, Contact Englishes result when speakers of English interact with speakers of another language in a context where English had previously not been used. Historically, language contact came about due to increased social interaction between people, for political or economic reasons, as in the case of colonial enterprises in Asia and Africa, or as illustrated by the development of plantations and international shipping. More recently, language contact with English has resulted from institutions that choose to privilege English, including governments, corporations, media enterprises, and schools, either in the form of mandated language policies (e.g., Choi 2015) or as the language of global capital and a resource for cosmopolitan identities (e.g., Park 2011). Contact with English is not necessarily a top-down process, of course, as individuals living in countries where English is not commonly spoken also demonstrate their own agency in bringing English into their lives through investing in private English education (e.g., Kim 2015) and through their consumption of English-dominant global media (Appadurai 1996).

Conventional language contact situations involve a variety of linguistic phenomena and classifications that are often used interchangeably, leading to considerable confusion when researching multilingual practices involving English. Some of these phenomena include *borrowing*, *pidginization*, *creolization*, *codeswitching*, and *language mixing*. Although many researchers have chosen to focus on the subtle differences that exist between these various terms, others have problematized their uses with attention to the question of boundaries between languages and the challenges that the localization of English brings to these typologies of language contact.

Borrowing

One of the most common phenomena that occurs in language contact situations is lexical *borrowing*. English is well known as a language that has benefited tremendously from borrowing, as its lexicon is heavily derived from French, Latin, and Greek, and new borrowings are noted four times a year by the *Oxford English Dictionary*. In March of 2016, among the 500 newly added words were Japanese-originated *enjo kosai*, a noun that refers to paid escort work provided by a young woman to an older man in exchange for money or luxury items, Sanskrit-originated *anudatta*, a noun that refers to the low tone of unaccented syllables, and *kaifong*, a Cantonese-originated word referring to a neighborhood association. As these three examples show, borrowing occurs when words and their associated concepts or ideas are adopted from one language or dialect into another. Borrowing of lexical items can occur in many forms including *loanwords*, *loan shifts*, and *calques* (Hoffer 2005).

When words and their related concepts are borrowed directly into another language, they are referred to as *loanwords*. A simple example of this might be the use of the word *painappuru* ('pineapple') in Japanese. When such borrowings occur, the recipient language makes the loanword fit into its phonological system, hence the shift from *pineapple* (/paɪnæpəl/) in the source language, English to *painappuru* (/painappɯɾɯ/) in the recipient language, Japanese. Another example is *supageti* ('spaghetti') in Swahili, which, similar to Japanese, requires a consonant-vowel syllable structure that reorganizes the phonology of the words, though the meaning stays the same.

Occasionally, when words are borrowed from one language to another there are shifts in meaning resulting in the phenomenon of *loan shifts*. For example, the semantics of the English word *meeting* became more narrow in 'Konglish,' or Koreanized English, as the word refers to a very specific type of meeting: a group date. Conversely, when Koreans borrowed *engineer*, its meaning widened to refer to a larger class of person who fixes and repairs things, including technicians, whereas in center Englishes, it only refers to professionally trained, white-collar individuals. In other cases, the shift does not involve broadening or narrowing, but simply indexes a culturally distinct concept. The Konglish word *mind control* is a good example, as it refers to the ability to be calm and keep one's mind clear even in stressful contexts, whereas it refers to the negative idea of brainwashing in center varieties of English. Loan shifts can also involve morphological modification, as illustrated by *konsento* in Japan ('concentric plug'), a clipping of the original English phrase that refers to an electrical outlet, and the more complex case of *hai*, a clipped form of *highball* used in Japan to refer to mixed drinks, which is also used in combination with other morphemes to refer to specific cocktails such as *uuronhai* ('oolong tea highball'). Another morphological phenomenon often found in loanwords is reduplication. In Hawai'i Creole, the word *taɾantaɾan* is a reduplicated borrowing from the Japanese *taran* ('lacking') that was often used to refer to people acting silly. Over time, the meaning of this word has shifted to also mean someone who is acting conceited, but this additional meaning is not present in the source language use of *taran*.

Sometimes a concept is borrowed from a source language to a recipient language, and rather than importing the original term into the phonology of the recipient language, the term is directly translated, resulting in a *calque*. The English term *blue-blood*, referring to someone who is of noble birth, is a calque from the Spanish *sangre azul,* which may have formed as an allusion to the visibility of veins in fair-skinned people. The meaning from the original Spanish remains the same but the term has been directly translated into English. Another example is *flea market*, which is a calque from French *marché aux puces* ('market of fleas') a term that references the old furniture sold at such markets that is likely to be flea-infested.

Research on lexical borrowing has often focused on categorizing linguistic items as belonging to one of the previously mentioned categories, but this focus ignores the complex ways that borrowed words get used in new, heteroglossic ways that construct identities and indicate affiliations. For example, the Japanese word *konpurekkusu* ('complex') is used to mean inferiority complex, but it coexists alongside the non-loan word *rettoukan*; some Japanese feel using the English-originated term makes them seem more sophisticated (Daulton 2008: 39). Similarly, French-originated loanwords are often utilized to display a sense of fashionable chic for businesses in the food industry in Japan (Tiersten 2001). One example of this can be seen in the naming of a chocolate specialty store Nina's Derriére in Tokyo (Blommaert 2010: 29). It is clear from the use of the grave accent in the word *derriére* that this is meant to be French, but as Blommaert points out, it is not being used in a literal way, as few people would be interested in eating an expensive chocolate that comes from someone's rear-end. Such examples are neither errors nor borrowings, but rather are localized and highly meaningful uses of language that have been transformed for their new environments.

Pidginization and creolization

When languages come into contact with each other, there is the possibility of new languages being formed under the right circumstances. One such language type is a *pidgin*. Pidgins are usually described as a type of 'reduced language' that is formed when two groups of people that do not share a common language are in contact with each other for an extended length of time, but also use their home language as their main source of communication (Holm 2010: 253). When this new language first forms, it takes the majority of the words in its new lexicon from one of the languages in contact; that language is referred to as either the *lexifier* language or *superstrate* language. In this early stage, the language is usually referred to as a *jargon,* but once the grammar becomes stabilized, it is then identified as a pidgin. At this stage, the language still has a quite small vocabulary and often no morphology (Siegel 2008: 3). The following example is from an English lexified pidgin from the Solomon Islands.

(1) *White man allsame woman, he no savee fight, suppose woman plenty cross she make plenty noise, suppose man-of-war he come fight me, he make plenty noise, but he allsame woman – he no savee fight.*

(Coote 1882: 206)

White men are just like women, they don't know how to fight. If a woman is really mad she'll just make a lot of noise. If a white soldier comes to fight me, he'll also make a lot of noise, but just like a woman, he doesn't know how to fight.

(translated by the authors)

Other well-known pidgins include Pidgin Fijian, Nigerian Pidgin, Kisettla (Kenya), and Pidgin Hawaiian (spoken in the nineteenth century). Pidgins are used as a means for communication between different groups of people but they are not anyone's native language.

If there is extensive interaction among the next generations of pidgin speakers, a pidgin can become a *creole*, thereby increasing its grammatical complexity, stability and gaining native speakers. Because creoles start off as pidgins, they may still be understood as and referred to as pidgins by their speakers, which is one reason why many people are confused about the distinctions between these two terms. This is the case in Hawai'i, where the language known by linguists as Hawai'i Creole is simply known as 'Pidgin' in everyday communication, even though this term actually refers to the language that first developed on sugar plantations at the turn of the twentieth century. The linguistic status of the language known as 'Pidgin' in Nigeria depends on the speaker; among its 40 million speakers, the language is a creole for those who speak it natively, and for others, it reflects a pidgin status since some speakers use it as a link language in a much more simplified fashion (Faraclas 1996). Confusingly, both ways of speaking are called 'Pidgin.'

Creoles are most often created in situations where people of different cultures and languages are transported far away to work as slaves or indentured servants, often on plantations (Siegel 2012: 530). The following samples are in Hawai'i Creole, which is an English lexified creole language.

(2) a. *I no like do dat – da garbage yo kuleana!*
I don't want to do that – the garbage is your job!

(Simonson et al. 2010: 22)

b. *You wen spahk da guy?*
Did you see that guy?

(Simonson et al. 2010: 34)

c. *Eh, no cockroach my job!*
'hey, don't steal my job'

(Higgins 2015: 155)

The creole in these samples has a developed grammatical system as seen by the use of both negative and past tense markers. Other well-researched creoles include Fitzroy Kriol (Australia), Tok Pisin (Papua New Guinea), Jamaican Creole, and Gullah (U.S.).

The categorizations of pidgin and creole are not always quite so simple. Examining the grammatical complexity and the existence of native speakers shows that several language varieties exist that bring this traditional dichotomy into question. Languages such as Singlish (Singapore) or Pitkern (Pitcairn Islands) have been often referred to as *creoloids*, given that they did not emerge from pidgins but have many continuum-like features that many creoles share (Platt 1975, 1977). Also, language varieties such as African American English, which is believed by some to have its origins in the creole Gullah, has qualities that make it difficult to distinguish (Mufwene 2001: 25).

Another topic of heated discussion in this area of linguistics is the idea of decreolization, the phenomenon where a creole's features such as syntax or phonology begin to change over time further resembling the lexifier language. The existence of a post-creole continuum is often given as evidence for this phenomenon where various *mesolects* – an intermediate variety on the continuum – exist between the *basilect* (the variety least similar to the lexifier language) version of the creole and the *acrolect* (the variety most similar to the lexifier language) (Sato 1993). On the other side of this issue, many creolists have argued that creoles may move in both directions towards or away from the acrolect (Mufwene 2004: 49–50). Additionally, there is evidence that the various *lects* have always coexisted with the acrolect and basilect (Winford 2000) and so the basic idea of decreolization, where a creole language changes becoming gradually more similar to the lexifier language, is called into question. In Hawai'i, as in other creole contexts, it is the case that people who speak Hawai'i Creole often mix and shift between this language and English, indicating that there is a coexistence of lects not only among speakers, but also within the linguistic repertoires of individuals.

Codeswitching, codemixing, and translanguaging

When speakers have access to two or more languages, it is common to shift between the languages in different ways. The multilingual practices that result have been described using a range of terms, including *codeswitching*, *codemixing*, and *translanguaging*. While codeswitching and codemixing are long-standing terms that became widely used in the 1970s, translanguaging is a term that has only gained traction in the past decade after scholars began to more regularly question the separability of languages as used by multilingual people (García and Li Wei 2013).

Codeswitching

Codeswitching has been of great interest to many linguists in terms of syntactic structure and pragmatic purposes. It is usually defined as 'the use of two (or more) languages by a single speaker in the same conversation' (Thomason 2001: 132). This broad definition has often led many linguists who specialize in bilingual communication to try to separate codeswitching into several distinct phenomena. Auer (1999) gives a typology of different types of bilingual speech found in these situations moving along from *codeswitching* to *language mixing* to *fused lects*. These three terms present a cline of pragmatic uses of languages in codeswitching to a grammaticalization of two or more languages in the form of fused lects, with codemixing in the middle. While codeswitching always implies a pragmatic effect, codemixing is seen to be a form of free variation of mixed languages. And while any two or more languages can be involved in codeswitching and codemixing, fused lects are created in contexts where speakers have formed a fixed way of using their languages. One case is Texas German (Salmons 1990), in which speakers have replaced the German system of discourse markers and conjunctions with English discourse markers and conjunctions in their otherwise German conversations.

A key distinction in codeswitching types was made by Blom and Gumperz (2000 [1972], who distinguished *situational* and *metaphorical* codeswitching in their research on two varieties of language used in northern Norway: Ranamål, a regional variety, and Bokmål, the standardized variety used in education. Situational codeswitching coincides with the context of the situation, such as location and participants. Many children studying in English as a Foreign Language (EFL) classrooms switch from English to their first language when doing pair work, for example. Auer (1999) refers to this as *participant-oriented codeswitching*, as it treats the participants' linguistic proficiencies and preferences as mitigating the language choice. On the other hand, *metaphorical* codeswitching (Blom and Gumperz 2000 [1972]: 116) is a form of discourse-related codeswitching that accomplishes a shift in footing or which projects a particular stance in conversation. A speaker may use codeswitching to disagree, or to take on the voice of another person, as in the case of reported speech (Gumperz 1982). Such codeswitching is metaphorical because it exploits associations between languages and their social functions to produce a metalinguistic communicative effect even though the situation itself is unchanged. In Blom and Gumperz's research in the context of northern Norway, a Ranamål phrase might be occasionally inserted into an otherwise Bokmål sentence to give the words a sense of secrecy (Blom and Gumperz 2000 [1972]: 118). In research on codeswitching among journalists in Dar es Salaam, Higgins (2009) found that switches from Swahili to English were often used to mitigate face-threatening acts, such as rejecting a suggestion or disagreeing with an assessment. In addition, the journalists also used English frequently for greetings in an apparent effort to create an atmosphere of conviviality and efficiency.

More recent research has called into question static distinctions between metaphorical and situational codeswitching. Scholars have made the argument that all contexts are constructed or ratified in the moment, and hence language alternation can best be analyzed in its microcontext, in interaction, with attention to the wider ethnographic context. This allows researchers to interpret the meanings that speakers bring with them to the interaction as well as those that are created in the act of codeswitching. These two types of meaning are often referred to as those that are 'brought along' and those that are 'brought about' (Auer 1999; Li Wei 1998; Rampton 1998). As more scholars frame their work in *translanguaging* frameworks, the relevancy of codeswitching as a concept remains somewhat murky, as we discuss below.

Codemixing

The second key term, *codemixing*, refers to the non-systematic use of more than one language in communication (Kachru 1978). Many examples of codemixing come from situations where English mixes with other languages, resulting in Contact Englishes such as Spanglish, Hinglish, Japlish, Konglish, and Germlish. In codemixing, the choice of the English morphemes or words is not rule-governed or obligatory; in the next instance or the next day, the same speaker who asks 'Hungry kya' ('are you hungry?') may well articulate the same question only using Hindi.

(3) a. *Hungry kya?*

('Are you hungry?')

(Hinglish, Bhatia 2009: 159)

b. *Konai eisei wo tugyazaa* ('together') *shiyou ze!*

('Let's take care of our oral health together!')

(Japlish, Takahata 2010)

c. *binil-bongtu*

('vinyl envelope')

(Konglish, McDonald 2010: 138)

d. *¿Piensas que mañana we could go to the beach after returning from la casa de mi abuelita?*

('Do you think that tomorrow we could go to the beach after returning from my grandmother's house?')

(Spanglish, Ardila 2005: 70)

The act of codemixing is more significant on the macrolevel than at the level of interaction. While codeswitching can be used for pragmatic effects such as upgrading one's stance or disagreeing more politely, codemixing itself does not yield pragmatic effects in interaction. Nonetheless, codemixing helps to construct a range of identities related to national identity, gender, ethnicity, and class. An example of (trans)national identity is presented in DeFina's (2013) study of Spanish radio broadcasts in the Washington, DC area, where codemixing often occurred at the level of pronunciation. When radio hosts pronounced local place names such as Kensington, Maryland with an English phonological system in an otherwise Spanish sentence, they were playfully admonished by their co-hosts and corrected to use a more Spanish accent, as in ['kenzinton]. Such gentle rebukes point to an underlying ideology of Spanish as located in a nationalist paradigm associated with Central and South America, rather than with the realities of multilingualism based on codemixing in the Washington, DC area in which many Spanish speakers mix phonological systems on a regular basis. Gender identities are also produced in relation to codemixing, as Higgins (2009) illustrated in her analysis of beauty pageant contestants' speech in Dar es Salaam, Tanzania. Young women who accidentally mixed their English self-introductions with Swahili, or who simply pronounced English words with a Swahili-influenced accent were interrupted by the audience with loud boos and dismissive clapping. At the same time, the hosts of the pageants and the young male rappers who entertained the audiences between segments of the pageants freely mixed their languages with no adverse responses. As representatives of Tanzania, the young women were being held to a different standard of language that does not occur outside of beauty pageants, as codemixing is the default way of speaking among those living in large cities. Codemixing with English in written forms can also construct cosmopolitan identities, particularly in advertising (e.g., Curtin 2014) and in social media (Sharma 2012). While codemixing lacks discernable pragmatic effects in speech and writing, Contact Englishes with *–lish* suffixes such as Hinglish, Spanglish, and Japlish signify that the language users are (or are aspiring to be) highly educated, upper class individuals with a global orientation and a relatively privileged position in society.

One interesting example of English language mixing leading to negative perceptions is the case of 'Conyo talk' in the Philippines, a way of speaking that mixes Spanish and English with Tagalog and which is a type of discourse that differentiates people of privilege from the rest of the population (Garvida 2013). Conyo talk is seen as emulating how English and Spanish native speakers talked to Filipinos, and hence, despite being a marker of socio-economic power, it is widely disparaged due to its strong associations with colonizers and forms of imperial arrogance. Presently, it has become associated with the middle class in the Philippines. It is distinct from other forms of language mixing such as Taglish in that grammatical elements like plurals come from English or Spanish (e.g., *yaya*s 'nannies') rather than Tagalog, and the English verb *make* is productively used with Tagalog verbs (e.g., *make* pila 'to queue') (Garvida 2013: 30).

Translanguaging

The term *translanguaging* encompasses all of the above concepts with reference to language contact phenomena, but it offers a framework that is not concerned with identifying typological differences in the forms of language contact. Instead of beginning with the view that languages are bounded by structures and then using those structures to analyze people's language use, translanguaging takes a practice-based orientation to language. As a fluid and dynamic phenomenon, translanguaging is what happens when multilingual people use their various linguistic resources to engage in activities and to engage in social worlds. Translanguaging has a liberatory quality in that it is 'the enaction of language practices that use different features that had previously moved independently constrained by different histories, but that now are experienced against each other in speakers' interactions as one *new* whole' (García and Li Wei 2013: 21; emphasis added). In other words, even though translanguaging involves more than one language from an outsider perspective, translanguaging is experienced more holistically by its users. In terms of language contact with English, researchers have investigated how translanguaging is part of how multilingual students engage in various academic practices such as participating in group work and demonstrating academic knowledge. For teachers, translanguaging allows them to encourage students, to raise questions, to convey content matter, and to develop pluriliteracies involving English and other languages (Canagarajah 2011; García and Li Wei 2013). In the same vein, Pennycook and Otsuji (2015) have investigated similar phenomena in workplace contexts such as restaurants and markets, where multilingual people's practices are at the center of commerce and customer service, and where their 'metrolingual' repertoires are drawn upon to support these mundane activities.

The idea of translanguaging is important because it problematizes conventional language contact concepts by focusing on the active and original use of multilingual speakers' linguistic resources as more of an integrated system rather than separate codes that are alternated for effect, or as separate codes with different lexifier languages. With translanguaging, the focus becomes less on describing the language itself and more on what the language use is being used to accomplish socially. One example of this can be seen in the use of stylized native speaker English (NSE) in Japan (Furukawa 2015). While conventional approaches might view such usage as borrowing, a more heteroglossic framing treats speakers' usage of stylized NSE as constructing identities for themselves and others by drawing upon the ideological connections that exist in Japanese society between English, Japanese, and the cultural capital of 'social cool.' When Japanese celebrities on television use hypercorrect pronunciations of English in their Japanese (such as overly aspirated voiceless consonants or unreduced vowels, akin to the audio tracks that accompany language textbooks), it is a form of careful manipulation of these symbolic connections.

Similar cases are documented in Sultana et al. (2015), who found that youth in Mongolia and Bangladesh often used translanguaging as means of creating a shared youth identity by transgressing and creatively appropriating linguistic and cultural boundaries. In one example from a Facebook conversation, Sabbir uses Bangla and English (in italics) in his post 'Ajke ami amar *4 hoobies* khuje pelam . . . *Women, Girls, Chicks and Babes . . . lol*' ('Today I have found my four hoobies [hobbies] . . . Women, Girls, Chicks and Babes . . . lol'). In response to his self-aggrandizing statement, Bonya, a female friend, posts in Bangla: 'mohila, meye, murgi r bachcha . . . :-/' ('Woman, girl, chicken and baby . . . :-/') (2013: 4). Rather than an act of codeswitching, Bonya's post in Bangla makes meaning through the metapragmatic frame produced by the translation. The interaction continues in a mix of English and Bangla with Bonya and other female friends teasing Sabbir by comparing him to popular culture icons Johnny Bravo (a hunky ladies' man in an animated American television show) and Johnny Gaddar (the protagonist of a 2007 Hindi film about a drug-dealing criminal) in an effort to reject his proposition and maintain a friendly relationship through parody and emoticons. Such complex heteroglossic uses of language cannot be sufficiently explained by only examining the interactional positioning of languages that individual linguistic items belong to; rather, they require the understanding that both languages may be drawn upon as complex social resources tied to intertextual meanings.

As more scholars use a translanguaging framework for the analysis of language contact, the relevance of terms such as *borrowing*, *codeswitching* and *codemixing* becomes rather murky. While some scholars continue to describe language practices involving pragmatic uses of language alternation as codeswitching or language practices involving the importation of English words as borrowing, the framework of translanguaging requires aligning with a constant critique toward the enumeration and compartmentalization of languages. Hence, most translanguaging work avoids these terms. Though García and Li Wei (2013) have argued that translanguaging is an umbrella term inclusive of these other language contact phenomena, they largely avoid integrating these terms into their discussion since they are embedded in an understanding of multilingualism as a system of multiple monolingualisms.

Future directions

As explained earlier in this chapter, the complexity of most language contact situations has led many researchers to question conventional approaches to this topic. Rather than treating languages as separate codes, practice-based approaches can more fully highlight the complex uses of language that speakers draw upon in everyday interaction. Seeing language as a practice means that it is not an abstract system which can easily be distinguished from other similar systems, but rather a social activity that speakers engage in together (Pennycook 2010: 13). Viewing language as a practice draws attention to the fact that language is a key element in how society and everyday life are structured and therefore focuses less on the structure of language or typologies of language contact.

In addition to studying the ways that practice-based understandings of language create opportunities to express identities and to challenge linguistic and social borders, practice-based approaches also present excellent opportunities for educators since they offer students of all disciplines the chance to critically engage with their own knowledge and experiences related to heteroglossic language contact situations and identity. As applied linguists with an interest in relating research on Contact Englishes to contexts beyond the research academy, we value current trends in the study of heteroglossic Englishes in which language researchers are seeking ways to invite students, teachers, and other professionals to engage in learning more about heteroglossic Englishes in real-life contexts. Below, we discuss two approaches that are relevant to a range of pedagogical contexts.

Critical language awareness

Critical language awareness (CLA) involves the development of the collective linguistic abilities of an oppressed or dominated group (Clark et al. 1991: 47–48). CLA is accomplished through activities that lead students, often speakers of Contact Englishes, to develop critical ideas and opinions about language ideologies that draw upon the experiences and knowledge that they bring with them to the classroom, leading to their own empowerment. Through CLA, students have the potential to be empowered through relating their personal experiences to language ideologies that exist in society, through using their own voices in their educational process, and through having their own knowledge valued and respected in the domain of education (Siegel 2006: 169–170).

One way CLA can be brought into the classroom is through the use of literacy narratives. Through a combination of classroom activities, peer commentary, interviews, and stimulated recall, Canagarajah (2011) was able to create an environment where university-level students could challenge dominant language ideologies regarding codeswitching. Through the act of *codemeshing*, or using their full linguistic repertoires in writing, they were able to increase their creativity and daring. Importantly, Canagarajah points out that teachers need to create a safe environment for students to feel free to codemesh and experiment in class. Since they are used to treating languages as compartmentalized, codemeshing is an unfamiliar academic practice. In his study, the teacher helped to create this safe environment by sharing his own examples of codemeshing in writing.

CLA can also be achieved through student ethnography. One example of this can be seen in the 'Real Talk' Project (Alim 2010) where secondary students' understandings of 'real talk' or 'straight talk' were utilized in class by first having them transcribe an interview with a well-known hip hop artist. The theme of 'real talk' continued as students continued to use hip-hop themed data for expanding their critical thinking and understanding by developing their own ethnographies of speaking (Hymes 1972) and by doing linguistic profiling exercises. Another ethnographic approach can be seen in Higgins et al. (2012) where young student filmmakers in Hawai'i were asked to create a documentary about Hawai'i Creole in a media program at a secondary school. In the end, the film contained a great many examples of borrowing, code-mixing, and translanguaging involving English, Hawaiian, and Hawai'i Creole. The project was accompanied by interviews, community viewings and discussions that provided a space in which students could respond to hegemonic language ideologies as enshrined by policies established by the state department of education. Such projects lead to high investment of energy from the students as well as allowing students to become teachers by sharing their knowledge with others.

Linguistic landscape research and ELT

Another practice-based approach which has classroom applications is the exploration of linguistic landscapes. Linguistic landscapes refer to the use of language in public spaces, with attention to both official and unofficial signage, but also increasingly to mobile signs such as T-shirts and bumper stickers, the role of sounds in the production of public spaces, and even the contribution of aromas in the form of 'scentscapes' (Pennycook and Otsuji 2016). Inviting students to analyze the surrounding linguistic landscapes gives them an opportunity to examine the range of Contact Englishes that are used for everyday purposes. Explorations of linguistic landscapes are relatively new but have been reported on with various student populations, including primary students in multicultural urban settings such as Vancouver, Canada (Dagenais et al. 2008), young indigenous students in Finland (Pietikäinen 2012), and adult learners of EFL in Japan.

A great deal of linguistic landscape research has investigated how English is used in heteroglossic ways in countries such as Japan, Mexico or Taiwan. Sayer (2010) used this approach to examine the use of English on signs in Oaxaca, Mexico and to develop some guidelines for language teachers to use with English learners in similar settings. By taking pictures of written English around the area locally, Sayer demonstrated that English has romantic and sexual associations in Oaxaca, and that it can be used as a subversive code. Importantly, his analysis drew attention to the many ways that English is used for intracultural (i.e., Mexican) purposes, as it is often presumed that English is a 'foreign' language in nations like Mexico. Although this project was not actually used in a classroom environment, Sayer provides useful suggestions for teachers so that they can make connections between classroom lessons and the outside world as well as leading students to think creatively and analytically about language.

Following up on Sayer's (2010) ideas, Rowland (2013, 2016) has tried similar approaches in adult EFL classes in Japan. By having students use basic qualitative analysis and motive analysis on the English on Japanese signs, Rowland (2013) discovered several benefits for using linguistic landscape activities. The activities were found to help with both multimodal and critical literacy skills while giving opportunities for incidental language learning and increasing pragmatic competency. Students were also able to understand the symbolic uses of English and developed personal connections between their English and Japanese knowledge.

Finally, using a literacy walk activity, Chern and Dooley (2014) also found that such activities are also beneficial for beginning learners of English. By taking adult students on a walk in Taipei and instructing them take pictures with their phones of the English in their environment, teachers were able to help increase the learners' awareness of orthography and local social uses of English. Chern and Dooley suggest the use of pre and post activities to help focus the students' awareness. These approaches can help with language learning as well as helping students to understand the interactive and ideological uses of English in their daily lives.

Both CLA and linguistic landscape projects provide an opportunity for language learners, teachers, and users to come to grips with the heteroglossic meanings of English in their societies. CLA can easily be combined with linguistic landscape projects as a means of interrogating language ideologies that perpetuate static understandings of English as a language attached to western culture, international cosmopolitanism, and academic purposes. Rather than seeing English as constantly attached to or associated with its historical locations or its institutionalized purposes, these approaches invite people to explore how English has become highly localized and fragmented, as it has become part of the fabric of their social lives in their own local contexts.

Further reading

Auer, P. (ed.) (1998) *Code-Switching in Conversation: Language, Interaction and Identity*. London: Routledge. This edited volume provides a framework for studying language alternation from a highly empirical, interaction-based approach drawing on conversation analysis and interactional sociolinguistics.

Canagarajah, S. (2012) *Translingual Practice: Global Englishes and Cosmopolitan Relations*. London: Routledge. Drawing on ideas from new literacy studies and applied linguistics, this book critically examines English within a global context to argue that multilinguals map their own languages and values onto English, thereby constructing new sociolinguistic norms.

García, O. and Li Wei (2013) *Translanguaging: Language, Bilingualism and Education*. London: Palgrave Macmillan. This state-of-the-art book is the first volume to provide a definitive description of translanguaging, an approach to multilingualism that places social practices as the center of multilingual analysis.

Pennycook, A. and E. Otsuji (2015) *Metrolingualism: Language in the City*. London: Routledge. This book takes a practice-based approach to the use of language in cities by examining the translingual practices in restaurants, shops, and markets in Sydney and Tokyo.

Related topics

- The idea of English
- World Englishes: disciplinary debates and future directions
- English and multilingualism: a contested history
- Media, power and representation
- Sociolinguistics: studying English and its social relations.

References

Alim, H. S. (2010) 'Critical language awareness', in N. H. Hornberger and S. L. McKay (eds), *Sociolinguistics and Language Education*. Bristol: Multilingual Matters, 205–231.

Appadurai, A. (1996) *Modernity at Large: Cultural Dimensions of Globalization*. Minneapolis: University of Minnesota Press.

Ardila, A. (2005) 'Spanglish: An anglicized Spanish dialect', *Hispanic Journal of Behavioral Sciences* 27 (1): 60–81.

Auer, P. (1999) 'From codeswitching via language mixing to fused lects: Toward a dynamic typology of bilingual speech',*The International Journal of Bilingualism* 3 (4): 309–332.

Bakhtin, M. M. (1981) *The Dialogic Imagination: Four Essays by MM Bakhtin* (M. Holquist, Ed.; C. Emerson and M. Holquist, Trans.). Austin: University of Texas Press.

Bhatia, T. K. (2009) 'English in Asian advertising and the teaching of world Englishes', in K. Murata and J. Jenkins (eds), *Global Englishes in Asian Contexts*. New York: Palgrave Macmillan, 154–171.

Blom, J. P. and J. J. Gumperz. 2000 [1972]. 'Social meaning in linguistic structure: Code-switching in Norway', in Li Wei (ed.), *The Bilingualism Reader*. London: Routledge, 102–126.

Blommaert, J. (2010) *The Sociolinguistics of Globalization*. Cambridge: Cambridge University Press.

Canagarajah, S. (2011) 'Codemeshing in academic writing: Identifying teachable strategies of translanguaging', *The Modern Language Journal* 95 (3): 401–417.

Chern, C. and K. Dooley (2014) 'Learning English by walking down the street', *ELT Journal* 68 (2): 113–123.

Choi, T. H. (2015) 'The impact of the 'Teaching English through English' policy on teachers and teaching in South Korea', *Current Issues in Language Planning* 16 (3):201–220.

Clark, R., N. Fairclough, R. Ivanic and M. Martin-Jones (1991) 'Critical language awareness part II: Towards critical alternatives', *Language and Education* 5(1): 41–54.

Coote, W. (1882) *Wanderings, South and East*. London: Sampson, Low, Marston.

Curtin, M. (2014) 'Mapping cosmopolitanisms in Taipei: Toward a theorisation of cosmopolitanism in linguistic landscape research', *International Journal of the Sociology of Language* 228:153–177.

Dagenais, D., D. Moore, C. Sabatier, P. Lamarre and F. Armand (2008) 'Linguistic landscape and language awareness', in E. Shohamy and D. Gorter (eds), *Linguistic Landscape: Expanding the Scenery*. New York: Routledge/Taylor & Francis Group, 253–269.

Daulton, F. E. (2008) *Japan's Built-in Lexicon of English-Based Loanwords*. Bristol: Multilingual Matters.

DeFina, A. (2013) 'Top-down and bottom-up strategies of identity construction in ethnic media', *Applied Linguistics* 34 (5): 554–573.

Faraclas, N. G. (1996) *Nigerian Pidgin*. London: Routledge.

Furukawa, G. (2015) "Cool' English: Stylized Native Speaker English in Japanese Television Shows', *Multilingua* 34 (2): 265–291.

García, O. and Li Wei (2013) *Translanguaging: Language, Bilingualism and Education*. London: Palgrave Macmillan.

Garvida, M. M. (2013) '"Conyo talk": The affirmation of hybrid identity and power in contemporary Philippine discourse', *Lingue e Linguaggi* 8:23–34.

Gumperz, J. J. (1982) *Discourse Strategies*. Cambridge: Cambridge University Press.

Higgins, C. (2009) *English as a Local Language*. Bristol: Multilingual Matters.

Higgins, C. (2015) 'Earning capital in Hawai'i's linguistic landscape', in R. Tupas (ed.), *Unequal Englishes: The Politics of Englishes Today*. New York: Palgrave Macmillan, 145–162.

Higgins, C., R. Nettell, G. Furukawa and K. Sakoda (2012) 'Beyond contrastive analysis and codeswitching: Student documentary filmmaking as a challenge to linguicism in Hawai'i', *Linguistics and Education* 23 (1): 49–61.

Hoffer, B. L. (2005) 'Language borrowing and the indices of adaptability and receptivity', *Intercultural Communication Studies* 14 (2): 53–72.

Holm, J. (2010) 'Contact and change: Pidgins and creoles', in R. Hickey (ed.), *The Handbook of Language Contact*. Malden, MA: Wiley-Blackwell, 252–261.

Hymes, D. (1972) 'Models of interaction of language and social life', in J. Gumperz and D. Hymes (eds), *Directions in Sociolinguistics*. New York: Holt, Rinehart and Winston, 35–71.

Kachru, B. B. (1978) 'Toward structuring code-mixing: An Indian perspective', *Journal of the Sociology of Language* 16: 27–46.

Kim, H. (2015) 'Private education as de facto language policy in South Korea', *Working Papers in Educational Linguistics* 30 (1): 87–104.

Li Wei (1998) 'The 'why' and 'how' questions in the analysis of conversational code-switching', in P. Auer (ed.), *Code-Switching in Conversation: Language, Interaction and Identity*. London: Routledge, 156–179.

McDonald, C. (2010) 'A pre-trial collection and investigation of what perceptions and attitudes of Konglish exist amongst foreign and Korean English language teachers in terms of English education in Korea', *Asian EFL Journal* 12 (1): 134–164.

Mufwene, S. S. (2001) 'What is African American English?', in S. L. Lanehart (ed.), *Sociocultural and Historical Contexts of African American English*. Amsterdam: John Benjamins, 21–51.
Mufwene, S. S. (2004) *The Ecology of Language Evolution*. Cambridge: Cambridge University Press.
Park, J. S. Y. (2011) 'The promise of English: Linguistic capital and the neoliberal worker in the South Korean job market', *International Journal of Bilingual Education and Bilingualism* 14 (4):443–455.
Pennycook, A. (2010) *Language as a Local Practice*. London: Routledge.
Pennycook, A. and E. Otsuji (2016) 'Making scents of the landscape', *Linguistic Landscape: An International Journal* 1 (3):191–212.
Pietikäinen, S. (2012). 'Experiences and expressions of multilingualism: Visual ethnography and discourse analysis in research with Sámi children', in S. Gardner and M. M. Jones (eds), *Multilingualism, Discourse and Ethnography*. London: Routledge, 163–178.
Platt, J. T. (1975) 'The Singapore English speech continuum and its basilect 'Singlish' as a 'creoloid'', *Anthropological Linguistics* 17 (7): 363–374.
Platt, J. T. (1977) 'The 'creoloid' as a special type of interlanguage', *Interlanguage Studies Bulletin* 2 (3): 22–38.
Rampton, B. (1998) 'Language crossing and the redefinition of reality', in P. Auer (ed.), *Code-Switching in Conversation: Language, Interaction and Identity*. London: Routledge, 290–320.
Rowland, L. (2013) 'The pedagogical benefits of a linguistic landscape project in Japan', *International Journal of Bilingual Education and Bilingualism* 16 (4): 494–505.
Rowland, L. (2016) 'English in the Japanese linguistic landscape: A motive analysis', *Journal of Multilingual and Multicultural Development* 37 (1): 40–55.
Salmons, J. (1990) 'Bilingual discourse marking: Code switching, borrowing, and convergence in some German-American dialects', *Linguistics* 28 (3):453–480.
Sato, C. J. (1993) 'Language change in a creole continuum: Decreolization?', in K. Hyltenstam and A. Viberg (eds), *Progression & Regression in Language: Sociocultural, Neurophysical, & Linguistic Perspectives*. Cambridge: Cambridge University Press, 122–144.
Sayer, P. (2010) 'Using the linguistic landscape as a pedagogical resource', *ELT Journal* 64 (2): 143–153.
Sharma, B. K. (2012) 'Beyond Social Networking: Performing Global Englishes in Facebook by College Youth in Nepal', *Journal of Sociolinguistics* 16 (4): 483–509.
Siegel, J. (2006) 'Language Ideologies and the Education of Speakers of Marginalized Language Varieties: Adopting a Critical Awareness Approach', *Linguistics and Education* 17: 157–174.
Siegel, J. (2008) *The Emergence of Pidgin and Creole Languages*. Oxford: Oxford University Press.
Siegel, J. (2012) 'Multilingualism, indigenization, and creolization', in T. K. Bhatia and W. C. Ritchie (eds), *The Handbook of Bilingualism and Multilingualism*. 2nd edn. Somerset: Blackwell Publishing Limited, 514–541.
Simonson, D., K. Sakata and P. Sasaki (2010) *Pidgin to da Max*. Honolulu: Bess Press.
Sultana, S., S. Dovchin and A. Pennycook (2015) 'Transglossic language practices of young adults in Bangladesh and Mongolia'. *International Journal of Multilingualism* 12(1), 93–108. doi: 10.1080/14790718.2014.887088.
Takahata, T. (2010) '*Shanai kou yougo no eigoka ni yoru kokusaika to Ruu Oshibaka*' Available at http://blogs.itmedia.co.jp/teppeitakahata/2010/07/post_2.html, accessed 24 April 2016.
Thomason, S. G. (2001) *Language Contact: An Introduction*. Edinburgh: Edinburgh University Press.
Tiersten, L. (2001) *Marianne in the Market: Envisioning Consumer Society in Fin-de-Siecle France*. Berkeley: University of California Press.
Winford, D. (2000) '"Intermediate" creoles and degrees of change in creole formation: The case of Bajan', in I. Neumann-Holzschuh and E. W. Schneider (eds), *Degrees of Restructuring in Creole Languages*. Amsterdam: John Benjamins Publishing Company, 215–246.

8

The phonology of English

Robert Fuchs

Keywords: Phonology, acoustic phonetics, laboratory phonology, pronunciation models, language teaching, World Englishes, English as a Second Language, English as a Foreign Language, variation, diachronic phonology, intelligibility.

Introduction

This chapter outlines some of the breadth and scope of the study of the phonology of English as well as its practical and social relevance. The definition of phonology adopted here is broad and includes not only the study of the sound system (phonology narrowly defined) but also its phonetic realisation and the production and perception of speech sounds. Some key terms relevant and necessary to the discussion that follows are described briefly in Figure 1. The definitions are partly based on Matthews (2014).

Approximant: A consonant that is produced by the articulators (e.g. the tongue) not moving as closely together as in the production of a fricative or plosive.

FATE vowel: The vowels of the English language are often referred to as belonging to specific lexical sets, i.e. a set of words including this vowel (a tradition that goes back to Wells 1982). One word from the set is used to refer to the whole set. For example, 'FATE' is used to refer to the set of words that include the vowel /eɪ/.

Fricative: A consonant that is produced by the articulators moving closer together than in the production of an approximant, but not completely blocking the airstream, as is the case for plosives.

Plosive: A consonant that is produced by the articulators moving closely together such that the airstream is completely blocked.

Coda (of a syllable): The consonants in a syllable that follow the vowel.

High vowel: A vowel that is articulated with the mouth opened to only a small degree (e.g. /i/).

Front vowel: A vowel that is articulated with the highest point of the tongue being positioned towards the front of the mouth (e.g. /a/).

Aspirated: A plosive that is followed by a short period during which the vocal folds do not vibrate.

The remainder of this section illustrates what implications the study of phonology has for other branches of linguistics as well as its relevance for society in general. The chapter then briefly sketches historical trends in phonology to provide a backdrop to the ensuing discussion of current approaches and key areas of dispute and debate as well as future directions in research on phonology.

Theoretical and practical relevance of the study of phonology

Studying the phonology of English is of interest for both theoretical and practical reasons. Firstly, at an academic level, scholars are in pursuit of a better understanding of the sound system and its articulatory and acoustic realisation. While the phonology of a language can be usefully understood as involving a limited number of discrete phonemes, such as the consonant /r/ or the vowel /i/, the way these phonemes are articulated and their acoustic characteristics can differ drastically. An example of articulatory variation can be found in Scottish English (Schützler 2015), where the consonant /r/ can be realised as a tap or trill produced with the tip of the tongue (sometimes popularly known as a rolled 'r') or, alternatively, as an approximant as in standard British or American English (produced by raising the tongue towards the roof of the mouth without touching it). In terms of their physical manifestation, tapped/trilled /r/ and approximant /r/ are completely different sounds, yet speakers of English from all over the British Isles usually face no difficulty in recognising both as instances of the phoneme /r/. On the other hand, there is also acoustic variation, which is particularly noticeable in vowels, chiefly due to the fact that their acoustic characteristics depend in large part on the size of the oral cavity of the speaker, which can differ substantially between individuals. Men tend to have overall larger oral cavities and some acoustic effects of this, such as a deeper voice, are easily noticeable to laypeople. Still, variation between individuals is substantial and also extends to the acoustic make-up of vowels and other phonemes. For example, the acoustic characteristics of the vowel /i/ articulated by two people speaking the same dialect still tend to differ substantially, in a way that is distinct from but has similarities with the difference between a low and a high voice. However, recognising two instances of the vowel /i/ as pertaining to the same phoneme is a challenge that listeners overcome easily in a process that operates below the level of consciousness.

This kind of variation and how listeners deal with it in communication continues to interest researchers on a theoretical level. However, phonological and phonetic variation also has practical consequences. Miscommunication can occur when listeners are not familiar with the phonology of the variety that their interlocutor speaks. For example, in Hong Kong and Singapore English, it is not uncommon to find a merger between the vowels in 'sheep' and 'ship' (Brown and Deterding 2005; Hung 2000), potentially leading to confusion (on the part of the listener) between any of the large number of minimal pairs involving these two vowels. Apart from such cases of merged phonemes, miscommunication can also arise because the phonetic realisation of a phoneme in one variety does not match that in another. A case in point is the realisation of the FATE vowel in Australian English as [aɪ], giving rise to a well-known joke about an Australian abroad pointing out that they 'came here to die' ('today').

Apart from variation at the segmental level (i.e. the level of the phoneme), variation at the suprasegmental level (above the level of the phoneme) may also have consequences for communication. Many postcolonial varieties of English are thought to have a tendency towards a syllable-timed rhythm, for example Singapore English (Deterding 2001) and Indian English (Fuchs 2016a). In these varieties, consecutive vowels tend to be less variable in duration and loudness than in British or American English, which are stress-timed. (For a non-technical introduction to speech rhythm, see Fuchs 2014.) It has been argued that for speakers of such syllable-timed varieties the stress-timed rhythm of British and American English decreases intelligibility (Kirkpatrick et al. 2008: 360). Put differently, a speaker of a syllable-timed variety might likewise find syllable-timed talkers easier to understand than stress-timed talkers.

Another sense in which phonological and phonetic variation transcends the purely theoretical is its social evaluation. Language is a powerful social marker, and we (mostly) subconsciously align our linguistic 'fingerprint' with individuals and groups that we feel close to. Over the long run, this process helps speakers express their social identity. This linguistic fingerprint can, in turn, be used by others to interpret our social affiliations. This process can give rise to pleasant occasions, such as when we recognise someone as originating from the same town or village. Nevertheless, the recognition that an interlocutor belongs to a different social or ethnic group can also lead to discrimination. As Squires and Chadwick (2006) found, even as little information as that contained in a single word may suffice. Conducted in the United States, this study showed that African Americans were recognised after saying 'hello' over the phone and invited significantly less often to view properties than Caucasian Americans by real-estate agents.

Historical perspectives

The dominant approach in phonology in the early 20th century was structuralism, which regarded language not as consisting merely of distinct, unorganised units (e.g. speech sounds), but viewed these units as belonging to an ordered system. Crucially, these units derive their function from being in opposition to each other. Thus, the English vowel /i/ is characterised by being in opposition to other vowels, e.g. /u/, in that there are minimal pairs that are distinguished by this contrast, e.g. 'beat' /bit/ and 'boot' /but/. Explaining the historical development of phonology was another important focus of structuralist research (see Salmons and Honeybone 2015). Historical change was described by reference to sound laws, and research also explored structural and functional factors causing sound changes. Thus, a factor contributing to the loss of the fricative /x/, which still existed in Old English, is thought to be the lack of a voiced counterpart. Today, some of the concepts central to the structuralist approach are once again considered to be relevant in finding explanations for phonological change.

However, during a period beginning in the middle of the 20th century, most concepts central to the structuralist approach were eclipsed by a new approach to phonology that broke with many traditional concepts. Phonology in the generative tradition sought to explain the sound system of a language by virtue of deriving its 'surface' structure from an underlying or 'deep' structure through the application of rules. A well-known example illustrating this concept is the absence of voiced obstruents (plosives such as /d/ and fricatives such as /z/) in the syllable coda in several languages such as German and Polish. Nevertheless, simply stating that voiced obstruents do not occur in syllable codas in these languages fails to account for an alternation between voiced and voiceless obstruents in cases such as German 'Hund' /hʊnt/ ('dog') and 'Hunde' /ˈhʊndə/ ('dogs'), where in the latter the consonant in question gets resyllabified and assigned to the onset of the syllable that includes the plural morpheme. Generative phonology accounts for such alternations by positing an underlying or deep phonological structure, from which the surface structure is derived through the application of rules. Thus, the surface form /hʊnt/ can be derived from the underlying /hʊnd/ by application of a rule that devoices voiced coda obstruents. Meanwhile, the plural /ˈhʊndə/ can be derived through the addition of the plural morpheme, so that the rule prohibiting voiced coda obstruents is not applicable since /d/ is now the onset of the second syllable.

While generative phonology as initially conceived is rarely practised any more, it gave rise to a plethora of frameworks often collectively referred to as 'formal' approaches to phonology. A particularly popular one is Optimality Theory, where the derivation of surface forms is resolved through a constraint-based selection of the optimal output among several candidates. Constraints can be understood as requirements imposed on the surface form. While they can be violated, they are ordered hierarchically, with violations of higher-ranked constraints being considered more severe. In addition, a particular group of constraints demands faithfulness to the underlying form, for example, in terms of features such as voicing. In the previous example, a 'no voiced coda obstruent' constraint would have to be ranked higher than a 'faithfulness in voicing' constraint so as to lead to /hʊnt/ winning out over /hʊnd/ for the singular 'dog'.

Current approaches and critical issues

Despite all their differences, what the approaches briefly described in the previous section have in common is that most research within these frameworks is based on empirical evidence that comes either from introspection (such as when a native speaker of German states that /hʊnd/ is not a permissible phonological string in this language, but /hʊnt/ is) or from simple observation of speakers without the help of any analysis of the acoustic signal. The latter is also called impressionistic analysis, a term that, despite its seemingly negative connotation, is usually used in a neutral way.

The alternative to the impressionistic method is instrumental or acoustic analysis, that is, the analysis of the physical properties of human speech with the help of specialised technology. When desktop computers became widely available in the 1990s, they not only enabled linguists to analyse large amounts of data on the syntax and lexis of human languages through the compilation of corpora, but also provided computing power for the analysis of human speech. Previously, the equipment required for this kind of research was not in widespread use in linguistics departments (although there certainly were exceptions), and a considerable amount of the work in this area came from the field of electrical engineering and telecommunications companies. While both continue to contribute to acoustic phonetics, the computing power available today has led to the spread of instrumental phonetics also among English linguists and philologists, and its use can be taught from the undergraduate level.

The basis of acoustic phonetics is an awareness of speech as a physical entity, consisting of variations in (air) pressure, or sound waves. Many of these sound waves are periodic in a way that is similar to the recurrent movement of a swinging pendulum. Intonation, for example, is realised through the vibration of the vocal folds, where fast vibration gives rise to high pitch and slow vibration to low pitch. In English, questions commonly end in high pitch and declarative sentences in low pitch. However, due to ongoing language change over the last decades, more and more speakers end some of their declarative sentences in high pitch, a phenomenon formally known as high rising terminals. More informally, it used to be called 'Valley girl talk', due to its origins among young female Californians, but has since spread to speakers of either gender in many native varieties of English (Britain 1992; Fletcher and Harrington 2001). Another periodic element of human speech is found in vowels and certain consonants (nasals and approximants). The complex signal of these periodic sounds can be decomposed into simpler components to yield a frequency profile for a particular segment. These profiles show that certain areas in the frequency spectrum are louder (i.e. have more energy) than others. Areas of high energy are called formants, and the first three of these are sufficient to distinguish vowel, nasal and approximant phonemes from each other.

Although it can make the research process more time-consuming, what makes acoustic phonetics arguably superior to impressionistic phonetics for many research questions is its objectivity. Acoustic measurements of a single sound can be repeated by several investigators and will generally lead to the same result, which is not necessarily the case with impressionistic phonetics. Moreover, acoustic analyses allow more fine-grained measures. For example, in modern British English and a number of other varieties, /l/ in codas (such as in 'hold') is sometimes not realised as [l], but as a vowel, a phenomenon known as l-vocalisation (Johnson and Britain 2007). While in some instances it may be easy to impressionistically categorise individual pronunciations as vocalised or not, in many cases a firm decision might be difficult. Acoustic measurements can resolve this, and can arrive at intermediate categorisations, thus placing a specific pronunciation somewhere along the continuum from fully vocalised to fully consonantal. Extending the analysis to measurements of several words and speakers, one could also ask whether other factors play a role, such as phonological context (Is l-vocalisation more pronounced/frequent after certain vowels?) or word frequency (Is l-vocalisation more pronounced/frequent in common words?) Eventually, an analyst may then rank speakers according to how frequently and strongly they vocalise their /l/s, and whether, say, younger speakers use this feature more consistently than older speakers, which could be an indicator of ongoing language change.

Acoustic measurements can also help researchers shed light on questions such as the merger between the vowels in words such as 'ship' and 'sheep' in varieties like Singapore and Hong Kong English (Deterding 2003; Sung 2015). This contrast is sometimes referred to as involving a short ('ship') and long vowel ('sheep'), but in fact the acoustic basis of the contrast in British and American English is both one of vowel quantity (the vowel has a longer duration in 'sheep' than in 'ship') and vowel quality (the vowel is higher and more front in 'sheep' than in 'ship'). Gathering reliable data on these two dimensions would be next to impossible with impressionistic methods. An acoustic phonetics approach, on the other hand, allows researchers to gather reproducible and quantitative data that can be subjected to statistical analysis in order to determine whether speakers of Singapore and Hong Kong English distinguish these vowels in terms of quantity and/or quality, or, alternatively, whether they are merged. Further, just as with the example of l-vocalisation discussed above, one might also ask whether these varieties are homogeneous in this respect, or whether the phenomenon under study is sensitive to factors such as exposure to English during childhood and education or socioeconomic background.

These examples illustrate how phonetic measurements (e.g. the duration and quality of the vowels in 'sheep' and 'ship') can shed light on phonological questions (whether these vowels are merged or maintained as separate phonemes). This approach is sometimes called laboratory phonology, and, more narrowly defined, associated with the *Journal of Laboratory Phonology* and an eponymous conference series. More broadly, much of the research published in leading phonetics journals such as the *Journal of Phonetics* and the *Journal of the Acoustical Society of America* operate within the same paradigm, as does most of the phonetic research published in journals concerned with the English language, such as *English Language & Linguistics*, *English World-Wide* and *World Englishes*. Laboratory phonology is characterised by the use of 'laboratory methods to discover and explain the sound structure of human language' and views language as 'a phenomenon of nature', which explicitly includes the social relevance of language (Pierrehumbert et al. 2000: 274), in contrast to the formal methods described earlier. In addition to studying the production of speech, laboratory phonology also encompasses the study of how speech is perceived.

Research based on this framework relies on a body of data, often audio recordings, and this data is sometimes gathered specifically for a single study. However, for well-researched languages such as English, it increasingly also comes from phonological corpora. Nevertheless, most corpora of natural language, in so far as they include spoken language, still only comprise an orthographic transcription of speech. The principal reasons for this are logistical and practical. A written corpus of several million words takes up, by today's standards, negligible amounts of disk space. By comparison, digital audio recordings of several million words of speech were until recently difficult to ship and store on standard computer equipment. This is because good quality audio data takes up large amounts of disk space. How much exactly depends on specific parameters, but with commonly used settings one minute of audio data takes up 10 MB, or 600 MB per hour (44.1 kHz, 32-bit, mono). A moderately sized corpus can comprise more than 100 hours of speech.

Reducing file sizes by compressing audio data with codecs such as mp3 is inadvisable for acoustic analysis since the compression process invariably involves loss of information. At higher bit rates (that is, retaining a better quality, implying larger files) it may be difficult to auditorily discern the difference between original and compressed files, but some acoustic information is invariably lost, which may affect the analysis. If the data is for some reason only available in a compressed format, results of acoustic analyses may still be reliable, but have to be interpreted with care (Fuchs and Maxwell 2016). If possible, lossy compression codecs such as mp3 should be avoided. Consequently, phonological corpora typically consist of uncompressed audio (as well as some level of annotation, e.g. a phonemic transcription that is time-aligned with the audio recordings) and an increasing number of such corpora is becoming available to researchers.

As this section has shown, acoustic analysis provides an empirical basis for the study of phonology. The following section will discuss how this approach currently impacts key areas of dispute and debate in research on World Englishes, pronunciation models and language teaching.

Key areas of dispute and debate

Phonological variation in World Englishes

English is currently the most widely spoken second language (see Pecorari, this volume). Its rise as the world's Lingua Franca is in large part due to a prolonged period of British colonial activity and the subsequent domination of the world economy first by the United Kingdom and later the United States of America. While the status of English as a Lingua Franca would suggest that its use mainly occurs when people from different countries interact, many former colonies have retained English for internal use, and in many of these countries it continues to be used alongside local languages (see Schneider, this volume). The geographical separation from the British mainland and the fact that the local population learnt English mostly as a second language led to the emergence of new varieties of English in these territories. Varieties spoken in these countries belong to what Kachru (1985) called the Outer Circle, whereas those spoken in countries where English is a native language for most of the population belong to the Inner Circle. Alternatively, Outer Circle varieties are also sometimes known as World Englishes or New Englishes (see Bolton, this volume). These varieties differ from each other and from British English, and such differences can be found on all levels of the language system, including pragmatics, syntax, lexis and phonology. It may be difficult to determine in any formal way whether differences on any of these levels are greater than on the others. Nevertheless, phonological differences are likely to play a major role. A case in point is that, on the acrolectal level (the subvariety used by educated speakers in formal contexts), syntactic differences are mostly a question of frequency. For example, the present perfect is more common in Indian English than in other varieties (Fuchs 2016b), but it is not completely absent from any acrolectal variety. By contrast, phonological differences abound even on the acrolectal level and may lead to communication breakdown when interlocutors are not familiar with each other's accents (see examples in the introduction).

The study of the phonology of World Englishes poses several theoretical and practical questions. On a theoretical level, there is a need to document the extent of variation and attempt to explain it. On a practical level, the existing variation has implications for international intelligibility and for what standards should be taught in various countries around the globe. These questions will be briefly discussed in turn.

The analysis of phonological variation in World Englishes started out by documenting the phonologies of individual varieties and was mostly of an impressionistic nature. A particularly early example is Bansal (1966/67), who found, for example, that voiceless plosives are unaspirated in all positions in Indian English, as they are in some other languages such as Spanish and French (whereas in British English, they are aspirated in simple onsets such as in 'ton'). Another example is that the phonemes /w/ and /v/ are merged, so that minimal pairs such as 'veal' and 'wheel' are pronounced the same. Impressionistic work continues to the present day. As recently as in 2004, the chapters on phonology in the to date most comprehensive reference work in the field, the *Handbook of Varieties of English* (Schneider and Kortmann 2004), are all based on impressionistic methods or approaches not described in any detail.

Nevertheless, the *Handbook* continues to be a valuable resource, as it provides information on phonological features and makes it easy to compare a large number of varieties. This allows researchers to form a somewhat more holistic picture of the extent of phonological variation in World Englishes. For instance, on the suprasegmental level, most Outer Circle Englishes tend to be syllable-timed, whereas most Inner Circle varieties of English show stress-timing (Fuchs 2016a: 87–96; Mesthrie 2008: 317). On the segmental level, many, though by no means all, Outer Circle varieties realise the GOAT and FACE vowels as the monophthongs [o] and [e] ([e] as in German 'F<u>e</u>hler' and French 'all<u>er</u>', not as in British English 'dress'), whereas many Inner Circle varieties realise these vowels as diphthongs.

As these examples show, there is great potential for more in-depth work based on rigorous methodologies such as acoustic phonetics on the one hand, and work that aims for a more holistic picture of phonological variation in varieties of English on the other. While efforts are being made to achieve these goals, similar initiatives in the area of morphosyntactic variation in varieties of English have arguably advanced further in this direction than research on phonological variation. For example, the electronic *World Atlas of Varieties of English* (eWAVE; Kortmann and Lunkenheimer 2013) contains information on 235 morphosyntactic features in 50 varieties of English and 26 English-based creoles and pidgins in the form of expert judgments (i.e. not empirical analyses). Users of the website can determine easily, for example, how widespread the extension of the progressive to stative verbs is (feature 88), such as in *What are you wanting?* (see also Gut and Fuchs 2013; van Rooy 2014). By contrast, no comparable resource on phonological variation exists.

One reason why research on phonological variation has arguably lagged behind work on morphosyntactic variation in varieties of English is, as argued in the previous section, that databases and corpora providing large amounts of data on various varieties have until recently not been available for phonological research. A case in point is that the *International Corpus of English* (ICE; Greenbaum 1991) contains 1 million words of written and (transcribed) spoken language for each of so far 12 varieties of English, and has become a widely used resource for work on morphosyntactic and lexical variation. By comparison, the Nigerian component of ICE is the only completed component of the corpus so far to include the audio data of the spoken part of the corpus together with time-aligned transcriptions, which allows researchers to use the corpus for phonological research on this variety (Wunder et al. 2010). However, several of the ICE components that are currently being compiled will include both audio data and time-aligned transcriptions. This data as well as other resources will likely lead to more work on phonological variation across varieties of English, including which factors (such as influence from local languages, status as first or second language variety, geographical distance from Britain) are responsible for what amount and what kind of variation.

Pronunciation models

Even though no complete analysis of this phonological variation exists as yet (and a 'complete' analysis may in any case be more of an ideal than a practically attainable goal), the existing evidence makes it clear that the amount of variation is substantial. As the examples discussed in the introduction suggest, this variation may lead to miscommunication or a breakdown in communication. From a practical perspective, this raises the question of how such a breakdown in communication can be avoided. The first section discussed the example of a speaker of Singapore English pronouncing the words 'ship' and 'sheep' in the same way. One solution to this might appear to be to urge speakers of Singapore English to pronounce these two words differently, perhaps in the way they are pronounced in British or American English. Indeed, many non-linguists might find this option attractive. Their case is bolstered by the fact that British and American English are the most widely used educational models and are by many non-linguists simply regarded as 'standard' or 'good' English. Even the Singaporean government seemed to agree with this perspective on standard English when (in the year 2000) it launched the 'Speak Good English Movement', encouraging Singaporeans to 'Get it Right' and 'Be Understood. Not only in Singapore, Malaysia and Batam' (Siemund et al. 2014). Thus, Singapore's government is clearly exonormatively oriented, i.e. it urges Singaporeans to adopt an outside norm instead of a locally based, endonormative standard.

However, the Speak Good English Movement was singularly unsuccessful if measured by any noticeable shift towards British or American English, for which there is no evidence. In fact, some citizens responded by launching the 'Save Our Singlish Campaign' (Wee 2005), Singlish being the term used within and outside of Singapore for colloquial Singapore English. The existence of this campaign indicates that at least some Singaporeans do not regard Singapore English as erroneous or British and American English as the only valid ways of speaking English, and instead uphold a local variety.

The question of what standards should be used when teaching English to second and foreign language learners inspired a vigorous debate also among linguists (Kachru 1991; Quirk 1990). As far as the scholarly literature is concerned, one part of the debate has largely been resolved: Few linguists would claim today that British and American English are the only useful norms to be followed in the teaching of English. In Inner Circle countries (where English is used as a native language), a pluricentric approach has won out, whereby the variety that is locally used in formal contexts serves as a model for teaching. These local formal varieties tend to be mutually intelligible (although intelligibility is a subjective notion and also depends on an individual's prior experience). Local colloquial varieties, on the other hand, diverge much more from each other and are in many cases not mutually intelligible. The local formal variety might be identified, for example, with the way newsreaders speak, whereas a more colloquial variety might be used in a local soap opera (although, as a broadcast and scripted programme, this might still be more formal than a conversation among friends). Thus, in Inner Circle countries, both policy and practice largely follow endonormative standards.

By contrast, there is a continuing debate over what standards should be used in Outer Circle and Expanding Circle countries where English is used as an institutionalised second language or foreign language respectively. Three different positions can be broadly distinguished. Where an emerging local dialect of English exists, a compromise between exo- and endonormative standards is to teach a local educated standard for local usage and an international standard for international usage (in practice, British English, American English, or a mixture of the two). The latter might be required only for some of the learners of English in Outer Circle countries, since many of them will not use English for international communication. In fact, in a number of countries, such as India, most people who speak English use it rarely or not at all for international communication. This is due to the size of these countries, the importance of English as a national link language, the orientation of a large part of their economies to the local market and the limited means that most people have for international travel.

Another approach consists of focussing teaching on those pronunciation features that most impair international intelligibility (Jenkins 2000; Sewell 2010). Learners of English with the same first language often differ in their pronunciation from British or American English in similar ways, and some of these pronunciation errors are more likely to lead to misunderstandings in communication than others. This is partly due to the fact that the phonemes of the English language differ in frequency. Other things being equal, consistently mispronouncing a frequent phoneme is more likely to impair intelligibility than mispronouncing an infrequent phoneme. An additional criterion that can be used to prioritise goals in pronunciation teaching is ease of learnability, that is, how challenging it is for a learner to overcome a pronunciation error, which again depends in part on a learner's first language.

An approach to pronunciation teaching that is based on international intelligibility is compatible with the needs of both Outer and Expanding Circle contexts. An early example of this approach in an Outer Circle country is Bansal (1966/67), who proposes a modified endonormative Indian English pronunciation standard. More recent work studies contexts where English is used as a Lingua Franca across the Outer and Expanding circles, such as Deterding's (2013) analysis, which focuses on Southeast Asia.

Impact on language teaching

It is difficult to estimate the impact of the recommendations formulated by linguists (for obvious reasons, we cannot compare our world to one where this debate has not taken place), and there is limited research on actual practices applied in pronunciation teaching. The existing research suggests that, in Expanding Circle countries, curricula and teaching practice tend to be relatively conservative and often explicitly or implicitly defer to British English, American English or native pronunciation norms that are not further defined. Intelligibility is accepted as a goal by some teachers (Grau 2005). Textbooks usually focus on communication among native speakers or learners with native speakers, but not Lingua Franca communication among non-native speakers. Some teachers and trainee teachers also tend to favour British or American pronunciation norms and feel that settling for intelligibility as the goal of pronunciation teaching would deprive students of the chance to achieve native-like pronunciation.

In many Outer Circle countries, the situation is more complex. There is a noticeable difference between policy and practice, the former usually being exonormatively oriented, whereas local teachers often speak with a local accent, which they then pass on to their students. Moreover, local practices appear to depend in part on how much money can be spent on education. Governments in wealthy territories such as Hong Kong and Singapore have set up schemes to invite persons (not necessarily qualified as English teachers) from Inner Circle countries to teach English at local schools and the vigorous private education sector also employs teachers from such countries. While this is officially portrayed as a strategy to attract native speakers (and thus an exonormative policy), private schools, at least, tend to identify native speakers of English with Caucasian-looking people. The source of this prejudice appears to be located not so much among local teachers and principals, but among parents. These take a great interest in and invest substantial amounts of money and effort in the education of their children in the rich and newly industrialised countries of East and Southeast Asia, including Expanding Circle countries, where English is taught as a foreign language.

By contrast, in less wealthy countries such as India, most schools cannot afford to hire English-speaking staff from Inner Circle countries. Thus, students are in practice taught a local standard as they learn the phonology of English from the model of their teachers. However, it is interesting to note that relatively wealthy upper-middle class Indians tend to send their children to expensive English-medium schools that could hire at least some teachers from Inner Circle countries and take other measures to teach exonormative pronunciation norms to their students. In these situations, an emerging endonormative model is adopted that local teachers call a 'neutral accent', by which they mean a general Indian English accent whose speakers do not show clear influence from their respective Indian first language. Thus, the practices of this section of the Indian education sector shed light on the increasing acceptance of Indian English because they have the means to adopt an exonormative standard, but clearly choose not to do so. Nevertheless, this is not explicitly acknowledged in official documents by clearly codifying this policy as an explicitly Indian, endonormative standard.

Future directions

Research on English phonology is a vibrant and changing field, making it particularly challenging to predict how it will develop in the future. Nevertheless, from the current perspective, it seems likely that the following trends will shape the field.

Semi-automatic annotation and corpus phonology

Now that large amounts of audio data can be stored on affordable computer systems, the present challenge is how more data can be annotated and analysed in ways that reduce the amount of human intervention required. This implies first of all the production of time-aligned phonemic transcriptions, i.e. an annotation of human speech that indicates which phonemes occur in what order, and where they start and end. This very time-consuming process can be partly automated by using a process called forced alignment, which requires as input the audio recording, an orthographic transcription and an acoustic model of the phonology of the language that is automatically generated on previously manually annotated data (Gut and Fuchs 2017). Currently the output of this process still requires checking by human annotators for most applications. If this process can be further automated so that even less manual intervention is required, the amount of data available for phonological analyses could be dramatically increased. The phonetic transcription of human speech can be further (semi)automated if the orthographic transcription that is required for forced alignment can be generated through the use of speech recognition software. The application of this technique is at an earlier stage than that of forced alignment, but experimental services exist, such as the Bavarian Archive for Speech Signals (available online, see references). In conjunction with data collection methods such as crowd-sourcing phonological data via smartphones (Leemann et al. 2016) and the wider availability of the equipment and software necessary to collect data, this could revolutionise the field. The emerging field of corpus phonology (Durand et al. 2014) is likely to play a crucial role in this process.

Diachronic phonology

While historical corpora of written English have been available for decades, the study of phonology from a diachronic perspective is hampered by the fact that facilities to record sound were not available before the second half of the 19th century. Previously, evidence on phonological change came principally from documents produced by people with little or no formal education among whom spelling variation can continue to reflect pronunciation to a certain degree even after the standardisation of English spelling. Another source of data previously available is observations from contemporaries.

However, both of these sources of evidence are limited in their breadth. One emerging line of research addressing the relative lack of diachronic evidence attempts to make use of existing audio recordings and apply instrumental methods to them in order to provide acoustic evidence on the historical development of English phonology as well as the extent of regional variation. For example, a collection known as the Berliner Lautarchiv, containing recordings of British prisoners recorded during World War I in Germany, provides direct evidence of regional and social variation in British English at the start of the 20th century (Hickey 2017). A challenge that needs to be overcome in this type of research is the limited quality of early recordings, both in terms of noise and the limited frequency and time resolution of early recording equipment.

A related line of research looks at sound change across the lifespans of individuals. Previously, it was assumed that linguistic patterns, including phonology, are largely fixed after the end of adolescence. However, Harrington et al. (2000) found substantial change over time in the vowel system of Queen Elizabeth II in the same direction as among the general population. Future work on phonological and phonetic change in individuals will resolve the question of whether public figures such as Queen Elizabeth II are exceptional in following ongoing sound change in the community or whether many speakers do so.

Variation within World Englishes

Research on phonological variation in dialects of English across the world has so far mostly concentrated on educated speakers, that is, people who have received English-medium education and a substantial amount of formal education, often including a university degree. This bias is closely tied to the origins of the field. World Englishes were often perceived in- and outside academia as highly variable and including a substantial number of errors due to first language influence. One crucial aim of the field was to establish that a subset of the population uses focussed, that is, relatively stable, varieties that are on the way to being, or have already implicitly been, established as local standards. Research on language and dialect standardisation in the early modern and modern world indicates that it is the variety used by the educated and ruling elite that is selected as the standard. This knowledge motivated the study of the phonologies of educated speakers of World Englishes, with the assumption that their way of speaking English will likely be the basis for each of the individual emerging standard varieties.

While this argument continues to be valid, the field has arguably matured so much that an exclusive focus on this group of speakers is no longer required. The idea that World Englishes are not simply learner varieties has by now been broadly accepted in English linguistics. However, besides educated speakers of, say, Indian English, who use English as a second language, there are also speakers with different backgrounds. In fact, English is used in many Outer Circle countries as a native language, as a second language, and as a foreign language by varying numbers of people. Singapore, for example, is perhaps the most widely known case of a society that recently started a transition towards children acquiring English as a (sometimes additional) native language. However, such cases also occur in countries like India. At the same time, English continues to be used by a certain section of the Indian population as a second language, but is also learnt as a foreign language by another part of the Indian population who need just a limited knowledge of English for specific purposes (such as in the service industry). Studying the linguistic processes and outcomes of these distinct uses of English, especially from a phonological perspective, will help us develop a more complete picture of the diversity of English phonology.

Intelligibility

As discussed previously, intelligibility is seen by many researchers and educators as an important aim when teaching English to foreign and second language speakers. This is a laudable goal, given that more than half of all cases of communication breakdown in English as a Lingua Franca communication are due to unintelligible pronunciations (Jenkins 2000; Deterding 2013). However, the notion of intelligibility is also problematic. A conceptual definition is straightforward: A word pronounced in an intelligible manner is one that a listener can identify. By contrast, drawing up a list of pronunciation features that are intelligible or not is challenging, yet educators need to know which features of their students' pronunciation they need to focus on in pedagogical work.

A list of (un)intelligible pronunciation features is difficult to come by because intelligibility depends on a range of factors. First of all, instead of stating that a certain speaker's accent is intelligible or not, it is more accurate to refer to specific pronunciation features as intelligible (Sewell 2010). For example, the realisation of the FATE vowel in Australian English as [aɪ], referred to earlier, might cause a loss of intelligibility for some listeners. More specifically, previous familiarity with this variety likely increases the intelligibility of this feature (Abeywickrama 2013: 61), pointing to a further variable that influences intelligibility. Finally, a question that is as yet unresolved is whether accents similar to the listener's own accent are more intelligible than dissimilar ones (Major et al. 2002).

It is clearly an important goal of research at the intersection of phonetics and English Language Teaching as well as English as a Lingua Franca to draw up specific and actionable lists of intelligible pronunciation features and curricula. Still, before this aim can be achieved, research on intelligibility will have to provide a more comprehensive account of which variables influence intelligibility. Without more research filling this gap, the principle of international intelligibility as a goal in English Language Teaching risks remaining so abstract that its full potential cannot be harnessed.

Conclusion

This chapter has illustrated the theoretical, practical and social implications of the study of English phonology. These include topics belonging to the core areas of English linguistics, such as the historical development of the English language, as well as areas of practical applications, such as English Language Teaching.

Further reading

Gut, U. (2009) *Introduction to English Phonetics and Phonology*. Frankfurt: Peter Lang. This textbook provides an accessible introduction to English phonetics and phonology for readers with some knowledge of English linguistics and little previous knowledge of phonetics and phonology.

Ladefoged, P. (1996) *Elements of Acoustic Phonetics*. Chicago: University of Chicago Press. An introduction to acoustic phonetics suitable for readers with no previous knowledge in this area.

Hayward, K. (2000) *Experimental Phonetics: An Introduction*. Abingdon: Routledge. This textbook discusses a variety of important concepts in acoustic phonetics and is recommended for readers with at least basic knowledge of acoustic phonetics.

Durand, J., U. Gut and G. Kristoffersen (eds) (2014) *The Oxford Handbook of Corpus Phonology*. Oxford: Oxford University Press. This handbook provides an overview of the emerging field of corpus phonology.

Schneider, E. W. and B. Kortmann (eds) (2004) *A Handbook of Varieties of English*. Berlin: Mouton de Gruyter. This handbook continues to be the most comprehensive source of information on variation, including phonological variation, in varieties of English.

Related topics

- English and colonialism
- World Englishes: disciplinary debates and future directions
- Contact Englishes
- Sociolinguistics: studying English and its social relations.

Acknowledgments

The author would like to thank Lukas Sönning, Lian-Hee Wee as well as the editors for their constructive feedback on an earlier version of this chapter.

References

Abeywickrama, P. (2013) 'Why not non-native varieties of English as listening comprehension test input?', *RELC Journal* 44 (1): 59–74.

Bansal, R. K. (1966/67) 'Spoken English in India. Suggestions for improvement', *Bulletin of the Central Institute of English* 6: 95–116.

Bavarian Archive for Speech Signals Available at www.clarin.phonetik.uni-muenchen.de/BASWeb-Services/.

Britain, D. (1992) 'Linguistic change in intonation: The use of high rising terminals in New Zealand English', *Language Variation and Change* 4 (1): 77–104.

Brown, A. and D. Deterding (2005) 'A checklist of Singapore English pronunciation features', in D. Deterding, A. Brown and E. L. Ling (eds), *English in Singapore. Phonetic Research on a Corpus*. Singapore: McGraw Hill, 7–13.

Deterding, D. (2001) 'The measurement of rhythm: A comparison of Singapore and British English', *Journal of Phonetics* 29: 217–230.

Deterding, D. (2003) 'An instrumental study of the monophthong vowels of Singapore English', *English World-Wide* 24 (1): 1–16.

Deterding, D. (2013) *Misunderstandings in English as a Lingua Franca: An Analysis of ELF Interactions in South-East Asia*. Berlin: de Gruyter.

Durand, J., U. Gut and G. Kristoffersen (eds) (2014) *The Oxford Handbook of Corpus Phonology*. Oxford: Oxford University Press.

Fletcher, J. and J. Harrington (2001) 'High-rising terminals and fall-rise tunes in Australian English', *Phonetica* 58 (4): 215–229.

Fuchs, R. (2014) 'You got the beat: Rhythm and timing', in R. Monroy-Casas and I. de J. Arboleda Guirao (eds), *Readings in English Phonetics and Phonology*. Valencia: IULMA-UV, 165–188.

Fuchs, R. (2016a) *Speech Rhythm in Varieties of English. Evidence from Educated Indian English and British English*. Singapore: Springer.

Fuchs, R. (2016b) 'The frequency of the present perfect in varieties of English around the World', in V. Werner, E. Seoane and C. Suárez-Gómez (eds), *Re-Assessing the Present Perfect*. Berlin: de Gruyter, 223–258.

Fuchs, R. and O. Maxwell (2016) 'The effects of mp3 compression on the measurement of fundamental frequency'. Proceedings of Speech Prosody 2016, Boston.

Grau, U. (2005) 'English as a global language—What do future teachers have to say?', in C. Guntzmann and F. Intemann (eds), *The Globalisation of English and the English Language Classroom*. Tübingen: Gunter Narr, 261–274.

Greenbaum, S. (1991) 'ICE: The international corpus of English', *English Today* 7 (4): 3–7.

Gut, U. and R. Fuchs (2013) 'Progressive aspect in Nigerian English', *Journal of English Linguistics* 41 (3): 243–267.

Gut, U. and R. Fuchs (2017) 'Exploring speaker fluency with phonologically annotated ICE corpora', *World Englishes* 36 (3): 387–403.

Harrington, J., S. Palethorpe and C. Watson (2000) 'Monophthongal vowel changes in received pronunciation: An acoustic analysis of the Queen's Christmas broadcasts'. *Journal of the International Phonetic Association* 30 (1–2): 63–78.

Hickey, R. (ed.) (2017) *Listening to the Past: Audio Records of Accents of English*. Cambridge: Cambridge University Press.

Hung, T. T. (2000) 'Towards a phonology of Hong Kong English', *World Englishes* 19 (3): 337–356.

Jenkins, J. (2000) *The Phonology of English as an International Language*. Oxford: Oxford University Press.

Johnson, W. and D. Britain (2007) 'L-vocalisation as a natural phenomenon: Explorations in sociophonology', *Language Sciences* 29 (2): 294–315.

Kachru, B. B. (1985) 'Standards, codification and sociolinguistic realism: The English language in the Outer Circle', in R. Quirk and H. Widdowson (eds), *English in the World: Teaching and Learning the Language and Literatures*. Cambridge: Cambridge University Press, 11–30.

Kachru, B.B. (1991) 'Liberation linguistics and the Quirk concern', *English Today* 7 (1): 3–13.

Kirkpatrick, A., D. Deterding and J. Wong (2008) 'The international intelligibility of Hong Kong English', *World Englishes* 27 (3–4): 359–377.

Kortmann, B. and K. Lunkenheimer (eds) (2013) *The Electronic World Atlas of Varieties of English*. Leipzig: Max Planck Institute for Evolutionary Anthropology. Available at www.ewaveatlas.org, accessed 23 July 2015.

Leemann, A., M. J. Kolly, R. Purves, D. Britain and E. Glaser (2016) 'Crowdsourcing language change with smartphone applications', *PloS One* 11 (1): e0143060.

Matthews, P. H. (2014) *The Concise Oxford Dictionary of Linguistics*. 3rd edn. Oxford: Oxford University Press.

Major, R., S. Fitzmaurice, F. Bunta and C. Balasubramanian (2002) 'The effects of nonnative accents on listening comprehension: Implications for ESL assessment', *TESOL Quarterly* 36 (2): 173–190.

Mesthrie, R. (2008) 'Synopsis: The phonology of English in Africa and South and Southeast Asia', in R. Mesthrie (ed.), *Varieties of English. Africa, South and Southeast Asia*. Berlin: de Gruyter, 307–319.

Pierrehumbert, J., M. E. Beckman and D. R. Ladd (2000) 'Conceptual foundations of phonology as a laboratory science', in N. Burton-Roberts, P. Carr and G. Docherty (eds), *Phonological Knowledge: Its Nature and Status*. Cambridge: Cambridge University Press, 273–304.

Quirk, R. (1990) 'Language varieties and standard language', *English Today* 6 (1): 3–10.

Schneider, E. W. and B. Kortmann (eds) (2004) *A Handbook of Varieties of English*. Berlin: Mouton de Gruyter.

Schützler, O. (2015) *A Sociophonetic Approach to Scottish Standard English*. Amsterdam/Philadelphia: John Benjamins.

Salmons, J. and P. Honeybone (2015) 'Structuralist historical phonology: Systems in segmental change', in J. Salmons and P. Honeybone (eds), *The Oxford Handbook of Historical Phonology*. Oxford: Oxford University Press, 32–48.

Sewell, A. (2010) 'Research methods and intelligibility studies', *World Englishes* 29 (2): 257–269.

Siemund, P., M. E. Schulz and M. Schweinberger (2014) 'Studying the linguistic ecology of Singapore: A comparison of college and university students', *World Englishes* 33 (3): 340–362.
Squires, G.D. and J. Chadwick (2006) 'Linguistic profiling: A continuing tradition of discrimination in the home insurance industry?', *Urban Affairs Review* 41 (3): 400–415.
Sung, C. C. M. (2015) 'Hong Kong English: Linguistic and sociolinguistic perspectives', *Language and Linguistics Compass* 9 (6): 256–270.
van Rooy, B. (2014) 'Progressive aspect and stative verbs in Outer Circle varieties', *World Englishes* 33 (2): 157–172.
Wee, L. (2005) 'Intra-language discrimination and linguistic human rights: The case of Singlish', *Applied Linguistics* 26 (1): 48–69.
Wells, J. C. (1982) *Accents of English.* Cambridge: Cambridge University Press.
Wunder, E. M., H. Voormann and U. Gut (2010) 'The ICE Nigeria corpus project: Creating an open, rich and accurate corpus', *ICAME Journal* 34: 78–88.

9

The grammars of English

Anne O'Keeffe and Geraldine Mark

Introduction

Grammar or grammars?

Most dictionary definitions of the word 'grammar' include some reference to 'system', 'structure', 'syntax' and 'morphology'. Many proceed with a description of the word as (1) a mass or uncountable noun referring to this system, sometimes modified to describe a theory of grammar (*Chomskyan grammar*), the grammar of a specific language (*Korean grammar*), or a set of prescribed rules (*poor grammar*) and (2) a count noun referring to a book about grammar or grammar rules (*nineteenth-century grammars*).

As the title of this chapter suggests, we deal with both grammar and grammars, discussing the overarching conceptual definition of grammar, and describing some of the key approaches to the models and theories of grammar. We take a historical look at prescriptions and descriptions of grammar, and the evolution of books about grammar. We illustrate how variation plays a central role in a discussion of grammar and grammars and finally, consider the issues relating to teaching and learning grammar.

Grammar, according to Carter and McCarthy, consists of two basic principles: 'the arrangement of items (syntax) and the structure of items (morphology)' (2006:2). However, as they go on illustrate, a reduction of grammar to its basic principles tells us only about its form or structure, not about its usage. Carter and McCarthy draw attention to the difference between grammar as structure and grammar as choice, pointing out that when we speak and write, we make choices from a range of options available to us to create meaning. These choices are dependent not just on the surrounding words, phrases, clauses, sentences and paragraphs, but on whole texts, or strings of discourse. Added to this, the choices reflect our surroundings, the time and place where the text or discourse is created and, crucially, the relationships between participants. We use grammar to create relationships, to interact and convey messages and meanings for our own communicative purposes (see McIntyre and Price, Philip, and Pihlaja, this volume). It is an ever-changing and dynamic resource which is at the disposal of its users, and yet it is viewed by many as a 'linguistic straitjacket' (Larsen-Freeman 2002: 103) filling many of its users with despair.

Definitions of grammar abound with references to 'rules', 'correct use', 'accepted principles', with prescriptions and proscriptions. Grammar is bound up with issues of acceptability. Some of these rules and principles are stable, others are dynamic and subject to change. Opinions on acceptability vary, and historically grammar rules have been socially contentious (see next sub-section). As Carter and McCarthy (2017: 2) aptly put it, 'grammar has long been a source of controversy, with age-old themes rearing their heads periodically'. In this chapter, we will attempt to explore some of these issues.

Books about grammar: a historical perspective

Historical perspectives on grammar are intrinsically linked to the evolution of reference books about grammar, where rules were kept and answers found. The lineage of books about English grammar is traced back to the 1500s. Their existence sprang from the desire to match the grammar books of Latin which were used at the time. In fact, many were written in Latin as this was seen as more scholarly (Linn 2006). Bullokar's *Pamphlet for Grammar,* published in 1586, is widely held to be the first proper book on the grammar of English and it shows us that the eight basic parts of speech that we are familiar with today are found to have been well established 400 years ago (Linn 2006; McCarthy 2017). As Linn (2006) notes, the Latin grammar cast a long shadow on the early history of English grammars. Latin was associated with learnedness and had a godliness associated with its use in the church. Any deviation from the description of a rule which did not fit with the Latin grammar paradigms was seen as an untruth (Linn 2006).

Bullokar's 1586 grammar was initially designed for and read by privileged, so-called learned, adult males (Linn 2006). However, as British commercial activity grew, especially towards the second half of the seventeenth century, the focus on writing grammar books for learned scholars was superseded by a more pressing need for material for an audience outside Britain, especially those learning English (Linn 2006). This motivation is reflected in the fact that by the end of the seventeenth century, there were 270 new English grammar books (Linn 2006). Robert Lowth's *A Short Introduction to English Grammar, with Critical Notes* (1762) is the grammar most widely known from the eighteenth century. Howatt and Widdowson (2004) say that though Lowth (who was Bishop of London) claims to have written the grammar for 'private and domestic use', it went on to make him the most famous grammarian of his time. The influence of his work extended into the nineteenth century through his disciples Murray and Corbett (discussed below).

An important innovation in Lowth's grammar is that he included possible errors as footnotes. These footnotes had an express pedagogical purpose and for Howatt and Widdowson (2004), tracing the origins of English Language Teaching (ELT), this was a very noteworthy characteristic. At the time, Lowth caused some controversy and disturbance in pointing out grammar errors as there were instances of such errors in prestigious works, implicating some eminent authors of the time, including Pope, Swift and Addison. Aitchison (2001: 11) notes that many grammar books in use today have 'laws of 'good usage' which can be traced directly to Bishop Lowth's idiosyncratic pronouncements as to what was 'right' and what was 'wrong'.

This concept of using footnotes to illustrate typical errors was taken up and further developed by Murray. McCarthy (2017) lists Murray's *English Grammar, Adapted to the Different Classes of Learners* (1795 1st Ed, 1809 16th Ed) as one of the most popular and influential works. Although Murray was a disciple of Lowth, it is interesting to note how the title indicates a change and broadening of target audience. This shift in audience is a defining feature of the nineteenth-century grammars and is in line with massification in education that was emerging at this time. This shift was often reflected in their titles; for instance, Edward Shelley's *The People's Grammar; or English Grammar without Difficulties for 'the Million'* (1848). Later editions of Corbett's work, *A Grammar of the English Language, in a Series of Letters* (originally published in 1818) had the fascinating sub-title *Intended for the Use of Schools and of Young Persons in General; But More Especially for the Use of Soldiers, Sailors, Apprentices, and Plough-boys. To Which are Added Six Lessons Intended to Prevent Statesmen from Using False Grammar and from Writing in an Awkward Manner.* Brown's (1823) *Institutes of English Grammar* became part of mainstream schooling in the US. Linn (2006) comments on its stern influence right into the twentieth century: 'Brown did more than anyone, at least in America, to cement the popular association of grammar study with inviolable rules and, by association, with rules of propriety and morals' (Linn 2006: 77).

From written to spoken

Another key shift is the move beyond solely focusing on written language as the baseline for grammar rules. Towards the end of the nineteenth century, attention turned more systematically to the spoken language and this was linked to the development of the field of phonetics (as well as a more scientific approach to linguistics in general). Most notable is the work of Sweet 1899, 1900). Both his 1900 *A new English Grammar: Logical and Historical. Part I: Introduction, Phonology, and Accidence* and his 1899 work *The Practical Study of Languages: A Guide for Teachers and Learners* underscored the importance of the inclusion of spoken language integral to any grammar work. Sweet's influential work at the turn of the twentieth century asserted the principle that spoken language was not a corrupt form of written language and that it should be the starting point of any language description. His early work described many of the core features of what we now refer to as spoken grammar, including parataxis (the placing of two phrases or clauses side by side without a connecting word), phrases (now often referred to as clusters) and ellipsis (Carter and McCarthy 2017). The work of Palmer (1924/1969) is seen as the most significant of the early twentieth century in terms of asserting the importance of the inclusion of the spoken word in descriptions of English grammar. His work *A Grammar of Spoken English* (1924) displayed an in-depth understanding of the grammar of speech and discourse, with insights like the greater use of coordination of clauses rather than subordination in informal spoken contexts.

The influence of corpora

Modern grammars are based on real samples of language in the form of language corpora. Corpora are large, principled collections of real spoken or written language that that allow for large-scale linguistic analysis using corpus software (see Philip, this volume). Two major impacts of the use of corpora on grammar were, firstly, a shift from prescription about what should be said or written to description about what is found in the empirical data (see next section), and secondly, a gathering momentum to work on spoken grammar as distinct from written grammar.

The seminal works which mark the beginning of this new era of empirically-based grammar books are Quirk et al. (1972) and Quirk et al. (1985). Randolph Quirk is seen as the father of modern grammar descriptions. His early corpus endeavours led to the Survey of English Usage, which in turn led to Quirk et al. (1972) and what Leech (2015) refers to as the 'mega-grammar', Quirk et al. (1985). Leech (2015) notes that with the ability to look and describe language using a corpus came the responsibility (and sometimes burden) of unbiased objectivity through the 'principle of total accountability' (2015: 146), that is, making use of all relevant data in the corpus and not shying away from data that does not appear to fit received paradigms. As Leech puts it, a grammarian using a corpus 'cannot ignore data that do not fit his/her view of grammar, as theoretically oriented grammarians have sometimes done in the past' (2015:147).

A major innovation in the evolution of corpus linguistic tools in terms of analysing grammar was automated Part-of-Speech (POS) tagging (Green and Rubin 1971). Leech (2015: 148) points out that this innovation meant that it became relatively simple to extract instances of even 'abstract categories such as progressive aspect or passive voice'. The next level up from POS tagging is to automatically parse a corpus syntactically, but as Leech puts it, this has 'proved a more difficult nut to crack' (Leech 2015: 149).

Until the advent of corpus linguistics, grammar books were largely socially derived prescriptions about the grammar one should use. Corpus linguistics brought a descriptive turn. This meant that large bodies of evidence about how grammar was used was laid before linguists. As a result, language could be studied in terms of how it varied across contexts and users. Most of all, what technology did was take away the subjectivity about how grammar was described. Those who wrote grammar books had to be objective. They simply had to detail what the data told them and not what they thought should be the case.

Current critical issues and topics

What is interesting about the current critical issues and topics relating to grammar is that they are those which are already referred to in a historical context. In other words, many aspects of grammar are perennial issues.

Prescription vs description

Many associate grammar with what one 'ought to' use, and this is referred to as 'prescriptive grammar'. Larsen-Freeman sees prescriptive approaches to grammar as contributing to a 'general unease', where 'even proficient users of a language fear making mistakes, such as using *me* instead of *I* or choosing *who* when they should have chosen *whom*' (2014: 257). Descriptive approaches, on the other hand, describe how language is actually used at a point in time, regardless of whether it conforms to what is prescribed (or even proscribed). Prescriptive views on grammar are often associated with a value judgement – classifying and polarising language use into 'good' and 'bad' grammar depending on whether it observes or violates pre-defined rules. There is a perception that if 'good' grammar is not upheld then it is a sign that our social fabric is decaying. The reality is that language is a dynamic system which is subject to change. Continual language change, according to Aitchison, is 'natural and inevitable' (2001: 221). As we have seen from the historical perspective set out in an earlier sub-section (Books about grammar), some of those structures and features that are considered to be indications of decay today were the rules and standards of yesterday.

Carter and McCarthy (2006) note that prescriptive rules are often social rules that are believed to 'mark out a speaker or writer as educated or as belonging to a particular social class' (2006: 6). They give two classic examples of prescriptive rules: 1) Do not end a sentence with a preposition (for example, *This is something you should not be involved* ***in***), and 2) do not split an infinitive (for example, *I except* ***to*** *shortly* ***welcome*** *him here.*)

(ibid). Throughout their grammar, Carter and McCarthy (2006) describe where, in reality, these and other prescriptive rules are broken. Interestingly, they concede,

> it is important that learners are aware of the social importance which attaches to certain prescriptive rules while at the same time being aware of the way in which English is used by real speakers and writers of the language.
>
> (2006: 6)

As the first section makes clear, historically, books about grammar were prescriptive but since the advent of language corpora, descriptive grammar books have become the norm. Leech (2015: 146) goes as far as saying that, since the electronic era, the term 'descriptive grammar' has become redundant. All corpus studies of grammar, he notes, inevitably make use of the evidence of grammatical usage as observed in corpora. However, the descriptions of grammar from language corpora, regardless of how impartially they are drawn, can still cause a social furore if they threaten the socially-accepted perceptions of what grammar should be.

Variation, varieties, standards and acceptability

Establishing a standard grammar, for some languages, has meant that one dialect has officially been chosen for standardisation. Crucially, this was not the case with English. As Trudgill and Hannah (2002: 1) detail, standard English has been through a process in which it has been 'selected, codified and stabilized', in a way that other varieties have not. Standard English, they say, acquired its status more gradually and in a more organic manner. It did not entail a standardising committee; rather, the upper classes wrote in their own dialect and then were in a position to impose this as the standard use (ibid).

Trudgill and Hannah (2002: 2) define standard English as the variety whose grammar has been described and given public recognition in grammar books and dictionaries, with its norms considered to be correct and constituting good usage. They note, however, that this codification, which aims for stabilisation and uniformity, is only relative and that the standard English used in different parts of the English-speaking world differs noticeably from one place to another. Trudgill and Hannah (2002: 2) indicate some of the grammatical peculiarities of standard English which distinguish it from most other varieties (see Table 9.1).

There is, of course, a circularity involved in concepts such as variation, varieties, standards and acceptability. What drives acceptability is a standard codified model of language, but a standard is socially-rather than empirically-derived and ultimately it is linked to status and power. The creation of, or orientation towards, a standard ultimately lays down what is acceptable and, most importantly, what is not. By revering a standard, one is placing some regional and national forms of English at a lower status of 'variety'. These non-standard forms can then be described in terms of their difference or 'deviation' from the socially-constructed norm of the standard grammar, lexis and phonology.

A by-product of the eighteenth-century drive towards the codification of what is standard and acceptable British and American English was the casting out of what was different to these standard varieties. Regional varieties, dialects (e.g. Cumbrian or Tyneside English) and national varieties (e.g. Scottish, Irish or Canadian English) have been described over the years in terms of their variation from the norm. To quote Hickey (2010: 3), 'the standard became more and more characterised by its non-regional character. The divorcing of preferred public

Table 9.1 Examples of standard English grammar rules which usually distinguish it from non-standard varieties

Feature of standard English	*Rule in standard English*	*Use in non-standard variety*
Past tense forms of auxiliary verb and main verb *to do*	There is no distinction between the past tense forms of the auxiliary verb *to do* and those of the main verb *to do* (i.e. *did* is used in both cases).	In most non-standard varieties, *done* is used as the past tense form of the main verb: *I done nothing today* (Irish English)
Negative concord	There is no negative concord in Standard English.	In most non-standard varieties, negative forms agree grammatically with one another throughout a clause: *Don't say nothing* (Irish English).
Reflexive pronouns	Reflective pronouns are formed in an irregular manner, with some forms based on the possessive pronouns, *myself, yourself, ourselves, yourselves,* while others are based on object pronouns: *himself, themselves.*	Many non-standard dialects use a regular system using possessive forms throughout, e.g. *myself, yourself, hisself, ourselves, yourselves, theirselves.* *He saved hisself.* (American English)
Irregular past forms of the verb *to be*	There is a distinction between singular and plural of the past form of the verb *to be*: *I was, he was* but *we were, they were*, etc.	Many non-standard dialects use the same form for singular and plural: *We was living on a navy base.* (American English)

usage from regionality and local identity meant that the emerging standard was an essentially non-regional form of English.'

In their major corpus-based grammar book Biber et al. (1999), referring to grammatical variation in English, note that it would be wrong to assume that standard English is fixed grammatically. Their descriptions of grammar account for this variation in terms of contextual factors. They say:

> the notion that the standard insists on 'uniformity' – allowing just one variant of each grammatical feature – is a serious fallacy, arising from a misleading application to language of the notion of 'standard' and 'standardization' taken from other walks of life. (1999: 19)

Larsen-Freeman (2014) observes that traditional morphosyntactic definitions of grammar overlook 'the thousands upon thousands of patterns that make up a speaker's knowledge of a language' (2014: 257) and that with increasing knowledge from the field of corpus linguistics, it has become clear that grammatical structures and lexical items occur in a large number of regularly-occurring patterns and many of these are fixed. This has brought to light the need to consider lexicogrammar rather than limit our view to morphosyntax alone.

The contemporary reality is that English is used globally, by billions, and as Schneider (2016: 339) points out,

> [It] is not only a variety or even a set of young varieties any longer – it is a globally available resource for speakers, including speakers with limited access to formal education, employing it for their own communicative purposes in creative ways. It is used in transnational interactions of whatever kind to which the participants bring their respective linguistic backgrounds and use it creatively.

Quirk (1990: 6) made a useful distinction between 'use-related' and 'user-related' varieties in English. He defines use-related as a variety that a speaker or writer 'assumes along with a relevant role', giving examples such as legal English or literary English and he states that a person may have 'mastery of several such varieties'. He contrasts this with user-related varieties where a person is 'tied to one only', citing as examples British English or American English (1990:6). Each of the use-related contexts brings with it a set of conventions. It is worth reconsidering this dichotomy years on and in light of the global use of English and the convergent role of the internet and social media. In an updated model, we can say that we use English in so many roles and personae now – private, institutional and virtual – that, more and more, there is a tendency for a blurring of the lines in terms of our user-relatedness to any one standard variety.

Spoken grammar vs written grammar

The advent of corpora, in combination with sophisticated recording and storage technology, facilitated the gathering and analysis of spoken language. Hitherto, descriptions of grammar had been largely generalised from the written form. McCarthy and Carter (2001) were at the forefront of identifying the need to describe the grammar of spoken language. McCarthy and O'Keeffe describe this spoken grammar as 'the grammar that we find in regular and repeated use by the majority of native- and expert-speakers of a language in the majority of their spoken interactions' (2014: 272). They distinguish between these everyday conversations and specialised types of speaking such as speeches, lectures, sermons and interviews, each with their own and shared characteristics. They point out that, in the 1970s and 1980s, at a time when ELT was encouraging a focus on 'the interpersonal functions of language', within a communicative and skills-led pedagogy, what was known about spoken language was 'hardly adequate' (McCarthy and O'Keeffe 2014: 273). Since this time language corpora have enabled new insights into defining a spoken grammar, 'offering evidence from spoken data that everyday conversations manifested common grammatical phenomena that were marginalised in description and neglected in pedagogy' (Carter and McCarthy 2017:1).

However, Leech (2000) argues that the grammar of speaking and writing is one and the same, and that grammatical divergence lies in differing contexts of use, both written and spoken, rather than its mode, written or spoken. He argues that grammar plays a more significant role in writing than in conversation/speaking, which he considers to be syntactically less complex, tending towards disjunctive construction. Carter and McCarthy acknowledge differing distribution across contexts of both written and spoken use but argue that the grammars used in spoken contexts should not be based on writing 'as a sort of spin-off' (Carter and McCarthy 2017: 6, see also first section). They point out that this unitary position does not account for those grammatical phenomena that are characteristic of the spoken language and 'differently distributed' or 'markedly more frequent' in spoken than written language. Nor does it account for grammatical phenomena that are exclusive to speaking and independent of writing.

Key areas of dispute and debate

Models of grammar

Many differing models and theories of grammar and approaches to grammatical analysis have evolved over the years. This section gives a brief overview of some of the key theories and approaches. The differences between these models and approaches can be simplistically categorised as those concerned with the internal formal structures of grammar – grammar on the inside – and those concerned with the usage of grammatical structures – grammar on the outside.

The generative grammar theory is a formalist theory which conceives grammar as a context-free set of rules and principles. This approach was first formalised by Chomsky in 1956. There have been many iterations of the generative grammar theory since the 1950s, though common to all is an effort to establish a set of rules that defines natural language. The Chomskyan view holds that all languages are variations of one Universal Grammar (UG) and that each individual possesses an innate system of rules able to form grammatical *sentences* in a given language. This is a formalist theoretical view of language which focuses on syntax and morphology and does not consider usage. It divorces linguistic *competence* from *performance*. In Chomsky's words the 'Generative grammar provides the systematic definition of a sentence. Grammatical sentences are those that are generated by the grammar' (Chomsky 1980: 27). The Chomskyan approach views grammar as a biologically-conceived system of the mind and a window into the language faculty of the mind. Generativists show that humans are able to distinguish things that are grammatical in a language from things that are ungrammatical, irrespective of context and meaning. A famous illustration of this is Chomsky's example of the contrast between '*colourless green ideas sleep furiously*' and '*furiously sleep ideas green colourless*'. The first example is deemed to sound grammatically 'correct' to the expert user and yet not meaningful, while the second sounds neither 'correct' nor meaningful. Establishing reliable universal finite rules to account for a vast array of infinite utterances is inevitably a complex undertaking and one which has dramatically evolved over the years and taken many different turns, many of which have been subsequently abandoned.

In taking this approach, Chomsky was moving away from the views of the structuralists and early applied linguistics who viewed language as a relational system emerging from patterns of usage. Grammar from a Chomskyan perspective is top-down and rule-governed, rather than bottom-up and emergent. He sees it as 'modularised, encapsulated and divorced from performance, lexis, social usage and the rest of cognition' (Ellis 2011: 655). Critics of generativism considered the approach to be overly theoretical, abstract and complex.

In contrast to the formalist approach, which dominated the 1950s and second half of the twentieth century, was the re-emergence of functionally-based theories of grammar which hold social context and usage at their core. Systemic Functional Linguistics (SFL), founded by Halliday in the 1960s and associated with the Prague School, is one such theory. It views language as a system of relationships, in which the structural features are described in relation to the functions they fulfil and the meanings they create within contexts of use. Unlike the generativist approach, SFL sees form, function and meaning as inseparable. According to Halliday, when children are learning grammar they are learning how to mean (Halliday 1975). While formalist theories viewed grammar as a mental state, from a nativist, biological perspective, Halliday views grammar as a structural resource which humans draw on for use in different environments. Halliday's model thus takes a social environmentalist perspective. According to the systemicists, language is an ongoing series of structural and lexical choices that fulfil different social and cultural functions. As the name suggests, SFL endeavoured to describe both the system of grammar and its activity or function. Emerging from SFL was the term lexico-grammar, which Halliday uses to describe the interdependence of lexis and syntax. The advent of corpus linguistics facilitated greater identification of lexico-grammatical patterning in language and from this came Sinclair's 'idiom principle' (Sinclair 1991), which proposes that written and spoken language consists of preconstructed phrases and that grammar is used as a back-up device. Central to Sinclair's work is the importance of colligation and collocation in a description of language.

Another model which counters the notion that grammar is wholly formal focuses on how meaning-based grammatical constructions emerge from acts of language use. Tomasello (2003), drawing on the work of antecedents, provides a usage-based theory of language acquisition which holds that children come to the process of language acquisition equipped with two sets of interlinked cognitive skills – they can identify what language is used for (function) and they can identify patterns of language used in specific functions and ultimately they learn to use these productively. In essence, this model holds that language structure emerges from observed language use. Through various cognitive processes, grammar, which Tomasello refers to as 'a structured inventory of linguistic constructions' (Tomasello 2009: 86) is formed from the language that we hear being used around us as children. This model has been adopted by Ellis and his associates to explore patterns of second language acquisition (SLA). The use of corpus data has proved useful in evidencing usage-based theories of language which, in an SLA context, hold that usage leads to commonly occurring form-meaning pairings becoming entrenched as grammatical knowledge in the learner's mind. More frequent forms are experienced more by learners and can become entrenched earlier in the language acquisition process (Ellis et al. 2015).

Grammatical knowledge: do we need it?

A BBC TV programme (2016), *School Swap*, documents the brief visit of three 18-year old state-educated pupils from South Wales to a South Korean school. During the programme one of the three English-speaking students is asked to explain the difference between the present perfect and the past simple. He simply can't. He appears deeply embarrassed and yet throughout the programme he uses both structures with ease. He is an articulate, confident user of his own language and his inability to name and explain the nuts and bolts of his first language does not stand in the way of his ability to use it fluently, competently and creatively.

The grammar that the student uses so proficiently is the set of principles and codes that he subconsciously refers to in order to create his language. The rules governing the differences that he cannot explicitly articulate are a set of consciously codified rules, the types of rules found in grammar books. Users of a first language frequently display implicit automatic knowledge of the language and its formulaic patterning while acknowledging a lack of explicit knowledge of the so-called rules. For many second language learners the reverse often seems to be true. Why is it so important to those learning a second language not just to learn the language but to also learn about it? What greater understanding of a language do you gain by explicitly learning and knowing the grammar and how does that explicit knowledge convert to implicit understanding and use?

Second language grammar teaching and learning has long been the subject of much debate and research. Since the infancy of SLA research there have been many discussions about how to teach grammar, what to teach, when to teach it and whether the teaching of grammar is necessary at all. What follows is a brief account of some of the key debates relating to grammar teaching and learning.

How do we learn the grammar of another language?

In line with a Chomskyan UG perspective, Krashen (1982) argued that teaching grammar had very little impact on subconscious language acquisition. Krashen argued for learners to be exposed to 'comprehensible input', believing that, given adequate and rich input, the grammar of a language will be unconsciously acquired. He contended that there was no interface between explicit teaching and implicit knowledge. Krashen's findings on a natural order of acquisition of English morphemes appeared to substantiate this perspective. (See Murakami and Alexopoulou (2016) for a recent alternative stance on order of acquisition.) Long (1991) later argued for a less extreme approach, taking the view that teaching grammar should not be ignored but it should be executed in a communicatively focused way that would not disturb the natural order of acquisition. He put forward a 'focus on form' perspective where learners attend to grammar forms as they meet them rather than a 'focus on forms' approach involving systematic treatment and attention to a traditional step-by-step syllabus of grammatical structures. The focus on form was designed to draw on the strengths of communicative language teaching by combining attention to both form and meaning. Teachers were encouraged to react to problems with comprehension or 'ungrammatical' utterances incidentally as they happened during the course of meaningful communication, with a brief diversion to attend to the grammar if necessary. An important aspect of this approach was to encourage students to notice. Noticing theories are grounded on the assumption that learning requires attention. Schmidt's (1990, 2012) Noticing Hypothesis is based on the belief that comprehensible input alone is not enough. Schmidt contended that, as an integral part of the process towards implicit knowledge, learners need to detect and take explicit notice of specific linguistic features of the input.

A review of many second language teaching contexts today would indicate that a traditional approach to the teaching of grammar appears to prevail. Even the shift towards communicative language teaching, with a focus on function over form, has not led to an abandonment of explicit and traditional grammar teaching. Larsen-Freeman (2015: 264), in an overview of the impact of SLA and applied linguistics research on grammar learning and teaching, attributes this to 'long-standing views on the importance of grammar teaching by teachers and by those who set educational policy' (2015: 264).

Assuming that grammar teaching in the classroom is not about to be abandoned (at least in the short term), there continues to be a debate over how to teach it: explicitly or implicitly, deductively or inductively, what types of tasks and input to use, and how best to go about error correction and feedback. Traditional grammar teaching adopted a structural syllabus, often delivered using a Present, Practice, Produce (PPP) model involving a presentation context for a chosen grammar point, followed by a series of controlled practice exercises of spoken drills and written exercises, and concluding with opportunities to use the grammar point in freer communicative contexts. A theory behind this approach involves automatizing the use of the rule to the point where the learner no longer consciously refers to the rule. There is a body of evidence which shows that, through practice and repetition, explicit knowledge can become implicit (DeKeyser 1997), but crucially, according to Pienemann (1989), the learner has to be developmentally ready to acquire it. Critics of this maintain that the means used to test the effectiveness of explicit knowledge on implicit knowledge were based on decontextualised tests of discrete items in contexts such as gap-fills and sentence reformulations. However, studies such as Swain and Lapkin (1998) and Spada and Tomita (2010) inter alia illustrate that an explicit focus on a given grammatical feature can lead to spontaneous, contextualised usage.

How should we teach grammar?

A central question in teaching grammar is whether rules about grammar should be given to learners through a teacher-led deductive approach or whether they should work them out for themselves taking a discovery-led inductive approach. Various studies have shown that different aspects of grammar lend themselves better to one approach over the other. DeKeyser (1997), for example, has shown that learners appear to learn morphosyntactic rules more effectively through explicit, deductive learning whereas more complex syntactic features are most effectively taught through an inductive approach. Willis (2003) argues that the approach adopted should be driven by the nature of the grammar point in question and that an explicit approach is likely to be more suitable for a point which is largely a matter of form, whereas a grammatical feature requiring more complex conceptual understanding may need a more awareness-raising approach. Timmis (2015) picks up on this, pointing out that in the otherwise inductively-driven corpus-informed course *Touchstone*, the authors take an explicit traditional PPP approach involving overt explanation and practice in their treatment of the interactive role of *though* as a linking adverbial in conversation, a high frequency feature of spoken language which has almost non-existent presence elsewhere in ELT materials. McCarthy, one of the *Touchstone* authors, asserts that for the very reason that their insights about *though* and other corpus-informed revelations are revolutionary, the ways in which these innovations are presented need to remain familiar (McCarthy 2004). Overall it would appear that despite many studies reviewing the value and efficacy of both approaches, neither a deductive nor inductive approach has been consistently favoured (Ellis 2006).

The field of SLA is populated with a lineage of experimental studies of how grammar is taught and how grammar is or is not learnt. What is striking from all of this body of work, over the last 30 years especially, is how little we still know about how best to teach and learn grammar and indeed what grammar to teach. There are so many variables involved in learning that it is difficult to standardize studies and make them comparable. What appears to work for one cohort may not be replicable in another group, at another age, language level, from a different educational background and culture, and so on.

Future directions

Language as a system is a dynamic entity. As part of this process, its grammar will never be entirely fixed and uniform. In the era of globalisation, and especially in the context of English, this change is all the more rapid and, at times, disparate. And yet, socially, there is often a plea for fixedness in English grammar. Advances in technologies that allow us to capture and store speech and writing language in mega-corpora have given linguists the capacity to monitor language variation and change. Through these tools, we can observe and describe how grammar has changed and is changing.

Language corpora are also bringing empirical insight into the process of first and second language acquisition. Surprisingly, given all of this innovation, grammar instruction appears to have been relatively unaltered by research findings. It remains traditional for the most part, with grammar teaching centred on accuracy of form and paradigmatic learning, where mechanical exercises are seen as the way of bringing about learning. Looking ahead, it is fair to assume that many more studies will enhance our understanding of the processes of grammar acquisition in first and second languages and yet we speculate that overt grammar teaching will not have gone away from first or second language classrooms.

What is certain about the future is that grammar will remain a contentious topic, but the furore comes more from the public than from linguists. As language scholars, our role in relation to grammar is to collect, observe and describe change and to be mindful of Crystal's (2011) warning that the only languages that don't change are dead ones. As he points out, all living languages change because they have to. They exist through the people who use them. And because people are changing all the time, their language changes too. For future linguists, the challenge is to describe the widely changing and varying grammar of English in its global contexts of use.

Further reading

Carter, R. A. and M. J. McCarthy (2017) 'Spoken grammar: Where are we and where are we going?', *Applied Linguistics* 38 (1): 1–20. This paper reflects on twenty years of corpus-based work on spoken grammar. It reinforces the importance of its inclusion in any pedagogical grammar.

Crystal, D. (2017) *Making Sense: The Glamorous Story of English Grammar*. Oxford: Oxford University Press. Crystal charts the development of grammar, its history, varieties irregularities and uses.

Howatt, A. P. R. and H. Widdowson (2004) *A History of English Language Teaching*. Oxford: Oxford University Press. This book has some really insightful descriptions of grammar and grammars in pedagogical contexts over the centuries.

McCarthy, M. J. (2017) *English Grammar: Your Questions Answered*. Cambridge: Prolinguam Publishing. This book is a highly accessible and entertaining description of present day standard English highlighting some of the current and ongoing concerns about grammar usage.

Linn, A. R. (2006) 'English grammar writing', in A. McMahon and B. Aarts (eds), *The Handbook of English Linguistics*. Oxford: Blackwell, 72–92. This chapter provides a really comprehensive history of grammars, moving from historical prescriptive grammars right up to modern corpus-based descriptive works.

Related topics

- The historical study of English
- World Englishes: disciplinary debates and future directions
- Standards in English
- The relevance of English in higher education
- Teaching English to Speakers of Other Langauges (TESOL)
- Corpus linguistics: studying language as part of the digital humanities.

References

Aitchison, J. (2001) *Language Change: Progress or Decay?* Cambridge: Cambridge University Press.

Biber, D., S. Johansson, G. Leech, S. Conrad, E. Finegan and R. Quirk (1999) *Longman Grammar of Spoken and Written English*. Cambridge, MA: MIT Press.

Brown, G. (1823) *Institutes of English Grammar*. New York: Samuel and Wood (reprinted by Downey, C. (1982) Delmar, New York: Scholars' Facsimiles and Reprints).

Carter, R. A. and M. J. McCarthy (2006) *Cambridge Grammar of English: A Comprehensive Guide to Spoken and Written Grammar and Usage*. Cambridge: Cambridge University Press.

Carter, R. A. and M. J. McCarthy (2017) 'Spoken grammar: Where are we and where are we going?', *Applied Linguistics* 38 (1): 1–20.

Chomsky, N. (1980) 'Rules and representations', *The Behavioural and Brain Sciences* 3: 1–61.

Crystal, D. (2011) *A Little Book of Language*. New Haven: Yale University Press.

DeKeyser, R. M. (1997) 'Beyond explicit rule learning', *Studies in Second Language Acquisition* 19 (2): 195–221.

Ellis, R. (2006) 'Researching the effects of form-focussed instruction on L2 acquisition', *AILA Review* 19 (1): 18–41.

Ellis, N. C. (2011) 'The emergence of language as a complex adaptive system', in James Simpson (ed.), *Handbook of Applied Linguistics*. London: Routledge, 666–679.

Ellis, N. C., M. O'Donnell and U. Römer (2015) 'Usage-based language learning', in B. MacWhinney and W. O'Grady (eds), *The Handbook of Language Emergence*. Hoboken, NJ: Wiley, 163–180.
Green, B. B. and G. M. Rubin (1971) *Automatic Grammatical Tagging of English*. Providence, RI: Department of Linguistics, Brown University.
Halliday, M. A. K. (1975) *Learning How to Mean: Explorations in the Development of Language*. London: Edward Arnold.
Hickey, R. (ed.) (2010) *Varieties of English in Writing: The Written Word as Linguistic Evidence*. Amsterdam: John Benjamins.
Howatt, A. P. R. and H. Widdowson (2004) *A History of English Language Teaching*. Oxford: Oxford University Press.
Krashen, S. D. (1982) *Principles and Practice in Second Language Learning*. New York: Pergamon.
Larsen-Freeman, D. (2002) 'The grammar of choice', in E. Hinkel and S. Fotos (eds), *New Perspectives on Grammar Teaching in Second Language Classrooms*. London: Routledge, 103–118.
Larsen-Freeman, D. (2014) 'Teaching grammar', in M. Celce-Murcia, D. M. Brinton and M. A. Snow (eds), *Teaching English as a Second or Foreign Language*. 4th edn. Boston, MA: National Geographic Learning, 255–270.
Larsen-Freeman, D. (2015) 'Research into practice: Grammar learning and teaching', *Language Teaching* 48 (2): 263.
Leech, G. (2000) 'Grammars of spoken English: New outcomes of corpus-oriented research', *Language learning* 50 (4): 675–724.
Leech, G. (2015) 'Descriptive grammar', in D. Biber and R. Reppen (eds), *The Cambridge Handbook of English Corpus Linguistics*. Cambridge: Cambridge University Press, 146–176.
Linn, A. R. (2006) 'English grammar writing', in A. McMahon and B. Aarts (eds), *The Handbook of English Linguistics*. Oxford: Blackwell, 72–92.
Long, M. H. (1991) 'Focus on form: A design feature in language teaching methodology', *Foreign Language Research in Cross-Cultural Perspective* 2 (1): 39–52.
McCarthy, M. J. (2004) *Touchstone: From Corpus to Coursebook*. Cambridge: Cambridge University Press.
McCarthy, M. J. (2017) *English Grammar: Your Questions Answered*. Cambridge: Prolinguam Publishing.
McCarthy, M. J. and R. Carter (2001) 'Size isn't everything: Spoken English, corpus, and the classroom', *TESOL Quarterly* 35 (2): 337–340.
McCarthy, M. J. and A. O'Keeffe (2014) 'Spoken grammar', in M. Celce-Murcia, D. M. Brinton and M. A. Snow (eds), *Teaching English as a Second or Foreign Language*. 4th edn. Boston, MA: National Geographic Learning, 271–287.
Murakami, A. and T. Alexopoulou (2016) 'L1 influence on the acquisition order of English grammatical morphemes', *Studies in Second Language Acquisition* 38 (03): 365–401.
Palmer, H. E. (1924/1969) *A Grammar of Spoken English on a Strictly Phonetic Basis, First Edition 1924 Third Edition 1969, Revised and Rewritten by R. Kingdon*. Cambridge: Heffer.
Pienemann, M. (1989) 'Is language teachable?', *Applied Linguistics* 10: 52–79.
Quirk, R. (1990) 'Language varieties and standard language', *English Today* 6 (1): 3–10.
Quirk, R., S. Greenbaum, G. Leech and J. Svartvik (1972) *A Grammar of Contemporary English*. London: Longman.
Quirk, R., S. Greenbaum, G. Leech and J. Svartvik (1985) *A Comprehensive Grammar of the English Language*. London: Longman.
Schneider, E. W. (2016) 'Hybrid Englishes: An exploratory survey', *World Englishes* 35 (3): 339–354.
Schmidt, R. (1990) 'The role of consciousness in second language learning', *Applied linguistics* 11 (2): 129–158.
Schmidt, R. (2012) 'Attention, awareness, and individual differences in language learning', *Perspectives on Individual Characteristics and Foreign Language Education* 6: 27.
Sinclair, J. McH. (1991) *Corpus, Concordance, Collocation: Describing English Language*. Oxford: Oxford University Press.
Spada, M. and Y. Tomita (2010) 'Interactions between type of instruction and type of language feature: A meta-analysis', *Language Learning* 60 (2): 263–308.
Swain, M. and S. Lapkin (1998) 'Interaction and second language learning. Two adolescent French immersion learners working together', *The Modern Language Journal* 82 (3): 320–337.
Sweet, H. (1899) *The Practical Study of Languages. A Guide for Teachers and Learners*. London: J. M. Dent and Co.

Sweet, H. (1900) *A New English Grammar, Logical and Historical*. Oxford: Oxford University Press.
Timmis, I. (2015) *Corpus Linguistics for ELT: Research and Practice*. Abingdon: Routledge.
Tomasello, M. (2003) *Constructing a Language: A Usage-Based Theory of Language Acquisition*. Cambridge, MA: Harvard University Press.
Tomasello, M. (2009) 'The usage-based theory of language acquisition', in E. L. Bavin (ed.), *The Cambridge Handbook of Child Language*. Cambridge: Cambridge University Press, 69–88.
Trudgill, P. and J. Hannah (2002) *International English: A Guide to Varieties of Standard English*. 4th edn. London: Arnold.
Willis, D. (2003) *Rules, Patterns and Words*. Cambridge: Cambridge University Press.

Part 2
The relevance of English

10

The relevance of English language studies in higher education

Ann Hewings

Introduction

My aim in writing this chapter is to contextualise the position of English language studies (ELS) in higher education (HE), and to offer views on why it is a relevant and important area of study in the 21st century. It is written from my institutional perspective of frequently needing to explain to others what ELS is and why it is worth studying. It is also written within a particular historical context. At the time of writing, the United Kingdom recently voted to leave the European Union, a decision which has caused many to reflect on the language of political discourse, and the need for an open, tolerant and informed electorate able to evaluate complex and conflicting information. Such qualities are ones many of us in education would seek to promote in all university-level study, but I argue that ELS is particularly well placed to promote informed critical reflection and has the methodological tools to interrogate complexity in an interconnected world. So, while much of this volume deals with what ELS is about, in this chapter I deal with why university students should study it and academics research it in the context of 21st century HE.

Motivations for researching or studying ELS are clearly contextual and contingent on the history and scope of the discipline in different HE systems. They reflect, among other things, the role of English as a national language, a medium of instruction or an academic lingua franca. They may be influenced by the prevailing market-orientated discourses of HE worldwide, where the purposes of study are linked to the perceived needs of the economy and institutions are urged to be competitive and entrepreneurial in a marketised HE system (Brown 2015). Motivations may be instrumental, reflecting the relevance or otherwise of the English language to a variety of careers, particularly in non-Anglophone dominant countries (Baxter 2012; Gupta 2016). They also depend on what is meant by ELS in different countries and institutions and what purpose HE is designed to serve. My main context is the UK, particularly England, but evidence from curricula and research elsewhere serves to broaden the perspective and provide contrasting rationales for ELS.

ELS in UK universities

Within HE in the UK, the study of English language has a pedigree stretching back to the philological approaches of the late nineteenth and early twentieth centuries (English 2012;

Gupta 2015), and the trace of this remains in studies of older varieties of English in some departments today. Often this is linked to the study of English literature from past eras and is part of the academic training of students studying for degrees in ELS, English literature and English language and literature. It often starts with sketching the roots of modern English from Anglo-Saxon or Old English through Middle English to current dialects and varieties of the UK and beyond. It can focus on understanding the language of Beowulf, Chaucer and Shakespeare or concern itself with issues such as spelling variation and vowel shifts.

Currently in the UK, ELS operates within the overall expectations of degree-level study set by the Quality Assurance Agency (QAA), which also aligns with the European Qualifications Framework incorporating 47 countries within the Bologna Process. Embedded within statements related to understanding key aspects and techniques of a field of study, honours degree graduates are expected to have 'an appreciation of the uncertainty, ambiguity and limits of knowledge' and be able to 'critically evaluate arguments, assumptions, abstract concepts and data (that may be incomplete), to make judgements . . . ' (QAA 2014a: 26). In addition, there is an emphasis on skills for employment such as analysis, problem-solving and effective communication, and qualities such as exercising personal responsibility and decision-making in complex and unpredictable situations (QAA 2014b: 26). Relevant specifically to ELS is the QAA description of English Language as one of the three contributing strands of the university subject 'English' which may be studied separately, together or in combination, and the relevance of the subject English to contemporary society lies in its ability to develop the 'capacity to understand the world from a variety of perspectives' through focusing on the 'production, interpretation and negotiation of meaning' (QAA 2015: 5). It is the understanding of how meanings are made and interpreted, and whose meanings are valued and by whom and in what specific contexts that ELS contributes to the wider understanding of the world in which English and other languages are used. ELS spans both the Arts/Humanities and Social Sciences and provides rigorous analytical tools and training alongside topics of personal and societal relevance. Applications of theoretical and real-world insights inform practice in areas as diverse as immigration policy, education and medical training. For students, it promotes critical reflection on and development of their own language use and that in the world around them. It fosters understanding of the power of language to entertain and to promote understanding, or to manipulate and dominate others. ELS graduates are equipped to enter careers that require attention to detail, good analytical and communication skills, and an understanding and appreciation of linguistic and cultural diversity. ELS researchers contribute to an understanding of society and culture through explorations ranging from the language of poetry, humour and political speeches to mental and physical health, and conflict resolution.

The wider educational potential of ELS as set out above is not that well understood in both HE and society in general. As a contributing strand to subject English in UK HE, 'brand recognition' of ELS is fuzzy and disciplinary networks are dispersed. English Language may be invisible as a label within English departments, or it may be allied to education, languages, communication, media or (applied) linguistics. This is in contrast to its position as a school subject in the UK where it has gained greater recognition with the advent of English Language as a choice for 'A' level examinations. The syllabus specification indicates that school students are expected to cover, for example, diverse methods of analysis – phonetics, phonology and prosodics, graphology, lexis and semantics, pragmatics, and discourse – and use them to understand language, the individual and society (Assessment and Qualifications Alliance; (AQA) 2014). Specifically, within the AQA syllabus, students study language diversity and variety with the aim of understanding how and why language varies because of 'personal, social and geographical contexts' (p.14), and through this to develop their critical knowledge and understanding of different views and explanations. The previous iteration of this syllabus (AQA 2013) tied the knowledge and understandings more closely to developing a critical perspective on communication and specifically referenced critical discourse analysis (CDA). While school students base understandings of a subject on what they are taught, which is largely circumscribed by examination syllabi, within HE the discipline area is often harder to demarcate. In 2010 a group of academics in the UK attempted to rectify this situation by producing an English language benchmark statement under the auspices of the Higher Education Academy (HEA), the English Subject Centre and the Language and Area Studies Subject Centre (HEA 2011). The benchmark statement aimed to help teachers advising on the choice of university courses, academics introducing or reviewing a degree in English language, and employers wishing to understand the qualification obtained by a job applicant with a degree in English Language. The defining principles were set out as follows:

> Students study the linguistic systems underlying English, as well as language in use and the relationship between language and context, the society and the individual. They typically study both written and spoken language, with multimodal texts also a focus on some programmes. English may be studied in its cultural, contemporary and historical background; it may be related to literary texts, everyday discourse, and the structure of languages other than English. Descriptive analysis will be combined with more critical and theoretical work which develops students' understanding of texts and/or language systems. (p.3)

Despite this effort, it is often difficult to find ELS on UK HE websites, to know what label to search for it under, or what university faculty or department to search for it within. For example, in the online subject information within The Complete University Guide (2016), ELS is invisible and 'English' is largely synonymous with English literature. However, one of the videos on the site in which students talk about their experiences of studying English features a person who was actually a student of Linguistics. This lack of clarity and visibility serves to obscure the potential and reach of the subject on its own and in combination with others.

ELS in non-UK university contexts

The situation in other English-dominant countries is somewhat different as ELS is not a recognised subject label, although elements of it may be embedded within the curriculum. In the USA, English as a designation in HE is mostly synonymous with literature; however, rhetoric and composition classes have kept a language focus that has had a history in university education since the 19th century (Russell 2016). Aspects of ELS are mostly distributed among other disciplines such as Linguistics and Education. Writing from within a US tradition English (2012), in his book looking at futures for English Studies, begins his discussion by conflating English with literature, but later expands from a US focus to a global examination of English which includes English as a foreign language, creative writing and cultural studies. The (in)visibility of ELS in HE qualifications continues in Australasia, where English is again mostly associated with the study of literature written in English, and in both Australia and New Zealand aspects of English language study are likely to be found in other schools and departments such as Linguistics or Arts and Media.

Moving from Anglophone settings to those countries with a colonial heritage of English as an additional language, the visibility of ELS is greater but its role is often different.

The National University of Singapore offers English Language and English Literature as single honours options, the University of Malaya offers English (literature) and English Language and Linguistics. The University of Hong Kong's School of English offers both English Studies, which combines language, literature and creative writing, and Language and Communication. In contrast, Hong Kong Polytechnic University focuses on applied English language skills with their English Studies for the Professions degree programme. This last signals the importance of developing proficiency in using the English language as a foreign or additional language. Despite English being a second or official language in many of these countries, there is still demand for it also to be taught at university as a foreign language. Gupta (2016), in a discussion of English in Indian universities, notes a tension between academics in English departments who are trained in literature and the demands of students, and to some extent governments, to focus on English language often for motives of future employment and economic advancement.

The role of English as a global language is reflected in the number of universities teaching it in parts of the world that have no strong historical ties to English-dominant countries. As a foundation for intercultural communication, language learning – and nowadays particularly *English* language learning – is significant in many HE contexts, either as a subject in its own right or in support of other curriculum areas. Like the study of modern foreign languages within Anglophone settings, it has an important role to play in pluricultural and plurilingual contexts. European English undergraduate degrees often contain study of both language and literature together with aspects of society or culture (English 2012; Gupta and Katsarska 2009; Hultgren 2016), often taught within a department or school of philology or languages. English Language at undergraduate level focuses on proficiency in English as a foreign or additional language, often alongside knowledge of Anglophone history, culture and politics. Increasingly, curricula around the globe are also taking account of the reality that most communication through English is between non-native speakers (Mauranen 2012; Xiaoqiong and Jing 2013).

While not specifically part of ELS, the desire or need for proficiency in English language has projected English in universities worldwide beyond the English department and into other subject areas where qualifications are increasingly being taught in English. In Europe, the growth in undergraduate and master's courses taught through the medium of English since the beginning of the century has been charted by Wächter and Maiworm (2014). The number has grown from 725 in 2002 to 2389 in 2007 and 8089 in 2014. Academics more often find themselves needing to use English in their teaching and/or their research, thereby contributing to the increasing demand for a working knowledge of the language which enables them to participate in the Anglophone-dominated education arena. While there is much to criticise about the dominance of English as an academic lingua franca (Lillis and Curry 2010), those students who study through it do have access to an additional linguistic and cultural lens. For most, its importance lies in having access to more resources related to their subject, but it may also contribute an additional view on their education more generally through the ability to critically consider the role of language and culture more broadly. Students, both Anglophone and non-Anglophone, rather than simply using the language, can use the opportunity of studying the English language and studying through the English language to reflect on views around the hegemony of English internationally, and/or to reflect on usage in their own and other contexts.

This brief snapshot of ELS within the university sector highlights the variety of conceptions internationally of the subject matter and the reasons behind some of the confusion about what exactly ELS is. However, it also begins to illustrate how it is well positioned to develop not just subject-specific knowledge and skills but also less tangible qualities of the type often listed as the generic or transferable skills so favoured by governments (Collini 2012; McMahon and Oketch 2013). Two of these transferable skills particularly relevant here are:

- the ability to assess the merits and demerits of contrasting theories and explanations, including those of other disciplines.
- the ability to think and reason critically, to evaluate evidence and argumentation, and to form a critical judgement of one's own work as well as the work of others, both in academic and non-academic domains. (HEA 2011: 6)

These come from the English Language Subject Benchmark document and help to encapsulate the current relevance of ELS to society. In the discussion of current critical issues and future directions that follows, it is these wider attributes that are the focus.

Current critical issues and topics

In this section, I review a number of research areas in ELS in relation to the curriculum choices that they permit and their influence on pedagogy. The choice of components for degrees in ELS is broad and continuing to evolve. The critical issue then is: what should be studied and why? The UK QAA subject benchmark statements for English (that is, English considered more broadly, not specifically English language) indicate that

> The study of English language addresses all types and varieties of English, including national, regional, social, historical and contemporary forms. Students investigate the structure, function and use of varieties of English, and the influence of historical, social, geographical, cultural, political, stylistic and other contextual factors.
>
> (QAA 2015: 6)

This breadth of both historical and geographical sweep alongside the ability to analyse personally relevant linguistic and multimodal contexts using a variety of means is arguably where current intellectual concerns cross with the traditional grounding in phonetics, phonology, pragmatics, syntax and so on. To narrow the focus, I look at two of the major influences affecting language study. The first, is headed 'Language, text and technology'. The ability to communicate using a variety of (new) media has influenced language practices, and the use of computers to collect and analyse data has expanded the questions that can be posed and the range and quantity of evidence that can be interrogated. Secondly, 'English language and power' highlights the increased significance that critical examination of language and power in the personal and private sphere, as well as the public and political, is having. I refer to this as a critical-social turn in ELS. It brings together work on the varieties of Englishes from an individual to an international level, together with concepts of ownership and identity over time and space, and the social, cultural, political and economic consequences of Englishes past, present and future. These two developments within ELS help to indicate how it accords with the focus noted earlier on contemporary relevance and the capacity to understand the world from a variety of perspectives (QAA 2015: 15). There are many other 'current' trends and developments, but I use these two specifically to address the aim I set for this chapter of justifying why ELS should be studied and researched in HE in the 21st century.

English language, text and technology

Much undergraduate training to enable analysis and reflection on language starts with elements of segmentation – phonology, grammar and lexis. This is where ELS is most closely allied to linguistics. However, the linguistic skills of analysis and the metalanguage acquired are applied within ELS to understanding texts in context, whether written, spoken or multimodal. Traditionally the application of English language study focused on texts in old versions of English, a practice that Cameron (2012) likened to the philological study of English which helped at its foundation to establish intellectual rigour. This has now been largely replaced by analyses of more contemporary literary and non-literary texts. Significantly, both the means of analysis and the focus of the analyses have evolved with texts such as courtroom discourse, web pages and tweets being as likely to be examined as literature.

The application of various technologies over the last 70 years or so has influenced research questions and the choices of texts, and subsequently influenced the subject matter in the ELS curriculum. An example is work on spoken language. The ability to record speech is arguably one of the most profound technological changes in language analysis, and one that is now often taken for granted. The large-scale study of naturally-occurring speech began in Britain with the Survey of English Usage launched in 1959. A significant output from this was Svartvik and Quirk's (1980) *A Corpus of English Conversation* which consists of over 700 pages, 170,000 words, of conversation orthographically transcribed and marked for prosodic features. Along with the prosodic information, each grammatical category was separately recorded on slips of paper and filed at University College London for the use of researchers from across the world. In 1975, academics at Lund University, Sweden, began the massive process of making all the information from the Survey of Spoken English available in machine-readable form on magnetic tape for those researchers who were beginning to have access to computers. For researchers of English language, spoken and written, this was the beginning of access to large amounts of naturally-occurring data and a move away from descriptions of the language based largely on introspection or small data sets. The availability of this data and other later corpora influenced both research and the wider community, particularly the embedding within educational contexts of an understanding and valuing of variety and difference, and the relationship between dialects and standard English (Crystal 1987).

Moving forward to the first decades of the current century, research at the University of Nottingham, for example, has taken forward the work of the Survey of English Usage, particularly with regard to speech. Powerful computers store, enable and enhance the interrogation of huge amounts of data. Researchers continued the work on aspects of speech, but rather than concentrate on dialect or prosody, their focus is grammar and specifically how the grammar of speech and writing differ (see also O'Keefe and Mark, this volume). Students studying English language now benefit from and work within the shifting understandings of language that are emerging, understandings that chime with the needs of the 21st-century citizen to work with uncertainty and ambiguity. Researchers, teachers and students are now able to appreciate that there are rules governing speech that are different from the rules governing written language. The dialogic, real-time, social and interpersonal constraints of conversation do not usually give rise to fully formed sentences. Rather, '[w]hat seems more important is the production of adequate communicative units and the taking of turns' (Carter and McCarthy 2006: 165). One of the outcomes of research on spoken and written grammar for English language curricula is an appreciation of difference. Variety is both celebrated and normalised. So-called 'non-standard language' is as interesting, if not more so, than standard English.

This type of work is enabled by the collection and description of huge amounts of data via corpus studies (see also Philip, this volume). The development of computerised corpora is also facilitating the study and comparison of various other Englishes, particularly via the International Corpus of English (ICE). This project, which began in the 1990s, illustrates the increasing attention paid to Englishes in different parts of the world, with currently 26 projects to collect, analyse and make available for non-commercial purposes English from countries around the world (ICE 2016). The ICE also illustrates the recognition of internal diversity within Englishes through its corpus design protocol. Corpora for this type of comparison are designed to contain a variety of text types, both spoken and written. Speech samples include spontaneous face-to-face and telephone conversations, classroom interaction, scripted and unscripted speeches, and news broadcasts, while written texts are drawn from both private and public writings, fiction and non-fiction. Many corpora now also comprise language used on a variety of digital platforms. These may be designed to focus on discrete interaction contexts (e.g. text messaging, Tagg 2012; micro blogging, Zappavigna 2012) or to enable comparisons of the features of a variety of digital media including discussion boards, blogs, SMS texts and emails (Knight et al. 2014).

These studies provide evidence of the ability of people to be creative with language and the constant evolution of language that is taking place. The point here is that variety in language form and use is now given parity in research with so-called standard English. Therefore, most students studying ELS are exposed to variety and diversity in language not as a deviation from an arbitrary standard, but as a communicative tool for interacting in the world. They learn to evaluate evidence and arguments about English and reason critically to assess theories and explanations in a context where complexity and difference are the norm.

English language and power

The above discussion of the role of technologies in widening the application of ELS has focused largely on the ability to search large amounts of data, and the understandings of linguistic varieties within Englishes that this has helped bring to light. This section moves away from a methodological focus to an ideological one. The two, however, are not separate as technology is a tool used in uncovering issues of power within language. The divide is therefore a convenience for dealing with broader aspects of ELS in HE today. Briefly touched upon above, and relevant here, is the potential of varieties of English, particularly accents, to be used to socially categorise a speaker. ELS is uniquely placed to analyse and challenge any stigmatisation or discrimination against people based on how they speak. In many uses of language the exercise of power, from persuasion to control, is not overt and it is the ability to interrogate language choices which is particularly powerful in helping students to evaluate evidence and arguments within and beyond the subject matter of ELS. Below I focus mainly on research involving critical analysis at the level of text and of linguistic practices and illustrate how it can enable students to recognising the power of language.

The focus on power in language studies in the UK has been closely associated with the work of Fowler and colleagues, and Fairclough and colleagues beginning in the 1970s. Fowler et al (1979) in *Language and Control* foregrounded the role of linguistic analysis in understanding the exercise of power in the developing field of critical linguistics. Fairclough (1989) in *Language and Power* presented a more radical view wherein CDA

> emphasises ideology rather than (just) persuasion and manipulation. It views discourse as a stake in social struggle as well as a site of social struggle . . . including class struggle.

> It [*Language and Power*] sets as an objective for CDA raising people's consciousness of how language contributes to the domination of some people by others, as a step towards social emancipation.
>
> (Fairclough 2014: 2)

While the details and methodology of Fairclough's approach have not found favour with all discourse analysts, critical or otherwise (Blommaert 2008; Slembrouck 2001; Widdowson 1995), the significance of language as a means of understanding, exercising or accessing power has been widely taken up in various guises throughout applied linguistics and ELS.

For students, the critical dimension has expanded the types of text which are analysed. Everyday language across a variety of media is studied alongside more traditional literary texts. A particularly powerful notion is that of reader positioning: how texts are constructed to naturalise a particular view, to encourage the reader or hearer to accept the positioning put forward by the writer or speaker. The power of the media to position readers and shape public and private discourse is an obvious example of where critical language analysis may be applied, but one where researcher bias needs to be guarded against. Coffin and O'Halloran (2005), in analysing media texts, advocate applying more than one methodological approach. They used corpus analysis and systemic functional text analysis to reach conclusions about the subtle and persuasive uses of language in *The Sun* (a UK tabloid newspaper with a large circulation) on the topic of European Union migrants. They built up a picture of how certain expressions become imbued with particular connotations for *The Sun* readership over time. As a result, they contend that particular words and phrases which on their own are not value laden take on particular semantic prosodies for a particular readership on the basis of past associations. Learning to systematically analyse language using a variety of methods provides students with the means to approach the everyday texts they encounter in a more critical and analytical way. More recent research on the dynamics of online interaction on Facebook explores how users contribute to and circumscribe the social space in which their communications take place and importantly how their views shape the kind of political debate that they see, not unlike that of regular newspaper readers. Tagg et al. (2017) argue that the internet bubbles in which users of social media have their own views reinforced is a phenomenon that needs to be more widely understood in order for people to evaluate the information that they are receiving, particularly in an era of so-called fake news. The ability to critically interrogate texts is a valuable transferable skill not just in employment terms, but also in enhancing students' capacity to become reliably informed members of the public, contributing to the life of their community.

Another contribution relates ethnography and the study of social practices to the study of language. Now often referred to as Linguistic Ethnography, it grew out of New Literacy Studies (NLS), which moved away from considering literacy as a set of mental process such as decoding information, making inferences and so on. Rather, in NLS readers and writers are seen as taking part in social and cultural activities or practices in which literacy is a part. By viewing literacy as a social practice and embedded within multiple practices, it is possible to problematise what counts as literacy. The question of whose literacies are valued and whose are marginalised or resisted is a central concern (Street 2012: 27). This 'practices' perspective has been applied to literacies in HE with Lea and Street's (1998) research into academic literacies in HE bringing into focus the deficit view of literacy, in which the 'literacy problem' is located with the student while no account is taken of the social or institutional context and the relations of power and authority in which academic literacies are practised. Lillis (2003) moves academic literacies toward a theoretically grounded pedagogic approach, building from a model based on 'critique' towards one based on 'design'. She highlights the need for students to understand that they are writing within institutional settings where power and authority are unequally distributed. Building on this understanding, she argues that students should be enabled to draw on approved bodies of work and models of writing, but also to move it forward in directions of their own choosing, to contribute to new designs for academic writing. The effective closing down of certain ways of contributing in the academy is not confined to students. Lillis et al. (2010), through ethnographic, bibliographic and corpus studies, have illustrated the ways in which scholars from non-Anglophone contexts are also disadvantaged by the academic literacy contexts and norms in which they are expected to write. This is closely tied up with the power of English as a global language.

The role of the English language in global politics and economics has prompted much polemical writing. Phillipson (1992) is particularly associated with the view that the spread of English is linguistic imperialism; that is, nations such as the USA and the UK encourage the spread of the English language in order to exercise power over less powerful nations and therefore increase their economic and political power. Samuelson and Freedman (2010), for example, chart the change to English-medium education in Rwanda, and Gray (2012) indicates the role of the quasi-governmental British Council in this switch. Such moves privilege English over indigenous languages, thereby diminishing their role and promoting that of English. Studies also indicate that schooling is negatively affected by the use of a language relatively unknown to the child, and Williams (2011) provides evidence of language policy adversely affecting educational attainment in a variety of African countries. While the degree to which governmental influence is responsible for the rise of English is disputed, the role of businesses is well documented. In a globalised economic system, the use of a single dominant language facilitates the work of multi- or transnational companies. A recent study by Lockwood and Forey (2016) uses CDA and systemic functional linguistics to capture some of the difficulties that this creates in virtual meetings held by multilingual teams. Their analysis demonstrates the exercise of power and dominance through English and the effect on opening up or shutting down discussion. Consideration of the political and economic impact of the English language is now an integral part of many ELS curricula (Hewings and Tagg 2012).

As noted above, academia has embraced the use of English as a lingua franca, particularly for publishing. This not only may disadvantage those forced to publish in a language that is not their own but also influences research agendas in favour of the linguistically dominant contexts of the USA and UK (Lillis et al. 2010). Alongside scholarly publication through English, there is a trend towards increasing use of English in education itself at all levels. The dominance of English as an HE subject sees the language studied alone or in combination with literature and Anglophone cultures in many universities across the world. Gupta and Katsarska's (2009) volume on English in Eastern Europe illustrates well the variety within English, American and Irish Studies and the motivations behind its popularity. Gupta's (2016) work on English Studies in HE in India concludes that motivations of economic advancement based on knowledge of English outweigh desires to learn about Anglophone culture or literature, a situation that is at odds with the outlook of many of the academics teaching the subject. Hadley (2015) draws attention particularly to the growth of teaching positions in English for Academic Purposes in both Anglophone and non-Anglophone institutions. English as an academic lingua franca also enables the establishment of branch campuses of Anglophone HE institutions across the world. In Malaysia, for example, three Australian and one British university have set up campuses offering a variety of degree courses (Malaysia University Portal n.d.).

The growth in English-medium HE instruction can be linked to the forces of globalisation and economics discussed above and is in part an attempt by both Anglophone and non-Anglophone institutions to attract students from across the globe through instruction delivered in the world's current lingua franca. Students and scholars across the world are not only reading research literature in English, but are publishing PhD theses, articles and books in English. Siiner (2010), in a discussion of university courses taught through the medium of English, writes of anxiety about the impact of English on relatively smaller languages such as Danish, particularly in terms of domain-loss relating to scientific language. Hultgren (2016) provides statistics on the number of enrolments on BA programmes in Denmark in 2013 which demonstrates that English Studies attracted nearly five times as many students as the next most popular language, French. While there is concern about certain languages, the use of English as a lingua franca may alternatively be seen as a benefit in that it may facilitate collaboration and knowledge exchange across multiple languages. Researching and teaching about the position and impact of the use of English around the world, as well as of the power of language in general to influence and persuade, to close down or open up choices are vital understandings for citizens of the future. The emphasis on the critical and the social within ELS today can contribute to those understandings.

Future directions

Much of the above is relevant in any discussion of future directions for ELS. Here I single out just three topics, from the many possible, to outline briefly: English as a lingua franca, superdiversity, and multimodality. First is the growing emphasis on English as a lingua franca (ELF) and English as an academic lingua franca (EALF) as a distinct variety. ELF refers to communication in English between speakers with different first languages, mostly between those who are additional language speakers of English. Its importance rests on the fact that there is more use of English between speakers of various other languages than between so-called 'native' speakers and others. Graddol (2006: 87) described the teaching and learning of ELF 'as probably the most radical and controversial approach to emerge in recent years'. Two significant implications are firstly that changes to the English language are emerging as a result of the huge numbers of English as an additional language speakers using the language, and secondly that the native speaker is therefore no longer in the same position of power vis-à-vis English. Scholars, particularly in European universities, have researched the characteristics of ELF (Jenkins 2000), including significant corpus investigation (Mauranen 2012; Seidlhofer 2012) and have applied their findings to the teaching of English. However, the concept of ELF is one that is vigorously debated (O'Regan 2014) and touches on many of the issues of power and ideology in English usage, together with its global status. Given the global reach of English, its potential to enable communication between many different language speakers, but also its association with forces of globalisation that favour richer nations, debates of this kind are likely to continue. An alternative trajectory sees different varieties of English become more separate and mutually incomprehensible.

Secondly, the notion that languages are fixed and bounded by particular geographical or national regions is the subject of much critical questioning by researchers (e.g. Blackledge and Creese 2008; Garcia 2009; Otsuji and Pennycook 2010). The concept of a discrete national language linked with national identity is viewed by many as imposing an ideology, bound up with the creation of new European nation states in the 18th century, on our understandings today. Ethnographic research into language in use, particularly in urban contexts where people from different cultures with different linguistic repertoires are mixing, is revealing the complexity of communication and the possibility of divorcing it from its fixed association with nations and national identity. Indeed, Simpson (2016: 2) notes examples of public statements by politicians in which the disturbance to 'notions of linguistic fixity and boundedness' are linked with undermining 'social homogeneity and even national cohesion'. ELS scholars (Blackledge et al. 2017) frame this in term of the sociological concept of superdiversity (Vertovec 2007), where the mixing of very large numbers of people of different cultures, religions, ethnicities and linguistic backgrounds makes existing sociological and linguistic categorisation of little explanatory value. Seen as a meaning-making resource in contexts of diversity, language (spoken, written and multimodal) is less a set of traditional rules and more a functional system for getting things done and for expressing feelings. The value for ELS students of this more fluid approach to language and communication is one of broadening perspectives. As it is a sufficiently distinct theoretical position from that which is likely to be held by many potential students, it can help to foster 'the ability to assess the merits and demerits of contrasting theories and explanations' as outlined by the HEA benchmark statements (2011: 16).

Finally, within ELS, language is increasingly studied multimodally alongside other semiotic resources as understandings of the communication process expand. Some might be surprised that multimodality is considered an area for the future, as it has been part of communications research and teaching for many years (see Ravelli, this volume). Kress and van Leeuwen (1996) highlighted the growing necessity of visual literacy alongside traditional print literacy, the pictorial as well as the verbal, in order to function effectively in the workplace, and Goodman (1996) made the case for understanding 'visual English' as part of ELS. Over two decades on, the pace at which semiotics is combining aspects of the visual and the verbal is increasing greatly. The ubiquity of online communication and the speed of delivery have increased the requirements for ways of conveying affect more concisely alongside information. Emojis in SMS texts, clip art in emails, combinations of different scripts, and font and colour changes in computer-mediated communications are all worthy of study towards a greater understanding of how English alongside, and often interwoven with, other languages functions in different environments. Multimodal texts often rely for their impact on the unusual, memorable or unexpected and therefore are often studied alongside the concept of creativity. Analysis of such texts develops critical appreciation of creative language use, and focuses on the techniques and skills which underpin verbal art. For students, this can provide structured opportunities to try out different forms of writing, to tackle unfamiliar genres and crucially to see multimodal verbal art and language use more generally as a product that they too can design. Analysis and production of multimodal texts can give students opportunities to play with language multimodally in order to entertain, shock, inform and persuade. Through such participation, students can also start to reflect on the messages that they are consuming, to analyse their form, function and impact (Demjén and Seargeant 2016; Hann and Lillis 2016).

Conclusion

ELS cannot lay claim to being the only subject that promotes generic skills such as critical reflection and critical judgement, evaluation of evidence and argumentation, or understandings of the individual, society and sociopolitical contexts. But it does have a very strong analytical framework with which to interrogate and critique the role of English and communication through English. Its research agendas have significant relevance in current societies and feed into the vibrant subject matter at school and university level. Work within this field provides academics and students with opportunities to systematically analyse and evaluate the texts that surround us and shape society: understanding the history of English, the politics that underpins its past and current evolution, and the value systems it contains and contributes to. ELS can promote consideration of concepts such as plurilingualism and the porosity of linguistic boundaries, as well as teaching how to critically analyse and create spoken, written and multimodal texts. Some of the knowledge and the perspectives gained from studying ELS can also be woven into teaching where 'English' means literature, creative writing or learning an additional language. For example, the tools of stylistics or conversation analysis are relevant to those wishing to truly understand dialogue in all its contextual variation. Those learning the English language can be challenged by discussion and choices of text to consider issues such as linguistic hegemony or the appropriateness of code-mixing. As researchers and educators in the field of English language, we are faced with making selections from the rich array of ELS materials, and I would argue that keeping in mind the wider goals of an educated citizen should influence those choices and maintain relevance for the future.

Further reading

Carter, R. (2004) *Language and Creativity: The Art of Common Talk.* London: Routledge. This introduces the systematic corpus study of conversation and argues that creativity is a feature of everyday language deployed by ordinary people in diverse social contexts.

English, J. F. (2012) *The Global Future of English Studies.* Chichester: Wiley-Blackwell. Written initially from an American perspective, this volume explores the history and future of English Studies including literature, language, creative writing and cultural studies. Taking data from around the world, James English challenges the view of the subject as in crisis and focuses on the transformations occurring to the subject globally.

Hewings, A., L. Prescott and P. Seargeant (eds) (2016) *Futures for English Studies: Teaching Language, Literature and Creative Writing in Higher Education.* London: Palgrave Macmillan. This volume brings together international scholars to consider the future of English as a discipline and its component parts. The strength of English Studies is illustrated in terms of its traditional breadth and depth, and also its readiness to adapt, experiment and engage with other subjects.

Hewings, A. and C. Tagg (eds) (2012) *The Politics of English: Conflict, Competition, Co-Existence.* Abingdon: Routledge. This undergraduate textbook explores policies and practices that affect the use and position of English both nationally and internationally and in combination with other languages.

Related topics

- The idea of English
- Literacy in English: literacies in Englishes
- Teaching English to Speakers of Other Languages (TESOL)
- The politics of English
- Multimodal English.

References

AQA (2013) *English Language A for Exams from June 2014 Onwards, Version 1.3.* Available at www.aqa.org.uk/subjects/english/as-and-a-level/english-language-a-2700, accessed 16 August 2016.

AQA (2014) *AS and A-level English language Specifications, Version 1.0 14 October 2014.* Available at www.aqa.org.uk/subjects/english/as-and-a-level/english-language-7701-7702, accessed 16 August 2016.

Baxter, A. (2012) 'Higher education mission and vision in Rwanda: A comparative and critical discourse analysis'. *Reconsidering Development* 2(2): 1–26. Available at https://pubs.lib.umn.edu/index.php/reconsidering/article/view/572, accessed 15 February 2018.

Blackledge, A. and A. Creese (2008) 'Contesting "language" as "heritage": Negotiation of identities in late modernity', *Applied Linguistics* 29 (4): 533–554.

Blackledge, A., A. Creese, with M. Baynham, M. Cooke, L. Goodson, Z. Hua, B. Malkani, J. Phillimore, M. Robinson, F. Rock, J. Simpson, C. Tagg, J. Thompson, K. Trehan and L. Wei (2017) '*Language and superdiversity: An interdisciplinary perspective (WP. 26)*' Available at www.birmingham.ac.uk/generic/tlang/index.aspx, accessed 9 August 2017.

Blommaert, J. (2008) 'Review of N. Fairclough 'Language and globalization' (2006)', *Discourse & Society* 19 (2): 257–262.

Brown, R. (2015) 'The marketisation of higher education: Issues and ironies', *New Vistas* 1 (1): 4–9. Available at www.uwl.ac.uk/sites/default/files/Departments/Research/new_vistas/vol1_iss1/vol1_iss1_art1_23April2015.pdf, accessed 16 August 2016.

Cameron, D. (2012) 'Not changing English: Syllabus reform at Oxford', *Changing English* 19 (1): 13–22. DOI 10.1080/1358684X.2012.649136, accessed 28 September 2016.

Carter, R. and M. McCarthy (2006) *Cambridge Grammar of English*. Cambridge: Cambridge University Press.

Coffin, C. and K. O'Halloran (2005) 'Finding the global groove: Theorising and analysing dynamic reader positioning using APPRAISAL, corpus and a concordancer', *Critical Discourse Studies* 2 (2): 143–163.

Collini, S. (2012) *What Are Universities For?* London: Penguin.

Crystal, D. (1987) *The Cambridge Encyclopedia of Language*. Cambridge: Cambridge University Press.

Demjén, Z. and P. Seargeant (eds) (2016) *Creativity in Language: From Everyday Style to Verbal Art*. Milton Keynes: The Open University.

English, J. (2012) *The Global Futures of English Studies*. Chichester: John Wiley and Sons.

Fairclough, N. (1989) *Language and Power*. London: Longman.

Fairclough, N. (2014) '*What Is CDA? Language and Power Twenty-Five Years On*' Available at www.academia.edu/8429277/What_is_CDA_Language_and_Power_twenty-five_years_on, accessed 23 August 2016.

Fowler, R., B. Hodge, K. Cress and T. Trew (1979) *Language and Control*. London: Routledge and Keegan Paul.

Garcia, O. (2009) *Bilingual Education in the 21st Century: A Global Perspective*. Chichester: Wiley-Blackwell.

Goodman, S. (1996) 'Visual English', in S. Goodman and D. Graddol (eds), *Redesigning English: New Text, New Identities*. London: Routledge.

Graddol, D. (2006) *English Next*. British Council.

Gray, J. (2012) 'English the industry', in A. Hewings and C. Tagg (eds), *The Politics of English: Conflict, Competition, Co-Existence*. Abingdon: Routledge, 137–178.

Gupta, S. (2015) *Philology and Global English Studies*. Basingstoke: Palgrave Macmillan.

Gupta, S. (2016) 'English studies in Indian higher education', in A. Hewings, L. Prescott and P. Seargeant (eds), *Futures for English Studies: Teaching Language, Literature and Creative Writing in Higher Education*. Basingstoke: Palgrave Macmillan, 99–119.

Gupta, S and M. Katsarska (eds) (2009) *English Studies on this Side: Post-2007 Reckonings*. Plovdiv: Plovdiv University Press.

Hadley, G. (2015) *English for Academic Purposes in Neoliberal Universities: A Critical Grounded Theory*. Heidelberg: Springer.

Hann, D. and T. Lillis (eds) (2016) *The Politics of Language and Creativity in a Globalised World*. Milton Keynes: The Open University.

Hewings, A. and C. Tagg (eds) (2012) *The Politics of English: Conflict, Competition, Co-Existence*. Worlds of English. Abingdon: Routledge in association with the Open University.

Higher Education Academy English Subject Centre (2011) English language subject benchmark statement. Available at www.english.heacademy.ac.uk/explore/resources/language/docs/EL_benchmarking_final.pdf, accessed 28 September 2016.

Hultgren, A. K. (2016) 'The role of policy in shaping English as a university subject in Denmark', in A. Hewings, L. Prescott and P. Seargeant (eds), *Futures for English Studies: Teaching Language, Literature and Creative Writing in Higher Education*. Basingstoke: Palgrave Macmillan, 120–138.

International Corpus of English (ICE) (2016) Available at www.ice-corpora.net/ice/, accessed 27 September 2016.

Jenkins, J. (2000) *The Phonology of English as an International Language*. Oxford: Oxford University Press.

Knight, D., S. Adolphs and C. Ronald (2014) 'CANELC – constructing an e-language corpus', *Corpora* 9 (1): 29–56.
Kress, G and T. van Leeuwen (1996) *Reading Images: The Grammar of Visual Design*. London: Routledge.
Lea, M. and B. Street (1998) 'Student writing in higher education: An academic literacies approach', *Studies in Higher Education* 23 (2): 157–173.
Lillis, T. (2003) 'Student writing as "Academic Literacies": Drawing on Bakhtin to move from critique to design', *Language and Education* 17 (3): 192–207.
Lillis, T. and M. J. Curry (2010) *Academic Writing in a Global Context: The Politics and Practices of Publishing in English*. London/New York: Routledge.
Lillis, T., A. Hewings, D. Vladimirou and M. J. Curry (2010) 'The geolinguistics of English as an academic lingua franca: Citation practices across English-medium national and English-medium international journals', *International Journal of Applied Linguistics* 20: 111–135.
Lockwood, J. and G. Forey (2016) 'Discursive control and power in virtual meetings', *Discourse & Communication* 10 (4): 323–340.
Mauranen, A. (2012) *Exploring ELF: Academic English Shaped by Non-Native Speakers*. Cambridge: Cambridge University Press.
Malaysia University Portal (n.d.) Available at www.malaysiauniversity.net/branch-campus/, accessed 8 August 2017.
McMahon, W.W. and M. Oketch (2013) 'Education's effects on individual life chances and on development: An overview', *British Journal of Educational Studies* 61 (1): 79–107.
Otsuji, E. and A. Pennycook (2010) 'Metrolingualism: Fixity, fluidity and language in flux', *International Journal of Multilingualism* 7 (3): 240–254.
O'Regan, J. P. (2014) 'English as a lingua franca: An immanent critique', *Applied Linguistics* 35 (5): 533–52.
Phillipson, R. (1992) *Linguistic Imperialism*. Oxford: Oxford University Press.
Quality Assurance Agency (2014a) '*UK quality code for higher education, part A: Setting and maintaining standards*' Available at www.qaa.ac.uk/assuring-standards-and-quality/the-quality-code/quality-code-part-a, accessed 28 September 2016.
Quality Assurance Agency (2014b) '*The frameworks for higher education qualifications of UK degree-awarding bodies*' Available at www.qaa.ac.uk/publications/information-and-guidance/publication?PubID=2843#.WYssw0uWybx, accessed 9 August 2017.
Quality Assurance Agency (2015) '*Subject benchmark statement: English*' Available at www.qaa.ac.uk/en/Publications/Documents/SBS-English-15.pdf, accessed 28 September 2016.
Russell, D. R. (2016) 'The literary and the literate: The study and teaching of writing in US English departments', in A. Hewings, L. Prescott and P. Seargeant (eds), *Futures for Englishnorth Studies: Teaching Language, Literature and Creative Writing in Higher Education*. Basingstoke: Palgrave Macmillan, 139–157.
Samuelson, B. L. and S. W. Freedman (2010) 'Language policy, multilingual education, and power in Rwanda', *Language Policy* 9: 191–215.
Seidlhofer, B. (2012) 'Corpora and English as a Lingua Franca', in K. Hyland, H. Chau Meng and M. Handford (eds), *Corpus Applications in Applied Linguistics*. London, New York: Continuum International Publishing Group, 135–149.
Siiner, M. (2010) 'Hangovers of globalization: A case study of laissez-faire language policy in Denmark', *Language Problems and Language Planning* 34 (1): 43–62.
Simpson, J. (2016). Translanguaging in the contact zone: Language use in superdiverse urban areas. *Working Papers in Translanguaging and Translation* (WP. 14). Available at www.birmingham.ac.uk/generic/tlang/index.aspx.
Slembrouck, S. (2001) 'Explanation, interpretation and critique in the analysis of discourse', *Critique of Anthropology* 21 (1): 33–57.
Street, B. (2012) 'New literacy studies', in M. Grenfell, D. Bloome, C. Hardy, K. Pahl, R. Jennifer and B. V. Street (eds), *Language, Ethnography, and Education: Bridging New Literacy Studies and Bourdieu*. Abingdon: Routledge, 27–49.
Svartvik, J. and R. Quirk (1980) *A Corpus of English Conversation*. Lund: Liber Läromedel.
Tagg, C. (2012) *The Discourse of Text Messaging: Analysis of SMS Communication*. London: Continuum.
Tagg, C., P. Seargeant and A. A. Brown (2017) *Taking Offence on Social Media: Conviviality and Communication on Facebook*. London: Palgrave Macmillan.

The Complete University Guide (2016) '*The complete university guide*' Available at www.thecompleteuniversityguide.co.uk/league-tables/rankings?s=English, accessed 25 April 2016.

Vertovec, S. (2007) 'Super-diversity and its implications', *Ethnic and Racial Studies* 30 (6): 1024–1054.

Wächter, B. and F. Maiworm (2014) *English-Taught, Programmes in European Higher Education. The Picture in 2014*. Bonn: Lemmens. Available at www.aca-secretariat.be/fileadmin/aca_docs/images/members/ACA-2015_English_Taught_01.pdf, accessed 25 April 2016.

Widdowson, H. (1995) 'Discourse analysis: A critical view', *Language and Literature* 4 (3): 157–72.

Williams, E. (2011) 'Language policy, politics and development in Africa', in H. Coleman (ed.), *Dreams and Realities: Developing Countries and the English Language*. London: British Council, Teaching English Series, 2–18.

Xiaoqiong, H. and Jing, X. (2013) 'Towards a more appropriate university English curriculum in China in the context of English as an international language', *Changing English* 20 (4): 388–394. DOI 10.1080/1358684X.2013.855565.

Zappavigna, M. (2012) *Discourse of Twitter and Social Media: How We Use Language to Create Affiliation on the Web*. London: Continuum (now Bloomsbury).

11

Literacy in English

Literacies in Englishes

Carolyn McKinney

Introduction

While a key topic for consideration in English language studies, literacy in English is not a field as such. The term could refer to pedagogy for developing literacy in English in different global contexts, although there is indeed no unified approach to English literacy pedagogy. This chapter will address the question 'what is literacy?' as well as 'what counts as literacy in English?' It will argue for a pluralisation of literacies, acknowledging the diverse, socially situated practices that constitute literacy in different contexts and the ways in which these are ideologically and politically defined. The construct of 'English' as a single, unitary, named language will also be problematised (see also Seargeant, and Bolton, this volume). Engaging with the teaching of literacy in English across a range of levels (primary and secondary schooling and higher education), the chapter argues that 'literacy in English' is a contested space, where the English literacy classroom commonly functions as a 'contact zone' (cf. Pratt 1991; Canagarajah 2015). Pratt's oft-cited definition of contact zones refers to

> social spaces where cultures meet, clash, and grapple with each other, often in contexts of highly asymmetrical relations of power, such as colonialism, slavery, or their aftermaths as they are lived out in many parts of the world today.
>
> (1991, 34)

Pedagogy for English literacy is equally contested, historically indexed by references to 'the literacy wars' (Prinsloo and Baynham 2013) between advocates of meaning-focused versus decoding and synthetic phonics-focused approaches to early literacy, as well as by debates between advocates of creative expression versus proponents of explicit, norm-oriented pedagogies such as genre. Current imperatives towards decoloniality ask us to question what literacy in English might mean when perceived and theorised from the position of the subaltern (Mignolo 2007).

In many parts of the world, being literate in English is synonymous with being literate and with being educated. Alongside this, what counts as literacy in English, and what kinds of English are recognised is a key concern. While what counts as high status English and high status literacy practices will change in different contexts, domains and spaces, high status language and literacy resources are always unequally distributed. Thus this chapter will explore how the semiotic resources associated with literacies in English are stratified and unequally distributed, though not always in predictable ways. At the same time, such privileged or powerful English literacy practices are themselves being contested, and shifting in high status domains such as published academic writing (Alim and Smitherman 2012). The chapter will show how, given the position of English/es globally, the study of literacy/ies in English and English literacy pedagogies provides a window onto the increasingly heteroglossic/multilingual and multimodal, as well as highly political nature of what constitutes literacy and literacy pedagogy more broadly.

Historical perspectives: from literacy in English to literacies in Englishes

What is literacy?

Since the early 1980s, understandings of literacy have changed substantially. Early approaches emphasised universal, and individual, cognitive effects as a result of becoming literate, pitting literate cultures against oral cultures and literacy against orality. This became associated with 'Great Divide' theories of societies which suggested that modes of thinking in literate and non-literate societies were fundamentally different (e.g. Goody, 1969, Ong, 1982 both cited in Prinsloo and Baynham 2013). However, a number of scholars contested the idea that becoming literate itself led to particular kinds of cognitive development, or social development, with Graff labelling this position as 'the literacy myth' (Graff 1979; Scribner and Cole 1981; Street 1984). For example, Scribner and Cole's (1981) research in Liberia identified different kinds of literacy that people were engaged in, including school literacy in English, religious literacy in Arabic, and literacy using an indigenous local language for record-keeping and letter writing. They were able to separate effects of schooling from effects that had been earlier attributed to literacy and, as Prinsloo and Baynham (2013) point out, argued 'that literacy is not a general technology that is the same thing with the same consequences regardless of what the contexts of its acquisition might be.' Rather, 'literacy was always constituted within socially organised practices'. (xxvii).

In line with Scribner and Cole's findings, Heath's (1983) ethnographic study of the language and literacy socialisation practices of three communities in the Piedmont Carolinas in the USA foregrounded the ways in which different communities socialised children into literacy in distinct ways. Heath demonstrated how these different 'ways with words' had negative consequences for children of non-dominant groups whose literacy practices most differed from the middle-class practices privileged in schooling. A further influential study unsettling Great Divide approaches as well as assumptions regarding the universal consequences of literacy as a singular, context-independent technology was Street's (1984) research in Iran. In particular, Street's research challenged the idea of an automatic causal relationship between literacy and social development, and argued that literacy practices needed to be studied ethnographically, as embedded in their social contexts, in order for us to understand how literacy is differentially constituted through different practices and social activities.

Taking a pedagogical perspective on literacies, Freebody and Luke (1990) outlined four central components of successful literacy (particularly with regard to reading) as demanded by Australian society in 1990. In what has become known as the four resources model, Freebody and Luke argued for four roles that successful reading required: 'code-breaker' (able to successfully decode letter-sound relationships); 'text-participant' (able to make sense of or comprehend the text); 'text-user' (knowing how to use and work with a text appropriately, e.g. reading a graphic representation to extract factual information versus reading a literary text in order to produce a character analysis); and 'text-analyst' (critical reading of a text in order to determine the choices that have been made in ideologies, positioning and representation). Freebody and Luke argued that the integration of all four of these roles was necessary for reading in formal education at any level, whether in early literacy or in higher/college education. In recent years the study of literacy has also drawn attention to changing modalities showing that literacy rarely involves exclusively script-based and print-based engagement with texts. Rather, literacy in English is increasingly multimodal (see Ravelli, this volume), an aspect of digital literacy practices (Spilioti, this volume) and multilingual practices (Garcia and Lin, this volume). The work of the New London Group (2000) introduced the idea of 'multiliteracies' arguing that an exclusive focus on verbal texts in literacy pedagogy was out of step with the increasingly visual semiotic landscape and the shift to multimodal representation in textbooks and media in daily life.

Given that literacies in English are most often accomplished through formal education, the predominant focus in this chapter will be on literacies in English in educational contexts, and pedagogies for literacies in English. The approach to literacy in this chapter is that alongside the development of particular print-based skills which will differ depending on specific literacy practices, literacy can be 'conceived as participation in a range of valued meaning-making practices (. . .) themselves nested within particular activity structures' (Hull and Moje 2012: 1). It is important to note that both print-based skills and practices will differ, depending on the kind and purpose of literacy activity; consider the different skills and practices involved in reading a graph to infer weather patterns, reading a poem to conduct literary analysis, writing a poem as a birthday gift, decoding Arabic script to recite the Quran, or writing in a local language to produce a record of a meeting. While literacy in English is more likely to be an outcome of formal schooling and education, the understanding of literacy as a context-embedded, social practice emphasises that there is no such single thing as 'literacy in English' or any other language.

Within the field of (New) Literacy Studies (Prinsloo and Baynham 2013), Academic Literacies (Lillis and Scott 2007; Thesen and van Pletzen 2006) has developed with the specific goal of understanding the ways in which writing (in English) mediates participation in the academy, and to make visible obstacles to participation for both students and academics as writers (Lillis et al. 2016). For some researchers and teachers within the field of Academic Literacies, understanding literacies *in English* is central to understanding how students and academics are both constrained and enabled to participate in knowledge making in the academy. See, for example, Thesen (1997) on the positioning of first-generation university students in post-apartheid South Africa in relation to their English literacy resources, and Lillis and Curry (2010) on how the specific ideologies of English filter processes of production and evaluation in writing for publication.

English and Englishes

Like literacy, the named language 'English' is also often (mis)treated as a stable and unified phenomenon, in applied linguistics generally and specifically in language and literacy pedagogy, standardised assessment and academic publishing. Lillis and Curry challenge this notion of 'English' 'as a single stable semiotic resource over which the "native" speaker is attributed a privileged evaluative position' (Lillis and Curry 2015: p127) and Pennycook (1994, 2006) has argued that the notion of 'English' is a fiction. The World Englishes paradigm (Bolton, this volume) and Kachru's well known three circles model of Englishes[1] has for some time emphasised the idea of multiple Englishes. But it has also been critiqued more recently for failing to take into account the unequal power relations entangled with World Englishes, as well as the significant variation that occurs *within* national borders. John Trimbur argues that

> English does not branch off into the indigenized national varieties found in Kachru's system of World Englishes (1990) so much as it shatters, fragmenting into local enactments of English, off the grid, in the unequal spaces of the splintered metropolis.
> (2013, 468)

While such 'local enactments of English' may count as literacy in English in their local or micro-context, what Blommaert (2010) has called a lower scale level, these resources are often not recognised as such outside of their micro-contexts, in Blommaert's terms at a higher scale level.

Within historically English-dominant national contexts such as the UK and USA, there are also debates about literacy in English and its relationship to standard English, sometimes called standard written English (Snell and Andrews 2016) or, in the USA, Mainstream United States English (MUSE, Lippi-Green 1997). In the UK, Snell and Andrews draw attention to the ways in which regional accents and dialects of children are perceived by some to negatively affect their ability to produce standard written English, i.e. high status literacy in English. They show how regional accents and dialect variation in English are problematised in the schooling system, despite the fact that most UK children will arrive at school with what is considered a 'regional accent'. The National Curriculum explicitly states that children are expected to learn to speak 'standard English'. Snell and Andrews show that there is 'no straightforward relationship between children's language background and their achievement in school literacy' (2016, 308), and that specific difficulties cannot commonly be attributed to regional accents or dialects. This is despite the common assumption that regional varieties of English will compromise children's ability to write standard English.

Showing the complexity of attempting to characterise a standard spoken English, Snell and Andrews argue that the notion of 'standard' should be confined to standard written English. Like UK students characterised as having regional dialects and accents and therefore problems with literacy, in the USA bilingual Spanish/English Latinos and speakers of African American English are frequently also positioned in deficit ways (Alim 2010; Dyson and Smitherman 2009) . While systematic linguistic variation and the principle of linguistic equality are well-established tenets of linguistics, standardised assessments of literacy in English impose a monolingual mainstream standard (e.g. MUSE) that has profoundly negative consequences for bilinguals and users of so-called 'non-standard' varieties of English (Garcia and Menken 2006; Dyson and Smitherman 2009; Wiley and Lukes 1996). In South Africa, racialised uses of English are differently valued (McKinney 2013), with a UK-derived exogenous variety of English that travelled to the South with British settlers most highly valued (Makalela 2004).

Critical issues

At least two issues have historically been, and are currently, of critical concern in the research and teaching of literacies in English. First is what I will call the 'politics of literacy in English' and the language ideologies that accompany this. I will explore this in relation to the role of English literacy in education in post-colonial contexts as well as in global practices of writing for publication. Second, and related to the former, is the positioning of English as a colonial language and carrier of master narratives as well as the literary canon. This positioning of 'English literacy' as conduit of high culture is often imposed on English home language speakers and speakers of 'other(ed)' languages alike. In contrast to this is the positioning of English literacy as a space for political conscientisation, and the development of critical language awareness or critical literacy (Janks 2010; López-Gopar 2016; McKinney 2004; Norton Peirce 1989). This latter positioning I will take further in a discussion of debates on pedagogies for English literacy later in the chapter.

The imposition of literacy in English

Prevalent in many parts of the world, and growing, is the disturbing fact that literacy itself, and being positioned as literate, is exclusively linked to literacy in English. In other words literacy in English is seen as equivalent to being literate, or even to being educated (McKinney 2017; Ngũgĩ wa Thiong'o 1986). A well-rehearsed debate in post-colonial English studies is that between the Nigerian novelist Chinua Achebe and Kenyan author Ngũgĩ wa Thiong'o. Whereas Ngũgĩ argued that African experience could only be rendered through African languages and committed himself to writing in Gikuyu, Achebe argued for the appropriation and adaptation of English by African writers:

> I feel that the English language will be able to carry the weight of my African experience. But it will have to be a new English, still in full communion with its ancestral home but altered to suit its new African surroundings.
>
> (Achebe 1965: 30)

Ngũgĩ's autobiographical narrative of the imposition of English medium schooling in Kenya by the colonial regime and his punishment for deviating from speaking English at school is notorious:

> one of the most humiliating experiences was to be caught speaking Gikuyu in the vicinity of the school. The culprit was given corporal punishment – three to five strokes of the cane on bare buttocks – or was made to carry a metal plate around the neck with inscriptions such as I AM STUPID or I AM A DONKEY. Sometimes the culprits were fined money they could hardly afford.
>
> (...)
>
> The attitude to English was the opposite; any achievement in spoken or written English was highly rewarded; prizes, prestige, applause, the ticket to higher realms. English became the measure of intelligence and ability in the arts, the sciences and all the other branches of learning. English became the main determinant of a child's progress up the ladder of formal education.
>
> (Ngũgĩ wa Thiong'o 1986: 11–12)

Ngũgĩ's disturbing account illustrates the language ideologies exclusively valuing 'spoken or written English' in schooling practice, and the power of such ideologies in determining the kinds of literacy practices that count in schooling. Elsewhere I have described such ideologies with the term *Anglonormativity*, referring to the expectation that people will be and should be proficient in English, and are deficient, even deviant, if they are not. Anglonormativity supports the compulsory or expected command of English, valuing literacy in standard written English alone (McKinney 2017). More recently we find new generation Nigerian author Chimamanda Adichie explaining how Anglonormative ideologies that exclusively valued literacy in English during Ngũgĩ's colonial schooling continue to flourish. In response to an interview question regarding why she has chosen to write in English, Adichie explains:

> I'm not sure my writing in English is a choice. If a Nigerian Igbo like myself is educated exclusively in English, discouraged from speaking Igbo in a school in which Igbo was just one more subject of study (and one that was considered 'uncool' by students and did not receive much support from the administration), then perhaps writing in English is not a choice, because the idea of choice assumes equal alternatives.
>
> (in Azodo interview 2008: 2)

For many people in the world, literacy in English is not a choice but is imposed though formal schooling, and becomes equivalent to being educated. Driven by the power of literacy in English, pedagogy and reading materials for local languages are often not made available, and not valued. In Anglophone post-colonial contexts, literacy in high status forms of standard written English provides students from elite communities with opportunities for mobility, e.g. further study in the 'centre' and writing for publication for international English reading audiences. On the darker side, however, many researchers have shown how for non-elite children in post-colonial contexts, the imposition of literacy in English results in their exclusion from meaningful participation in schooling (Heugh and Skutnabb-Kangas 2012; McKinney 2017). Williams (1996) has referred to 'reading-like' behaviour where school children in Malawi chant (rather than read) English texts written on the chalkboard.

Appropriation of English

However, the history of the global spread and use of literacy in English is highly complex and often contradictory, such that the imposition of literacy in English and its exclusionary effects is only part of the story. Alongside discourses of the imposition of English and linguistic imperialism (Phillipson 1992) are accounts of the appropriation of literacy in English for local, and sometimes liberatory, purposes. As mentioned earlier, Achebe argued for the appropriation of English, and the shaping of the resources of written English in ways that would carry his 'African experience' (1965). During the anti-apartheid struggle in 1980s South Africa, Norton Peirce (1989) drew attention to the 'People's English' movement where the teaching of English in a way that 'expose[d] (. . .) inequalities and (. . .) help[ed] students explore alternative possibilities for themselves and their societies' was advocated (Norton Peirce 1989, 407). 'People's English' offered a counterdiscourse to English as a colonial language. Here we see how literacy in English can be severed from the cultural baggage to which it had historically been tied. As Norton Pierce argued in relation to People's English in South Africa, 'English like all other languages, is thus a site of struggle over meaning, access and power' (1989, 405). The extent to which literacy in English can be appropriated for liberatory and empowering purposes, for widening participation in quality schooling and higher education, rather than for domestication or gate-keeping purposes both in post-colonial and English dominant countries is centrally tied to pedagogy and curricula for literacy in English. Such pedagogies have historically been, and continue to be, a site of contestation.

Current debates

I foreground three current areas of debate in relation to literacy in English. Firstly, what kinds of English literacy resources are made accessible, or are distributed through schooling systems in different parts of the world? This is captured by what some authors have referred to as the semiotics of mobility, i.e whose English literacy resources can 'travel', and 'count' in different local and global contexts (Blommaert 2008, 2010; Canagarajah 2015). Secondly, I consider the ways in which what counts as literacy in English has become prescribed by national and international standardised assessments, such as the Progress in Reading Literacy Study (PIRLS[2]). Finally, I outline some of the debates regarding pedagogies for literacy in English, showing how this pedagogical space has been used for conflicting purposes: as a site of assimilation into a unitary, homogenous use of language, access to dominant genres and the traditional literary canon versus a site for transformative pedagogies and political conscientisation.

The (im)mobility of English literacy resources

Semiotic mobility, or the relative mobility of literacy resources in English developed in peripheral contexts has recently been the focus of debate. Using a poorly resourced school on the South African Cape Flats as an example, Blommaert (2010) has argued that while the majority of students in peripheral contexts aspire to master English literacy to improve their economic mobility, the English resources that are available to and acquired by such students are organised by norms generated in the periphery that have limited mobility. That is, while these norms are valued at the relatively low scale level of the local school, or local community, they do not count as 'proper English' outside of this local context, i.e. at a higher scale level. Linking it to work on 'grassroots literacy' in Central Africa, Blommaert labels this kind of 'sub-elite literacy' in English that has limited mobility as 'peripheral normativity'. He defines this as the 'systemic, normal and hence normative' use of 'orthographic, syntactic, lexical and pragmatic peculiarities'; from a standard language perspective, what would be considered as 'errors' (Blommaert et al. 2005, 378; Blommaert 2008).

Prinsloo and Stroud (2014) and Canagarajah (2015) take issue with the use of Blommaert's scales theory, that is, the notion of lower and higher scale levels operating across local and global sites, to describe the lack of mobility of students' English literacy repertoires beyond their local site. They argue that Blommaert's analysis bypasses the particular meanings of learners' English literacy practices within their local contexts, and neglects to pay attention to the potential ability of learners to deploy different (and differently valued) resources and practices at different times. Canagarajah argues that rather than be 'locked' into one scale level, 'people could be shuttling between different scale levels in the same location' (2015, 36). However, what seems to be left out of this debate is the way in which students' English literacy practices are enabled or curtailed as a consequence of extremely restricted literacy pedagogies in most South African schools. Such students have limited opportunities to read and write English texts in classrooms where discourses and practices are primarily oral (Dornbrack and Dixon 2014; Kapp 2004). These students are also subjected to a very early transition to English as a medium of instruction in their fourth year of schooling, and have thus had extremely limited opportunities to develop literacy resources in English before having to use it as their sole linguistic tool for learning. It is often restricted pedagogies and harmful language policy decisions that result in the kind of 'sub-elite literacy' or peripheral normativity that Blommaert (2010) describes.

Outside educational contexts, Trimbur (2013) draws our attention to some of the consequences of grassroots literacy using the resources of English in the political activism of the Asbestos

Interest Group (AIG) in the Northern Cape of South Africa. The AIG is a non-governmental organisation that was established to access compensation for victims of asbestos-related disease. Analysing both the 'local economy in which they were produced' and their 'translocal' uptake (Blommaert 2008), Trimbur shows how the AIG's 'grassroots literacy negotiates the paperwork of officialdom' (2013, 463). In one example he examines how minutes of a meeting recorded in English were not taken seriously on account of their deviations from conventionally accepted norms of standard written English. This example draws attention to the significant consequences of literacies in Englishes as unequally valued (and distributed) sets of semiotic resources.

Standardised assessment and literacy in English

Scholars in the UK (Jewitt et al. 2005; Maybin 2013) and the USA (Garcia and Menken 2006; Menken 2008) have drawn attention to the powerful effects of standardised assessments (national and international) on what counts as literacy in English in educational settings, as well as on pedagogies for English literacy. In the analysis of a primary English class in England, Maybin (2013) argues that standardised assessments such as the international PIRLS and the National Key Stage 2 SATs (Statutory Assessment Tests) have a narrowing effect on the teaching of literacy in English. In the literacy classrooms she observed, affective engagement, debate and pleasure were stripped away with literacy defined as a narrow set of skills that can be reliably assessed. Assessments then impose a restricted set of literacy practices onto teachers, learners and pedagogy. Similarly, in high school English classrooms, Jewitt et al. (2005) observed teachers' relentless focus on teaching students to tie their interpretations of literary texts to evidence from the text, which was driven by the requirements of the GCSE (General Certificate of Secondary Education) examination. In parallel with Maybin's research, affect and 'text to life connections' were ignored in this singular goal to achieve well on the GCSE.

In the USA, researchers have drawn attention to the negative consequences of standardised testing of literacy and language for students speaking non-mainstream varieties of English such as African American English (Dyson and Smitherman 2009) and Latino students who are Spanish dominant or speakers of Chicano English (Garcia and Menken 2006; Menken 2008). As Garcia and Menken point out, most Latinos in the United States are English speakers but not users of 'standard English' or MUSE. They are better described as 'moving along a *bilingual and bidialectal continuum*, using linguistic resources from the other language [English or Spanish] or from other English varieties or Spanish varieties when needed and possible' (2006, 172). Menken gives an example of the exclusionary effects of standardised testing for Latinos with the English Regents examination required for graduation from New York City High Schools. The 2002 cohort had only a 41.1% graduation rate for Latino students with an accompanying 26% drop-out rate. The emphasis on the production of standard written English in the heavily weighted essay requirement of this examination is a particular challenge for Latino students. The systemic exclusion of Latino/a children from US education is clearly evident in national throughput rates: 'for every 100 Latina/o children who enter school, a mere 53% will actually graduate from high school and only 11% will graduate from college' (Huber et al. 2006 in Pacheco 2010, 76). Literacy in English as defined and imposed by standardised assessments has powerful exclusionary effects.

Pedagogies for literacies in English

Different conceptions of literacy, and different conceptions of English, inevitably lead to different pedagogical approaches. The pedagogical space for the development of literacy in general, and of literacy in English in particular, is a contested one. This is the case whether the context is one of early literacy (cf. the reading or literacy wars, Gooch and Lambirth 2007), high school English, academic literacies in higher education, and whether the students are monolingual English speakers, or bilinguals and emergent bilinguals (also called English language learners). Much of the contestation is captured in the opposition between pedagogies which focus on discrete skills (such as phonics and decoding in early literacy) and dominant textual conventions versus pedagogies which privilege meaning-making and work with 'authentic texts' (such as whole language approaches to early literacy). At the upper primary and secondary school levels, genre approaches have been pitted against those that privilege creative expression and/or the production of transformative texts (Cope and Kalantzis 1993). There is also tension between the goals of literacy in English as assimilationist, where the aim is for students to conform to a single standardised written English and to the rules of 'powerful genres', as against the idea of using the pedagogical space to enable students to resist norms and to produce transformative or transgressive texts. The latter tension is echoed in higher education where traditional English for Academic Purposes as well as Systemic Functional Linguistics-inspired Genre approaches aim to induct students into disciplinary registers and genres, while academic literacies approaches aim to engage critically with dominant registers, genres and monoglot notions of a single standard English (see Coffin and Donohue 2012 for an overview).

Synthesis models of literacy pedagogy, such as Janks' (2010) critical literacy model and the New London Group's (2000) multiliteracies framework, explicitly aim at bringing together the seemingly incompatible goals of access to powerful forms of language and literacy, and the recognition of diverse language and literacy resources. In her four-dimensional critical literacy model, Janks (2010) highlights access, diversity, domination and design. She argues for a literacy pedagogy that

- gives students access to powerful uses of language and literate genres (access)
- recognises marginalised resources and works to expand what counts as powerful language and literacy use (diversity)
- develops students' critical ability to interrogate relations of power (domination)
- enables students to design new texts and transform language and literacy resources (design).

The multiliteracies framework operates with a similar logic, advocating situated practice, overt instruction, critical framing and transformed designs (New London Group 2000). It should be recognised that critical approaches to literacy in English remain on the margins of officially sanctioned curricula and materials. Currently, as discussed above, standardised testing works against the goals of critical literacy approaches and critical literacies have been subject to government restrictions. This was the case with the Language in the National Curriculum (LINC) project for English teacher education led by Ronald Carter in 1989–1992 in England and Wales. The LINC project was a UK government-funded response to shortcomings identified in two earlier reports on the state of English teaching in England and Wales (the Cox and Kingman reports). The LINC project was reviewed in 1991 by the Conservative government of that time, leading to the withdrawal of formal government support. Significantly, a decision not to publish the materials that had been generated and positively received by teachers was taken (Carter 1996).

Finally, within debates on pedagogy for literacy in English, there are also differing perspectives on the affordances of digital literacies in English and the consequences of digital resources for the teaching of English. A number of studies emphasise the creative potential of tapping into young people's digital literacy practices, such as blogging, texting, fanfiction writing and general use of social media (Mills 2010).

Mills (2010) highlights the finding that studies in North America, the UK and Australia 'consistently show that broadening literacy curricula to include multimodal and digital forms of representation results in significant English language learning gains for multilingual students' (261). In Uganda, Kendrick et al's research shows how the use of digital and multimodal literacies in an after-school English journalism club built learners' confidence as well as their literacy in English (Kendrick et al. 2013). However there are also studies in the global South (e.g. Prinsloo and Sasman 2015) showing that when multimedia are brought into the pedagogical space of English literacy, traditional, restricted pedagogies that were previously used can be merely transferred to the screen. Classrooms can also become silent theatres where students consume images without engaging interactively or critically with these. In line with an understanding of literacy as context-embedded social practice, digital literacies are recognised as having a range of affordances which can be taken hold of in many different ways with a range of different effects, depending on their context and specific use.

Future directions

Despite synthesis models of literacy pedagogy (such as multiliteracies) that aim to provide access to dominant literacy practices and textual genres, as well as to challenge and expand this repertoire, we have not taken seriously enough the need to critique what *counts* as powerful literacies in English. In other words, whose English language and literacy resources are dominant and whose language and literacy practices are effectively denied the status of resource, has not been sufficiently interrogated. Some scholars are drawing attention to the racialised implications of what are considered powerful literacies (e.g. in the USA, Dyson and Smitherman 2009; Flores and Rosa 2015, and in South Africa, McKinney 2017). Increasingly, scholars are concerned with the limitations for global citizenship of people who are monolingual in one variety of English (Garcia and Sylvan 2011). As Garcia and Sylvan put it, 'monolingual education is no longer relevant in our globalised world' (2011, 398). Alim and Smitherman provide a convincing analysis of how Barack Obama's ability to style-shift across Dominant American English and African American English, as well as his strategic use of Spanish at certain moments, gave him the competitive edge in his 2008 election campaign (Alim and Smitherman 2012). Attention has also been drawn to the range of varieties and increasing multilingualism of literacies in English in digital spaces (Deumert 2014; Lankshear and Knobel 2014; Black 2008).

There are at least two responses emerging from the recognition that literacy in English cannot be understood and/or taught as literacy in a single mainstream variety. Firstly, there are teacher-researchers who are using the English literacy pedagogical space for a particular kind of critical literacy work that enables students to become critically aware of language ideologies and of how they and their language and literacy resources are positioned by these. Such pedagogies encourage learners to use literacies in different registers, styles and varieties of English to challenge and resist deficit positioning. Alim's (2010) work with high school students in the San Francisco Bay area of California conducting their own ethnographic research into African American language in their communities is an excellent example of this. Alim draws attention to the dominant language ideologies in the school, which positioned Black Language as deficient, inappropriate and abnormal. Drawing on critical language awareness (CLA), Alim designed a series of projects to disrupt this deficit positioning of African American students' linguistic resources. CLA enables teachers to show students 'that it is the language and communicative norms of those in power' that are privileged (Alim 2010, 209). Alongside CLA, Alim capitalised on the students' interest in hip hop culture, music and language.

In the first student project introduced, Alim aims to develop the students' awareness of sociolinguistic variation as well as their research skills. He also raises the status of Black Language and hip hop language by making these legitimate objects of study in the language arts classroom. In the second project, 'Language in my life', students are introduced to Hymes' ethnography of speaking framework, and to the accompanying sociolinguistics concepts of speech situation (e.g. a music concert), speech event (e.g. an interview backstage at the concert) and speech act (e.g. a joke told during an interview). An audio-recorded interview with a hip hop artist is used to guide students through an ethnography of speaking analysis (see Alim and Smitherman 2012, 181, Table 6.1). Students are then tasked with researching their own language use, using an ethnography of communication approach and creating journal entries which account for specific events in their daily lives. Through this project, students develop metalinguistic awareness of their own language use, and of themselves as 'style-shifters'; the activity also validates students' out of class and out of school language practices. Students continue to apply and extend their newly developing sociolinguistic research skills in the third project, in which they focus on language use in their peer group and peer culture, beginning with a focus on 'lexical innovations within hip hop culture' (Alim 2010, 218).

With its explicit focus on the relationships between language and power and the working of ideology through language practices, CLA (Fairclough 1992) is an ideal approach for transgressive literacy education. Alim's use of hip hop culture enables him to reposition Black Language as a significant resource in the classroom while at the same time engaging his students in challenging research activities and academic discourse. His own translanguaging across academic language, MUSE and Black language models powerful examples of languaging for students. Following in the footsteps of Smitherman, Alim continuously pushes the boundaries of academic language in his own published writing, regularly drawing on resources of Black Language and moving seamlessly between Black Language and MUSE as the following paragraph from his article in *Educational Researcher* shows:

> While the media and public discourse attacked Black Language (BL) and Black people for so-called 'deficiencies', a generation of young Hip Hop Headz (including me) spent hours crafting linguistic skillz and pushin the boundaries of the English language in rhyme ciphers, battles and freestyles. Wasn't no way in the world you could get me to see Black Language as deficient!
>
> (Alim 2005, 24)

Alim's translanguaging flies in the face of critics who argue that students need to be socialised into the exclusive use of 'standard written English' or MUSE, as these are the only resources with power and the only ones that are accepted in high stakes writing. His own literacy pedagogy and literacy practices are thus transgressive, designed to produce students as creative and powerful languagers, adept style-shifters with the potential not just to play the game but to change it (Alim and Smitherman 2012, 193).

Secondly, research on literacies in English in educational contexts, whether at school level (e.g Newfield and Maungedzo's (2006) work with high school students in Soweto South Africa; Manyak's (2008) work on young Spanish/English bilingual learners in the USA) or in higher education (Canagarajah 2013), shows that pedagogies are becoming increasingly multilingual. López-Gopar's (2016) work on decolonising Primary English Language

Teaching (PELT) with indigenous and mestizo children in Oaxaca, Mexico is an inspirational example of this. López-Gopar describes a project which uses PELT to intervene in a situation where indigenous children are struggling and discriminated against in the schooling system, and have become ashamed of their indigenous languages and cultures. Working together with a group of student teachers, López-Gopar describes English classes where the lives and socio-cultural context of children drive the curriculum and where children are involved in the co-creation of multilingual identity texts. Enabling children to work with indigenous languages, Spanish and English simultaneously has made the PELT space a liberating one which challenges monolingualism and monolingual literacies in English particularly. Multilingual and heteroglossic approaches are also a recent focus in English composition studies in the USA with scholars calling for a 'translingual' approach (e.g Horner et al. 2011; Canagarajah 2013). Conceiving of literacy as translingual means recognising that heterogeneity is the norm rather than the exception, and designing pedagogies that 'foreground strategies of production and reception of texts' rather than 'codes and norms' (Canagarajah 2013, 4).

Conclusion

I have argued in this chapter that a narrow and homogenous understanding of both what counts as 'literacy' and what counts as 'English' is a highly contested product of coloniality that has had negative consequences in many parts of the world. This is especially the case for education in post-colonial contexts where being educated has become synonymous with being literate in a narrow repertoire of standard written English. However, examples such as the liberatory appropriation of English in 'People's English', the decolonising of English language and literacy teaching with indigenous children in Mexico and CLA with varieties of English as well as translingual composition in the USA provide wonderful contrasts to the imposition of literacy in English as a narrowly defined 'representational repertoire of the invaders' (Pratt 1991, 36). These examples draw attention to the unique responsibilities and opportunities of teachers of literacies in Englishes in a wide range of contexts and levels to challenge asymmetrical relations of power by giving students access to what counts in a particular context as powerful use of literacy in English, as well as to critique and expand restricted notions of literacy in English.

Notes

1 The inner circle of 'Native English' speaking countries that are norm providing; the outer circle of countries with English as an official language and additional language speakers developing new norms for English; and the expanding circle of norm-dependent speakers in countries where English was characterized as a 'foreign language' (Kachru 1990). Dynamics of globalisation and interaction over the internet has complicated this model substantially.

2 For more information on the international literacy assessment PIRLS, please see http://timss.bc.edu/

Further reading

Canagarajah, A. S. (ed.) (2013) *Literacy as Translingual Practice: Between Communities and Classrooms*. London and New York: Routledge. This edited collection conceptualises writing in higher education through a multi- or translingual lens challenging monolingualist approaches to writing pedagogy.

Janks, H. (2010) *Literacy and Power*. New York and London: Routledge. Janks explores the relationships between literacy and power in educational settings and draws attention to the opportunities for developing CLA or critical literacy in pedagogies for English literacy.

Dyson, A. H and G. Smitherman (2009) 'The right (write) start: African American language and the discourse of sounding right', *Teachers College Record* 111 (4): 973–998. Dyson and Smitherman present research on the relationship between African American children's language resources and their writing in English highlighting the myths about African American language that negatively shape writing pedagogy for these children.

Newfield, D. and R. Maungedzo (2006) 'Mobilising and modalising poetry in a Soweto classroom', *English Studies in Africa* 49 (1): 71–93. This paper provides insights into an innovative multilingual and multimodal pedagogical approach to literacy in English with marginalised youth.

Related topics

- The idea of English
- English and multilingualism: a contested history
- The relevance of English language studies in higher education
- Teaching English as an additional language in Anglophone and Brazilian contexts: different curriculum approaches
- Sociolinguistics: studying English and its social relations.

References

Achebe, C. (1965) 'English and the African writer', *Transition* 18: 27–30.

Alim, H. S. (2005) 'Critical language awareness in the United States: Revisiting issues and revising pedagogoies in a resegregated society', *Educational Researcher* 34(7): 24–31.

Alim, H. S. (2010) 'Critical language awareness', in N. H. Hornberger and S. L. McKay (eds), *Sociolinguistics and Language Education*. Bristol: Multilingual Matters, 205–231.

Alim, H. S. and G. Smitherman (2012) *Articulate while Black: Barack Obama, Language and Race in the U.S.* Oxford: Oxford University Press.

Azodo, A. U. (2008) Interview with Chimamanda Ngozi Adichie: Creative Writing and Literary Activism, 1–5. Available at www.iun.edu/~minaua/interviews/interview_chimamanda_ngozi_adichie.pdf, accessed March 2016.

Black, R. (2008) *Adolescents and Online Fiction*. New York: Peter Lang.

Blommaert, J. (2008) *Grassroots Literacy, Writing and Identity: Voice in Central Africa*. London and New York: Routledge.

Blommaert, J. (2010) *The Sociolinguistics of Globalisation*. Cambridge: Cambridge University Press.

Blommaert, J., N. Muylaert, M. Huysmans and C. Dyers (2005) 'Peripheral normativity: Literacy and the production of locality in a South African Township school', *Linguistics and Education* 16 (4): 378–403.

Canagarajah, A. S. (ed.) (2013) *Translingual Practice: Global Englishes and Cosmopolitan Relations*. London and New York: Routledge.

Canagarajah, A. S. (2015) 'Negotiating mobile codes and literacies at the contact zone: Another perspective on South African Township schools', in C. Stroud and M. Prinsloo (eds), *Language, Literacy and Diversity: Moving Words*. London and New York: Routledge, 34–54.

Carter, R. (1996) 'Politics and knowledge about language: The LINC Project', in R. Hasan and G. Williams (eds), *Literacy and Society*. London: Longman, 1–21.

Coffin, C. and J. Donohue (2012) 'Academic literacies and systemic functional linguistics how do they relate?' *Journal of English for Academic Purposes* 11: 64–75.

Cope, B. and M. Kalantzis (1993) *The Powers of Literacy: A Genre Approach to Teaching Writing*. London: Falmer Press.

Deumert, A. (2014) *Sociolinguistics and Mobile Communication*. Edinburgh: Edinburgh University Press.

Dornbrack, J. and K. Dixon (2014) 'Towards a more explicit writing pedagogy: The complexity of teaching argumentative writing', *Reading and Writing* 5(1):1–8. DOI 10.4102/rw.v5i1.40.

Dyson, A. H and G. Smitherman (2009) 'The right (write) start: African American language and the discourse of sounding right', *Teachers College Record* 111 (4): 973–998.

Fairclough, N. (ed.) (1992) *Critical Language Awareness*. London: Longman.

Flores, N. and J. Rosa (2015) 'Undoing appropriateness: Raciolinguistic ideologies and language diversity in education', *Harvard Education Review* 85 (2): 149–171.

Freebody, P. and A. Luke (1990) 'Literacies programs: Debates and demands in cultural context', *Prospect: An Australian Journal of TESOL* 5 (3): 7–16.
Garcia, O. and K. Menken (2006) 'The English of Latinos from a plurilingual transcultural angle: Implications for assessment and schools', in S. Nero (ed.), *Dialects, Englishes, Creoles, and Education*. Mahwah, NJ: Lawrence Erlbaum Associates, 167–184.
Garcia, P. and C. Sylvan (2011) 'Pedagogies and practices in multilingual classrooms: Singularities in pluralities', *Modern Language Journal* 95 (3): 385–400.
Gooch, K. and A. Lambirth (2007) *Understanding Phonics and the Teaching of Reading*. Maidenhead: Open University Press.
Graff, H. (1979) *The Literacy Myth: Literacy and Social Structure in the Nineteenth Century City*. New York: Academic Press.
Heath, S. B. (1983) *Ways with Words*. Cambridge: Cambridge University Press.
Heugh, K. and T. Skutnabb-Kangas (2012) *Multilingual Education and Sustainable Diversity Work: From Periphery to Centre*. New York: Routledge.
Horner, B., M. Z. Lu, J. J. Royster and J. Trimbur (2011) 'Language difference in writing: Towards a translingual approach', *College English* 73 (3): 303–320.
Hull, G. A. and E. B. Moje (2012) 'What is the development of literacy the development of? *[Stanford Understanding Language: Language, Literacy and learning in the content areas]*' Available at www.ell.stanford.edu/sites/default/files/pdf/academic-papers/05-Hull%20%26%20Moje%20CC%20Paper%20FINAL.pdf.
Janks, H. (2010) *Literacy and Power*. New York and London: Routledge.
Jewitt, C., K. Jones and G. Kress (2005) 'English in classrooms: Only write down what you need to know: annotation for what?' *English in Education* 39 (1): 5–18.
Kachru, B. (1990) 'World Englishes and applied linguistics', *World Englishes* 9 (1): 3–20.
Kapp, R. (2004) '"Reading on the line": An analysis of literacy practices in ESL classes in a South African Township school', *Language and Education* 18 (3): 246–263.
Kendrick, M., M. Early and W. Chemjor (2013) 'Integrated literacy in a rural Kenyan Girl's Secondary school journalism club', *Research in the Teaching of English* 47 (4): 391–419.
Lankshear, C. and M. Knobel (2014) 'Englishes and digital literacy practices', in C. Leung and B. V. Street (eds), *The Routledge Companion to English Studies*. New York: Routledge, 977–1002.
Lillis, T. and M. J. Curry (2010) *Academic Writing in a Global Context*. London: Routledge.
Lillis, T. and M. J. Curry (2015) 'The politics of English, language and uptake: The case of international academic journal article reviews', *AILA Review* 28: 127–150.
Lillis, T., C. McKinney and L. Thesen (2016) Academic Literacies as a Transformative Project: Re-imagining English, language and knowledge. Colloquium presentation, *Sociolinguistics Symposium, Murcia, Spain.*
Lillis, T. and M. Scott (2007) 'Defining academic literacies research: Issues of epistemology, ideology and strategy', *Journal of Applied Linguistics* 4 (1): 5–23.
Lippi-Green, R. (1997) *English with an Accent: Language, Ideology and Discrimination in the United States*. London: Routledge.
López-Gopar, M. E. (2016) *Decolonising Primary English Language Teaching*. Bristol: Multilingual Matters.
Makalela, L. (2004) 'Making sense of BSAE for linguistic democracy in South Africa', *World Englishes* 23 (3): 355–366.
Manyak, P. (2008) 'What's your news? Portraits of a rich language and literacy activity for English language learners', *The Reading Teacher* 61 (6): 450–458.
Maybin, J. (2013) 'What counts as reading? PIRLS, EastEnders and the man on the flying trapeze', *Literacy* 47 (2): 59–66.
McKinney, C. (2004) '"A little hard piece of grass in your shoe": Understanding student resistance to critical literacy in post-apartheid South Africa', *Southern African Linguistics and Applied Language Studies* 22 (1&2): 63–73.
McKinney, C. (2013) 'Orientations to English in post-apartheid schooling', *English Today* 29 (1): 22–27.
McKinney, C. (2017) *Language and Power in Post-Colonial Schooling: Ideologies in Practice*. New York and London: Routledge.
Menken, K. (2008) *English Learners Left Behind: Standardised Testing as Language Policy*. Clevedon: Multilingual Matters.

Mignolo, W. (2007) 'Introduction', *Cultural Studies* 21 (2–3): 155–167.
Mills, K. A. (2010) 'A review of the 'Digital Turn' in the new literacy studies', *Review of Educational Research* 80 (2): 246–271.
Newfield, D. and R. Maungedzo (2006) 'Mobilising and modalising poetry in a Soweto classroom', *English Studies in Africa* 49 (1): 71–93.
New London Group (2000) 'A pedagogy of multiliteracies: Designing social futures', in B. Cope and M. Kalantzis (eds), *Multiliteracies: Literacy Learning and the Design of Social Futures*. London: Routledge, 9–37.
Ngũgĩ wa Thiong'o (1986) *Decolonising the Mind: The Politics of Language of African Literature*. London: James Currey.
Norton Peirce, B. (1989) 'Toward a pedagogy of possibility in the teaching of English internationally: People's English in South Africa', *TESOL Quarterly* 23 (3): 401–420.
Pacheco, M. (2010) 'Performativity in the bilingual classroom: The plight of English learners in the current reform context', *Anthropology and Education Quarterly* 41 (1): 75–93.
Pennycook, A. (1994) *The Cultural Politics of English as an International Language*. London: Longman.
Pennycook, A. (2006) 'The myth of English as international language', in S. Makoni and A. Pennycook (eds), *Disinventing and Reconstituting Languages*. Bristol: Multlingual Matters, 90–115.
Phillipson, R. (1992) *Linguistic Imperialism*. Oxford: Oxford University Press.
Pratt, M. (1991) 'Arts of the contact zone', *Profession* 33–40.
Prinsloo, M. and M. Baynham (eds) (2013) *Literacy Studies Volume 1: Great Divides and Situated Literacies*. Los Angeles: Sage.
Prinsloo, M. and F. Sasman (2015) 'Literacy and language teaching and learning with interactive whiteboards in early schooling', *TESOL Quarterly* 49 (3): 533–554.
Prinsloo, M. and C. Stroud (2014) 'Introduction', in M. Prinsloo and C. Stroud (eds), *Educating for Language and Literacy Diversity: Mobile Selves*. Basingstoke: Palgrave Macmillan, 1–19.
Scribner, S. and M. Cole (1981) *The Psychology of Literacy*. Cambridge, MA: Harvard University Press.
Snell, J. and R. Andrews (2016) 'To what extent does a regional dialect and accent impact on the development of reading and writing skills?', *Cambridge Journal of Education* 47(3): 297–313. DOI 10.1080/0305764X.2016.1159660.
Street, B. (1984) *Literacy in Theory and in Practice*. Cambridge: Cambridge University Press.
Thesen, L. (1997) 'Voices, discourse and transition: In search of new categories in EAP', *TESOL Quarterly* 31 (3): 487–511.
Thesen, L. and E. van Pletzen (2006) *Academic Literacy and the Languages of Change*. London and New York: Continuum.
Trimbur, J. (2013) 'Grassroots literacy and the written record: Asbestos activism in South Africa', *Journal of Sociolinguistics* 17 (4): 460–487.
Wiley, T. and M. Lukes (1996) 'English-only and standard English ideologies in the U.S', *TESOL Quarterly* 30 (3): 511–535.
Williams, E. (1996) *Bridges and Barriers: Language in African Education and Development*. Manchester and Kinderhook: St Jerome Publishing.

12

Teaching English as an Additional Language in Anglophone and Brazilian contexts

Different curriculum approaches

Paula Tatianne Carréra Szundy and Constant Leung

Introduction

The continuing global spread of English has made English Language an important school curriculum subject in a large number of educational jurisdictions in many parts of the world. Following Stenhouse's (1975) argument that curriculum can be seen as a selective reflection of cultural and political values in society, the focus of this chapter is on the ways in which the conceptualization of English as an Additional Language (EAL), influenced by ideas associated with a socio-historical perspective, is understood and taken up by policymakers and educators in diverse local national and/or regional curriculum environments. Our main aim is to show that while EAL teaching has been broadly influenced by a collection of internationalized ideas associated with the concepts of communicative competence and Communicative Language Teaching, specific historical and policy factors in different social and cultural environments can have a significant impact on the actual curriculum design and practice.

The concept of communicative competence was attributed to Hymes (1972, 1977) who, as an ethnographer, was interested in the ways in which people accomplish actual communication in context, beyond the use of words and other grammatical resources. This concept has been further elaborated by a whole host of applied linguists and language educators in relation to additional/second[1] language teaching (for a more detailed discussion see Leung and Lewkowicz, in press). The seminal work of Canale and Swain in the 1980s made a significant contribution to the consolidation of this development and laid the foundations for subsequent expansions and refinements (Canale 1983, 1984; Canale and Swain 1980a, 1980b). Their rendering of communicative competence for additional/second language education is made up of four components: grammatical competence (vocabulary and grammar rules), socio-linguistic competence (socio-cultural conventions of language use), discourse competence (cohesion across the components of a spoken/written text and content meaning coherence) and strategic competence (making use of all available language and other semiotic resources to achieve communication). These competences, mainly modelled on native speakers, have been consolidated into a teaching approach widely known as Communicative Language Teaching (CLT). In many ways CLT has become the orthodoxy in the language teaching profession in many parts of the world; indeed it has been assumed as the dominant international paradigm, particularly by textbook publishers, English language testing organizations, private sector English language teaching (ELT) providers, and transnational educational agencies. For instance, elements of CLT can be found in the Common European Framework of Reference for Languages (CEFR) (Council of Europe 2001). The CEFR is a language teaching and assessment framework initially developed for education systems within Europe but it has now been widely adopted internationally. The CEFR (Council of Europe 2001: 9) 'views users and learners of a language primarily as "social agents" (. . .) who have tasks (. . .) to accomplish in a given set of circumstances, in a specific environment, and within a particular field of action'. Therefore the goals of language education and language teaching are to provide learners with the opportunity to develop the desired capacity and the knowhow to communicate with others in real world contexts.

The assumptions and principles underlying CLT are necessarily formulated at a very high level of abstraction. We cannot assume that the highly abstract principles are translated in the same way at different times and in different places. In practice, language teaching takes place in schools, universities and other educational contexts that are subject to a variety of cultural, social and political influences. As Stenhouse (1967: 57) argues, 'the curriculum may most profitably be regarded as a selection of culture, it must be seen in relation both to the social life of the classroom, of which it is the medium, and to the background of the culture of our society as a whole'. To understand any particular curriculum development or pedagogic practice, we need to take account of the specific 'local' conditions and histories.

With this perspective in mind, we will look at the conceptualizations and educational values underlying the curriculum provision for the teaching of EAL in two different contexts. These two situated accounts will help make the point that CLT principles can be interpreted and enacted in different ways; the specific character of EAL in any education system is shaped, at least in part, by a confluence of the perceived educational needs of students, prevailing pedagogic approaches, social values and attitudes, and societal priorities. In the next part of this discussion we will provide a brief account of the ways in which EAL has been conceptualized and realized as curriculum provision in school education in England.[2] After that we will focus on English in the Brazilian school curriculum, paying attention to the national policy framework and its translation into a particular state level curriculum, as a context-specific conceptualization of EAL in a Latin American setting. We will conclude with some remarks on the need to construe EAL as a situated curricular artefact, the characteristics of which can only be understood in terms of a confluence of local and trans-local intellectual, socio-cultural sensibilities and practical considerations.

English as an Additional Language in England

EAL is a significant educational issue in England. At the present time over 20% of the primary school population and over 15% of the secondary school population are classified as learners of EAL (Department of Education/Office for National Statistics 2016). These students are from linguistic minority communities and they attend regular state-funded schools. Under the current policy all students with EAL backgrounds are integrated into their age grades, irrespective of their English language proficiency. This policy is known as 'mainstreaming'. In England, the language of schooling is English, so EAL learners are expected to learn the age-appropriate curriculum content and English Language at the same time. To understand the current provision of EAL it is necessary to understand the background developments.

Curriculum provision of EAL first attracted attention in the 1950s when large numbers of workers were recruited to the manufacturing industries and public services from (then) British Commonwealth countries such as Jamaica and India.[3] When the children of these workers arrived at local schools with little English or speaking a different variety of English, the educational response was to make them 'become "invisible", a truly integrated member of the school community . . . as soon as possible' (Derrick 1977: 16). In practice, the newly arrived students were, where resources and staffing allowed, put into specially instituted full-time or part-time English language classes, separate from the mainstream curriculum and school. The pedagogic approach to the teaching of English was underpinned by elements of a language-as-structure view and pragmatic everyday language use. For instance, the Ministry of Education (1963: 18) advised that

> The teacher, through his [or her] own clear and natural speech should act as a constant example of the normal intonation, rhythm and pitch of ordinary conversation, using pictures, objects, actions and improvised dialogues to ensure comprehension and to enlarge vocabulary . . . Most teachers . . . would stress the importance of basing oral work on a carefully graded vocabulary and carefully introduced sentence patterns.

There was no national uniformity in this provision. The length of time spent by students in these English language classes varied between a few weeks and 18 months, depending on the policy and resources of the local (county level) education authorities. This separate provision was seen, for a time, as the most efficacious way to teach English to migrant children; it also served the purpose of reducing the visibility of the presence of ethnically different EAL learners in the mainstream school which triggered outcries of 'lowering standards' in some quarters (see Leung and Franson 2001).

However, the educational merits of this separate English teaching provision, first instituted in the 1950s and 1960s, were beginning to be questioned in the 1970s. Emerging evidence suggested that these English classes did not provide the students with an adequate preparation for integration into mainstream schooling (Department of Education and Science 1971, 1972). At this time changing social attitudes were beginning to be sensitive to issues such as equal opportunities and racial discrimination. The practice of teaching EAL learners in separate classes was seen as potentially socially problematic. An official government statement advised that

> the Secretary of State wishes to emphasise that on suitable occasions the children should join from the beginning in the normal social life of the school and gradually take their place in the ordinary classes as their command of English allows.
>
> (Department of Education and Science 1965: 2)

Another important educational policy statement suggested that

> Common sense would suggest that the best arrangement is usually one where the immigrant children are not cut off from the social and educational life of a normal school . . . Specialist language teachers need to work in close liaison with other teachers . . . they should . . . be in touch with the child's education as a whole.
>
> (Department of Education and Science 1975: 289–290)

This move away from separate ELT was re-affirmed and emphasized in yet another official policy statement a decade later:

> We believe that the language needs of an ethnic minority child should no longer be compartmentalised ... and seen as outside the mainstream of education since language learning and the development of effective communication skills is a feature of every child's education. In many respects, ethnic minority children's language needs serve to highlight the need for positive action to be taken to enhance the quality of language education provided for all pupils ... since ... we have the additional resource within our society of bilingual ... communities, it is surely right and proper that the education system should seek to build on the opportunities which this situation offers.
>
> (Department of Education and Science 1985: 385–386)

By the mid-1980s, this separate English language provision had been dismantled because official opinion, reflecting community sentiments, had deemed this form of EAL provision represented a form of racial discrimination (Commission for Racial Equality 1986). This shift in social attitudes was accompanied by a fundamental curricular and pedagogic reorientation. EAL was no longer regarded as a separate subject; it was now to be acquired as part of the everyday curricular communication and learning. The following statement by Bleach (1990: 63) expressed this view clearly:

> In English lessons, when students are working on the comprehension of texts, we already know that sensitive questioning can lead them to the heart of the text. It is clear that we could learn to write questions in such a way that our students would be given the necessary support to code their answers to the questions. Within this sort of task, too, we should be able to ensure that some systematic work on new structures was being done in the mainstream English lesson.

In this view the opportunities to develop English proficiency in all subject lessons were to be exploited for EAL learners. Indeed this approach was extended to all areas of the school curriculum to form what was (and is), in effect, an EAL across-the-curriculum policy and practice. The theories of Krashen (1982, 1985) and Cummins (1984, 1993, 2000) have been drawn on to lend intellectual support. Krashen's distinction between 'language acquisition' and 'language learning' was seen as particularly important. In one official curriculum document 'acquisition' is interpreted as follows:

> the acquired system is a subconscious process very similar to that which children undergo when they acquire their first language. It requires meaningful interaction in the target language where the focus is on natural communication.
>
> (Department for Education and Skills 2006: 12)

'Language acquisition' through meaningful use is preferred to 'learning' which is likened to conscious efforts to master vocabulary and grammar rules (which by extension harks back to separate language classes). The appeal to the 'naturalness' of this approach can also be seen in the allusion to first language development in the above quote. (For a fuller discussion see Leung 2016.)

In a way, EAL in the school curriculum in England can be seen as a particular form of CLT. The principle of 'acquisition through meaningful use' is embedded in the statutory National Curriculum. Paradoxically, because EAL is completely embedded into the content and activities of the mainstream curriculum, little explicit attention has been paid to issues related to EAL-sensitive content-language integrated teaching, learning outcomes, teacher education and so on in the past 30 years. No specialist qualification is needed to teach EAL. The quality and amount of EAL provision for these students are largely in the hands of individual schools and teachers.

English as an Additional Language within foreign modern languages provision in the Brazilian public educational system

Given the territorial extension of the country, its large school population and diverse educational provision, it would be beyond the scope of this chapter to offer a general account of how English is taught in schools in Brazil. Instead, as with the focus on schools only in England within the United Kingdom, we will focus on national and state level policies designed to set out curricular orientations for modern foreign language teaching. By focusing on these policies, we intend to offer an informed account of the conceptualization and curriculum realization of the subject 'English' in Brazilian public (state) schools, where it is the additional language most frequently taught to the large and heterogeneous public school population. An account of how the curricular goals and teaching process of modern foreign languages, of which EAL is one, is envisaged in national and state curricular framework can be seen as a telling contrast to EAL in England. Terminologically, we have chosen to use the term 'Additional Language' (instead of 'foreign/second') when we refer to English within the Brazilian modern foreign languages curriculum. As the analysis will illustrate, this choice is justified by the fact that languages are usually conceptualized as additional resources to students' linguistic repertoires in the target documents. That said, the umbrella term 'modern foreign language/s' will be used when referring to Brazilian language education policies and frameworks to reflect the terminological use in the relevant documents and legislations.

While additional languages may be introduced as early as kindergarten in private education and in the earlier years of elementary schools in a few public-funded schools, it is not until the sixth grade of elementary school (at the age of 10/11) that modern foreign languages should be compulsorily introduced in schools, according to the legislation LDBEN 9394/96 (Brasil 1996), the law that lays down the foundations for Brazilian education today. This law requires that at least one modern foreign language should be included in the curriculum from the sixth grade of elementary school to the third year of high school (at the age of 14/15). It also states that the language to be taught should be chosen by the school community, taking into consideration the local needs and institutional characteristics.

A study conducted by the British Council (2015) in ten states reveals that, except for Pará, a state in the north of Brazil where the teaching of Spanish is the most sought-after provision in schools, English is the most taught language in public schools in the other nine states included in the study. This study also shows that the number of English classes in most states tends to be limited to two 45 or 50 minute classes a week, and in some schools, especially in the North and Northeast regions, a single class a week is offered. The 2013 educational census showed that only 39% of English teachers in public schools hold a specific major in English from their pre-service training. This relatively low level of teacher proficiency in English, together with the small number of classes a week provided to students, has engendered a widespread perception that the quality of the teaching in English is generally low. Within this context, the national policies are intended to provide educational leadership and to inform curricular developments, teacher education and textbook choices through the establishment of principles aimed at promoting the learning of modern foreign languages. In addition to asserting that modern foreign languages can and should be learned in public schools, these policies emphasize their importance as a means of fostering wider participation in the social world, which is understood as a *sine qua non* for the exercise of a more participatory and transformative citizenship.

Expanding the notion of citizenship from civic awareness to the competence of understanding, producing and transforming meanings in diverse social spheres, the national curriculum framework (*parâmetros nacionais* in Portuguese), first established to orient modern foreign language curricula across the 26 states of Brazil, is largely framed by a socio-interactional view of teaching-learning additional/foreign languages, a socio-historical perspective of language, and a critical stance towards (multi)literacies. These three theoretical pillars emphasize the role of interaction with other people and cultural artefacts in diverse social institutions (Vygotsky 1930 [1998], 1934 [1998]). Therefore, in the socio-interactional perspective advocated by these documents, first and/or additional languages should be taught/learned through the engagement of participants in situated language uses and practices. According to this view, meanings expressed in language are socio-historically (trans)formed by interlocutors to account for and reflect changes in society and culture (Voloshinov 1929 [1986]; Bakhtin 1953 [1986]). In this sense, the assumptions that orient the Brazilian curricula frameworks for language teaching seem to lie on clearer ideological and pedagogical principles than those in the Anglophone documents loosely based on CLT.

Framed by these perspectives, the next two subsections will examine the curriculum conceptualizations that inform the teaching of EAL in the public sector schools and how they are translated into the Minimum Curriculum designed by the state of Rio de Janeiro.

National framework for modern foreign languages in Brazil: curriculum conceptualizations

Building on the aforementioned views of how languages should be taught/learned, the Brazilian Ministry of Education policies (Brasil 1996, 1998, 2006, 2014, 2016) set out the expectations of the central curriculum authorities in terms of pedagogic orientations (Szundy and Cristóvão 2008). Therefore, these policy texts can be regarded as prescriptive statements on the approach and organization of the teaching-learning processes for languages (Machado and Cristóvão 2005). To capture the kind of ELT legitimated by curriculum policies in Brazil, we proceed to the analysis of specific excerpts from the policies mentioned above. Taking into consideration the time span involved in the publication of three of these official documents, PCN-LE (1998), OCEM-LE (2006) and BNCC (2016), and by examining some of the key passages in each of these policies concerned with teaching-learning processes, we can glimpse a view of the historical trajectory of how EAL (and other languages) has been understood in Brazilian public education.

The Brazilian curricular approach has been strongly influenced by a socio-historical perspective, in turn strongly influenced by Vygotskian and Bakhtinian views of languages as semiotic instruments which are constantly (re)shaped through human interactions. This perspective can be seen in the excerpts below.[4] They point to the ways in which modern foreign language teaching-learning processes are conceptualized in terms of social interaction, situated learning and identity (de-/re)construction.

Excerpts 1, 2 and 3 – PCN-LE (1998)

> [. . .] Every meaning is dialogic, that is, constructed by the participants of discourse. In addition to that, every interactional encounter is crucially determined by the participants' social world: by institutions, history and culture.
>
> (p. 27)

[...] The markers that define social identities (as poor, rich, women, men, black, white, homosexual, heterosexual, elderly, youngsters, people with special needs, speakers of (non)stigmatized varieties, speakers of languages enjoying more or less social prestige etc.) are intrinsically connected with how people can act through discourse or with how other people can act with them in the various oral and written interactions in which they engage. It is worth saying that the exercises of power and resistance in discourse are typical of daily experienced interactional encounters.

(p. 27)

[...] In order to make the construction of socio-interactional meanings possible, people use three kinds of knowledge: systemic knowledge, world knowledge and textual organization knowledge. These three kinds of knowledge compose the student's communicative competence and prepare him/her for the discursive engagement.

(p. 29)

Excerpts 4 and 5 – OCEM-LE (2006)

[...] In such a conception [of grammar], language can be described, taught and learned as an abstract system composed of abstract rules – all of this distant from any specific socio-cultural context, community of practice and distinct group of users.

(p. 107)

[...] by imposing normativity and a sole model, the homogeneity marginalizes and eliminates the sociocultural and linguistic variations that constitute a natural part of any language.

(p. 108)

Excerpts 6 and 7 – BNCC (2016)

[...] In its educational dimension, the curricular component Modern Foreign Language contributes to the appreciation of the sociocultural and linguistic Brazilian plurality so as to stimulate respect to differences. Working with texts in other language(s) places the student in contact with diversity.

(p. 121)

[...] The focus is not on comprehending a set of theoretical concepts and linguistic categories for later application, but on learning, for use and through use, linguistic discursive and cultural practices that may be added to other knowledge that students already carry in their repertoires in Portuguese, indigenous languages, heritage languages, sign languages, among others.

(p. 121)

In the seven excerpts above, the socio-historical premise, found in the works by Vygotsky (1930 [1998], 1934 [1998]), Voloshinov (1929 [1986]) and Bakhtin (1953 [1986]), can be clearly seen. In particular, a strong theoretical principle for curricular development is that individual students' conscience and identities are (re)shaped through and in interactions with other(s) in different social spheres. In this sense, teaching English or any other language at schools is largely justified by the possibility of exposure to and construction of otherness: other interactional encounters and dialogues (excerpt 2), other linguistic and cultural varieties (excerpt 5), knowledge about other areas and other possibilities of social interactions (excerpt 7). The incorporation of a responsive attitude to otherness as a condition for discursive engagement in the additional language portrays the influence of the dialogic conception of language (Bakhtin 1953 [1986]) in the design of these curricular policies. Whereas dialogism is understood as engagement in institutionally, historically and culturally located meaning construction processes in the curricular policy published in 1998 (excerpt 1), in the ensuing documents, published in 2006 and 2016, the scope of dialogism is widened to encompass plurilingualism, interpreted as cultural-linguistic heterogeneity (see excerpts 5 and 6). This extended scope has clear interconnections with the view of languages as additional situated resources interacting with students' multilingual repertoires. It can thus be related to current focuses of EAL research on how 'teaching and learning work in local, situated practices in different schools, classrooms and local education authorities' (Leung 2016: 166).

Because language is understood in terms of its socio-interactional and dialogic dimensions, traditional pedagogic practices in which grammar is taught for its own sake are not promoted by the three policy documents. Instead the focus is on situated language use. Although the term communicative competence is only explicitly used in the third excerpt from PCN-LE, the Hymesian ethnographic precept that 'competence in language use is not just a question of an abstracted knowledge of grammar residing in the individual, it also involves social conventions of use in actual contexts of communication' (Leung and Street 2012: 85) seems to be present in all three documents, reflecting what Leung (2013) defines as a widened notion of the 'social' in the teaching of EAL. Therefore, rather than restricting it to users' competence to apply different language functions in a variety of contexts, the scope of the social in these three curricular policies is enlarged to include 'the markers that define social identities', 'the exercises of power and resistance in discourse' (excerpt 2); '[. . .] specific socio-cultural context, community of practice and distinct group of users' (excerpt 4), and 'the contact with diversity' (excerpt 6). In this more complex and diverse view, communicative competence in a language should be accomplished both through students' engagement in language use and through their reflections on the processes of use (Rojo 2000), which are informed by the view that meanings are constructed through 'three kinds of knowledge: systemic knowledge, world knowledge and textual organization knowledge' (excerpt 3), and that learning comprises linguistic-discursive and cultural practices 'in the use and for the use' of language (excerpt 7).

In face of the dynamic social views of uses, practices, (inter)actions, identities and meanings that characterize the views that these three national policies embrace, the term 'foreign' to qualify languages other than the mother tongue seems less appropriate than 'additional'. While the main reason for privileging the term 'foreign' in official documents lies in the fact that the name of this curricular component in the law that founded the premises for these policies (LDBEN 9394 – Brasil 1996) is 'Modern Foreign Language', the educational perspective that is voiced in the excerpts above seems closer to the concept of additional language, which recognizes that 'pupils have other linguistic resources before learning English' (Leung 2016: 159). This perspective, however, is only indirectly expressed through the idea of plurality of oral and written interactions emphasized in the first two documents, but it is clearly voiced in the position expressed in the third document that learning should take place through 'linguistic-discursive and cultural practices that may be added to other knowledge that students already carry in their repertoires in Portuguese, indigenous languages, heritage languages, sign languages, among others' (excerpt 7).

Taking the curricular framework of the second biggest state in Brazil as an example, the next section focuses on how these wider national curriculum statements are translated into learning objectives in curricular policies that should orient additional language teaching in public schools in Rio de Janeiro.

Curricular frameworks at state level: the Minimum Curriculum of Rio de Janeiro

Taking into consideration the learner's identity as a speaker of Brazilian Portuguese, the Minimum Curriculum of Foreign Language (Secretaria Estadual de Educação do Rio de Janeiro 2012) aims to provide students with opportunities to learn and experience different varieties of the foreign language in conjunction with the mother tongue, Brazilian Portuguese. The cross-curricular work is realized through the selection of speech genres (*gêneros discursivos*, in the original Portuguese text) that constitute both oral and written competence in the foreign language. In addition, the Minimum Curriculum also emphasizes that the speech genres may trigger interdisciplinary dialogues with other areas.

The reference in the Minimum Curriculum (Secretaria Estadual de Educação do Rio de Janeiro 2012) to the notion of speech genres as varieties of texts and utterances that organize and influence people's participation in different situations of interaction can be clearly related to the Bakhtinian definition of speech genres as relatively stable types of utterances developed by each sphere in which language is used (Bakhtin 1953 [1986]). Framed by this notion of genres, the Minimum Curriculum lists the genres that should orient the provision of English and/or Spanish as additional languages in each term of the school year. Since the school year is divided into four terms of two months in duration, the Curriculum indicates an average of four genres to cover written and oral production/comprehension in each grade of primary and secondary school. In addition to listing the genres, the Curriculum requires that understanding and producing written/oral language should be regarded as the main competences (under 'axis' in Table 12.1 below) to be developed; it also sets out the goals to be accomplished in each of these competences in respect of each genre/groups of genres.

Table 12.1 presents an overview of the speech genres that integrate the Minimum Curriculum that establishes frameworks for ELT in public schools in the state of Rio de Janeiro.

With the organization of language teaching in speech genres and the variety of genres listed in Table 12.1 in mind, it is possible to infer that, similar to the national policies analysed in the previous section, the Minimum Curriculum of Rio de Janeiro is also informed by a socio-historical view of language and the teaching-learning processes. In the interpretation of national policies in this state curriculum framework, the socio-historical purview is locally translated into a syllabus that covers social (inter)actions in different speech genres. As these overlap with the students' other curricular activities in Portuguese, the oral and written topics seem to be regarded as additional resources to be added to a linguistic repertoire students already hold and/or are developing in their first language.

However, the translation of the dynamic socio-historic view of language into curriculum practice has shown signs of reification. Whereas Bakhtin's emphasis on the patterned but also contingent nature of the utterances can be related to a situated and ideological perspective of literacies (Oliveira and Szundy 2014), the Minimum Curriculum appears to treat the concept of genre in additional language teaching as a static phenomenon. The reification of the social dimension through the objectification of speech genres in the state curriculum of Rio de Janeiro is illustrated in the content defined for the first term of the sixth grade of elementary school in Table 12.2.

In Table 12.2 the descriptors for the written and oral production/comprehension of the genre comics/comic strips seem to suggest that language use can be replicated across contexts and tasks in a stable way. There is a strong sense that the 'autonomous' language model – in which linguistic forms and functions are stable and neutral irrespective of the context of

Table 12.1 Speech genres in the Minimum Curriculum for Modern Foreign Language

ELEMENTARY SCHOOL					
TERM	*SIXTH GRADE*	*SEVENTH GRADE*	*EIGHTH GRADE*	*NINTH GRADE*	*AXIS*
First	Comics/comic strips	Diaries/blogs	Advice letters	Encyclopaedia entries/science-popularization articles	– written and oral competence – language in use – written and oral production
Second	Tales (fairy tales/ legends/fables)	Advertisements	News/reports	Readers letters	
Third	Game rules/recipes/ instruction manuals	Adventure narratives/science fiction	Interviews	Opinion articles	
Fourth	Instant messages, notes, mailbox messages	Songs and poems	Cartoons	Short stories	

Table 12.2 Content for the first term of the sixth grade (Minimum Curriculum: 5)

Foreign language	*Sixth grade of elementary school*
Axis **Abilities and competences**	**Comics/comic strips** WRITTEN AND ORAL COMPREHENSION • Comprehend the interaction between reader, discourse and iconic element and the use of linguistic resources. • Comprehend the nature of humour present in the genre.
Axis **Abilities and competences**	**Comics/comic strips** LANGUAGE IN USE • Recognize the linguistic marks of colloquial register and figures of speech that create humorous effect (irony, comparison) • Recognize the linguistic resources to describe people (adjectives, comparisons, etc.) and the elements that characterize dialogues in this genre, such as: answers, questions and verbal structures. ORAL AND WRITTEN PRODUCTION • Produce a comic/comic strip arising from a daily or imagined situation. • Role play the dialogues of this comic/comic strip.

Note: The table was translated from its original version in Brazilian Portuguese by one of the authors.

use – is being adopted here (for a discussion see Street 2014, 2009). By interpreting the context as a fixed and stabilized entity, the Minimum Curriculum depicts a monolithic and universal rather than a dialogic and locally situated understanding of speech genres. Amorim (2014) suggests that there is a difference between such a position and the Bakhtinian view that context determines the characteristics of the genre. For Bakhtin (1953 [1986]), the relationship between genres and contexts is always dialectical, which means that they are mutually constituted and (trans)formed. Although descriptors such as 'comprehend the interaction between reader, discourse and iconic element and the use of linguistic resources', 'comprehend the nature of humour present in the genre' and 'recognize the linguistic marks of colloquial register and figures of speech that create humoristic effect (irony, comparison)' indicate the connection of the Rio de Janiero curriculum with the socio-interactional perspective advocated by national curricular principles, the scope of the social is considerably more limited than that envisaged in the national documents. This is so because, despite the rhetoric in the Minimum Curriculum, we cannot see in the curriculum content (e.g. see Table 12.2) any descriptors that propose the use of comics to problematize, for instance, issues of stereotypes, prejudice and identities, which would engage with the national curriculum view of citizenship as the engagement with and construction of plural meanings.

The reduction of the scope of the social in the Minimum Curriculum is also reflected in the definition of a list of pre-determined speech genres, which seems to ignore the participants' agency in choosing and (re-)shaping linguistic repertoires locally in school and in the classroom. By merely listing the genres and the competences that should be developed through them, the tendency to regard language as abstracted linguistic norms criticized in the national policies is reiterated as genre. In a way, the more traditional emphasis on grammar for the sake of grammar is merely replaced by the emphasis on genres for the sake of genres, which can become objectified units in the curriculum that can be replicated in many different contexts. In this sense, the dynamic agentive plurilingualism, embedded in the three national curricular policies analysed in the previous section, seems to be absent in the interpretation of 'autonomous' speech genres privileged by the Minimum Curriculum. This absence of contingency and dynamism is felt in the attempt to homogenize the learning-teaching contents and processes of additional languages across the state of Rio de Janeiro. This approach would disregard the diverse socio-cultural semiotic resources of the students, many of whom are familiar with the innovations and hybridization of genres that populate lives in the heterogeneous local communities in Rio de Janeiro.

Concluding remarks

At a very high level of abstraction the teaching of EAL in both England and Rio de Janeiro would seem to fit the 'international' CLT paradigm. However, a close-up examination suggests that the curriculum principles are built on very different intellectual and ideological foundations. Arguably the 'international' CLT paradigm follows the dictum 'when in Rome, do as the Romans do', or better still for this discussion, 'do as the native speakers do'. In other words, a (if not *the*) main goal of language teaching is to help students learn what other speakers, particularly native speakers of the focal language, do with the language. In this view language teaching should aim, first and foremost, to inculcate the capacity to produce/reproduce a pre-existing knowledge and model of use. The approach in the English school system is communicative in that EAL is completely embedded in the everyday English-medium classroom and school activities. At the same time little attention is paid to language pedagogy beyond 'acquisition through meaningful use'; in other words, the immersion of students in an English-speaking language environment is assumed to provide most, if not all, of the support needed for EAL development. By this reckoning teachers of all subjects are also, by default, teachers of English because they teach in English. There is little discussion of language learning goals beyond helping EAL learners to engage in curricular activities. EAL in the English school system is thus a diffused idea that has no curricular focus and visibility. We can say that at the curriculum level, the concept of CLT is largely understood in terms of communicative language use in school contexts; the language teaching dimension is, at best, left to individual teachers and schools.

In contrast, the Brazilian approach, by our account, appears to aim at individual and social transformations. The purpose of language teaching and learning is thus to help students to be decentred, to learn to be the 'other/s'. In a way CLT is seen as having the potential to assist students to realize their transformative capacity. It is perhaps a little ironic that the transformative agenda in the Minimum Curriculum of Rio de Janeiro may well be hindered by a somewhat monolithic assumption that specified 'speech genres' are static and context-neutral. We would contend that unless the 'speech genres' are themselves open to critique and transformation, students would merely be taught to reproduce what the curriculum planner and policymakers have chosen for them.

Unlike the approach to EAL in England, the Minimum Curriculum of Rio de Janeiro attempts to translate wider linguistic and pedagogic principles into concrete learning goals. However, a common challenge shared by England, Brazil and probably many other contexts where EAL is taught/learned, seems to reside in the inability of policy and curriculum designers to take proper account of the complexity involved in the enactment of situated language use in relation to student needs and pedagogic practice. While the diverse educational settings clearly call for context-sensitive pedagogic approaches, the internationalized CLT principles do not seem to speak to the local complexities and contingencies found in different world locations. This is so because in the pedagogic recontextualization of the

Hymesian ethnographic concept, CLT has rendered the 'social' in EAL in terms of pre-existing native speaker models and practices; in effect the 'local', a key concern in ethnographic perspectives, has been drained out of the concept. This conceptual reduction has meant that the CLT orthodoxy has little analytic purchase on 'local' conceptualizations and practices of EAL situated in diverse social and historic contexts. Thus, we argue that the conceptual *re-localizing* of CLT principles in EAL curriculum development and teacher education is a prerequisite for making the principles of CLT relevant in different educational contexts.

In practice, the relocalizing of CLT principles would encourage teachers and policymakers to abandon the idea that there is a context-free model of communicative competence and a universal pedagogic template for its development (e.g. the teaching materials represented by internationally marketed ELT textbooks). Teachers and curriculum developers should be encouraged to pay attention to the kind/s of issues/topics that would be educationally salient in their local context and how such issues/topics should be rendered into teaching materials and activities at different levels or stages of language learning. The materials development process should take account of different views of language development (e.g. naturalistic acquisition, instruction-based learning) and teaching approaches (e.g. using the target language only, using all languages available in the classroom as appropriate, and so on). Teachers and materials writers should be encouraged to consider different approaches to teaching and views on language development with broad CLT principles in mind. Ultimately though, if the concept of communicative competence is fundamentally about capturing the ways in which people do things with words and other semiotic means in particular contexts, then CLT should regard local communicative practices as the starting point in designing curriculum and pedagogy.

Notes

1 We are aware of the fact that the lexical choices used to refer to English Language Teaching (English as a Second Language, English as a Foreign Language, English as an Additional Language etc.) link authors with distinct views about language. When reviewing different scholars, we are loyal to the term a specific researcher chooses to refer to ELT. Nevertheless, we opt for the term *additional* to refer to ELT. Such an option is justified by our belief that other languages constitute additional linguistic resources to students' as well as teachers' linguistic repertoires.
2 Given the devolved nature of the governance in the United Kingdom, the education systems in England, Northern Ireland, Scotland and Wales are run by their respective local administrations. While these four systems share some broad similarities, there are also local differences. For this reason this discussion will refer to the developments and events in England only.
3 At that time EAL was labelled English as a Second Language.
4 The excerpts were extracted from three official national curricular policies: PCN-LE (1998), OCEM-LE (2006) and BNCC (2016).

Further reading

Burns, A. (ed.) (2005) *Teaching English from a Global Perspective*. Alexandria, VA: Teachers of English to Speakers of Other Languages, Inc. This edited volume provides a non-parochial discussion on the need to move away from a monolithic view of English, and to reconsider the importance of taking diversity into account.

Conteh, J. (2015) *The EAL Teaching Book: Promoting Success for Multilingual Learners in Primary and Secondary Schools*. 2nd edn. London: Sage. This text provides a helpful account of how teachers can respond to linguisitic diversity in their classrooms.

Cummins, J. (2000) *Language, Power and Pedagogy: Bilingual Children in the Crossfire*. Clevedon: Multilingual Matters. This is a very useful text in setting out the arguments for the promotion of bi/multi-lingualism in education, particular with reference to linguisitic minority students.

Leung, C. (2013). 'Second/additional language teacher professionalism – What is it?', in M. Olofsson (ed.), *Symposium 2012: Lärarrollen I svenska som andraspräk*. Stockholm: Stockholms universitets förlag, 11–27. This text addresses the key professional issues facing additional language teachers in contemporary contexts where ethnic and linguistic diversity is the norm.

Leung, C. (2014) 'Communication and participatory involvement in linguistically diverse classrooms', in S. May (ed.), *The Multilingual Turn: Implications for SLA, TESOL and Bilingual Education*. New York: Routledge, 123–146. This discussion demonstrates that the contingent language use in actual classrooms demands a more complex lanugage model than the conventionally accepted view of communicative competence (as represented by many internationally marketed ELT tests and textbooks).

Related topics

- English and multilingualism: a contested history
- The relevance of English language studies in higher education
- Literacy in English: literacies in Englishes
- Teaching English to Speakers of Other Languages (TESOL)
- English and social identity
- Sociolinguistics: studying English and its social relations.

References

Amorim, M. A. (2014) 'Documentos oficiais, currículo e ensinagem de I/LE: possíveis (inter-) relações sócio-históricas', *Trabalhos em Linguística Aplicada* 53 (2): 357–380.

Bakhtin, M. M. (1953 [1986]) 'The problem of speech genres', in M. M. Bakhtin (ed.), *Speech Genres and Other Late Essays*. Austin: University of Texas Press, 60–89.

Bleach, J. (1990) 'Finding a voice and conversational competence: Mixed ability English, a social base for negotiated learning', in J. Levine (ed.), *Bilingual Learners and the Mainstream Curriculum*. London: Falmer Press, 60–81.

Brasil (1996) *Lei de Diretrizes e Bases da Educação Nacional. Lei n° 9394, de 20 de dezembro de 1996*. Brasília, DF: Estabelece as diretrizes e bases da educação nacional.

Brasil (2014). *Guia de livros didáticos PNLD: Língua Estrangeira Moderna*. Brasília, DF: MEC.

Brasil, SEB/MEC (2006) *Orientações Curriculares para o Ensino Médio: linguagens, códigos e suas tecnologias*. Brasília, DF: SEB/MEC.

Brasil, SEB/MEC (2016) *Base Nacional Comum Curricular. Prosposta Preliminar. Segunda Versão*. Brasília, DF: SEB/MEC.

Brasil, SEF/MEC (1998). *Parâmetros Curriculares Nacionais* – 3° e 4° ciclos do Ensino Fundamental – Língua Estrangeira. Brasília, DF: SEF/MEC.

British Council (2015) *O ensino de inglês na educação pública brasileira*. São Paulo: Elaborado com exclusividade para o British Council pelo Instituto de Pesquisa Plano CDE.

Canale, M. (1983) 'From communicative competence to language pedagogy', in J. Richards and J. Schmidt (eds), *Language and Communication*. London: Longman, 2–27.

Canale, M. (1984) 'A communicative approach to language proficiency assessment in a minority setting', in C. Rivera (ed.), *Communicative Competence Approaches to Language Proficiency Assessment: Research and Application*. Clevedon: Multilingual Matters, 107–122.

Canale, M. and M. Swain (1980a) *A Domain Description for Core FSL: Communication Skills*. Ontario: Ministry of Education.

Canale, M. and M. Swain (1980b) 'Theoretical bases of communicative approaches to second language teaching and testing', *Applied Linguistics* 1 (1): 1–47.

Commission for Racial Equality (1986) *Teaching English as a Second Language*. London: CRE.

Council of Europe (2001) *Common European Framework of Reference for Languages: Learning, Teaching, Assessment*. Cambridge: Cambridge University Press.

Cummins, J. (1984) *Bilingualism and Special Education: Issues in Assessment and Pedagogy*. Clevedon, Avon: Multilingual Matters Ltd.

Cummins, J. (1993) 'Bilingualism and second language learning', in W. Grabe (ed.), *Annual Review of Applied Linguistics*. Vol. 13. Cambridge: Cambridge University Press, 51–70.

Cummins, J. (2000) *Language, Power and Pedagogy: Bilingual Children in the Crossfire*. Clevedon: Multilingual Matters.

Department of Education and Science (1965) *The Education of Immigrants (Circular 7/65)*. London: HMSO.

Department of Education and Science (1971) *The Education of Immigrants: Education Survey 13*. London: HMSO.

Department of Education and Science (1972) *The Continuing Needs of Immigrants. Education Survey 14*. London: HMSO.

Department of Education and Science (1975) *A Language for Life: Report of the Committee of Inquiry Appointed by the Secretary of State for Education and Science under the Chairmanship of Sir Alan Bullock/Committee of Inquiry into Reading and the Use of English*. London: HMSO.

Department of Education and Science (1985) *Education for All: The Report of the Committee of Inquiry into the Education of Children from Ethnic Minority Groups (The Swann Report)*. London: HMSO.

Department for Education and Skills (2006) *Secondary National Strategy: Pupils Learning English as an Additional Language*. London: DfES.

Department of Education/Office for National Statistics (2016) *Schools, Pupils and their Characteristics: January 2016*. England: DofE/ONS.

Derrick, J. (1977) *Language Needs of Minority Group Children*. Slough: NFER.

Hymes, D. (1972) 'On communicative competence', in J. B. Pride and J. Holmes (eds), *Sociolinguistics*. London: Penguin, 269–293.

Hymes, D. (1977) *Foundations in Sociolinguistics: An Ethnographic Approach*. London: Tavistock Publications.

Krashen, S. (1982) *Principles and Practice in Second Language Acquistion*. Oxford: Pergamon.

Krashen, S. (1985) *The Input Hypothesis*. New York: Longman.

Leung, C. (2013). 'The "social" in English language teaching: Abstract norms versus situated enactments', *Journal of English as a Lingua Franca* 2 (2): 283–313.

Leung, C. (2016) 'English as an additional language – a genealogy of language-in-education policies and reflections on research trajectories', *Language and Education* 30 (2): 158–174.

Leung, C. and C. Franson (2001) 'England: ESL in the early days', in B. Mohan, C. Leung and C. Davison (eds), *English as a Second Language in the Mainstream: Teaching, Learning and Identity*. London: Longman, 153–164.

Leung, C. and B. Street (2012) 'Linking EIL and literacy: Theory and practice', in L. Alsagoff et al. (eds), *Principles and Practices for Teaching English as an International Language*. London and New York: Routledge, chapter 6. Kindle Edition.

Machado, A. R. and V. L. L. Cristóvão (2005) 'Representações sobre o professor e seu trabalho em proposta institucional brasileira para a formação docente', in *Congresso Internacional Educação e Trabalho: Representações Sociais, Competências e Trajectórias Profissionais*. Aveiro. *Anais*. Aveiro: Universidade de Aveiro, 1–14.

Ministry of Education (1963) *English for Immigrants*. London: HMSO.

Oliveira, M. B. F. and P. T. C. Szundy (2014) 'Multiliteracies practices at school: For a responsive education to contemporaneity', *Bakhtiniana*, São Paulo 9 (2): 191–210.

Rojo, R. H. R. (2000) 'Modos de transposição didática dos PCNs às práticas de sala de aula: progressão curricular e projetos', in R. H. R. Rojo (org.) (ed.), *A prática de linguagem em sala de aula: praticando os PCNs*. Campinas, SP: Mercado de Letras, 27–38.

Secretaria Estadual de Educação do Rio de Janeiro (2012) *Currículo Mínimo: língua estrangeira*. Rio de Janeiro: SEE-RJ.

Stenhouse, L. (1967) *Culture and Education*. London: Thomas Nelson and Sons Ltd.

Stenhouse, L. (1975) *An Introduction to Curriculum Research and Development*. London: Heinemann.

Street, B. (2009) 'Ethnography of writing and reading', in D. R. Olson and N. Torrance (eds), *The Cambridge Handbook of Literacy*. Cambridge: Cambridge University Press, 329–345.

Street, B. (2014) *Letramentos sociais: abordagens críticas do letramento no desenvolvimento, na etnografia e na educação*. Trad. de Marcos Bagno. São Paulo: Parábola Editorial.

Szundy, P. T. C. and V. L. L. Cristóvão (2008) 'Projetos de formação pré-serviço do professor de língua inglesa: seqüências didáticas como instrumento no ensino-aprendizagem', *Revista Brasileira de Linguística Aplicada* 8 (1): 115–137.
Voloshinov, V. N. (1929 [1986]) *Marxism and the Philosophy of Language*. USA: Harvard University Press.
Vygotsky, L. S. (1930 [1998]) *A Formação Social da Mente*. São Paulo: Martins Fontes.
Vygotsky, L. S. (1934 [1998]) *Pensamento e Linguagem*. São Paulo: Martins Fontes.

13

Teaching English to Speakers of Other Languages (TESOL)

Diane Pecorari

Introduction

English is used by large numbers of people around the world. Arriving at an accurate estimate of just how many people speak English is a highly problematic enterprise, but a British Council report put the number of people who speak it at 'a useful level' at 1.75 billion (British Council 2013: 5), a figure which matches Crystal's estimate of 'in the direction of 2 billion' (Crystal 2008: 5). The number of people who speak English as a first language (L1) is estimated by Ethnologue (Lewis et al. 2016) at 339 million, so approximately 1.66 billion people in the world use it as a second (L2) or foreign language. TESOL, or Teaching English to Speakers of other Languages, is the area of English studies which serves the needs of such learners. This area is also sometimes known as English Language Teaching (ELT), Teaching English as a Second Language (TESL) or Teaching English as a Foreign Language (TEFL).

The scope of TESOL

With a focus on the learning and teaching of English, TESOL has traditionally had an affinity for areas of applied linguistics and has been less influenced by literary studies, or by work which is primarily descriptive. However, within that focus, a broad range of activities are included under the TESOL umbrella. An indication of this breadth can be seen in the special interest groups within the professional organisation also called TESOL (TESOL International Association n.d.). Members of the organisation have formed 21 such groups to address topics as diverse as intensive English programmes, second language writing, teacher education, materials writing, intercultural communication and social responsibility.

TESOL involves both pedagogical practice and research. As with any other language, teaching English as a second or foreign language involves teaching the forms of the language, (i.e., vocabulary, grammatical structures, pronunciation, etc.), the skills required to use the language (reading, writing, speaking and listening) and various types of metalinguistic knowledge and skills, such as the pragmatic competence involved in selecting the most appropriate way to make a request from a number of possibilities. Courses in general English typically survey those areas broadly, selecting target vocabulary, structures, etc., which are appropriate to the learners' level. In addition, more focused teaching addresses areas of English for Specific Purposes (ESP) such as business English, English for academic purposes (EAP) or specific learner needs such as exam preparation.

Teaching English (like any other language) involves the pedagogical skills to plan, deliver and assess learning, so TESOL involves activities such as curriculum design, assessment and materials writing. The last two of these are particularly prominent. Several large international publishers, along with many smaller ones, produce a voluminous selection of textbooks, workbooks, reference books and other materials for learners of English. Many commercial tests of English proficiency are available as well, including the International English Language Testing System (IELTS) and the Test of English as a Foreign Language (TOEFL), both of which are used by universities around the world to assess the suitability of students for study through the medium of English, and the Cambridge Preliminary, First and Advanced exams, which test general English proficiency at various stages of study.

As an area within applied linguistics, research in TESOL is intended to inform and benefit the way the language is taught or learned. Research topics include the forms of instruction which best promote learning; the frequency with which particular linguistic forms occur, as a basis for understanding what needs to be taught; and effective ways of assessing what has been learned. The training of English teachers has also been in focus, including the experiences of teachers in training and the provisions at institutions for their continuing professional development. Another strand of research in TESOL has a focus on the needs and characteristics of the learners, so for instance the particular needs of young learners or adults have been the subject of research. Similarly, a body of work looks at the concerns of learners in a vulnerable position, such as immigrants and refugees. The various types of motivation which learners possess has been the object of a large body of research.

This description of the areas of research and teaching interest which come under the heading of TESOL is far from complete, but it serves to illustrate the breadth, richness and variety of the field. (For a deeper perspective on the kinds of activities which come under the heading of TESOL, useful resources are the tables of contents of two journals published by TESOL, a membership organisation representing the profession. *TESOL Quarterly* has a focus on research issues, while *TESOL Journal* is oriented toward the interests of teachers.)

The development of TESOL

The development of TESOL could in a sense be dated back to the point at which people with another language first had a need to learn English, and this was, according to Howatt (1984), the result of a process in several steps. The first development, starting from the end of the 14th century, was when English began to replace French as the language used in official and business contexts. The result of this trend was that fewer people in England could speak French, and French speakers who wanted to sell to the English found it advantageous to learn English. The 16th century saw the arrival in England of French-speaking refugees. To serve the demands of these groups which now had an incentive to learn English, materials and teachers became available. The end of the 15th century saw the publication of 'double manuals' with content in both French and English, acting as a sort of phrasebook and useful to English people wanting to communicate in French as much as to French speakers wanting to communicate in English. In the mid-to-late 16th century, three language teachers (two with French as a first language and one with Italian) are documented as working in London, teaching English to the refugee community, and the first textbooks for English as a foreign language were published (Howatt 1984: 3–22).

However, in the sense in which the acronym is usually used 'the emergence of TESOL . . . is firmly located in the mid-twentieth century' (Gray 2016: 82). It was in the period following World War II that the position of English as a global lingua franca was firmly established, leading to the rapid rise, documented above, in the need for people worldwide to learn English. The earliest citation in the Oxford English Dictionary (2017) for TESOL dates back to 1969, and for TEFL and TESL it is 1963 and 1967, respectively.

During this early period the field which came to be called TESOL was being invented, as evidenced by the proceedings of an early conference on University Training and Research in the Teaching of English as a Second/Foreign Language held in 1960 (Wayment 1961). Some of the themes raised at that conference are ones which, as will be seen below, have had perennial relevance for the field. For example, Firth (1961) pointed out the need to investigate the relationship between the rise of English in developing countries and the status and use of the countries' indigenous languages. A representative of the British Council pointed out that while the elite had previously had best access to English, widening access to English could in turn create opportunities which would confer some of the privileges of the elite more widely, so that using English was

> no longer a question of the sons of Maharajahs, but of the sons of the cultivators. People want English because English is the badge of the middle class, the language of good jobs.
>
> (King 1961: 24)

One presenter invoked a commercial metaphor in which students were the consumers, teachers the retailers and teacher trainers the wholesalers (Catford 1961: 37).

A common theme in a number of papers at this early conference was the role which linguistics departments could play in developing the field of ELT by providing an empirical and scholarly foundation for teaching practice. The novelty of the idea at the time is demonstrated not only by the fact that several linguists felt the need to argue for it, but also by the exceedingly modest estimate of the growth potential:

> If many more than four or five universities turn out to be interested in one way or another in the problem of English language teaching, a plan should be worked out in which these various universities assume responsibility for different tasks.
>
> (McIntosh 1961: 29)

Current critical issues and topics

Language is so inextricably bound up with what makes us human that it is impossible entirely to separate it from social structures and relationships. The English language in particular is closely associated with a history of colonialism, and as a result 'English language teaching cannot be isolated from the cultural and political contexts in which it is embedded' (Pennycook 1994: 692). Among many members of the TESOL community there is a strong awareness of these issues, and of the need to engage with them and consider their implications for English teaching practice.

Critical approaches to TESOL

A trend dating approximately to the 1990s is important to TESOL; that is, an awareness of issues with social relevance. A critical approach to TESOL is characterised by two key features: 'a focus on the inequitable contexts in which language education takes place' and 'a pedagogical focus on changing those conditions' (Pennycook 1999: 335). Topics meriting a critical approach are any which have the potential to create or inform inequalities, including race, gender, sexuality and sexual orientation, and migration status. The following short descriptions of two studies taking a critical approach to TESOL can illustrate the nature of work in this area.

The first is an ethnographic study (Ibrahim 1999) set in a French-language school in an English-speaking part of Canada. The focus of the study were sixteen Francophone immigrants from African countries, all of whom were multilingual, speaking an African language and English to some extent in addition to French. In this setting – with English as the dominant language of the city in which they were living, and French, the language of instruction in school, associated with its colonial legacy – the opportunities for asymmetries among these languages was substantial. A finding of the study was that the participants were enthusiastic adopters of aspects of Black North American culture, despite having limited contact with Black North Americans. They favoured 'rap, hip hop, and the corresponding dress' (p. 360) and their speech included features associated with African American Vernacular English. The significance of this finding is that 'identity. . . governs what ESL learners acquire and how they acquire it', leading the author to suggest 'rap and hip-hop (and Black popular culture in general) as curriculum sites where learning takes place and where identities are invested'. Ibrahim goes on to question

> whose language and identity are we as TESOL professionals teaching and assuming in the classroom if we do not engage rap and hip-hop? That is, whose knowledge is being valorized and legitimated and thus assumed to be worthy of study, and whose knowledge and identity are left in the corridors of our schools?
>
> (Ibrahim 1999: 366)

This study is characteristic of the critical turn in that it is concerned with a fundamental aspect of (in)equality, i.e., whose English is worth learning and teaching, and is also concerned with exerting change, in that an argument for introducing Black culture into the curriculum is presented.

Those themes – social asymmetry and a focus on exerting change – are also present in an account of a critical approach to needs analysis: that is, the process by which courses are planned following an analysis of the pedagogical situation and the outcomes needed by the learners. In this account (Benesch 1996), two traditional instances of needs analysis are presented. They involve describing, but not questioning the demands which the setting makes on learners. These are then contrasted with a set of interventions which Benesch designed to address a problematic situation in her own teaching context. ESL learners faced significant challenges in a psychology course which had an ambitious body of content, much of which was delivered through lectures. As in a more traditional needs approach, Benesch developed some interventions designed to help the learners adapt to the needs of the curriculum, such as working with their note-taking during lectures. However, adopting a critical approach required going further, and this involved creating two additional sorts of interventions 'which challenged the requirements, and . . . worked outside the requirements to create possibilities for social awareness and action' (1996: 733). These included counterbalancing the monologic nature of a lecture by creating spaces in which the students could address the teacher, and engaging students in the political processes which had brought about budget cuts, thus leading to more large-group lectures and fewer small-group discussion sessions.

Because the English language has global reach, so does TESOL, and inevitably in many of the settings in which it is taught, issues of social inequality are present. Language is rarely a neutral choice, and so the questions of whether and how to teach English are related to other questions of societal importance. Advocates of a critical perspective on TESOL seek to foreground those relationships to create positive change.

English as lingua franca

A closely related issue is the impact of the status of English as a lingua franca (ELF), that is, the language used when people needing to communicate do not share a common first language. The rise of ELF has brought with it a number of problems. It is the status of ELF which is the factor underlying the large numbers of people learning English as a second or foreign language, but the movement toward English has entailed a corresponding movement away from other languages. For example, a report by the European Commission (2012) looked at the language skills attained by students in 16 language communities in Europe. In the large majority, English was the primary foreign language in the school system, meaning that more pupils studied English, or studied it for a longer period of time. Not surprisingly, pupils' skills were stronger in the primary foreign language than in the secondary foreign language. In other words, English is studied in European schools in greater numbers, for a longer period of time, and to a higher degree of proficiency than other foreign languages. In this sense, it is fair to speak of other languages competing with English – and usually losing.

Phillipson (1992) distinguishes between different degrees of competition between English and other languages. The movement toward English and away from other foreign languages is an example of what he terms *replacing*. In other settings, English *displaces* other languages in some domains only. For instance, research results are reported in academic journals overwhelmingly in English (and research published in other languages is difficult for other scholars to access, and as a result tends to be used and cited less often). As a consequence of the tendency to use English in academic communication, other languages have either lost, or risk losing, certain features of language, such as a specialised terminology related to an academic area. Domain loss (as this situation is called) is another consequence of ELF.

Other consequences of ELF are felt by individual users. While a common language for communication is of itself beneficial, communicating in a foreign language generally takes more effort, is more time-consuming, and has greater potential to be less effective or satisfying. Even people with strong proficiency in a second language report that they find it difficult to find nuanced forms of expression, or to be spontaneous, or to use and respond to humour in an interaction. As a result, in interactions which involve some people who have English as a first language and others for whom it is a foreign language, the advantage is generally to the former: the native speaker has a better chance of achieving communicative objectives effectively, comfortably and with relatively less effort.

The L1 user of English benefits from an additional advantage as well. The native speaker has traditionally been identified as the standard for what constitutes good use of English (or indeed any other language). In that sense, the ultimate objective of language teaching is often assumed to be to raise the learner's proficiency in the target language as close as possible to that of a native speaker of the language (even though for most learners this is an unrealistic objective; only a small proportion of language learners ever achieve native-like proficiency in the target language). The native-speaker norm has come under sustained criticism from several directions, including from scholars working from a World Englishes perspective (see Bolton, this volume) who point out that the numerous varieties of English spoken in the world make it difficult to assign a normative role to a single variety, or a small handful of them. Yet an adherence to the native-speaker norm persists; for example, a recent study showed that students in Hong Kong assigned higher status to native-speaker pronunciation (favouring UK, US and Australian pronunciation, in descending order), while perceiving Hong Kong speakers of English as having higher status than those from the Philippines or mainland China (Chan 2016). In other words, even when the communicative competence of a non-native user of English is unproblematic, the relative judgements about subjective aspects of an interaction tend to be made in favour of the native speaker.

What are the implications of this situation for TESOL? One view is that these inequalities are the inevitable consequence of the use of any lingua franca – some people will always be more skilled in the language than others – but that they are outweighed by the benefits of having a lingua franca. In any event, the status of English as a world language is not a situation created by the field of TESOL; in fact the opposite is closer to the truth. From this pragmatic perspective it has also been suggested that whether the advantages outweigh the costs or not, the status of English is firmly entrenched, and therefore is a reality which cannot be altered and must be accepted.

An alternative position is that because the potential for these inequities is always present, the TESOL community has a responsibility to consider whether to teach English, how to teach it, and which English(es) to teach. Awareness of these critical issues can promote beneficial change. Informed and thoughtful choices can be made about which materials and methods to use in order to bring a diversity of voices into the classroom. Recognising the diversity of Englishes used in the world and bringing them into the TESOL classroom has the potential not only to remove the unrealistic model of the native speaker as the sole target of instruction, but also to tap into the resources which English language learners have as multilinguals. In other words, TESOL can deliver

> a message of hope for students. . . . do not see yourselves as failures always trying to be like native speakers; see yourselves as successes, achieving things as L2 users that are out of the reach of monolinguals.
>
> (Cook 2016: 187–188)

Debates in TESOL

In its relatively short history over the post-World War II period, two issues have been perennial sources of debate: the question of who teaches TESOL, and the related matter of TESOL as a commercial enterprise.

The teachers of TESOL

As noted above, the native-speaker norm has been criticised from several perspectives but it has also proven to have considerable sticking power. Native-speaker status frequently plays an important, indeed sometimes decisive, role in the recruitment of English teachers. Like teachers of all languages, English teachers require a range of skills and knowledge, and one which is essential is the ability to use the target language well. To the extent that using English 'well' has frequently been construed to mean using it like a native speaker, there has been a tendency to view native speakers of English as better equipped to teach the language than non-native speakers. Indeed, a belief in the native-speaker norm is so deeply entrenched that the preference for first-language users of English has frequently gone beyond the qualification 'all other things being equal;' it is not unusual for a native English speaker with few qualifications in language teaching (or none at all) to be selected for a teaching position in preference to another candidate with superior teaching credentials but who is a second-language user of English.

Many TESOL professionals have taken an activist stance, challenging this state of affairs and working for more equitable hiring practices. A body of scholarly literature supports efforts to challenge the prioritising of native speakers. Nonetheless, it remains common, as this vignette illustrates:

> One of my students from a Southeast Asian nation came to my office on the day of her graduation. On a day when she should be full of joy and laughter, she was crying. Instead of rejoicing at the completion of her studies, she was regretting it because she realized that the time had come for her to go home and face the ground reality there. She was one of my best students, full of potential, but still was afraid to return home because English language teaching in her country is the proud privilege of expatriates from the UK and the US. According to her, it is difficult for even well-qualified citizens with foreign degrees to compete with expatriates, and if they do manage to get a job at an institution of their liking, their salary and service conditions are not on par with those of the expatriates, nor do they enjoy the same respect and recognition accorded to native speakers. They are treated as second-class citizens in their native land. I fully understood what my student was saying about her country because, just a few months before her graduation, I was in her country to give a keynote address at a conference. On the first day, just before my talk, there was a function to inaugurate the conference. Sharing the stage with me and other invited speakers were nearly half a dozen office bearers of the association that organized the conference. I looked around—all expatriates, not a single local professional on the stage. The non-natives were, of course, sitting in the audience. It was apparent that they were not running the show in their own country.
>
> (Kumaravadivelu 2016: 68–69)

If native speaker status is not a necessary part of the skill set of an English teacher, what is? Good knowledge of the language is essential, but it must be complemented by metalinguistic knowledge. So, for example, an English teacher needs a good vocabulary, but also an awareness of which vocabulary items are very common, and therefore suitable to introduce to elementary learners, and which are less common and may need to be explained if elementary learners encounter them. Similarly, the fact that 'hook,' meaning a kind of blow in boxing, is related by metonymic association to the physical object called a hook is not something which necessarily needs to be presented to a group of learners in explaining the term, but a teacher who can access that and other semantic relationships has more tools available for understanding what learners need to know about the word and for finding effective ways of presenting it to them. A good foundation in English linguistics is therefore indispensable for an English language teacher. Valuable tools for a teacher include the descriptive tools of syntax, semantics and phonetics and phonology, and approaches to examining language such as discourse analysis and corpus linguistics.

Teachers also need a grounding in how languages are learned. Although a deep understanding of the processes of second-language acquisition is not necessary to be effective in the classroom, such an understanding can often be a valuable resource in making principled pedagogical decisions about what content to introduce, when to introduce it, and how to follow up effectively to consolidate learning.

A related skill set is the ability to manage learning effectively in the classroom and beyond. To keep learners engaged and motivated, teachers need to have a wide range of teaching and learning activities in their tool boxes. Pedagogical skills are also needed outside of the classroom, in planning curriculum, course content and learning objectives, for example, and in designing assessment activities which accurately measure students' attainment of the learning objectives.

In other words, as a discipline within applied linguistics, TESOL is situated at the point at which English studies intersects with applied linguistics, and teachers need skills and knowledge from both domains. This suggests that institutions which provide instruction in TESOL should be highly attuned to recruiting staff with strong backgrounds in both these areas, and promoting their continuing professional development. This, however, is not always the case (e.g., Crookes 1997), and one reason for that is that the salaries which well qualified teachers command are not compatible with the budgetary constraints – or the profit imperative – which is associated with much TESOL instruction.

TESOL as an industry

ELT is big business, and the speed with which TESOL has become such a large enterprise is particularly remarkable. As noted above, as recently as 1961 there was speculation about whether as many as four or five universities in the UK would be interested in training English teachers (McIntosh 1961). Within a very short time, that cautious speculation was shown to be a wild underestimate. As of 2016, the British Council's website listed approximately 40 universities in the UK alone offering degrees in teaching English as a second or foreign language. This large body of institutions preparing teachers is explained by a commensurately large number of courses needing to be staffed: the same website listed 352 universities, language schools or other institutions in the UK offering general English courses. While large, this figure also underestimates the amount of ELT as it does not account for teaching happening on specialised courses, at institutions which are not listed by the British Council, one-on-one lessons provided by individuals not affiliated with an educational institution, etc.

It would be difficult if not impossible to produce similar, accurate figures for the rest of the world, but the situation in the UK is indicative of the fact that TESOL is a large industry, and that is hardly surprising; the estimate of 1.66 billion people who use English as a second or foreign language given at the beginning of this chapter is also an estimate of the number of people who receive, or have received, tuition in English.

Nor does the TESOL industry consist solely of the provision of instruction: a wealth of related products and services exist as well. ELT-related publications are a significant source of revenue for several large international publishers and innumerable smaller ones. For example, the Cambridge University Press ELT catalogue for 2016 (n.d.) was 104 pages long. Its offerings included textbooks for learners ranging in age from pre-primary school to adults; graded readers; exam preparation guides; workbooks for practicing grammar, vocabulary, listening skills, pronunciation, etc.; and professional literature for teachers. According to the annual report of another of the big publishers, English course materials generated £185 million in revenue for the company in 2015 (Pearson 2016).

English language testing is another profitable area of TESOL. Learners frequently need or want to produce an assessment of their English language proficiency, either for a specific purpose, such as showing they meet the entry requirements for a university course, or generally in order to add specificity to a skill listed on a curriculum vitae. A number of organisations administer commercial tests designed to provide scores which allow the relative abilities of test-takers to be compared and benchmarked against statements about what someone with a stated proficiency level can do. Two tests which are used extensively for university admissions are TOEFL and IELTS. Suites of exams like the Cambridge Preliminary, First and Advanced provide tests suitable for a broad range of learner levels. According to the TOEFL website, over 30 million people have taken the TOEFL, and the fee, which varies from one testing centre to another, is around $200, giving an indication of the scale of the revenues generated by English language testing (ETS n.d.).

Unsurprisingly, the major publishers and testing organisations in ELT are based predominantly in English-speaking countries (especially the UK, the US and Australia), and these are also popular destinations for studying English, and popular sources of English teachers. At one level this is unremarkable; Germany is a likely place to look for German textbooks, and France for French textbooks. However, the sheer scope of TESOL means that English is a particularly valuable commodity which is consumed by the entire world, but controlled primarily by just a few countries.

Future directions

Looking to the future, three issues are likely to play a prominent role in the development of TESOL: the way that the use of educational technology is incorporated into TESOL; the extent to which English continues to maintain a prominent status vis à vis other languages; and implications of ELF.

Technology and TESOL

Technological developments have wrought sweeping changes on the educational landscape. Virtually all subjects have felt the impact of these, and TESOL is no exception. Course platforms enable teachers to provide large amounts of supplementary materials and activities to students, including materials created and hosted by other educational institutions, and to engage and interact with students outside of lessons. In the classroom, apps allow students to participate in activities, polls or assessments via their own mobile devices. The development of massive open online courses (MOOCs) means that the shape of the classroom itself is changing; students can attend lectures from all parts of the world. Online courses, such as Duolingo's (n.d) suite of language courses, provide instruction and practice whenever and wherever the learner wants them. Language learning in particular requires a great deal of exposure and practice, and the internet provides this to an extent which language learners in earlier centuries could not imagine. Films, television programmes, books and music can be streamed online or downloaded, allowing varied forms of exposure to the target language. Social media platforms permit interaction in English; in other words, truly authentic communicative activities.

Some technological innovations have now been part of language learning for a considerable time, and have become thoroughly integrated into teaching practice, at least in those parts of the world fortunate enough to have access to them. However, the speed with which innovations occur mean that this situation is subject to change. In a review of technology in language teaching published in 2006, Kern observed that

> the rapid convergence of functionality across digital devices, and our growing reliance on such devices for communication, means we may soon need to refer broadly to information and communication technologies rather than specifically to computers in our research.
>
> (Kern 2006: 185)

It took very little time for that tentative prediction to be realised, and tablets and mobile phones are now frequently used for instructional purposes, and indeed are the devices of preference to a younger generation who see computers as archaic. The potential of future technological developments to change TESOL is considerable.

Will English retain its dominance?

The crucial element sustaining the large TESOL industry described above is the status of English as the pre-eminent global lingua franca, and some question how long English will retain that status. It is easy to find predictions of other languages 'overtaking' English on the basis of the number of speakers they have and are projected to have in the future. Based on figures from the Ethnologue website (Lewis et al. 2016), the 339 million first-language users of English are dramatically outnumbered by the 1,302 million who speak Chinese. Spanish, with 427 million speakers, is also ahead of English, and Arabic, with 267 million, is not far behind.

However, the factors which make it likely that a language will achieve global reach and lingua franca status go beyond the number of people who use it. Commercial importance is another factor, and is part of the reason for Chinese frequently being named as the language most likely to usurp the position of English. The Chinese population is not only large, it has a growing middle class with disposable income; in other words, it has a population of consumers. Much as the French-speaking merchants of the 16th century found it expeditious to be able to communicate with their English customers in English, the desire to tap into the Chinese consumer market may favour those who can communicate in Chinese, thus setting up a situation which could lead to a demand for Chinese speakers, and making Chinese a popular language to learn – possibly more popular than English.

While the logic of this scenario is clear, commercial strength is also clearly not the only driver behind the creation of a world language, as evidenced by the position of Germany as an economic force within Europe in the last part of the 20th century, precisely the time period when the number of pupils studying German in school was decreasing sharply.

If the number of people wishing to learn English were to drop dramatically in favour of another language, that would have an indelible impact on TESOL, but whether this will happen, or what the pace of such a change would be, are at present unanswerable questions.

Will ELF change English?

For the foreseeable future then, English will continue to be widely used around the world. The majority of people who use English in their daily interactions will continue to be those who have a different first language. As the previous section on ELF noted, this sometimes disadvantages L2 users of English. On the other hand, given the number of second-language English speakers, communication in English is frequently between speakers of a variety of languages other than English. In such situations, the ability to make oneself understood and negotiate meaning may advantage the L2 speaker. This has led those who work from an ELF perspective to take the view that it is desirable to distinguish between non-standard features in the English of second-language users which disrupt communication and those which do not. It is those which disrupt communication that become the focus of teaching. This is part of the rationale for denying the native speaker a privileged status: there are many differences between native and non-native speakers of English, but not all of the differences should be regarded as problematic. From this perspective there is a case to be made for cultivating an acceptance of the features of non-native speaker English, such as the omission of the final 's' on third-person singular verbs in the present, or treatment of the countability of nouns. If those features are accepted, then it is possible that as part of the natural process of language change, they may come to be regarded as standard. In other words, there is an argument that the use of English by speakers of other languages may lead to changes in the language itself.

Whether this will come to pass is difficult to predict (for a discussion, see MacKenzie 2015). However, the prospect raises important questions for TESOL: should a focus on accuracy (e.g., standard grammatical forms, word choice, pronunciation) be abandoned in favour of an emphasis on communicative competence? Should textbooks represent non-native usage of English, on the basis that it is most common? Is it meaningful to speak of a non-native variety of English? These are questions which closely relate to key issues in sociolinguistics. Regardless of the answers which are ultimately found for them, the fact that they are being asked opens up an opportunity for TESOL to engage with and feed back into the sociolinguistic curriculum and research agenda, thus allowing TESOL to inform its parent discipline.

In just over half a century, TESOL has established itself, claimed a place within applied linguistics and English language studies, and seen rapid expansion and a degree of commercial impact which is atypical of language teaching generally. It has found itself at the heart of pressing questions about colonialism and its aftermath, globalisation and social equality, and is now positioned to observe the next stage in the development of the English language. The next half century of TESOL promises to be as eventful as the first.

Further reading

Jenkins, J. (2007) *English as a Lingua Franca: Attitude and Identity*. Oxford: Oxford University Press. This book provides an in-depth treatment of issues relating to the use of ELF, which, as discussed above, have significant implications for TESOL.

Nunan, D. (2015) *Teaching English to Speakers of Other Languages: An Introduction*. London: Routledge. This volume, which is aimed at future teachers of English, provides an introduction to key topics in TESOL.

Pennycook, A. (ed.) (1999) 'Special Issue on Critical Issues in TESOL', *TESOL Quarterly* 33 (3). This special issue features articles investigating some of the critical issues described above, and contains an introduction which orients the reader to the critical perspective on TESOL.

Phillipson, R. (1992) *Linguistic Imperialism*. Oxford: Oxford University Press. This book sets the teaching and learning of English, in the context of the dominant status of the English language around the world.

Snow, D. B. (2007) *From Language Learner to Language Teacher: An Introduction to Teaching English as a Foreign Language*. Alexandria, VA: Teachers of English to Speakers of Other Languages (TESOL). This volume provides a resource for English language teachers who have another first language than English.

Related topics

- English and colonialism
- World Englishes: disciplinary debates and future directions
- The relevance of English language studies in higher education
- Literacy in English: literacies in Englishes.

References

Benesch, S. (1996) 'Needs analysis and curriculum development in EAP: An example of a critical approach', *TESOL Quarterly* 30 (4): 723–738.

British Council (2013) *'The English effect: The impact of English, what it's worth to the UK and why it matters to the world'* Available at www.britishcouncil.org/sites/default/files/english-effect-report-v2.pdf.

Cambridge University Press (n.d.) *English Language Teaching 2016*. Cambridge: Cambridge University Press.

Catford, J. C. (1961) 'Training in the teaching of English', in H. G. Wayment (ed.), *English Teaching Abroad and the British Universities: Extracts from the Proceedings of the Conference on University Training and Research in the Teaching of English as a Second/Foreign Language held at Nutford House, London, W1 under the Auspices of the British Council on December 15, 16 and 17*, 1960. London: Methuen, 33–37.

Chan, J. Y. H. (2016) 'A multi-perspective investigation of attitudes towards English accents in Hong Kong: Implications for pronunciation teaching', *TESOL Quarterly* 50 (2): 285–313. DOI 10.1002/tesq.218.

Cook, V. (2016) 'Where is the native speaker now?' *TESOL Quarterly* 50 (1): 186–189. DOI 10.1002/tesq.286.

Crookes, G. (1997) 'What influences what and how second and foreign language teachers teach?' *Modern Language Journal* 81 (2): 67–79.

Crystal, D. (2008) 'Two thousand million?' *English Today* 24 (1): 3–6. DOI 10.1017/S0266078408000023.

Duolingo (n.d.) www.duolingo.com

ETS (Educational Testing Service) (n.d.) '*ETS TOEFL. About the TOEFL ibt test*'. Available at www.ets.org/toefl/ibt/about, accessed 15 February 2017.

European Commission (ed.) (2012) *OCLC: 846980477. First European Survey on Language Competences: Final Report*. Luxembourg: Publishing Office of the European Union.

Firth, J. R. (1961) 'The study and teaching of English at home and abroad', in H. G. Wayment (ed.), *English Teaching Abroad and the British Universities: Extracts from the Proceedings of the Conference on University Training and Research in the Teaching of English as a Second/Foreign Language held at Nutford House, London, W1 under the Auspices of the British Council on December 15, 16 and 17*, 1960. London: Methuen, 11–21.

Gray, J. (2016) 'TESOL and the discipline of English', in A. Hewings, L. Prescott and P. Seargeant (eds), *Futures for English Studies: Teaching Language, Literature and Creative Writing in Higher Education*. Basingstoke: Palgrave, 81–98.

Howatt, A. (1984) *A History of English Language Teaching*. Oxford: Oxford University Press.

Ibrahim, A. E. K. M. (1999) 'Becoming black: Rap and hip-hop, race, gender, identity, and the politics of ESL learning', *TESOL Quarterly* 33 (3): 349–369.

Kern, R. (2006) 'Perspectives on technology in learning and teaching languages', *TESOL Quarterly* 40 (1): 183. DOI 10.2307/40264516.

King, A. H. (1961) 'The nature of the demand for English in the world to-day, as it affects British Universities', in H. G. Wayment (ed.), *English Teaching Abroad and the British Universities: Extracts from the Proceedings of the Conference on University Training and Research in the Teaching of English as a Second/Foreign Language held at Nutford House, London, W1 under the Auspices of the British Council on December 15, 16 and 17*, 1960. London: Methuen, 22–25.

Kumaravadivelu, B. (2016) 'The decolonial option in English teaching: Can the subaltern act?' *TESOL Quarterly* 50 (1): 66–85. DOI 10.1002/tesq.202.

Lewis, M. P., G. F. Simons and C. D. Fennig (eds) (2016) *Ethnologue: Languages of the World*. 19th edn. Dallas, TX: SIL International. Available at www.ethnologue.com, accessed 15 February 2017.

MacKenzie, I. (2015) 'Will English as a lingua franca impact on native English?' in C. Sanchez-Stockhammer (ed.), *Can we Predict Linguistic Change? Studies in Variation, Contact and Change in English*. Helsinki: Varieng. Available at www.helsinki.fi/varieng/series/volumes/16/mackenzie/

McIntosh, A. (1961) 'Contemporary English language and general linguistics', in H. G. Wayment (ed.), *English Teaching Abroad and the British Universities: Extracts from the Proceedings of the Conference on University Training and Research in the Teaching of English as a Second/Foreign Language held at Nutford House, London, W1 under the Auspices of the British Council on December 15, 16 and 17*, 1960. London: Methuen, 26–33.

Oxford English Dictionary (2017) '*Oxford University Press*', Available at www.oed.com, accessed 15 February 2017.

Pearson Plc. (2016). *Focused on Delivery: Pearson Annual Report and Accounts 2015*. London: Pearson.

Pennycook, A. (1994) 'Critical pedagogical approaches to research', *TESOL Quarterly* 28 (4): 690–693.

Pennycook, A. (1999) 'Introduction: Critical approaches to TESOL', *TESOL Quarterly* 33 (3): 329–348.
Phillipson, R. (1992) *Linguistic Imperialism*. Oxford: Oxford University Press.
TESOL International Association (n.d.). '*TESOL interest sections*'. Available at www.tesol.org/connect/interest-sections, accessed 15 February 2017.
Wayment, H. G. (ed.) (1961) *English Teaching Abroad and the British Universities: Extracts from the Proceedings of the Conference on University Training and Research in the Teaching of English as a Second/Foreign Language helt at Nutford House, London, W1 under the Auspices of the British Council on December 15, 16 and 17*, 1960. London: Methuen.

14

English and social identity

Esther Asprey and Robert Lawson

Introduction

Language is a powerful tool for communicating to the world who we are, where we have come from, and even where we want to go in the future. When people speak to one another, judgements are often made about social background, life history, character and more. Sometimes, this link between 'who we are' and how we speak is clear-cut. If you were from the UK and heard a speaker talking about their 'wee pinkie' instead of their 'little finger', you would be confident of placing that speaker as having some sort of Scottish background. Similarly, if you heard a speaker listening to the 'wireless' or describing something as a 'dumpster fire', it is typically going to be the case that one speaker is older and the other younger.

That said, how we speak does not always map neatly onto other aspects of who we are. For example, our sexual orientation, our gender and our social class are not always easily determined just on the basis of our speech. In times of social mobility and diversity, as reflected in much of the late 20th century, the links between how we sound and who we are have become more tenuous (Coulmas 2015: 143). This, of course, does not stop people making inaccurate, imprecise, or socially damaging assumptions about a speaker's character, personality and background.

What underpins all of this is the idea that how we speak, and the linguistic resources that make up our talk, is related to who we are. In other words, when we speak, we are telling the world something about our *identity*. This notion of identity has been a central concern of linguists for the past 50 years (cf. Watt and Llamas 2009; Preece 2016). Linguists are interested in the intersection between language and identity because so much of what we do on a day-to-day basis is about crafting identity through our talk. And how people understand the kinds of identity projects that we undertake has significant implications for how speakers are judged, evaluated and accepted by others.

In this chapter, we examine the concept of identity as it relates to research in English language (with a particular focus on the field of sociolinguistics, perhaps the one sub-area of linguistics which has most enthusiastically taken up issues of identity as they relate to language use). We discuss the methods adopted by linguists in their investigations, in both examining language structure and change and interpreting such structure and change, particularly in the context of interaction. We first give an account of the arrival of identity in linguistics, moving on to outline some of the core issues and topics within language and identity research, ranging from the nature of identity (an often hotly contested term), to the tensions between self-identity and group identity, and to the possibility that both kinds of identity are in play at any given time. We also discuss the tension between viewing identity as something monolithic, unchanging and fixed, to something which is more negotiable, easier to adopt, and easier to shed, drawing on work on indexicality, enregisterment and social meaning (see also Deumert, this volume). We finish by bringing the chapter up to date with an account of some of the latest developments in the field, including stance, multimodality, bi/multi/translanguaging, speech and embodiment, linguistic landscapes, language learning and teaching, and researcher reflexivity.

Historical perspectives on identity – early work

The concept of identity has been of interest to the academic community for quite some time. At the heart of many discussions of identity has been an interrogation of what the term actually covers, and much ink has been spilled over the years debating this point. For example, Edwards (2009: 16) is particularly critical of the 'labyrinthine treatments' of identity in linguistics, while Norris (2011: xiii) makes the point that 'in most of the literature, the notion of identity appears to be fleeting, ephemeral and transitory. Identity appears to be something that we can talk about, but we cannot grasp.' Similarly, Ladilova (2015: 177) argues that there is a 'crisis' in identity work and suggests a number of alternative terms to more finely distinguish the various kinds of social orientations in which people participate, including *commonality*, *connectedness* and *groupness*.

Most contemporary work on language and identity has since adopted a 'social constructionist' approach, where identity is something that speakers *do* rather than something speakers *have*. Influenced by the work of scholars like Judith Butler, this theoretical position was introduced by Eckert and McConnell-Ginet (1992), in what has since come to be one of the most cited papers in sociolinguistics. Although Eckert and McConnell-Ginet's focus was primarily on how language is a key way through which gendered identities are socially constructed, their work sparked a groundswell of research into the relationship between language and other aspects of identity, and particularly how identity is co-constructed through interaction (cf. Bucholtz and Hall 2005).

As Edwards (2009: 14) explains, the earliest conceptions of identity focused on notions of 'groupness' and *sameness* versus *difference* (as we discuss later, definitions of identity end up going beyond these rather binary categories of belonging). This concept of sameness versus difference was to underpin much of the early sociological work about group identity, most notably the programme of research undertaken by Tajfel and Turner (1979). In particular, they were concerned with the question of how and why individuals *identified with* specific groups of people, particularly through the processes of categorisation, social comparison and social differentiation.

Ideas about social differentiation were at the heart of Labov's (1972) influential work on Martha's Vineyard, a popular summer holiday island located off the coast of Massachusetts in the Northeastern USA. This study, which focused on the relationship between code choice and attitudes to place, space, ways of life and other people, investigated the realisation of differently articulated diphthongs in the English of communities on the island. Labov described the effects social, economic and political shifts had on the identity a person wished to adopt, and the way they made this clear through their language, arguing that '[b]y correlating the complex linguistic pattern with parallel differences in social structure, it will be possible to isolate the social factors which bear directly on the linguistic process' (Labov 1972: 1).

In this work, he identified a number of different groups of people on the island, one of which was the fishing community from the Chilmark area. This community formed a tightly-knit social group, set apart from other groups by their occupation and low income level. Furthermore, Labov claimed that the islanders fell broadly into two groups; those who felt a strong allegiance to the island and its way of life, and those whose allegiance was not as strong. Of particular importance in this study was the argument that these groups on the island differed in their linguistic usage, particularly in differing rates of diphthongisation, and that these differences carried social significance (Labov 1972).

The groups which wished to identify strongly with island life viewed groups such as the Chilmark fishermen, together with their linguistic usage, as a reference point. Labov argued that centralised starts to a diphthong correlated with an on-island identity because they were forms associated with the older and less mobile generation who had never left the island. As such, linguistic features could be used to express an identity. Indeed, many of the informants discussed Martha's Vineyard in binary opposition to mainland America. One proposed Vineyard English as a separate variety of English, remarking that 'I think perhaps we use [an] entirely different . . . type of English language . . . [We] think differently here on the island . . . it's almost a separate language within the English language' (Labov 1972: 29). Labov's reporting of speakers' own thoughts on their speech and their social circumstances was innovative, and he used it to feed directly into his explanations of their high levels of use of variants which were 'part of a weaker tendency in the older generation'. Crucially, though, he viewed speakers' choices as unconscious, even though some speakers appeared to recognise at interview that their speech differed from that of mainland America.

From the 1960s onwards, sociolinguists began to grapple with the concept of identity independently of sociological theory, placing language more centrally to proceedings. One key contributor to the field is Hymes (1974), who introduced the idea of the speech community as a way of conceptualising the link between identity and its ramifications for language. For him, the concept of speech community was important because it permitted those within it to have access to *different* 'codes'. Equating one code with a speech community, Hymes argued, removed its methodological usefulness since it stripped the term 'speech community' of its ability to recognise that communities' internal and external boundaries cannot be defined by language alone. Coupland and Thomas (1990) echo this point in their work on Welshness. Though there are those within the Welsh speech community who argue that command of the Welsh language is central to a Welsh identity, many also dispute this. It is the concept of speech community rather than linguistic codes used which is more useful in defining Wales, since as a nation it contains two codes (English and Welsh), one of which is economically and educationally dominant (English) and the other (Welsh) which is arguably declining in use and in influence despite the wishes and efforts of many Welsh speakers. Coupland and Thomas (1990: 3) captured this struggle between language and identity, remarking that 'it is demonstrably the case that minority ethnic groups can, among their own members, adopt quite polarised and often internally very complex positions towards majority languages'. The second wave of sociolinguistics began to address these complex positions theoretically, as we shall see.

Identity becomes agentive – the second wave

The exploration of the notion of speakers making conscious identity choices initially came to the fore in situations where identity and language had previously been conflated and were becoming complicated as colonial forces withdrew from states, in work by creolists like Le Page and Tabouret-Keller (1985), who carried out research in Belize. The country had been the British Crown Colony of British Honduras since 1836, having first been part of the Spanish Empire. It gained independence in 1981 as their work was coming to a close. Creolists work, by definition, in communities where the different codes in play are often discrete and unrelated, rather than being two ends of a continuum (as they are, for example in mainland and Vineyard English). This may have made the concept of speakers actively choosing one variety over another easier to observe. Belize had been subject to Spanish and British influences as well as Creole influences for the sake of everyday communication. The influence of the different countries was just one factor which they claimed influenced the inhabitants' choice of languages, ethnic groups and identities. Many languages, including Spanish, English, Maya, Carib, and Creole, were spoken in Belize in the 1950s, reflecting the ethnic and cultural complexity of the country. Le Page and Tabouret-Keller recorded comments made by those they interviewed concerning identity and language use. The status of Creole was lower than that of Spanish or English due to its origins in the slave trade. Le Page (1992: 75) recorded some 'informants who could not conceal their distaste and regret at "Creole" replacing Spanish as the lingua franca of their District'. During the time that Le Page and Tabouret-Keller conducted fieldwork, attitudes towards certain ethnic groups and languages shifted, and with them, the way speakers identified themselves. Some became less reluctant to identify themselves as Creole speakers, and began to distinguish Creole usage from English usage. A young male informant in the 1970s admitted that he and his siblings 'understand the English but we usually speak Creole. Most useful . . . the Creole' (Le Page 1992: 77).

The results Le Page and Tabouret-Keller discovered led them to formulate the theory that speakers can express identity and solidarity through their language choice, and that speakers behave according to the behavioural patterns of the groups they find it desirable to identify with (Le Page and Tabouret-Keller 1985). They further outlined a series of constraints which they argue govern how and why a particular individual will orientate towards a group (such constraints being that potential members are able to identify the group, have access to the group, and have motivation to join the group). These constraints set the scene for a linguistics which now (at least at the multilingual level) acknowledged the possibility that speakers actively chose for themselves certain varieties in order to identify themselves with, or distance themselves from, other groups of speakers.

From the mid-1990s onwards, research started to move identity theory towards issues of indexicality – that is, what meaning speakers assign to linguistic structures within their own community, and later, second-order reevaluations of that meaning as linguistic forms are reencountered and reevaluated by speakers and listeners (Silverstein 2003). Rather than merely noting that, for example, glottalling in English is something which appears at high levels in working class communities, and labelling glottalling a 'working class' phenomenon, researchers have acknowledged competing evaluations of the social currency of variants. That is to say, they realised that simply imposing categories onto linguistic variants was not enough; that if middle-class speakers use glottal stops, albeit at lower levels than do working class speakers, then it was not enough to label the phenomenon as 'working class' (cf. Trudgill 1974; Lawson 2015). Instead, the motivations of speakers in using glottal stops becomes a subject of enquiry. If, as traditional studies suggested, variants from the lower social scales are seen as socially undesirable, then explaining why middle-class speakers use them at all becomes problematic. Any approach which is to explain linguistic behaviour must account for all linguistic behaviour, however unexpected.

Agentive identity and the 'second wave'

One of the key discussions of English language and identity work is set out in Eckert (2012), where she outlines a framework for structuring developments in variation and identity research over time in the Western world. Eckert discusses what she terms three 'waves' of sociolinguistic study which, she explains, are not 'strictly ordered historically . . . no wave supersedes the previous, rather all three waves are part of a whole. But I think of them as waves because each represents a way of thinking about variation and a methodological and analytic practice that grew out of the findings of the previous one' (Eckert 2005: 1). Each of these waves has had a significant impact on how English Language Studies has developed, both in terms of focus and methodology.

The first wave she examines is typified by large scale, rapid survey work in urban locations like New York City (Labov 1972), Norwich (Trudgill 1974), and Glasgow (Macaulay 1977). This work was influential in laying a framework for the study of variation by establishing broad correlations between linguistic variables and the primary social categories of socio-economic class, sex class and age, particularly for English speakers. Importantly, these studies suggested that socioeconomic status was an important factor in determining language behaviour and identity shaping. They tended to confirm a regular and replicable pattern of socioeconomic stratification of variables, in which the use of non-standard, and geographically and ethnically distinct variants, correlates inversely with socioeconomic status. In Western society, the standard language accrued economic capital, and speakers of all social classes were aware of this and responded to it (although to varying extents).

The advantage of the survey method's 'broad brush' approach is that by using categories identifiable for communities across the Western world – class, gender, age – studies can easily be replicated, and tell us something about the effect of belonging to certain social groups – females, working class, over 60s – on one's language; that is, variables are treated as 'markers of primary social categories . . . carrying class-based prestige/stigma' (Eckert 2005: 3). What eventually pushed those working in the first wave paradigm towards change was the discovery in every community of patterns which went against the accepted model of class-based prestige/stigma (Eckert 2005: 4) and which could not be explained using a traditional Marxist understanding of the concept of class as rooted in conflict, with middle-class status as something to aspire to, and working-class status as something to avoid.

Focusing on the fact that innovation is not usually undertaken by the lowest members of the socioeconomic hierarchy (the lower working class), but by the upper working class and lower middle class, leaves us questioning why the lower working class would choose to continue using high levels of vernacular and stigmatised variants which, according to this model, serve only to perpetuate their status as the lowest in the social hierarchy. Eckert (2005: 10) explains that 'while the vernacular may be stigmatised on a global level, its association with local values and practices gives it positive value on the local level'. This theory was also put forward by other second wave linguists, including Gal (1979) in Oberwart/Felsoör, Austria and Milroy (1980) in Belfast. Milroy (1980: 148) reconciles the first wave approach with that of the second and points out how much more identity work the second approach can uncover in a speaker's choices (see also Mendoza-Denton 2002: 476).

The primary difference between the first and second waves of research, then, is that the second wave has moved on from considering that all style shifts are designed to elevate speakers towards prestigious form of speech and a more coveted identity, and has instead promoted the idea that speakers can wish to identify with other groups considered prestigious and worth indexing through their use of English language *within* their own speech communities. That is, they had moved from the global to a more local focus.

The third wave and beyond – identity linguistics today

The research tradition of the third wave began by shifting away from general categories like age, class and gender towards the concept of the *Community of Practice* (CoP) (cf. Lave and Wenger 1991), which investigates the ties and social practices that bind communities. While researchers involved in its development acknowledge some overlap with the term 'speech community', it has since become clear that the CoP approach has built on, and diverged from, more established sociolinguistic concepts. A key idea put forward by advocates of the CoP approach was that speakers play multiple roles in society, and that although speakers occupy fixed categories such as biological sex and age, they typically belong to more than one social group. Eckert and McConnell-Ginet (1992: 464) define the CoP as

> an aggregate of people who come together around mutual engagement in an endeavor. Ways of doing things, ways of talking, beliefs, values, power relations – in short, practices – emerge in the course of this mutual endeavor. As a social construct, a [CoP] is different from the traditional community, primarily because it is defined simultaneously by its membership and by the practice in which that membership engages.

Eckert's work in the Detroit school she called Belten High (Eckert 1988, 2000) is perhaps the most well-known example of the CoP approach. Drawing on long-term ethnographic fieldwork, coupled with participant interviews, Eckert found that opposition between the 'Jock' group and the 'Burnout' group in Belten High was exemplified by their differing interests, priorities and mutual engagement in social practice among their groups. The Jock group, for example, participated in school-based activities such as after-school clubs and sports societies and was comprised primarily of middle-class students who enjoyed prominence and faculty favour in elementary school (Eckert 1988: 188). The Burnouts, on the other hand, orientated more towards urban Detroit and participated in a range of 'taboo' social practices, including skipping school, drug-taking and under-age drinking. Eckert found that the different CoPs she identified marked their differences in their use of English, with Burnouts using higher levels of variants typical of urban Detroit speakers.

The crucial point about the work conducted within the CoP framework, and what places it in the third wave of English variation studies, is that it sheds light on social fluidity. Within her speaker sample, Eckert found not only differing levels of usage of the linguistic variants she examined among her speakers, but a category of speakers who she termed 'In-betweens'. The pupils classed as 'In-betweens' had levels of use of the Detroit variants which fell below those of the Burnout CoP and above those of the Jock CoP. This finding correlated with the In-betweens' social position as students with, so to speak, a foot in both camps.

The move, then, has been away from the notion of the speaker as a mirror of wider society. This has been replaced by a notion of the empowered speaker, one who possesses choices and agency, a shift that is reflected in much third wave work (Mendoza-Denton 2008; Zhang 2008; Lawson 2011; although see Bell 2016: 402 for a critique of the 'wave' model and the role of agency in sociolinguistic variation). Woolard (1992: 241) explains that Silverstein's explanation of 'language ideology' is that 'ideological tenets are derived from some aspect of experience and then generalized beyond that core and secondarily imposed on a broader category of phenomena' (see also Seargeant, this volume). In other words, communities and speakers may impose ideological frameworks beyond the social structure onto other phenomena such as language. Ironically, through their noticing and rationalising of linguistic phenomena, they may change the social meanings which those linguistic phenomena have first had imposed on them. First-order indexicality is 'the association by social actors of a linguistic form or variety ... with some meaningful social group such as female, Asian, Spanish, working class, aristocratic, and so forth' (Milroy 2004: 167). Second-order indexicality, on the other hand, is a metapragmatic concept, describing the noticing, discussion and rationalisation of first-order indexicality. It is these second-order indexical processes that emerge as ideologies. Crucially, however, language varieties are likely to be differently noticed, rationalised and evaluated from community to community and from nation to nation. In different communities, different varieties are foregrounded, and the kind of people who speak these varieties are differently ideologized. Particular ideologies need to be explained in terms of local histories and local social, political and economic conditions.

The schema of indexicality enables links between the global and the local to be made, and makes the links between the first, second and third waves of variation which Eckert (2005) discussed clearer. If different speaker groups rationalise the same linguistic structures in different ways, then it can be expected that the relationship between linguistic structures and the construction of identity using those linguistic structures will vary between groups of speakers.

Current research directions

As the field of language and identity research has progressed, we have seen the integration of more qualitative approaches, including developments in stance (Jaffe 2009, 2016; Kiesling 2009), bi/multi/translanguaging (Blackledge and Creese 2017), and speech and embodiment (Bucholtz and Hall 2016; Soulaimani 2017). We have also seen language and identity research shift into new contexts of English Language Studies, such as linguistic landscapes (Blackwood et al. 2016), language learning and teaching (Barkhuizen 2017), and reflective accounts of researcher practice (Giampapa 2016). These developments offer more nuanced ways of investigating the intersection between English language and identity.

Stance has been crucial in showing how particular sociolinguistic variants coalesce over time to construct a socially recognisable identity (or *persona*, to use a term from Coupland 2001). Stance, first outlined in Ochs' (1993) seminal article on language socialisation, and further elaborated by Kiesling (2009), Snell (2010) and others, has come to be one of the central tenets of language and identity research in recent years. Drawing on a range of established critical theories, including Peirce's *sign theory*, Silverstein's (2003) notion of *orders of indexicality*, Agha's (2005) work on *enregisterment* and Eckert's (2008) idea of the *indexical field*, stance seeks to explain why speakers adopt particular linguistic variants, how these variants become imbued with social meaning, and how the use of interactional resources become part of identity construction. By interrogating the processes which link the micro (that is, specific grammatical, phonological or lexical linguistic features) with the macro (that is, general social variables like age, class, gender, ethnicity and so on), it is possible to show the paths through which language comes to mean something beyond its denotational referent.

In relation to identity construction in speech, Kiesling (2009: 172) notes, stance is 'a person's expression of their relationship to their talk', categorised into *epistemic* (a speaker's relational orientation towards their own talk, e.g. confident, unsure etc.) and *interpersonal* (a speaker's relational orientation towards their interlocutor, e.g. friendly, threatening, etc.). By combining these elements, speakers can establish different stances towards their talk, such as flirting, arguing, agreeing, sympathising, questioning, (dis)affiliating, through to more specific and interactionally bound stances like 'cool' masculinity (Kiesling 2004) or the expression of cultural elitism by British newspaper journalists (Jaworski and Thurlow 2009). As such, there is a link between stance and personal/collective *styles*, where 'stancetaking is the main constitutive social activity that speakers engage in when both creating a style and "style-shifting"' (Kiesling 2009: 175).

While recent research has focused on how stance is an interactional resource for the construction of self-identity, Coupland and Coupland (2009: 229) have argued that more attention be paid to the other side of the interaction, rather than solely to the analysis of *authorial identity*. For example, they suggest that utterances like 'you must be lying' and 'you must be thinking' are strategies for speakers to do *other stance attribution*, and by extension discursively construct their interlocutor's identity. This kind of treatment of stance moves us towards a fuller consideration of the dialogic nature of conversation and how issues of power, hierarchy and asymmetry are bound up with the kinds of identity projects in which interlocutors are engaged.

Other work has also moved analysis beyond the immediate speaker context, focusing on multimodal communication and the non-discursive elements of an interaction (see Ravelli, this volume). Goodwin (2007), in particular, has been a key figure in promoting the use of audiovisual methods within linguistic anthropology and sociolinguistics to investigate English language use and identity, an approach also forwarded by, for example, Norris (2011). Audiovisual recordings have also recently been used in Podesva et al. (2015) to explore the relationship between positive/negative affect and vowel fronting, suggesting productive means to investigate sociophonetic variation in conjunction with visually communicative elements like smiling.

This work has led to calls to think more explicitly about the role of the body in language and identity work, explored more fully in research on embodiment (Bucholtz and Hall 2016; Mondada 2016), gesture (Müller et al. 2013) and materiality (Irvine 2017). While a focus on embodiment may seem to move us away from English language, Bucholtz and Hall (2016: 188) argue that attending to bodily praxis (aspects like gaze, hand movements, body position, bodily presentation and so on) furthers our understanding of indexicality, discourse and agency, all integral elements of identity construction/production in language use. Indeed, Fairclough (2003: 159) makes the prescient point that 'who you are is partly a matter of how you speak, how you write, as well as a matter of embodiment–how you look, how you hold yourself, how you move, and so forth'.

Fairclough's observation has since been taken up in a variety of work, and researchers are now starting to tackle the question of how the physical body is implicated in conversational interaction, drawing on approaches in kinesiology, biomechanics, physiology and anatomy. For example, Mendoza-Denton et al. (2017) examine the intersection of the body and materiality through the analysis of the language of a group of gamers who are connected to devices which measure electrodermal activity (EDA), where higher sweat levels caused by either physical or physiological stimuli lead to increased skin conductivity. Their analysis concentrates on a moment during a multiplayer game of Mario Party 8 where two of the male gamers (Bob and Ross) use a Wii-mote controller to simulate male masturbation. Not only do Ruth and Joey's accompanying speech, bodily movements and eye gaze show disaffiliation with the joke, Joey has a demonstrable negative psychophysiological EDA response, a finding the authors argue is the result of 'second-hand sexism', whereby 'sexism and exclusion are felt not only by the target, but also physiologically by aligned bystanders/overhearers, a reflection of the sort of processes that Bell (1984) identified as overhearer effects' (Mendoza-Denton et al. 2017: 568).

The analysis shows how such inclusionary/exclusionary stances can reify existing social inequalities and thus contribute to ongoing constructions of gender. This analysis is augmented through measuring bodily responses to external stimuli, gaze and body positioning, alongside attention to ongoing interactional processes. Indeed, there is substantial potential for integrating physical and physiological measurements alongside the analysis of ongoing talk-in-interaction in future linguistic research of all kinds, particularly in collaboration with psychology, physiology, biology and other fields concerned with the examination of the body.

Mendoza-Denton et al. (2017) also call into question the divide between technology and body, a point similarly raised by Bucholtz and Hall (2016: 186–188), who suggest that technology 'changes not only the way we interact but also our sense of self'. This integration of technology (in large and small ways) as an aspect of identity in our everyday lives has variously been taken up by a range of scholars, including those working in the fields of multilingualism and translanguaging (see Otheguy et al. 2015: 281). These are particularly prescient in English Language Studies, as statuses of different varieties of English vary (see Bolton, García and Lin, and Higgins and Furukawa, this volume). Schreiber (2015) focuses on the digital translanguaging practices of a Serbian university student (Aleksander) as he uses Facebook. Through his strategic deployment of multiple linguistic codes drawn from English, Serbian and African American Vernacular English, embedding these elements of discourse into a new context and giving them new social meanings, Aleksander uses Facebook as a multimodal site to construct his identity not only as Serbian, but also as a member of a global hip-hop community. As Schreiber (2015: 70) points out, 'students' digital literacy practices in English, involving high levels of code-mixing, invented spellings and transliterations, and other forms of linguistic creativity, express new, often hybrid identities'. Moreover, Aleksander's use of multiple digital affordances demonstrates how the artificial divisions between languages can be unified as part of a holistic semiotic repertoire, furthering our understanding of how strategic linguistic diversity can be deployed as a way of bridging local and global contexts.

While language and identity research has existed in its traditional enclaves, we are now starting to see more attention to issues of identity in areas of research where it has typically been overlooked. For example, the collected chapters in Blackwood et al. (2016) show how our understanding of dynamic linguistic landscapes can be augmented by attending to identity and agency, while Tufi and Blackwood (2015) focus on how in transcultural spaces normative, transgressive and subversive acts of identity are performed and embedded (with particular reference to Italian and French coastal cities). Particularly relevant in the recent global context of increasing political and social upheaval, Said and Kasanga (2016) show how civil protest in the Arab Spring Revolution is bound up with identities that encompass national, patriotic and revolutionary elements. Similar issues are investigated by Brannick (2016), who offers an analysis of historical and contemporary bilingual signs, monuments and other geosemiotic resources in relation to language, identity, hegemony and the production of social space in northern Italy, demonstrating how these signs and monuments become sites of contestation between speakers of Italian and German. All of this work shows how personal, political and national identities are constructed both by self-authored talk and through the language practices that are inscribed in the world around us.

There has also been an uptake of language and identity perspectives by researchers in language learning and teaching, an area which typically has not engaged with the role of identity. Martel and Wang (2014: 290) point out that 'language teachers' identities are shaped in interaction with significant others, personal biographies and contexts' and argue that such interactions can have important ramifications for teaching style, approach to language content and the construction of professional identity. By way of evidence, they cite a number of examples of teachers whose pedagogical practice was fundamentally shaped by their personal histories and experiences, from one teacher who avoided using a particular French grammar book because he disliked learning from it in high school, to a Chinese-speaking teacher of English in a TESOL (Teaching English to Speakers of Other Languages) class whose status as a non-native speaker was raised as a problem for teaching English (Martel and Wang 2014: 291). Barkhuizen (2017) develops this strand of Language Teacher Identity research in a wide-ranging set of narrative reflections from 41 language teaching practitioners and academics. For example, Donato (2017) argues that examining, discussing and reflecting on how language teachers construct their own professional identities not only humanises teacher education by moving the focus away from learning processes and policies, but also helps teachers improve their practice and facilitate teacher resilience over the course of their career.

Similar kinds of reflective accounts of practice have made their way into other strands of English language research, particularly in terms of examining researcher influence on identity projects, a research trajectory which builds on existing work in linguistic ethnography and linguistic anthropology (see Mendoza-Denton 2008: 43–49). Who we are as researchers cannot be untangled from the research we do and being an objective observer while conducting linguistic research in a social context is difficult, if not impossible. Researchers fundamentally influence what happens in their research site, particularly in ethnographic fieldwork. Furthermore, a researcher will always have an effect on the kinds of topics that are discussed, the kinds of relationships that are developed, and the kinds of speech events that occur. While it can be tempting to simply ignore the difficulties that researcher positionality brings, recent research argues that this is a misguided approach. In a wide-ranging discussion concerning data collection, analysis and interpretation, Giampapa (2016) highlights the benefits that can be accrued through a critical examination of the role of the researcher, including methodological robustness, improved triangulation of research findings, and the development of new forms of research reporting (such as research vignettes and audio recordings of team research meetings). Kirkham and Mackey (2016) also show how attention to the role of the researcher in the co-production of data can lead to further insights into how particular sociolinguistic variants pattern in a community (in the case of Kirkham's research, how the happY vowel was used among male and female adolescent speakers with pro/anti-school orientations).

Future directions

In the context of growing international instability, more attention is being given to issues of belonging and community (as evidenced in recent debates surrounding the UK's decision to leave the EU), and there is ever-increasing media attention on the intersection of sex, gender, power and language. In this section, we sketch out three main areas we believe will be productive research avenues in identity as it relates to English language over the next five to ten years. We should note, though, that this list is not at all exhaustive. English Language Studies moves quickly and new approaches, methods and theories could come along which shift the field in ways that we cannot predict.

First, as noted above, stance, affect and social meaning are now core concepts in English language and identity research. While much of this work examines face-to-face interaction, there is potential for this intersection to be explored in new online contexts, particularly through the lens of digital messaging services (Sánchez-Moya and Cruz-Moya 2015), social media (Tagg et al. 2017) and online gaming (Collister 2013; Newon 2015). As these online elements become more integrated into our everyday lives, and as new online industries such as e-sports come into the mainstream, questions will emerge on the influence such technologies will have on our communicative practices, how interaction is managed and negotiated in online contexts and how we use these disparate technological resources to do identity work.

The second area of future research is concerned with the role of language in mediating and constructing conceptualisations of national identity, belonging, and community. Scholars have been interested in these issues for some time (Edwards 2009), but the rise of right-wing politics, Brexit, and increased attention to religious fundamentalism and online radicalisation, means that how people position themselves in relation to the their local community, the nation state and beyond will continue to be a major focus for English language researchers. This includes arguments over who gets to claim membership of local communities and adopt particular national identities and how these national identities are policed. Further, the extent to which membership of these communities is dictated by linguistic performance will continue to be of interest to linguists, including how linguistic discrimination plays out in superdiverse contexts. And finally, how 'radicalised' identities constructed is likely to remain an important topic as long as terrorism continues to dominate news and media.

Third, a focus on gender politics is likely to continue as a central focus in English language and identity, given the position it occupies in modern-day society, both in online and offline contexts. For example, the analysis of hashtags like #notbossy, #mansplaining, #metoo and more sheds light on the ways in which language is implicated in the maintenance of gender relations in online spaces, while research on toxic masculinities (Hess and Flores 2016) and the language of sexual harassment (Bailey 2017) is becoming increasingly important, particularly amid contemporary debates about gender roles, privilege, and power. We expect that such research will continue to make key contributions concerning the linguistic practices of men, women and non-binary individuals and particularly how language is used to do relational work within and across these groups.

Conclusion

Research in English language and identity has furthered our understanding of some of the key questions in linguistics – why do speakers adopt particular patterns of use? How are these patterns of use inflected with social meanings at a local and a global level? And, to come back to one of the points made at the outset of this chapter, how are these patterns of use ultimately part of a speaker's semiotic repertoire to show the world 'who they are'? While we are now closer to having the answers to some of these questions, there remain outstanding areas for further investigation, particularly in terms of cross- and interdisciplinary research on language and identity. Indeed, the integration of insights from a variety of analytical and theoretical perspectives will not only allow us to investigate how language is part of identity construction/production, but also how language is bound up with other aspects of being.

Further reading

Blackwood, R., E. Lanza and H. Woldemariam (eds) (2016) *Negotiating and Contesting Identities in Linguistic Landscapes*. London: Bloomsbury. This volume sets out a number of explorations of identities in different socioeconomic, political and cultural contexts. Of particular interest to the contributing authors is how linguistic landscapes – rural/urban, public/private, open/institutional – become places where identities are managed, negotiated and contested, drawing on the analysis of protest signs, street art, football banners, monuments and public signs.

Nortier, J. and Svendsen, B. (eds) (2015) *Language, Youth, and Identity in the 21st Century*. Cambridge: Cambridge University Press. This volume presents research which tackles issues of identity, representation and community among young people in the 21st century. Drawing on data and speakers from a range of international cities in Africa, Canada, Europe and the USA, the chapters deal with questions of contemporary language use, including the effects of social media on language use, the processes of linguistic differentiation, hybridisation and homogenisation in communities of young speakers, and the interplay between local and global linguistic resources.

Preece, S. (ed.) (2016) *The Routledge Handbook of Language and Identity*. London: Routledge. This handbook covers the history of identity theory as it relates to linguistics and brings us up to the present day, examining identity in multilingual communities and on the internet. It includes chapters by key authors such as John Earl Joseph and Tope Omoniye, as well as case studies of gender, class, and religion.

Related topics

- Contact Englishes
- Language, gender and sexuality
- Sociolinguistics: studying English and its social relations
- Linguistic ethnography: studying English language, cultures and practices.

References

Agha, A. (2005) 'Voice, footing, enregisterment', *Journal of Linguistic Anthropology* 15 (1): 38–59.

Bailey, B. (2017) 'Greetings and compliments or street harassment? Competing evaluations of street remarks in a recorded collection', *Discourse and Society* 28 (4): 353–373.

Barkhuizen, G. (ed.) (2017) *Reflections on Language Teacher Identity Research*. London: Routledge.

Bell, A. (2016) 'Succeeding waves: Seeking sociolinguistic theory for the twenty-first century' in N. Coupland (ed.), *Sociolinguistics: Theoretical Debates*. Cambridge: Cambridge University Press, 391–416.

Blackledge, A. and A. Creese (2017) 'Translanguaging in mobility', in S. Canagarajah (ed.), *The Routledge Handbook of Migration and Language*. London: Routledge, 31–46.

Blackwood, R., E. Lanza and H. Woldemariam (eds) (2016) *Negotiating and Contesting Identities in Linguistic Landscapes*. London: Bloomsbury.

Brannick, P. J. (2016) *Bilingualism in Bolzano-Bozen: A Nexus Analysis* (Unpublished doctoral dissertation, University of Birmingham).

Bucholtz, M. and K. Hall (2005) 'Identity and interaction: A sociocultural linguistic approach', *Discourse Studies* 7 (4–5): 585–614.

Bucholtz, M. and K. Hall (2016) 'Embodied sociolinguistics', in N. Coupland (ed.), *Sociolinguistics: Theoretical Debates*. Cambridge: Cambridge University Press, 173–200.

Collister, L. B. (2013) *Multimodality as a Sociolinguistic Resource* (Unpublished doctoral dissertation, University of Pittsburgh).

Coulmas, F. (2015) *The Study of Speakers' Choices*. 2nd edn. Cambridge: Cambridge University Press.

Coupland, N. (2001) 'Dialect stylization in radio talk', *Language in Society* 30 (3): 345–375.

Coupland, N. and J. Coupland (2009) 'Attributing stance in discourses of body shape and weight loss', in A. Jaffe (ed.), *Stance: Sociolinguistic Perspectives*. Oxford: Oxford University Press, 227–250.

Coupland, N. and A. Thomas (eds) (1990) *English in Wales*. Clevedon: Multilingual Matters.

Donato, R. (2017) 'Becoming a language teaching professional: What's identity got to do with it?' in G. Barkhuizen (ed.), *Reflections on Language Teacher Identity Research*. London: Routledge, 24–30.

Eckert, P. (1988) 'Adolescent social structure and the spread of linguistic change', *Language in Society* 17 (2): 183–207.

Eckert, P. (2000) *Language Variation as Social Practice: The Linguistic Construction of Identity in Belten High*. Oxford: Wiley-Blackwell.

Eckert, P. (2005) Variation, convention, and social meaning. Paper presented at the Annual Meeting of the Linguistic Society of America, 6–9 January, Oakland, California.

Eckert, P. (2008) 'Variation and the indexical field', *Journal of Sociolinguistics* 12 (4): 453–476.

Eckert, P. (2012) 'Three waves of variation study: The emergence of meaning in the study of sociolinguistic variation', *Annual Review of Anthropology* 41: 87–100.

Eckert, P. and S. McConnell-Ginet (1992) 'Think practically and look locally: Language and gender as community-based practice', *Annual Review of Anthropology* 21: 461–490.
Edwards (2009) *Language and Identity*. Cambridge: Cambridge University Press.
Fairclough (2003) *Analysing Discourse: Textual Analysis for Social Research*. London: Psychology Press.
Gal, S. (1979) *Language Shift: Social Determinants of Linguistic Change in Bilingual Austria*. San Francisco: Academic Press.
Giampapa, F. (2016) 'The politics of researcher identities: Opportunities and challenges in identities research', in S. Preece (ed.), *The Routledge Handbook of Language and Identity*. London: Routledge.
Goodwin, C. (2007) 'Participation, stance and affect in the organization of activities', *Discourse and Society* 18 (1): 53–73.
Hess, A. and C. Flores (2016) 'Simply more than swiping left: A critical analysis of toxic masculine performances on Tinder Nightmares', *New Media and Society* 1461444816681540.
Hymes, D. (1974) *Foundations in Sociolinguistics: An Ethnographic Approach*. Philadelphia: University of Pennsylvania Press.
Irvine, J. T. (2017) 'Afterword: Materiality and language, or material language? Dualisms and embodiments', in J. Cavanaugh and S. Shankar (eds), *Language and Materiality: Ethnographic and Theoretical Explorations*. Cambridge: Cambridge University Press, 277–294.
Jaffe, A. (ed.) (2009) *Stance: Sociolinguistic Perspectives*. Oxford: Oxford University Press.
Jaffe, A. (2016) 'Indexicality, stance and fields in sociolinguistics', in N. Coupland (ed.), *Sociolinguistics: Theoretical Debates*. Cambridge: Cambridge University Press, 86–112.
Jaworski, A. and C. Thurlow (2009) 'Taking an elitist stance', in A. Jaffe (ed.), *Stance: Sociolinguistic Perspectives*. Oxford: Oxford University Press, 195–226.
Kiesling, S. F. (2004) 'Dude', *American Speech* 79 (3): 281–305.
Kiesling, S. F. (2009) 'Style as stance: Stance as the explanation for patterns of sociolinguistic variation', in A. Jaffe (ed.), *Stance: Sociolinguistic Perspectives*. Oxford: Oxford University Press, 171–194.
Kirkham, S. and A. Mackey (2016) 'Research, relationships and reflexivity: Two case studies of language and identity', in P. Costa (ed.), *Ethics in Applied Linguistics Research*. London: Routledge, 103–120.
Labov, W. (1972) *Sociolinguistic Patterns*. Philadelphia: University of Pennsylvania Press.
Ladilova, A. (2015) 'Language and identity of migrants: The role of the heritage language in the process of collective identity construction in a migration situation', in R. Săftoiu (ed.), *Constructing and Negotiating Identity in Dialogue*. Amsterdam: John Benjamins, 176–193.
Lave, J. and E. Wenger (1991) *Situated Learning: Legitimate Peripheral Participation*. Cambridge: Cambridge University Press.
Lawson, R. (2011) 'Patterns of linguistic variation among Glaswegian adolescent males', *Journal of Sociolinguistics* 15 (2): 226–255.
Lawson, R. (2015) 'Fight narratives, covert prestige and performances of "tough" masculinity: Some insights from an urban centre', in T. Milani (ed.), *Language and Masculinities: Performances, Intersections, Dislocations*. London: Routledge, 53–76.
Le Page, R. (1992) '"You can never tell where a word comes from": Language contact in a diffuse setting', in E. Jahr (ed.), *Language Contact: Theoretical and Empirical Studies*. Berlin: Mouton de Gruyter, 71–102.
Le Page, R. and A. Tabouret-Keller (1985) *Acts of Identity: Creole-based Approaches to Language and Ethnicity*. Cambridge: Cambridge University Press.
Macaulay, R. (1977) *Language, Social Class and Education: A Glasgow Study*. Edinburgh: Edinburgh University Press.
Martel, J. and A. Wang (2014) 'Language teacher identity' in M. Bigelow and J. Ennser-Kananen (eds.), *The Routledge Handbook of Educational Linguistics*, Oxon: Routledge, 289–300.
Mendoza-Denton, N. (2002) 'Language and identity', in J. K. Chambers, P. Trudgill and N. Schilling-Estes (eds), *The Handbook of Language Variation and Change*. Oxford: Blackwell Publishing Ltd., 475–499.
Mendoza-Denton, N. (2008) *Home Girls. Language and Cultural Practice among Latina Youth Gangs*. Malden: Blackwell.
Mendoza-Denton, N., S. Eisenhauer, W. Wilson and C. Flores (2017) 'Gender, electrodermal activity, and videogames: Adding a psychophysiological dimension to sociolinguistic methods', *Journal of Sociolinguistics* 21 (4): 547–575.

Milroy, L. (1980) *Language and Social Networks*. Oxford: Blackwell.
Milroy, L. (2004) 'Language ideologies and linguistic change', in C. Fought (ed.), *Sociolinguistic Variation: Critical Reflections*. Oxford: Oxford University Press, 161–177.
Mondada, L. (2016) 'Challenges of multimodality: Language and the body in social interaction', *Journal of Sociolinguistics* 20 (3): 336–366.
Müller, C., A. Cienki, E. Fricke, S. Ladewig, D. McNeill and S. Teßendorg (eds) (2013) *Body – Language – Communication: An International Handbook on Multimodality in Human Interaction*. Berlin: De Gruyter Mouton.
Newon, L. (2015) 'Online multiplayer games', in A. Georgakopoulou and T. Spilioti (eds), *The Routledge Handbook of Language and Digital Communication*. London: Routledge, 289–304.
Norris, S. (2011) *Identity in (Inter)action: Introducing Multimodal (Inter)action Analysis*. Berlin: Mouton De Gruyter.
Ochs, E. (1993) 'Constructing social identity: A language socialization perspective', *Research on Language and Social Interaction* 26 (3): 287–306.
Otheguy, R., O. García and W. Reid (2015) 'Clarifying translanguaging and deconstructing named languages: A perspective from linguistics', *Applied Linguistics Review* 6 (3): 281–307.
Podesva, R. J., P. Callier, R. Voigt and D. Jurafsky (2015) 'The connection between smiling and GOAT fronting: Embodied affect in sociophonetic variation', *Proceedings of the International Congress of Phonetic Sciences* 18. Available at https://nlp.stanford.edu/pubs/ICPHS0343.pdf.
Said, S. and B. Kasanga (2016) 'The discourse of protest: Frames of identity, intertextuality, and interdiscursivity', in R. Blackwood, E. Lanza and H. Woldemariam (eds), *Negotiating and Contesting Identities in Linguistic Landscapes*. London: Bloomsbury, 71–83.
Sánchez-Moya, A. and O. Cruz-Moya (2015) '"Hey there! I am using WhatsApp": A preliminary study of recurrent discursive realisations in a corpus of WhatsApp statuses', *Procedia-Social and Behavioral Sciences* 212: 52–60.
Schreiber, B. R. (2015) '"I am what I am": Multilingual identity and digital translanguaging'. *Language Learning and Technology* 19 (3): 69–87.
Silverstein, M. (2003) 'Indexical order and the dialectics of social life', *Language and Communication* 23 (3): 193–229.
Snell, J. (2010) 'From sociolinguistic variation to socially strategic stylisation', *Journal of Sociolinguistics* 14 (5): 630–656.
Soulaimani, D. (2017) 'Embodiment in Moroccan Arabic storytelling: Language, stance and discourse analysis', *Text and Talk* 37 (3): 335–357.
Tagg, C., P. Seargeant and A. Brown (2017) *Taking Offence on Social Media: Conviviality and Communication on Facebook*. Basingstoke: Palgrave Macmillan.
Tajfel, H. and J. Turner (1979) 'An integrative theory of intergroup conflict', in W. G. Austin and S. Worchel (eds), *The Social Psychology of Intergroup Relations*. Monterey, CA: Brooks/Cole Publishing Company, 33–47.
Trudgill, P. (1974) *The Social Differentiation of English in Norwich*. Cambridge: Cambridge University Press.
Tufi, S. and R. Blackwood (2015) *The Linguistic Landscape of the Mediterranean French and Italian Coastal Cities*. London: Palgrave Macmillan.
Watt, D. and C. Llamas (eds) (2009) *Language and Identities*. Edinburgh: Edinburgh University Press.
Woolard, K. A. (1992) 'Language ideology: Issues and approaches', *Pragmatics* 2 (3): 235–249.
Zhang, Q. (2008) 'Rhotacization and the "Beijing Smooth Operator": The social meaning of a linguistic variable', *Journal of Sociolinguistics* 12 (2): 201–222.

15

Language, gender and sexuality

Melissa Yoong

Introduction

Language and gender is a rapidly expanding field within the larger study of sociolinguistics. Although language and gender studies are not always feminist in orientation, this is an area of academic enquiry with feminist roots, emerging in the early 1970s, possibly as a result of the women's liberation movements. While work on gender and the English language had existed prior to this, it was during this period that the interface between language and gender began to be examined in a systematic way (Mills and Mullany 2011), often with a political purpose. The majority of language and gender studies today continues to share the political goal of gender equality. While researchers are united by emancipatory aims, there is now a broad spectrum of research in a wide range of social contexts from a variety of theoretical positions.

This chapter will commence with a broad overview of early research that looked for differences between women's and men's language use, before turning to leading current perspectives that place emphasis on agency and diversity in the linguistic construction of gender identities. It will then discuss two crucial lines of inquiry within scholarly work applying these contemporary theoretical frameworks: how women leaders negotiate their professional identities through the use of language, and the various ways masculinities are linguistically constructed and inflected by sexuality. Following this, there will be a discussion of selected areas of debate, in particular those relating to the interactional salience of gender, and the use of the masculine/feminine dichotomy in the analysis of speech styles. The final section will put forward a series of recommendations for future language and gender research concerning the topics and issues examined in the chapter.

Early approaches and pioneering research

The main theoretical frameworks in early language and gender research are commonly known as the deficit, dominance and difference approaches (see Talbot 2010). While these paradigms are useful for tracing the field's chronological advancements, empirical work often drew on elements from more than one approach, and some did not fall under any particular theoretical category (Mullany 2010). Initial studies were driven by feminist concerns regarding the sociopolitical disparities between the sexes, and aimed to reveal the social subordination of women that was reflected in their linguistic subordination. Lakoff's (1975) *Language and Woman's Place* hypothesises that there is a distinct 'women's language' characterised by a lack of confidence, superpoliteness and weakness, mirroring women's subordinate status in society. This account is largely based on anecdotal observations, and unintentionally reinforces stereotypes and the deficit model of women's speech. Nevertheless, it was valuable as a springboard for academic research in the 1970s and 1980s that analysed the linguistic features of 'women's language', such as affective adjectives, hedges and tag questions.

Like *Language and Woman's Place*, Spender's (1980) *Man Made Language* focuses on differences between women's and men's language use. The theme of male dominance is central to this work, and its fundamental claim is that the English language is literally man-made and manifests a patriarchal social order. The book popularised the study of language and gender, and introduced a large audience to conventionalised sexism in the English language, highlighting examples such as male generics. However, it was widely criticised for its determinist notion of the relationship between language and reality as well as its highly monolithic view of language, male power and gender relations (see Black and Coward 1981).

Feminist linguists argued against the negative portrayal of women's language as weak and women as victims, and in the 1980s, research began to take a new perspective that conceived the differences in male and female language patterns not as male oppression of women, but as a 'cross-cultural' phenomenon arising from the single-sex sociolinguistic subcultures in which women and men are socialised as children. This 'two cultures approach' was initiated by Maltz and Borker (1982), who reinterpreted interactional difficulties between the sexes in earlier studies as miscommunication due to differing expectations of discourse. This offered linguists a way to conduct research beyond a dominance and oppression framework, and to celebrate 'women's talk'. Tannen (1991) adopted Maltz and Borker's explanatory framework in the bestseller *You Just Don't Understand*, in which she polarised and stereotyped women's and men's conversational styles, claiming, for example, that women look for intimacy through conversation, whereas men seek status. Tannen carefully maintained a neutral position, and received strong criticism for disregarding broader sociopolitical considerations and power asymmetries in gender relationships (Cameron 1992). The cross-cultural communication analogy was also questioned since women and men share linguistic worlds, including as children (Troemel-Ploetz 1991).

Contemporary approaches

While early research differentiated gender (learned behaviour) from sex (biologically based), 'the latter [was] implicitly assumed to provide the grounding for the former', resulting in the polarisation of women and men into homogenous groups (Cameron 2005: 484). Current investigations into language and gender predominantly adopt social-constructionist perspectives, which regard gender as something people do rather than have. The paradigm shift, observed in the 1990s, was influenced by Butler's (1990) model of performativity, which represents gender as dynamic, fluid and performatively constituted in interaction, rather than an inherent trait. Individuals are constantly negotiating and renegotiating their social identities, including their gender identity, and one of the ways of producing themselves as gendered beings is through their linguistic practices. In this sense, linguistic behaviour does not arise from a pre-existing gender identity, but rather, it is through repeated linguistic acts over time that gender identities are produced. However, while these practices are not automatically determined by biological sex, they are also not freely chosen, but constrained and conditioned by 'a rigid regulatory frame' (Butler 1990: 33). Deeply rooted social expectations of gender behaviour affect how an individual speaks in a particular context, and the 'masculine' and 'feminine' speech styles identified in research can be conceived as the congealed result of repeated enactments of what is considered socially acceptable gender identity (Cameron 1997). At the same time, Butler emphasises the individual's agency and ability to subvert societal norms and forces, sometimes with negative consequences.

Eckert and McConnell-Ginet's (1992) Communities of Practice framework complements the performativity model as it not only views gender as something that emerges from interaction, but also reconnects language use to social practices in local communities. Eckert and McConnell-Ginet (1999: 186) define a community of practice (CofP) as 'an aggregate of people who, united by a common enterprise, develop and share ways of doing things, ways of talking, beliefs, and values: in short, practices'. This framework allows analyses to be more sensitive to situation-specific expectations of linguistic behaviour and localised language patterns, and their relationship to the distinct and diverse gender identities constructed.

Two important theoretical developments bridge local language practices with the wider gender order, and are often integrated with the performativity approach and the CofP framework: Ochs's (1990, 1992) theory of 'indexicality', and the notion of gendered discourses (Sunderland 2004). Ochs argues that few lexical items have a direct indexical relationship with gender. On the other hand, manhood or womanhood tend to be indirectly indexed through language features that carry gendered meaning due to regular association with men or women. In order to interpret a speech pattern as indexing maleness or femaleness, the sociocultural context must be considered. Discourses, in this chapter, refer to 'practices that systematically form the objects of which they speak' (Foucault 1972: 49). 'Gendered discourses' can be seen as systems that 'carry' ideology and regulate gendered behaviour in society (Sunderland 2004: 3). Gendered discourses, such as the persistent discourse of gender differences, both constitute and are constituted by the social world.

The emphasis on context and local meanings has moved feminist linguistics from stereotyping male and female speech patterns to taking into account how the interlocutors' various social attributes, such as ethnicity, age, religion and social class, operate together with gender in complex ways to produce their linguistic behaviour. Within this approach, termed 'intersectionality', identity is viewed not only as dynamic, but also as multidimensional, where different facets of social identity are instantiated and indexed via the use of language.

Current critical issues and topics

Language and women's leadership in professional settings

Language and gender studies largely have feminist intentions and aim to redress the gender disparities in society that are reflected in, and perpetuated by, language use. One significant aspect of gender inequality that continues to receive a great deal of attention in this field has been the lack of women in leadership roles in professional contexts, often referred to as the 'glass ceiling'. Although there has been an increasing number of female leaders in the workplace in recent decades, women's advancement still lags behind that of their male counterparts, and language is a powerful contributing factor behind the under-representation of women at leadership level (Baxter 2008).

Leadership discourse has two important functions: to promote organisational goals (transactional behaviour) and maintain good working relationships within the team (relational behaviour). Transactional behaviours that 'primarily aim at getting things done, solving problems and achieving set goals' are typically indexed for masculinity, whereas more relational practices that focus on 'ensuring group harmony and creating a productive working environment' are ascribed to femininity. In other words, the language and performance of leadership are gendered (Schnurr and Mak 2011: 348), despite growing evidence that women and men leaders utilise both stereotypical 'masculine' and 'feminine' linguistic behaviour, depending on their interactional context and aims (e.g. Holmes 2006; Mullany 2007). Holmes (2005: 49) argues that these 'gendered discourse patterns typically emphasise the power of the male, and underline the supportive role of the female in workplace interaction'.

In many workplaces, it is stereotypical 'masculine' discourse strategies, such being direct, assertive and outcome-oriented (Holmes and Stubbe 2003) that tend to be associated with leadership. Women moving into professional contexts where normatively masculine speech styles predominate sometimes adopt the masculine interactional behaviour of their CofP (Holmes 2006). However, this has not been successful in breaking the glass ceiling due to prevailing discourses of gender differences that 'systematically attribute quite rigid styles of speech and behaviour to males and to females', leading to women being judged differently from men for adopting equivalent communicative strategies (Baxter 2008: 201). For example, since assertiveness indexes masculinity, women are viewed as going against their gender when they are assertive in their language use (Holmes 2006), which can cause their behaviour to be perceived as threatening and unfeminine by their colleagues (Mullany 2007).

Researchers have found that women in positions of authority often face a 'double bind' (e.g. Marra et al. 2006; Mullany 2011), that is:

> if they interact in a stereotypically feminine manner they will be negatively evaluated for being an incompetent professional, whereas if they interact in a stereotypically masculine manner, using 'marked' linguistic forms, they will be negatively evaluated for being overly aggressive.
>
> (Mullany 2007: 32)

This is arguably why some women make the pragmatic choice to use tentative and indirect speech, rather than assert themselves, in the workplace (Crawford 1995). Barrett's (2004) study is an important example of this. She found that senior women in Australian workplaces, including those with high confidence, believe that the masculine model of communication is more valuable for achieving particular goals, but less effective for women in certain situations. Thus, even senior women favour more indirect, 'feminine' approaches. As Mills and Mullany (2011: 55) state,

> women engage in a complex process whereby they assess others' stereotypical beliefs about gender and then tactically adopt strategies which will be most likely to achieve their ends; and some of those strategies may well be ones stereotypically associated with feminine language.

Nevertheless, it is becoming increasingly evident in research that many interactional styles associated with 'effective' leadership are indexed for femininity (Eagly and Carli 2003), and a more 'feminised' workplace culture that values relational leadership behaviour is emerging in international corporations (Cameron 2000). In such workplaces, discourse strategies typically associated with femininity, such as being indirect, conciliatory, supportive and collaborative (Holmes and Stubbe 2003), have been neutralised of their associations with gender, and institutionalised as integral management skills (Cameron 2000; Baxter 2008).

However, the shift towards a management style that combines transactional and relational aspects of leadership has not benefitted senior women (Baxter 2012). This is evident in Baxter's (2008: 217) study on how British business leaders discursively construct their leadership identities. She found that in addition to being celebrated for using relational forms of discourse, the men are tolerated or admired when they display authoritative behaviour, but the women are negatively assessed for doing the same and have to deploy a range of strategies to 'observe, regulate, police, review and repair the way they appear and sound to their colleagues', including preparing rigorously and using humour, mitigated commands and apologies. This pattern has also been identified in the Wellington Language in the Workplace Project, which analysed a corpus of over 1,500 recorded workplace interactions in New Zealand (e.g. Holmes and Stubbe 2003). Baxter (2008: 217) argues that this can weaken the impact of the women's talk, which 'may offer a linguistic reason why females still struggle to "make it to the top"'.

This is not to imply that women are hapless victims in the workplace. Kendall (2003: 604) argues that some senior women who linguistically downplay status differences are not reluctant to exert authority, but are in fact exercising their authority 'by speaking in ways that accomplish work-related goals while maintaining the faces of their interlocutors'. Empirical evidence shows that women managers are capable of drawing on a wide repertoire of discursive styles in order to get certain business accomplished (Holmes and Stubbe 2003). Therefore, it is important to recognise women's agency in negotiating with an array of disabling constraints in order to meet their professional goals.

The linguistic construction of masculinities

Due to the political aims of language and gender research, studies in this field have largely focused on women's linguistic behaviour and the construction of women's identities through the use of language. Furthermore, women have been traditionally contrasted to men, who have been regarded as the norm or default as well as a homogeneous group. The lack of problematisation of men's language use, as Kiesling (2007) argues, has rendered men relatively invisible, and partly contributed to male dominance in society. However, scholarly work into the varied ways men use language to construct their multiple subjectivities and how these are shaped by discourses of masculinity has increased since the late 1990s.

Research has demonstrated that men often index hegemonic masculinity through an array of linguistic strategies (e.g. Coates 2003), where hegemonic masculinity is 'the qualities defined as manly that establish and legitimate a hierarchical and complementary relationship to femininity and that, by doing so, guarantee the dominant position of men and the subordination of women' (Schippers 2007: 94). These characteristics typically include leadership, heterosexuality and physical strength, though the culturally dominant notion of masculinity and how it is linguistically expressed is context-dependent. For example, in Wetherell and Edley's (1999) study, male students in a British university discursively position themselves as 'ordinary' (i.e. normal or average) or 'rebellious' (i.e. non-normative) rather than 'macho', thereby reinforcing their personal autonomy, which is a hegemonic ideal. On the other hand, in a fraternity party in a US university, members of this 'hypermasculine' CofP use competitive speech genres, such as insults, which Kiesling (2005) posits are the products of the conflict between achieving dominance and developing homosocial ties with other men. In a Malaysian phone-in radio show, the hegemonic features of idealised masculinity indexed by married male callers' talk include economic power and control over the household (Yoong 2017). Even though multiple masculinities exist, many men strive to emulate hegemonic masculinity as it is considered the ideal and allows them to tap into certain social privileges, and language is an important resource to articulate hegemonic masculine identities.

Hegemonic masculinity is ideologically intertwined with heterosexuality. For instance, in order to construct their masculinity, the fraternity members in Cameron's (1997) work gossip about another man and construct him as gay, implying that they are not. By doing so, they are not only performing gender, but also doing sexuality. Although current scientific and political discourses categorically differentiate between gender and sexuality, the two dimensions inflect one another (Cameron 2005), and one recent development in the field of language and gender is the increasing focus on the relationship between gender and sexual identities, including non-normative identities.

Research into queer men's and trans men's linguistic behaviour has provided a richer and more nuanced perspective of the myriad of ways masculinity can be achieved through the *adoption* of language indexical of the speaker's sexual identity. Various studies have described the range of ways gay men use language to index homosexuality rather than hegemonic, heteronormative masculinity (see Jones 2016). Conversely, Hazenberg's (2016: 289) study shows how *avoidance* strategies are central to the linguistic constructions of gender by straight men and transsexuals in Ottawa due to social stigma. While the former avoided sounding gay or effeminate to prevent any loss of social capital associated with heteronormative masculinity, the latter, who were at risk of violence, chose linguistic features that are 'neither markedly feminine nor markedly masculine, but nevertheless [fall] within the acceptable ranges of both' to ensure their gender performance was taken at face value.

By demonstrating that 'the performance of the gendered selves' were socially driven, Hazenberg's work picks apart the essentialist view that men (and women) possess inherent traits. As Milani (2011: 183) reminds us, alongside the important research on language, gender and 'liminal' sexual identities, critical analyses of heterosexual masculinities performed by men are necessary because

> from the point of view of queer theory, we should not only pay attention 'to the cases in which bodies/relations/desires 'deviate' from the norm ... it is through the deconstruction of what counts as 'normal' that we can undermine claims of biological and/or cultural essentialism, revealing instead the deeply social roots of such 'normality'.

Nevertheless, gender and sexuality is not the only potentially relevant combination of social identity categories. Language and masculinity studies adopting an intersectional perspective have been relatively rare, and Milani (2011: 181) makes the crucial observation that 'we still know too little about the ways in which ... social "othering" (Jaworski 2007) [along the lines of class and race] operates through language/discourse'. In one intersectional analysis, Baker and Levon (2016: 134) examine representations of various racialised and classed masculinities in the British print media between 2003 and 2011 to understand how these situate against each another within the broader ideological field of masculinity, and observe that 'black, Asian, working- and upper-class men are marginalised not (or not only) because of their race or social class, but because of the gendered connotations of these racial and social class positions'. Given that black and Asian masculinities 'realise a "patriarchal dividend" in certain contexts' (Baker and Levon 2016: 135) and upper-class men wield a considerable amount of social and material power over women and other men, it can be argued that there are multiple hegemonies, where certain masculine identities that are linked to social categories such as class and race exercise particular types of power over femininities and other masculinities depending on the context (Hearn and Morrell 2012). Therefore, more intersectional analyses of masculinities are needed in language and gender research to understand the ideological organisation of specific configurations of masculinity with other axes of inequality.

Key areas of debate

Interactional salience of gender

In current theoretical approaches, gender is recognised as one of the several relevant analytical categories in the linguistic construction of complex social identities. Many researchers share the perspective that gender is an omni-relevant social category, including Holmes and Schnurr (2006: 33), who maintain that

> gender is . . . an ever-present influence on how we behave, and how we interpret others' behaviour, even if our level of awareness of this influence varies from one interaction to another, and from moment to moment within an interaction.

However, this is not wholly accepted, and over the past decades there has been an extensive discussion on gender salience in interactions. Schegloff (1997) argues against assuming that gender is always relevant as this could lead to scholars imposing their political concerns and their own ideas of what constitutes context onto interactions. Therefore, in order to remain objective, analysts should examine conversational behaviour from the micro-linguistic level of interactions and, if required, work up to the macro-level of political inequality, rather than the reverse. In other words, gender can only be considered as interactionally salient if it is explicitly signalled by the interlocutors, such as through self-repairs of gendered pronouns, and then becomes the topic of the conversation. In fact, for some researchers, even the use of gendered terms does not necessarily make gender a salient social variable. For example, in Kitzinger's (2007: 43) analysis of a recorded conversation on a helpline for women in trauma after childbirth, she argues that uses of 'women' and 'we women'

> have less to do with gender and are much more directly related to the business of the helpline in delivering its advertised service. Gender is certainly not irrelevant to the interactional business being pursued here, but it is subordinated to, and in the service of, it.

Critics of this approach, on the other hand, assert that broader sociocultural forces are at work within interactions, alongside the context explicitly invoked by the speakers (Mills and Mullany 2011). Holmes (2005) provides examples of workplace interactions in which gender is never made explicit, but operates in the background. In one case, a senior woman would speak authoritatively, and then mitigate the impact of her 'masculine' behaviour with a humorous comment – a pattern found in many studies, as discussed in the previous section. Therefore, to disregard the effects of implicit gendered expectations on interpersonal speech styles 'would be to miss out a crucial step in the analytical process, particularly when attempting to engage in politically active research' (Mills and Mullany 2011: 168). Weatherall (2000) also maintains that it would be unrealistic to expect feminist researchers not to draw on their values and political concerns. In fact, to focus on isolated segments of a conversation that explicitly orient to gender while ignoring the rest of the surrounding talk can be itself a non-neutral analytic decision (Stokoe and Smithson 2001). For certain researchers, such as Wetherell (1998), micro- and macro-analysis each informs and lends meaning to the other, and rather than choosing between the two, they have successfully combined them in their studies.

Another issue with relying on the explicit mention of gender references is that since few English words directly index gender (Ochs 1992), this would limit admissible research data. Schegloff (1997: 182) addresses this by proposing that 'orientation to gender can be manifested without being explicitly named or mentioned'. Indirect indices of gender could include references to gendered activities, as well as 'ambiguous words with possible references to sexuality; reference to female appearance or male appearance; or references to female demeanor or male demeanor' (Hopper and LeBaron 1998: 171). Given that such terms are not intrinsically gendered, this would pose a conflict with Schegloff's overall stance since, as Stokoe and Smithson (2001) point out, it requires analysts to draw on implicit cultural knowledge. However, they also argue that despite the risk of misinterpretation, the inferential resources of analysts must be taken into account in order to produce an analytic study rather than a descriptive one.

Additionally, the habitual and repetitive re-enactments of 'feminising' or 'masculinising' acts, including through language behaviour, render the performance of gender invisible (Butler 1990). Therefore, even when gender may not be a conscious focus of identity performance, it may still be constructed linguistically. One could argue that if speakers uphold gender ideologies without being aware of making such language choices, this is all the more insidious for being instinctive (Widdowson 2007) as the more an ideology is taken for granted, the more powerful it becomes (Phillips 2003). Hence, it is the role of the analyst to expose gender discrimination and inequality that may have been previously unnoticed by the interactants. Nevertheless, in order to ensure their work is empirically grounded, it is important for researchers to think 'reflexively' about how their positions, values, experiences and biases may influence their research and interpretative capacity.

Approaches to analysing gendered speech styles

Earlier in this chapter, we discussed how contemporary language and gender studies have adopted a more constructionist stance, where feminist linguists are concerned about how gender is negotiated locally within interaction, including through the use of gendered speech styles. Consequently, current research largely theorises speakers with reference to sociocultural stereotypes of femininity and masculinity. For example, stereotypically 'feminine' interactional styles include being indirect, deferent and facilitative, whereas 'masculine' speech is direct, assertive and competitive. This draws on the notion of categorical dichotomy in which 'there are two and only two categories (men and women, masculinity and femininity), and they are stereotypically opposite and homogeneous' (Kiesling 2007: 656).

Masculinity and femininity are not only defined in relation to each other, but also to men and women (Paechter 2006). This eliding of 'feminine' and 'masculine' speech styles with femaleness and maleness, which Butler (1990) argues are also cultural constructs, is problematic since 'by emphasizing language which reflects the [biological female-male dichotomy], linguists may be reinforcing biological essentialism, even if they emphasize that language, like gender, is learned behaviour' (Bing and Bergvall 1996: 18). It has also been subjected to critique for (inadvertently) reifying the gender binary, which 'glosses over the myriad identities within the broad categories of "masculine" and "feminine". It also ignores the gendered experiences of participants, particularly transsexuals' (Hazenberg 2016: 270). The trans men in Zimman's (2012) study, for example, do not switch from using aspects of language indexical of femininity to those indexing heteronormative cis (i.e. non-trans) masculinity, but perform complex gender identities that are specific to their personal experiences and how they see themselves, and do not fall on either side of the masculine/feminine dichotomy perfectly.

Another problem with referencing stereotypical models of femininity and masculinity is that this could further entrench the association of feminine language with weakness and powerlessness. While masculinity and masculine language are conferred cultural power (Kiesling 2007), femininity is constructed as 'a variety of negations of the masculine' due to the dualistic relation between masculinity and femininity (Paechter 2006: 256). Consequently, as Holmes and Schnurr (2006) note, femininity is often associated with a lack of power and influence, and perceived as a negative attribute, which can have adverse implications. Their examination of interactional data from the Wellington Language in the Workplace Project, for example, demonstrates how men can face derision for using normatively feminine ways of talking within certain workplace cultures.

Critics have questioned if what have been termed as 'masculine' language features really index power and dominance, as claimed in previous research (see Coates 2003), given the indeterminacy of meaning for specific formal linguistic features (Toolan 1996). For instance, in early theorising, interrupting was viewed as a powerful strategy (Mills and Mullany 2011), and it was assumed that men not only interrupt more than women, but also interrupt women more than men (Kiesling 2007). However, the results of studies investigating this feature and gender have been inconclusive (see James and Clarke 1993). On the other hand, it has been found that speakers in positions of power tend not to interrupt since they are given more 'space' to speak. In contrast, those attempting to claim power use this linguistic form more (Diamond 1996; Manke 1997). Conversely, 'powerless' features may not be the simple markers of powerlessness as has been maintained (Mills 2012). Silence, which can be viewed as submissive and the opposite of interruption, may be a powerful feature when deployed by a man (Sattell 1983), whereas silence from a woman may be interpreted as weakness (Kiesling 2007). Likewise, O'Barr and Atkins (1980) found that women who do not use 'feminine' linguistic forms indexing deference are still perceived as speaking in a powerless way.

Mills and Mullany (2011) suggest developing new terms that transcend stereotypical feminine/masculine opposition and do not associate speech characteristics with gender. Rather than evaluating linguistic behaviour as masculine or feminine, Mills (2012) proposes the term 'discourse competence' to describe speech that applies co-operative and competitive strategies appropriately. She argues that 'feminine' and 'masculine' speech styles cannot be viewed as homogenous groupings of characteristics since both cover negative as well as positive elements. Therefore, discourse competence is achieved through a combination of co-operative and competitive strategies, and not normative masculinity. This can provide theorists with the space to classify the linguistic behaviour of strong female speakers as discursively competent, rather than deviant or 'masculine'. It also allows for the possibility to 'identify and describe women and men speakers who are displaying features of neither feminine or masculine speech behaviour, but who are simply competent speakers' (Mills 2012: 236) (see Sznycer 2013).

At the same time, Mills and Mullany (2011: 165) point out that 'developing non-gendered terms risks ignoring the meaning that those styles still have for many of the interactants'. As we have seen earlier, such as in our discussion of the 'double bind', the binary notion of gendered speech norms has deep social roots and greatly influences expectations of gender-appropriate language behaviour. While a large amount of language and gender scholarship has focused on women who adopt masculine speech norms, thereby 'challeng[ing] the notion that these are in fact masculine norms at all' (Mills 2012: 250) and 'dislocating masculinity' from men (Milani 2011: 183), Holmes (2007: 56–57) reminds us that 'most of the world continues to treat "women" and "men", "female" and "male" as fundamental social categories, not least in describing interpersonal communication style'. Stereotypical feminine and masculine speech patterns are indirectly gender-indexed, and therefore strongly influence how we judge the linguistic behaviour of others. Speakers who 'fail to stay within the boundaries of gendered speech norms, Butler's (1990: 33) "rigid regulatory frame", . . . may well be subject to negative evaluation or abuse' (Mills and Mullany 2011: 53). Hence, although feminist academics may regard 'feminine' and 'masculine' speech norms as socially constructed, in order to challenge stereotypes and sociocultural expectations of female and male speech styles, references to stereotypical models of femininity and masculinity may be necessary.

Future directions

One significant area of research that needs to be given attention in the field of language and gender is the relationship between language, gender and postfeminism. Postfeminism is a sensibility that both invokes and rejects feminism with an emphasis on individualism, choice, empowerment, self-regulation, consumerism and sexual agency (Gill and Scharff 2011). It has been criticised for promoting myths that sustain the status quo, including the notion that gender equality has been achieved. Postfeminist narratives co-opt and universalise feminist discourses highlighting women's progress in certain societies while rejecting political aspects of feminism that direct attention to gender inequality since these hinder women from embracing their empowerment (Budgeon 2011). Lazar (2007: 154) criticises the seemingly emancipatory message that women can now 'have it all' if they try hard enough, as

> [this] reframes women's struggles and accomplishments as a purely personal matter, thus obscuring the social and material constraints faced by different groups of women . . . A self-focused 'me-feminism' of this sort shifts attention away from the collective 'we-feminism' needed for a transformational political program.

While many scholars from various disciplines in the arts, humanities and social sciences have highlighted the widespread proliferation of postfeminist rhetoric, and critiqued the resignification of freedom and agency and the resulting depoliticisation of gender equality (e.g. Gill and Scharff 2011), relatively little research into the ways that language is used to construct postfeminist narratives and subjects has been done in the field of language and gender, and this gap needs to be addressed.

As most language and gender studies have focused on cisgender people, or those implicitly presumed to be cisgender, due to their cultural privilege (Jones 2016), it is of crucial importance that research into the interplay between language, gender and sexual identities that have been typically perceived as deviant continues to expand. Linguists working within LGBT communities need to attend to an important concern that Hazenberg (2016) raises with regards to an intersectional conceptualisation of gender. For some researchers, gender and sexual identities, though not interchangeable, are closely linked. For example, in Cameron's (1997) analysis of interactions between fraternity members discussed earlier, hegemonic masculinity and heterosexuality are enacted simultaneously and inflect each other. However, Hazenberg (2016: 271, emphasis in original) argues that viewing gender and sexuality as inextricably intertwined is problematic:

> From the perspective advanced by many gender and queer activists (e.g. Burke 1996; Beasley 2005) – the two are clearly distinct: gender is an aspect of identity, of *self*, while sexuality is an aspect of desire, of attraction to *others*. Trans people in particular have fought long and hard to have their gender identities recognised as distinct from their

> sexual orientations ... For researchers working within marginalised communities, this can present a problem: do we recognise and maintain the separation that is so important to the people we are working with, or do we capitulate to the more widespread academic understanding of these phenomena, for the sake of clarity and consistency?

These are questions that require further consideration in the field. In Hazenberg's (2016) own study, discussed in the previous section, he uses a six-way gender split, categorising his participants as straight men, straight women, queer men, queer women, transsexual men and transsexual women. In so doing, Hazenberg (2016: 271) 'consolidate[s] the independent axes of gender and sexual orientation into a multi-dimensional space where both are equally important'.

The issue of self-identity and self-definition is related to the next recommendation. Given the unrelenting 'domination and exclusion based on people's gender and sexual identities' (Caldas-Coulthard and Milani 2016: 147), it is of utmost importance that feminist linguists continue to feed developments in intellectual thought into practices both within and beyond academia to promote a better understanding of human diversity and bring about re-enactments of public policies. We need to pose more questions on how findings from intellectual inquiry can be translated to 'real world' contexts and eliminate gender and sexual discrimination. As Cameron (2007: 22) reminds us,

> I did not become a feminist academic so I could talk to other feminist academics in our own intellectual space; I became a feminist academic because I wanted to challenge sexism. If we cease to do that, then in my view, nothing else we do will matter.

Finally, although the English language is used in most, if not all, parts of the world, studies have predominantly been conducted in Western locations. Research assessing the role that the English language plays in sustaining stereotypes and gender disparity has gradually expanded into previously under-researched countries and cultural contexts, and it is imperative that this continues so that gender inequalities globally are better represented, understood and deconstructed. This includes ensuring the complex intersection between language, gender and the fullest range of social identity categories is taken into consideration. For example, Mullany and Yoong's (2016) lexico-grammatical analysis of Malaysian media coverage of a parliamentary by-election demonstrates how a Malay Muslim politician's religion, race, sexuality and age intersected with her gender to constitute her as the less suitable candidate compared to her older, ethnically Chinese male opponent. Such research acknowledges that the ways that different groups of women materially experience gender discrimination vary according to their local context. Feminist linguistics needs to continue examining the diverse ways in which gender intersects with other social identity variables and systems of power.

Further reading

Gray, J. (2016) Language and non-normative sexual identities, in S. Preece (ed.), *The Routledge Handbook of Language and Identity*. Oxon: Routledge, 225–240. This chapter examines the roles that language plays in the representation and performance of non-normative sexual identities.

Kiesling, S. (2007). 'Men, masculinities, and language', *Language and Linguistics Compass* 1: 653–673. Kiesling explores how men use language to express masculinity and how language becomes associated with masculinities.

Mullany, L. (2007). *Gendered Discourse in the Professional Workplace*. Basingstoke: Palgrave. Drawing on interactional data from UK workplaces, Mullany examines the crucial role that gendered discourses play in maintaining the 'glass ceiling'.

Talbot, M. M. (2010). *Language and Gender*. 2nd edn. Cambridge: Polity Press. This key textbook provides an overview of foundational research as well as an insightful discussion of current trends in the field.

Zimman, L. (2014). 'The discursive construction of sex: remaking and reclaiming the gendered body in talk about genitals among trans men', in L. Zimman, J. Davis and J. Raclaw (eds), *Queer Excursions: Retheorizing Binaries in Language, Gender, and Sexuality*. Oxford: Oxford University Press, 13–34. Zimman explores how trans men discursively transcend their assigned sex in the absence of radical bodily transformation.

Related topics

- English and social identity
- Media, power and representation
- Sociolinguistics: studying English and its social relations
- Discourse analysis: studying and critiquing language in use.

References

Baker, P. and E. Levon (2016) '"That's what I call a man": Representations of racialised and classed masculinities in the UK print media', *Gender and Language* 10 (1): 106–139.

Barrett, M. (2004) 'Should they learn to interrupt? Workplace communication strategies Australian women managers forecast as effective', *Women in Management Review* 19 (8): 391–403.

Baxter, J. (2008) 'Is it tough talking at the top? A post-structuralist analysis of the construction of gendered speaker identities of British business leaders within interview narratives', *Gender and Language* 2 (2): 197–222.

Baxter, J. (2012) 'Women of the corporation: A sociolinguistic perspective of senior women's leadership language in the U.K', *Journal of Sociolinguistics* 16 (1): 81–107.

Beasley, C. (2005) *Gender and Sexuality: Critical Theories, Critical Thinkers*. London: Sage.

Bing, J. M. and V. L. Bergvall (1996) 'The question of questions: Beyond binary thinking', in V. L. Bergvall, J. M. Bing and A. F. Freed (eds), *Rethinking Language and Gender Research: Theory and Practice*. New York: Longman, 1–30.

Black, M. and R. Coward (1981) 'Linguistic, social and sexual relations: A review of Dale Spender's *Man Made Language*', *Screen Education* 39: 69–85.

Budgeon, S. (2011) 'The contradictions of successful femininity: Third wave feminism, postfeminism and "new" femininities', in R. Gill and C. Scharff (eds), *New Femininities: Postfeminism, Neoliberalism and Subjectivity*. Basingstoke: Palgrave Macmillan, 279–292.

Burke, P. (1996) *Gender Shock: Exploding the Myths of Male and Female*. New York: Anchor Books/Doubleday.

Butler, J. (1990) *Gender Trouble: Feminism and the Subversion of Identity*. New York: Routledge.

Caldas-Coulthard, C. R. and T. M. Milani (2016) 'Ten years of gender and language', *Gender and Language* 10 (2): 145–148.

Cameron, D. (1992) 'Review of Tannen 1991', *Feminism and Psychology* 2 (3): 465–489.

Cameron, D. (1997) 'Performing gender identity: Young men's talk and the construction of heterosexual masculinity', in J. Coates (ed.), *Language and Gender: A Reader*. Oxford: Blackwell, 270–284.

Cameron, D. (2000) *Good To Talk: Living and Working in a Communication Culture*. London: Sage.

Cameron, D. (2005) 'Language, gender, and sexuality: Current issues and new directions', *Applied Linguistics* 26 (4): 482–502.

Cameron, D. (2007) 'Unanswered questions and unquestioned assumptions in the study of language and gender: Female verbal superiority', *Gender and Language* 1 (1): 15–25.

Coates, J. (2003) *Men Talk: Stories in the Making of Masculinities*. Oxford: Blackwell.

Crawford, M. (1995) *Talking Difference: On Gender and Language*. London: Sage.

Diamond, J. (1996) *Status and Power in Verbal Interaction: A Study of Discourse in a Close-Knit Social Network*. Amsterdam and Philadelphia: John Benjamins.

Eagly, A. H. and L. L. Carli (2003) 'The female advantage: An evaluation of the evidence', *The Leadership Quarterly* 14: 807–834.

Eckert, P. and S. McConnell-Ginet (1992) 'Think practically and look locally: Language and gender as community-based practice', *Annual Review of Anthropology* 21: 461–490.

Eckert, P. and S. McConnell-Ginet (1999) 'New generalisations and explanations in language and gender research', *Language in Society* 28 (2): 185–201.

Foucault, M. (1972) *The Archaeology of Knowledge*. London: Routledge.

Gill, R. and C. Scharff (eds) (2011) *New Femininities: Postfeminism, Neoliberalism and Subjectivity*. Basingstoke: Palgrave Macmillan.

Hazenberg, E. (2016) 'Walking the straight and narrow: Linguistic choice and gendered presentation', *Gender and Language* 10 (2): 270–294.

Hearn, J. and R. Morrell, (2012) 'Reviewing hegemonic masculinities and men in Sweden and South Africa', *Men and Masculinities* 15: 3–10.

Holmes, J. (2005) 'Power and discourse at work: Is gender relevant?', in M. M. Lazar (ed.), *Feminist Critical Discourse Analysis: Gender, Power and Ideology in Discourse*. Basingstoke: Palgrave, 31–60.

Holmes, J. (2006) *Gendered Talk at Work*. Oxford: Blackwell.

Holmes, J. (2007) 'Social constructionism, postmodernism and feminist sociolinguistics', *Gender and Language* 1 (1): 51–78.

Holmes, J. and S. Schnurr (2006) 'Doing femininity at work: More than just relational practice', *Journal of Sociolinguistics* 10 (1): 31–51.

Holmes, J. and M. Stubbe, (2003) 'Feminine workplaces: Stereotype and reality', in J. Holmes and M. Meyerhoff (eds), *The Handbook of Language and Gender*. Oxford: Blackwell, 573–599.

Hopper, R. and C. LeBaron (1998) 'How gender creeps into talk', *Research on Language and Social Interaction* 31 (3): 59–74.

James, D. and S. Clarke (1993) 'Women, men, and interruptions: A critical review', in D. Tannen (ed.), *Gender and Conversational Interaction*. New York: Oxford University Press, 231–280.

Jaworski, A. (2007) 'Language in the media: Authenticity and othering', in S. Johnson and A. Ensslin (eds.), *Language in the Media: Representations, Identities, Ideologies*. London: Continuum, 271–280.

Jones, L. (2016) 'Language and gender identities', in S. Preece (ed.), *The Routledge Handbook of Language and Identity*. Oxon: Routledge, 210–224.

Kendall, S. (2003) 'Creating gender demeanors of authority at work and at home', in J. Holmes and M. Meyerhoff (eds), *The Handbook of Language and Gender*. Oxford: Blackwell, 600–623.

Kiesling, S. (2005) 'Homosocial desire in men's talk: Balancing and recreating cultural discourses of masculinity', *Language in Society* 34: 695–727.

Kiesling, S. (2007) 'Men, masculinities, and language', *Language and Linguistics Compass* 1: 653–673.

Kitzinger, C. (2007) 'Is "woman" always relevantly gendered?' *Gender and Language* 1 (1): 39–49.

Lakoff, R. (1975) *Language and Woman's Place*. New York. Harper and Row.

Lazar, M. M. (2007) 'Feminist critical discourse analysis: Articulating a feminist discourse praxis', *Critical Discourse Studies* 4 (2): 141–164.

Maltz, D. and R. Borker (1982) 'A cultural approach to male–female miscommunication', in J. J. Gumperz (ed.), *Language and Social Identity*. Cambridge: Cambridge University Press, 196–216.

Manke, M. (1997) *Classroom Power Relations: Understanding Student–Teacher Interaction*. Mahwah, NJ and London: Lawrence Erlbaum Associates.

Marra, M., S. Schnurr and J. Holmes (2006) 'Effective leadership in New Zealand: Balancing gender and role', in J. Baxter (ed.), *Speaking Out: The Female Voice in Public Contexts*. Basingstoke: Palgrave, 240–260.

Milani, T. M. (2011) 'Introduction: Re-casting language and masculinities', *Gender and Language* 5 (2): 175–186.

Mills, S. (2012) *Gender Matters: Feminist Linguistic Analysis*. London: Equinox.

Mills, S. and L. Mullany (2011) *Language, Gender and Feminism: Theory, Methodology and Practice*. Oxon: Routledge.

Mullany, L. (2007) *Gendered Discourse in the Professional Workplace*. Basingstoke: Palgrave.

Mullany, L. J. (2010) 'Gender and interpersonal pragmatics', in M. A. Locher and S. L. Graham (eds), *The Handbook of Interpersonal Pragmatics*. Berlin: Mouton de Gruyter, 225–250.

Mullany, L. J. (2011) 'Discourse, gender and professional communication', in J. P. Gee and M. Handford (eds), *The Handbook of Discourse Analysis*. London: Routledge, 509–522.

Mullany, L. and M. Yoong (2016) 'Language, gender and identities in political life: A case study from Malaysia', in S. Preece (ed.), *The Routledge Handbook of Language and Identity*. Oxon: Routledge, 428–442.

O'Barr, W. and B. Atkins (1980) '"Women's language" or "powerless language"?' in S. McConnell-Ginet, R. Borker and N. Furman (eds), *Women and Language in Literature and Society*. New York: Praeger, 93–110.
Ochs, E. (1990) 'Indexicality and socialisation', in J. W. Stigler, R. A. Schweder and G. Herdt (eds), *Cultural Psychology: The Chicago Symposia*. Cambridge: Cambridge University Press, 287–308.
Ochs, E. (1992) 'Indexing gender', in A. Duranti and C. Goodwin (eds), *Rethinking Context: Language as an Interactive Phenomenon*. Cambridge: Cambridge University Press, 335–358.
Paechter C. (2006) 'Masculine femininities/feminine masculinities: Power, identities and gender', *Gender and Education* 18 (3): 253–263.
Phillips, S. U. (2003) 'The power of gender ideologies in discourse', in J. Holmes and M. Meyerhoff (eds), *The Handbook of Language and Gender*. Oxford: Blackwell, 252–276.
Sattell, J. (1983) 'Men, inexpressiveness and power', in B. Thorne, C. Kramarae and N. Henley (eds), *Language, Gender and Society*. Rowley, MA: Newbury House, 118–124.
Schegloff, E. (1997) 'Whose text? whose context?' *Discourse & Society* 8 (2): 165–185.
Schippers, M. (2007) 'Recovering the feminine other: Masculinity, femininity, and gender hegemony', *Theory and Society* 36 (1): 85–102.
Schnurr, S. and B. Mak (2011) 'Leadership in Hong Kong: Is gender really not an issue?' *Gender and Language* 5 (2): 343–371.
Spender, D. (1980) *Man Made Language*. London: Routledge & Kegan Paul.
Stokoe, E. H. and J. Smithson (2001) 'Making gender relevant: Conversation analysis and gender categories in interaction', *Discourse & Society* 12 (2): 217–244.
Sunderland, J. (2004) *Gendered Discourses*. Basingstoke: Palgrave.
Sznycer, K. (2013) 'Strong female speakers: The resistant discourse of tennis players', *Gender and Language* 7 (3): 303–332.
Talbot, M. M. (2010) *Language and Gender*. 2nd edn. Cambridge: Polity Press.
Tannen, D. (1991) *You Just Don't Understand: Women and Men in Conversation*. New York: William Morrow.
Toolan, M. (1996) *Total Speech: An Integrational Linguistic Approach to Language*. Durham, NC: Duke University Press.
Troemel-Ploetz, S. (1991) 'Selling the apolitical', *Discourse and Society* 2 (4): 489–502.
Weatherall, A. (2000) 'Gender relevance in talk-in-interaction and discourse', *Discourse & Society* 11 (2): 286–288.
Wetherell, M. (1998) 'Positioning and interpretative repetoires: Conversation analysis and post-structuralism in dialogue', *Discourse & Society* 9 (3): 387–412.
Wetherell, M. and N. Edley (1999) 'Negotiating hegemonic masculinity: Imaginary positions and psycho-discursive practices', *Feminism and Psychology* 9 (3): 335–356.
Widdowson, H. G. (2007) *Discourse Analysis*. Oxford: Oxford University Press.
Yoong, M. (2017) 'Men and women on air: Gender stereotypes in humour sequences in a Malaysian radio phone-in programme', *Gender and Language* 11 (1): 30–50.
Zimman, L. (2012) *Voices in Transition: Testosterone, Transmasculinity, and the Gendered Voice among Female-to-Male Transgender People* (Unpublished PhD thesis, Boulder, Colorado: University of Colorado).

16

The politics of English

Joe Spencer-Bennett

Introduction

Politics has to do with the decisions we make about how to live together, how to distribute resources, and what course of action to take on significant collective issues. It is a response to the fact that we live in complex societies in which there exist people and groups with different – often opposing – values, interests, and practices. As Bernard Crick puts it, politics is a 'solution to the problem of social order' (1964: 18). And it is a particular kind of solution; one that involves, or at least aims to involve, a degree of *dialogue* between those people and groups. It is therefore a phenomenon that cannot help but involve language. Indeed, without language, it is difficult to see how we could have politics at all (Aristotle 1951). This chapter discusses some of the key relations between the English language and politics. My focus will be on the ways in which contemporary researchers in English Language have understood these relations, the concepts they have used to explore them, the questions they have asked, and the disputes that they have entered into.

Current issues: ideology, power, and normativity

Perhaps the two most prominent concepts in recent linguistic thought about politics are *ideology* and *power*. I will discuss each of these concepts in turn, before outlining the significance of an equally fundamental – but less often explicitly addressed – concept in the politics of English: the *normativity* of both language and politics.

Ideology

The language that people encounter, have, or use provides them with ways of conceptualising the world around them. In terms of linguistic theory, this idea was central to the structuralist linguistics of Saussure (1983), for whom a language was to be understood as a structured conceptual network shared by members of a society. It was also key to early twentieth-century developments in American linguistics, articulated most famously in the work of Whorf and Sapir, and later known as the Sapir-Whorf hypothesis. As Sapir put it, 'Language and our thought-grooves are inextricably interwoven, are, in a sense, one and the same' (1921: 232). A version of this view was shared by the Marxist linguist Volosinov, who in most other respects was fiercely opposed to Saussure's anti-materialist 'abstract objectivism'. Volosinov saw human consciousness as the internalisation of social communication that takes place using language. Therefore, the linguistic sign was, for Volosinov, 'the ideological phenomenon par excellence' (Volosinov 1973: 13).

The political implications of this view were that ideas about what the world is like (and about what it should and should not be like) do not originate in direct understanding of that world. They are powerfully mediated by, and in some strong formulations, fully *shaped by*, language. This academic theorising about language had echoes in a much wider conception of language as an instrument by which 'the masses' could be controlled through processes of linguistic manipulation and 'brain-washing'. The spread of mass democracy in the early twentieth century and advances in communications technology such as radio and television led to concerns that political elites could increasingly manipulate such opinion and 'manufacture consent' (Lippmann 1932). The most famous articulation of such fears is that of Orwell in his novel *Nineteen Eighty-Four* (Orwell 1954) and in essays such as 'Politics and the English Language' (Orwell 2004 [1946]). Orwell put forward a view of political language which is now often referred to simply as 'Orwellian', and which sees political language as a means by which those in positions of power mask the reality of the political situation by propagating a radically simplified or euphemistic linguistic representation.

In the case of *Nineteen Eighty-Four*, this simplified linguistic representation is 'Newspeak', a semi-artificial language promoted by the tyrannical regime to control the thought of the population. In the fictional world that Orwell creates, 'The purpose of Newspeak was not only to provide a medium of expression for the world-view and mental habits [of the regime] . . . but to make all other modes of thought impossible' (Orwell 1954: 241). Given this broad emphasis on the relations between language and ideological manipulation, it is not surprising that many political activists in the late twentieth century saw the critique of language as part of their political project. For example, Spender challenged what she saw as the patriarchal nature of English in her book *Man-Made Language* (1980). For Spender, English itself was a *man*-made language, and was thus structured in ways that embodied a patriarchal ideology. Features of English such as the *-ess* morpheme in words like *actress*, *waitress*, and *lioness* contributed to a naturalisation of male–female binaries, and of the idea that to be male is normal, while to be female is to be *marked*. (For further debate see Cameron 1992).

For many late twentieth-century scholars of English Language, an effect of such tendencies was to suggest that to investigate language was to investigate something saturated with ideology. This was a major impetus behind the development of critical linguistics (Fowler et al. 1979) and later critical discourse analysis (Van Dijk 1993; Fairclough 1995, 2015). In such work, the language in focus is generally that of explicitly political people and institutions – or 'elites' – as in the case of Fairclough's (2000) investigation of the discourse of the British Prime Minister (1997–2007) Tony Blair and his New Labour Party. For Fairclough, New Labour's language was characterised by a merging of traditionally right-wing and left-wing representations of the world, an attempt to linguistically tread what the party called (following Bill Clinton's Democrats in the US) 'the Third Way' (see also Farrelly 2010; Mulderrig 2011). Another prominent strand of work in this area has taken as its focus xenophobic, nationalist, and fascist ideologies in political and media discourse on immigration and Islam (e.g. Van Dijk 2015; Gabrielatos and Baker 2008; Richardson 2008). Such work shows how national and cultural groups are, to a significant extent, constructed or 'imagined' (Anderson 1983) using language.

Recently, Fairclough and Fairclough (2012) have criticised the emphasis on language as a medium of ideological representation. What is important about political language, they suggest, is not what it says about the world, but what it is used to *do*. And what it is used to do is, for them, to engage in argument. Their emphasis on argumentation is a useful point of connection between critical linguistic research and the essentially deliberative nature of politics outlined at the beginning of this chapter. However, what is key about the broad-ranging focus on language and ideology that I have discussed in this section is that it highlights the extent to which the very language in which political actors argue – and which those with whom they are arguing use, as well as the audience for whom they argue – is saturated with ideology (Finlayson 2013). Since politics itself – obviously including practical argumentation – significantly takes place through language, the kinds of things that political actors say and write, and the ideologies that they articulate, or perpetuate, in doing so shape the kinds of political decisions that they are able to make. Language is constitutive of political possibilities; it is *the* medium in which political 'imaginaries' are articulated (Jessop 2004), even as politics necessarily involves reflecting on, developing, and, indeed, arguing about these possibilities.

Power

Like ideology, *power* has been subject to a great deal of attention in accounts of the politics of language. In particular, it is recognised that language is a means by which power can be claimed, maintained, and challenged (Van Dijk 2008; Thornborrow 2013; Fairclough 2010). This is implicit in much of the above discussion of ideology. For example, Spender argued that the 'man-made' nature of English was problematic not simply because it was imbued with ideas about the world, but also because these rules serve the interests of a powerful group – men – at the expense of a less powerful – women. These were not just any ideas, they were ideas in the service of *power*. In Thompson's classic formulation, they were 'ways in which meaning ... serves to sustain relations of domination' (1984: 4). That is to say that they are not just ideological in the 'neutral' sense of the term, whereby all socially significant points of view on the world might be deemed ideologies. They were also ideological in the 'negative' or 'critical' sense, whereby to identify something as ideological is to say that there is something *wrong* with it, and usually that it contributes to relations of power and inequality (see Woolard and Schieffelin 1994).

The critique of power has also been applied to elements of communication that are less easily understood in terms of ways of talking or thinking about the world, and more to do with social identities or forms of social action. For example, the language that political leaders and institutions use is a means by which they are able to construct or present a political ethos, identity, style or 'message' (Aristotle 1951; Silverstein 2003; Coupland 2007). In this connection, a contemporary tendency identified by many political and cultural commentators (Fairclough 2000; Pearce 2005) is for an 'informalisation' or 'conversationalisation' of language. This involves political leaders using language associated with less formal registers in their public discourse, and is generally interpreted as a means by which these leaders are able to construct an identity as 'ordinary people', and an attempt to make a rhetorical appeal on the grounds of social solidarity, rather than superiority. Power is first relevant here in the obvious sense that the designers of such informalised political discourse clearly recognise that language is a means by which social relations of hierarchy and solidarity can, at least to some extent, be negotiated. But it is also relevant because, aside from the semiotic details of markers of 'ordinariness' such as constructions associated with spoken registers or with 'non-standard' dialects, the power relations between the informalised political leader and their audience are unaltered; they remain thoroughly hierarchical. Talking in (what is supposed to be) the language of everyday life does not break down the relations of power that characterise representative democracies (and many other political institutions), and it may serve to obscure those relations by giving the appearance of an equality that does not really exist. It is, as Fairclough puts it, '*synthetic* personalisation' (2015, emphasis added).

Power is also at issue when it comes to the workings of the genres and institutions of political communication. Shaw (2000) shows evidence, for example, that male Members of Parliament in the UK are disproportionately more likely to interrupt other speakers than their female colleagues, and, as such, 'have more control over the interaction ... and therefore more power in debates than female MPs' (416). Thornborrow (2001) investigates a rather different genre of political communication, BBC radio phone-ins where members of the public are invited to call in and put questions to Margaret Thatcher, who, at the time of the research, was British Prime Minister. Thornborrow finds that the host of such programmes mediates the interaction so as to reinforce the institutional power of the prime minister and limit the capacity of the callers to challenge her. A clear implication of such research is that people in positions of power are able to use language to limit and skew the decision-making practices of democratic politics in their own favour. This in turn warns against any conception of politics that sees such decision making as a *pure* matter of rational argumentation or abstracted deliberation. Power struggles shape who gets to say what and when. Who gets to use language to do politics is itself a political matter.

Normativity

Alongside power and ideology, a yet more fundamental – but less often explicitly acknowledged – concept that is central to understanding the politics of English is *normativity*. This term is used to capture the fact that politics involves taking an evaluative – normative – position on the world. It means saying things about what it is like, how good or bad that is, and how it should or should not be (Crick 1964; Sayer 2006). Ideology and power certainly matter politically, but they do so in so far as they relate to the articulation and enactment of normative conceptions of how the world should be. For Aristotle, it was the normative potential of language that allowed human beings to develop political practices and institutions, to argue about how things should be. This essentially Aristotelian point is emphasised in Fairclough and Fairclough's (2012) argumentation-based approach, mentioned above. For Fairclough and Fairclough, political language is 'practical argumentation'. It involves claims about what should be done. Such normative claims need not necessarily take the form of extended argumentative oratory. Huntington (2016), for instance, shows how visual internet memes consisting of a picture and a few words are used in contemporary online communication to make condensed arguments. Such memes may include little in the way of high-flown rhetoric or lengthy disposition of claims and premises. What makes them political is their essentially normative nature. In common with other political uses of language, they have something to say about what we should, or should not, do, or about how our world should, or should not, be.

Language as political instrument and object

So far, this chapter has been concerned with ideology, power, and normativity as they are communicated or enacted in language use itself. In such cases, language is an *instrument* of politics. However, it is also often an *object* of politics. This is clearest to see in official, state-enforced language policy. For example, in the United Kingdom, citizens are subject to legislation and guidance in relation to a range of linguistic phenomena. Some of these have been the focus of a good deal of research. Others have not, but are worthy of investigation. They include:

- the linguistic incitement of racial and religious hatred and violence (Hate Speech legislation, see e.g. Waldron 2012)
- the structures, sounds and uses of 'correct English', as well as the best way in which this should be learned (the National Curriculum in England and Wales, e.g. Milroy 2001)
- what can and cannot be said on television and radio, by whom and when (Ofcom broadcasting guidelines)
- the English language competence required of applicants for British visas and citizenship (Home Office Visa entry requirements, citizenship test, e.g. Piller 2001; Blommaert 2009)
- what counts as an acceptable personal name (deed poll regulations)
- what counts as verbal evidence of 'radicalisation' and 'extremism' and what the limits are on the discussion of 'controversial topics' in schools (Prevent strategy)
- the ownership of words, phrases and texts (copyright laws).

In all of these cases, particular ideologies of language – understandings of what language is like and how it should work – are backed by the bureaucratic, legislative powers of the state. For example, the teaching and assessment of English as specified in the National Curriculum for England and Wales embodies ideologies of 'standard English' (Milroy 2001). Pupils – or, indeed, teachers – who are unable or unwilling to 'live up to' these standards will suffer in terms of educational qualifications, which it is within the power of the state to distribute. In the case of relations between English and immigration, the policies of the British government can be understood largely in terms of longstanding 'monoglot' ideologies, whereby a nation state is held to be a unit of linguistic order (Blommaert 2009). In the case of the British government, this monoglot conception is marked by an assumption – with a few exceptions in 'devolved' Wales and Scotland – of English monolingualism. The vast majority of people applying for a visa for 'skilled work' in the United Kingdom, for example, are subject to the following restriction:

> You must score 10 points for your English language skills ... If you are unable to score 10 points for English language skills, your application will be refused, even if you have scored 50 points or more for attributes and have met all the other Tier 2 requirements.
>
> (UK Home Office 2015 Tier 2 of the Points Based Visa System – Policy Guidance, 131–132)

The political power that is important here is the power to shape the world in accordance with this normative ideological perspective, and the power to reward and punish people according to how well their practice fits with such a perspective.

Not all political decisions about language take this codified state-backed form. Cameron (1995) discusses numerous cases of 'verbal hygiene', normative debates about language in the media, education, the workplace, and day-to-day life that are also debates about a range of political issues, such as social inequalities. The Occupy movement of 2011 provides a good example of non-state action to shape language. The movement's 'retaking and rediscovering of words and language' (Sitrin and Azzelini 2012: 19; Graeber 2014) involved finding new ways of doing political debate. Many involved in the Occupy movement believed that representative democracy (whereby we elect political representatives to debate political issues on our behalf) should be replaced by direct democracy (whereby we all have an equal right – and ability – to speak for ourselves). To facilitate this direct democracy within the movement itself, new forms of communication were developed and codified, including sets of hand signals to indicate various types of agreement and disagreement. The idea behind these hand signals was that they afford 'horizontal' consensus-decision making in ways that traditional forms of political debate do not. A speaker, looking at a crowd, can supposedly quickly gauge the extent of (dis)agreement with what she is saying, and the communicative hierarchies associated with traditional forms of democratic discussion can be avoided. This was a political project that involved work on and with language, and shows how political processes are often productive, or constitutive of language itself. National languages, such as English, are formed in practices of nation building, by the printing press, dictionaries, and education and immigration policy (Hobsbawm 1992). The Occupy movement involved using language to say things about how the world should be. But it also involved arguments about how language itself should be. Language is itself a political 'product', and not just an instrumental part of the process (Cameron 2006). We can relate this to Crick's idea of politics as a 'solution to the problem of social order'. Using language is part of the solution. But it is a 'solution' which itself raises further problems, such as whose language is to be considered 'right' or 'appropriate' to particular practices and forms of identity (including national identity), what the right way of talking about the environment or economic inequality is, or how political debate should be carried out.

Current disputes and future directions

The politics of language is, by its very nature, constantly heading off in new directions and becoming embroiled in new disputes. Since the study of language and politics is always the study of historically and culturally situated practices, and it is always conducted by researchers who are themselves historically and culturally situated, this means that academic research in the field is likely to respond to these changes. At the same time, there are a number of striking continuities between Ancient Greece and Rome and contemporary thought. Throughout the years, for example, we have seen debates between those who would conceive of political language as an exercise in manipulation and those who would conceive of it as a more open deliberative process. Recently Chilton (2004) has called these the Machiavellian and Aristotelian conceptions of political language, respectively. In what follows, I do not hope to do justice to the full range of concerns and debates in which current and future researchers of the politics of English (will) find themselves involved, but I do wish to point to a few key tendencies.

The normativity of English language research

Perhaps the most prominent area of dispute when it comes to the politics of English has to do with the normativity of linguistic research itself. I have said above that politics itself is necessarily normative. Political actors make evaluations of the world in their language and in their other actions. That includes making evaluations of language. But should the academic study of language be normative in this way, too? Should, we, as linguists, make judgements about how language should and should not be used? For most of the scholars discussed so far in this chapter, the answer to both of these questions would be 'yes'. But it is not an uncontroversial answer. Avowedly normative, political researchers of language have often been criticised for being so by researchers who see no place for the supposedly subjective commitments of politics in linguistic research. Quirk (1990), for instance, disparagingly refers to 'liberation linguistics' in debates about English around the world, and the discourse analyst Widdowson (1995) considers the field of critical discourse analysis to rest on a contradiction in terms; one cannot be 'critical' *and* do 'analysis', since analysis cannot be 'subjective' (and political commitments are, he seems to assume we all agree, 'subjective' things). Both of these writers have been answered by scholars for whom there is simply no other way of researching the spread of English around the world or the uses of English to communicate politically significant world views than to be, in some way or another, politically committed (Kachru 1991; Fairclough 1995, respectively). Even to seek to avoid political commitment would be simply to reinforce the status quo, and that, in the end, is just as political as challenging it. From this perspective, questions about the politics of English are necessarily themselves political questions. When we see language in its social and political situation, the idea that we could – or should – simply *describe* that situation is as limited as the idea that we could – or should – simply describe any other aspect of human life, be it town planning, medical care, furniture design, music, or theatre. However, it might still be argued that many such critical researchers risk blunting their political edge somewhat by reproducing Widdowson's assumption that there exists something basically subjective about the normative stances they bring to bear (e.g. Fowler 1996), as if to be political about language is simply to be open about your own bias, rather than to claim that there is any particular merit in that supposed bias.

In relation to this equation of researcher normativity with bias and subjectivity, Sayer's (2011) critique of the avoidance of ethical argument in the social sciences offers a useful perspective. Sayer has suggested that a lot of social research is guilty of what he calls 'cryptonormativity'. By this he means that scholars write with a vague sense of political and ethical normativity, but without explicit and developed arguments about what is good, what is bad, or why. This goes too for explicitly critical work, which, as Sayer observes, often either simply takes the relativising position, 'Yes, I am bringing my political stance to bear, but I am doing so just because it is my political stance, not because I make any claim that it is right', or it avoids the need for ethical justification by assuming a shared political perspective in its audience rather than arguing for the particular form of socialist, feminist, anti-racist or whatever politics it is that underlies the critique. Sayer's own response to this is to suggest that critical social and political research be grounded in a more explicit sense of the moral or ethical significance of human life (2011). Others suggest that a form of 'immanent critique' is the best basis for political normativity, identifying and questioning *contradictions* in the existing linguistic, social, and political order (e.g. Fairclough 2010; Herzog 2016).

Reflexivity

Much of what I have written in this chapter so far is indicative of an important fact about the politics of language: it is not only we, as academic researchers, who are reflecting on and, potentially, evaluating it (e.g. Cameron 1995; Agha 2007; Zienkowski 2017) This has been a central tenet of recent linguistic anthropological research into political language (Hill 2008; Lempert and Silverstein 2012), as well as some discourse analytic work (e.g. Schröter 2013). Such work has shown how the meanings of speeches, interviews, press conferences, and other canonically political uses of language are continually recontextualised, remediated, and to a significant degree actually constituted by their discussion in the media. Hill's study of the racist 'gaffes' of US politicians is particularly revealing of the relationship between the things that political agents say and the language ideologies available to the media and public to make sense of their language. Such 'ethnoblooperology', as Lempert and Silverstein (2012) term it, is a useful measure of the significance of ideologies of interpretation that may otherwise go unnoticed. This, and more broadly naturalistic investigation of existing political meta-language, can also be a useful theoretical and methodological corrective to text-focused approaches to political language which sometimes treat political discourse as if it is not ordinarily subject to sophisticated practices of interpretation and critique (see Jones 2007).

Pride and profit

'Pride' and 'profit' are terms used by Heller and Duchêne (2012) to name two basic ideological orientations towards political choices about language, especially as made by nation states. The shift from 'pride' to 'profit' is of particular interest to contemporary scholars of the politics of English. As Heller and Duchêne see it, pride-based, or 'ethnonationalist' (Heller 2003) ideologies of language have played a vital role in the development of the nation state over the past few hundred years. Such ideologies see language as rooted in the tradition of a people, and suggest that political choices about language in the nation state and its institutions (parliament, courts, education, broadcasting, immigration office, etc.) should be geared towards the maintenance of such a tradition. More recently, though, profit-based, or 'commodified' ideologies have risen to prominence. These see language as an economic asset, and political choices about language as strategic profit-oriented decisions. These two ideologies in turn relate to wider political ideologies of ethnonationalism and neoliberalism respectively, and the relationship of commodified ideologies of language to neoliberal political ideologies is of particular contemporary concern. While, as Holborow (2015) shows, language has long been conceptualised in vaguely economic turns – Saussure, for instance, saw words as being like coins, and as having 'value' – this seems to be being intensified in many contemporary contexts, where whole languages, and particular linguistic competences, are evaluated by political actors largely in terms of what is perceived to be their actual market value. Such evaluations of language are in accord with, and constitutive of, the broader 'commodification of everything' that Harvey (2005) identifies in neoliberal politics. However, even while language is increasingly commodified, such commodification remains in complex relations with the better established, ethnonationalist ideologies. 'Traditional' languages and linguistic practices are part of what is being sold when language is commodified, for instance (Heller and Duchêne 2012). There is future work to be done in tracing the ongoing relations between these two (and other) ideologies of language, and in relating them to wider political changes. The recent intensification of nationalist politics in the United States and much of Europe presents a particular challenge in this regard.

As a broader point, it is worth noting here that if we conceive of politics as a solution to the problem of social order, then simply pointing out that these two ideologies *are* ideological is not a solution. The question, for political actors, including politically interested linguists, must also be how we *should* understand relations between language and national identity, or at least what is *wrong* with these particular ways of understanding it. This is likely to take us outside the boundaries of linguistics or English Language studies as currently conceived, but it will not take us outside politics or ideology more generally. This is because the politics of English is tied up in political debate more generally, and uses of English or arguments about English cannot be understood, assessed, or critiqued independent of this. If we want to argue with nationalist ideologies of English, for example, then we are arguing with a kind of nationalism. This may involve engaging with arguments of the kind that geographers, historians, political scientists, and philosophers are used to making. Yet more generally, to refer back to some other relations between politics and language, if we identify articulations of particular world views or constructions of leadership style in English, then evaluating these world views and styles is not simply a linguistic matter, and if we are critical of the linguistic practices of particular institutions, such as parliament, then that involves arguing about what those institutions should be like in a broader sense; for example, about how the power to speak ought to be distributed. In each of these cases, and any other that we might encounter, we cannot assume that the critical 'solutions' to situations that we find so troubling are simply obvious or that they are going to be matters of consensus. All of this might seem to be taking us very far from the 'linguistics' of things. Certainly, members of the public critical of the language of political debate have little concern for whether their criticisms are essentially 'linguistic' or 'political'. Discussing the politics of English is much like discussing the politics of anything else, an essentially normative, ideological matter, with little time for institutional boundaries (Graham 2003).

New media and political change

Another recent development that has caught the interest of English language researchers is the invention and rapid growth of online 'digital', 'new' and/or 'social' media (see Deumert (2014) on the terminology; see also Spilioti, and Neary and Ringrow, this volume). Few are in any doubt that such media have changed the ways in which many people do political talk, and have raised new questions about how political talk is, and should be, institutionalised. To give a single example, for the political theorist van Reybrouck, the fact that this new technology 'gives people a voice' makes 'the electoral system [of Western representative democracy] creak at the seams' (van Reybrouck 2016: 53). However, there is less agreement on how we should respond to such changes, and indeed on many of the communicative details of the changes themselves. It is these communicative details that English language researchers have tended to hone in on, asking what exactly people are doing with their apparently newfound online voices. Such research has often answered that social media communication is used in order to construct relations of identity and community (e.g. Zappavigna 2011; Seargeant and Tagg 2014). There is a challenge, perhaps, in bringing this perspective together with the larger political questions, so that we can understand the ways in which social media communication feeds into more macro-level political debate, if it does so at all (though see Fairclough and Fairclough (2012) for discussion of readers' comments on online news articles as political argumentation). It may give people a voice – though under some regimes it does not even do this – but how and under what conditions it allows those voices to be *heard as* contributions to large scale political debate is another question. What kind of political agency does engaging in online debate give people? How does what ordinary citizens say on Facebook or Twitter relate to the decisions made by political leaders? In one form or another, these are questions that have always been central to the politics of language. They are raised with particular intensity by forms of new media, but they are continuous with long-standing questions about who is to speak, and how. Democracy itself is centrally a theory of who should speak (and who should listen, Green 2010), and necessarily involves making decisions about the arrangements of rights and opportunities for people – the 'demos' – to speak and to be heard.

Conclusion

Politics is never very far away from the things that we say and write, in English or in any other language. Political decisions have shaped, and continue to shape, the language that we have learnt in schools and that we hear on television. They shape what we can and cannot be punished for saying and writing, and how the things that we say are evaluated as 'good' or 'bad' English. Such political decisions are ongoing, essentially normative, ideological, and inflected by and constitutive of social relations of power. Conversely, without us saying and writing things, we could not have politics at all. Politics depends on language, on our ability to use it to articulate conceptions of what the world is like, what it could be like, and what it should be like. This chapter has covered some of the key concepts and controversies in the ways that English language researchers (and some other scholars) have dealt with this complex but necessary relationship between language and politics. However, while some of these concepts and controversies are of considerable vintage, both politics and language are essentially open phenomena, bound to enter into new relations and to raise new difficulties and arguments.

Further reading

Joseph, J. E. (2006) *Language and Politics*. Edinburgh: Edinburgh University Press. This book takes in both political uses of language, and political debates about language. Joseph puts forward the argument that language is 'political from top to bottom', and, true to this claim, provides a wide-ranging account.

Chilton, P. (2004) *Analysing Political Discourse*. London: Routledge. This book puts forward a general approach to analysing political discourse. It is influenced by cognitive linguistics, but sufficiently broad that its insights can be put to use by researchers working in other fields too.

Fairclough, I. and N. Fairclough (2012). *Political Discourse Analysis*. London: Routledge. This book argues for an argumentation-based approach to political discourse, drawing on insights from linguists, philosophers, theorists of rhetoric, and political scientists. Empirically, it focuses on British political discourse from the period following the 2007/8 financial crisis, but the real drivers of the book are the wider theoretical and methodological arguments about what political discourse is and how we should investigate it.

Cameron, D. (1995) *Verbal Hygiene*. London: Routledge. This is a seminal text which remains the best discussion of politics of debates about language. Those debates are generally slightly more 'micro' in their politics than the ones discussed in this chapter, but Cameron's general argument that language is necessarily subject to normative discussion is one that is useful for the investigation of the politics of language very generally.

Related topics

- English and colonialism
- Persuasive language
- Media, power and representation.

References

Agha, A. (2007) *Language and Social Relations*. Cambridge: Cambridge University Press.
Anderson, B. (1983) *Imagined Communities*. London: Verso.
Aristotle (1951) *The Politics*. Trans T. A. Sinclair. Harmondsworth: Penguin.
Blommaert, J. (2009) 'Language, asylum, and the national order', *Current Anthropology* 50 (4): 415–441.
Cameron, D. (1992) *Feminism and Linguistic Theory*. 2nd edn. Houndmills: Palgrave Macmillan.
Cameron, D. (1995) *Verbal Hygiene*. London: Routledge.
Cameron, D. (2006) 'Ideology and language', *Journal of Political Ideologies* 11 (2): 141–152.
Chilton, P. (2004) *Analysing Political Discourse*. London: Routledge.
Coupland, N. (2007) *Style*. Cambridge: Cambridge University Press.
Crick, B. (1964) *In Defence of Politics*. Harmondworth: Penguin.
Deumert, A. (2014) *Sociolinguistics and Mobile Communication*. Edinburgh: Edinburgh University Press.

Fairclough, N. (1995) 'A reply to Henry Widdowson's "Discourse analysis: a critical view"', *Language and Literature* 5 (1): 49–56.
Fairclough, N. (2000) *New Labour, New Language?* London: Routledge.
Fairclough, N. (2015) *Language and Power.* 3rd edn. London: Routledge.
Fairclough, N. (2010) *Critical Discourse Analysis.* 2nd edn. London: Routledge.
Fairclough, I. and N. Fairclough (2012) *Political Discourse Analysis.* London: Routledge.
Farrelly, M. (2010) 'Critical discourse analysis in political studies: An illustrative analysis of the "empowerment" agenda', *Politics* 30 (2): 98–104.
Finlayson, A. (2013) 'Critique and political argumentation', *Political Studies Review* 11 (3): 313–320.
Fowler, R. (1996) 'On critical linguistics', in C. R. Caldas-Coulthard and M. Coulthard (eds), *Texts and Practices.* London: Routledge, 3–14.
Fowler, R., R. Hodge, G. Kress and T. Trew. (1979) *Language and Control.* London: Routledge and Kegan Paul.
Gabrielatos, C. and P. Baker (2008) 'Fleeing, sneaking, flooding: A corpus analysis of discursive constructions of refugees and asylum seekers in the UK press, 1996–2005', *Journal of English Linguistics* 36 (1): 5–38.
Graeber, D. (2014) *The Democracy Project.* London: Penguin.
Graham, P. (2003) 'Critical discourse analysis and evaluative meaning', in G. Weiss and R. Wodak (eds), *Critical Discourse Analysis.* Basingstoke: Palgrave, 110–129.
Green, J. (2010) *The Eyes of the People.* Oxford: Oxford University Press.
Harvey, D. (2005) *A Brief History of Neoliberalism.* Oxford: Oxford University Press.
Heller, M. (2003) 'Globalization, the new economy, and the commodification of language and identity'. *Journal of Sociolinguistics* 7(4): 473–492.
Heller, M. and A. Duchêne (2012) 'Pride and profit: Changing discourses of language, capital and nation-state', in A. Duchêne and M. Heller (eds), *Language in Late Capitalism: Pride and Profit.* London: Routledge, 1–21.
Herzog, B. (2016) *Discourse Analysis as Social Critique.* Basingstoke: Palgrave Macmillan.
Hill, J. (2008) *The Everyday Language of White Racism.* Oxford: Wiley-Blackwell.
Hobsbawm, E. (1992) *Nations and Nationalism since 1780.* Cambridge: Cambridge University Press.
Holborow, M. (2015) *Language and Neoliberalism.* London: Routledge.
Huntington, H. E. (2016) 'Pepper spray cop and the American dream: Using synecdoche and metaphor to unlock internet memes' visual political rhetoric', *Communication Studies* 67 (1): 77–93.
Jessop, B. (2004) 'Critical semiotic analysis and cultural political economy'. *Critical Discourse Studies* 1(2): 159–174.
Jones, P. (2007) 'Why there's no such thing as "critical discourse analysis"', *Language & Communication* 27 (4): 337–368.
Kachru, B. (1991) 'Liberation linguistics and the Quirk concern', *English Today* 7 (1): 3–13.
Lempert, M. and M. Silverstein (2012) *Creatures of Politics.* Bloomington: Indiana University Press.
Lippmann, W. (1932) *Public Opinion.* London: George Allen & Unwin.
Milroy, J. (2001) Language ideologies and the consequences of standardization. *Journal of Sociolinguistics* 5(4): 530–555.
Mulderrig, J. (2011) 'The grammar of governance', *Critical Discourse Studies* 8 (1): 45–68.
Orwell, G. (1954) *Nineteen Eighty-Four.* Harmondsworth: Penguin.
Orwell, G. (2004 [1946]) 'Politics and the English language', in *Why I Write.* London: Penguin, 102–120.
Pearce, M. (2005) 'Informalization in UK party election broadcasts 1966–97', *Language and Literature* 14 (1): 65–90.
Piller, I. (2001) 'Naturalization language testing and its basis in ideologies of national identity and citizenship', *International Journal of Bilingualism* 5 (3): 259–277.
Quirk, R. (1990) 'Language varieties and standard language', *English Today* 6 (1): 3–10.
Richardson, J. E. (2008) '"Our England": Discourses of "race" and class in party election leaflets', *Social Semiotics* 18 (3): 321–335.
Saussure, F. de (1983) *Course in General Linguistics.* Trans. R. Harris. London: Duckworth.
Sayer, A. (2006) 'Language and significance – or the importance of import', *Journal of Language and Politics* 5 (3): 449–471.
Sayer, A. (2011) *Why Things Matter to People.* Cambridge: Cambridge University Press.
Schröter, M. (2013) *Silence and Concealment in Political Discourse.* Amsterdam: John Benjamins.
Seargeant, P. and C. Tagg (eds) (2014) *The Language of Social Media.* Basingstoke: Palgrave Macmillan.

Shaw, S. (2000) 'Language, gender and floor apportionment in political debates', *Discourse & Society* 11 (3): 401–418.
Silverstein, M. (2003) *Talking Politics: The Substance of Style from Abe to 'W'*. Chicago: Prickly Paradigm.
Sitrin, M. and D. Azzelini (2012) *Occupying Language*. New York: Zuccotti Park Press.
Spender, D. (1980) *Man-Made Language*. London: Routledge & Kegan Paul.
Thornborrow, J. (2001) 'Questions, control and the organization of talk in calls to a radio phone-in', *Discourse Studies* 3 (1): 119–143.
Thornborrow, J. (2013) *Power Talk*. London: Routledge.
Waldron, J. (2012) *The Harm in Hate Speech*. London: Harvard University Press.
Widdowson, H. (1995) 'Discourse analysis: A critical view', *Language and Literature* 4 (3): 157–172.
Woolard, K. and B. Schieffelin (1994) 'Language ideology', *Annual Review of Anthropology* 23 (1): 55–82.
Van Dijk, T. (1993) 'Principles of critical discourse analysis', *Discourse & Society* 4 (2): 249–283.
Van Dijk, T. (2008) *Discourse and Power*. Basingstoke: Palgrave Macmillan.
Van Dijk, T. (2015) *Elite Discourse and Racism*. London: Sage.
Van Reybrouck, D. (2016) *Against Elections: The Case for Democracy*. London: Penguin.
Volosinov, V. (1973) *Marxism and the Philosophy of Language*. Trans. I. R. Titinuk. Cambridge, MA: Harvard University Press.
Zappavigna, M. (2011) 'Ambient affiliation: A linguistic perspective on Twitter', *New Media & Society* 13 (5): 788–806.
Zienkowski, J. (2017) 'Reflexivity in the transdisciplinary field of critical discourse studies', *Palgrave Communications* 3:17007.

17

Persuasive language

David Hann

Introduction

Human beings are highly social animals who use talk as their primary means of communication. It is hardly surprising then that they dedicate a good deal of their energy to attempting to persuade others to a particular action or a particular way of seeing the world. After all, negotiating conflicting viewpoints without recourse to such strategies as intimidation or violence is crucial to a tolerable and civilised existence. It could be argued that persuasion is the true measure of the power of language in that it can effect change without recourse to anything but the strength of its own resources.

This chapter examines persuasive language by, firstly, exploring its nature. It then provides a brief historical perspective on persuasion by looking back to its study by Aristotle, whose influence in the Western tradition of thought can be felt to the present day. The different ways in which persuasion has been understood and conceptualised in the field of applied linguistics are then explored. The chapter also discusses how the field is reacting to a changing world where the place of English as the world's lingua franca, together with rapid advances in telecommunications in the twenty-first century, have cemented its place as the pre-eminent language of political and commercial persuasion. Finally, possible avenues of future investigation are mooted.

What is persuasion?

It is important to establish initially exactly what sort of communicative phenomenon we are dealing with. A reflection on the meanings of two everyday sentences provides a starting point:

a) 'She asked me to postpone the meeting.'
b) 'She persuaded me to postpone the meeting.'

Sentence (b) suggests the possibility of initial resistance and an overcoming of that resistance. As such, it foregrounds the importance of the receiver of the message in a way which sentence (a) does not. After all, if the receiver does not comply, there is no persuasion. This explains the difficulty there would be in hazarding a guess at the linguistic form(s) persuasion would take in a particular instance compared to that for a request. Accommodating to the needs of a receiver and the context of its reception results in a process rather than a single act. In this regard, an associated but rather different meaning of persuasion is helpful. The notion of persuasion as a belief system, as when referring to someone's 'political persuasion', hints at an important element in persuasion itself. The process involves tapping into another's beliefs or viewpoints and moving them in some way. Perhaps, then, it is unsurprising that researchers looking into children's developing 'theory of mind', i.e. the ability to attribute feelings and beliefs to others, can effectively do so by investigating how their young subjects persuade another to an action (e.g. Bartsch et al. 2011). Persuasion, then, can encompass more than mere argumentation. As Charteris-Black points out, '[the] language of persuasion appeals both to our conscious rational judgements and to our unconscious emotional responses' (2005: xi). So, persuasive language can move us to change our minds, or at least modify our outlook, which may well involve moving us emotionally. As such, it is necessarily a two-way and interactive process even when it takes a monologic form such as someone standing at a podium delivering a speech. Indeed, the fact that persuasion foregrounds the relationship between the communicative trinity of sender, receiver and text makes it of particular interest to the applied linguist. As will be seen, different approaches place different emphases on these three elements. The interactive and intersubjective dimensions to persuasion, along with the means used in its execution, are all returned to in the course of this chapter.

Before looking at the different ways in which persuasion has been explored in the field of linguistics, however, it is instructive to look briefly at how it was first studied by the Ancient Greeks.

An historical perspective: Aristotle

Aristotle's (2004 [350 BCE]) *Rhetoric* is probably the most influential treatise on the art of persuasion to have been written, certainly in the Western world. The preceding discussion about persuasion appealing to the heart and head are central to its ideas. Aristotle saw rhetoric as comprising three persuasive elements: an appeal to reason (*logos*); an appeal to emotion (*pathos*); and an appeal to the good reputation of the speaker (*ethos*). He also regarded the craft of persuasion as being vital to the functioning of society, something central to the life of a community (BBC Radio 4 2004). It is perhaps no coincidence that it came to be regarded as a discipline worthy of study at a time when early democratic institutions were taking root in the Athenian state. After all, its acknowledgement of the requirement to take account of the needs and wants of an interlocutor is democratic in spirit. Indeed, some have argued that the importance of the persuasive arts has waxed and waned in societies in reverse proportion to the autocratic tendencies of those societies (Cockcroft and Cockcroft 2005: 8ff).

In the Aristotelian tradition, the study of rhetoric was looked at in the context of public speaking, where its practitioners can draw on a number of rhetorical devices that enhance the appeal of their message. These include the use of figurative language, such as metaphors and similes, and the manipulation of rhythm by various means, such as the use of repetition. These features are readily acknowledged as rhetorical devices to this day.

Key areas of investigation and relevant linguistic frameworks

The formal characteristics of effective rhetoric that Aristotle identified (2004 [350 BCE] Book III) have much in common with the properties of language which Roman Jakobson and the

Russian Formalists in the twentieth century saw as being characteristic of literary texts. Jakobson (1960: 356) sees language as having six principal functions, one of which is the poetic. This function allows language to draw attention to its own semantic, phonological and grammatical properties through the use of figures of speech, repetition and so on, features which Aristotle singled out as effective tools in the art of persuasion. In current linguistic approaches, interest in the rhetorical features in communication is most prominent in stylistics, an approach which has grown significantly in recent years and one which can trace its lineage directly back to the formalist school of literary criticism. Below is a very brief extract from one such example of stylistic analysis by David Crystal as he reflects on Barak Obama's victory speech when he first became American president in 2008:

> The rhetorical 'rule of three' is an important feature of the speech. It's something that all famous speech-makers use. Churchill was brilliant at it. But all public speakers know that they can get a round of applause if they use a triptych with structural parallelism:
>
> *I was with you yesterday*
> *I am with you today*
> *And I shall be with you tomorrow!*
>
> (Crystal 2008)

Crystal then goes on to look at how the following paired lines contrast with the triptych to provide variety and pace. Indeed, the linguistic features of the text itself are at the centre of his analysis, something which is typical of the stylistics approach in general. Although the discipline has broadened its focus in recent years to encompass an interest in contextual factors, the text remains its key concern. Nevertheless, it needs to be remembered that even within the formalist frameworks of analysis there are concepts such as foregrounding (Mukarovsky 1970 [1932]) and defamiliarisation (Shklovsky 1998 [1917]) which relate to how people react to texts and thus recognise, at least to a degree, the importance of the receiver in the persuasive process.

Another major approach to persuasion which retains the text as its main analytical focus is genre analysis. This sees the recognisable features of particular genres as being shaped by the communicative purposes to which they are put. Bakhtin (1981 [1935]: 289) sees genres as emerging in the repeated realisation of particular types of communication. Swales (1990) posits that genres are typified by certain types of 'move'. Moves can be defined as 'rhetorical instruments that realise a subset of specific communicative purposes associated with a genre' (Bhatia 2001: 84) and, as this definition implies, they are central in the process of persuasion. So, for example, Cheung (2008), in an analysis of emailed sales literature, identified various moves such as 'establishing credentials', each with their own subset of possible 'steps' (Cheung 2008: 168). This illustrates how the text is shaped, in part, by an anticipation of an audience's needs. This idea is integral to Mikhail Bakhtin's theorising of language, where he sees it as being infused with previous intentions and anticipating responses to come (1981 [1935]: 276–277). His contention that language is fundamentally dialogical and heteroglossic is helpful in explaining the interactive nature of persuasion and how it can be shaped to accommodate the needs of both sender and receiver. However, despite its recognition of the receiver, genre analysis retains a primarily textual focus, maybe in part because it tends to focus on written communication.

For persuasion to succeed, it has to have, in Austin's (1962: 101) terms, a 'perlocutionary effect'. In other words, it has to influence the listener's outlook or behaviour and thus, an analysis of its impact actually lies beyond the persuader's own language. Indeed, it has been argued by some that herein lies the difference between rhetoric and persuasion: 'Rhetoric refers to the act of communicating the hearer's perspective while persuasion refers both to speaker intentions and to successful outcomes' (Charteris-Black 2005: 8–9). As such, successful persuasion is more immediately identifiable in face-to-face interaction than written communication, as the reaction of the targeted audience is usually evident. However, when an analysis of persuasion moves into the area of spontaneous spoken interaction, everything becomes more complicated. There can, of course, be a tension between the desires and needs of the sender of a persuasive message and its recipient, and the moves in spoken interactions are often less premeditated and less predictable than in the written mode, emerging in the process itself.

The potential tension between the needs of the interlocutors in the persuasive process foregrounds the importance of protecting face, the immediacy of which is evident in spoken interactions. Goffman's (1990 [1959]) notion of face, a preferred self-image which speakers present to the world and which, ordinarily, they and their interlocutors seek to safeguard, is one which can be threatened in persuasion. In Brown and Levinson's (1987: 62) seminal politeness framework, persuasion can be seen as a threat to someone's 'negative face', the need that his or her 'actions be unimpeded by others'. Given the face threat that persuasion entails, some speakers may choose to be indirect, allowing their interlocutors to infer meanings that lie beneath the semantic surface. These off-record utterances have the advantage of being deniable. The philosopher Grice (1975) coined the term 'implicatures' to describe the ways in which inferences can be triggered when what he sees as the default cooperative maxims of conversation are flouted, as, for instance, when there is an inherent face threat in a communicative act.

The lasting legacy of the ideas of Goffman, Brown, Levinson and Grice can be witnessed in the analyses of influential contemporary figures in the area of persuasion, such as Culpeper and Haugh (2014). For instance, when exploring the to-ing and fro-ing of an interaction between a counsellor and pregnant client where the former is attempting to persuade the latter to stop smoking, the authors refer to Brown and Levinson's notions of off-record utterances and negative politeness while also drawing on Grice's concepts of implicature and the flouting of the maxims of Relation and Quantity (Culpeper and Haugh 2014: 212–214). However, the limitations of these influential frameworks have also been much discussed and both politeness theory and the cooperative principle have been criticised for underplaying the importance of cultural variation and the open-ended and contingent nature of communication. Indeed, Culpeper and Haugh themselves question politeness theory on these grounds (2014: 202 – 212). It also needs to be remembered that an important dimension to politeness and, by extension, persuasion, is the crucial role that paralinguistic features such as tone of voice play in the process. The cultural dimension to communication and its multimodal nature are returned to later in this chapter.

Persuasion as storytelling

An aspect of our everyday communications which can be an effective vehicle for persuading others to our view of the world and of ourselves, and one which is often collaborative in nature, is storytelling. The idea of the narrative has come to be seen as important, not only in academia, but also in everyday discourse, especially in relation to persuasive texts such as adverts and political speeches. The typical ways in which we narrate our experiences are structured in persuasive ways. It has been noted, for example, that Labov's influential model of the component parts of everyday narrative structure (Labov and Waletzky 1997) has clear parallels with the classical Roman rhetoricians' recommended sequencing for persuasive texts (Cockcroft and Cockcroft 2005: 137).

Recalling Crystal's analysis, mentioned earlier in this chapter, of part of a speech at the beginning of Obama's presidential career, an examination of one at the end of it illustrates the close parallels between classical rhetorical structures and the narrative structures associated with Labov's framework. These extracts are from the President's last State of the Union address in 2016. Although only a small part of the speech is presented here, the extracts provide an insight into its overall structure. The brief analysis which follows looks at each of the sections in turn:

a) Tonight marks the eighth year that I've come here to report on the State of the Union. And for this final one, I'm going to try to make it a little shorter. (Applause.) I know some of you are antsy to get back to Iowa. (Laughter.) I've been there. I'll be shaking hands afterwards if you want some tips. (Laughter.) And I understand that because it's an election season, expectations for what we will achieve this year are low. (. . .)
b) We live in a time of extraordinary change – change that's reshaping the way we live, the way we work, our planet, our place in the world. (. . .) America has been through big changes before – wars and depression, the influx of new immigrants, workers fighting for a fair deal, movements to expand civil rights. Each time, there have been those who told us to fear the future; who claimed we could slam the brakes on change; who promised to restore past glory if we just got some group or idea that was threatening America under control.
c) And each time, we overcame those fears. We did not, in the words of Lincoln, adhere to the 'dogmas of the quiet past.' Instead we thought anew, and acted anew. We made change work for us, always extending America's promise outward, to the next frontier, to more people.
d) And because we did – because we saw opportunity where others saw only peril – we emerged stronger and better than before.
e) What was true then can be true now.

Section a), the introduction is, in classical rhetoric, where rapport with the audience needs to be established, one dictated by the structuring principle of *ethos.* Obama clearly does this through his use of humour and by his deliberately relating his own experience to that of his audience ('I've been there'). This is reinforced by his informal 'antsy', an American English word for impatient. In terms of Labov's narrative structure, the story hasn't really started at this point, although it could be argued that it forms part of what is classified as 'orientation' – some background to the story he's about to tell. He frames the speech in terms of it being his final hurrah and nobody expects his administration to achieve much in the coming year.

Section b) could be classified in rhetorical terms as a combination of the 'statement of facts' and 'the point at issue' (Cockcroft and Cockcroft 2005: 136). Of course, how facts are presented has a big effect on how they are perceived and there is a clear setting up here of an oppositional narrative ('there have been those who told us to fear the future'). In Labov's terms, this recounting of what had happened is part of the story's orientation.

Section c) is a combination, in classical rhetorical terms, of the 'proof of the case' and the 'refutation of the opponent's case' where 'we' overcame the fears that others had expressed. In Labov's terms, this is the 'complicating action' – the things that happened without which there would be no story. Note how Section c) comes as no surprise, as the expectation of such an outcome has already been seeded in the preceding section.

Section d) is, in rhetorical terms, part of the conclusion which the previous discussion leads to. Labov would classify it as the 'evaluation' of the story; that is, the lesson to be learnt from it. However, although positing evaluation as a possible stage of a narrative, Labov recognises that speakers' explicit and implicit evaluations pervade the stories they tell through such means as lexical choices (Labov 1972: 370–375).

Section e) is again part of the conclusion. Labov, however, defines it as a separate stage of the narrative – its 'coda', where the narrator relates what has been said to the here and now.

Although each stage of both classical rhetoric and Labovian narrative is somewhat fuzzy in its boundaries and may not even be present in a particular persuasive or narrative text, the brief analysis above shows the parallels between the two and how narrative is often used for persuasive ends. This is hardly surprising as stories are imbued with particular viewpoints and the very objective of persuasive texts is to seek to influence viewpoint.

The Cognitive Turn

The persuasive power of the narrative form is evident at the individual cognitive level, and work in this area focuses much of its attention on the receiver of the persuasive text. The importance of storytelling to cognition has been increasingly recognised in various disciplines, especially since the twentieth-century philosopher Walter Fisher reacted against the notion of a rational or scientific approach to knowledge. He maintained in his Narrative Paradigm theory that all meaningful communication is a form of storytelling where we understand the world through the stories we tell about it (Fisher 1984). For example, the concept of schemata (patterns of expectation shaped by our experiences), first mooted in psychology by Bartlett (1932), indicates that we bring a generic mini-narrative, a script of what-happens-when, to the situations we meet in our everyday lives. Memory is not merely receptive but constructive in nature and we make sense of the world by generalising from the specific. Thus, we relate new experiences to expectations based on what has gone before. These expectations can be exploited by the skilful persuader: 'Messages become persuasive when they evoke things that are already known or at least familiar' (Charteris-Black 2005: 10). This relates to the similarity model of argument (Cockcroft and Cockcroft 2005: 91). where the speaker or writer evokes similarities between one situation and another in order to convert an audience to their view. In Obama's State of the Nation address featured above, the story of people being presented with obstacles and then overcoming them against the odds is a universally recognised one which traverses cultures. The similarity model of argument links to another important area of cognition that the persuader can exploit to his or her own ends: the use of metaphor.

As previously mentioned, metaphor is something identified by Aristotle as one of the tools at the disposal of the rhetorician. It allows the speaker to liken an idea or concept to another, possibly more familiar one and, through forging a novel resemblance, deepen the audience's understanding of the former. However, Lakoff and Johnson's (1980) notion of cognitive metaphor conceptualises metaphor not so much as a figure of speech but as a figure of thought, something central to our understanding of the world. They claim that we make sense of abstract concepts through relating them to the physical world around us. This is important in persuasion because metaphor, it is argued, can subconsciously frame and constrain the ways in which an audience perceives an issue. Lakoff (2004: 3–34) himself noted how, for example, the concept of the nation can be understood using one of two related but competing metaphors: the stern father or the nurturing parent. Through the parent/nation metaphor, the abstract and imagined community of the nation is made accessible by relating it to our everyday experiences of the family. However, these two frames carry within them two very different ideological viewpoints. The stern father model values discipline, hard work and self-reliance while the nurturing parent model prizes cooperation and protection (see Lakoff 2016 for an application of this framework to the American presidential campaign of that year). Needless to say, these metaphorical understandings of the nation envisage very different roles for the state in people's lives. Thus, the use of metaphor to frame a description or discussion in a particular way can be seen as a powerful weapon in the persuader's arsenal. Other features of language that appear in persuasive discourse such as hyperbole and irony, which are traditionally regarded as rhetorical tropes, can usefully be looked at through the cognitive lens (e.g. Burgers et al. 2016).

Insights from social psychology can throw light on the conscious and subconscious cognitive processes at play in persuasion. Following an influential paper by Tversky and Kahneman (1974), a dual process theory of reasoning has held sway in the field of psychology. This posits that human beings have two distinctive systems which they use to make sense of the world: one which is largely subconscious, automatic and determined by biases and past experiences, and another which is conscious, effortful and employs logical reasoning. We might like to think that we usually use the latter but, in practice, it is the former which we more frequently rely on – in part because we don't have the cognitive stamina to do otherwise. Various theoretical models based around the dual process theory have been hypothesised (e.g. Sloman 1996; Petty and Cacioppo 1986). These models, though often quite different in detail, retain a notion of the two systems at work, one conscious and the other predominantly subconscious.

An appreciation of the importance of the subconscious system of cognition provides an insight into the effectiveness of particular textual features in an audience's reception of a message. For example, McGlone and Tofighbaksh (2000) found that messages which rhyme have a greater chance of being believed than those that don't. Repetition, often employed in persuasive texts from political speeches to adverts, has been shown to be an important means of ensuring a message is not only remembered but believed in what is known as the 'illusion-as-truth' effect (Kahneman 2011: 59ff). The very name of this phenomenon communicates an underlying uneasiness, a wariness of the power of persuasion to exploit which goes back to the birth of the study of persuasive language as a discipline in Ancient Greece.

Persuasion: skill or spell?

The boundary between persuasion and manipulation is a fuzzy one and the former has been viewed by some as a dark art. Even before Aristotle, Plato was wary of rhetoric, regarding it as a form of flattery that could sway the ignorant (Plato 1961 [fourth century BCE]). This suspicion of the art of persuasion lingers to this day. Words that frequently collocate with 'rhetoric' such as 'empty' or 'mere' point to an attitude where the features of persuasive language are regarded as indicative of show rather than substance. In Plato's day, this distrust of the persuasive speaker was directed towards the likes of the sophists – teachers of the arts of philosophy and rhetoric. Nowadays, such scepticism is more likely to be generated by the words of politicians, spin doctors, advertisers and, today's propagandists, the PR industry. Invariably, the accusation, to put it in Aristotelian terms, is that too much emphasis is placed on *ethos*, an appeal to the speaker's good name, as can be found in celebrity endorsements and the cultivation of corporate identities, and *pathos*, an appeal to the emotions, while not enough is put on *logos*, our logic and reasoning.

An approach in linguistics which reflects this general wariness about the tools of persuasion is Critical Discourse Analysis (CDA). It sees its job as one of uncovering the ideological workings of language which exercise power through 'consent', a power which it regards as perpetuating the status quo and, thus, social inequalities. It is an approach which seeks to reveal how a text can work on people's perceptions through its ideology, that is, the embedded assumptions about hierarchy and power that lie within it (Fairclough 2001: 2). One of CDA's aims is to bring this process of manipulation (be it intentional or not) to consciousness.

CDA draws on a number of methodologies in its analysis. At the textual level, it tends to favour a functional approach, examining, for example, how particular elements within a text are assigned grammatical roles which present 'reality' in a particular way. Beyond the text itself, it looks at the ways in which texts are produced and consumed and how they perpetuate existing societal structures. Ideologically driven, it tends to concentrate on institutional, commercial and political discourses.

CDA has attracted criticism from various quarters. It has been accused, for example, of finding only what it wants to find, of lacking secure theoretical underpinnings and having a tendency to overlook important contextual factors such as the intersubjectivity at the heart of people's interactions (Jones 2007; Widdowson 2004). Nevertheless, some of its main practitioners retain a powerful influence in the applied linguistics field (e.g. Fairclough 2001; Van Dijk 2008; Wodak 2015). Furthermore, it has been argued that the accusation of bias levelled at it can be countered, at least to a degree, by the application of corpus software which provides a systemised means of revealing the ways in which readers can, over time, be ideologically positioned by texts such as newspaper articles (Coffin and O'Halloran 2010).

A new environment: implications for the researcher into persuasive language

The previous mention of corpus software reminds us that the study of persuasive language does not stand still but is inevitably influenced by technological and social changes that feed into and shape each other. One of the most significant developments of recent times in the media landscape has been the advent of the internet, and particularly social media, which has provided the first opportunity for ordinary citizens to broadcast to the many and receive responses in return without having to do so through channels controlled by others. This shift in the balance of receptive and productive activity in the new media has profound implications for the study of persuasion both in terms of the social effects of the widespread use of digital technologies and in terms of the aspects of persuasion which this new environment brings to the fore for analysis.

The fact that anyone can tweet or retweet a message or can post a video to YouTube is blurring the line in the political arena between the politician, the activist and the electorate, and, in the commercial sphere, between the advertiser and the consumer. As a result, the relationship between the persuader and their audience is becoming more complex and the former is having to adapt accordingly. In the commercial world, the ease with which a consumer can avoid advertising in the new media environment means that the producer/advertiser must find new ways to reach and engage their target audience. One strategy for doing this is to endeavour to build a long-term relationship with the consumer. This can be done through the consumer encountering a brand or product across multiple platforms and media. This enables the construction of a brand story, with the essential element of *pathos* that this can bring to selling a product: 'The emotions are a serious opportunity to get in touch with consumers. And best of all, emotion is an unlimited resource' (Kevin Roberts, CEO of Saatchi & Saatchi, quoted in Jenkins 2006: 70). In this regard, the affordances of the digital environment mean that advertisers are able not just to create sales texts but to build an architecture of hyperlinks around the text, bringing together multimedia and multimodal experiences for the consumer that can appeal to the senses and trigger a direct emotional response. Furthermore, they can encourage or incentivise potential consumers to send links to their own networks of friends and family (Cheung 2008: 162).

In the political field, the ability of citizens to tweet about events as they unfold allows the real-time dissemination of news and is as often a means of speaking to the outside world as it is to a domestic audience (Murthy 2013: 104). In this regard, the use of English on banners and posters during street protests in predominantly non-English speaking countries reveals an awareness among the politically active of the importance of influencing global opinion and the role that English, as the world's main lingua franca, inevitably plays in that process (e.g. Aboelezz 2016).

The mixing of English and local languages on protest banners is indicative of the way an interconnected world has facilitated the meeting and fusing of the global and the local. This process of 'glocalisation' can be seen in the ways that the prevailing political discourse, heavy with the ideological terminology of 'knowledge economies' and 'flexibility', is adapted or resisted at national and local levels (Wodak 2005). Glocalisation is evident in the commercial arena where multinational companies attempt to retain the power of their global brands and products, yet adapt their advertising and marketing to suit local cultural conditions (e.g. Kobayashi 2012). Commercial enterprises are, like street protestors, well aware of English's global reach. And this global reach gives it a symbolic significance as the language of modernity (e.g. Hasanova 2010); its use, as much as its semantic content, can have the power to persuade. Therefore, in a globalised context, it comes to function emblematically as much as it does linguistically (Blommaert 2010: 30–43). As a result, a common feature of adverts, packaging and labels is to mix English with local language(s) in order to trigger positive associations (e.g. Luna and Peracchio 2005).

The very media that allow commercial and political vested interests to promote their messages also allow an opposing discourse. The digital revolution has allowed people to reproduce, repurpose and recontextualise texts with ease, opening up officially vetted materials to parody and ridicule. As a result, 'memes' that take content and subvert it in some way are a common feature of online political discourse. They encourage resistance to established authority and are part of a transgressive discourse. To take just one example, a poster that came out in 2014 in response to the then Prime Minister of Turkey, Recep Tayyip Erdoğan's attempt to ban Twitter (Taylor 2014) featured a picture of Erdoğan with the words 'Yes, we ban'. This was an intertextual reference to Obama's original electoral slogan 'Yes, we can', contrasting the small-minded dictatorial action by the Turkish Prime Minister with the high-minded idealism that the latter phrase encapsulated.

The preceding discussion reinforces the idea that language is dialogical and heteroglossic. The digital environment brings into relief the multi-layered, multi-voiced, complex and contingent nature of communication, one which researchers into persuasive language need to accommodate through the approaches that they use, such as linguistic ethnography which endeavours to provide a detailed account of local interactions within their broader social contexts (Blackledge 2012) and a CDA approach based on 'ethical subjectivity' which attempts to uncover the voices of the powerless through using a corpus tool (O'Halloran 2014). The internet also highlights the issue of how persuasive language manifests itself in different cultural soils and, indeed, what happens when different rhetorical styles encounter each other.

Contrastive Rhetoric has been one response to the need to move away from an exclusively Anglo-Saxon notion of rhetorical norms in order to explore how persuasive texts are realised in different cultures. However, the contrastive approach is seen by some as risking an essentialist and reductive view of culture which privileges the national dimension and ignores the fact that cultures are multi-faceted, fluid and complex entities (Conor et al. 2016). The new globalised, interconnected world which many people now inhabit brings to the fore the fact that individuals are not just members of one culture but inhabit different social, professional and familial cultures. Indeed, some would argue that culture is best studied and understood by focusing on the individual rather than the group (e.g. Atkinson and Sohn 2013), thereby highlighting the contextually-dependent nature of rhetorical norms.

One aspect of the digital age which is pertinent to current and future analyses of persuasive texts is the increasingly multimodal nature of such texts. Of course, ever since persuasion was first deemed worthy of study, the importance of elements beyond language itself has been recognised. Classical rhetoric acknowledged the crucial effect that a speaker's delivery has on the persuasiveness (or otherwise) of the words uttered. The role of images that accompany words in advertising has been central to the genre since its inception. Yet, although multimodality is not new in itself, new technologies have facilitated the growth of multimodal, multimedia texts. One of the challenges for the researcher, even one focused primarily on the language of persuasion, is how to accommodate and talk about other semiotic resources such as image, colour and layout (Kress and van Leeuwen 2006) and how these interact with language to produce meaning. There is not the space to discuss multimodality in detail here. However, it is worth noting that, as with other current approaches, its focus is on situated action, on the fact that communication in different modes has been shaped by its sociocultural functions in those modes, and on the interaction of modes as part of the meaning-making process (Jewitt 2015: 69–70). Because of the complexity of factors at play in multimodal analysis, it often involves sampling videoed interactions and the use of analytical software (e.g. O'Halloran et al. 2013).

Finally, technological developments mean that the researcher has increasingly sophisticated tools at their disposal. The well-established use of corpus software has already been mentioned and is now core to much linguistic study. There are other technologies which have recently been developed that can be of aid to the researcher. Indeed, the commercial field has been quick to pick up on eye-tracking devices, MRI scans and electroencephalography (EEG), all of which have now become part of the marketing researcher's toolbox, allowing a glimpse into what is going on in our heads as we think and react to what we see and hear around us. These developments have intensified the age-old fears of the persuasive dark arts that Plato warned against (Garvey 2016). However, although eye-tracking devices have quickly been adopted in the research into how readers comprehend texts in educational settings (e.g. Was et al. 2016), this technology is yet to be exploited by scholars in understanding how texts can be used to sway an audience's viewpoint. It seems reasonable to assume that such exploitation is only a matter of time.

Conclusion

It is undeniable that we are living through interesting times for the analysis of persuasive language. Primarily due to technological advances in communication that have grown exponentially in recent years, there is the potential for individuals with limited resources to access audiences, however remote they might be culturally and geographically, and seek to influence them. They will often do so in English, which, given its current status as the world's lingua franca, looks set to retain an important role in such persuasion for some time to come. Persuaders can now reach their audiences across a range of platforms, using a range of media and adapting existing materials for their own ends. Research into persuasion needs to be able to encompass this multimodal, multi-voiced and often multilingual environment. At the same time, new tools are emerging which can be used to measure the effectiveness of persuasive texts. These tools can be used in the refashioning of such texts for commercial or political ends, but also have potential to facilitate academic research into them. However, despite the undoubted impact of the digital age on this and many other fields of communication, new debates are, in many ways, previous debates in modern guise. One of these is to do with the degree to which persuasive language can be trusted. Yet persuasion is essential to healthy private and public debate. The effective persuader must be able to appreciate how their audience views the world, and needs to understand the possible objections and arguments that can be raised to counter their own messages. In short, an effective persuader needs to appreciate both logical argument and empathy. As Aristotle himself asserted, the key to effective yet socially responsible persuasion is a balance between *logos*, *pathos* and *ethos*. As citizens, we need to be vigilant when it comes to detecting imbalances in the persuasive messages that surround us. Linguistic knowledge and analysis are key to this vital process.

Further reading

Charteris-Black, J. (2005) *Politicians and Rhetoric: The Persuasive Power of Metaphor*. Basingstoke: Palgrave Macmillan. This book focuses specifically on political discourse and demonstrates how a cognitive framework can throw light on the mechanisms at work in persuasion in the public arena.

Cockcroft, R. and S. Cockcroft (2005) *Persuading People: An Introduction to Rhetoric*. Basingstoke: Palgrave Macmillan. A useful introduction to the skills of rhetoric and how established linguistic frameworks and approaches can inform an analysis of the tools of effective persuasion.

Hann, D. and T. Lillis (eds) (2016) *The Politics of Language and Creativity in a Globalised World*. Milton Keynes: The Open University. The chapters in this collection focus on creativity and the shift from reception to production in the digital age. It looks at creative language as a resource for political activity as well as the politics surrounding the production, ownership and evaluation of creative output.

Jenkins, H. (2006) *Convergence Culture: Where Old and New Media Collide*. New York: New York University Press. Using a series of mostly American case studies, Jenkins explores the effect of 'convergence culture' on areas such as politics, advertising and education. While acknowledging the potential pitfalls of the digital age, he sees it primarily as empowering and democratising.

Related topics

- Metaphor studies and English
- The politics of English
- The language of social media
- Discourse analysis: studying and critiquing language in use.

References

Aboelezz, M. (2016) 'Creating a counter-space: Tahrir Square as a platform for linguistic creativity and political dissent', in D. Hann and T. Lillis (eds), *The Politics of Language and Creativity in a Globalised World*. Milton Keynes: The Open University, 103–112.

Aristotle (2004 [350 BCE]) *Rhetoric* (trans. R. W. Roberts). Mineola, NY: Dover Publications.

Atkinson, D. and J. Sohn (2013) 'Culture from the bottom up', *TESOL Quarterly* 47 (4): 669–693.

Austin, J. L. (1962) *How to Do Things with Words*. Oxford: Oxford University Press.

Bakhtin, M. (1981 [1935]) *The Dialogic Imagination*. Austin: University of Texas Press.

Bartlett, F. C. (1932) *Remembering: A Study in Experimental and Social Psychology*. Cambridge: Cambridge University Press.

Bartsch, K., C. Wade and D. Estes (2011) 'Children's attention to others' beliefs during persuasion: Improvised and selected arguments to puppets and people', *Social Development* 20 (2): 316–333.

BBC Radio 4 (2004) 'Rhetoric', programme first broadcast 28th October 2004 as part of *In Our Time* series. Available at www.bbc.co.uk/programmes/p004y263, accessed 13 August 2016.
Bhatia, V. K. (2001) 'Analyzing genre: Some conceptual issues', in M. Hewings (ed.), *Academic Writing in Context: Implications and Applications*. Birmingham: University of Birmingham Press.
Blackledge, A. (2012) 'Discourse and power', in J. P. Gee and M. Handford (eds), *Routledge Handbook of Discourse Analysis*. Abingdon: Routledge.
Blommaert, J. (2010) *The Sociolinguistics of Globalisation*. Cambridge: Cambridge University Press.
Brown, P. and S. Levinson (1987) *Politeness*. Cambridge: Cambridge University Press.
Burgers, C., E. A. Konijn and G. J. Steen (2016) 'Figurative framing: Shaping public discourse through metaphor, hyperbole, and irony', *Communication Theory* 26 (4): 410–430.
Charteris-Black, J. (2005) *Politicians and Rhetoric: The Persuasive Power of Metaphor*. Basingstoke: Palgrave Macmillan.
Cheung, M. (2008) '"Click here": The impact of new media on the encoding of persuasive messages in direct marketing', *Discourse Studies* 10 (2): 161–189.
Cockcroft, R. and S. Cockcroft (2005) *Persuading People: An Introduction to Rhetoric*. 2nd edn. Basingstoke: Palgrave Macmillan.
Coffin, C. and K. O'Halloran (2010) 'Finding the global groove: Theorising and analysing dynamic reader positioning using APPRAISAL, corpus, and a concordancer', in C. Coffin, T. Lillis and K. O'Halloran (eds), *Applied Linguistic Methods: A Reader*. Abingdon: Routledge; Milton Keynes: The Open University, 112–132.
Conor, U., E. Ene and A. Traversa (2016) 'Intercultural rhetoric' in K. Hyland and P. Shaw (eds.) *The Routledge Handbook of English for Academic Purposes*. Abingdon: Routledge, 270–282.
Crystal, D. (2008) 'On Obama's Victory Style', *DCBlog* [Online], Available at www.david-crystal.blogspot.co.uk/2008/11/on-obamas-victory-style.html, accessed 7 December 2016.
Culpeper, J. and M. Haugh (2014) *Pragmatics and the English Language*. Basingstoke: Palgrave Macmillan.
Fairclough, N. (2001) *Language and Power*. 2nd edn. Harlow: Pearson Education Ltd.
Fisher, W. R. (1984) 'Narration as human communication paradigm: The case of public moral argument', *Communication Monographs* 51: 1–22.
Garvey, J. (2016) *The Persuaders: The Hidden Industry that Wants to Change Your Mind*. London: Icon Books Ltd.
Goffman, E. (1990 [1959]) *The Presentation of Self in Everyday Life*. London: Penguin Books Ltd.
Grice, H. P. (1975) 'Logic and conversation', in P. Cole and J. Morgan (eds), *Syntax and Semantics, 3: Speech Acts*. New York: Academic Press.
Hasanova, D. (2010) 'English as a trademark of modernity and elitism', *English Today* 26 (1): 3–8.
Jakobson, R. (1960) 'Closing statement, linguistics and poetics', in T. Sebeok (ed.), *Style in Language*. Cambridge, MA: MIT Press.
Jenkins, H. (2006) *Convergence Culture: Where Old and New Media Collide*. New York: New York University Press.
Jewitt, C. (2015) 'Multimodal analysis', in A. Georgakopoulou and T. Spilioti (eds), *The Routledge Handbook of Language and Digital Communication*. Abingdon: Routledge, 69–84.
Jones, P. (2007) 'Why there is no such thing as "critical discourse analysis"', *Language and Communication* 27: 337–368.
Kahneman, K. (2011) *Thinking, Fast and Slow*. London: Penguin.
Kobayashi, K. (2012) 'Corporate nationalism and glocalization of Nike advertising in "Asia": Production and representation practices of cultural intermediaries', *Sociology of Sport Journal* 29: 42–61.
Kress, G. and T. van Leeuwen (2006) *Reading Images: The Grammar of Visual Design*. 2nd edn. London: Routledge.
Labov, W. (1972) *Language in the Inner City: Studies in the Black English vernacular*. Philadelphia: University of Pennsylvania Press.
Labov, W. and J. Waletzky (1997) 'Narrative analysis: Oral versions of personal experience', *Journal of Narrative and Life History* 7: 3–38.
Lakoff, G. (2004) *Don't Think of an Elephant: Know Your Values and Frame the Debate*. White River Junction: Chelsea Green Publishing.
Lakoff, G. (2016) '*"Understanding Trump" (published 23rd July 2016) in Lakoff's blog*' Available at www.georgelakoff.com/2016/07/23/understanding-trump-2/, accessed 24 August 2016.
Lakoff, G. and M. Johnson (1980) *Metaphors We Live By*. Chicago: University of Chicago Press.

Luna, D. and L. Peracchio (2005) 'Advertising to bilingual consumers: The impact of code-switching or persuasion', *Journal of Consumer Research* 31 (4): 760–765.
McGlone, M. S. and J. Tofighbaksh (2000) 'Birds of a feather flock conjointly (?): Rhyme as reason in aphorisms', *Psychological Science* 11(5): 424–428.
Mukarovsky, J. (1970 [1932]) 'Standard language and poetic language', in D. Freeman (ed.), *Linguistics and Literary Style*. New York: Holt, Rinehart and Winston.
Murthy, D. (2013) *Twitter*. Cambridge: Polity Press.
O'Halloran, K. (2014) 'Counter-discourse corpora, ethical subjectivity and critique of argument: An alternative critical discourse analysis pedagogy' in *Journal of Language and Politics* 13 (4): 781–813.
O'Halloran, K. L., K. L. E. Marissa, A. Podlasov and S. Tan (2013) 'Multimodal digital semiotics: The interaction of language with other resources', *Text & Talk* 33 (4–5): 665–690.
Petty, R. and J. Cacioppo (1986) 'The elaboration likelihood model of persuasion', *Advances in Experimental Social Psychology* 19: 123–181.
Plato (1961 [fourth century BCE]) 'Laws' (trans. A. E. Taylor), in E. Hamilton and H. Cairns (eds), *The Collected Dialogues of Plato*. Princeton: Princeton University Press, 11.937d–11.938a.
Shklovsky, V. (1998 [1917]) 'Art as technique', in J. Rivkin and M. Ryan (eds), *Literary Theory: An Anthology*. Malden: Blackwell Publishing Ltd.
Sloman, S. A. (1996) 'The empirical case for two systems of reasoning', *Psychological Bulletin* 119: 3–22.
Swales, J. M. (1990) *Genre Analysis: English in Academic and Research Settings*. Cambridge: Cambridge University Press.
Taylor, A. (2014) Why Turkey Banned Twitter (And Why Banning Twitter Isn't Working)', *The Washington Post*, 21 March 2014, Available at www.washingtonpost.com/news/worldviews/wp/2014/03/21/why-turkey-banned-twitter-and-why-banning-twitter-isnt-working/, accessed 16 August 2016.
Tversky, A. and D. Kahneman (1974) 'Judgement and uncertainty: Heuristics and biases', *Science* 185: 1124–1131.
Van Dijk, T. (2008) *Discourse and Power*. Houndsmills: Palgrave.
Was, C., F. Sansosti and B. Morris (eds) (2016) *Eye-Tracking Technology in Educational Research*. Hershey, PA: IGI Global.
Widdowson, H. G. (2004) *Text, Context, Pretext: Critical Issues in Discourse Analysis*. Oxford: Blackwell Publishing.
Wodak, R. (2005) 'Global and local patterns in political discourses – "Glocalisation"', *Journal of Language and Politics* 4 (3): 367–370.
Wodak, R. (2015) *The Politics of Fear: What Right-Wing Populist Discourses Mean*. London: Sage.

18

Literature and the English language

Geoff Hall

Background

Literature influenced earlier understandings and valuations of English, an influence that continues today in English studies in the UK and beyond. English-language literary texts typically use language in recognisable but at times unusual ways to prompt responses in readers or auditors. In this chapter I focus on the 'literary use' of English language which can sometimes be unusual or noticeable, but which also exists on a continuum with other uses of language. I make a distinction between literature as *text,* with identifiable linguistic tendencies, and literature as *discourse*, meaning texts that offer distinct challenges and satisfactions to particular readers when compared with other texts. The chapter also reports some historical perspectives on the development of the English language traceable through literary texts, with the aim on contextualising contemporary Literary Linguistics in a broader study of English and showing how recent work offers empirical evidence to support claims about particular authors and 'literary language' more generally.

To begin focusing the wider discussion we may sample some utterances taken from English language literature:

1 That was a way of putting it – not very satisfactory.
2 Sit ye down father. Rest ye.
3 I will do such things. What they are, yet I know not.
4 Their heads are green, and their hands are blue, And they went to sea in a sieve.
5 Woman much missed, how you call to me, call to me.
6 I wake and feel the fell of dark, not day.

All of these quotations are easily remembered by me from some of my own favourite uncontroversially literary texts, from poetry and drama more specifically (compare Tambling 1988, examples and discussion). The memorability of some literary text is itself an interesting feature, indicating careful design and appropriacy to recognisable meanings. A reader may wish then to consider what might be specifically 'literary' about these instances of language use, or whether indeed they are particularly literary at all. At first sight the extracts contain some obviously less frequent vocabulary items such as 'sieve' (text), but we also note that what is really original is going to sea in a sieve (discourse), and perhaps also the surprising colours of the actors, and the challenge to our usual narrative expectations of cause and effect or logical sequence of some kind ('And'). '[Y]e' is old fashioned or dialectal language (2), though the invitation is otherwise entirely everyday and unremarkable. Old-fashioned too, probably, is the sequence of 'yet I know not' (3). In the case of (6) from G. M. Hopkins's late sonnets, 'fell' is ambiguous, likely to be noticed as both dialectal and old-fashioned ('fell' for 'fall') but also exploiting the less common and traditional meaning of 'skin', 'fur', 'pelt of animal'. Examples (1), (3) and (6) use negative structures for ideas difficult to express, unsatisfactory or counter-intuitive. You may also note that parallel structures commonly found in literature, repetitions or near repetitions come to our attention, such as 'ye'/ 'ye' (2), 'call to me' (5), alliteration as repetition ('feel'/ 'fell'; 'much' 'missed'/' me'), or poetic metre pushing a reader to consider relations between 'green', 'blue' and 'sieve' (4). Example (1) contains a metalinguistic reflection on its own adequacy or felicity; much literature is overtly concerned with itself in this way. In form, however (1) looks like conversational ordinary language use.

In sum, I would submit that utterances like these are fascinating both for their apparent ordinariness and readability, and the fact that at the same time they can also be seen as slightly unusual, highly designed and suggestive instances of language use. Some language items are 'foregrounded' (Garvin 1964), designed to catch a reader's attention. They are more fundamentally highly meaningful in context, including emotional charge. Importantly, any linguistic literariness they may display or that may be discerned lies as much in their uses in context (what I have labelled 'discourse') as in intrinsic formal features and patternings ('text'). Literature is a linguistic textual phenomenon, but also a sociocultural phenomenon, and a cognitive phenomenon offering readers particular challenges that many report enjoying and valuing. (Maybin and Pearce 2006 introduce each of these perspectives carefully in turn).

Literature as text and discourse

Variation is the most basic characteristic of language use in literature and a wider range of variation is typically found in literary texts than in any other text type or genre. Any language can be used in literature, whereas most other text types and genres are more constrained. For example, a weather forecast or a sales letter will not normally feature the same range of vocabulary, grammar, rhetorical and other devices as a literary text – though it is important to note that *some* of the same features will be found. There is no hard and fast dividing line between the literary and the non-literary, whether textually or more widely. More interesting still, a story, novel, poem, drama or other literary work may well include within it apparently faithful representations or even actual 'found' reproductions of weather forecasts, sales letters, dialogues in the street and in the boardroom and much more besides, recontextualised for new aesthetic, reflective purposes. Literature is a kind of 'supergenre' in this sense, able in principle to include any other genre to do a different job from the one the language used was originally designed to do. Language will typically be less standard in form in literature than in most other forms of communication. Or more accurately, literature, particularly in more modern times, can be expected to contain a mix of the standard and the non-standard. This mix and variation of language features is so distinctive that it can be claimed to be a distinguishing and defining feature of a literary text even in a time when genres in general seem to be less fixed and formal than they once were. Certainly all linguists who have looked at English language literature have agreed for some time that the language used is characteristically non-standard (Blake (1981) remains a classic early study with multiple examples).

To extend this idea of variation, Carter and Nash (1990) coined the useful term *re-registration* to point to the way literary works use a wide range of registers and deliberately bring them into contact or even conflict with each other (another example of 'foregrounding') so that literature can be defined, in this view, at least literature in English in more modern times, as texts which employ an unusually wide range of differing styles and registers, where most genres (a business letter, a tax form, a notice in a hospital) will typically display a more monochrome style. In re-registration, meaning is generated precisely from shifts and contrasts of register. Bakhtin (1981) had anticipated this point in the earlier part of the 20th century with his ideas of 'heteroglossia', in 'Discourse in the Novel' [1934-35] tracing a wide range of 'languages' (registers and styles) in character speech as well as in narration in classic 19th-century novels by Dickens and Dostoevsky. Adamson (1998), Jeffries (1993) and others have shown how this 'novelisation' as Bakhtin termed it, today extends to poetry, drama and indeed all the literary genres and forms, with very few exceptions. A poet like Philip Larkin characteristically structures his poetry precisely upon register clashes to foreground (typically) a metaphysical or spiritual point with 'poetic' marked language against the banality of everyday experience represented by more everyday language (see, for example, Larkin's 'Sad Steps'; on register, see Biber and Conrad 2001, but also Butler 1999).

A further and related distinctive feature of literary texts to be noted, however, is that functionally, where a sales letter or weather forecast, job interview or even chatting with a friend in a café has identifiable purposes or functions, the function of a literary text – another way to know one when you read or hear it – is likely to be less obvious, or at least 'socially and historically variable' (Burton and Carter 2006), valued by different groups for different reasons at different times, with inferential work expected and required rather than any immediately obvious surface meaning to be easily taken away. The purpose may be aesthetic, social or cultural, political, educational, or indeed produced almost involuntarily for the sheer pleasure, satisfaction or need of creative self-expression. The purpose of a literary utterance may not be known even to the author and crucially, unlike other forms of communication we experience, it is not obviously directed specifically and purposefully at the reader who reads it or auditor who hears it, sometimes hundreds of years later in contexts which could never have been predicted. Even an advertisement (closely related linguistically to literature in its tolerance for variation) has a clear purpose: to engage with your desires, wishes and anxieties in ways more directive than the literary work, and you were certainly intended to notice it if not immediately act upon it. What, by contrast, is a reader of a novel supposed to do when they have read it, as a result of this reading? What is the value of the reading of a text never in the first place particularly intended for this particular reader? Indeed it is remarkable, given how vague or varied the functions of literature reading often are, on a first glance, how many people over so many centuries have been prepared to give so much time and other resource to such a poorly defined activity, whether as producers or consumers or both, and how highly the activities associated with literature production and consumption have often been valued. The source of this value, and the extent to which the valuation is linguistic, must be a concern for this chapter and takes us into the idea of literature as sociocultural discourse (language use considered in contexts of use).

Literature, then – to offer a working definition – is a vague and generic term usually given to a large and somewhat miscellaneous range of texts, usually fictional or imaginative, that a given group values particularly highly for aesthetic or cultural reasons (after Eagleton 1983). These texts are linguistically distinct, if at all, only in their eclectic range of use of language forms and features and a tendency to self-awareness of forms used. Returning to the examples with which I began, it may be noticed how repetition or partial repetition is a typical feature of literary texts. But again, those opening quotations were also intended to prompt the reader to consider whether this is a distinctive or perhaps just a more pronounced feature of the literary utterance than of more obviously non-literary language use. Readers will have their own prototypes associated with 'literature', perhaps including notions of pleasure and recreation, creativity and ingenuity, even moments of profound insight into some aspect of the human condition; or sometimes less pleasant and more strenuous memories of difficult reading and assignments in school, puzzling to make sense of unusual language forms or use or combinations of forms.

English literature typically has for its central object of study a group of texts historically valued, or found to be of particular interest at least, often for ethnic, nationalist or purportedly linguistic reasons. Other claims relate to ethical or related benefits to be gained from literary experience by individuals and societies. Many now prefer to use the term 'literatures in English' rather than 'English literature' precisely to emphasise the growing global diversity and variety of both English language use, as explored elsewhere in this Handbook, but also the growing diversity of literary production, distribution and consumption of such literatures even as that very fact sometimes provokes politicians or educationalists to a new attempt at control, limitations and prescriptivism. Thus Carter (2016; after Bakhtin 1981) usefully prompts us to consider competing 'centripetal' and centrifugal' swings and tensions in relation to English use and study through history and beyond the purely educational field. Orthodoxy in modern literary studies values diversity over standardisation, the centrifugal rather than the centripetal features of English use, with ever-increasing diversity in English language use and in literatures written in English an evident fact (see also Burton and Carter 2006).

Prize-winning novels or other works of literature represent varied experience from around the world, of varied authors from around the world, with differing identities and with experimentation with literary form also commonly found. Importantly, such prizes are typically controversial and disputed. Allington (2016) among others reports characteristic suspicion of the publishing and prize awarding industry on the part of self-identifying 'ordinary readers' in book groups or on websites. Assignation of value and consequent rewards is typically contested with regard to literary creation. It is interesting to note, however, that when disputes threaten in book groups, readers will often refer other readers back to the precise language of the text under discussion (Peplow 2016). Similarly, the fundamental contention of scholars working in the area of linguistics known as stylistics, is that the experience of the precise language of the literary text is where understandings and interpretations begin and will typically return to. Readers of literature will often notice more consciously and carefully the surface linguistic forms in a literary text than they do when processing other forms of linguistic communication (Zwaan 1994).

Historical perspectives

In education, a qualification in English at school in the UK by the mid-20th century, required for white collar jobs, university entry and many other more advantageous pathways in life meant certified knowledge of and ability to write essays about classical literary works, rather an odd requirement at first sight. Very few jobs would require literary reading skills understood as the ability to read poems, plays or stories, or to write critically about them. Nevertheless, literature was felt to be central to understandings of and competence in using English language and even to English identity for many of those awarding certificates and offering or withholding jobs. A singular and clearly knowable English language, to be located, it seemed, somewhere in the realm of literature, was pretty much taken for granted, with the abundant evidence suggesting that the situation was not actually so simple pretty much ignored. Similarly, the idea that literature or English literature is a straightforward knowable body of knowledge or experience came to be widely challenged even as advocates tried to elaborate its contents and ways of working, mainly through the 20th century. Modern understandings of *literature*, at first programmatic, increasingly more nuanced and empirically informed, and then critical, emerged from the 19th century in Europe and the US with the governing class's anxieties around decline of Christian faith, class tensions and gender, and not least deriving from the demands of empire (Viswanathan 1989). (for useful overviews see Eagleton 1983; Williams 1977; Baldick 1983). Literature was posited or presented by influential 19th-century cultural pundit Matthew Arnold as the 'best' uses of English and so a model to study and to imitate in schools and beyond. Valued culture, for Arnold, was 'the best which has been thought and said', notably in classic literature (Arnold 2006 [1869]). Poetry is still commonly seen as 'the best words in the best order', in the aphorism widely attributed to English Romantic writer Samuel Coleridge.

Literature was also the authoritative source of knowledge of the English language as philology emerged, notably from the 18th century in Europe. For example, Murray's first edition of the Oxford English Dictionary (OED) on historical principles took the majority of its citations used to illustrate the English language from literary works and from the King James Authorised translation of the Bible and the Book of Common Prayer, from Shakespeare in particular (and from *Hamlet* in particular from within that corpus: 'in my mind's eye' etc.). Such facts have much to tell us about a culture's preoccupations: see Winchester (2003). Our lifespan is still for many marked as 'a vale of tears' as we move, Christian by belief or not, 'to love and to cherish' someone 'till death us do part', 'for richer, for poorer', 'in sickness and in health', toward 'ashes to ashes and dust to dust' (*Book of Common Prayer*). Today we find it surprising how much language from literature still occurs in everyday speech. However, the supposed 'standard' form and the 'literary' form were much the same thing for respected early scholars. Just as literary scholars were attempting to fix the canon of English literature, so too the philologists and lexicographers were attempting to fix the standard language, and the two projects were mutually intertwined. Racist and nationalist ideologies of England and the English were also being constructed with the help of such notions of pure, essentialised English language and literature, and the supposed shared culture of the English. Ironically, however, the historical approach of what became known as the Oxford English Dictionary, to give the date of first written use and meaning and then show how these meanings change over time, of course already began to undermine the idea that any simple and unchanging 'truth' about the English language can be definitively established by consulting the OED. Critiques of this 'fixing' have come from linguists but also from within literary studies itself in more recent times. Multiple and contested understandings of English as well as of (English) literature now exist. This is partly because of the historical development of ideas of English language and partly by dint of the very nature of literary uses of language as themselves by definition linguistically reflexive, inclusive and culturally central. Literature, as is generally agreed by those who have studied these issues, 'foregrounds' for our attention language and language use, whether in English or any other language. Scholars of language and educators have thus predictably often been drawn to the study of language in literature, even though modern linguistics would argue that this is to mistake the part for the whole.

One key reason for the variation found in literature is simply because it is a historical collection of texts. Languages vary over time. Adamson (1998) is the best single source for understanding the historical and changing nature of the language used in English language literature. (See also for historical English language studies and literature, including a brief introduction to Adamson's research, Auer et al. 2016). Adamson traces an ordinary-language impulse in literary writers in English from the 19th century at least, undoubtedly complicated by modernism with its notoriously difficult literary texts, but consistently resisting and struggling against artificially literary heightened or 'poetic' (in a denigratory sense) style. Increasingly colloquial or demotic and/ or mixed styles, including representations of non-standard language use are characteristic of much contemporary literature, not least that which is most highly valued, one aspect of contemporary cultural 'conversationalisation', through dialects and other vernacular strategies (Hodson 2014) as in writers like Larkin, Harrison or the present Poet Laureate in the UK, Carol Ann Duffy (examples in Hall 2000; Jeffries 1993). While the prototype of literature for many will be a written text, literature was originally oral (early ballads, legends and epics) and in many cases still is. The winner of the Nobel Prize for Literature 2016 is Bob Dylan, whose lyrics will be known to most as sung, not as written. It is interesting to consider from Adamson's account, the way in which the spoken 'ordinary everyday language' is returned to again and again in literature as a resource for creative use and improvisation, though this may also be changing with the affordances of modern technology to record, reproduce, sample and then broadcast sounds ever more easily and creatively.

Literary language

Jakobson's classic 1960s linguistic essay on 'poetic language' was arguably the beginning of modern stylistics and has been much discussed elsewhere in print. There Jakobson posited, in essence, that 'poetic language' is found predominantly in literature, where it is to be understood functionally as language that in one way or another draws attention to itself. Standard devices for doing this are repetition or near repetition ('parallelism' is Jakobson's term) and deviant uses of language (neologism, archaic language, unusual collocations, innovative uses of figurative language, dialect forms in standard contexts (or vice versa) and so on. See, for example, discussions in Goodman and O' Halloran 2006; Jeffries 1996; Tambling 1988). Many of these ideas remain very fertile sources of understanding of how language in literature works. Cognitive poetics has taken up such ideas as 'foregrounding' as a defining characteristic of literature; salient forms or uses are likely to be noticed and found meaningful by the literary reader (see Stockwell 2002 for an introduction to foregrounding and cognitive poetics more widely.) Also interesting, for example, is Jakobson's idea that because of this concentration on language forms literature can be driven by language as much as by meaning (unlike the weather forecast or a sales letter). Thus popular musician Ian Dury wrote lyrics for his songs with the aid of a rhyming dictionary, with the rhyme word then driving the backward formation of the rest of the line. Sound driving sense, as Jakobson would say. Most of us who have tried to do any extended writing recognise the truth of E. M. Forster's widely quoted adage, 'How do I know what I think until I see what I say?' It is basic to literature to be particularly concerned with form, perhaps especially when reading and writing poetry. A genre like the sonnet can be extended and played with (16 line sonnets in sequence in the cases of George Meredith and Tony Harrison rather than the usual 14 lines) but here as elsewhere form (rhyme, rhythm, metre) is found by many to be creatively enabling as well as sometimes constraining. Creative literary writing can be a key space for such experimentation and play with form and meaning.

Early stylistics showed how revealing attention to the 'language of literature' could be. Halliday (1967) on linguistics of agency in William Golding's novel *The Inheritors* is still highly illuminating analysis. Later stylistics went on to raise important sociocultural issues in literary writing through close and informed examination of the language used. Nash (1990), for example, showed how close the language of popular romances sometimes was to the much more highly valued literary language of D. H. Lawrence, as well as suggesting some interesting differences. Staying with studies in language and gender, stylisticians investigated claims from critics, literary theorists and writers themselves that women somehow 'write differently' from men. Woolf's idea of the 'female sentence' was empirically shown to be at best highly problematic, textually speaking (e.g. Mills (1995), 'The Gendered Sentence'.) Others have looked at linguistic constructions of gender in literature, for example Hermione in the best-selling Harry Potter series (Eberhardt 2017). Sotirova's (2011) subtle studies of free indirect speech have shown the value of attention to language as a primary fact of any literary experience. Most recently, a stylistics of discourse has necessarily concerned itself with actual acts of literary reception and literary reading practices where traditional stylistics and literary criticism tended to speculate or assert without evidence on the effects of language in literature on a purely textual basis (Allington and Pihlaja 2016; Allington and Swann 2009; Peplow et al. 2016).

Stories are also to be found in everyday conversation with much the same features and structure as in literature. When does storytelling become recognisable as literary fiction? What features of a story may lead to a higher valuation than for some others? Is life writing (for example) 'literature' (biography or autobiography)? Children's or teenage fiction? Graphic novels? Most important for the present discussion, how far are these evaluations based on language use alone? Toolan (2001) offers an informed introduction to the worlds of narrative and its study (narratology), which serves as another area of enquiry for those who wish to investigate what literature is, or how it works, and the role of language in that working. The answers lie in awareness of language use as discourse: who is writing for whom about what, as much as what they are writing. Educational or other powers and authorities, publishers and exam boards, critics and teachers, will play a crucial role in generating or promoting wider evaluations of stories. Toolan (2012) specifically investigates the fascinating question of the linguistics of 'bad literature', when unconvincing or clumsy language use disqualifies a text from the label of literature. (See Toolan 2012 on valued creative use of repetition versus repetition as irritating or ineffective writing).

Thus the basic point needs to be clearly reiterated that literary language is recognised and valued as such as discourse. That is, utterances are literary because of the context in which they occur, the co-text of utterances or sentences preceding and following, the larger context of the whole poem/play/ novel, and larger contexts such as the literature lesson at school, the reading circle or public performance. Taken alone and out of context, any of the examples with which I began could have been found in non-literary contexts. 'Non-literature' is an interesting thought experiment, but for that reason is not meaningfully considered in terms of isolated sentences. The non-literary, in so far as it can be found or imagined, is language used (by author or reader) for non-literary purposes. (See Carter (2004), for example, on the surprisingly pervasive poetic nature of everyday discourse.) There is nothing or little literary or non-literary but thinking makes it so. No literary readers, no literature, as some would have it. Zwaan (1994) again offers strong empirical evidence for such a position.

Recent research

In this section I report briefly on some instances of linguistic or stylistic research into language use in literature to illustrate the advances and advantages a more scientific approach to our topic can bring.

Corpus linguistics research on literary language

As has been argued already, there is no single linguistic feature distinguishing the supergenre Literature from the non-literary, nor does a single feature distinguish a novel from a poem, a sermon from a lecture. Rather, as Biber and colleagues notably show through computational linguistic analysis (Biber and Conrad 2001), clusters of tendencies suggest the presence of the literary or a specific genre and the likelihood of its being taken for literature by a given group and even valued as a strong exemplar of literature. It was already established by the 1990s (Carter and Nash 1990; Adamson 1998) that what is unusual about language in literature is actually not only unusual (or 'deviant') uses of forms, but also the very range of styles and registers to be found in literary works, particularly in modern times. Language variation includes dialect (regional, class) style (gender, identity, idiolect) and register. Register is a term used by linguists to label uses of language (media news, sports commentary, legal document, adult talking to child and so on) which experienced users of a language can recognise as identifying or even constructing a situation of language use. (Montgomery et al. 2013, Chapter 7 is a good basic introduction to the idea with reference to literary texts.) Corpus linguistic work of Biber and colleagues went on to identify statistically systematic 'dimensions' of a language use in literature use (clusters of 'features', we might say, such as particular pronoun use co-occurring with particular tenses or sentence structures) which co-occur and come to show relative tendencies of a particular genre in comparison with other genres (see Biber and Conrad 2001; more recent examples in Biber and Conrad 2009). Overall Biber's work statistically supports Adamson or others who argue that literature and indeed English language use generally has become more vernacular and less formal over time to the present day. (Biber and Finegan 1989 was an important first sketch). Fictional literary texts such as the novel are shown to typically share many features with personal phone conversations or examples of written interpersonal communication. The more closely a genre is specified ('19th-century realist novel', 'Victorian narrative poetry', etc.) the more easily and reliably linguistic dimensions can be identified. 'Literature'– even 'English literature' – is not identifiable purely linguistically but probabilistic tendencies can be identified for specific literary genres. There is no 'literary language' then, in any useful generalised sense, but some typical uses of language, particularly in relation to specific literary genres. Corpus linguistics has now shown this systematically and extensively, beyond the single qualitatively 'hand-harvested' examples of the earliest linguists who looked at this question.

Shakespeare's language

A second example of more recent scholarship on language use in literature can refer to advances in Shakespeare studies. The writings usually attributed to William Shakespeare have often been taken as the paradigmatic instance of literature in the English language in modern times. Here if anywhere is highly valued literary use of language. It is therefore worth pausing to examine more carefully some of the claims that have been made for Shakespeare's language by non-linguists and then to show what more recent linguistic research can add to such claims and understandings. Once again, it can be seen that inflated claims for the distinctive nature of literary language use have to be carefully qualified. Probably the most persuasive and impressive single volume on Shakespeare's language to date is Kermode (2001). The eye of an experienced editor has carefully examined speeches and exchanges with the detail of the Shakespeare canon and contexts fully in mind, and the results are fascinating and illuminating. Nevertheless, the method is frustratingly impressionistic. Why look at this speech or word(s) rather than another? The examination is driven by literary judgments of dramatic value rather than by issues of language description or analysis, despite the book's title *Shakespeare's Language*. We learn a lot about Shakespeare's writing but only incidentally about his language. The account is highly selective without the principles for selection being made explicit. The focus is firmly on describing characters and plot first and foremost; the language in which this is done actually remains secondary. Historical understanding of Elizabethan rhetoric is the discipline used through most of the book with very little evidence of any knowledge or interest in what linguistics since the 17th century might have to offer one of the most sophisticated Shakespeare scholars in the world at that time. It is an unfortunate missed opportunity. Later plays, we are told at one point, in a fascinating cataloguing of repetitions and near repetitions in Shakespeare's writings, are 'unlike the rhetoric of earlier rhetoric' (Kermode 2001: 216). Earlier plays have characters who talk like the rhetoric books Shakespeare would have studied at school (35). I would trust Kermode's highly informed intuition, or at least find it worth investigating. Unfortunately, unable or unwilling to apply linguistic methodologies, Kermode seems to have no resource beyond this impression to analyse and describe in what way exactly the repetition differs between earlier and later plays. Interesting quotations are offered, but no systematic account, a good example of the difference between literary criticism and stylistics (Hall 2014).

More promising for those wishing to explore systematically and scientifically Shakespeare's use of English is research related to Culpeper's (2016) 'Shakespeare Encyclopedia' project based at Lancaster University, UK. Through a computational corpus-linguistic approach features of Shakespeare's word use, grammar, semantics and more can be highlighted both in their own right, and importantly against a background of contemporary uses. This analysis allows us to see what might have been distinctive about Shakespeare's writing and could have contributed to his being noticed and valued by some contemporaries as a leading playwright even before the near canonisation that took place from the 18th century onward, where sociocultural factors are obviously an important part of the bard's growing reputation beyond any purely linguistic virtues (Taylor 1989). Although some commentators historically have pointed to the size and range of Shakespeare's vocabulary as a source of his greatness, Elliott and Valenza (2011) show that this statistical claim is not valid. The impression of an unusually large vocabulary can be explained both against the general growth of English vocabulary during the period in which Shakespeare wrote and in which he inevitably participated and the demands of dramatic writing, where other contemporary dramatists were using a similar or even larger range. Similarly, examining a myth largely promoted by OED's pervasive quoting of Shakespeare as 'first' user of a new word meaning or word, Goodland (2011) shows that Shakespeare's reputation for coining new words has been much exaggerated because of weaknesses in the original gathering and recording of first usages. Such research implicitly raises interesting questions about the sometimes unreflecting high valuation of originality of language use and forms in the overall valuation of creativity. While there is no space here to discuss the issue, computational linguistics also makes increasingly sophisticated contributions to authorship attribution studies (e.g. Vickers 2004 on Shakespeare). Even if qualitative judgements of scholars will always also be finally inescapable, they can be usefully informed by such statistics. Elsewhere, Hoover (2007), for example, uses computational methods in thoughtful ways to deepen our understanding of the evolving style and techniques of Henry James.

Metaphor in literature

Literature is thought to be particularly prone to metaphor and other non-literal uses of language. Once again, however, modern linguistics gives a more precise and nuanced picture.

Metaphor is pervasive through all kinds of language use (Lakoff and Johnson 1980). What varies is what kinds of metaphor are used and how. Metaphor in literature is typically innovatory and elaborated rather than conventional and passing, not more frequent than in other text types, but interestingly, often self-consciously signalled as such (Lakoff and Turner 1989; Dorst 2015). It may be convenient here to instance Sylvia Plath's poem 'Metaphors'. This is another instance of the central argument of this chapter, that the language found in literature is not fundamentally different from other uses of language, but may be deployed in original ways for primarily creative purposes. Our understanding of these specificities has grown with recent research (see also Semino and Steen 2008). For modern cognitive linguistics, metaphor is thinking as much as it is language use, or the two are indivisible, so that the novel metaphors of literary works naturally are used to explore innovatory thought and expression, once again moving understandings on from linguistic surface form text to discourse and meanings.

Dispute and debate: why read literature?

If, then, literature is linguistically different in its range and exploitation of the resources of English, but not completely different, what might be the value or advantages of continuing to read literature when there are ever more distractions, and less demanding, often more immediately attractive ways to spend our time? The literature fan whose attention to literature has been rewarded in past experience will need no convincing but a new generation of readers are clearly not reading the same things in the same way as their parents did. Literature reading (broadly understood) is widely agreed to lead to an expanded vocabulary and general language awareness enhancement, and those who read more, unsurprisingly, become more fluent readers and usually also better readers on a variety of measures. Further claims for writing skills advantages are made, most convincingly where creative writing and other more active approaches to literature reading are used. Advocates for stylistics or looser language-based approaches to literature reading argue that evidence-based approaches to literature through its language increase accessibility for those who find literary texts difficult or confusing, giving them a way in from which more rewarding literary experiences may grow. The relative success and growth in popularity in the UK of various English language and literature 'A level' (school leaving) syllabuses in recent years suggests many teachers and students find something in such claims (Stockwell 2016: 220; for further statistics, see reports of the UK English Subject Group). Literary critics see a need to engage with the language of literary texts in scholarship, criticism and education, but at the same time express hostility to purportedly reductive linguistic approaches or stylistics without offering any alternative (Hall 2014). As with Kermode's (2001) sophisticated ruminations on Shakespeare's writings, much literary criticism and linguistic research in such areas could and should be mutually informing, but sadly this occurs too infrequently. A 'keyword' (for example) for a literary critic is thematic and intuitive, but far more nuanced and contextual than the frequency statistics of the linguist's 'keyword' (a word occurring more frequently in a text than probability would predict). For computers 'what you see is what you get'; critics will always be better at inferencing and interpretation. The challenge is to produce an account of the language of literary texts that can bring insights and findings of the two parties into dialogue. These enquiries can and should be complementary rather than conflictual.

It is probably uncontroversial now to recognise the need for flexible understandings of literature. Culture wars and battles over the canon are largely a matter of the past for educators if not for politicians. Literature for those in education is widely understood to be an appropriate way to engage in formal education or in wider life-issues such as migration, diaspora, globalisation, race and ethnicity. Not long ago UK Education Minister Michael Gove upset many such educators by insisting on removing American literature titles by John Steinbeck from school study in favour of Shakespeare and 19th-century English poetry with a declared nationalistic agenda. A difficulty readers like Gove have with the expanded canon of literatures in English is increasing globalisation in English language literary creation and the obvious non-standard uses of English in many writers with a wide range of variation. The shortcoming of such views, as we have seen, is that variation and non-standard uses have been central to works recognised as literature from the beginning and increasingly so in more recent times. The problem of accessibility of Shakespeare is partly of outdated language, but as Kermode (2001) points out, no audience of Shakespeare ever understood or indeed listened to every word of his plays. One mistake is to approach literature with inappropriate expectations. England and the English were only ever an imagined community. The same applies to novels or stories from Africa, Asia or the many places in between: to be sometimes puzzled in our reading is not a bad thing. Creativity in English language use was ever thus. Reading literature problematises notions of one correct or standard English, both now and across history; it cannot possibly teach such mistaken notions. The UK school standards auditing body Ofsted worries in recurrent reports that too many 'non-fiction' texts are being used and studied, that their value is not clear, and they can be studied in other subjects anyway. As this chapter argues, however, the only way to appreciate what literary writings might offer that is different or new is precisely to study them against the background of other genres from which they are thought to differ and on which they draw.

Future directions

Space only allows a very brief highlighting here of some more obvious topics for future research, already touched on in this account. Hewings et al. (2016) can fill out some of these topics further for those interested as well as my own references included below.

- Corpus linguistics (e.g. Mahlberg; Culpeper et al., Biber) and 'digital humanities' generally prompts new questions as well as deepening understanding of older ones. Its contribution has already been important but there is still clearly much to offer. Thus Mahlberg (2013) studies repetition and parallelism in Dickens as a creative technique in ways facilitated by software and digitised storage of the work. A similarly repetitive and even obsessive writer like D. H. Lawrence would benefit from such an approach too.
- Related are studies of literature and new media, new technologies, Kindles, audio books and more. New technologies are prompting new reading and writing practices, particularly among younger readers (Deegan and Hayler 2016). Language study needs necessarily to give way to more multimodal studies of semiotic creativity and reception as new technologies affect composition and consumption of creative texts in ways we are only beginning to study and understand.
- Literary reading research (compare Peplow and Carter 2014) is a relatively new area for the investigation of how readers make literary meanings from words. Growing awareness of which words are noticed, for what purposes and how deployed in interpretation is one immediate benefit from this stream of research and the role of language in literary meaning making. Some aspects of the account of literary language in this chapter may well need to be modified as these findings extend.
- New Englishes, postcolonial Englishes, transnational and translingual creative uses, and hybridity are the norm in much new literature in English. Remarkably little has been

written to date on code-mixing and related phenomena in English literary works, or perhaps rather in works with a 'matrix' of English language (Sebba et al. 2012). The phenomenon is not entirely new, of course – consider the multilingual realities of medieval England, to be seen as late as Chaucer's early attempts at vernacular English-language literature in the 14th century; Wolf (2017) has explored George Eliot's use of French in her classic English Victorian novels. Taylor-Batty (2014) has begun to explore the pervasive multilingualism informing classic modernist literature in English. There is no doubt however that such practices are becoming ever more common and seem likely to continue or increase into the foreseeable future. 'English', as elsewhere in this Handbook, is not a straightforward idea, but nationalistic and monolingual approaches have limited understandings of literature as of language to date.
- Cognitive and neurolinguistic advances are prompting new understandings and new understandings of literary linguistic practices. One fascinating example (Garrard et al. 2005) expands our understanding of Alzheimer's as well as of literature by charting a narrowing vocabulary in the later novels of Iris Murdoch.
- New interest in ethics and literature reading – e.g. educational research into 'empathy' and emotions in the literary reading experience is also being driven by cognitive linguistics (Sklar 2013). Language is a way of relating to each other, understanding each other and building relations. This traditional role of literature is increasingly investigated rather than just taken for granted or asserted and undoubtedly feeds into the educational arguments for engagement with literature and 'English studies'.

Cultural and linguistic creativity generally, including creative writing, has never been more popular than it is today. 'Other people' used to write 'literature' and tell us how to read it. Now more and more ordinary people participate in various ways in literary creativity across a range of sites. Literature has been a demonstrably important source for many expressions and usages in English historically, though the importance of literature as such a source may now be declining even as classic literature reading is arguably declining, or at least broader and looser notions of the literary are coming into play. A recent study found British people could more readily quote fragments of advertising than they could recall classic literary texts ('I'm lovin' it', 'Does exactly what it says on the tin', etc.) (Guardian 2008). Advertising undoubtedly uses literary linguistic strategies and devices quite extensively and appeals in some of the same ways at times (Cook 2001), and we live in a culture of promotional messages. Literature has also played a crucial part in historical efforts to 'fix' a standard English language, and in attempts by those in power through education and other cultural mediation to enforce norms of best or 'proper' English language use, broadly in foredoomed attempts to hold back language change (Aitchison 2013). There is much research still to be done in this demanding and still rapidly evolving area even as our understandings of literature and of the English language continue to evolve. Literature is a 'site of struggle' as Bakhtin (1981) rightly observed, and these struggles take place in and through language use in literature. In debates over literary language are to be found key indicators of who readers want and don't want to be and how they want to live. If literature didn't matter, these often emotional and controversial debates would have ceased long ago. They matter.

Further reading

Adamson, S. (1998) 'Literary language', in S. Romaine (ed.), *The Cambridge History of the English Language*. Vol 4. 1776–1997. Cambridge: Cambridge University Press. 7: 589–692. A classic, but not yet surpassed, informed introduction to modern literary language and its evolution toward more vernacular standards in recent times. Also raises many other relevant areas for those interested by this chapter.

Hall, G. (2014) 'Stylistics as literary criticism', in P. Stockwell and S. Whiteley (eds), *The Cambridge Handbook of Stylistics*, Ch. 7, Cambridge: Cambridge University Press, 87–100. Language as an issue in literary criticism and linguistic or stylistic approaches to English literature. The argument is that unhelpful hostilities and misunderstandings which are illustrated can and should be overcome in the interests of the value of both approaches.

Hall, G. (2015) *Literature in Language Education*. 2nd edn. Basingstoke: Palgrave Macmillan Ch. 1 Literary language and ordinary language. Discusses some of the issues raised here in more depth and with further references.

Pope, R. (2012) *Studying English Literature and Language. An Introduction* [*The English Language Studies Book*]. 3rd edn. London: Routledge. A lively, sometimes provocative introduction to many of the themes broached here and their centrality to 'English studies'. Can be read selectively or opportunistically as a reference book rather than a straightforward textbook, and contains many useful examples to explore and stimulate new insights and connections.

Language and Literature (Sage journal) ISSN: 0963-9470 Online ISSN: 1461-7293. The leading international research journal for issues in language and literature will give a taste of the range of issues and approaches that currently exist.

Related topics

- The idea of English
- World Englishes: disciplinary debates and future directions
- Standards in English
- The language of creative writing
- Stylistics: studying literary and everyday style in English.

References

Adamson, S. (1998) 'Literary language', in S. Romaine (ed.), *The Cambridge History of the English Language*. Vol. 4. 1776–1997. Cambridge: Cambridge University Press, 7: 589–692.

Aitchison, J. (2013) *Language Change. Progress or Decay?* 4th edn. Cambridge: Cambridge University Press.

Allington, D. (2016) '"Power to the reader" or "degradation of literary taste"? Professional critics and Amazon customers as reviewers of *The Inheritance of Loss*', *Language and Literature* 25 (3): 254–278.

Allington, D. and S. Pihlaja (eds) (2016) 'Special issue. Reading in the age of the internet', *Language and Literature* 25 (3) 201–307.

Allington, D. and J. Swann (eds) (2009) 'Special issue. Researching literary reading as social practice', *Language and Literature* 18 (3): 219–334.

Arnold, M. (2006) [1869] *Culture and Anarchy*, in J. Garnett (ed.), Oxford: Oxford World's Classics.

Auer, A., V. Gonzalez-Diaz, J. Hodson and V. Sotirova (eds) (2016) *Linguistics and Literary History*. Amsterdam: Benjamins.

Bakhtin, M. M. (1981) *The Dialogic Imagination. Four Essays*, in M. Holquist (ed.). Trs. C. Emerson and M. Holquist, Austin: University of Texas Press.

Baldick, C. (1983) *The Social Mission of English Criticism 1848–1932*. Oxford: Oxford University Press.

Biber, D. and S. Conrad (2001) 'Register variation: A corpus approach', in D. Schiffrin, D. Tannen and H. E. Hamilton (eds), *Handbook of Discourse Analysis*. Malden, MA: Blackwell, 175–196.

Biber, D. and S. Conrad (2009) *Register, Genre and Style*. New York: Cambridge University Press.

Biber, D. and E. Finegan (1989) 'Drift and the evolution of English style. A history of three genres', *Language* 65: 487–517.

Blake, N. F. (1981) *Non-Standard Language in English Literature*. London: Andre Deutsch.

Burton, B. and R. Carter (2006) 'Literature and the language of literature', in K. Brown (ed.), *Encyclopedia of Language and Linguistics*. 2nd edn. Oxford: Elsevier: 267–274.

Butler, L. S. J. (1999) *Registering the Difference*. Manchester: Manchester University Press.

Carter, R. (2004) *Language and Creativity. The Art of Common Talk*. London: Routledge.
Carter, R. (2016) 'English pasts, English futures', in A. Hewings, L. Prescott and P. Seargeant (eds), *Futures for English Studies*. Basingstoke: Palgrave Macmillan, 11–18.
Carter, R. A. and W. Nash (1990) *Seeing through Language: Styles of English Writing*. Oxford: Blackwell.
Cook, G. (2001) *The Discourse of Advertising*. 2nd edn. London: Routledge.
Culpeper, J. (2016) '*Encyclopedia of Shakespeare's language*'. Available at www.research.lancs.ac.uk/portal/en/projects/encyclopaedia-of-shakespeares-language%280c9c75c4-d2f5-4a85-97fc-2fba-fedc922c%29.html.
Deegan, M. and M. Hayler (2016) 'Digital humanities and the future of the book', in A. Hewings, L. Prescott and P. Seargeant (eds), *Futures for English Studies*. Basingstoke: Palgrave Macmillan, 161–178.
Dorst, A. G. (2015) 'More or different metaphors in fiction? A quantitative cross-register comparison', *Language and Literature* 24 (1): 3–22.
Eagleton, T. (1983) *Literary Theory*. Oxford: Blackwell.
Eberhardt, M. (2017) 'Gendered representations through speech: The case of the *Harry Potter* series', *Language and Literature* 26 (3): 227–246.
Elliott, W. E. Y. and R. J. Valenza (2011) 'Shakespeare's vocabulary: Did it dwarf all others?', in M. Ravassat and J. Culpeper (eds), *Stylistics and Shakespeare's Language*. London: Continuum, Ch 2, 34–57.
Garrard, P., L. M. Maloney, J. R. Hodges and K. Patterson (2005) 'The effects of very early Alzheimer's disease on the characteristics of writing by a renowned author', *Brain* 128 (2): 250–260.
Garvin, P. L. (ed.) (1964) *A Prague School Reader on Aesthetics, Literary Structure and Style*. Washington: Georgetown University Press.
Goodland, G. (2011) 'Strange deliveries': Contextualizing Shakespeare's first citations in the *OED*', in M. Ravassat and J. Culpeper (eds), *Stylistics and Shakespeare's Language*. London: Continuum. Ch. 1, 10–33.
Goodman, S. and K. O'Halloran (eds) (2006) *The Art of English: Literary Creativity*. Basingstoke: Palgrave Macmillan.
Guardian (2008) Available at www.theguardian.com/media/organgrinder/2008/dec/19/ad-slogans-blog, accessed 19 January 2017.
Hall, G. (2000) 'Coining phrases: Cliché and creativity in the poetry of Tony Harrison', in L. Jeffries and P. Sansom (eds), *Contemporary Poems: Critical Approaches to Recent British and Irish Poetry*. Huddersfield: Smith/Doorstop Books, 38–53.
Hall, G. (2014) 'Stylistics as literary criticism', in P. Stockwell and S. Whiteley (eds), *The Cambridge Handbook of Stylistics*. Cambridge: Cambridge University Press Ch. 7, 87–100.
Halliday, M. A. K. (1967) 'The linguistic study of literary texts', in S. Chatman and R. S. Levin (eds), *Essays on the Language of Literature*. Boston: Houghton Mifflin, 217–223.
Hewings, A., L. Prescott and P. Seargeant (eds) (2016) *Futures for English Studies. Teaching Language, Literature and Creative Writing in Higher Education*. Basingstoke: Palgrave Macmillan.
Hodson, J. (2014) *Dialect in Film and Literature*. Basingstoke: Palgrave Macmillan.
Hoover, D. (2007) 'Corpus stylistics, stylometry, and the styles of Henry James', *Style* 41 (2): 174–203.
Jeffries, L. (1993) *The Language of Twentieth-Century Poetry*. Basingstoke: Macmillan.
Jeffries, L (1996) 'What makes English into art?', in J. Maybin and N. Mercer (eds), *Using English. From Conversation to Canon*. London and New York: Routledge/The Open University, 162–197.
Kermode, F. (2001) *Shakespeare's Language*. London: Penguin Allen Lane.
Lakoff, G. and M. Johnson (1980) *Metaphors We Live By*. Chicago: University of Chicago Press.
Lakoff, G. and M. Turner (1989) *More Than Cool Reason. A Field Guide to Poetic Metaphor*. Chicago: University of Chicago Press.
Mahlberg, M. (2013) *Corpus Stylistics and Dickens's Fiction*. London: Routledge.
Maybin, J. and M. Pearce (2006) 'Literature and creativity in English', in S. Goodman and K. O'Halloran (eds), *The Art of English Literary Creativity*. Basingstoke, UK: Palgrave Macmillan with the Open University, 3–24.
Mills, S. (1995) *Feminist Stylistics*. London: Routledge.
Montgomery, M., A. Durant, T. Furniss and S. Mills (2013) *Ways of Reading*. 4th edn. London: Routledge.
Nash, W. (1990) *Language in Popular Fiction*. London: Routledge.
Peplow, D. (2016) *Talk about Books. A Study of Reading Groups*. London: Bloomsbury.

Peplow, D., J. Swan, P. Trimarco and S. Whiteley (2016) *The Discourse of Reading Groups*. London: Routledge.
Peplow, D. and R. Carter (2014) 'Stylistics and real readers', in M. Burke (ed.), *The Routledge Handbook of Stylistics*. London and New York: Routledge, 455–470.
Sebba, M., S. Mahootian and C. Jonsson (2012) *Language Mixing and Code-Switching in Written Discourse*. London: Routledge.
Semino, E. and G. Steen (2008) 'Metaphor in literature', in R. Gibbs (ed.), *The Cambridge Handbook of Metaphor and Thought*. New York: Cambridge University Press, 232–246.
Sklar, H. (2013) *The Art of Sympathy in Fiction. Forms of Ethical and Emotional Persuasion*. Amsterdam: Benjamins.
Sotirova, V. (2011) *D. H. Lawrence and Narrative Viewpoint*. London: Continuum.
Stockwell, P. (2002) *Cognitive Poetics. An Introduction*. London: Routledge.
Stockwell, P. (2016) 'English language studies from rhetoric to applied English', in A. Hewings, L. Prescott and P. Seargeant (eds), *Futures for English Studies. Teaching Language, Literature and Creative Writing in Higher Education*. Basingstoke: Palgrave Macmillan, 215–232.
Tambling, J. (1988) *What is Literary Language?* Milton Keynes: Open University Press.
Taylor, G. (1989) *Reinventing Shakespeare. A Cultural History from the Restoration to the Present*. London: Hogarth Press.
Taylor-Batty, J. (2014) *Multilingualism in Modernist Fiction*. Basingstoke: Palgrave Macmillan.
Toolan, M. (2001) *Narrative. A Critical Linguistic Introduction*. 2nd edn. London: Routledge.
Toolan, M. (2012) 'Poems: Wonderfully repetitive', in R. Jones (ed.), *Discourse and Creativity*. London: Pearson, 17–34.
Vickers, B. (2004) *Shakespeare, Co-Author. A Historical Study of Five Collaborative Plays*. Oxford: Oxford University Press.
Viswanathan, G. (1989) *Masks of Conquest. Literary Study and British Rule in India*. London: Faber and Faber.
Williams, R. (1977) *Marxism and Literature*. Oxford: Oxford University Press.
Winchester, S. (2003) *The Meaning of Everything. The Story of the Oxford English Dictionary*. Oxford: Oxford University Press.
Wolf, A. J. E. (2017) 'In search of lost hybridity: The French *Daniel Deronda*', *Language and Literature* 26 (2): 213–226.
Zwaan, R. (1994) 'Effects of genre expectations on text comprehension', *Journal of Experimental Psychology: Learning, Memory and Cognition* 20 (4): 920–933.

19

The language of creative writing

Jeremy Scott

Introduction: definitions and historical perspectives

The inclusion of a chapter on creative writing in a handbook of English Language Studies may raise some eyebrows. It should not. That it might, points to an important issue: that the subject and its practice are usually approached more from the context of literary studies. Further, if creative writing engages with a critical infrastructure at all, that infrastructure tends to be literary in provenance and scope. The art of composition and consideration of rhetoric have been aspects of language studies for a long time; however, these kinds of *linguistic* focus on the mechanisms that underpin the creation of a literary text have been notably absent from most creative writing discourses. This is eminently understandable, given that the primary focus of the discipline of creative writing is the creation of literary texts. However, this chapter will take what might currently be viewed as an unorthodox approach to the discussion of creative writing practice by asserting that the discipline can also be approached from the perspective of the study of language as well as, or even instead of, the context of literary studies. The argument I wish to make here could be summarised as follows: to write is to engage, inexorably, self-consciously, with language and its mechanics. Thus, a better understanding of these mechanics must be of enormous benefit to the creative writer. I will justify this assertion using a critical framework drawn from stylistics: the analysis of discourse using frameworks drawn from linguistics (Short 1996; Toolan 1998; Simpson 2004).

As a summarising justification for an approach to creative writing practice through stylistics, it will be useful to turn to Toolan (1998: ix):

> [One of the] chief feature[s] of stylistics is that it persists in the attempt to understand technique, or the craft of writing. . . . Why these word-choices, clause-patterns, rhythms and intonations, contextual implications, cohesive links, choices of voice and perspective and transitivity etc. etc., and not any of the others imaginable? Conversely, can we locate the linguistic bases of some aspects of weak writing, bad poetry, the confusing and the banal? Stylistics asserts we should be able to, particularly by bringing to the close examination of the linguistic particularities of a text an understanding of the anatomy and functions of the language. . . . Stylistics is crucially concerned with excellence of technique.

Toolan's remarks refer to study and analysis of extant, completed literary texts. I am suggesting here a reversal of that paradigm. What applications might a critical and reflective stylistic awareness have in the *creation* of texts, not just in their analysis after they have been written? Stylistics, as Toolan suggests, can help identify and, crucially, account for moments of 'excellence' as well as parts of the work which are less successful. I would like to suggest that such stylistic awareness can become an integral part of creative practice itself. As Eliot (1980) acknowledges in his essay 'The Function of Criticism':

> the larger part of the labour of an author in composing his work is critical labour, the labour of sifting, combining, constructing, expunging, correcting: this frightful toil is as much critical as creative.
>
> (30)

A note of caution, though: it is in no way the intention of this chapter to suggest that creative writers *must* engage with stylistics and/or language studies in general. Such a proposition would be patently absurd. You do not need to understand complicated linguistic concepts to be an accomplished writer. My hope, though, is to point to the various ways in which a practical exploration of the mechanics of language in general and stylistics in particular through writing rather than just reading texts can benefit both the creative writer and the student of language. Rather than showing the only way to write well, combining stylistics and creative writing provides opportunities to explore how you *can* write, how to avoid certain common pitfalls and, at the very least, to consider critically the question posed by Toolan above: why *these* words, and not others?

There are two key issues which should be explored before continuing: the first is an issue of definition, the second of technique.

In a broad sense, creative writing can be characterised as writing that moves beyond the strictures of journalistic, technical, academic and other professional genres (which are analytic and pragmatic in scope), is in some sense original (it draws on the imagination to convey meaning) and is concerned with self-expression. I would like to advance a more specific, tripartite definition which, as should be expected given the orientation of this chapter, draws on linguistic concepts.

1 Creative writing harnesses the natural *playfulness* to be found in everyday language use: a bending of rules and norms, innovative expression, repetition, reworking and intertextuality (Carter 2004: 8–9). Swann et al. (2011: 11) support this proposal that linguistic creativity should be seen as an essential function of language itself, as inherent in every act of meaning-making and as a universal feature of everyday spoken language, accessible to all (see also Chomsky 1965).
2 *Creative* writing, in comparison to more instrumental discourses, is characterised by the fact that processes of writing and reading become analogous. It is possible to envisage situations where we 'just write': a shopping list, a quick email at work, a jotted-down reminder to do something. In these examples, the process of writing is in the ascendant, and reading is backgrounded. More often, though, we write and read at the same time; Oatley (2003) terms this combination of processes *writingandreading*. I have just re-read the two previous sentences and made some changes (I added the words 'at work' to the email example, and then deleted a further example of pure writing: the instructions on how to operate a coffee maker). Creative writing, then, foregrounds the act of reading – and re-reading. Morley (2011: 25) also posits this equivalence: 'reading is a kind of rewriting

but by many hands and eyes. Writing is only a more exacting form of reading, individual in its action and exactions.' In further support of this definition, Swann et al. (2011: 9) broaden the term 'rereading' to capture a notion of 'reusing' the potentialities of language:

> [A]ll reading is in some sense a form of rewriting (recasting what one reads in one's own mind), and ... much writing is a form of rereading (recasting the resources of the language and texts as found into what one makes of them).

3 Creative writing cues up cognitive processes of world-building in the mind of the reader – worlds which may or may not have counterparts in reality. It (almost) always refers to states of affairs that are 'not here' and 'not now'. If I write 'The man sat in the armchair by the fire reading a book', the reader builds a mental representation (the metaphor of a 'world' is used to describe it) based upon conceptual knowledge gathered from the real world. Pause now and examine the world this sentence builds in your imagination. What age is the man? (Elderly?) What is the armchair made of? (Leather?) What colour is it? (Red? Perhaps green?) What time of day is it? (Evening?) What type of book is it? (Hardback?) Individual answers may or may not have matched the suggestions in brackets, but I would suggest that it is highly likely that they did. Further: none of this information is given in the sentence; it is inferred by the reader from a pre-existing mental schema[1] (Bartlett 1995). This cognitive linguistic process is crucial to the effect of creative writing and a defining characteristic of it.

To summarise: creative writing draws on the playfulness inherent in spoken language, treats writing and reading as equiponderant processes and exploits the world-building properties of discourse.

The second issue to be explored concerns the relationship between 'showing' and 'telling', a technical distinction much beloved of creative writing workshops and a concept which can be greatly elucidated through a principled understanding of how language works.

There is a fundamental quality of human language that separates it from other forms of communication across the natural world. Chimpanzees have been taught to use sign language to a basic level. The sounds dolphins make have been shown to communicate specific messages: danger, food here, come this way. However, there is one crucial difference between these kinds of communication and those that are possible through human language: *the capacity of human language to refer to situations, contexts and even worlds that are 'other' than the here-and-now of the communicative situation.* The chimpanzee can ask for food because it is hungry *now*, but (as far as we know) it cannot reference the food it had yesterday, or the food it would prefer to have tomorrow. The clicks of dolphins can warn of an approaching killer whale in the present moment, but cannot subsequently relate what happened to friends later in the day. In short, human language creates worlds that are different to and other than the present moment in which the exchange takes place. It can build a world that does not exist in the here and now.

These worlds are created by virtue of two distinctive but complementary functions of language, which creative writing discourse refers to as *showing* and *telling* (Boulter 2007: 77). The easiest way to illustrate the difference is through an example. Which is the more effective of these two mediations of an action in the story world?

1 She was very angry so she left the room.
2 She left the room, slamming the door behind her.

The same thing 'happens' in the world of the story in each case. However, the way the action is mediated for the reader differs significantly. Sentence 2 is arguably more effective; the reason why should be familiar to all students of creative writing. It is (nearly) always better to aim to *show* an emotion, a reaction or a character trait than to describe it. The reasons why this is so are complex, but the insights afforded by stylistics, particularly cognitive stylistics, go a long way towards explaining them in terms of schema theory (Lakoff 1987; Bartlett 1995) and the concept of foregrounding (Harber & Hershenson 1980). Accordingly, I would suggest the terms *mimesis* and *diegesis* as a better alternative to 'showing' and 'telling' as they capture the essence of what is happening as the reader builds a world in response to the linguistic cue. The features of the world are either portrayed, objectively, or described, with inevitable slant, by the narrating voice; in the latter case, there is more mediation, more intervention, between the action in the story world and the reader's apprehension of it. The cline between mimesis and diegesis is a fundamental paradigm of a language-based approach to writing.

The two terms are classical in origin, but their influence can be traced in the etymology of many current English words: to *mimic*, to *imitate*, to *mime* – all these words are concerned with the representation of reality. For Plato, the terms are used very specifically: diegesis is representation of action 'in the poet's voice', while mimesis is representation of action in the 'voice(s) of characters'. Their use in the context of creative writing must be more nuanced, though. Accordingly, I also want to capture their wider reference: the representation of an imaginary world through language (Auerbach 1968) uses *mimesis* to refer to the representation of reality in art), but, as Lodge (1990: 25–44) points out, it is not a straightforward matter to differentiate between them nor to distinguish between their two effects (see also Booth 1983 and Rimmon-Kenan 1989). The taxonomy which stylistics proposes to categorise literary presentation of discourse can help here. It ranges from Narration, pure diegesis ('She opened the door and walked into the room, seeing him standing by the window') to Free Direct Discourse, as close to a pure mimesis as written language can get ('Here she comes'). Thus, stylistics addresses Lodge's valid objection, mapping the distinction between mimesis and diegesis, and thus between showing and telling, more rigorously (Scott 2013: 93–94).

To return to the example given earlier: instead of 'She was very angry', we prefer 'She left the room, slamming the door behind her' because the second mediation of the story world event is closer to the conceptual space of the character. There is no external voice of mysterious provenance explaining what the character is feeling on her behalf. Rather, her behaviour speaks for itself. To be glib for a moment: actions speak louder than words. The description of a character's behaviour leaves space for the reader to interpret it, as he or she would in the actual world, based on everyday familiarity with the kinds of mood that slamming a door indicates (in cognitive terms, the reader has a 'losing one's temper' schema which is activated by the slamming of the door; we have seen someone do this before, or, indeed, we have done it ourselves; we know why it happens, and we know what it signifies: anger). Straight diegetic description bypasses that space, enervating the reader's processes of world-building. Rather than seeing *through* language, the reader is *looking at* the narrative voice. In short, as cognitive linguistics can demonstrate, the narrative discourse should aim (unless there are very good reasons not to – and there may well be) for proximity to the sphere of character rather than narrator. We can also argue here for a connection to the *connotative* as opposed to *denotative* functions of language; mimesis corresponds to the former, while diegesis draws upon the latter.

The lesson for creative practice is straightforward. Do not 'lay the table' or 'manage the stage' too diligently, or in too much detail. Let the reader's imagination do its work. Much of interest can be gleaned from the gaps in texts, from ellipsis, from the unsaid, from the unexplained.

The reading experience will be richer and more nuanced – more personal, more lifelike – and thus, the opening discussion of this chapter comes full circle. Creative practice (writing) and creative engagement with the output of that practice (reading) are two sides of the same coin. Rather than simply writing or only reading, it helps to think of ourselves as writing and reading at the same time. Thus, we become both agents simultaneously, each attuned to the needs and actions of the other.

The rest of this chapter will home in on two of the many potential areas of enquiry available for this topic: the concept of language as a representative medium, and the significant insights to be gained from narratology.

Current critical issues and topics 1: seeing through language

In this section I will discuss the language of creative writing using another world-based metaphor: the text as window into an imaginary world. As already proposed, the literary text arises from two essential materials: language, and the imaginary worlds that language cues up in the mind of the reader. Of course, the worlds created will vary from reader to reader, even though the language from which they are built is identical. So, the discussion in this chapter so far has implied the presence of two 'worlds': the one imagined by the writer, and the one imagined by the reader.

However, it is not strictly (or not always) correct to say that the creative writer first imagines a world and then writes about it. Indeed, it is possible to argue, as Derrida (1976) did, that the text refers to nothing at all outside of itself: that its 'meaning' resides at the centre of an unattached web of words with no external anchoring. Prior to this, Abrams (1953) had proposed that language *can* mediate both material and interior (mental) worlds, but that this – mere representation – is not the primary purpose of art. Rather, verbal art focusses and directs attention. Unlike Hamlet's 'mirror held up to nature', it should not reflect; nor should it simply 'imitate', a function of verbal art that Plato also disparages in *The Republic*. Instead, it should *illuminate* like a lantern.

It is easier, probably, for most writers to accept the assertions of Abrams than those of Derrida. However, while it is self-evidently useful for the creative writer to reflect upon the representational aims of the text that she or he is writing and its essential inter-relationship with the 'real world' (wholly fictitious, semi-autobiographical, science-fictional, fantastical, objective, subjective), it is also an interesting thought experiment – if nothing else – to dwell for a moment on Derrida's infamous pronouncement that '*Il n'y a pas de hors-texte.*' The process of translating this phrase into English has (appropriately enough) proved to be a contentious process. '*There is nothing outside the text*' is often used, but disputed (see, for example, Deutscher 2009). For our purposes, it will be sufficient to render it as 'There is no such a thing as out-of-the-text', or, more arguably: 'There is no such thing as context.' I introduce the notion of context to complicate the previous discussion of the ways in which creative writing uses language to mediate between an imaginary world and a reader. Creative language use need not always involve mediation or an imagined context; as the second part of the definition of creative writing which opened this chapter should make clear: *creativity can arise from within language itself.* The two processes of imagining a world and mediating it through language are not necessarily antecedent one to the other. Often, it is in the very act of writing that the imaginary world is created. This makes the act of writing an act of thought, and we think through the physical performance of it. Creative writing 'happens' in the interplay between language and world, but also within language itself. From the one, we gain access to the other, and the two are interdependent. *We see through language,* hence the metaphor of text as window, into a world beyond. This happens whether we are writers or readers – and creative writers are both.

Of course, the process of seeing through language can happen in many different ways, and exploring this assertion opens the door to a range of available techniques. It will be useful now to focus on some examples. Here are two extracts through which the reader 'sees' in fundamentally different ways.

Text 1

No sweat, we'll never win; other choirs sing about Love, all our songs are about cattle or death!

Fionnula (the Cooler) spoke that way, last words pitched a little bit lower with a sexyish sideways look at none of the others. The fifth-year choir all laughed.

Orla, still so thin she had her legs crossed to cover up her skinniness, keeked along the line and says, When they from the Fort, Hoors of the Sacred Heart, won the competition last year, they got kept down the whole night and put up in a big posh hotel and . . . everything, no that I want that! Sooner be snogged in the Mantrap.

Know what the Hoor's school motto is? Fionnula spoke again, from the longest-legs-position on the wall. She spoke louder this time, in that blurred, smoked voice, It's 'Noses up . . . knickers DOWN'!

The Sopranos all chortled and hootsied; the Seconds and Thirds mostly smiled in perusual admiration.

Text 2

It was when she ate that Lin was most alien, and their shared meals were a challenge and an affirmation. As he watched her, Isaac felt the familiar trill of emotion: disgust immediately stamped out, pride at the stamping out, guilt, desire.

Light glinted in Lin's compound eyes. Her headlegs quivered. She picked up half a tomato and gripped it with her mandibles. She lowered her hands while her inner mouthparts picked at the food her outer jaw held steady.

Isaac watched the huge iridescent scarab that was his lover's head devour her breakfast.

These two extracts[2] illustrate two fundamentally different ways in which readers see through language. The stylistically-aware writer should be considering the following questions:

- Who is 'witnessing' the imagined story world (i.e. from what perspective does the reader see the world)?
- Whose voice is telling the reader about the story world? Does it have any foregrounded (linguistically deviant)[3] qualities?
- What is the effect of foregrounded narrative voice on the way the reader sees through language into the story world?

When reading Text 1, the reader will 'see' a quotidian situation: a group of schoolgirls sitting on a wall, talking together. Note, however, that this information is not 'told' to the reader directly. There is no description of the wall; it is introduced with a definite article, 'the', signalling that the story begins *in medias res*. 'The' does not refer anaphorically back to a previous indefinite article and thus its use, deictic in this instance, assumes a shared mental space (compare the effect if 'a' is substituted for 'the') – a world in common. The reader pictures schoolgirls because of the character names, the references to the 'Hoors of the Sacred Heart' (another school) and the phrase 'fifth-year choir'; the term 'fifth year' is culturally specific to the UK and, as it happens, now obsolete, positioning the scene within a particular time period. A reader familiar with this cultural context will also be able to infer that the school is a Catholic one (from its name, and, perhaps, from the Irish-origin girls' names: Fionnula, Orla), and the use of 'hoors' (whores) signals an all-girls school. In terms of setting: the names signal Ireland, but the language signals Scotland (the use of dialect terms such as 'keeked', 'hootsied' and 'hoors'). Thus, we as readers also infer a particular place, culture and time, from very sparse textual cues.

The narrative voice of Text 1 is clearly not standard English; neither does it follow the conventions for presenting direct speech (inverted commas). It is third-person, but uses a spoken register more akin to a first-person voice (as well as the dialect words, notice the deviant compound adjectives 'longest-legs' and 'per-usual'). The narrator exists, both ontologically and linguistically, on the same plane as the characters rather than speaking on their behalf from an omniscient perspective. We see through the language to a world beyond, but at the same time both the particular detail of that world and our view into it are conditioned fundamentally by the distinct attributes of the narrative voice, which is linguistically 'other' than standard English, and thus foregrounded. It is also 'other' when compared to the 'mainstream' third-person voice of English literature, which tends to be in standard English (Scott 2009: 145–148). The world being described by it, however, is familiar.

By comparison, the narrative voice of Text 2 is standard English. There is nothing deviant about its use of words or grammatical structures, although the syntax of the opening sentence does bear examination. Compare 'It was when she ate that Lin was most alien' to the (arguably) more usual 'Lin was most alien when she ate.' The act of eating, expressed by the verb phrase in subject position, is the focus in the original, rather than the fact that Lin is non-human. The syntax has the dual effect of drawing the reader's attention to the act (which is the focus of the rest of the paragraph), and also of maintaining suspense. We engage with the everyday act of eating food *before* we come to the realisation that Lin is 'other' than Isaac. The form of the sentence used in the extract is more effective in expressive terms than its more 'normalised' version – another example of the advantages to the creative writer of a keen stylistic awareness. The narrative situation is also third-person, as in Text 1, but, in this instance, is more 'transparent': we see through the discourse into the world of the story without becoming unduly interested in or distracted by the language use itself (in opposition to the situation in Text 1, where the demotic cadences, lack of speech marks and slang words drew attention to themselves; they *foreground* the narrative discourse). However, the scenes and characters described are anything but matter-of-fact: a human character, Isaac, sharing food with his alien lover, Lin, who has a scarab – complete with mandibles – for a head. In Text 1, the discourse is foregrounded while the story world is quotidian. In Text 2, the discourse is quotidian but the story world is fantastical, and foregrounded.

The various linguistic features of these two texts and the contrasts between them demonstrate one of the central paradigms justifying this chapter's assertion that critical linguistic awareness sits at the heart of reflective creative writing practice. It is helpful to envisage a cline between 'standard' discourse, which aspires towards transparency, and more linguistically deviant modes of expression which draw attention to themselves as well as the world they mediate. In the former, we are seeing as if through a clear, flawless window pane to a world beyond (as in Text 2, say); in the latter, the pane is cracked, or stained, or distorted (as in Text 1). The creative writer may situate his or her narrative discourse at either end of this cline, at a point somewhere along it, or even as fluctuating back and forth across it. The choice is a crucial one, though, and consideration of these methodological options should automatically become an aspect of creative practice.

Current critical issues and topics 2: narrative and structure

Narrative is a substantial subject within both language and literary studies. It lies at the core of many literary texts, be they fiction or poetry. Narratives surround us in our daily lives, and in our daily language use. They are crucial to the structure of media discourse, for example, and so shape the way that we understand the world beyond our immediate experience. Narratives can also be continuous or serial, and, indeed, very long and complex, such as serialised TV dramas or soap operas. They may also be mini-narratives, or narrative 'snapshots', limited or single narrative events which leave the viewer to fill in the gaps. News stories in particular are shaped and mediated by the wider 'meta-narratives' into which they are situated (think 'national decline', 'economic catastrophe', 'social breakdown', 'environmental collapse'). We cannot avoid *storying* our lives. It is what human beings do in order to make sense of a highly complex and confusing world.

Prototypical narratives begin with the presentation of an initial stable situation which is in some way disturbed, disordered or upset due to a particular obstacle or problem. This is often set up by a particular desire or wish that a character will have, and an obstacle that stands in the way of them achieving that goal. The particular nature of the obstacle and how it is overcome is a key feature of genre: finding the killer, solving the mystery, giving the villain his comeuppance or obtaining the sought-after thing or person. As should be predictable from the assertions made so far in this chapter, this universal narrative form is by no means unique to literary texts; it can also be found in the ways in which newspapers and the media in general present the news (who is to blame for this problem which has disrupted our lives? how will it be resolved?) The same structure may be found in TV quiz shows (who will win the cash prize?) or in sport (who will win the match?). Even advertisements make use of this fundamental structure. This is the problem you have (less-than-white teeth), or this thing is lacking in your life (a sexual partner). Here is how you solve the problem (whitening toothpaste), or fill the gap (perhaps the same product). The achievement (or otherwise) of this goal is what brings about some sort of *change* or *transformation* in the initial situation – a fundamental attribute of narrative. Narratives, in short, have to be about change, disturbance, transformation and/or disorder.

Burroway (2014) models this basic structure as made up of *conflict* (between characters, between a character and her inner self, between a character and something she desires), *crisis* (the situation comes to a head in some way, and the tension peaks) and *resolution* (the crisis is resolved, as is the conflict). Baldwin (1987) describes a similar approach, what he calls the 'angel cake' approach to crafting fiction, but preferring the terms *exposition*, followed by *complication* and ending in *resolution*. Other models add a fourth stage, *climax*, which comes in between the complication and the resolution. To define these terms in more detail:

1 *Exposition*: the part of the story which sets the scene and introduces the character.
2 *Complication*: the part of the story where the lives of the character(s) are complicated in some way.
3 *Climax*: the point where suspense is highest and matters are at their most threatening.
4 *Resolution*: a solution to the complication is introduced (it need not be a happy one).

According to structuralist narratology, *all* narratives have these essential structures (some models are more complex but advance the same kinds of arguments). The sociolinguist Labov (1972) found that similar patterns naturally occurred in oral narratives in everyday speech. The structure is universal, and can be found in texts ranging from the Bible to Medieval mystery plays, the Koran to *The Hobbit*, and soap operas to *The Arabian Nights*. If structuralist approaches to narratology are correct, narrative has a grammar or syntax of its own, just like the language of which it is made up, and that structure is universal: it applies across cultures and in all situations. Just as a sentence will have a subject and a verb, and perhaps an object (no matter how these are represented orthographically or phonologically), so narrative, which, like the sentence, is an attempt to mediate between humans and the world, has a beginning, a middle and an end. So, from the stories we tell each other every day to novel sequences to the highly-crafted narratives of video games, the same essential pattern can be discerned. All involve the transformation and mediation of experience via the syntax of narrative, no matter whether they are presented orally, via text or via a screen.

An essential methodological choice must be made with regard to the many ways in which the elements of a narrative can be presented. An aspect of the successful mediation of a story world comes (although this is certainly not true of all narratives) through the use of tension and momentum, most obviously in narrative fiction. Thus, the plot begins with the exposition, moves up a slope where suspense and tension gradually increase in response to the complication (or series of complications), reaches a point of climax, and then quickly descends and ends in the resolution. The concept is often presented as an inverted tick shape, with the climax at the 'point' of the tick. This pattern of suspense need not, of course, be as neat as the inverted tick image would suggest. In a novel or longer piece of writing, it may well resemble a staircase up until the point of the climax, with tension rising and falling at different stages of the story.

To further develop this idea of tension through structure above: it is crucial to grasp that the relentless progression of the plot *need not necessarily be matched by the ordering of the mediating discourse of the text*. The language of the text can mediate the story in any order that the writer wishes it to, including by starting at the beginning and simply following it through to the end. It would equally be possible, of course, to begin with the climax, move to the beginning, and then come back to the end – or, indeed, start at the end. Genette (1983: 33–35) called this aspect of narrative *order*, and it concerns structure at the level of story. For example, imagine the event sequence that makes up a murder mystery. Someone is murdered (call this Event A). The corpse is discovered (Event B). A series of clues revealing the identity of the murderer are uncovered by the detective (Event C). Finally, the sleuth identifies the murderer and brings him or her to justice (Event D). Assuming the story is to be narrated chronologically, it would be notated as follows: A, B, C, D. First comes the murder, then its discovery, then the investigation, then the revelation of the killer's identity. However, these events could be mediated in a different order as follows: B (discovery), A (flashback), C (investigation) and finally D (the revelation). The disjunction between story (what happened) and discourse (how it is represented) is full of creative potential, heightening suspense, causing the reader to ask questions and to want to read on. It is helpful to the creative writer, then, to envisage a separation between narrative discourse itself and the story being mediated by that discourse; this idea of the story or plot as distinct from the discourse which mediates it was termed the *fabula* by formalists such as Propp (1968). Order can play a crucial role in how a story works. It can even function as an actor in the story itself – a kind of 'plot' in its own right, running alongside that of the story. Interest occurs in the way in which (when and how) the details of the *fabula* are revealed to the reader.

These structures can be even more complex, particularly in longer novels which often contain several different, interlocking narrative structures. To facilitate illustration of this point, the various narratives of a complex structure will be labelled with letters (A, B, C and so on) and the order in which they are mediated by the discourse (the point at which they are revealed to the reader in discourse time) will be indicated by a numerical value. So, if the narrative discourse simply follows the chronological order of the narrative in the story world (in fabula time), it would run as follows: A1, A2, A3 and so on. The structure of Book Two of *The Lord of the Rings* ('The Two Towers') contains at least three such narratives: the story of Frodo and Sam and their journey to Mount Doom (A), the fate of Merry and Pippin after they are kidnapped by orcs (B) and the tribulations of Aragorn, Gimli and Legolas and later Gandalf, who are pursuing them in a rescue attempt (C). The discourse of the novel mediates each stage of each narrative in series. This relatively simple structure would be notated as follows: A1, B1, C1, A2, B2, C2, A3, B3, C3 and so on. Quentin Tarantino's film *Pulp Fiction*, on the other hand, makes use of a structure which is highly complex. For illustrative purposes, it will be assumed that there are three principal narrative threads (there are more, in fact): A (the story of two hired assassins), B (the story about a boxer who refuses to 'fix' a fight for a gang leader) and C (the story of two robbers holding up a diner). Approximately, the structure looks like this: C1, B2, A1, A2, A3, B1, B3, C3. This is complex, and very effective. The viewer will engage in significant cognitive work in putting the various narrative strands 'back together' from their broken-down sections. At one point, a character appears in the film who has already been killed *in the world of the fabula* (in story time). In the narrative discourse, though, he is alive and well, but his character is leant a tragic air by the fact that the viewer knows what will eventually happen to him. This ironic effect (a kind of reverse foreshadowing) would be impossible without the complex structure. Another example from fiction: in Martin Amis's novel *Time's Arrow* (2003) the discourse runs backwards, from the protagonist's death to his birth, while the fabula itself runs forwards. Characters walk backwards, speak backwards, and eat backwards. There are intriguing ideological reasons for this, connected to the book's subject matter: the Holocaust. In one sense, this novel is an attempt to 'un-write' a horrific chapter of European history and this effect is entirely due to Amis's creative manipulation of the relationship between discourse and fabula (story).

As a final word on the subject of narrative, Genette's (1983: 86–88) concept of *duration* should also be mentioned. As noted, narratives involve a discourse time and a story (or fabula) time – which may or may not coincide. Genette called the relationship between them *duration*. 'Twenty years passed' is a long time in story world terms, but is a short piece of language which takes only a second to write or read. Conversely, James Joyce's *Ulysses* is set in a relatively short story period of twenty-four hours; however, it takes a great deal longer than that to read. In short, it has a long discourse time. Again, duration can be exploited by creative writers to great effect in terms of creating suspense, ironic distance, and in summarising lengthy information which is important in plot terms but need not be represented in detail by the discourse. *Time's Arrow* also exploits this facet of narrative discourse and the tension it creates between discourse and fabula in terms of compression and reversal.

Understanding and exploiting the relationship between 'discourse' and 'fabula' leads to reflection on the concept of *mediation*: the fact that there is an inevitable intercession in any act of communication between an object of representation and its representation, be that an image, a film or, in this case, discourse. Every utterance entails that linguistic choices be made from the (to all intents and purposes) infinite resources of the language. Transmitting experience through narrative form is an everyday facet of human communication (as the work of Labov 1972, makes clear) as well as a key aspect of writing poetry or stories. Thus, a fundamental linguistic insight drawn from everyday language use can be brought to bear on the practice of creative writing.

Future directions

The intersections between the practice of creative writing and the study of language are numerous and fascinating, but rigorous and principled research into the field is still in its infancy. Notable early work in this area includes *The Language of Fiction* by Lodge (1966), himself a successful novelist; his collection of essays explicitly engages in detailed analysis of narrative methodology from a linguistic perspective. Subsequently, the work of Nash (1980), Carter and Nash (1990) and Pope (1995, 2005) has explored the notion of creativity in terms of linguistic theory, including, as in this chapter, consideration of the interchange between language as it is used in quotidian contexts and the processes involved in crafting prose and poetry. My own *Creative Writing and Stylistics* (2013) contains specific discussion of the insights stylistics and linguistics might bring to creative practice. All of this work has attempted to broaden the usual academic and, indeed, pedagogical contexts of creative writing and argues for its status as a significant part of English Language Studies, and not just a branch line from the main track through literary studies. This is not to dismiss or in any way diminish the self-evident importance of the attentive, critical reading and study of literature that any creative writer should undergo in furtherance of the understanding of their art, be that of 'the canon' of poetry, plays and fiction, the postcolonial, the 'popular', world literature, and literary theory.[4] Rather, it is to assert that, at its most fundamental level, creative writing is *verbal* art, built from language. Accordingly, it will benefit those interested in its practice to engage with disciplines that explore and account for language in a principled and rigorous manner. It will be useful now to speculate on the kinds of future directions that research and practice in this area could take. I have identified three for brief discussion here: cognitive poetics, texts in performance and 'anatomising inspiration'.

Cognitive poetics draws on both cognitive linguistics and traditional poetics, and its ambition is to provide a rigorous account of the mechanics of reading. The field makes use of cognitive concepts from Gestalt psychology (Kohler 1992), such as figures and grounds,[5] and schema theory to develop rigorous models of what happens when we read literary texts (Stockwell 2002; Gavins and Steen 2003). One of the most relevant branches of cognitive poetics in terms of creative practice is Text World Theory (Werth 1999; Gavins 2007). In its delineation of the various conceptual spaces which a reader creates as she or he engages with a literary text, as well as the myriad of ways in which these spaces (text worlds) interact, Text World Theory gives the writer the tools to devise an invaluable conceptual map, depicting both the ways in which his or her text might be read (or, more precisely, imagined, conceptualised and envisaged) and, from the point of view of craft, the position of a narrative or poetic voice in relation to this text-world: within it or without it, integral to the story or removed from it and so on, thus keeping the writer attuned to the epistemological status of that voice (see Scott 2016 for further discussion).

A second area deserving of exploration is that of the text in performance. Plenty of work has been done on the stylistics of play texts, especially on how they create character (Culpeper 2001) and in terms of the use of pragmatics-based frameworks to analyse dialogue (Short 1996), but little from the perspective of the playwright (however, see Castagno 2001). To what extent could an understanding of pragmatics (for example, politeness frameworks and conversational maxims) aid and inform the writing of authentic-sounding dialogue, rather than just its analysis? Also of potential relevance here is the ways in which modern stylistic approaches and, indeed, studies of linguistic creativity in general, are embracing analysis of non-textual media, for example film, TV, plays and poetry in performance (Swann et al. 2011). This could certainly inform creative practice, for example in devised approaches to theatre and in other forms of improvisation.

Third, and perhaps most speculatively, it would be interesting to investigate what stylistics, especially its cognitive branches, has to say about the process of 'poetic inspiration' – or perhaps, to put it less contentiously, about the relationships between language and creativity. As should be clear by now, it has long been my ambition to inculcate stylistic awareness into creative practice, not only as a post-composition editorial facility but as part of the process of writing. The most promising route for this investigation would appear to be through research into language and creativity. One example can be found in the process referred to by Keith Oatley (Gavins and Steen 2003) as *writingandreading*. When reading a text, we perform it, and thus we mentally 'write' it. In what ways can this experience of writingandreading be mined for insights into the processes involved in creating texts?

Conclusion

The central proposition of this chapter is simple, and syllogistic. Creative writing is made from language. Stylistics is the principled study of this language. Therefore, an understanding of stylistics should be of benefit to creative writers. Among the vast number of potential topics, this chapter has focussed on the notion of 'seeing through language', on mimesis and diegesis, on narrative structure and on linguistic mediation. As an attempt to summarise the discussion: usually, we think of a context or reference coming first, and the language to mediate it second. This may well be the case, but the purpose of this chapter has been to consider that in creative writing, the opposite can also be true. Words flow, and ideas come. Thus, the usual paradigm can be reversed, so that a context or reference is mapped onto language. By emphasising the 'language' side of this equation, it is hoped that this chapter will have done at least a small part of the work required in arguing for the study of language as key to the study of creative writing.

Notes

1 *Schema* are 'packets' of pre-existing contextual information which we bring to bear when processing language. The concept was originally developed in connection with research into artificial intelligence in order to overcome the barrier of conceptual dependency. In other words, when we process language, we do not rely solely on a series of dictionary-like definitions and denotations of words, but rather on a pre-learned set of associations with a particular term or concept. Good examples are 'pub' and 'restaurant'; both words come with a set of associations and expectations that do not need to be fleshed out in discourse (see Stockwell 2002: 76–77).

2 The provenances of these two texts were omitted deliberately. This was to encourage analytical focus on the texts' language in complete isolation from any knowledge of the respective author or novel. For the curious: Text A is from Warner's (1999) novel *The Sopranos* whilst Text B is taken from *Perdido Street Station* by China Miéville (2000).

3 Linguistic deviation as it occurs in literary discourse is defined by Carter and Nash (1990: 31) as follows:

> According to deviation theory literariness or poeticality inheres in the degrees to which language use departs or deviates from expected configurations and normal patterns of language, and thus defamiliarises the reader. Language use in literature is therefore

different because it makes strange, disturbs, upsets our routinised normal view of things, and thus generates new or renewed perceptions.

4 See Boulter 2007 for an excellent exploration of the relevance of literary theory to creative writers.
5 *Figure* refers to that which is foregrounded against a static *background*, such as a moving object in an otherwise stationary scene. In discourse, this could be non-standard linguistic usage which foregrounds itself (stands out) against the background of standard linguistic norms (see Stockwell 2002: 14–18).

Further reading

Carter, R. and W. Nash (1990) *Seeing Through Language: A Guide to Styles of English Writing*. Oxford: Blackwell. A comprehensive discussion of how linguistics and language studies shed light on the creation of texts, and a corrective to these disciplines' main focus on spoken language.

Scott, J. (2013) *Creative Writing and Stylistics: Critical and Creative Approaches*. Basingstoke: Palgrave Macmillan. An exploration of how an understanding of stylistics and its related concepts can aid and influence creative writing practice.

Scott, J. (2016) 'Worlds from words: Theories of world-building as creative writing toolbox', in J. Gavins and E. Lahey (eds), *World Building: Discourse in the Mind*. London: Bloomsbury. This chapter speculates on the ways in which an understanding of cognitive poetics could be relevant to fictional methodology.

Related topics

- Literature and the English language
- Stylistics: studying literary and everyday style in English
- Discourse analysis: studying and critiquing language in use.

REFERENCES

Abrams, M. H. (1953) *The Mirror and the Lamp: Romantic Theory and the Critical Tradition*. Oxford: Oxford University Press.

Auerbach, E. (1968) *Mimesis: The Representation of Reality in Western Literature*. Princeton: Princeton University Press.

Baldwin, M. (1987) *The Way to Write Short Stories*. London: Hamish Hamilton.

Bartlett, F. C. (1995) *Remembering: A Study in Experiential and Social Psychology*. 2nd edn. Cambridge: Cambridge University Press.

Booth, W. C. (1983) *The Rhetoric of Fiction*. Chicago, IL: The University of Chicago Press.

Boulter, A. (2007) *Writing Fiction: Creative and Critical Approaches*. Basingstoke: Palgrave Macmillan.

Burroway, J. (2014) *Writing Fiction: A Guide to Narrative Craft*. 9th edn. New York: Barnes and Noble.

Carter, R. (2004) *Language and Creativity: The Art of Common Talk*. London: Routledge.

Carter, R. and W. Nash (1990) *Seeing Through Language: A Guide to Styles of English Writing*. Oxford: Blackwell.

Castagno, P. C. (2001) *New Playwriting Strategies: A Language-Based Approach to Playwriting*. London: Routledge.

Chomsky, N. (1965) *Aspects of the Theory of Syntax*. Cambridge, MA: The Massachusetts Institute of Technology Press.

Culpeper, J. (2001) *Language and Characterisation: People in Plays and Other Texts*. Harlow: Longman.

Derrida, J. (1976) *Of Grammatology*. Baltimore, MD: John Hopkins Press.

Deutscher, M. (2009) 'Some friendly words for the postmodern', *Crossroads: An Interdisciplinary Journal for the Study of History, Philosophy, Religion and Classics* 4 (1): 5–12.

Eliot, T. S. (1980) 'The Function of Criticism', in *Selected Essays*. London: Faber and Faber.

Gavins, J. (2007) *Text World Theory: An Introduction*. Edinburgh: Edinburgh University Press.

Gavins, J. and G. Steen (eds) (2003) *Cognitive Poetics in Practice*. London: Routledge.

Genette, G. (1983) *Narrative Discourse: An Essay in Method*. New York: Cornell University Press.
Harber, R. and M. Hershenson (1980) *The Psychology of Visual Perception*. 2nd edn. New York: Holt, Rinehart and Winston.
Kohler, W. (1992) *Gestalt Psychology: An Introduction to New Concepts in Modern Psychology*. 2nd edn. New York: Liveright Publishing Company.
Labov, W. (1972) *Language in the Inner City*. Philadelphia: University of Pennsylvania Press.
Lakoff, G. (1987) *Women, Fire and Dangerous Things: What Categories Reveal about the Mind*. Chicago, IL: University of Chicago Press.
Lodge, D. (1966) *The Language of Fiction*. London: Routledge.
Lodge, D. (1990) *After Bakhtin: Essays on Fiction and Criticism*. London: Routledge.
Miéville, C. (2000) *Perdido Street Station*. London: Pan Macmillan.
Morley, D. (2011) *The Cambridge Introduction to Creative Writing*. Cambridge: Cambridge University Press.
Nash, W. (1980) *Designs in Prose*. London: Longman.
Oatley, K. (2003) 'Writing and reading: The future of cognitive poetics', in J. Gavins and G. Steen (eds), *Cognitive Poetics in Practice*. London: Routledge. 161–171.
Pope, R. (1995) *Textual Intervention: Critical and Creative Strategies for Literary Studies*. London: Routledge.
Pope, R. (2005) *Creativity: Theory, History, Practice*. London: Routledge.
Propp, V. (1968) *The Morphology of the Folktale*. Austin: University of Texas Press.
Rimmon-Kenan, S. (1989) *Narrative Fiction: Contemporary Poetics*. London: Routledge.
Scott, J. (2009) *The Demotic Voice in Contemporary British Fiction*. Basingstoke: Palgrave Macmillan.
Scott, J. (2013) *Creative Writing and Stylistics: Creative and Critical Approaches*. Basingstoke: Palgrave Macmillan.
Scott, J. (2016) 'Worlds from words: Theories of world-building as creative writing toolbox', in J. Gavins and E. Lahey (eds), *World-Building: Discourse in the Mind*. London: Bloomsbury. 127–145.
Short, M. (1996) *Exploring the Language of Poetry, Plays and Prose*. Harlow: Longman Pearson.
Simpson, P. (2004) *Stylistics: A Resource Book for Students*. London: Routledge.
Stockwell, P. (2002) *Cognitive Poetics: An Introduction*. London: Routledge.
Swann, J., R. Pope and R. Carter. (2011) *Creativity in Language and Literature*. Basingstoke: Palgrave Macmillan.
Toolan, M. (1998) *Language in Literature: An Introduction to Stylistics*. London: Arnold.
Warner, A. (1999) *The Sopranos*. London: Vintage.
Werth, P. (1999) *Text Worlds: Representing Conceptual Space in Discourse*. London: Longman.

20

Media, power and representation

Clara Neary and Helen Ringrow

Introducing Media English

As the ubiquity and potential influence of the media increase, the language and imagery used to create meaning in this domain are of continued and enhanced interest to English Language researchers. While 'the media' or even 'the English-speaking media' is not one homogenous entity, the term is used throughout this chapter to refer broadly to a collection of media types such as newspapers, television, radio and so on. Media English can be understood as referring to the ways in which reality is linguistically constructed through these platforms. Additionally, media institutions play a significant role not only in terms of communication but also by way of 'mediating society to itself' (Matheson 2005: 1) in that the media helps to construct societal norms and values. Media language is distinctive because media discourses can be 'fixed' (i.e. recorded for posterity) as well as being interactive (people can react to subject matter, often using media forms to publically share their response(s), themselves becoming producers of media content). In investigating Media English, scholars analyse overall styles or genres in order to explore and challenge particular choices of language and/or imagery within a given media text.

This chapter commences with a consideration of some key contemporary media terminology. It then considers the dominance of *English* in Media English. Following this is a discussion of research into media representation(s) in terms of social class, race, ethnicity, gender and so on. The chapter then focuses on the range of text types the study of Media English currently encompasses, from 'traditional' media genres such as print and broadcast media, to 'new' media genres with an emphasis on online contexts. Recent developments in more 'traditional' media genres will also be considered, such as the increasing public participation and interactivity facilitated by digital communication and social media in particular. Throughout, key areas of dispute and debate in the field will be outlined. The chapter will close with a look towards future directions in the study of Media English, highlighting new and developing trends in the investigation of the communicative choices and shifting contexts of media output.

Contemporary media research

Academic study of the media results from what Scannell (2007) identifies as two 'key historical moments' on both sides of the Atlantic: firstly, the development of a 'sociology of mass communication' in the United States between the mid-1930s and the mid-1950s, and secondly, from the mid-1960s to the end of the following decade, the splintering of a branch of Cultural Studies in Britain to form what we now term 'media studies' (1). The 1970s also witnessed a surge in academic interest in language analysis – exemplified by Levi-Strauss's work in structuralist anthropology, neo-Marxian explorations into the concept of ideology and Barthes and Eco's work in the field of semiotics – which was followed, in the 1980s, by an increasing awareness of the importance of contextual factors in the act of textual interpretation (see Corner 1998). In combination, these developments have generated a field of contemporary academic research into Media English which endeavours to analyse language within the context of both its production and reception.

Every communicative medium possesses its own grammar, that is, a set of rules and conventions by which it operates and according to which it is interpreted; in each case, the nature of these rules and conventions is determined by the specific characteristics of the medium in question. At this juncture, it is practicable to outline the characteristics of mass media, firstly because this facilitates identification of the differences and similarities between media types, and secondly because these characteristics determine how each medium, and the language it uses, is produced and consumed and, therefore, how its language should be analysed. Mass communication is defined as 'a form of communication that constitutes its audience and speaks to it as a mass' (Scannell 1991: 3) and its chief characteristics are as follows: *audience; time; distance; display and distribution; interactivity;* and *storage* (see Medoff and Kaye 2017: 8–9).

Firstly, *audience* refers to the manner in which a medium reaches its audience, with some media, such as print newspapers, communicating via a simple person-to-person or one-to-one mechanism, while others such as radio and television are considered monological, i.e. they follow what is called a 'one-to-many' broadcast model. The second characteristic of *time* essentially focuses on the speed with which media output is received; this is, of course, directly related to the *distance* which the media output has to travel for delivery. Print newspapers can be considered asynchronous as relative distance causes a delay between their production and receipt by a reader, while radio and television output is essentially synchronous due to the near-immediacy of its broadcast technology. Next to consider is *display and distribution*: display is akin to communicative mode in that it refers to the substance through which the text is transmitted, while distribution refers to how substance transmission takes place; for example, the audio-visual mode of television is largely distributed via cable or satellite transmission. The extent to which media are *interactive* also varies; television, for example, was traditionally known as a 'technical' medium in that viewers were unable to interact with it directly while radio has long availed of the 'phone-in' as a means of inviting audience interactivity. Finally, media differ in terms of how they are *stored*; traditionally, print newspapers were archived in hard copy while television programmes were stored on reels of film.

The mainstream popularisation of the internet from the 1990s onwards has had a clearly discernible impact upon these characteristics of mass media. In terms of how it reaches its audience, the internet is the first simultaneously mass and individual medium, capable of broadcasting on both a one-to-one and one-to-many basis. Its immediate distribution via wireless connection or mobile phone signal means it offers both synchronous and asynchronous transmission according to whether one wishes to view electronic output immediately or record it to access at a later date. However, its most dramatic effect upon media consumption is in terms of interactivity. In the pre-digital age, radio and television were predominantly non-interactive media genres, with the only opportunity for real-time interaction with their output coming in the form of occasional phone-ins. However, the increasing levels of interactivity facilitated by digital transmission and internet use mean that a traditionally one-to-many broadcast mode is at times transformed into a one-to-one broadcast mode, for example when comments or questions asked by individual audience members are addressed in real time; solicited audience input can also shape large swathes of a programme's content (for example, audience voting on reality television talent shows). This heightened interactivity has caused a reconfiguration of pre-existing media audience models, one where the boundaries between media producer and media consumer are increasingly porous as audience members become (at least partial) producers. Though developed for application to online social media platforms, Bruns and Jacobs' (2006) term 'produser' – a conflation of producer and user – captures the changed nature of participant roles as a result of the increasing interactivity of much digital media output.

The rapidly increasing and ever-evolving influence of the internet has also generated a multitude of new text types which, while utilising some of the linguistic and discursive strategies associated with their 'traditional' or 'old media' predecessors, have also had to cultivate many more such strategies; in so doing, they are effectively redefining these media genres. The resultant output cumulatively comes under the umbrella term 'new media', a not unproblematic term which largely refers to all communication taking place via digital technologies (though see Manovich 2001 for a fuller discussion of the term). This term has become somewhat contentious largely because many 'new media' are not actually 'new': radio and television have been around for a considerable period of time but as they are now solely transmitted via digital technology in the UK (following the completion of the 'analogue switch-off' in 2012), both are technically defined as 'new media'. Similarly, the fact that a typical 'legacy media' genre such as the newspaper – extant since the latter decades of the seventeenth century – is increasingly read in digital form would suggest its not unproblematic recategorisation as 'new media'. This blurring of boundaries between print and electronic media, known as *convergence* (Jenkins 2006), has considerably complicated the nature of contemporary media genres.

'English' in Media English

The original language of the internet, English (especially as a North American first language or L1) remains largely dominant on a global stage, demonstrating a hegemonic presence in relation to other languages. With the increase of globalisation and related socioeconomic changes, the internet has, however, become increasingly multilingual. The growing prevalence of Chinese on the internet, reflecting to some extent 'off-line' social, political and economic developments, may point to future changes in terms of which language is likely to rival the online presence of English – or indeed which *variety* of English will dominate (see Crystal 2006, 2011). Within the framework of UNESCO's commitment to a multilingual internet, the potential consequences of the steady increase of internet penetration in Africa are noteworthy, considering the continent is home to approximately one-third of the world's languages (Crystal 2011: 80–84). However, future developments within these new settings may become increasingly connected to questions of internet censorship, which have not previously been a major issue in many English-as-L1 contexts.

If we consider how minority and/or endangered languages fare online, to some extent the internet has been beneficial for both preservation and promotion, particularly amongst a younger generation. Of particular relevance here are minority languages in contexts where English is the dominant language (for example, Irish, Welsh, Scottish Gaelic) and in which motivation and ease of online communication therefore needs to be considered. For minority languages in the process of developing an online presence, there are often questions over how (and in what contexts) they can co-exist with English.

Within non-English advertising, English vocabulary is often used symbolically to 'connote a social stereotype of modernity, global elitism and the free market' (Piller 2011: 101), while a heightened demand for English media more broadly has resulted from an increase in people crossing borders for work and leisure. Machin and van Leeuwen (2007) show how Vietnamese journalists writing for an English-language newspaper have adapted to more Western styles, thereby raising questions regarding language hybridity in media contexts. Recent research into the language of the media has largely prioritised English-language media outputs and is generally published in English. As this chapter specifically focuses on Media English, it cannot, unfortunately, help in redressing this balance (see, however, Danet and Herring 2007). Future directions in this research area, however, may continue to explore non-English texts and contexts.

Media representation(s)

For a range of complex reasons (spatial and time constraints; perceived newsworthiness; dominant societal norms; audience considerations; political views of media outlets and so on), the mainstream media can never offer us a full and unbiased picture, but instead uses language and imagery to provide us with representations of reality. Something which has been of key concern to many media discourse scholars is how media texts represent individuals and/or certain groups (sometimes called 'social actors', following van Leeuwen 2008). Through naming and visual strategies, certain aspects of identity can be foregrounded, often in quite subtle ways. Media communications often reinforce – or at least correspond to – various societal hierarchies or groupings, as Gill (2007: 7) argues: 'We live in a world that is stratified along lines of gender, race, ethnicity, class, age, disability, sexuality and location, and in which the privileges, disadvantages and exclusions associated with such categories are unevenly distributed.' These privileges, disadvantages and exclusions are, to a large extent, reflected in mainstream media discourse.

English Language researchers working in these areas of media representation tend to use methods typically (although not exclusively) associated with Critical Discourse Analysis (CDA). As Media English research is concerned with exactly *how* and *why* particular language is used in authentic contexts, it draws upon Foucault's (1972) concept of discourse. Foucault posits that society and societal practices shape language use; therefore, analysis of language use should reveal the users' ideology, that is, the system 'of ideas, beliefs and practices' of that individual or social group (Mayr 2008: 10). Both within and beyond English Language study, there exist various definitions of what power is and what it might entail in different contexts. Power is often viewed at both individual and group levels. These levels are especially relevant when we consider how much power individual citizens have in relation to wider societal structures which can be, to a large extent, greatly outside of their control. In general terms, power can be conceptualised as privileged access to social resources such as education and wealth.

Within most broadly democratic societies, power tends to refer to the somewhat nuanced ways in which groups legitimise this privilege (see Simpson and Mayr 2010). Broadly, this conceptualisation of power connects to Gramsci's (1971) concept of hegemony, as the 'naturalisation' of these ideas helps to reinforce the existing power structures. Within this context of power relations in Media English, the producer of the discourse should also be carefully considered. According to various metrics (e.g. the Reporters Without Borders World

Press Freedom Index), the press is relatively 'free' in many English-speaking contexts, in terms of the lack of overt censorship. However, the picture becomes complicated when we consider the political leanings of various media outlets which are often owned or funded by political parties or influential individuals. For certain newspapers, for example, there will therefore be reader expectations in terms of the content and style. Thus, consideration of language and power affects many levels of media texts.

This connection between language and power is significant for Media English research as it is often via mainstream media's communication systems that some groups' ideas are legitimised whilst others are delegitimised (Simpson and Mayr 2010: 2). However, dominant views may shift over time and according to socioeconomic developments. Media institutions therefore have power in that their positions, viewpoints and ideologies can be both privileged and disseminated widely. This power can be challenged and/or negotiated to a certain extent, both in terms of producing alternative media content – consider, for example, the rise of non-mainstream and social media sources, which will be explored later in this chapter – and by contesting disseminated ideas. Historically, studies of the media have considered two opposing power differentials – 'media power' versus 'people power' – although the reality tends to be more complex. Early constructions of the reader/addressee/viewer as somewhat passive and receptive (the so-called media 'effects' audience research model) have been superseded latterly by constructions of a more active, critical and inquiring media consumer (the 'uses and gratifications' model). This emphasis on reader autonomy is reflected, to some extent, in Reader Response research which considers the role and views of the text's audience(s). However, when discussing the reader in Media English, a careful balance must be struck: in according the reader agency, the ubiquity of media discourse and the often problematic assumptions found there – especially in terms of discursive representations of particular groups or individuals – must be acknowledged.

Particular groups or individuals may be portrayed in a range of ways in media texts. These portrayals do not necessarily reflect lived realities. In terms of gender, research into the area of media representation has examined how ideas about masculinity and femininity are reproduced, most often in gender-targeted media texts. Scholars have considered the construction of the female body in magazine and advertising discourse (e.g. Jeffries 2007; Talbot 2010) and explored how norms about masculinity are circulated in the mainstream media (e.g. Benwell 2004). The highly gendered domain of cosmetics advertising language in particular has also been examined from this perspective, with research exploring how dominant conceptualisations of the body are reproduced and reinforced (e.g. Harrison 2008; Ringrow 2016). Similarly, media representations of sexuality have also been explored within the expanding field of language and sexuality studies (see Baker 2008). In many cases, media representations of sexuality often intersect with discourses about gender norms.

In the current sociopolitical climate in which 'difference' is often (over)emphasised, the media's representation of race and ethnicity is subject to much scrutiny. Following Islamist attacks throughout the world, media scholars are increasingly interested in the portrayal of perpetrators, of Islam itself, and of Muslims more widely, generally in the context of increasing concern over Islamophobia in the Western media. Research into the (mis)representation of Muslims and Islam in contemporary British press – often using corpus linguistic approaches – reveals how language contributes to this notion of 'difference' or 'othering' (e.g. Baker et al. 2013). Similarly, investigations into media representations of immigration reveals discourses of fear and exclusion (e.g. Gabrielatos and Baker 2008; Hanson-Easey et al. 2014). Media depictions of (perceived) class can also be extremely revealing, with much contemporary research focused on representations of people from lower socioeconomic backgrounds which often give rise to claims of misrepresentation and tend to obscure issues of social inequality, thereby 'preserv[ing] the dominance of those in powerful political positions' (Bennett 2013: 161; see also Jones 2011). Mainstream media representations of political movements and political figures tend to intersect with dominant ideas about class, social structure and economics (see for example the LSE's Media and Communication research project on mainstream media representations of the Labour party leader Jeremy Corbyn, 2016; see also Wodak 2015).

The potential effects of media representation on both the various groups and individuals themselves (for example, whether they have been fairly represented) and on the reader/addressee of the text (in terms of how they engage with the ideas portrayed) must also be considered. If we consider the area of gender and advertising, the relationship between media, gender and identity is incredibly complex but certainly most scholars agree that it is highly unlikely that media ideals have no effect whatsoever on at least some of the target audience. Although many consumers are increasingly critical, the constructs represented in advertising and other media discourses are often pervasive. As such, alternative ways of thinking and being may involve substantial conceptual shifts (Jeffries 2007). Media representations of people who appear 'different' may reinforce what van Dijk (1991) calls 'us/them' discourses, in which similarities are ignored and binary opposites are often preferred (see Davies 2013).

Traditional print media

Analyses of what we might term 'traditional' print media within English Language studies have focused predominantly on the discourse of newspapers. These analyses have often approached newspaper language from the perspective of CDA and/or SFL (Systemic Functional Linguistics), especially in terms of power and ideology (see Fowler 1991; Fairclough 1995a, 1995b; Richardson 2006). Newspapers are generally stratified in terms of (perceived) social class, education level, political leanings and so on. Media scholars have therefore historically been interested in exploring how, though text and imagery, print publications appeal to their demographics and how they represent certain social groups, especially groups with limited social power (e.g. Richardson and Machin 2008). Some studies of print newspaper discourse have considered evaluation (in SFL terms), exploring possible distinctions between tabloid and broadsheet newspapers (see Bednarek 2006). Within this context, much research has also investigated what makes certain stories more likely to appear in news media than others, i.e. the *news values* that help to explain both news content, salience and editorial stances in particular social, cultural and national contexts (e.g. Bell 1991; Bednarek and Caple 2017). These news values have recently been adapted to apply to online as well as traditional forms of news discourse, particularly in the context of the now 24-hour news cycle (e.g. Clarke 2017). Further contemporary research within Media English has considered the influence of 'new' media on these older forms, which often leads to hybrid, interactive texts (e.g. readers' online comments on newspaper articles). This interactivity is having an increasing impact upon discourse and communication conventions, not least in terms of im/politeness and in/civility (e.g. Neurauter-Kessels 2011) and in terms of why and how readers engage with news articles (e.g. Blom and Reinecke Hansen 2015 on 'clickbait'). It is worth considering whether traditional print media will see drastic overhauls in terms of style, content and format as a consequence of the increase of online news media, and thinking more about how these different media affect one another. For example, Fairclough's comments on the 'conversationalisation' of public discourse (the creation of a 'public colloquial' language; see Fairclough 1995a) could be revisited, given the likelihood of further developments in print newspaper discourse as a result of its increasingly popular online counterpart.

Another area of traditional print media focus within Media English research has been advertising discourse, especially the examination of print advertising from critical linguistic and stylistic perspectives (see Cook 2001). This kind of research has broadly considered how advertisers identify strategies to tailor their content towards their target demographic, often (although not exclusively) in terms of gender and lifestyle (e.g. Williamson 1978; Goffman 1979). Multimodal approaches to printed advertising texts have also considered how visual grammar works with textual grammar in the often image-saturated domain of print advertising (see for example Forceville 1996). With regards to female-targeted advertisements in particular, women's bodies tend to be constructed in these kinds of texts as always needing 'work' in order to fix 'problems' and therefore conform to particular beauty standards (Lazar 2011; Ringrow 2016). In adherence to these standards, the fat female body symbolises a lack of discipline and control (Murray 2008) and ageing is seen as something which is unwanted and needs to be disguised (Coupland 2007). With male-targeted print advertisements for cosmetics, linguistic analyses have explored the general lack of emphasis on ageing in addition to an attempt on behalf of advertisers to appeal to homo- and heterosexual audiences (e.g. Coupland 2007; Harrison 2008, 2012). In a similar vein, print lifestyle magazines are often highly gendered in terms of both text and imagery (e.g. Jeffries 2007; Benwell 2004), and thus address a certain kind of reader/audience.

As a consequence of the effects of digitisation on print media, contemporary research in the area focuses as much – if not more – on its online counterparts. As such, insights into language use in digitial communication, and in particular the consequences of its characteristic interactivity, are increasingly drawn upon when investigating what was once the most ubiquitous form of media text but is now a rapidly-mutating genre.

Broadcast media

As mentioned above, the increasing digitisation of media output has resulted in a generic hybridity which increasingly confounds categorisation and renders a distinction drawn on the basis of 'new' versus 'traditional' increasingly problematic. As such, this distinction is not applied here; rather, the current section will focus on broadcast media – applying the term in its narrower sense to refer to radio and television – while the following section focuses on social media.

From the 1920s onwards, radio rapidly grew in popularity, with the first British Broadcasting Corporation (BBC) radio broadcast taking place in 1922. In its coverage of a wide range of subject matter – from news and entertainment to factual programming – radio began to generate a vast array of varying text types, including talk shows, radio phone-ins, documentary programmes and advertisements, many of which were subsequently adapted for television. Television was first broadcast in the UK in 1936 and by the late 1970s it was integral to most people's daily lives, outstripping radio as the dominant source of news and entertainment (Branston and Stafford, 2010: 261). Unlike, perhaps, other media forms, the ideological underpinnings of these new media platforms were made fiercely explicit, at least in the UK. From the outset, the BBC monopolised both British radio and television broadcasting and while its core mission to 'inform, educate and entertain' audiences was deemed patronisingly middle-class and elitist by many, it was nonetheless an ideology to which all subsequent new UK television and radio stations had to adhere. While such ideological transparency is not unproblematic, its absence is undoubtedly more so; the objectivity of US television's Fox News Channel, for example, is consistently compromised by its deep-rooted yet largely unacknowledged political biases.

Consideration of contextual factors is crucial to all discourse analysis, and particularly in the case of broadcast media; Goffman (1967) referred to its output as 'talk' – meaning the casual and everyday exchange of conversation – rather than language, asserting that the former term situates language firmly in its context of use. The development of the internet has had a significant impact upon all aspects of radio and televisual communication, largely due to its alteration of their contexts of production and consumption, as noted above. All broadcast talk is intended for public consumption and marked by its 'double articulation', i.e. it is a 'communicative interaction between those participating in discussion, interview, game show or whatever and, at the same time, is designed to be heard by absent audiences' (Scannell 1991: 1). While broadcasters cannot control the context in which their output is received, successful broadcasting involves using language which shows understanding of these contexts. The preference, primarily dictated by the domestic sphere in which broadcast talk is received, is for language which mimics the intimacy and interaction of informal conversation; interestingly, in their mimicry of a one-to-one broadcast mode, radio and television are considered to constitute 'the end, not the extension, of mass communication' (see Scannell 1991: 3–4).

Latterly however, contexts of production and consumption are frequently conflated as a result of the unprecedented interactivity facilitated by the digital age, with many television programmes adopting internet-enabled technology to encourage participation from audiences seated in the comfort of their own living rooms. The traditionally 'absent' audience is becoming increasingly present as listeners and viewers are invited to engage further with and/or comment upon programme content by using their electronic devices to access, for example, a programme's Facebook and/or Twitter accounts. The arrival of the digital age, while not changing the primacy of radio or television within the domestic sphere, has however dramatically altered the ways in which audiences access broadcast output. For example, cameras are increasingly installed in radio studios, thereby encouraging radio listeners to simultaneously become viewers of the radio presenters and their guests; similarly, the increase in online television viewing prompted the Broadcast Audience Research Board (BARB) – the official source for UK audience viewing figures since 1981 – to include online television viewing figures from September 2015.

Despite its longevity and popularity, radio has suffered a comparative degree of investigative neglect, being, as Tolson notes, a 'relatively "forgotten" medium' (Tolson 2006: 3). And while television broadcasting has been the subject of a considerable degree of academic enquiry, mainly within the fields of media and cultural studies, the focus has largely been on its subject matter rather than its discursive practices. In particular, and despite the centrality of language – and spoken discourse in particular – to their output, there is a paucity of research on the *form* of both radio and television discourse when compared to other media genres. As Lorenzo-Dus (2009: 2–3) notes, this is in part because researchers are acutely aware of the difficulties of paying sufficient attention to the all-important contexts of production and consumption when investigating broadcast media texts.

While both radio and television are generically 'slippery' media, television, with its increased multimodality, is characterised by 'fluid formats and self-reflexive economy' which enable it to fulfil its function as 'the prime purveyor of a postmodern sensibility' (Stempel-Mumford 1995: 20). However, this also makes television a difficult object of formal study as effective analysis of such a multimodal genre requires interdisciplinary expertise which many researchers, up to now, did not have. None of this is aided by the perception that, as Tolson notes, '[t]he products of TV and radio seem transitory and ephemeral and at best their consumption is a routine form of leisure' (Tolson 2006: 5). What has been overlooked until recently is that radio and television output simultaneously shapes and is shaped by our discursive practices, and, as is the case with all media, studying their communicative mechanisms affords scholars yet another means of interrogating the relationship between language and societal practice.

Early media theorists such as Fiske and Hartley (1978) constructed television as fulfilling the traditional social role of storyteller within a community – a role which can also be attributed to radio – assisting not in the generation but rather in the dissemination and, crucially, interpretation of news and information; in the role of storyteller, mediation is foregrounded. Within this model, broadcast media output takes on a distinctly narrative form operating on two levels: firstly, using terms taken from Young (1987), each programme can be considered a 'taleworld' in that it tells its own story which is driven by a plot and peopled by characters; secondly, these characters themselves tell stories, forming their own metanarratives or 'storyrealms' (see Lorenzo-Dus 2009). These narratives in turn act as purveyors of identity, encouraging audiences to either identify with or 'against' the ideals of the social groups represented.

Much research into broadcast media discourse draws upon a combination of these techniques. Scannell (1991) is one such early example, with most contributions to this edited collection analysing the narrative structure of radio or television discourse in terms of how identity is performed, from the identity of the broadcast personality to the politician's self-representation through talk (for more contemporary but similar examples see Bednarek 2010; Piazza et al. 2011). Research into how talk acts as a marker of control and/or identity has, in the past, largely focused on non-fiction television, and talk shows in particular (e.g. Thornborrow 2007); however, such research has extended into the increasingly popular genres of realist crime fiction and new non-fiction genres such as 'true crime', which are loaded with discursively-constructed power play (see Gregoriou 2011; Statham 2015).

In terms of audience, earlier research on broadcast media audiences largely identified their role as that of 'overhearing recipient of a discourse' (Montgomery 1986: 428) or 'eavesdroppers on a cosy chat' (Moss and Higgins 1979: 291); however, this is problematic given that these audiences, though absent, are nonetheless authorised. Contemporary research increasingly constructs audiences as legitimised, though absent, participants in a conversation, and endeavours to develop communication models which go beyond the traditionally dyadic to accommodate the unique interactional strategies typical of broadcast media. As a result, much of this research adopts a structural, largely Conversation Analysis perspective, often focusing, as noted by O'Keeffe, on 'the discourse of interactions in broadcast settings' and how this differs from casual conversation (O'Keeffe 2006: 1).

While textual analyses of the genre of reality television – also known as 'popular factual entertainment', or 'actuality-based' television – tend to mimic that of fictional television, they must nonetheless take into account a more diverse set of complexities when doing so, including the genre's hybridity and problematic engagement with the notion of 'real', both of which affect how the participants in these programmes are represented. Indeed, the genre's concern with participant performativity and display has ensured that much of the academic focus – coming not from linguistic but media and cultural studies' perspectives – is on assessing how 'real' reality television is. Lorenzo-Dus and Blitvich (2013)'s work constitutes one of a limited number of linguistic approaches to reality television discourse. Here, reality television output drawn from an impressively diverse range of countries, including Argentina, Israel and China, is analysed, not only in terms of how social, national and individual identities are linguistically represented, but also how aggression and conflict – crucial elements in successful reality television programming – are constructed in these texts through linguistic im/politeness.

Social media

Many newer digital text types come under the genre of social media, a term referring to all online platforms which encourage social interaction (Mandiberg 2012). Social media tends to be differentiated from mass media on the basis of interactivity: while the latter communicates via an indiscriminate 'one-to-many' broadcast mode, social media's targeting of specific individuals/networks of individuals results in its characteristic interactivity. As noted elsewhere, this interactivity has changed the nature of much traditional print and broadcast media output, as digital media platforms are increasingly appropriated into their broadcast mechanism. The heterogeneity of social media genres, which includes a range of forums and platforms, reflects a corresponding hybridity of form, comprised as it is of both written and spoken discourse features.

Research on language use in digital communication developed along three distinct strands (see Barton and Lee 2013). Firstly, emphasis was placed on investigating the structural features seen as unique to online language use. This was followed by a more context-orientated strand of research, in which the theoretical observations of the first wave were augmented by situating them within their contexts of use. The findings of much of this research indicate the continuity between offline and online language use, as well as a continued interest in the narrative dimensions of new media typical of the research on broadcast media (see Zappavigna 2012; Seargeant and Tagg 2014). It also foregrounds the existence of new digital communities which use particular linguistic and interactional strategies to create online identities, including gender, sexual and ethnic (see Page 2012; Tagg 2012, 2015). The darker side of this online linguistic identity performance is manifest in the increasingly rampant phenomenon of 'trolling' or cyber-bullying (see Pihlaja 2014; Hardaker 2015). The final strand is two-fold. Firstly, it focuses on language ideologies, addressing common misconceptions of the effect of digital communication on language standards or what Barton and Lee refer to as 'techno panics' (Barton and Lee 2013: 7). Secondly, it investigates the way language is talked about online, i.e. metalanguage. Cumulatively, these strands represent the primary purposes of analysing online language use: to investigate the extent to which these perplexingly hybrid media outputs represent unique and innovative language use at the structural level; to analyse online strategies of linguistic representation and self-presentation; and finally, to investigate the effect of online language use on language 'standards' overall. The extent to which language shapes reality is, in an online context, particularly evident. As such, the study of Media English online not only analyses how we use language in digital communication – and indeed, given that we do so largely as a means of identity performance and forging interpersonal bonds, such use is largely contiguous with its use in offline contexts – but how digitally mediated communications 'extend and transform what people are already doing with language' (Tagg 2015: 9).

Finally, much has been made of the collaborative nature of new media construction, a phenomenon encapsulated in descriptive terms such as 'participatory media' (Mandiberg 2012), which emphasise the perceived democratisation of the internet. This is perhaps most obvious in the rise of 'citizen journalism' – which takes place largely though not exclusively via online media platforms – where the public actively participate in the various information gathering, analysis and dissemination processes previously carried out exclusively by journalists (for more on citizen journalism see Allan 2013). However, in analysing new media, it is important to note that this purported democratisation only holds true up to a point, given the presence of editorial 'gatekeeping' in citizen journalism websites. This is also the case with social media; the content of wikis, though created wholly through collaboration, is nevertheless decided upon by an elite team of administrators, while the creators of a blog decide which comments are suitable to remain on their site and which are deleted. As such, though new media genres – and social media in particular – may smooth out the hierarchies found in mass media broadcasting, they often re-establish them in alternative ways.

Future directions

In the past two decades, changing sociocultural norms coupled with numerous technological developments have triggered seismic shifts in how media institutions operate, as touched upon throughout this chapter. The wide range and increasing variety of text types has altered the nature of our relationship with the media, replacing a largely unidirectional broadcast mechanism with one characterised by a bidirectional interactivity which increasingly blurs the boundaries between producer and consumer. Simultaneously because of and despite this increased interactivity, the influence of the media in today's society has arguably never been stronger. As such, the study of Media English remains buoyant, with a number of key trends in future research likely to dominate, namely, interdisciplinary studies; the politics of media representation; and research into language abuse, especially in the digital domain.

Research into Media English is expanding in an increasingly interdisciplinary fashion and is likely to continue in this vein. This is evidenced in a number of areas within the study of Media English. For example, increasing awareness of the importance of non-linguistic semiotic modes – including colour, sound and movement – has stimulated much research into the visual and auditory grammar of media communication. Proponents of what has become known as Multimodal Critical Discourse Analysis have analysed the various means by which non-linguistic semiotic modes communicate individually, in tandem with each other and alongside a text's linguistic modes to communicate meaning (see Machin and Mayr 2012; see also Kress and van Leeuvwen 1996; Kress 2010; Dancygier and Sweetser 2012). This multimodal research also takes numerous forms; for example, one recent study analyses multimodality in the context of the effects of digitisation on traditional media (see Bednarek and Caple 2016 on print media). Finally, multimodal approaches themselves are, in turn, becoming increasingly interdisciplinary. Lukes and Hart (2007), for example, integrate insights from cognitive linguistics into multimodal and linguistic CDA approaches while Bednarek (2015) uses corpus-assisted techniques in her analysis of the multimodal construction of television and film narratives.

Research in the field also continues to interrogate the politics of media representation, as issues of personal, social, cultural, national and political identity are increasingly discursively constructed (see Stoegner and Wodak 2016). As suggested in the fourth section, political tensions and developments on a global stage have led to an increased interest in interrogating representations of Muslims and of Islam, especially in media discourses. In this vein, Törnberg and Törnberg (2016) examine the (largely homogenous and extremist) representation of Muslims and Islam in social media over time, while Pihlaja and Thompson (2017) use focus groups to investigate how young British Muslim students respond to and engage with negative media narratives about Muslims, especially in the aftermath of terrorist attacks. Another area of increased interest to Media English researchers is the representation of marriage, romantic relationships and parenting, especially in online media contexts. This interest can perhaps in part be attributed to societal changes, such as the increased popularity of online dating sites; the progression of legalising same-sex marriage in many parts of the world; the increased visibility of what we might broadly call 'non-traditional' relationships (cohabiting couples, civil partnerships, same-sex parents, polyamorous relationships, etc.); and the growth in online spaces for parenting discussions (via dedicated blogs and discussion forums). Recent linguistic research in these areas includes Mackenzie's (2017) work on the discursive construction of parenting on the UK Mumsnet website and Jones et al.'s (2017) research on the identity politics of naming (including name-changing) practices for British couples.

As a phenomenon which raises issues of authenticity, authorship and audience reception, 'fake news' is also likely to generate new research from media linguistics. In essence, fake news involves the purposeful dissemination of false information via traditional broadcast media. As a form of political propaganda, its use dates back to ancient times but was greatly facilitated by the rise of mass media communication in the twentieth century. Its notoriety has, however, substantially increased in recent times, largely due to the purported impact of fake news upon events of national and international import, such as government elections and national referendums (though the disseminators of fake news in such cases have tended to be members of small-scale groups rather than state-sponsored propagandists). Social media is very much implicated in the contemporary rise of fake news. In their investigation into the effect of fake news on the 2016 US presidential elections, Allcott and Gentzkow (2017), for instance, note the pivotal role played by social media in its circulation and ultimate impact.

The anonymity typical of many channels of digital communication has generated a 'darker side' of language use in online contexts. As delineated above, the study of Media English is increasingly orientated towards investigation of the language and shifting contexts of digital and, in particular, social, media, with the latest research in the field replacing traditional linguistic concepts with bespoke terms more adept at capturing the nuances of internet language use, and placing these terms within various societal contexts. As a result, research into the origins, contextual use and, as appropriate, effects of bespoke internet language will no doubt abound. Of relevance here, for instance, is Thurlow's (2017) recent semiotic analysis of 'sexting', in which he explores how mainstream media discourses are used to both represent and discipline sex and sexuality. In addition, the internet's darker side is beginning to attract the attention of Media English scholars interested in the language used to construct these online communities. Lawson and McGlashan (2017), for example, investigate gender identity performance in online 'pick up artist' communities while Hardaker and McGlashan (2016) analyse the linguistic and identity politics of Twitter rape threats.

Conclusion

Media English is a problematic category, comprised of disparate and at times indistinguishable bodies of texts whose hybridity has increased rapidly as a result of digitisation. It is a broad term referring to the ways in which the English language is used to construct reality through media platforms, such as the front cover of a print newspaper, the advertisements in a magazine, a radio programme, a text message or a tweet. Contemporary media research increasingly addresses the impact on the media landscape brought by digitisation, which has resulted both in the creation of new media platforms and the reformation of the old. One of the most significant changes has been in terms of media interactivity, resulting in the transformation of a previously unidirectional broadcast mechanism to one which is bidirectional and increasingly dialogic. Yet such interactivity is not unproblematic, resulting in an increasing abuse of the privileges of online communication. In the future, research in this field will no doubt continue to investigate the media's evolution and diversification into increasingly more interactive and multimodal forms, as well as investigating the challenges wrought by the increasing complexities of media forms and outputs. Language, however, continues to be a core communicative and discursive tool which mirrors the changing society in which contemporary media operates. The language of the media, in particular, simultaneously creates and refracts our reality; as such, it will always constitute a worthy and indeed crucial area of English Language study.

Further reading

Fairclough, N. (1992) *Discourse and Social Change*. Cambridge: Polity Press. Explicitly laying out the central tenets and methods of CDA, this is an erudite introduction to the relationship between discourse and society.

Fowler, R. (1991) *Language in the News: Discourse and Ideology in the Press*. London: Routledge. Fowler examines how language mediates reality, focusing on how newspaper representations reflect social constructions of power, ideology, gender and authority.

Tagg, C. (2015) *Exploring Digital Communication*. London: Routledge. A key text representing current and future directions in the flourishing medium of digital communication.

Related topics

- World Englishes: disciplinary debates and future directions
- Language, gender and sexuality
- Persuasive language
- The language of social media.

References

Allan, S. and H. Caple (2013) *Citizen Witnessing: Revisioning Journalism in Times of Crisis*. Cambridge: Polity.

Allcott, H. and M. Gentzkow (2017) 'Social media and fake news in the 2016 election', *Journal of Economic Perspectives* 31: 211–236.

Baker, P. (2008) *Sexed Texts: Language, Gender and Sexuality*. London: Equinox.

Baker, P., C. Gabrielatos and T. McEnery. (2013) *Discourse Analysis and Media Attitudes: The Representation of Islam in the British Press*. Cambridge: Cambridge University Press.

Barton, B. and C. Lee (2013) *Language Online: Investigating Digital Texts and Practices*. London: Routledge.

Bednarek, M. (2006) *Evaluation in Media Discourse: Analysis of a Newspaper Corpus*. London: Continuum.

Bednarek, M. (2010) *The Language of Fictional Television: Drama and Identity*. London: Continuum.

Bednarek, M. (2015) 'Corpus-assisted multimodal discourse analysis of television and film narratives', in P. Baker and T. McEnery (eds), *Corpora and Discourse Studies: Integrating Discourse and Corpora*. Basingstoke: Palgrave Macmillan, 63–87.

Bednarek, M. and H. Caple (2016) 'Rethinking news values: what a discursive approach can tell us about the construction of news discourse and news photography', *Journalism: Theory, Practice and Criticism* 17 (4): 435–455.

Bednarek, M. and H. Caple (2017) *The Discourse of News Values*. Oxford: Oxford Academic Press.

Bell, A. (1991) *The Language of News Media*. Oxford: Blackwell.

Bennett, J. (2013) Chav-spotting in Britain: The representation of social class as private choice. *Social Semiotics* 23 (1): 146–162.

Benwell, B. (2004) 'Ironic discourse: Evasive masculinity in British men's lifestyle magazines', *Men and Masculinities* 7 (1): 3–21.

Blom, J. N. and K. Reinecke Hansen (2015) 'Click bait: Forward-reference as lure in online news headlines', *Journal of Pragmatics* 74: 87–100.

Branston, G. and R. Stafford (2010) *The Media Student's Book*. 5th edn. London: Routledge.

Bruns, A. and J. Jacobs (2006) *Uses of Blogs*. New York: Peter Lang.

Clarke, B. (2017) '"We're hearing from Reuters that . . . ": The role of around-the-clock news media in the increased use of the present progressive with mental process type verbs', in S. Gardner and S. Alsop (eds), *Systemic Functional Linguistics in the Digital Age*. Sheffield: Equinox Publishing, 68–84.

Cook, G. (2001) *The Discourse of Advertising*. 2nd edn. London: Routledge.

Corner, J. (1998) *Studying Media: Problems of Theory and Method*. Edinburgh: Edinburgh University Press.

Couldry, N. and B. Cammaerts (2016) Journalistic representations of Jeremy Corbyn in the British press: From watchdog to attackdog. www.lse.ac.uk/media-and-communications/assets/documents/research/projects/corbyn/Cobyn-Report.pdf.

Coupland, J. (2007) 'Gendered discourses on the "problem" of ageing: Consumerized solutions', *Discourse and Communication* 1 (1): 37–61.

Crystal, D. (2006) *Language and the Internet*. 2nd edn. Cambridge: Cambridge University Press.

Crystal, D. (2011) *Internet Linguistics: A Student Guide*. London: Routledge.

Dancygier, B. and E. Sweetser (eds) (2012) *Viewpoint in Language: A Multimodal Perspective*. Cambridge: Cambridge University Press.

Danet, B. and S. Herring (eds) (2007) *The Multilingual Internet: Language, Culture, and Communication Online*. New York: Oxford University Press.

Davies, M. (2013) *Oppositions and Ideology in News Discourse*. London: Bloomsbury.

Fairclough, N. (1995a) *Critical Discourse Analysis: The Critical Study of Language*. London: Routledge.

Fairclough, N. (1995b). *Media Discourse*. London: Hodder Arnold.

Fiske, J. and J. Hartley (1978) *Reading Television*. London: Methuen.

Forceville, C. (1996) *Pictorial Metaphor in Advertising*. London: Routledge.

Foucault, M. (1972) *The Archaeology of Knowledge* (Translated from the French by A. Sheridan). London: Tavistock.

Fowler, R. (1991) *Language in the News: Discourse and Ideology in the Press*. London: Routledge.

Gabrielatos, C. and P. Baker (2008) 'Fleeing, sneaking, flooding: A corpus analysis of discursive constructions of refugees and asylum seekers in the UK press, 1996–2005', *Journal of English Linguistics* 36 (1): 5–38.

Gill, R. (2007) *Gender and the Media*. Cambridge: Cambridge University Press.

Goffman, E. (1967) *Interaction Ritual: Essays on Face-to-Face Behaviour*. Garden City: Anchor.

Goffman, E. (1979) *Gender Advertisements*. London: Macmillan.

Gramsci, A. (1971) *Selections from the Prison Notebooks*. London: Lawrence and Wishart.

Gregoriou, C. (2011) *Language, Ideology and Identity in Serial Killer Narratives*. London: Routledge.

Hanson-Easey, S., M. Augoustinos and G. Moloney (2014) "They're all tribals": Essentialism, context and the discursive representation of Sudanese refugees', *Discourse and Society* 25 (3): 362–382.

Hardaker, C. (2015) '"I refuse to respond to this obvious troll": An overview of responses to (perceived) trolling', *Corpora* 10 (2): 201–229.

Hardaker, C. and M. McGlashan (2016) '"Real men don't hate women": Twitter rape threats and group identity', *Journal of Pragmatics* 91: 80–93.

Harrison, C. (2008) 'Real men do wear mascara: Advertising discourse and masculine identity', *Critical Discourse Studies* 5 (1): 55–73.

Harrison, C. (2012) 'Studio5ive.com: Selling cosmetics to men and reconstructing masculine identity', in K. Ross (ed.), *The Handbook of Gender, Sex and Media*. London: Wiley-Blackwell, 189–204.

Jeffries, L. (2007) *The Textual Construction of the Female Body: A Critical Discourse Analysis Approach*. Basingstoke: Palgrave Macmillan.

Jenkins, H. (2006) *Convergence Culture: Where Old and New Media Collide*. New York: New York University Press.

Jones, O. (2011) *Chavs: The Demonization of the Working Class*. London: Verso.

Jones, L., S. Mills, L. Paterson, G. Turner and L. Coffey-Glover (2017) 'Identity and naming practices in British marriage and civil partnerships', *Gender and Language* 11 (3): 309–335.

Kress, G. (2010) *Multimodality: A Social Semiotic Approach to Contemporary Communication*. London: Routledge.

Kress, G. and T. van Leeuvwen (1996) *Reading Images: The Grammar of Visual Design*. London: Routledge.

Lawson, R. and M. McGlashan (2017) Discourses of neoliberal masculinity: A corpus-based discourse study of an online 'Pick Up Artist' community. BAAL SIG on Language, Gender and Sexuality, University of Nottingham, 27 April 2017. Slides downloaded from www.bcu.academia.edu/RobertLawson/Talks.

Lazar, M. M. (2011) 'The right to be beautiful: Postfeminist identity and consumer beauty advertising', in R. Gill and C. Scharff (eds), *New Femininities*. Palgrave Macmillan, London, 37–51.

Lorenzo-Dus, N. (2009) *Television Discourse: Analysing Language in the Media*. Basingstoke: Palgrave Macmillan.
Lorenzo-Dus, N. and P. Blitvich (eds) (2013) *Real Talk: Reality Television and Discourse Analysis in Action*. Basingstoke: Palgrave Macmillan.
Lukes, D. and C. Hart (2007) *Cognitive Linguistics in Critical Discourse Analysis: Application and Theory*. Cambridge: Cambridge Scholars Publishing.
Machin, D. and A. Mayr (2012) *How to Do Critical Discourse Analysis: A Multimodal Introduction*. London: Sage.
Machin, D. and T. van Leeuwen (2007) *Global Media Discourse: A Critical Introduction*. London: Routledge.
Mackenzie, J. (2017) '"Can we have a child exchange?" Constructing and subverting the "good mother" through play in Mumsnet Talk', *Discourse & Society* 28 (3): 296–312.
Mandiberg, M. (ed.) (2012) *The Social Media Reader*. New York: New York University Press.
Manovich, L. (2001) *The Language of New Media*. Cambridge: MIT Press.
Matheson, D. (2005) *Media Discourses: Analysing Media Texts*. Maidenhead: Open University Press.
Mayr, A. (2008) *Language and Power: An Introduction to Institutional Discourse*. London: Continuum.
Medoff, N.J. and B.K. Kaye (2017) *Electronic Media: Then, Now and Later*. 3rd edn. New York: Focal Press.
Montgomery, M. (1986) 'DJ talk', *Media, Culture and Society* 8(4): 421–440.
Moss, P. and C. Higgins (1979) 'Radio voices', in G. Gumpert and R. Cathcart (eds), *Inter/media: Interpersonal Communication in a Media World*. Oxford: Oxford University Press, 282–299.
Murray, S. (2008) *The 'Fat' Female Body*. Basingstoke: Palgrave Macmillan.
Neurauter-Kessels, M. (2011) 'Im/polite reader responses on British online news sites', *Journal of Politeness Research* 7 (2): 187–214.
O'Keeffe, A. (2006) *Investigating Media Discourse*. London: Routledge.
Page, R. (2012) *Stories and Social Media: Identities and Interaction*. London: Routledge.
Pihlaja, S. (2014) *Antagonism on YouTube: Metaphor in Online Discourse*. London: Bloomsbury.
Pihlaja, S. and N. Thompson (2017) '"I love the Queen": Positioning in young British Muslim discourse', *Discourse, Context & Media* 20: 52–58.
Piller, I. (2011) *Intercultural communication*. Edinburgh: Edinburgh University Press.
Piazza, R., M. Bednarek and F. Rossi (eds) (2011) *Telecinematic Discourse: Approaches to the Language of Films and Television Series*. Amsterdam: John Benjamins, 161–183.
Richardson, J. E. (2006) *Analysing Newspapers*. Basingstoke: Palgrave Macmillan.
Richardson, J. E. and D. Machin (2008) 'Renewing an academic interest in structural inequality', *Critical Discourse Studies* 5 (4): 281–288.
Ringrow, H. (2016) *The Language of Cosmetics Advertising*. London: Palgrave Macmillan.
Scannell, P. (ed.) (1991) 'Introduction: The Relevance of Talk', in P. Scannell (ed.), *Broadcast Talk*. London: Sage, 1–13.
Scannell, P. (2007) *Media and Communication*. London: Sage.
Seargeant, P. and C. Tagg (eds) (2014) *The Language of Social Media: Identity and Community on the Internet*. Basingstoke: Palgrave Macmillan.
Simpson, P. and A. Mayr (2010) *Language and Power*. London: Routledge.
Statham, S. (2015) '"A guy in my position is a government target ... You got to be extra, extra careful": Participation and strategies in crime talk in *The Sopranos*', *Language and Literature* 24 (4): 322–337.
Stempel-Mumford, L. (1995) *Love and Ideology in the Afternoon: Soap Opera, Women and Television Genre*. Bloomington: Indian University Press.
Stoegner, K. and R. E. Wodak (2016) '"The man who hated Britain": The discursive construction of "national unity" in the *Daily Mail*', *Critical Discourse Studies* 13 (2): 193–209.
Tagg, C. (2012) *The Discourse of Text Messaging*. London: Continuum.
Tagg, C. (2015) *Exploring Digital Communication*. London: Routledge.
Talbot, M. (2010) *Language, Intertextuality and Subjectivity: Voices in the Construction of Consumer Femininity*. Saarbrücken: Lambert Academic Publishing.
Thornborrow, J. (2007) 'Narrative, opinion and situated argument in talk show discourse', *Journal of Pragmatics* 39 (8): 1436–1453.

Thurlow, C. (2017) '"Forget about the words"? Tracking the language, media and semiotic ideologies of digital discourse: The case of sexting', *Discourse, Context & Media* 20: 10–19.
Tolson, A. (2006) *Media Talk: Spoken Discourse on TV and Radio*. Edinburgh: Edinburgh Univerity Press.
Törnberg, A. and P. Törnberg (2016) 'Muslims in social media discourse: Combining topic modeling and critical discourse analysis', *Discourse, Context & Media* 13:132–142.
van Dijk, T. (1991) *Racism and the Press*. London: Routledge.
van Leeuwen, T. (2008) *Discourse and Practice*. Oxford: Oxford University Press.
Williamson, J. (1978) *Decoding Advertisements*. London: Marion Boyars.
Wodak, R. (2015) *The Politics of Fear*. London: Sage.
Young, K. (1987) *Taleworlds and Storyrealms: The Phenomenology of Narrative*. Dordrecht: Martinus Nijhoff.
Zappavigna, M. (2012) *Discourse of Twitter and Social Media*. London: Continuum.

21
The language of social media

Tereza Spilioti

What is social media?

The chapter aims to provide a critical review of current research on the language of social media and point to its developing research agendas. After defining what is commonly understood by 'social media' and delineating its key distinctive properties, I will first position research on the language of social media vis-à-vis recent developments in studies of digitally mediated language and communication. I will then shed light on current research foci, particularly the study of language and social variation, on the one hand, and language practices, on the other. Issues of self-presentation, identity, and community will be revisited in light of current debates in the field. The chapter concludes by reviewing points of contention regarding methodological issues and developing agendas related to critical and ethical research on social media.

Although there is no consensus about who coined the term 'social media', it is almost certain that academics cannot take credit for it: the term appeared and was popularised first among the creators and developers of the very internet sites and services which are today known by the term (Bercovici 2010). Following, to some extent, technologists' use of the term, academics have also defined social media broadly as referring to a range of internet-based sites and applications that promote, are designed for, and/or are adopted for social interaction between participants (Page et al. 2014; Seargeant and Tagg 2014; Georgakopoulou 2015; Leppanen et al. 2017). The use of such a broad definition has the advantage of bringing together research on various sites and services, ranging from instant messaging apps to social network sites and virtual worlds, and contributes to the development of a critical mass for research on the language of social media. Nevertheless, assuming that technologies for social interaction, such as email, TV, radio, telephone, postcards, and epistolary writing, predate the so-called social media, we need to clarify further some of the distinctive qualities associated with academic and lay understandings of the specific internet-based sites.

In order to clarify what is distinctive about social media, we will focus on three elements that have been hailed as the hallmarks of web 2.0; namely, participation, convergence, and social network architecture. Unlike mass media communication (e.g. newspapers, radio, TV), social media content 'is as much a product of participation as it is of traditional creative and publishing/broadcast processes' (Seargeant and Tagg 2014: 4). *Participation* for social media users involves generating and sharing content either publicly or to a selected group of people in a collaborative and often creative manner. Such participation takes place in complex communicative environments that display *convergence* of previously distinct technologies and afford the integration of multiple semiotic modes for user-generated content. For example, Facebook users can move across distinct spaces affording either one-to-many posts (e.g. Facebook wall; News Feed) or one-to-one messaging (e.g. Messenger) and they can also combine a range of modalities by integrating text, image, audio, and video in their status update or chat. At the same time, participation is afforded by a *social network architecture* which

> allow[s] individuals to (1) construct a public or semi-public profile within a bounded system, (2) articulate a list of other users with whom they share a connection, and (3) view and traverse their list of connections and those made by others within the system.
> (boyd and Ellison 2008: 211)

The social network architecture may vary from site to site. For example, the *connections* between the members of a social network can range from symmetrical ones (e.g. Facebook connections, where the user has to accept the invite and thus ratify the connection) to asymmetrical ones (e.g. Twitter, where a user can follow another user, without any ratification from the other party). As a result, the extent to which connections can be visible and clearly articulable also varies between these two platforms, with Facebook affording a more explicit articulation of connections within the network. Nevertheless, one of the elements that remain constant across most social media sites and services concerns the creation of a *personal profile* that enables the user to generate content, link with other profiles, and participate in the network. The generation of a personal profile usually involves providing information about one's self in the form of (user)names, pictures, demographic information (such as age, gender, location), and answers to questions about personal interests, beliefs, and likes. Last, but not least, the social network architecture also affords communicative environments where multiple contexts collapse and previously distinct audiences are brought together into single platforms ('*context collapse*' Marwick and boyd 2011: 115). For example, if the average Facebook user has about 338 Facebook friends (Smith 2014), the potential readers and thus audience of a status update include a large amount of people who probably belong to distinct social groups, ranging from professional to family contacts and friends.

Research on digitally mediated language: historical perspectives

In order to understand the theoretical and methodological momentum of current advances in social media research, we need to contextualise contemporary studies within the short, yet rapidly developing, historical trajectory of the field. Early interest in human communication via networked computers (or computer-mediated communication, henceforth CMC) can be traced as far back as the 1980s and 1990s. The interdisciplinary scope of the then emerging field offered fertile ground for linguistic studies to appear and develop in parallel with CMC research in related areas of sociology, computer science, and media and cultural studies. Although marginalised compared to more mainstream areas of linguistic research, language-focused CMC studies continued to proliferate. Despite their fragmentation in terms of analytical foci and methods, they began to cluster together into a relatively identifiable research strand under the umbrella term 'Computer-Mediated Discourse Analysis' (CMDA,

Herring 2004). To use Androutsopoulos's (2006) waves metaphor, the first wave of CMC research is preoccupied with formal and functional properties of text-based communication in primarily English-speaking internet settings, such as email, echat, online forums and multi-player online games. The focus on issues related to the position of CMC vis-à-vis speech and writing, creativity and play, generic norms and textual coherence reveals the field's early attempts to understand the presumed 'new' and 'novel' in juxtaposition with the 'old' norms (Georgakopoulou 2006). In early CMDA studies, such understandings are often constrained by a logic that sees the medium and its technological properties as key shaping factors for language and communication in digital media ('technological determinism' Hutchby 2001).

The field's growing familiarity with the 'novelties' of the medium, as well as opening up to concurrent methodological and theoretical advances in socially-minded linguistics, paved the way for the so-called second wave of CMC research, coined as such in Androutsopoulos (2006). From formal and functional properties of digitally mediated texts, the focus shifts to users, their language practices and the ways in which identities, relations, and communities are formed in a range of internet contexts, including discussion forums, text and instant messaging, social media profile pages, and online games. At the same time, there is a move from the earlier monomodal and monolinguistic research on primarily English-speaking texts towards studies that examine the combination of multiple modes (mainly image and text) and multiple languages, varieties, and styles on the internet. Furthermore, although not widely acknowledged, the second wave also critically engages with metalinguistic discourses about digitally mediated language and communication that are circulated in 'old' media (e.g. press, radio and TV), frame folk understandings of the internet, and interplay with wider language and social ideologies.

After the first and second wave, voices now converge towards the realisation that a third wave is currently sweeping through the field (Georgakopoulou and Spilioti 2016). Social media and their communicative exigencies play a key role in shaping the foci and methods of recent research. Following on from the second wave, the focus on users and their practices remains, with a heightened attention to practices that are intimately linked with the design and techno-social environment of social media platforms (e.g. sharing, liking, tagging). Identities, relations, and communities are still central foci of interest but they are revisited in light of the various audiences and global networks afforded by social media and, most importantly, in relation to the interplay and mutual embeddedness of face-to-face and mediated (or offline and online) contexts. Furthermore, there is a proliferation of multimodal and multilingual research that attempts to gauge the increased reliance on the visual mode, on the one hand, and the creative and dynamic manipulation of varieties, styles, and language forms, on the other. As argued in the last section, the critical engagement with wider discourses and ideologies moves away from framings of new technologies in old media and puts under the microscope the discourses and scripts of social media platform templates and algorithms that mediate user-to-user interaction.

The language of social media I: English language and social variation

Drawing on the key premise that language is heterogeneous, research on the language of social media explores variation in the realisation of language forms associated with the English language system. In this line of research, linguistic variation at any level of language description, including spelling, morphology, lexis, syntax, or pragmatics, is often associated with external factors ranging from properties of the technology (e.g. character limit or platform prompts) to social categories such as participant gender, age, or ethnicity. The latter preoccupation that explores language variation in relation to social aspects of the user's identity or the specific situation is more typical of what we have identified as the second wave of CMC research.

In one of the earliest book-length examinations of social media discourse, Zappavigna (2012) points out a range of alternative spelling forms that vary from standard orthography, such as emoticons, repeated letters or punctuation marks, vowel omission, and phonetic respellings. In her data, it proves difficult to discern specific patterns or to correlate non-standard variants with social factors, as usage is highly variable even within single tweets. As Zappavigna (2012) points out, this can be understood as a sign of fluidity and instability of established norms in the then emerging communicative context of Twitter. Indeed, research on more established genres such as blogs and multi-player online games has fruitfully pointed out how alternation between standard and non-standard spellings correlates with social factors, such as the blogger's gender and residence (Hinrichs 2012) or the player's role status and virtual proximity with another player in the game world (Iorio 2009). Beyond spelling, Herring and Paolillo (2006) explored stylistic variation in blogs and indicated that blog genres (i.e. diary vs. filter entries) co-vary with stylistic features associated with 'female' and 'male' language (regardless of the author gender).

Similarly, more recent research on Twitter offers further insights into sociolinguistic variation in social media. Gender is one of the key social variables that have received due attention. Bamman et al. (2014) focus on lexical variation in order to study gendered language styles in a large corpus of 14,000 Twitter users. Their results reveal that although there are some strong gender orientations (e.g. higher frequency of personal pronouns and emotion words in female authored tweets), there are some 'outliers' that do not fit mainstream language and gender classifications. They suggest that cluster analysis of lexical variables can provide a more nuanced understanding of other potential factors at play. More specifically, the gender make-up of the wider social network emerges as a key social factor, as lexical and stylistic choices are found to co-vary with the gender composition of the network, rather than the writer's assumed gender ('homophily effect').

The role of the network audiences and potential addressees in understanding stylistic variation is further supported by Squires's (2014) study of a mass media novel phrase and its adoption, circulation and diffusion on Twitter. Her findings reveal that non-standard spellings and informality markers were most frequently used in tweets that were not directed at the celebrity associated with the novel phrase. Similarly, Eisenstein (2015) notes that alternation between non-standard and standard spellings depends on whether tweets are addressed to individual users or tweeted to the general Twitter audience.

In addition to metadata about authors' and addressees' gender and status (e.g. celebrity, ordinary) in social media, analysts can also have access to information about the geographical location of the author, if the latter has activated the GPS or location function. The study of geolocated tweets or Facebook messages has the potential of using social media research to explore the interplay between regional and spelling variation. An example of such research is Eisenstein's (2015) study on the demographics of neography (broadly defined as unconventional spelling), whereby non-standard spellings (e.g. g-deletion in <ing>) are mapped against geographical regions in the US, based on metadata from geolocated tweets. His findings reveal that non-standard spellings are more frequent in tweets from areas populated by more individuals who identify as African Americans, whereas standard spellings appear more among tweets from areas where the majority includes individuals who identify as White. This pattern of sociolinguistic variation is strikingly similar with how the equivalent phonological variables (e.g. g-dropping in <in>) behave in the corresponding geographical regions, suggesting potentially a more profound connection between spelling and phonological variation (Eisenstein 2015).

The language of social media II: language and social practices

Beyond associations between language and social factors, research on the language of social media has focused on language and social practices that are afforded by particular exigencies in social media environments, such as (i) the design of the specific platform and (ii) the users' agency and engagement with particular aspects of the design. The relation between the two is bidirectional, with examples where not only do the design features shape user practice (e.g. 'like' buttons for positive evaluation on Facebook) but also user practice shapes the development of design interface (e.g. the creation of Twitter 'reply' button as a result of @username practices to respond to a tweet). More so than in other areas, this line of research develops through cross-fertilisations between media/cultural theory and discourse analysis, operationalising and adapting concepts introduced in media and cultural studies to the needs of a more (micro) language-focused approach to communication in social media. In this section, we will focus primarily on the practices of addressing, tagging, sharing, and meming.

Having a conversation on social media: addressing and tagging

Maintaining a sustained conversation between two parties can be a challenge in 'noisy' social media environments (Honeycutt and Herring 2009) populated by millions of users and by large volumes of continuously updated content (e.g. texts, images, videos). Nevertheless, it appears that social media users often target particular addressees, rather than an undifferentiated mass, with their messages. The consideration of specific addressees and their social characteristics (e.g. gender or celebrity status) is implied in findings about spelling and style variation discussed in the previous section. In addition, practices of addressivity (i.e. prefacing a message with the username of the intended addressee) that predate the birth of social media (Herring 1999) also enable users to maintain one-to-one conversations in public multiparty and multi-network environments. For example, Twitter users employ @mentions (that is, @username) to target specific addressees and 'establish [. . .] the conditions for threading multiple tweets together as a "conversation"' (Squires 2016: 242). Similarly, in one of the few studies of turn management and conversational coherence in YouTube comments, Bou-Franch et al. (2012) demonstrate how cross-turn addressivity and turn entry/exit devices (such as discourse markers like 'listen', 'that's all', question tags, and aphorisms) are used as turn management signals and capitalise on the conversational potential of the site.

Another practice for attracting the attention of another user and marking content as relevant or salient is through tagging. Tagging can be broadly defined as the use of a hyperlinked keyword that attaches a label to user-generated texts, images, audios, and videos. In the context of Facebook, tagging another user in photos or status updates results in notifying the other party about what is shared and opens up the potential for social interaction. In social media platforms like Twitter, Instagram and Flickr, tagging can take the form of hashtags where the label-word/phrase is prefaced by the # symbol. Unlike the Facebook type of user-tagging, hashtags have an organisational function as they are based on topics or ideas. Clicking on a particular hashtag results in threads of uploaded tweets or photos that cohere around a particular label-word/phrase. In other words, as Zappavigna (2012) puts it, hashtags result in 'searchable talk' and contribute to the organisation and flow of social media content.

In one of the earliest studies on Twitter discourse, Page (2012) has broadly identified two types of hashtags: 'topic-based' when the tag specifies a topic (e.g #brexit) and 'evaluative' when the tag offers an evaluative comment on the topic discussed (e.g. #brexshit).

Participating in social media: sharing

In his seminal paper about the emergence of 'sharing' as a keyword, John (2013) argues about the centrality of sharing as a defining practice in the so-called social media. By tracing the meanings and uses of 'share' in social network sites over a decade, he concludes that sharing in social media involves two main activities: (i) distributing content by making texts, links, photos, videos available to others, and (ii) communicating thoughts, emotions, and big and small events of one's everyday life. Starting with the first understanding of sharing as distributing content, we can discern a number of technologically afforded acts that aim at (re)distributing content. In the communicative dynamics of Twitter, for example, sharing can be achieved through a range of acts: 'tweeting' for broadcasting and thus making content available to others, 'retweeting' for rebroadcasting another user's content through one's own stream, 'modified tweeting' for selecting and commenting on parts of another user's tweet, and 'embedding' by rebroadcasting tweets within a different communicative context (e.g. a blog or a newspaper website). All these practices of sharing also indicate a further quality of social media, namely the portability of texts and any elements they consist of. As noted by Squires (2016: 244) in her discussion of tweets, 'they come with a detachability that makes them particularly amenable to de-and re-contextualization'.

In an attempt to unpack further John's second understanding of sharing as communicating, Androutsopoulos (2014: 17) probes into processes of de/recontextualisation and defines sharing on Facebook 'as a set of practices by which individuals entextualize significant moments for, and with, their networked audience'. Taking as unit of analysis the Facebook 'wall event' that consists of the user's initiating post (i.e. Facebook status update) followed by 'likes' and one or more responses by members of the audience, he outlines three stages in social media sharing: '*Selecting* refers to the choice of moments to share; *styling* concerns how to entextualize what is being shared; and *negotiating* refers to the audience engagement that follows up on acts of sharing' (Androutsopoulos 2014: 8). In other words, research on sharing practices involves analysing (i) what is selected to be shared (e.g. routine activities or life events; completed events or moments on the go); (ii) the range of resources used for styling the selected shareables (e.g. styles, language forms, photos, links, etc); and (iii) the audience responses following up the shareable and the ways in which they impact on overall wall event's style and content. An application of such an approach to sharing is offered by Giaxoglou (2015), who examines mourning practices online and draws attention to the ways in which participants select, style, and negotiate significant moments in the mourning process on public RIP Facebook walls.

Although there is a growing body of research on sharing as entextualising significant moments in social network sites, there is less attention to related phenomena of virality and memicity where particular signs are shared and spread at an astonishing speed by – and to – large numbers of people. From a media and cultural studies perspective, Shifman (2012) makes a distinction between virality and mimecity and sees the degree of sign modification as a key difference between the two. For example, a viral YouTube video is spread without significant change, whereas a memetic video 'lures extensive creative user engagement in the form of parody, pastiche, mash-ups or other derivative work' (Shifman 2012: 190). Varis and Blommaert (2014) show how a socio-discursive perspective that approaches such phenomena as social semiotic activities offers a more nuanced perspective, blurring the boundaries between virality and memicity. Beyond (re)entextualisation, the study of sharing in memes invokes the concept of 'resemiotization' which

> refers to the process by means of which every 'repetition' of a sign involves an entirely new set of contextualization conditions and thus results in an entirely 'new' semiotic process, allowing new semiotic modes and resources to be involved in the repetition process.
>
> (Varis and Blommaert 2014: 8)

Memes illustrate this process by establishing some generic recognisability through repetition of certain sign elements, on the one hand, and producing different communicative effects through modification and adjustment to specific situations and for different audiences, on the other. As a result, a language-focused approach to memes can investigate the range of resources that are mobilised in the complementary processes of establishing recognisability while producing different effects. Such resources include the visual architecture of the meme (e.g. design, layout, colour), its speech act format (e.g. 'keep calm and [*directive*]'), its textual-stylistic features (e.g. lolspeak), or, in the case of mashup memes, a combination of the above originating in different established memes (Varis and Blommaert 2014).

The language of social media III: identity & community

Social identities and the study of language as indexical of belongingness to wider social groupings (such as gender, geographical location, and ethnicity) have preoccupied research on language and social variation on social media. At the same time, though, there is a wealth of studies that have undertaken a more discourse-oriented approach and explored identity not as a stable or fixed property but as multiple, fluid, and constructed through discourse and in interaction with others (Bucholtz and Hall 2005). Shying away from pre-existing social categories and paying attention to the ongoing social construction and negotiation of identities are also appropriate for environments that have often been hailed as anonymous and, more importantly, display a social network architecture that capitalises on the reflexive design of personal profiles for multiple audiences. What research on the language of social media can contribute to the study of reflexive performances of identity for networked audiences is attention to the ways in which verbal and other semiotic resources are mobilised to achieve such performances.

The mobilisation of multiple languages and scripts – or, to be more precise, of multiple forms associated with particular languages and scripts as sociocultural constructs (e.g. English, French, Latin, or Greek alphabet) – have attracted the attention of language scholars. From earlier studies of code-switching and language choice to more recent research on trans-languaging and trans-scripting, English-related forms have been noted to appear among the linguistic repertoires of social media users in very diverse contexts (e.g. Chinese and Spanish Flickr users, Lee and Barton 2011; Nepalese undergraduate students on Facebook, Sharma 2012; members of Finland-based football web forums and Finnish footballers on Twitter, Kytola 2016). Although English-related forms are used with varying and ambivalent indexical values and meanings, this line of research converges in foregrounding the multiple and hybrid identities performed in social media: from the negotiation of 'glocal' identities on Flickr (Lee and Barton 2011) to the varying 'translocal' positions projected by users with real or aspirational transnational trajectories (Sharma 2012; Androutsopoulos 2014; Kytola 2016).

In addition to linguistic codes and scripts, previous literature has paid attention to time and space, especially explicit references to and markings of time and physical or geographical space as resources for identity formation on social media (Georgakopoulou 2015). For example, spatio-temporal references contribute to the construction of expert identities in online reviews (Vasquez 2015), to the authentication of diasporic identities (Heyd and Honkanen 2015), and to the maintenance and affirmation of friendship (Cohen 2015). Platform-specific discursive features, such as hashtags on Twitter, can also be mobilised as resources for self-presentation. For example, Page (2012) and Lorenzo-Dus and Di Cristofaro (2016) demonstrate how the varying types of hashtags (e.g. topic-based vs. evaluative) and their thematic co-occurrence contribute to different ways of self-branding among celebrities, corporations, ordinary people, and influential citizens on Twitter. The mobilisation of visual resources for self-presentation remains relatively under-explored in language-focused research. A notable exception is Georgakopoulou's (2016: 300) study of pictures and selfies by adolescent women on Facebook where she concludes that 'far from being narcissistic expressions of "ideal selves", selfies emerge as contextualized and co-constructed presentations of self'.

With social media platforms increasingly marketing new services as tools for sharing stories (e.g. from Storify to Snapchat or Instagram Stories app), narrative is emerging as one of the key modes for participating and relating with others. Of course, such narratives seldom have the form of prototypical, long, and monologic stories; instead, they are often fragmented, non-linear, co-constructed and open-ended (cf. small stories approach Georgakopoulou 2007). It is during such acts of story-telling that social media users create particular roles for themselves in interaction with their networked audiences (Dayter and Muhleisen 2016). For example, various forms of story-telling enable users to construct a counselling or advisor persona in online health contexts (Thurnherr et al. 2016), a credible and authentic persona in online dating ads (Muhleisen 2016), or a figure of authority in the reading and interpretation of the Bible among Evangelical Christian YouTube users (Pihlaja 2016).

It goes without saying that any identity projections or claims invoke wider groupings and collectivities. In other words, it is impossible to study identity without referring to the concept of 'community'. Similarly to identity, assumptions about community as static, fixed, and delineated by specific (and pre-existing) geographical or temporal boundaries have been challenged by social media research. Instead, identity projections and claims online contribute to the participants' alignment with strangers on the basis of shared interests, topics, and experiences (e.g. photography, Lee and Barton 2011; football fandom, Kytola 2016; interpretation of religious texts, Pihlaja 2016). In such affinity spaces, language researchers can explore the development and negotiation of shared repertoires of rituals, routines, vocabulary, and styles that contribute to the emergence and formation of local communities of practice. For example, Potts (2015) demonstrates how the introduction of homosocial meaning and homosexual innuendo by prominent gamers contributes to the formation of a self-policing community of practice that is more tolerant and rejects bigotry in YouTube comments by heterosexual male fans. Furthermore, increased attention has been given to the so-called 'hashtag communities' of Twitter and social media 'where people have an "ambient affiliation" (Zappavigna 2012) to a topic or issue around which they interact' (Seargeant and Tagg 2014: 12). In such communities, connections between people and content are felt to exist but they are not necessarily defined or visible in a clear manner. Hashtags play a key role in making such connections findable and searchable but it is the feeling of ambient sociability rather than any clear articulation of such connections that is of the essence in such environments. For Varis and Blommaert (2014), memes as signs almost empty of semantic meaning represent prime resources for achieving ambient sociability and generating temporary collectives. If we accept that social media groups display loose bonds around transient and superficial interests, then memes and, more importantly, the practice of meme sharing offer 'brief moments of focusing on perceived recognizable and shareable features'. The exact meaning of such features in a given context is highly indeterminate but the recognisable act of innocuous sharing creates a 'structural level of conviviality' and generates transiently focused collectives (Varis and Blommaert 2014: 18–19).

Researching the language of social media: mixed methodologies

The rapid development of the field has left it rather fragmented in terms of the range of methodologies used for researching and analysing the language of social media. Nevertheless, one could argue that the multiplicity of perspectives brought about by such fragmentation is one of the field's strengths: the lack of convergence towards a single dominant paradigm has enabled research to develop simultaneously across a range of linguistic research traditions, on the one hand, and facilitated the use and application of mixed methodologies to the study of social media discourse, on the other. In fact, a commitment towards 'mixed methods' research arguably represents a current point of convergence in the field (Bolander and Locher 2014: 20–22), although the term is used for various stages of the research process and in relation to various combinations of existing methodologies.

In terms of data collection, a mixed methods approach is often equated with the complementary use of log file data (i.e. 'the stored, static records of message sequences that have been put into their particular order by a server feature and that are displayed as a message protocol on the users' screens' Beisswenger 2008) and interviews with the people participating in the social media platforms from which the log file data are extracted. In Androutsopoulos's (2013) terms, it combines 'screen-based' with 'user-based' data and it develops in line with the wider shift in the field's preoccupations from formal, functional and textual properties of social media to users' practices for self-presentation, (dis)identification and community building online. Some notable examples of such work include Lee and Barton's (2011) study of multilingual writing practices on the photo-sharing site Flickr, Tagg and Seargeant's (2016) research on language choice as audience design on Facebook, and Georgalou's (2015) study of time and age identities on Facebook.

There is also a wealth of research where the process of collecting log file data and interviews is paired with systematic observation and immersion in the communities and cultures of social media users (either online only or both online and offline). Some recent examples of this type of 'virtual fieldwork' (Androutsopoulos 2013) or, more broadly, 'digital ethnography' (Varis 2016) can be found in research on player communities in virtual games (e.g. Newon 2011), as well as on Twitter communities of practice based around shared interests (e.g. ballet in Dayter 2016).

Beyond the combination of various methods for data collection, mixed methods research has also been used to refer to 'multi-sited' approaches to the study of social media. The multi-sited element is evident in research that attends to the multiple sites for user participation and engagement afforded by social media platforms. For example, YouTube research may involve the study of language resources and practices within and across three inter-related but distinct sites: (i) the video clip uploaded by the user, (ii) the 'comments' space populated by other users' responses to the video and to one another, and (iii) the 'hosting space', that is 'the individual webpage on which each video is framed with additional information' (Androutsopoulos and Tereick 2016). Such multi-sited and mixed methods studies also attend to the multiple semiotic resources mobilised in the respective spaces of social media, undertaking a multimodal perspective or, at least, committing to the study of the interplay between the verbal and the visual. Furthermore, the term multi-sited is also increasingly used to refer to research that spans across multiple web sites and social media platforms; for example, the study of a particular hashtag, its meanings and potential for affiliation and community building, can take the researcher to a journey across social media, from Twitter to Facebook to its further embeddings in online news streams. Although still in its infancy, the mobility in the research process of exploring links and moving around in the networks has potential as it replicates the ways in which users engage with the openness, diversity, and connectivity of social media (cf. 'guerrilla ethnography' Yang 2003; and Deumert 2014).

In terms of data analysis, a mixed methods perspective entails not only the combination of qualitative and quantitative methodologies but also the development of eclectic approaches that draw on more than one framework for analysing language. For example, attention to both visual and verbal aspects in social media environments has given rise to studies that combine social semiotics with (critical) discourse analysis. The relative ease of access to large bodies of text-based data, generated for social interaction but still persistent on screen, has paved the way for an increased use of language corpora and corpus linguistics tools. Either alone or in combination with other frameworks from sociolinguistics or discourse analysis, corpus analysis is often used to address quantitatively-oriented research questions about language use on social media. Nevertheless, the field is still trying to grapple with appropriate ways for combining the smallness of qualitative micro-linguistic research with big data and their potential for quantitative analysis of not only user-generated texts but also abundant meta-contextual information (metadata) generated with such texts (Page 2016).

Future directions

Reflecting upon the future of research on language and social media brings forward the realisation that the age of innocence has long passed both for the field and for social media. It is by now a truism that social media is not only a means for communication but also a means for surveillance. Taking the practice of sharing as an example, it is not always clear what we share, with whom, and under what circumstances, when we 'check in' on our favourite hangouts or when we agree with the Terms and Conditions of the various platforms and apps. What I suggest as a loss of innocence or, perhaps, a sign of maturity for the field is manifest in the call for critical approaches to the discourse of social media users and, primarily, to the discourse of media platforms and design (e.g. Georgakopoulou and Spilioti 2016: 5).

Research on language and surveillance practices is still in its infancy but studies are already pointing to the role of discourse analysts and sociolinguists in enriching surveillance studies with insights from language theory (e.g. inferential pragmatics Jones 2016; Goffmanian interaction order, as well as contextualisation and inferencing processes Rampton 2016). More specifically, Jones (2016: 409–410) proposes an approach to social media texts as 'information gathering devices' that not only collect information about people but also construct discourse positions and social identities for them. This type of surveillance work is achieved by means of 'subtexts' (e.g. algorithms, default templates), 'pretexts' (e.g. rhetorical strategies that precondition users to opt for a preferred option), and new 'contexts' where the circumstances for participation, monitoring, and control over information may be obscure or subject to change (for example, privacy default settings are often updated as social media platforms develop or change corporate hands). Out of the three, we find some preliminary work on subtexts and pretexts: for example, Eisenlauer's (2014) study on Facebook software and text automation processes as the 'third author' intervening between profile owner and profile recipients, and Blommaert and Omoniyi's (2006) research on 'phishing' strategies of fraud emails. There is still ample scope for further research in this area, particularly in the role of users' agency in interacting with platform sub/pretexts and in the wider and rather complex contextualisation processes on social media. Although social media platforms deserve a more detailed and critical study, the loss of innocence does not need to shift the field towards an a-critical dystopic view of technologies, especially since, as Seargeant and Tagg (2016) remind us, 'the filter bubble isn't just Facebook's fault – it's yours' as well.

Recent developments that have foregrounded the need for language-focused research into surveillance and privacy have also been coupled with a renewed interest towards ethics. Once restricted to the realm of philosophers and ethicists, questions about selfhood, privacy and responsibility now feature in public debate and popular discourse: for example, they are present in users' everyday practices while choosing the privacy settings of their personal profile, as well as in web designers' development of such choices for them. Issues of privacy and responsibility, though, are also central to the academic community and debates about research ethics in a changing world.

Although research on social media is developing fast within and across disciplines, research ethics procedures seem to be lagging behind, still driven by a dichotomous understanding of private versus public sphere and by a checklist rationale that orients primarily to prevention of harm. The complex, dynamic, and, at times, unexpected participation formats afforded in social media environments challenge prior understandings of public and private, informed consent and its limitations in online environments, as well as the researcher's responsibility towards the various stakeholders (users as producers/consumers, platform owners and, of course, the wider public). For issues related to research ethics, the Association of Internet Researchers offers the most up-to-date, complete, and authoritative recommendations for general research on social media (Markham and Buchanan 2012). Similar recommendations for language-focused research can be found in the relevant professional associations, such as the BAAL (British Association for Applied Linguistics) Recommendations on Good Practice (BAAL 2016). Dominated by ethicists and philosophers, issues related to the field of internet research ethics are marginally addressed in applied linguistic research. Nevertheless, linguists and discourse analysts can offer important insights into how privacy and/or publicness are constructed, (re)negotiated and oriented to by participants in – and through – social media discourse. The special issue on the ethics of online research in applied linguistics (Spilioti and Tagg 2016) provides a first step and brings together a range of primarily qualitative studies that have addressed some of these challenges through an approach to ethics as a contextualised, reflexive, and iterative process of decision-making at critical junctures. There is still, though, ample scope for language researchers to engage with internet ethics debates by further unpacking social media discourses and bringing in disciplinary-specific sensitivities to issues of power and control in researcher–researched relationships and networks.

Further reading

Georgakopoulou, A. and T. Spilioti (eds) 2016 *The Routledge Handbook of Language and Digital Communication*. London and New York: Routledge. This 29-chapter edited volume showcases critical reviews of established literature in language-focused research on digitally mediated communication, while engaging with cutting edge research and pointing to new directions for study.

Page, R., D. Barton, J. W. Unger and M. Zappavigna (2014) *Researching Language and Social Media: A Student Guide*. London and New York: Routledge. A highly accessibly book that offers useful guidance to undergraduate and postgraduate students on how to design, undertake, and engage with language-focused research on social media.

Seargeant, P. and C. Tagg (eds) (2014) *The Language of Social Media: Identity and Community on the Internet*. Basingstoke: Palgrave Macmillan. This 11-chapter volume represents one of the first comprehensive collections of original research on the language of social media, with a focus on identity and community issues in such environments.

Related topics

- English and social identity
- Media, power and representation
- Sociolinguistics: studying English and its social relations
- Multimodal English.

References

Androutsopoulos, J. (2006) 'Introduction: Sociolinguistics and computer-mediated communication', *Journal of Sociolinguistics* 10 (4): 419–438.

Androutsopoulos, J. (2013) 'Online data collection', in C. Mallinson, B. Childs and G. Van Herk (eds), *Data Collection in Sociolinguistics: Methods and Applications*. London and New York: Routledge, 236–250.

Androutsopoulos, J. (2014) 'Moments of sharing: Entextualization and linguistic repertoires in social networking', *Journal of Pragmatics* 73: 4–18.

Androutsopoulos, J. and J. Tereick (2016) 'YouTube: Language and discourse practices in participatory culture', in A. Georgakopoulou and T. Spilioti (eds), *The Routledge Handbook of Language and Digital Communication*. London and New York: Routledge, 354–370.

BAAL. (2016) '*Recommendations on good practice in applied linguistics*'. Available at www.baal.org.uk/goodpractice_full_2016.pdf.

Bamman, D., J. Eisenstein and T. Schnoebelen (2014) 'Gender identity and lexical variation in social media', *Journal of Sociolinguistics* 18 (2): 135–160.

Beisswenger, M. (2008) 'Situated chat analysis as a window to the user's perspective', *Language@Internet* 5, article 6. Available at www.languageatinternet.org/articles/2008/1532.

Bercovici, J. (2010) Who Coined Social Media? Web Pioneers Compete for Credit, *Forbes*, 9 December, Available at www.forbes.com/sites/jeffbercovici/2010/12/09/who-coinedsocial-media-web-pioneers-compete-for-credit/2/.

Blommaert, J. and Omoniyi, T. (2006) 'Email fraud: Language, technology, and the indexicals of globalisation', *Social Semiotics* 16 (4): 573–605.

Bolander, B. and M. Locher (2014) 'Doing sociolinguistic research on computer-mediated data: A review of four methodological issues', *Discourse, Context & Media* 3: 14–26.

Bou-Franch, P., N. Lorenzo-Dus and P. Garces-Conejos Blitvich (2012) 'Social interaction in YouTube text-based polylogues: A study of coherence', *Journal of Computer-Mediated Communication* 17 (4): 501–521.

boyd, d. and N. Ellison (2008) 'Social network sites: Definition, history, and scholarship', *Journal of Computer-Mediated Communication* 13: 210–230.

Bucholtz, M. and K. Hall (2005) 'Identity and interaction: A sociocultural linguistic approach', *Discourse Studies* 7 (4–5): 585–614.

Cohen, L. (2015) 'World attending in interaction: Multitasking, spatializing, narrativizing with mobile devices and Tinder', *Discourse, Context & Media* 9: 46–54.

Dayter, D. (2016) *Discursive Self in Microblogging: Speech Acts, Stories and Self-Praise*. Amsterdam: John Benjamins.

Dayter, D. and S. Muhleisen (2016) 'Telling stories about self in digital contexts: Same, same, but different?' *Open Linguistics* 2: 572–576.

Deumert, A. (2014) *Sociolinguistics and Mobile Communication*. Edinburgh: Edinburgh University Press.

Eisenlauer, V. (2014) 'Facebook as a third author – (semi-)automated participation framework in social network sites', *Journal of Pragmatics* 72: 73–85.

Eisenstein, J. (2015) 'Systematic patterning in phonologically-motivated orthographic variation', *Journal of Sociolinguistics* 19 (2): 161–188.
Georgakopoulou, A. (2006) 'Postscript: Computer-mediated communication in sociolinguistics', *Journal of Sociolinguistics* 10 (4): 548–557.
Georgakopoulou, A. (2007) *Small Stories, Interaction and Identities*. Amsterdam: Benjamins.
Georgakopoulou, A. (2015) 'Introduction: Communicating time and place on digital media – multi-layered temporalities & (re)localizations', *Discourse, Context & Media* 9: 1–4.
Georgakopoulou, A. (2016) 'From narrating the self to posting self(ies): A small stories approach to selfies', *Open Linguistics* 2 (1): 300–317.
Georgakopoulou, A. and T. Spilioti (eds) (2016) 'Introduction: Language and digital communication', in A. Georgakopoulou and T. Spilioti (eds), *The Routledge Handbook of Language and Digital Communication*. London and New York: Routledge, 1–16.
Georgalou, M. (2015) 'Beyond the timeline: Constructing time and age identities on Facebook', *Discourse, Context & Media* 9: 24–33.
Giaxoglou, K. (2015) "Everywhere I go, you're going with me': Time and space deixis as affective positioning resources in shared moments of digital mourning', *Discourse, Context & Media* 9: 55–63.
Herring, S. (1999) 'Interactional coherence in CMC', *Journal of Computer-Mediated Communication*, 4: 0. doi: 10.1111/j.1083–6101.1999.tb00106.x
Herring, S. (2004) 'Computer-mediated discourse analysis: An approach to researching online behaviour', in S. A. Barab, R. Kling and J. Gray (eds), *Designing for Virtual Communitities in the Service of Learning*. Cambridge: Cambridge University Press, 338–376.
Herring, S. and J. Paolillo (2006) 'Gender and genre variation in weblogs', *Journal of Sociolinguistics* 10 (4): 439–459.
Heyd, T. and M. Honkanen (2015) 'From *Naija* to *Chitown:* The New African Diaspora and digital representations of place', *Discourse, Context & Media* 9: 14–23.
Hinrichs, L. (2012) 'How to spell the vernacular: A multivariate study of Jamaican e-mails and blogs', in A. Jaffe, J. Androutsopoulos, M. Sebba and S. Johnson (eds), *Orthography as Social Action: Scripts, Spelling, Identity and Power*. Boston/Berlin: De Gruyter Mouton, 325–358.
Honeycutt, C. and S. Herring (2009) 'Beyond microblogging: Conversation and collaboration via Twitter', *Proceedings of the Forty-Second Hawai'i International Conference on System Sciences (HICSS-42)*. Los Alamitos, CA: IEEE Press. Available at www.ella.slis.indiana.edu/~herring/honeycutt.herring.2009.pdf.
Hutchby, I. (2001) 'Technologies, texts and affordances', *Sociology* 35 (2): 441–456.
John, N. (2013) 'Sharing and web 2.0: The emergence of a keyword', *New Media & Society* 15 (2): 167–182.
Jones, R. (2016) 'Surveillance', in A. Georgakopoulou and T. Spilioti (ed.), *The Routledge Handbook of Language and Digital Communication*. London and New York: Routledge, 408–411.
Iorio, J. (2009) 'Effects of audience on orthographic variation', *Studies in the Linguistic Sciences: Illinois Working Papers 2009*: 127–140. Available at hdl.handle.net/2142/14815.
Kytola, S. (2016) 'Translocality', in A. Georgakopoulou and T. Spilioti (eds), *The Routledge Handbook of Language and Digital Communication*. London and New York: Routledge, 371–388.
Lee, C. and D. Barton (2011) 'Constructing glocal identities through multilingual writing practices on Flickr.com®', *International Multilingual Research Journal* 5 (1): 39–59.
Leppanen, S., S. Kytola, E. Westinen and S. Peuronen (2017) 'Introduction: Social media discourse, (dis)identifications and diversities', in S. Leppanen, E. Westinen and S. Kytola (eds) *Social Media Discourse, (Dis)identifications and Diversities*. New York and London: Routledge, 1–36.
Lorenzo-Dus, N. and M. Di Cristofaro (2016) #Living/minimum wage: Influential citizen talk in Twitter', *Discourse, Context & Media* 13 (Part A): 40–50.
Markham, A. and E. Buchanan (2012) 'Ethical decision-making and internet research: Recommendations from the AoIP ethics working committee', Available at www.aoir.org/reports/ethics2.pdf.
Marwick, A. and d. boyd (2011) 'I tweet honeslty, I tweet passionately: Twitter users, context collapse, and the imagined audience', *New Media & Society* 13 (1): 114–133.
Muhleisen, S. (2016) '"More about me" – Self-presentation and narrative strategies in Carribean online dating ads', *Open Linguistics* 2 (1): 437–449.
Newon, L. (2011) 'Multimodal creativity and identities of expertise in the digital ecology of a *World of Warcraft* guild', in C. Thurlow and K. Mroczek (eds), *Digital Discourse: Language in the New Media*. Oxford: Oxford University Press, 203–231.

Page, R. (2012) 'The linguistics of self-branding and micro-celebrity in Twitter: The role of hashtags', *Discourse & Communication* 6 (2): 181–201.

Page, R. (2016) 'Moving between the big and the small: Identities and interaction in digital contexts', in A. Georgakopoulou and T. Spilioti (eds), *The Routledge Handbook of Language and Digital Communication*. London and New York: Routledge, 403–407.

Pihlaja, S. (2016) '"What about the wolves?" The use of scripture in YouTube arguments', *Language and Literature* 25 (3): 226–238.

Potts, A. (2015) "Love you guys (no homo)": How gamers and fans play with sexuality, gender, and Minecraft on YouTube', *Critical Discourse Studies* 12 (2): 163–186.

Rampton, B. (2016) 'Foucault, Gumperz and governmentality: Interaction, power and subjectivity in the 21st century', in N. Coupland (ed.), *Sociolinguistics: Theoretical Debates*. Cambridge: Cambridge University Press, 303–328.

Seargeant, P. and C. Tagg (2014) 'Introduction: The language of social media', in P. Seargeant and C. Tagg (eds), *The Language of Social Media: Identity and Community on the Internet*. Basingstoke: Palgrave Macmillan, 1–21.

Seargeant, P. and C. Tagg (2016) The Filter Bubble Isn't Just Facebook's Fault – It's Yours, *The Conversation*, 5 December 2016, Available at www.theconversation.com/the-filter-bubble-isnt-just-facebooks-fault-its-yours-69664.

Sharma, B. K. (2012) 'Beyond social networking: Performing global Englishes in Facebook by college youth in Nepal', *Journal of Sociolinguistics* 16 (4): 483–509.

Shifman, L. (2012) 'An anatomy of a YouTube meme', *New Media & Society* 14 (2): 187–203.

Smith, A. (2014) 6 New Facts About Facebook, *Pew Research Center*, Available at www.pewresearch.org/fact-tank/2014/02/03/6-new-facts-about-facebook/.

Squires, L. (2014) 'From TV personality to fans and beyond: Indexical bleaching and the diffusion of a media innovation', *Journal of Linguistic Anthropology* 24 (1): 42–62.

Squires, L. (2016) 'Twitter: Design, discourse, and the implications of the public text', in A. Georgakopoulou and T. Spilioti (eds), *The Routledge Handbook of Language and Digital Communication*. London and New York: Routledge, 239–256.

Spilioti, T. and C. Tagg (2016) 'The ethics of online research methods: Challenges, opportunities, and directions in ethical decision-making', *Applied Linguistics Review* 8 (2–3): 163–167.

Tagg, C. and P. Seargeant (2016) 'Facebook and the discursive construction of the social network', in A. Georgakopoulou and T. Spilioti (eds), *The Routledge Handbook of Language and Digital Communication*. London and New York: Routledge, 339–353.

Thurnherr, F., M.-T. von Rohr and M. Locher (2016) 'The functions of narrative passages in three written online health contexts', *Open Linguistics* 2 (1): 450–470.

Varis, P. (2016) 'Digital ethnography', in A. Georgakopoulou and T. Spilioti (eds), *The Routledge Handbook of Language and Digital Communication*. London and New York: Routledge, 55–68.

Varis, P. and J. Blommaert (2014) 'Conviviality and collectives on social media: Virality, memes and new social structures', *Tilburg Papers in Culture Studies*, Paper 108: 1–21. Available at www.tilburguniversity.edu/upload/83490ca9-659d-49a0-97db-ff1f8978062b_TPCS_108_Varis-Blommaert.pdf.

Vasquez, C. (2015) *'Right now* versus *back then:* Recency and remoteness as discursive resources in online reviews', *Discourse, Context & Media* 9: 5–13.

Yang, G. (2003) 'The internet and the rise of a transnational Chinese cultural sphere', *Media, Culture & Society* 25: 469–490.

Zappavigna, M. (2012) *Discourse of Twitter and Social Media: How we Use Language to Create Affiliation on the Web*. London: Continuum.

Part 3
Analysing English

22

Stylistics

Studying literary and everyday style in English

Dan McIntyre and Hazel Price

Introduction

Stylistics is often defined as the linguistic study of style in language; but what does this mean in practice? The first point to note is that style arises from motivated choice (motivated in the sense of there being a range of linguistic options from which to choose rather than that choice necessarily being a conscious one). It is only when we have such a choice that it is possible for a style to emerge. As an example of what this means, consider this statement from the American actor Clint Eastwood, made in response to an interviewer's suggestion that the Republican 2016 US presidential candidate, Donald Trump, had been trying to emulate Eastwood's tough-guy persona:

> Maybe. But he's onto something, because secretly everybody's getting tired of political correctness, kissing up. That's the kiss-ass generation we're in right now. We're really in a pussy generation.
>
> (Clint Eastwood, quoted in Hainey 2016)

Eastwood's phrase 'pussy generation' garnered widespread attention and was widely quoted in reports of the interview in other news outlets. One reason for this is that the soundbite is both provocative and acts as an exemplar of Eastwood's public persona; i.e. that of the forthright everyman who sticks to his straight-talking style whatever the context. There is nothing unusual about Eastwood's turn of phrase to anyone familiar with the way he typically presents himself. Why, then, should this particular part of the interview have been quoted so much when others could also have been chosen to convey his straight-talking style? Part of the answer is that Eastwood's lexical choice generates additional effects. *Pussy* is a euphemism for female genitalia and to use this as a term of abuse, as Eastwood does, is outside the politeness norms of public discourse. That Eastwood chooses to use the phrase is indicative of his either not considering or not caring how this might be interpreted by readers. His stylistic choice creates an interpretative effect which, depending on the reader, may lead to him being perceived as misogynistic, crass, foolish or even, if the reader shares his viewpoint, admirable. The extract is therefore attention-grabbing as a result of being highly provocative; and in the world of internet journalism this makes it perfect clickbait.

This example illustrates some of the fundamental concepts of stylistics. Style arises from motivated choice and choices have consequences. Stylistic analysis necessitates both linguistic description and an assessment of the interpretative consequences of whatever choice has been made. The functions of stylistic choice might be to construct particular styles (e.g. genre style, authorial style), to generate particular literary effects (such as point of view), to convey certain ideologies or to trigger particular emotional responses in the reader. These are just some of a wide range of possibilities and it is important to note that these effects can be created in both fiction and non-fiction texts. There is, then, no reason why stylistic analysis should be confined to literary fiction, though it is undeniably the case that most contemporary stylisticians are particularly interested in literature (we discuss the issue of 'literary' and 'non-literary' stylistics in more detail in at the start of the third section).

At the heart of stylistics is the concept of foregrounding. This originates in the work of the Russian Formalists (see, for example, Mukařovský 1964 [1932] and Shklovsky 1965 [1917]), who hypothesised that the elements of a text that readers will pay most attention to are those that in some way deviate from an expected norm (i.e. are foregrounded against a perceived background). Van Peer (1986) provides experimental support for the notion of foregrounding, demonstrating too that what is likely to be perceived as foregrounded can be predicted. Miall and Kuiken (1994a, 1994b) have also shown experimentally that the extent to which linguistic deviation is present in a text can be used as a predictor of what readers will perceive to be foregrounded. Furthermore, they show that foregrounded features of a text provoke emotional responses and prolong reading time. Unsurprisingly, then, foregrounding theory is central to stylistics since its predictive power gives stylisticians a means of accounting for why particular stylistic choices might elicit particular responses in readers. Ultimately, this is what stylisticians are concerned with doing. This chapter introduces some of the key areas and practices within stylistics today, focusing particularly on how these areas and practices relate to the concept of foregrounding. We begin by outlining classic and recent work in foregrounding theory before going on to consider how its central tenets can be observed in current work in cognitive and corpus stylistics. We then discuss two particular issues that we believe are crucial to contemporary conceptualisations of stylistics. One of these – the issue of objectivity in analysis – has been both widely debated and greatly misunderstood. We aim to clarify what objectivity means and how this impacts on stylistic analysis. The second issue is one which we believe has not been discussed enough by stylisticians. This is the issue of what is meant by the terms *literary* and *non-literary stylistics*. Our view is that this distinction is unhelpful and contradicts one of the basic premises of stylistics, namely that there is no distinction to be made on formal grounds between the language of literature and the language of everyday discourse. Finally, we discuss what we believe to be the likely future directions for stylistics.

Current critical issues and topics

Foregrounding, deviation and parallelism

Choice is fundamental to the composition of style in many areas of everyday life. For example, our clothing and musical choices all form part of how we style our own identity. In the same way, linguistic choices give rise to particular stylistic effects in language. Foregrounding occurs when our linguistic expectations are not met. It is caused by two phenomena: linguistic deviation and linguistic parallelism. Deviation 'is essentially the occurrence of unexpected irregularity in language and results in foregrounding on the basis that the irregularity is surprising to the reader' (Jeffries and McIntyre 2010: 31); by contrast, parallelism is 'unexpected regularity' (2010: 32). The concepts of deviation, parallelism and foregrounding are central to stylistic analysis, even in contemporary sub-fields such as cognitive stylistics and corpus stylistics, as we will show. In the next section we demonstrate the application of foregrounding theory analytically as a precursor to discussing its psychological validity, as demonstrated through experiment.

Foregrounding and levels of language

Foregrounding can occur at any linguistic level, from those at the formal end of the scale (e.g. phonology) to those that are more functional in nature (e.g. pragmatics). In this section we demonstrate by reference to a selection of linguistic levels how deviation from linguistic norms can generate foregrounding effects.

Semantics

Semantic foregrounding exploits expectations about lexical or sentence-level meaning. Consider the lyrics below from the Joanna Newsom song, 'Peach, Plum, Pear':

> you were knocking me down with the palm of your eye
>
> (Joanna Newsom,
> 'Peach, Plum Pear', 2004)

The line 'with the palm of your eye' is foregrounded as a result of semantic deviation; eyes do not have palms. Newsom appears to be describing a situation in which the narrator is attempting to work out the intentions of someone she is romantically interested in through the way they look at her. The impact on the narrator is described in terms of a conceptual metaphor (A LOOK IS PHYSICAL FORCE; see Lakoff and Johnson 2003), which is made novel by the semantic deviation which suggests that eyes are constituted like hands (i.e. they have palms) and can be used to physically push people. The literary effect of the foregrounding is to emphasise the effect of a single look from the narrator's object of desire.

Pragmatics

While semantics is concerned with lexical and sentence-level meaning, pragmatics is concerned with meaning in interaction, and how this is shaped by context. The study of pragmatic meaning in stylistics makes extensive use of Grice's (1975) Cooperative Principle, which stipulates that interactants make their 'conversational contribution such as is required, at the stage at which it occurs, by the accepted purpose or direction of the talk' (Grice 1975: 45). Grice's Cooperative Principle is based on the maxims of quality, quantity, relation and manner (Grice 1975: 45–46).

The extract below is from *The Curious Incident of the Dog in the Night-time*, a novel by Mark Haddon. The story is narrated in the first person by the main character, 15-year-old Christopher. Although the novel does not label Christopher as autistic, Haddon has since commented that Christopher's character does have a form of autism and the book was widely acclaimed for its depiction of the condition. At the start of the novel, Christopher is found at the side of his neighbour's dog, Wellington, who has been killed with a garden fork. When the police arrive, Christopher is suspected of having killed the dog and is taken to the police station to be questioned about his role in the death of Wellington:

> They asked me if I had any family. I said I did. They asked me who my family was. I said it was Father, but Mother was dead. And I said it was also Uncle Terry, but he was in Sunderland and he was Father's brother, and it was my grandparents, too, but three of them were dead and Grandma Burton was in a home because she had senile dementia and thought that I was someone on television.
>
> (Haddon 2003: 17)

In his questioning of Christopher, the police officer asks if he has any family, and Christopher confirms that he does. Given Christopher's young age and our schematic knowledge about police protocols, we can assume that the policeman needs to find out from Christopher who his guardians are in order to contact them and tell them that he is with the police. The illocutionary force of the police officer's utterance is a command ('Give me the details of an adult to contact'). However, Christopher does not understand the implicature and instead simply confirms that he does have a family. In effect, Christopher infringes (Thomas 1995) the Gricean maxim of quantity, as his response does not give the police officer enough information (note here that *infringe* rather than *flout* is used as Christopher is not intentionally breaking the maxim). Given that the police officer has not achieved the desired perlocutionary effect (i.e. Christopher revealing his father's name), he reframes his question to be more explicit. In answer to this reframed question, Christopher infringes two maxims: (i) quantity, by not interpreting the question as 'who are your immediate family', therefore giving too much information, and (ii) relation, by giving information that is not relevant to the current exchange (e.g. that his Grandma is senile and does not recognise him).

The foregrounding that arises from Christopher's pragmatic deviation generates the sense of the character having a deviant mind style (Semino 2014). Christopher is unable to interpret the illocutionary force and intended perlocutionary effect of the policeman's questions. A typical conversational participant (by the terms of Grice's Cooperative Principle) would be able to do this. Moreover, the manner in which Christopher tells the police officer about the death of his mother and his grandparents, and describes his only living grandparent as not recognising him, shows that Christopher deals in facts and does not appear distressed by issues that would typically be upsetting, such as death and being unrecognisable to a close relative. This example usefully demonstrates both external and internal deviation. For Christopher's character, this way of behaving is entirely internally consistent with what is normal for him. However, for typical participants, Christopher's behaviour deviates from external pragmatic norms of attributing intentions to interlocutors and communicating via the Cooperative Principle.

Orthography

Orthography refers to spelling conventions. Consider the following extract:

> The sweat wis lashing oafay Sick Boy; he wis trembling. Ah wis jist sitting thair, focusing oan the telly, trying no tae notice the cunt. He wis bringing me doon.
>
> (Welsh 1993: 3)

This example is the first line of *Trainspotting*, a novel by Irvine Welsh. The novel is set in Edinburgh and in this extract, Renton, the main character and first-person narrator, is describing his friend Sick Boy. Both Sick Boy and Renton are users of heroin. Throughout the novel, Welsh uses non-standard orthography to present Renton's thought and speech. The effect of this is to suggest a regional pronunciation, which we assume to be the Edinburgh vernacular used by Renton. Foregrounding Renton's way of speaking in this way aids characterisation as it emphasises something that would typically go unsaid. Some stylisticians might consider this example to constitute phonological deviation, since it is concerned with pronunciation. We argue that it is ultimately how the text is experienced that determines how we should characterise the type of deviation. If the text is read aloud then the reader will experience phonological deviation; if the text is read silently then the reader will experience orthographic deviation.

Phonology

The issue of how the term *phonology* is often used in stylistics is worth commenting on here. Unlike the technical meaning of phonology in linguistics more broadly, in stylistics the term tends to be used to describe sound in a more specific sense (see, for example, Short's 1996 use of the term to encompass rhyme schemes, assonance, alliteration and consonance). In line with the argument we made in relation to orthography, we argue that the extract below is concerned with the phonological level of language, as it is intended to be performed.

> I'll tell you now and I'll tell you firmly
> I don't never want to go to Burnley
> What they do there don't concern me
> Why would anybody make the journey?
>
> [. . .]
>
> I'll tell you now and I'll tell you briefly
> I don't never want to go to Keighley
> I'll tell you now, just like I told Elsa Lanchester . . .
> I don't ever want to go to . . . Cumbernauld

(Cooper Clarke, no date)

Above is the first and last stanza of 'Burnley' a poem performed by the spoken word 'punk' poet, John Cooper Clarke. Cooper Clarke was born in the city of Salford in the North of England, close to the city of Manchester. When performing, Cooper Clarke recites his poetry in his native Salford accent. In each of the four stanzas of the poem, Cooper Clarke introduces new locations around the North of England and describes why he does not wish to visit them.

Each stanza has four lines and each of the four lines shares the same rhyme; i.e. each line ends on the [ɪ] phoneme. Furthermore, each of the lines in the poem features between seven and 11 syllables, which sets up a rhythm for reciting it. Moreover, the repetition of the rhyme suggests that the listener can expect this rhyme pattern (AAAA, AAAA etc.) for the rest of the poem. This phonological parallelism is only deviated from in the last stanza, when the last phoneme in the penultimate line is not [ɪ], but [ə]. It is also in this line that the first indication that the rhyme scheme may change comes, as it features more syllables than the lines that have come before it. By doing this, Cooper Clarke deviates from an internal phonological norm and as a result foregrounds the last sound in the penultimate word 'Lanchester'. Despite the change in rhyme, the listener expects the next line to rhyme with 'Lanchester' and when this does not, it has a foregrounding effect as it preserves neither the rhyme scheme nor the phonological patterns set up in the poem generally; clearly, most listeners will expect 'Manchester'. Furthermore, as well as being foregrounded phonologically, Cumbernauld is also marked against the towns Cooper Clarke has previously mentioned as it is not a Northern English town, but a town in Scotland. The effect of the foregrounding is comedic, partly because Manchester is a much more well-known place than the towns mentioned earlier in the poem. The humour is likely to be heightened if listeners have the contextual knowledge that Salford (Cooper Clarke's home town) is often seen as secondary in importance to the neighbouring city of Manchester; in effect, by playing with listeners' expectations, Cooper Clarke is able to reduce Manchester's importance for a change.

Syntax and morphology

Below is an extract from *The BFG*, a children's story written by Roald Dahl. In the story, the BFG (or Big Friendly Giant) takes Sophie from the orphanage where she lives after she sees him blowing dreams into children's bedrooms. In the extract, Sophie does not know that the giant is friendly and begs him not to eat her:

> The Giant let out a bellow of laugher. 'Just because I is a giant, you think I is a man-gobbling cannybull!' he shouted. 'You is about right! Giants is all cannybully and murderful!'
>
> (Dahl 1984 [1982]: 25)

This example is rich in linguistic deviation. As well as being a prime exemplar of morphological deviation, it deviates on the syntactic level ('I is a giant') and the semantic level ('cannybully'). The BFG is incredulous that Sophie could think that he would eat her and explains how he is different from other giants, describing them as 'murderful'. This non-standard adjective is formed by combining a free morpheme, 'murder' with the derivational suffix '-ful' to increase the intensity of the root (the neologism suggests that giants are full of murder).

Dahl's decision to have the BFG frequently use neologisms aids the characterisation of him as someone who is isolated from the 'human bean' world and therefore not fluent in standard English, instead having to rely on his ability to combine words and morphemes in unusual ways, in order to speak to Sophie. The use of nonsense words and morphological deviation also works as a minor plot device, allowing Sophie to correct the BFG's use of English, thereby adding an educational dimension to the story. Moreover, the BFG's foregrounded neologisms, which often feature non-standard morphology, foregrounds the process of language learning, making it both memorable and fun for children.

Graphology

Graphology is the level of language concerned with how a written text looks and how the choices made about features of the layout or design contribute to the composite meaning of a text. Figure 22.1 is a poster from the 'We Listen' campaign launched by the Samaritans (a UK charity supporting people in emotional distress) and Network Rail to advertise and raise awareness of the work of the Samaritans.

Figure 22.1 The Samaritans: We Listen (2016)

The poster features a triadic layout of text, image and logo. One of the features of the poster likely to catch the eye is the deviant stance of the subject who is facing away from the viewer, preventing the viewer from being able to read his facial expression, something which is vital in human interaction. (Typically in advertisements, the subject maintains the gaze (Kress and van Leewen 2006) of the viewer in order to create [or assume] a closer relationship between them and the service or product being depicted in the advertisement). This external graphological deviation foregrounds the stance of the subject and pushes the viewer to interpret the significance of this design choice. As is normative in advertisements that feature a subject, the text element of the poster is written in the first person, which has the effect of attributing a voice to the subject in the image by suggesting that it is he who is declaring that he is going to be alright and is fine spending a lot of time alone. The text above the image of the subject deviates from an internal norm in that the darker coloured font is foregrounded against the lighter coloured font. Through this deviation, two voices are created for the subject which suggests that there is a conflict between what the subject is saying and what the subject is actually feeling. By doing this, the Samaritans foreground the social stigma around admitting loneliness and the issue of males in particular as a high risk group that are not accessing services like the Samaritans due to this stigma. This interpretation of the text is also supported by having the subject look away from the viewer, which is suggestive of him hiding his feelings by physically turning away from help.

The duality of voice created by the change in font colour is also present in the text underneath the image of the subject. In this instance, however, the voices are not attributed to the subject, but instead to the viewer and the Samaritans as an institution. This is indicated by the second-person pronoun 'you', which addresses anyone viewing the poster, and the first-person plural pronoun 'we'. The use of two font colours here also sets up the words 'hear' and 'listen' as being in opposition to each other and suggests that when others merely hear, the Samaritans listen. The use of colour is also graphologically parallel with the text at the top of the advert; the 'we listen' clause is the same colour as the implied propositional content 'I'm so alone'. This parallelism pushes the viewer to see these two elements of the poster as connected, suggesting that, by listening, the Samaritans are able to hear the implied meaning behind their callers' words.

Experimental work on foregrounding

The previous sub-section demonstrated the application of foregrounding theory analytically. But do readers really notice and attach significance to particular linguistic choices? The answer, based on experimental work that has tested the psychological reality of foregrounding, is a clear yes. This important experimental work was initiated by van Peer (1986) in a groundbreaking book which is an attempt to validate foregrounding theory by experiment rather than through the simple discussion of examples. In brief, van Peer (1986) began by analysing a series of texts, identifying the deviation, parallelism and resultant foregrounding in them. He then asked 153 participants to mark what they took to be particularly noticeable elements in the texts. Van Peer found that these participants identified the same textual elements as he himself had done, thereby establishing that readers' attention is attracted by foregrounding. Van Peer's participants also claimed that passages containing high degrees of foregrounding were more significant and worthy of discussion (validating Leech's 1969 claim for the importance of what he termed congruence of foregrounding). Moreover, van Peer's findings were statistically significant, meaning that the results were generalisable beyond the particular sample of participants studied. Van Peer's (1986) study was therefore able to establish both the affective value of foregrounding and the predictive power of foregrounding theory. Subsequent experimental work has built on these initial findings. Miall and Kuiken (1994a), for example, were able to replicate van Peer's (1986) findings and show that participants read textual passages that contained foregrounding more slowly. Hakemulder's (2007) study provided similar support for van Peer (1986). Other studies have concentrated on specific aspects of foregrounding. For example, Emmott et al. (2006) have demonstrated the foregrounding potential of sentence fragments (e.g. incomplete sentences in the form of short noun phrases), showing through experiment that depth of processing is increased when readers' attention is caught by such fragments.

Experimental work on foregrounding has not been confined to literary texts, however. As stylistics has diversified into the study of texts of all types (consider our analysis of the Samaritans advert in the previous section), so too has experimental work. Hakemulder (2007), for example, has investigated the issue of foregrounding in film. In many respects this is a natural step for stylistics given that one of its founders, Viktor Shklovsky, was a noted screenwriter and critic and close compatriot of the early Russian film director Sergei Eisenstein. Indeed, the influence of Shklovsky's Russian Formalist approach can still be seen in the work of contemporary film critics such as David Bordwell (see, for instance, Bordwell et al. 2016).

Hakemulder's (2007) study was designed to replicate van Peer's findings concerning the effects of foregrounding. In addition, Hakemulder aimed to test the background/foreground hypothesis; that is, the notion that to perceive foregrounded elements, readers/viewers must be aware of normal conventions. (The background/foreground distinction is also a prime concern for cognitive stylisticians and maps on to their concepts of figure and ground; see next sub-section for more details on this). To test whether perceptions of foregrounding were enhanced by recognition of a background, Hakemulder enlisted 65 participants, with a mean age of 19–26 (Standard Deviation = 1.89), and divided them randomly into two groups. The first group was shown a scene from the 1953 film *Moulin Rouge*. The scene in question takes place in a restaurant and in cinematic terms is a conventional portrayal. Participants were then asked to describe what they had seen and indicate what they found most striking about the scene. Participants were then shown a second restaurant scene, this time from the 1983 film *E la nave va*, and asked the same questions. The scene from *E la nave va* was chosen for its unusual filmic techniques: in the section that takes place in the restaurant kitchen, fast motion is used, whereas when the waiters enter the dining room, slow motion is employed to reflect the change of pace from the frenetic atmosphere of the kitchen.

The second group followed the same procedure, except that rather than viewing the scene from *Moulin Rouge* prior to watching the scene from *E la nave va*, they were instead shown a scene from the 1985 film *Witness*. This scene is of a shooting in an underground car park. Hakemulder's (2007) hypothesis was that Group 1, having been made more aware of the conventional representation of a restaurant than Group 2, would be likely to perceive a greater degree of foregrounding in the unusual restaurant scene.

Participants were asked to compare the scenes they had watched in terms of the degree to which they found them striking, beautiful, interesting, poetic, surprising, artful and attention-grabbing. Group 1 (the experimental group) considered scene 2 (*E la nave va*) to be more striking, beautiful, interesting, surprising, artful and attention-grabbing than scene 1 (*Moulin Rouge*). There was no significant difference between scenes for the 'poetic' variable. Group 2 (the Control Group) considered scene 2 to be more striking, beautiful, poetic, surprising and artful than scene 1 (*Witness*). There was no significant difference between scenes for the 'attention-grabbing' and 'interesting' variables. There is, then, some support in these results for the background/foreground hypothesis. Group 1 found scene 2 to be more interesting and attention-grabbing than did Group 2. Hakemulder's (2007) results also demonstrate that foregrounding can be perceived in film, just as it is in writing.

Experimental work continues in stylistics and some of the most interesting recent research has aimed to test cognitive stylistic accounts of how readers engage with narrative. For instance, Sanford and Emmott's (2012) groundbreaking book *Mind, Brain and Narrative*, provides neuroscientific evidence for a range of phenomena related to foregrounding. In the next section, we outline how the cognitive stylisticians whose work is currently being tested have engaged with the concept of foregrounding.

Cognition

Much contemporary stylistics is informed by insights from cognitive linguistics concerning the processing of language (key work in this area includes Emmott 1997; Stockwell 2002; Burke 2011). Given that stylistics aims at 'relating linguistic facts (linguistic description) to meaning (interpretation) in as explicit a way as possible' (Short 1996: 5), the value of cognitive stylistics (or cognitive poetics as it is sometimes known) is that it offers a principled framework within which to hypothesise about how interpretation is likely to stem from textual choices. Cognitive stylistics (if practised well) does not dispense with the linguistic element of stylistics. Rather, it brings together two endeavours: (i) description of the stylistic characteristics of a text using linguistic theories, models and methods, and (ii) assessment of the interpretative significance of these using theories and models from cognitive linguistics (and, sometimes, from cognitive science more generally).

The particular value of cognitive approaches for our understanding of foregrounding stems from an ambiguity in the term. Emmott and Alexander (2014: 330) explain that foregrounding 'can apply either to the linguistic devices used to create prominence or to the effect of bringing parts of a mental representation to the forefront of attention'. In 2.2 we focused on the linguistic triggers of foregrounding but it is insights from cognitively-oriented work that allow us to explain how such devices prompt attention. Key to explaining this is the concept of figure and ground, which originates in the work of the Danish psychologist Edgar Rubin.

Rubin's (1915) work on visual perception proposed that we make a distinction between what he termed figures and the background against which they are made prominent. In visual terms, figures have form (as opposed to the formlessness of the ground), and may be brighter, larger or more colourful than the ground. Figures attract our attention and, as a result, we assume they are meaningful in a way that the ground isn't. This saves cognitive effort; we do not need to process the whole of an image to the same degree that we process figures. As West (2011: 242) explains, when you read a book you focus on the marks on the page (i.e. the words) rather than the white spaces around them. As a result of figure/ground segregation (Ungerer and Schmid 1996: 157), the illusion is created that the black words are *on* the white page, as opposed to the reality of the page being a combination of black and white shapes.

Ungerer and Schmid (1996: 160) explain that locative relations (e.g. up, down, in, out, over, under, next to, behind, in front of, etc.) are an important aspect of figure/ground segregation. And a key explanatory concept for understanding the cognitive processing of locative relations is the image schema. Image schemas are basic cognitive structures derived from our everyday experiences. We use them to understand and make sense of the world around us. OVER, for instance, is an example of an image schema that distils our experience of a particular relationship between objects, where one is the trajector and the other is the landmark. *Trajector* and *landmark* are terms used when figure and ground exist in a locative relationship to each other. The trajector in an OVER image schema is the element that moves above the landmark; that is, it is figural against the ground of the landmark. In stylistic analysis, image schemas can be drawn on to hypothesise about how we make interpretative sense of particular stylistic choices. Consider the following striking image from Lisa Klaussmann's novel *Tigers in Red Weather*:

> The oak tree in the backyard cut pieces from the moon[.]
>
> (Klaussmann 2012: 4)

In linguistic terms, this sentence is foregrounded. Oak trees have neither volition nor dexterity, so it is semantically deviant for the noun phrase 'The oak tree' to form the subject of the dynamic verb 'cut'. Combined with our schematic knowledge, which renders impossible the idea that the moon might have pieces literally cut from it by a tree, this forces us to interpret the sentence as metaphorical. Our IN FRONT OF image schema enables us to make sense of the description. The moon is a landmark partially covered by the trajector that is the oak tree; and the tree's branches moving in front of the moon give the impression that parts of the moon have been cut away (rather like black ink cuts away the whiteness of a page in West's 2011 example). However, the proposition conveyed by the syntactic structure of the sentence contradicts the cognitive structure stored in our IN FRONT OF image schema, thereby disrupting the image schema by forcing us to reconceptualise the relationship between trajector and landmark. The foregrounding effect of the semantic deviation is that it makes us focus attention on the landmark (the moon) rather than the trajector, which gives rise to a defamiliarising effect (just as if we were to try to focus on the page rather than the writing on it).

Corpora

Alongside developments in cognitive stylistics, one of the most significant advances of recent years has been the use of corpora and corpus linguistic analytical techniques to support stylistics. Corpora can be large-scale, such as the Global Web-based English (GloWbE) corpus of 1.9 billion words of written language (see http://corpus.byu.edu/glowbe/), or they can be smaller-scale, such as the West Yorkshire Regional English Database (WYRED) of Northern British English speech currently being developed at the University of Huddersfield to support forensic phonetic analysis (see Gold et al. 2017). Corpus methods have revolutionised stylistics because they offer a means of identifying the statistical significance of foregrounded features of language. They do this by providing a means of determining the norms against which foregrounded features are figural. In effect, corpora offer a way of identifying both figure and ground in language. This is an important development as Mukařovský's (1964 [1932]) concept of foregrounding depends on the notion of what he calls the 'standard language' (i.e. linguistic norms) against which foregrounded features are prominent. However, until the advent of electronic corpora, determining what these norms were was remarkably difficult to do with any degree of confidence. Moreover, some linguists doubted the value of frequency information at all. Freeman (1970: 3), for instance, states that 'even if [frequencies] could be ascertained they would constitute no real insight into either natural language or style'. Corpus stylistic studies have conclusively shown this not to be the case and, consequently, Freeman's view no longer has credence within stylistics.

One area of stylistics in which quantitative information has been invaluable is the study of speech and thought presentation. In their groundbreaking book *Style in Fiction*, Leech and Short (1981: 324) introduce what they term a 'cline of interference' with regard to the options for presenting character talk in fiction. At one end of the cline are categories that purport faithfulness to a perceived original utterance. The most obvious of these is direct speech (or thought), where the exact words of the character in question are reported in inverted commas; e.g. *'Who the hell are you?' asked a very military voice.* (Le Carré 1974: 7). At the opposite end of the scale is very minimal presentation, where all we know is that speech (or thought) took place, as in *The two young men spoke for a long time, one into the ear of the other.* (Gorriti 2003: 65). Leech and Short (1981: 334) point out that in fiction direct speech is the norm for speech presentation, whereas indirect rather than direct thought is the norm for thought presentation (e.g. *He thought that they had established some kind of mutual respect [.]* [de Bernières 1994: 196]). This is on the grounds that thoughts are not formulated verbally and so cannot be reported word for word. Semino and Short's (2004) corpus-based study of speech, writing and thought presentation in a 250,000 word corpus of English writing (fiction, news and biography) offers a means of testing these proposed norms. Semino and Short's corpus was manually annotated to identify all the speech, writing and thought presentation techniques present in the data. This allowed for the calculation of frequency information for each category. While they found that direct speech was indeed the quantitative norm for speech presentation, free indirect thought (FIT) rather than indirect thought was the quantitative norm for thought presentation (FIT mixes features of narration with features of direct presentational forms; Leech and Short (1981: 25) use the example *He would return there to see her again the following day*). Semino and Short (2004) point out that one reason for this apparent overuse of FIT in the corpus is the opportunities it affords for dramatising thoughts in a way that avoids the artifice of presenting thought directly. Support for this comes from the fact that in their corpus, while FIT was the most frequent thought presentation category in the corpus generally, it was only in the fiction section that it dominated.

In a later study, McIntyre and Walker (2011) built a corpus of Early Modern English writing (fiction and news) and annotated it for speech, writing and thought presentation using Semino and Short's (2004) categorisation system. What they found was that, in contrast to Semino and Short's 20th-century data, *indirect* thought was the quantitative norm in the Early Modern period, with FIT only emerging much later in the period. The value of these particular corpus-based projects is that they offer an insight into how norms shift across time with regard to the presentation of speech, writing and thought. This increases our ability to judge what counts as deviant usage in particular periods. McIntyre and Walker (2011) also suggest that their results are indicative of how genre styles develop over time. In more general terms, the use of corpora in stylistics enables the testing of ideas originally developed without recourse to empirical data.

Corpus stylistics, however, is not limited simply to quantifying norms. Corpora can also be used to test intuitions about particular interpretations. And the issue of interpretation applies equally to everyday discourse as it does to literary texts. The following example is text taken from a tweet that went viral with over 35,000 Twitter 'likes' at the time of writing. It is often some level of foregrounding that causes such posts to go viral, as can be seen here:

> People who are offended when I breastfeed in public need to STFU. What I'm doing is natural and strengthens the bond between me and my dog.

The first sentence of this tweet invokes a societal argument about breastfeeding (i.e. that people exist who are offended about others breastfeeding in public) and then plays on this in the second sentence. The foregrounding arises because of a collocational clash; the final noun phrase 'my dog' contradicts our schematic expectations of who or what is breastfed as well as how the bond between a dog and its owner is usually 'strengthened'. The foregrounding that occurs here is as a result of external semantic deviation from collocational norms. Corpus analysis demonstrates this. In the British National Corpus, for instance, which comprises 100 million words of British English, the only statistically significant noun collocates of 'breastfeeding' are 'counsellor', 'pregnancy', 'baby', 'child' and 'women'. 'Dog', unsurprisingly, is nowhere to be seen. Corpus data, in this case, provides evidence of collocational behaviour that allows us to determine the norms against which the semantic foregrounding is made prominent.

Corpus stylistics continues to develop, with recent work exploring the potential for integrating cognitive analytical frameworks and corpus methods (see, for example, Stockwell and Mahlberg's 2015 work on characterisation in Dickens, and McIntyre's 2015 discussion of the integration of cognitive and corpus methods generally).

Key areas of dispute and debate

Having outlined the fundamental concept of foregrounding, in this section we discuss two issues in particular that continue to be the cause of debate in stylistics. These are the distinction between literary and non-literary stylistics, and the notion of objectivity in stylistic analysis.

Literary and non-literary stylistics

Stylistics is often perceived to be the linguistic analysis of literature, not least because that is how many stylisticians describe it (see, for example, Stockwell and Whiteley's (2014: 1) claim that 'Stylistics is the proper study of literature'). However, while it may be true that many stylisticians concentrate exclusively on the analysis of literary texts, there is nothing about stylistic methods that prevent them being applied in the analysis of non-literary texts. Moreover, it is important that stylistics is recognised as being the study of style in both literary and non-literary texts, since early stylistic work that aimed to discern the linguistic properties of literature was quickly abandoned when it became apparent that no such formal distinction existed. To define stylistics exclusively as the linguistic analysis of literature is therefore not only misleading but counterproductive, since it fails to acknowledge one of the most important contributions that stylistics has made to our understanding of the nature of literature itself; namely that there is no formal distinction between literary and non-literary language. Contemporary claims that stylistics is the linguistic analysis of literature also overlook the long history of research within stylistics into style in non-literary texts, such as that by Crystal and Davy (1969), Enkvist (1973), Short (1988), Carter (2004), McIntyre et al. (2004), Semino and Short (2004), Jeffries (2010), Browse (2016) and many others.

A related issue is that the terms *literary* and *non-literary stylistics*, which are still commonly used by stylisticians, are confusing. They tend to be used to distinguish between the analysis of fiction and non-fiction (as we have done in the previous paragraph) rather than between the analysis of texts that are literary and those that are not. To this end, there is little need to use them, since the methods employed in the analysis of fiction and non-fiction are essentially the same. Added to this is the fact that literariness, as Carter and Nash (1983) have demonstrated, is a point on a cline. It is not determined solely by reference to linguistic features, nor is it a property exclusive to fictional texts. Carter (2004), for instance, has shown conclusively that the creativity often associated with literary writing is just as prevalent in everyday discourse (see also Swann et al. 2011). As he puts it, 'Creativity is not simply a property of exceptional people but an exceptional property of all people' (Carter 2004: 13). There is, then, a compelling argument for abandoning the terms *literary* and *non-literary stylistics*, at least as they are currently used.

Objectivity

Because many stylisticians (e.g. Stockwell 2002, Montoro 2012, Gavins 2013) are interested in the analysis of literary fiction, and because the approaches used in stylistics are often seen as anathema to non-linguistically inclined literary critics, stylisticians have tended to be unusually defensive in the way they explain their approaches. Nowhere is this seen more than in the ongoing debate about objectivity in stylistic analysis. Other areas of linguistics (and, indeed, the sciences and social sciences generally) do not regularly engage in protracted arguments about whether their methods are rigorous and replicable, probably because it should be obvious from the outcomes of analysis whether this is the case. Stylisticians, on the other hand, are often drawn into debates about the nature of objectivity in relation to stylistic analysis. This is in part because of an attempt to persuade literary critics of the value of stylistics but also as a result of the attacks that have been made on stylistics over the years by critics whose views have been that literature is not susceptible to objective analysis. In defending their approach, stylisticians have been forced into defending the concept of objectivity itself.

Perhaps the earliest such discussion was that between the linguist Roger Fowler and the literary critic F. W. Bateson, whose debate (see Fowler 1971) about the merits of applying linguistic methods in the analysis of literature reached its nadir when the discussion was reduced to the level of personal insult, not to mention shocking sexism: Bateson responded to a hypothetical question concerning whether he would 'allow' [sic] his sister to marry a linguist by replying that he would prefer not to have one in the family. Bateson's complaint was that literature is by its nature not amenable to objective analysis because responses to it are so subjective. Stylisticians reject this claim on the grounds that it dismisses the notion that it should ever be possible to investigate the nature of art and the human condition and make claims about these with any degree of certainty. If we take Bateson's position, then every reader's opinion is equally valid and any claims we choose to make about literature can never be proved right or wrong. In effect, this position repudiates the very notion of critical inquiry and at a stroke makes the practice of literary criticism redundant. In contrast to this view, stylisticians claim that literature is, like any other object of study, open to objective analysis. Furthermore, stylisticians reject the notion that anything goes when it comes to interpreting texts. Instead, they (and by definition we) would argue that there is a finite set of reasonable responses to a text. Moreover, any supposedly different readings of a text are likely to be minor variants of a relatively stable higher order interpretation (see Short et al. 2011 for a discussion of this issue).

In a later debate, Mackay (1996), also a literary critic, went further than Bateson by taking issue with the concept of objectivity generally. On the grounds that objectivity is never fully achievable (as stylisticians freely admit; see, for example, Carter 1982), Mackay rejects the view that we should aim for objectivity at all in stylistic analysis. But if we reject objectivity then we are left with nothing but subjective intuition, the problems with which we have already described in the previous paragraph. Mackay overlooks this problem and instead, in response to Short's (1996: 358) claim that no stylistic analysis is objective in the sense of being true for all time, complains:

> I read this as meaning that an analysis can be objective but not in the particular sense 'that it is true for all time'. So in what sense are we to assume that an analysis is or can be objective? How long is its shelf-life? Five years? One year? Can such an analysis be true for a fortnight?
>
> (Mackay 1999: 61)

The problem here is that Mackay fundamentally misunderstands the nature of objectivity. As Short and van Peer (1999: 272) point out, the only claims that are likely to be true for all time are analytically true statements, such as 'all triangles have three sides' (and it is possible to imagine circumstances in which even these might no longer hold). Given that this is the case, it makes little sense to ask how long a supposedly objective claim ought to hold for. The answer is, of course, until someone else is able to demonstrate that it is wrong.

The other aspect of being objective that can be difficult to grasp is the fact that it is not possible to be 100% objective. This is because there will always be variables that we are unable to control. This is a problem even in the natural sciences. In stylistics, our analyses might be affected by sociological parameters such as our schematic knowledge of the world or our cultural upbringing. This does not mean that we should abandon the idea of objective inquiry. Rather, we need instead to identify potentially confounding variables and prevent these having a bearing on our results as far as is possible, for example through triangulation (see Miller and Brewer 2003: 326). In stylistics, this might involve, say, using corpus stylistic methods to support the notion of what might constitute ground (that is, norms) in a cognitive stylistic account of figural elements in a text.

In their reply to Mackay (1999), Short and van Peer (1999) summarise the concept of objectivity as follows:

> In trying to be objective, one tries to be (a) clear, detailed and open (so that one's position is unambiguous) and (b) ready to change one's mind if the evidence or a subsequent counter-argument demands it. This is why it makes sense to talk of trying to be objective, and trying to be more objective. Objectivity is not like a light-switch, having only two positions, on or off. It involves a complex of interrelated factors and, as a consequence, is more suitably measured on a sliding scale.
>
> (Short and van Peer 1999: 273)

To this we would add that being clear and detailed necessitates being systematic in analytical terms. This means applying analytical frameworks rigorously and not ignoring inconvenient data or cherry-picking examples to suit a particular argument. There is nothing in this approach that is remotely controversial to linguists, or indeed to social scientists or natural scientists generally. It is perhaps because of stylistics' focus on literature, and the fact that these theoretical and methodological standards do not tend to apply in literary studies, that the debate about objectivity in stylistics has been such a long-running one (see West 2008 and McIntyre 2011 for most recent discussions of the argument).

Future directions

What we hope to have shown in this chapter is that fundamental to stylistics is the notion of choice. Style, whether literary or non-literary, is dependent on this. And central to understanding the functional significance of choice is foregrounding theory. Despite the many significant advances in stylistics over the years, the concept of foregrounding remains at the heart of all stylistic analysis. Theories and models from linguistics remain key to describing how and why features of language are foregrounded. Advances in cognitive stylistics have provided principled mechanisms for explaining the functional significance of foregrounding to readers. And developments in corpus stylistics have provided methods for determining norms, calculating the statistical salience of foregrounded features and testing intuitions about texts.

As stylistics moves forward, we envisage a number of possible developments. In recent years, the analysis of multimodal texts has become more prevalent. We saw above how experimental stylisticians such as Hakemulder (2007) have engaged with multimodality. Other stylisticians have begun to explore how paralinguistic and non-linguistic elements of texts combine with language to project meaning. Forceville (2011), for instance, has explored how meaning is constructed from both image and text when reading comic books. Nørgaard's work (summarised in Nørgaard 2014), by contrast, has investigated the meaning potential of the graphological and typographical form of language itself, paying attention to such issues as font and colour. McIntyre (2008), on the other hand, has developed an approach to the stylistic analysis of drama that aims to make the analysis of performance as systematic as the analysis of the dramatic text. One aim for the future would be to improve the replicability of such work by developing more reliable frameworks for multimodal analysis. As such work continues, we would also hope that stylisticians turn their attention to speech; there is no reason why stylistics should remain a text-based subject. Certainly, the analysis of dramatic performance is one which would benefit considerably from the insights of phonetics as well as pragmatic methods.

In more general terms, we would advocate that stylistics stop framing itself as the linguistic analysis of literature, and instead adopt a more general definition that sees it as the analysis of style and its functional significance in all discourse types. Constant justification of stylistics to non-linguistically oriented literary critics is one of the practices that has led to defensiveness with regard to methodological approaches. Shifting the focus of stylistics so that it is not exclusively about analysing literature would reduce the need to argue about the value of rigour and replicability; instead, this could be demonstrated simply through analytical practice.

Further reading

Jeffries, L. and D. McIntyre (2010) *Stylistics*. Cambridge: Cambridge University Press. An accessible postgraduate-level overview of stylistics, covering key areas of the field from cognitive to corpus stylistics.

Leech, G. and M. Short (2007) *Style in Fiction*. 2nd edn. London: Pearson. A seminal study of the language of fictional prose.

Nowottny, W. (1962) *The Language Poets Use*. London: The Athlone Press. One of the earliest textbooks in stylistics and still valuable to contemporary stylisticians.

Simpson, P. (2014) *Stylistics: A Resource Book for Students*. 2nd edn. Abingdon: Routledge. An undergraduate-level task-based introduction with lots of examples and exercises.

Sotirova, V. (ed.) (2015) *The Bloomsbury Companion to Stylistics*. London: Bloomsbury. A handbook providing a broad-ranging overview of the field, including a historical perspective.

Related topics

- Literature and the English language
- The language of creative writing
- Corpus linguistics: studying language as part of the digital humanities.

References

Bordwell, D., Thompson, K. and Smith, J. (2016) *Film Art: An Introduction*. 11th edn. New York: McGraw-Hill.

Browse, S. (2016) 'Revisiting Text World Theory and extended metaphor: Embedding and foregrounding metaphor in the text-worlds of the 2008 financial crash', *Language and Literature* 25 (1): 8–37.

Burke, M. (2011) *Literary Reading, Cognition and Emotion*. Abingdon: Routledge.

Carter, R. (1982) *Language and Literature: An Introductory Reader in Stylistics*. London: George Allen & Unwin.
Carter, R. (2004) *Language and Creativity: The Art of Common Talk*. London: Routledge.
Carter, R. and W. Nash (1983) 'Language and Literariness', *Prose Studies* 6 (2): 124–141.
Cooper Clarke, J. (no date) 'Burnley'. Unpublished poem.
Crystal, D. and D. Davy (1969) *Investigating English Style*. London: Longman.
Dahl, R. (1984) [1982] *The BFG*. London: Puffin.
de Bernières, L. (1994) *Captain Corelli's Mandolin*. London: Secker and Warburg.
Emmott, C. (1997) *Narrative Comprehension*. Oxford: Oxford University Press.
Emmott, C. and M. Alexander (2014) 'Foregrounding, burying and plot construction', in P. Stockwell and S. Whiteley (eds), *The Cambridge Handbook of Stylistics*. Cambridge: Cambridge University Press, 329–343.
Emmott, C., A. J. Sanford and L. Morrow (2006) 'Capturing the attention of readers? Stylistic and psychological perspectives on the use and effect of text fragmentation in narratives', *Journal of Literary Semantics* 35 (1): 1–30.
Enkvist, N. E. (1973) *Linguistic Stylistics*. The Hague: Mouton.
Forceville, C. (2011) 'Pictorial runes in *Tintin and the Picaros*', *Journal of Pragmatics* 43 (3): 875–890.
Fowler, R. (1971) *The Languages of Literature*. London: Routledge & Kegan Paul.
Freeman, D. C. (1970) 'Linguistic approaches to literature', in D. C. Freeman (ed.), *Linguistics and Literary Style*. New York: Holt, Reinhard and Winston, 3–17.
Gavins, J. (2013) *Reading the Absurd*. Edinburgh: Edinburgh University Press.
Gold, E., K. Earnshaw and S. Ross (2017) 'An introduction to the WYRED database', *Transactions of the Yorkshire Dialect Society* 23: 1–8.
Gorriti, J. M. (2003) 'The treasure of the Incas', in F. Masiello (ed.), *Dreams and Realities: Selected Fiction of Juana Manuela Gorriti*. Oxford: Oxford University Press, 41–68.
Grice, H. P. (1975) 'Logic and conversation', in P. Cole and J. Morgan (eds), *Syntax and Semantics, Volume III: Speech Acts*. New York: Academic Press, 41–58.
Haddon, M. (2003) *The Curious Incident of the Dog in the Night-Time*. London: Jonathan Cape.
Hainey, M. (2016) 'Clint and Scott Eastwood: No holds barred in their first interview together', *Esquire*. September: 116–120.
Hakemulder, J. (2007) 'Tracing foregrounding in responses to film', *Language and Literature* 16 (2): 125–139.
Jeffries, L. (2010) *Critical Stylistics*. Basingstoke: Palgrave.
Jeffries, L. and D. McIntyre (2010) *Stylistics*. Cambridge: Cambridge University Press.
Klaussmann, L. (2012) *Tigers in Red Weather*. London: Picador.
Kress, G.R. and T. van Leeuwen (2006) *Reading Images: The Grammar of Visual Design*. 2nd edn. New York: Routledge.
Lakoff, G. and M. Johnson (2003) [1980] *Metaphors We Live By*. Chicago: University of Chicago Press.
Le Carré, J. (1974) *Tinker Tailor Soldier Spy*. London: Hodder and Stoughton.
Leech, G. (1969) *A Linguistic Guide to English Poetry*. London: Longman.
Leech, G. and M. Short (1981) *Style in Fiction*. London: Longman.
Mackay, R. (1996) 'Mything the point: A critique of objective stylistics', *Language and Communication* 16 (1): 81–93.
Mackay, R. (1999) 'There goes the other foot: A reply to Short et al.', *Language and Literature* 8 (1): 59–66.
McIntyre, D. (2008) 'Integrating multimodal analysis and the stylistics of drama: A multimodal perspective on Ian McKellen's *Richard III*', *Language and Literature* 17 (4): 309–334.
McIntyre, D. (2011) 'The place of stylistics in the English curriculum', in L. Jeffries and D. McIntyre (eds), *Teaching Stylistics*. Basingstoke: Palgrave, 9–29.
McIntyre, D. (2015) 'Towards an integrated corpus stylistics', *Topics in Linguistics* 16 (1): 59–68.
McIntyre, D., C. Bellard-Thomson, J. Heywood, T. McEnery, E. Semino and M. Short. (2004) 'Investigating the presentation of speech, writing and thought in spoken British English: A corpus-based approach', *ICAME Journal* 28: 49–76.
McIntyre, D. and B. Walker (2011) 'Discourse presentation in Early Modern English writing: A preliminary corpus-based investigation', *International Journal of Corpus Linguistics* 16 (1): 101–130.
Miall, D. and D. Kuiken (1994a) 'Beyond text theory: Understanding literary response', *Discourse Processes* 17 (3): 337–352.

Miall, D. and D. Kuiken (1994b) 'Foregrounding, defamiliarization, and affect: Response to literary stories', *Poetics* 22: 389–407.
Miller, D. L. and J. D. Brewer (2003) *The A-Z of Social Research: A Dictionary of Key Social Science Research Concepts*. London: Sage.
Montoro, R. (2012) *Chick Lit: An Analysis of Cappuccino Fiction*. London: Continuum.
Mukařovský, J. (1964) [1932] 'Standard language and poetic language', in P. L. Garvin (ed.), *A Prague School Reader on Esthetics, Literary Structure, and Style*. Washington, DC: Georgetown University Press, 17–30.
Newsom, J. (2004) *'Peach, Plum, Pear'*, on *The Milk-Eyed Mender*. Chicago: Drag City.
Nørgaard, N. (2014) 'Multimodality and stylistics', in M. Burke (ed.), *The Routledge Handbook of Stylistics*. Abingdon: Routledge, 471–484.
Rubin, E. (1915) *Synsoplevede Figuere*. Copenhagen: Gyldendalsde: Boghandel.
Sanford, A. and C. Emmott (2012) *Mind, Brain and Narrative*. Cambridge: Cambridge University Press.
Semino, E. (2014) 'Pragmatic failure, mind style and characterisation in fiction about autism', *Language and Literature* 23 (2): 141–158.
Semino, E. and M. Short (2004) *Corpus Stylistics: Speech, Writing and Thought Presentation in a Corpus of English Writing*. London: Routledge.
Shklovsky, V. (1965) [1917] 'Art as technique', in L. T. Lemon and M. J. Reiss (eds), *Russian Formalist Criticism: Four Essays*. Lincoln: University of Nebraska Press, 3–24.
Short, M. (1988) 'Speech presentation, the novel and the press', in W. van Peer (ed.), *The Taming of the Text*. London: Routledge, 61–81.
Short, M. (1996) *Exploring the Language of Poems, Plays and Prose*. London: Longman.
Short, M., D. McIntyre, L. Jeffries and D. Bousfield (2011) 'Processes of interpretation: Using meta-analysis to inform pedagogic practice', in L. Jeffries and D. McIntyre (eds), *Teaching Stylistics*. Basingstoke: Palgrave, 69–94.
Short, M. and W. van Peer (1999) 'A reply to Mackay', *Language and Literature* 8(3): 269–275.
Stockwell, P. (2002) *Cognitive Poetics: An Introduction*. London: Routledge.
Stockwell, P. and M. Mahlberg (2015) 'Mind-modelling with corpus stylistics in *David Copperfield*', *Language and Literature* 24 (2): 129–147.
Stockwell, P. and S. Whiteley (2014) 'Introduction', in P. Stockwell and S. Whiteley (eds), *The Cambridge Handbook of Stylistics*. Cambridge: Cambridge University Press, 1–9.
Swann, J., R. Pope and R. Carter (2011) *Creativity in Language and Literature: The State of the Art*. Basingstoke: Palgrave.
Thomas, J. (1995) *Meaning in Interaction*. London: Longman.
Ungerer, F. and H. J. Schmid (1996) *An Introduction to Cognitive Linguistics*. London: Longman.
van Peer, W. (1986) *Stylistics and Psychology*. London: Croom Helm.
Welsh, I. (1993) *Trainspotting*. London: Secket & Warburg.
West, D. (2008) 'Changing English: A polemic against diversity and fragmentation', *Changing English* 15 (2): 137–143.
West, D. (2011) 'Teaching cognitive stylistics', in L. Jeffries and D. McIntyre (eds), *Teaching Stylistics*. Basingstoke: Palgrave, 239–254.

23

Sociolinguistics

Studying English and its social relations

Ana Deumert

Introduction: what do sociolinguists study?

In a book titled *What Is Sociolinguistics?*, the Canadian scholar Gerhard van Herk (2012) answered his own question, somewhat tongue-in-cheek, as follows: 'It depends who you ask.' That sociolinguistics is best understood as a pluralized discipline is also reflected in Alan Bell's (2013) *Guidebook to Sociolinguistics*. Bell titles the opening chapter to the book 'What *are* sociolinguistics?' (my emphasis). Pluralization is an important aspect, and strategy, of academia in the twenty-first century, as disciplines are fragmenting and epistemological projects of 'disciplinary disobedience' are gaining popularity (Smith 1999; Mignolo 2008). Consequently, to articulate even a minimalist definition of what it is that sociolinguists study quickly runs into problems. Consider the following attempt: sociolinguistics is the study of linguistic practices within the context of human social relations. At first glance this seems to be uncontroversial and rather basic. Yet even this minimalist definition raises questions: Are we only looking at *linguistic* practices? Should we not look at communication more broadly and include multimodal practices, which are central to, especially, new media communication (Machin 2014)? And should we emphasise 'human relations', given that post-humanist scholars are paying increasing attention to human–machine interaction as well as human–animal interaction (see Haraway 2008; Kirksey and Helmreich 2010; Kohn 2013)?

It's not only the subject matter of sociolinguistics that is diverse, but also its theoretical foundations. The field occupies a broad interdisciplinary – as well as transdisciplinary – space, drawing on a wide range of disciplinary knowledges in the investigation of communicative practices. Thus, sociolinguists draw on sociology (considering, for example, how ways of speaking reflect class positions or other group identities), literary theory (in discussions of voice, heteroglossia, performance and style), critical theory (in analysing discourse and language ideologies) and human geography (for example, when studying linguistic, or semiotic, landscapes, that is, the visual presence of language(s) in public spaces). Important theoretical innovations have also come from (linguistic) anthropology, resulting in a renewed engagement with meaning and semiotic theory. More recently, the field's strongly Euro-American orientation has been discussed critically (Smakman and Heinrich 2015). These debates reflect a broader academic project of centring the global south as an important, and unique, epistemic site. Thus, while in the past 'the South' was seen as a space for fieldwork and data collection (Hountondji 1997), it is now emerging as a space where existing (Euro-American) theories are critiqued and new theories are formulated (Ndlovu-Gatsheni 2013).

Debate and contestation notwithstanding, sociolinguists across the world tend to be united in their rejection of the asocial abstractions that underlie most structuralist and formal approaches to language; that is, the idea that we can – even just in principle and for the sake of argument – understand 'language' by focusing our attention on 'the ideal-speaker listener, in a completely homogenous speech-community, who knows its language perfectly' (Chomsky 1965: 3). Homogeneity is not what sociolinguists are ever interested in, and if anything unifies sociolinguistics, it is a commitment to heterogeneity. Thus, for a sociolinguist 'English', or any other language, is never a unitary object; it is an internally diverse practice and exists within complex sociopolitical and historical, as well as linguistic, relations. This chapter explores these relations and is structured as follows: the next section outlines the history of the field; the third section contributes to current critical debates by discussing examples of Southern sociolinguistic theory. The fourth, fifth and sixth sections focus on three core topics in sociolinguistics: indexicality, ideologies, and diversity and inequality. The conclusion reflects briefly on the future of sociolinguistics.

Historical perspectives: North and South

Sociolinguistics is commonly described as having emerged as a distinct field of inquiry in the United States during the 1960s and 1970s (Figueroa 1994; Murray 1998). It is no coincidence that this was also the time of the civil rights movement, and it was not unusual for sociolinguists – in the past and today – to also be political activists. The North American scholar Gregory Guy (1996: x) reflects on these early days more than a quarter of a century later:

> [T]he things I was studying in synchronic linguistics ... were pale and bloodless ... Linguistic form has its own appeal, but I was beginning, as an undergraduate, to be nagged by uneasy questions such as: Where are the people? What happened to communication? I was also feeling, in 1970, a lack of relevance in the field. I was a social activist, deeply involved in the anti-war movement, civil rights and social justice and it made me uneasy that the linguistics I was studying seemed to be so remote from these concerns.

It is in this political context that conferences and workshops brought together scholars who were interested in the social and political aspects of language use. Not all of these scholars were linguists; some had a background in anthropology, others in sociology, and resulting debates and conversations were thus, from early on, of an interdisciplinary nature. As a result of their different disciplinary backgrounds, scholars focused in their work on different aspects of language use and social meaning, and adopted different methodologies, ranging from large-scale, quantitative surveys to fine-grained ethnographic studies.

Even though North American scholars such as Joshua Fishman, William Labov, Dell Hymes and John Gumperz are often foregrounded in historical overviews of sociolinguistics (e.g. Bell 2013), their work constitutes but one – admittedly highly influential – strand of sociolinguistic work. A comprehensive history of sociolinguistics would be considerably longer, as well as more rhizomatic and global. This history includes early studies of language contact (e.g. the work of the Austrian scholar Hugo Schuchardt), European dialectology (e.g. publications by Herman Paul and Louis Gauchat), the early tradition of linguistic anthropology in the

United States (e.g. Franz Boas and Edward Sapir), as well as the language-philosophical work of scholars in Eastern Europe, especially Russia (e.g. Mikhail Bahktin and Valentin Voloshinov, but also Roman Jakobson). For the second part of the twentieth century, it also includes work on language and power (by, for example, Basil Bernstein in the United Kingdom, and Pierre Bourdieu as well as Michel Foucault in France), and functionalist, that is, meaning-centred approaches to grammar (evident in the contributions by J. R. Firth and M. A. K. Halliday; see Deumert (2013) for a discussion of some of these strands).

Sociolinguistic theories developed not only in diverse locations and at different times in Euro-America, but also in the global South; that is, those parts of the world that have been the object of European colonialism since the fifteenth century, and that constitute the so-called 'majority world' (which is home to about 80 percent of the world's population). Scholarly contributions coming out of Africa, Asia and South America have, so far, received limited attention in the academy. The social theorist Raewyn Connell (2007), for example, argued in her book *Southern Theory* that colonialism has been suspiciously absent from social – and by extension sociolinguistic – theorizing. Yet colonialism, and its enduring consequences, have shaped the modern world-system, and are particularly important for the study of English, a language that was deeply implicated in the colonial project (Pennycook 1998), and continues to be the object of neo-imperialist practices (Phillipson 1992, 2013). Built on violent systems of exploitation and racial domination, colonialism created hierarchical relations not only between people, but also between languages, leading to the formation of a unique interaction order (Go 2013). The long-term effects of colonialism are experienced not only in the former colonies, but also in the metropole: twentieth and twenty-first century migration to Euro-America stems to a large extent from the former colonies, and the present-day multilingual ecologies of metropolitan cities such as New York, Amsterdam or London are shaped by the *longue durée* of the colonial situation. To centre colonialism is one of the contributions a Southern perspective can make to contemporary sociolinguistics.

In the next section I discuss examples of work by scholars from Africa and the African diaspora. Similar discussions could be offered for scholars from Asia and Latin America, as well as from marginalized, indigenous communities from across the world (Santos 2014). And a final caveat: like most academic disciplines, sociolinguistics is, historically, male-dominated and male linguists have been foregrounded in historical accounts of the discipline. This is clearly visible in the canonical names mentioned above. Yet, as Julia Falk (1999) has shown us in her work on American female linguists, women were always there, even before their numbers began to grow from the mid-twentieth century onwards. To uncover their contributions reflects a project akin to that of southern theory; the aim is to surface marginalized voices and to disrupt hegemonic disciplinary histories.[1]

New debates: Southern theories in sociolinguistics

A well-known, and indeed classic, source for southern thinking about language is the work of the anti-colonial Caribbean scholar Frantz Fanon. In his book *Black Skin, White Masks* ([1952] 2008), Fanon reflects on colonialism, race and language, identity and alienation, inferiorization and inequality, the link between individual experience and social processes, the promise of liberation and agency, as well as the ways in which language, and certain ways of speaking a particular language, call us into being as a (racialized) subject (a theory that was further developed in Althusser's (1971) work on interpellation; on Fanon's contribution to sociolinguistics, see Mazrui (1993, 2006)). For Fanon, colonial subjects (and other subordinated groups) cannot avoid reflecting themselves to themselves through the language of domination;

that is, the colonial language. This creates a double-consciousness: the colonial subjects cannot simply 'return to the source' and re-instantiate pre-colonial practices, but have to live with the fact that they will always experience a certain 'two-ness' or multiplicity: they have 'black skins' but are forced to wear 'white masks' (the term 'double-consciousness' was first used by Du Bois (1903), in *The Souls of Black Folk*). For Fanon, a return to the past – linguistically or culturally – is not possible, and only radically new forms of speaking will allow the 'wretched of the earth', the 'damned', to articulate liberation, political emancipation and revolution; that is, to overcome the colonial experience (Fanon [1961] 1967; for a comprehensive discussion of anti-colonial language politics see Pupavac (2012: 144–168)). Fanon's work is important for sociolinguists: he formulates a sociolinguistics of, and for, those who find themselves in positions of subordination and oppression (the *damnés*), giving voice to their experiences and struggles, to the humanity that has been denied to them.

Another Southern thinker whose work is of relevance to sociolinguistics is the Algerian-born philosopher Jacques Derrida. Derrida's work, which is commonly described as post-structuralist, touches on many themes that are relevant to sociolinguists, including speech and writing, speech act theory and intertextuality, as well as the fundamental diversity, plurality and indeterminacy of all language and meaning (McNamara 2010; Chow 2014). In *Monolingualism of the Other,* Derrida ([1996] 1998) reflects on his own experience of growing up under French colonialism. He positions language as central to our sense of being (and belonging) in the world, while at the same time destabilizing the idea of a 'mother tongue' as a single, inherited and original language. He discusses the ways in which language is violent, imposed on us, and, consequently, is never fully ours; yet to make it ours – to claim and appropriate it – is a strong, never-ending, never fulfilled desire. Derrida's text is an early example of linking language and biography (as reflected also in recent sociolinguistic work, e.g. Busch (2012) and Blommaert and Backus (2013)), and emphasizes the way in which languages exist in hierarchical relationships to one another.

As in the case of Fanon, Derrida's argument is influenced by his own experience of colonial domination: the monolingualism of the other is, first and foremost, a Euro-centric monolingualism that is imposed in the historical context of colonialism. Derrida sees coloniality as a fundamental social condition, rather than a specific historical process of racialization and exploitation (he differs from Fanon in this respect). Thus, according to Derrida, all cultural forms are essentially colonizing, and language is never fully ours: it always comes from others, it is given to us, but it also subjects us and controls us. Because of this fundamental coloniality, no one – even the so-called 'native speakers' – can ever be a full master of their own language. Derrida describes a radical linguistic homelessness, a homelessness which is most clearly visible in the colonial encounter where the language of the colonizer was imposed and diversity silenced. Thus, colonialism emerges as an epistemological lens, which allows us to see the 'homo-hegemony' (Derrida's term) that has been at the core of European modernity: the creation of a linguistically unified nation state, the imposition of monolingualism, and the reduction of diversity and plurality to homogeneity. Rey Chow (2014: 41) captures this in her work on the postcolonial experience as follows:

> The colonial situation has, if unwittingly, conferred upon the colonized the privilege of a certain prescience – the grasp how artificially and artifactually, rather than naturally, language works and can work in the first place.

Another recent strand of sociolinguistic theorizing that comes out of Africa and the African diaspora emphasizes, via the philosophical concept of ubuntu, the deep and fundamental *relationality* of all being and all agency.[2] Thus, while Guy, a North American scholar, sees a strong need to bring 'speakers' back into our linguistic explanations – a view that we might call anthropocentric – ubuntu philosophy emphasizes communication not as the agency of individuals, but as the complex ethical expression of our relations to others, including humans and animals as well as diverse 'objects' (things, places, time, practices, languages; see Wiredu 2008; Chirindo 2016; Makalela 2016). The focus, in other words, is not on the intentions and agency of individuals, but on interactions between people, as well as between people and the object/natural world.

The notion of relation is also fundamental to the work of the Caribbean philosopher Glissant (1997, also Britton 1999). He links relation – the fact that we exist first and foremost as part of a plurality, not as singularities – to that of entanglement (Fr. *intrication*). Relation and entanglement refer to an intimate sense of being twisted together: not as separate bodies (as speakers and social agents who do things), but in a complex togetherness of bodies, objects and ideas. Neither relation nor entanglement is something we can move in and out of, something we can choose or resist; rather, it is fundamental to our being in the world. And not only is it ontological, it is also the basis of an ethical life. Bringing ethics back into the social sciences is a fairly recent move, a break with the traditions of positivism and descriptivism, and a return to a social science which aims to contribute to a better life (Keane 2016). The very title of this chapter 'English and its social relations' could thus be read as 'English and all that [languages, people, animals, spaces, objects, technologies, etc.] it is in some form of ethical relation with'. Disentanglement from these relations is impossible and our task as sociolinguists is to understand them, theoretically and practically.

The idea of relation expresses a sense of lived, everyday philosophy. Drawing on folk knowledges (also referred to as 'Indigenous Knowledge Systems') in the formulation of social theory is not limited to southern contributions to knowledge, but also informs, for example, Bent Flyvbjerg's (2001, also Flyvbjerg et al. 2012) idea of 'real social science'; that is, social (and sociolinguistic) theory, that is rooted in the everyday wisdom, morality and ethics of those who participate in social life. In other words, when trying to understand language, we should not only listen to the theories articulated by scholars, but also to everyday, practical theories that are articulated by social actors. And we should not forget that scholars are social actors as well: they are not looking in from the outside, they are co-participants in social life. In the remainder of this chapter I will look at three core topics in sociolinguistics: indexicality, ideologies and inequalities. These are topics which have shaped the history of the discipline, and which remain central to contemporary work.

Core issues 1: indexicality, variation and social meaning

Penny Eckert (2016) has described variation as central to language because it allows speakers to express diverse meanings in interaction. In a nutshell, different linguistic forms carry, or index, different meanings. For example, referring to a traffic light as a 'robot' might suggest that the speaker comes from South Africa, or has spent time there. In other words, the choice of a particular lexical item suggests that the speaker is a person from Y, or a person who has been to Y, or maybe a person who has heard about linguistic practices in Y and tries to emulate them. Drawing on the semiotic theories of the American philosopher Charles Sanders Peirce, sociolinguists refer to such forms as indexicals (Silverstein 2003). An important characteristic of indexicals is that the meanings they express are non-denotational: they do not simply reference something that exists in the world (a traffic light), but additionally index, or 'point to', sociocultural or affective meanings. Thus, by referring to a traffic light as a 'robot', speakers might index a particular geopolitical space in which English was acquired, and thus point to an aspect of their linguistic biography. They might also index belonging to a group, a sense of identity and/or a feeling of solidarity. In this sense, indexicals do not simply reflect pre-existing contexts ('a person who has been to, or knows about, Y'), but also create new contexts and communities (and thus new meanings, 'a person who has an emotional attachment to Y'). It is important to realize that all linguistic forms index meaning: while 'robot' indexes local identities, speaking about a 'traffic light' in South Africa might index awareness of standard norms, and thus also produces a certain type of speaker, a social persona. As noted by Michael Silverstein (2016: 56): '[i]n every possible communicative situation, one is at all times speaking *as someone*, that is, indexing all manner of sociological category-types made relevant' (emphasis in the original).

Indexical meanings can also be carried by linguistic units smaller than a word or a morpheme. Consider the pronunciation of the fricative /th/ as a stop /d/. Saying [də] instead of [ðə] does not change the referential meaning of the utterance (both pronunciations refer to the determiner 'the'), but carries with it other types of meaning. It can, for example, indicate a second-language speaker of English, a speaker of African American English (or a speaker who wishes to sound like a speaker of African American English), a speaker of Nigerian Pidgin, and so forth. This list of possible or potential meanings suggest that meanings are always under-specified or indeterminate: linguistic forms can mean different things in different contexts. Thus, to say [də] can be an affirmation of identity, the expression of a desire for an identity, or the mocking of a stigmatized identity. Meaning can also be emergent: to say [də] might not be part of my habitual way of speaking, but to produce [də] in interaction might echo my interlocutor's pronunciation – a process social psychologists call 'accommodation' – and thus become a sign of reaching out and creating communality and relation (Giles et al. 1991).

While early work has typically focused on individual variables, recent work has begun to look at the ways in which diverse of linguistic forms work together in the formation of registers (Agha 2007). Register is a musical metaphor, originally referring to the range (relative height) of a voice or an instrument. Thus, the same melodic sequence can be rendered differently, depending on the register of the performer. Similarly, the same denotational or interactional content (for example, a greeting) can be articulated differently, and we have distinct, indexically contrastive ways of saying (or writing) the same (e.g. 'good morning, madam' versus 'hi there'). Moreover, these ways of speaking/writing co-vary with other aspects of our social presentation (such as dress and bodily demeanour). Thus, what we call 'languages' are in reality complex assemblages of diverse registers, which tend to co-vary with other contextual factors, in different local settings and at different times (Silverstein 2016; see also Eckert (2016) on the relationship between register and style). Moreover, registers exist not only within languages, but also across languages. Examples of this are 'mixed' registers such as Singaporean English, Spanglish (US) or Sheng (Kenya).

Indexicalities are often contested and even contradictory. It is for this reason that Jane Hill (2005, 2008, following Ochs 1990) makes a distinction between 'direct indexicality' and 'indirect indexicality' in her work on language and racism. Direct indexicality refers to the overtly intended meaning of linguistic forms. Indirect indexicality, on the other hand, refers to meaning that is not directly acknowledged, but rather works through implicit associations. Consider the Spanish word *mañana* ('tomorrow', 'morning') in the following branding example for an annual music festival:

> *Mañana Mañana. Het meest relaxte festival van Nederland* ('Mañana Mañana. The most relaxed festival in the Netherlands'; www.mananamanana.eu).

Hill (2005) has shown that *mañana* is an old borrowing in American English (going back to the nineteenth century), and is commonly used to index a sense of laid-backness. Thus, for a monolingual White speaker of American English to say something like 'I'll do that *mañana*' indexes a social persona to the audience who is relaxed and laid-back, with a cosmopolitan sense of humour (direct indexicality). Similarly, the *Mañana Mañana* festival, drawing on these globalized meanings of *mañana,* is all about being relaxed and chilled, enjoying 'dancing, drinking, making fire and even to catch a fish' (*dansen, drinken, vuurtje stoken en zelf een visje vangen*). Or consider the webpage *alwaysmanana.com*, which provides a portal for English-speaking expatriates in Spain, and shows on its logo a smiling donkey, a bright sun and a palm tree with a hammock. Again, associations of relaxation, of being unhurried, are intended and clearly visible. These meanings, argues Hill, are not innocent, but linked to long-standing racist stereotypes of Latin American laziness and procrastination. Thus, by uttering a phrase such as 'I'll do that *mañana*', the speaker not only indexes laid-backness, but also reproduces – and thus normalizes – a racial stereotype (indirect indexicality). *Mañana,* and other forms of what Hill calls 'Mock Spanish', work similar to 'blackface' performances; they are linguistic examples of the hegemonic appropriation (and indeed some may say 'theft') of black cultural resources by white people. According to Hill, indirect indexicality is important for understanding racism (and other *-isms*, such as sexism or ageism) in language: few people still resort to racist slurs, yet pejorative racial stereotypes linger, and their indexicalities work even when speakers claim (with all sincerity) that they did not intend to offend anyone, that they did not intend to be racist (on language and racism see also Weber (2015), Alim et al. (2016); on mock language, see also Deumert (2014, chapter 4)).

Core issues 2: language ideologies

For much of the twentieth century, sociolinguists approached language as a social fact; that is, as a communal practice which is characterized by cross-individual regularities and patterns of usage. In order to uncover these regularities of usage, sociolinguists were advised to record what Labov (1972) called 'the vernacular': maximally unselfconscious, 'natural' or unmonitored, ways of speaking. Moreover, sociolinguists were advised not to trust what people themselves said about language. People's views about language(s) were seen as unreliable and reflecting prejudice, thus standing in opposition to the expert academic knowledge produced by linguists (a view that goes back to Boas (1911)).

Assumptions about method and what counts as data changed quite fundamentally in the 1980s and 1990s, when scholars began to pay attention to people's ordinary ability to step back and reflect on language and linguistic practices. They also began to be interested in non-habitual uses of language. Influenced by work in linguistic anthropology on performance, sociolinguists became interested in those moments in interaction where a speaker would 'put on' a particular accent, play around with language, or engage in 'spectacular' and 'artful' linguistic displays (Bauman 1977; Rampton 1995; Coupland 2007; Finnegan 2015). Often these displays are short-lived events, removed from the flow of ordinary interaction, but they are nevertheless important for understanding the ways in which social meaning can be expressed by drawing, quite strategically and self-consciously, on the complex indexicalities of language. In addition to documenting and analysing habitual and non-habitual language practices, sociolinguists are also turning their attention to the beliefs, or ideologies, people hold about language in general, and specific languages in particular. People's views about language are no longer seen as unreliable, but as shaping the social world, including the ways in which language is used, and changes (Kroskrity 2010).

Thinking about English and its social relations brings to mind a particular relation, a relation that is hierarchical and infused with power. This is the relation between UK/US standard English and a multitude of other ways of speaking English that exist around the world. For sociolinguists, the 'standard' – the type of language that is taught in school and evaluated as 'correct' – is just one way of speaking among many; it is neither worse nor better than other ways of speaking. Yet it is also a sociolinguistic fact that standard English is often seen as being 'better', and other ways of speaking English might be described as 'illogical', 'uneducated', 'lazy' and so forth (Lippi-Green 2012; Milroy and Milroy 2012). Such evaluations are reflexive rationalizations of social indexicals as discussed in Section 4.

In the processes of colonialism and globalization standard English came to carry additional meanings such as being 'developed', 'civilized', 'modern' or 'fashionable', while local languages were often seen as 'backward' and 'traditional'. However, ideologies, like anything else in the social world, are never uniform and one-dimensional: thus English might be 'modern', but it can also be experienced as 'alienating' or 'cold'; local languages might be 'backward', but they can express solidarity and identity. Janet McIntosh (2010: 339) describes such a situation for Kenya, with particular reference to language choices in text messages:

> English and local African languages can become foils for each other in particularly vivid ways, suggesting that ... English ... contrasts with Kigiriama [one of the local languages]: It dramatizes a fantasy of unfettered freedom, whereas Kigiriama comes to dramatize the local, the social, and the respectful.

Ideologies can be explicitly formulated as corrections ('don't say x'), as value judgements ('X is a beautiful/ugly language'), or as moral evaluations ('what a friendly voice!'). In other cases, ideologies are more implicit: they can be seen in the reaction to certain ways of speaking, they are evident in the choices we make, and in the ways in which we rationalize ways of speaking as 'desirable' or 'appropriate' for specific social personae. For example, Eckert (2016: 73) reflects on certain linguistic choices she made in the context of her professional career. When she obtained her first academic position following her PhD in 1978, she was one of just a few female academics at the university, and in order to be taken 'seriously' she lowered her pitch, made her voice sound deeper. This choice was not the result of a personal preference, but reflected beliefs and ideologies about what counts as authoritative language. At the time, academic authority was still firmly in the hands of men, and men have a deeper pitch than women; consequently, an authoritative voice became associated with – was indexed by – a certain pitch range (on gender and language ideologies, see Cameron (2014)). These examples show clearly that ideologies and indexicals work closely together: indexicals are able to do the communicative work they do because they are tied to explicit or implicit ideologies about language. The examples also show that ideologies about language are rarely about language alone: they are commentaries on social questions (ranging from education and class to modernity and tradition, gender and voice), and often serve to justify and naturalize existing inequalities and hierarchies.

An interesting aspect of language ideologies is that they often attribute sensuous or experiential qualities to language (Gal 2013). For example, some words in English might be seen as 'hard' or 'big'; a style that favours short sentences might be considered 'plain', while a smooth-talking style that makes use of many embellishing adjectives might be described as 'sugary' or even 'oily'. Sensuous qualities are also projected onto whole languages: English speakers might perceive German as 'harsh', Italian as 'musical', and French as 'sexy'. Similarly, speakers of other languages also project ideologies onto English. In nineteenth-century

South Africa, the Afrikaner nationalist du Toit (1891) argued that the imperialist character of the British colonial government was directly reflected in the English language, including its visual representation (orthography). Thus, du Toit sees, for example, the capitalization of 'I' not simply as an orthographic convention, but as a reflection of 'arrogance and selfishness' (*anmatiging en selfsug*). The further fact that English orthography does not reflect pronunciation was seen as an example of 'untrustworthiness' (*onvertroubaarheit*); and what he perceives as an abundance of /s/ sounds in English reminds him of the hissing of a snake (an animal that, in Christian mythology, is of a cunning nature). Thus, du Toit imbues linguistic forms with meaning that, in turn, is projected onto speakers. This is an instantiation of the familiar nineteenth-century European ideology that languages reflect, quite directly and indeed stereotypically, perceived national culture and characteristics. This example also illustrates the fact that language ideologies (just like any other linguistic practices) exist in time and place: they are not universal, but changeable. Today, du Toit's arguments might sound amusing, but at the time they echoed with deeply held beliefs about language and national identity.

The turn to language ideologies is a move that is in line with a sociolinguistics that recognizes speakers/hearers as theorists of language (see Section 3). As noted by Susan Gal (2016: 131):

> Language ideological approaches resist the temptation that the 'linguist knows best' or that there is 'a view from nowhere' . . . It forces analysts to listen to the valuations of speakers.

Language-ideological approaches also draw attention to the ideologies of linguists. An example of this is the way in which changing designations reflect not only academic preoccupations and interests but also assumptions and beliefs about language. For instance, there has been a move away from the idea of 'languages' (as countable objects and rule-based systems) to 'repertoires' (reflecting combinations of linguistic resources that are strategically employed in interactions). Getting away from seeing language as a bounded object is generally felt to be an important move, but the notion of repertoires brings with it its own problems and blind spots. As argued by Jon Orman (2013), 'repertoire' carries with it individualistic and mentalistic approaches to language, whereas 'language' emphasizes the communal and social aspects of language use.

Core issues 3: diversity and inequality

The philosopher Kwame Anthony Appiah (1991: 356) once described social scientists, especially those writing about the global South and other historically marginalized populations, as 'otherness-machines', 'with the manufacturing of alterity as our principal role'. This is an important observation. The methodological shift away from habits and patterns of speech, and the attention directed at unusual and spectacular language (discussed in the previous section), carries with it the danger of an ideology of exoticism, a belief that difference rather than similarity is interesting and worth writing about. This is evident, for example, in the study of youth languages, which are often positioned as unique and unusual in their hybridity (combing diverse linguistic forms) and creativity (the invention of new forms; Cornips et al. 2015). Yet youth languages are only unique and unusual if we assume something else to be normal; in this case, the standard norm of a language and the speech habits of middle-class adults. In other words, difference needs the foil of normality to become visible, and this reinforces existing stereotypes of us-and-them.

Appiah links the manufacturing of difference to one of the core effects of modernity: the fundamental economization of everyday life. In modern, capitalist economies, differentiation is central to economic success: products – including cultural products – must be distinguished from other products to be valuable. A focus on such economic-ideological processes is evident in much recent work on multilingualism (Duchêne and Heller 2012; Park and Wee 2012; on linguistic markets see also the foundational work by Bourdieu (1986)). In contemporary consumer societies, cultural diversity – understood as the harmonious co-presence of difference – is highly valued, and diversity discourses abound in politics, management studies and education (Piller 2016). Consider the online self-representation of Henkel, a German company, which positions diversity as a competitive advantage:

> As a globally operating company, Henkel employs people from 125 nations in more than 75 countries. More than 80 percent of them work outside of Germany ... The diversity of our employees and their individual differences, whether regarding their cultural origins, gender, generation, religious orientation or differing values, abilities and experiences, is essential to our strength and innovative capabilities.[3]

A commitment to diversity is generally seen as 'good' because it positions the speaker (or the institution) as tolerant, cosmopolitan, open and inclusive, and in this case also 'innovative'. In other words, portraying oneself as respectful of diversity creates a particular social persona (and of course, rejecting diversity creates a social persona too). Henkel does not mention language, and indeed linguistic diversity is strangely absent from the short text. Other companies, however, foreground language and linguistic diversity. An example of this is Delta's 2016 in-flight video, *Global Safety*.[4] In the video, passengers are greeted by a racially diverse crew in English, Spanish and Japanese. This is followed by the safety instructions which are communicated in English, spoken with various non-native accents.

A helpful concept when analysing examples of multilingual advertising is Helen Kelly-Holmes's (2014: 139) idea of the 'linguistic fetish', a concept that she developed in conversation with Karl Marx's well-known work on the 'commodity fetish'. Consider this example: a chair, made by a carpenter, is an object to sit on. In paying money for it, I reward the carpenter for their labour. However, if I start desiring a particular chair, which might have a unique shape but did not take longer to be produced, and I am willing to pay more money for it because of its distinctive look, then I am entering the world of commodity fetishism. This is a world where the value of an object is no longer simply linked to its use-value, and its production time, but to its difference from other objects. Kelly-Holmes argues that similar processes also work in language. Fetishization creates symbolic value that goes beyond what is communicated referentially: it draws on the broader indexicalities of language and imbues them with economically productive value. Thus, if the greetings in the Delta video were all in English, it would fail to communicate the kind of cosmopolitanism that is intended by saying: *hola* or *kon'nichiwa*. Fetishization commercializes indexicality, and the inclusion of different languages positions Delta in particular ways: we are a global airline, we are inclusive, we are cosmopolitan, be our customer, fly with us!

In the Delta video diversity is represented not only through the fetishization of different languages, but also through the fetishization of accents. In principle this is a positive move: by including different ways of speaking English, the video normalizes the historically stigmatized and marginalized persona of the migrant, and recasts English-with-an-accent as cosmopolitan and global; gone are associations of lack of education or other negative stereotypes. The video thus contrasts positively with an earlier video produced by United Airlines (*Safety Is Global* 2014). The latter also includes greetings in different languages and boasts a racially diverse flight crew. Yet otherwise its language is monolithic: everyone speaks standard American English. However, a closer look at the Delta video reveals that the diversity presented is of a particular kind. Quite invisible, for example, are accents of English that are not the result of migration-related (adult) second language acquisition, but that represent the appropriation of English by people of colour. Jade, the black flight attendant from the UK, speaks in a rather posh British accent (described by a YouTube commentator as 'typically British'); Queshan, the Black flight attendant from the US, uses standard American English; and, much to the disappointment of one of the YouTube commentators, Imran (from India) doesn't 'even have an Indian accent'. This can be seen as a progressive decision as it breaks with stereotypes of racially typical ways of speaking. Yet at the same time it is also an example of linguistic whitewashing. Thus, the very real linguistic histories of colonialism and slavery are elided. English is either standard in its pronunciation, or the 'accent' is the result of second language acquisition. It is an accent that does not challenge the norm too much as it is transient: it is the voice of the foreigner, or the first generation migrant (whose children will grow up speaking the local American way). It is not the sedimented reminder of centuries of oppression and marginalization, a shibboleth that defines 'the other' and reminds us of the fact that, throughout history, certain types of difference have been dealt with in violent ways.

However, long-standing inequalities and injustices don't disappear easily. They cannot be glossed over with a good soundtrack and the celebration of a globalized diversity. In its representation of a specific form of diversity the Delta video also excludes: that is to say, not all accents, and not all languages, are equally welcomed. In December 2016, a new theme appeared in the YouTube comment section of the video: language-linked discrimination and racism. One comment reads:

> Delta Airlines Sucks ... They kick 2 guys out of the plane just because they spoke in different language DELTA AIRLINES SUCKS.

The comment was posted in reaction to a claim made by Adam Saleh, a well-known YouTube vblogger, that he was removed from a Delta flight after speaking Arabic on the plane. Saleh's statement has since been debunked as a prank. However, other people were indeed removed from flights (and one could argue that Saleh, by performing such a removal, meant to draw attention to these cases). An example is Khairuldeen Makhzoomi who was, reportedly, escorted off a Southwest Airlines flight in early 2016. A fellow passenger had reported him because she believed that he had made threatening statements while speaking Arabic on the phone. There was also the experience of Nazia Ali and her husband who, for the same reason, were escorted off a Delta flight from Paris to Cincinnati. In both cases the phone conversations had been to relatives and nothing threatening was said.[5]

Diversity, in other words, is a troubling concept: it sounds good and progressive, but in the end only certain diversities count, and deep inequalities persist. Thus, the American journalist Jeff Chang (2016) asked recently: 'What would diversity that liberated *everyone* look like?' (my emphasis). We might rephrase this with a linguistic slant: What does it mean to have linguistic justice? What kind of ideal or vision might we be striving towards? In a chapter titled *Report from an Underdeveloped Country,* Dell Hymes (1996: 64) provides a critical perspective on linguistic justice in the United States and outlines his vision for linguistic social justice as follows:

> Two ingredients of a vision [for linguistic social justice] are longstanding. One is a kind of negative freedom, freedom from denial of opportunity due to something linguistic, whether in speaking or reading or writing. One is a kind of positive freedom, freedom for satisfaction in the use of language, for language to be a source of imaginative life and

> satisfying form. In my own mind I would unite the two kinds of freedom in the notion of voice: freedom to have one's voice heard, freedom to develop a voice worth hearing. One way to think of the society in which one would like to live is to think of the kinds of voices it would have.

What is important in Hymes' reflection is the idea of 'voice': linguistic justice is not only about different languages and their place in the world (for example, by granting official status to more languages, designating them as medium of instruction in schools, or making them visible in public spaces), but also about being able to articulate oneself; it is about expression, just as much as it is about representation and visibility. In other words, a diversity that liberates everyone is not an exercise in impression management, but a commitment to creating voice, to enabling people to communicate in the ways they wish to communicate, without experiencing inequalities, or a sense of alienation (*pace* Fanon; see also the idea of linguistic citizenship, developed by Stroud (2001, 2015)).

To return to the question of English and its social relations: the Delta video visualizes a sub-set of these relations as part of a marketing exercise; it affirms certain diversities and silences others. It presents a comfortable and comforting view of diversity, a view that Emi Otsuji and Alistair Pennycook (2010: 244) have called 'happy hybridity'. Yet if we could bring in all relations together, if we could give equal voice to everyone, the picture might not be quite as 'happy' or 'harmonious'. There might be contestation, there might be critique. The voices we develop when we grant the freedom to be heard, and the freedom to 'develop a voice worth hearing', might sometimes jar, they might disrupt one another and challenge one another, they might sometimes make us feel uncomfortable or even anxious, but in allowing them we might get a bit closer to linguistic social justice.

Conclusion: old and new

In his article 'Why decoloniality in the 21st century?', Sabelo Ndlovu-Gatsheni (2013: 11) argues that mainstream academic work often reflects 'knowledges of equilibrium', and contrasts this with what he calls decoloniality or 'knowledges of disequilibrium':

> [Knowledges of equilibrium] do not question methodologies as well as the present asymmetrical world order. In decoloniality research methods and methodologies are never accepted as neutral but are unmasked as technologies of subjectivation if not surveillance tools that prevent the emergence of another-thinking, another-logic and another-worldview.

Sociolinguistics – reflecting a diversity of research topics, methodologies and theories – seems well-suited to such an approach, for a stance of epistemological disobedience. Yet at the same time, many scholars remain deeply invested in existing paradigms and often limit the development of a more global sociolinguistics to a critical refinement of existing (northern) theories and approaches (as evident in, for example, Ball 2010). The view of sociolinguistics presented in this chapter is, in part, deliberately unorthodox, emphasizing scholars (Fanon, Derrida, Glissant) who are not usually part of 'introductions' to the discipline. At the same time more orthodox and established themes have been discussed (indexicality, ideologies, inequality). This dialectic between that which is established and known, and that which is developing and new, suggests that, like many other disciplines in the social sciences, sociolinguistics will continue to be driven by a mix of the old and the new, by 'knowledges of equilibrium' and 'knowledges of disequilibrium'. We might want to think not simply about 'English and its social relations', but about 'sociolinguistics and its social relations'. These relations stretch in space and time; they include early thinkers on language and society, as well as contemporary theorists. They draw on data from diverse contexts (metropolitan and postcolonial) as well as theories about language from these places. The future of sociolinguistics is global.

Notes

1 A first step in this direction was made in 2016 at a British Academy conference: 'Distant and Neglected Voices. Women in the History of Linguistics' (www.britac.ac.uk/events/distant-and-neglected-voices-women-history-linguistics).
2 *Ubuntu*, like most philosophical concepts 'defies a single definition' (More 2004: 156); in its most basic meaning it refers to the ethical quality of being human-in-relation-with-others. Its root is *-ntu*, which indicates an ontological state of being in the world (and this root is shared among a large number of southern African languages).
3 www.henkel.com/sustainability/put-into-practice/our-diversity-is-our-strength.
4 www.youtube.com/watch?v=IFG-XllVS7w.
5 www.independent.co.uk/news/world/americas/muslim-passenger-southwest-airlines-khairuldeen-makhzoom-arabic-phone-uncle-baghdad-cair-statement-a7347311.html; www.pastemagazine.com/articles/2016/12/muslims-traveling-by-air-in-the-united-states-are.html.

Further reading

Agha, A. (2007) *Language and Social Relations*. Cambridge: Cambridge University Press. Explores the role of language in social life, drawing on examples from a wide range of social and geopolitical contexts.

Bell, A. (2013) *The Guidebook to Sociolinguistics*. Oxford: Wiley/Blackwell. A comprehensive and accessible introduction to the field of sociolinguistics.

Coupland, N. (ed.) (2016) *Sociolinguistics: Theoretical Debates*. Cambridge: Cambridge University Press. Provides an overview of current debates and discussions in sociolinguistics.

Piller, I. (2016) *Linguistic Diversity and Social Justice. An Introduction to Applied Sociolinguistics*. Oxford: Oxford University Press. Discusses, through various case studies, the ways in which language is implied in structures of inequality in society.

Related topics

- English and colonialism
- English and multilingualism: a contested history
- English and social identity
- Language, gender and sexuality.

References

Agha, A. (2007) *Language and Social Relations*. Cambridge: CUP.

Alim, S., J. R. Rickford and A. Ball (2016) *Raciolinguistics*. Oxford: OUP.

Althusser, L. (1971) 'Ideology and ideological state apperatuses', in L. Althusser, *Lenin and Philosophy and Other Essays*. New York: Monthly Review Press, 121–176.

Appiah, K. A. (1991) 'Is the post- in postmodernism the post- in postcolonial?', *Critical Inquiry* 17: 336–357.

Ball, M. J. (2010) *Handbook of Sociolinguistics Around the World*. London: Routledge.

Bell, A. (2013) *The Guidebook to Sociolinguistics*. Oxford: Wiley/Blackwell.

Bauman, R. (1977) *Verbal Art as Performance*. Prospects Heights, IL: Waveland.

Blommaert, J. and A. Backus (2013) 'Superdiverse repertoires and the individual', in I. Saint-Georges and J. J. Weber (eds), *Multilingualism and Multimodality*. Dordrecht: Sense Publishers, 11–32.
Boas, F. (1911) 'Introduction', in F. Boas (ed.), *Handbook of North American Indian Languages*. Bureau of American Ethnology: Bulletin 40. Washington: Government Print Office, 1–83.
Bourdieu, P. (1986) 'The forms of capital', in J. Richardson (ed.), *Handbook of Theory and Research for the Sociology of Education*. New York: Greenwood, 241–258.
Britton, C. (1999) *Eduard Glissant and Postcolonial Theory*. Charlottesville/London: University of Virginia Press.
Busch, B. (2012) 'The linguistic repertoire revisited', *Applied Linguistics* 33: 503–523.
Cameron, D. (2014) 'Gender and language ideologies', in S. Ehrlich, M. Meyerhoff and J. Holmes (eds), *Handbook of Language, Gender and Sexuality*. 2nd edn. Oxford: Wiley, 281–296.
Chang, J. (2016) *We Gon' Be Alright. Notes on Race and Resegregation*. London: Picador.
Chirindo, K. (2016) 'Bantu sociolinguistics in Wangari Maathai's peacebuilding rhetoric', *Women's Studies in Communication* 39: 442–459.
Chomsky, N. (1965) *Aspects of the Theory of Syntax*. Cambridge, MA: MIT Press.
Chow, R. (2014) *Not Like a Native Speaker. On Languaging as a Postcolonial Experience*. New York: Columbia University Press.
Connell, R. (2007) *Southern Theory: The Global Dynamics of Knowledge in the Social Science*. Cambridge: Polity.
Cornips, L., J. Jaspers and V. de Rooij (2015) 'The politics of labelling youth vernaculars in the Netherlands and Belgium', in J. Nortier and B. A. Svendsen (eds), *Language, Youth and Identity in the 21st Century. Linguistic Practices across Urban Spaces*. Cambridge: Cambridge University Press, 45–70.
Coupland, N. (2007) *Style: Language Variation and Identity*. Cambridge: CUP.
Derrida, J. ([1996] 1998) *Monolingualism of the Other or the Prosthesis of Origin*. Stanford: Stanford University Press.
Du Bois, W. E. B. (1903) *The Souls of Black Folk. Essays and Sketches*. Chicago: A.C. McClurg & Co.
Deumert, A. (2013) 'Language, culture and society', in K. Allan (ed.), *The Oxford Handbook of the History of Linguistics*. Oxford: Oxford University Press, 655–674.
Deumert, A. (2014) *Sociolinguistics and Mobile Communication*. Edinburgh: EUP.
Duchêne, A. and M. Heller (eds) (2012) *Language in Late Capitalism: Pride and Profit*. London: Routledge.
Du Toit, S. J. (1891) *Afrikaans Ons Volkstaal. 72 theses, of Stellinge, Neergeleg en Verklaar*. Paarl: D.F. du Toit.
Eckert, P. (2016) 'Variation, meaning and social change', in N. Coupland (ed.), *Sociolinguistics: Theoretical Debates*. Cambridge: CUP, 68–85.
Falk, J. (1999) *Women, Language and Linguistics. Three American Stories From the First Half of the Twentieth Century*. London: Routledge.
Fanon, F. ([1952] 2008) *Black Skin, White Masks*. London: Pluto.
Fanon, F. ([1961] 1967) *The Wretched of the Earth*. New York: Grove.
Figueroa, E. (1994) *Sociolinguistic Metatheory*. Oxford: Pergamon.
Finnegan, R. (2015) *Where is Language? An Anthropologist's Questions on Language, Literature and Performance*. London: Bloomsbury.
Flyvbjerg, B. (2001) *Making Social Science Matter: Why Social Inquiry Fails and How it Can* Succeed Again. Cambridge: CUP.
Flyvbjerg, B., T. Landman and S. Schram (2012) *Real Social Science: Applied Phronesis*. Cambridge: CUP.
Gal, S. (2013) 'Tastes of talk: Qualia and the moral flavor of signs', *Anthropological Theory* 13: 31–48.
Gal, S. (2016) 'Sociolinguistic differentiation', in N. Coupland (ed.), *Sociolinguistics: Theoretical Debates*. Cambridge: CUP, 113–138.
Giles, H., J. Coupland and N. Coupland (eds) (1991) *Contexts of Accommodation: Developments in Applied Sociolinguistics*. Cambridge: CUP.
Glissant, É. (1997) *The Poetics of Relation*. Translated by B. Wing. Ann Arbor: University of Michigan Press.
Go, J. (2013) 'For a postcolonial sociology', *Theory and Society* 42: 25–55.
Guy, G. R. (1996) 'Preface', in G. R. Guy, C. Feagin, D. Schiffrin and J. Baugh (eds), *Towards a Social Science of Language: Papers in Honor of William Labov. Volume 2: Social Interaction and Discourse Structures*. Amsterdam/New York: Benjamins, ix–xiv.

Haraway, D. (2008) *When Species Meet*. Minneapolis: University of Minnesota Press.
Hill, J. (2005) 'Intertextuality as source and evidence for indirect indexical meanings', *Journal of Linguistic Anthropology* 15: 113–124.
Hill, J. (2008) *The Everyday Language of White Racism*. Oxford: Wiley/Blackwell.
Hountondji, P. J. (1997) *Endogenous Knowledge: Research Trails*. Dakar: COSESRIA.
Hymes, D. (1996) *Ethnography, Linguistics, Narrative Inequality: Toward an Understanding of Voice*. London: Taylor Francis.
Keane, W. (2016) *Ethical Life: Its Natural and Social Histories*. Princeton: Princeton University Press.
Kelly-Holmes, H. (2014) Linguistic fetish: The sociolinguistics of visual multilingualism', in D. Machin (ed.), *Visual Communication*. Berlin: De Guyter, 135–152.
Kirksey, S. E. and S. Helmreich. 2010. 'The emergence of multispecies ethnography', *Cultural Anthropology* 25: 545–576.
Kohn, E. (2013) *How Forests Think: Towards an Anthropology Beyond the Human*. Berkeley: University of California Press.
Kroskrity, P. V. (2010) 'Language ideologies—evolving perspectives', in J. Jaspers, J.-A. Östman and J. Verschuren (eds), *Society and Language Use*. Amsterdam/New York: Benjamins, 192–211.
Labov, W. (1972) *Sociolinguistic Patterns*. Philadelphia: University of Pennsylvania Press.
Lippi-Green, R. (2012) *English with an Accent. Language, Ideology and Discrimination in the United States*. 2nd edn. London: Routledge.
Machin, D. (2014) (ed.), *Visual Communication*. Berlin: De Guyter.
Makalela, L. (2016) 'Moving out of linguistic boxes: The effects of translanguaging strategies for multilingual classrooms', *Language and Education* 29: 200–217.
Mazrui, A. (1993) 'Language and the quest for liberation in Africa: The legacy of Frantz Fanon', *Third World Quarterly* 14 (2): 351–363.
Mazrui, A. (2006) 'A sociolinguistics of "double-consciousness": English and ethnicity in the black experience', in J. Brutt-Griffler and C. E. Davies (eds), *English and Ethnicity*. New York: Palgrave, 49–74.
McIntosh, J. (2010) 'Mobile phones and Mipoho's prophecy: The powers and dangers of flying language', *American Ethnologist* 37: 337–353.
McNamara, T. (2010) 'Reading Derrida: Language, identity and violence. *Applied Linguistics Review* 1: 23–44.
Mignolo, W. D. (2008) 'Epistemic disobedience, independent thought and de-colonial freedom', *Theory, Culture and Society* 26: 1–23.
Milroy, J. and L. Milroy (2012) *Authority in Language. Investigation Standard English*. London/New York: Routledge.
More, M. P. (2004) 'Philosophy in South Africa under and after apartheid', in K. Wiredu (ed.), *A Companion to African Philosophy*. Oxford: Blackwell, 149–160.
Murray, S. O. (1998) *American Sociolinguistics: Theory and Theory Groups*. Amsterdam/New York: John Benjamins.
Ndlovu-Gatsheni, S. (2013) 'Why decoloniality in the 21st century?', *The Thinker* 48: 10–15.
Ochs, E. (1990) 'Indexicality and socialization', in J. W. Stigler, R. A. Shweder and G. Herdt (eds), *Cultural Psychology*. Cambridge: CUP, 287–308.
Orman, J. (2013) 'New lingualisms, same old codes', *Language Sciences* 37: 90–98.
Otsuji, E. and A. Pennycook. (2010) 'Metrolingualism: Fixity, fluidity and language in flux', *International Journal of Multilingualism* 7: 240–254.
Park, J. S-Y. and L. Wee (2012) *Markets of English. Linguistic Capital and Language Policy in a Globalizing World*. London: Routledge.
Pennycook, A. (1998) *English and the Discourses of Colonialism*. London: Routledge.
Phillipson, R. (1992) *Linguistic Imperialism*. Oxford: OUP.
Phillipson, R. (2013) *Linguistic Imperialism Continued*. London: Routledge.
Piller, I. (2016) *Linguistic Diversity and Social Justice. An Introduction to Applied Sociolinguistics*. Oxford: OUP.
Pupavac, V. (2012) *Language Rights: From Free Speech to Linguistic Governance*. London: Palgrave.
Rampton, B. (1995) *Crossing: Language and Ethnicity among Adolescents*. London: Longman.
Safety Is Global (2014) United Airlines inflight safety video. Available at: www.youtube.com/watch?v=dXsUrFJ3n6E.
Santos, B. de S. (2014) *Epistemologies of the South: Justice Against Epistemicide*. London: Paradigm/Routledge.

Smith, L. T. (1999) *Decolonizing Methodologies. Research and Indigenous People*. London/New York: Zed.

Silverstein, M. (2003) 'Indexical order and the dialectics of sociolinguistic life', *Language & Communication* 23 (3): 193–229.

Silverstein, M. (2016) 'The "push" of Lautgesetze and the "pull" of enregisterment', in N. Coupland (ed.), *Sociolinguistics: Theoretical Debates*, 37–67. Cambridge: CUP.

Smakman, D. and P. Heinrich (eds) (2015) *Globalizing Sociolinguistics. Challenging and Expanding Theory*. London: Routledge.

Stroud, C. (2001) 'African mother-tongue programmes and the politics of language: Linguistic citizenship versus linguistic human rights', *Journal of Multilingual and Multicultural Development* 22: 339–355.

Stroud, C. (2015) 'Linguistic citizenship as Utopia', *Multilingual Margins* 2: 20–37.

Van Herk, G. (2012) *What Is Sociolinguistics?* Oxford: Wiley.

Weber, J.-J. (2015) *Language Racism*. London: Palgrave.

Wiredu, K. (2008) 'Social philosophy in postcolonial Africa: Some preliminaries concerning communalism and communitarianism', *South African Journal of Philosophy* 27: 332–339.

24

Corpus linguistics

Studying language as part of the digital humanities

Gill Philip

Introduction

Corpus linguistics is a computer-aided approach to the study of language based on the search for regularities in word use. Such regularities may feature the habitual co-occurrence of two or more words (collocation), of a word with a grammatical or syntactic feature (colligation), a word's consistent use within a particular semantic field (semantic preference), or couched within contexts that suggest connotative or evaluative meanings (semantic prosody). The focus is firmly placed on the word, or more specifically, the word *form*, since even singular and plural forms of a noun are of preference viewed as different 'words'. At first glance this might seem an unnecessarily pedantic distinction to make, but its relevance can be appreciated from a simple example: 'eye' co-occurs (collocates) with the words 'blink', 'opener', 'cast', 'private', and 'witness', amongst others (Sinclair 2003: 168), while 'eyes' counts amongst its collocates colours, body parts, and vision verbs (ibid.). From this information it can be appreciated that the plural tends to refer to the physical feature or organ of sight, and that the singular form is, instead, more typically involved in compounds and idiomatic expressions, e.g. 'an eye-opener', 'cast an eye over something', 'an eye-witness account'.

Observations such as this lay bare typical features of language use which speakers often recognise only in retrospect – a phenomenon Louw (1993: 173) has described as 'twenty-twenty hindsight'. Declarative knowledge of the language is not necessarily unreliable, but it is selective: all users of language, linguists included, tend to focus on salient forms and meanings with the result that much is overlooked. Corpora make it possible to overcome this partial blindness, thus enriching descriptions of language with detail that is normally inaccessible to our intuitions (ibid.: 157). Since the salient meaning of 'eye(s)' is the organ of sight, it is reasonable to assume that both singular and plural refer to a person's facial features or to the act of seeing. The data reminds us that other meanings exist, and allows us to identify how they are realised via combination with other words. It is this sense of discovery that lies at the heart of corpus linguistics.

This chapter will focus on the main contributions of corpus linguistics to English Language studies. Part 2 looks at what a corpus is and how it is compiled, the main functions found in concordancing software, and how these are used in corpus linguistics. Part 3 addresses current issues in the use of corpus linguistics in the study of English. It introduces the three broad approaches currently in use, namely corpus-driven, corpus-based, and corpus-assisted, and goes on to discuss the ways in which they have been applied to the study of English language, discourse and literature. Part 4 outlines the main areas of debate within corpus linguistics, in particular which approach is best for different kinds of research, and the integration of corpus linguistics with existing theoretical and methodological practices. Part 5, by way of conclusion, suggests likely future developments in terms of data (what can be studied), tools (how to study it) and theory (outstanding issues requiring attention).

Studying language through electronic text: corpora and concordancing software

What is a corpus?

The term 'corpus' is used in many branches of linguistics, as a general term meaning 'a collection of examples'. In corpus linguistics, a corpus is defined as a *principled* collection of *naturally-occurring texts*. The texts may be written or spoken (or, more recently, multimodal), of varying lengths, and represent any range of text types, genres and subject matter. What differentiates a 'corpus' from a 'text collection' is that its composition is based on specific guidelines, aimed at ensuring breadth of coverage and balance (no single text or author may be included disproportionately). A large archive of texts, such as www.gutenberg.org is a 'text collection' rather than a 'corpus', since it is not concerned with offering such breadth and balance: it makes available all it can. The Internet, used by many as a corpus, is for the same reason more accurately described as a text collection. However, a corpus can be *drawn* from a text collection or repository:

> The data were collected through an online interface of newspaper and periodicals (LexisNexis) by way of the following search query:
>
> refugee* OR asylum* OR deport* OR immigr* OR emigr* OR migrant* OR illegal alien* or illegal entry OR leave to remain AND NOT deportivo AND NOT deportment
>
> Data were collected from nineteen UK newspapers, including six daily tabloids (*Sun, Daily Star, People, Daily Mirror, Daily Express, Daily Mail*) and their Sunday editions (*Sunday Express, Mail on Sunday, Sunday Mirror, Sunday Star*), five daily broadsheets (*Business, Guardian, Herald, Independent, Telegraph*), two Sunday broadsheets (*Observer, Independent on Sunday*), and two regional newspapers (*Evening Standard, Liverpool Echo*). Data were obtained for most of the newspapers from January 1996 through October 2005, although in a few cases data were not available until 1999 (*Business*), 2000 (*Sun, Daily Star, Sunday Star*), or 2001 (*Liverpool Echo*).
>
> (Gabrielatos and Baker 2008: 9)

The corpus whose composition is described above is an illustration of a new generation of specialised corpora. Once known as small corpora – small both in size and in coverage – such specialised corpora can now be very large (e.g. '140 million words, containing 175,000 full newspaper articles spanning ten years', ibid. 6). The specialised focus is ensured by specifying which key words should appear in the texts; and the genre (news) is likewise

```
<w lemma="why" type="AVQ">Why </w>
<w lemma="can" type="VM0">ca</w>
<w lemma="not" type="XX0">n't </w>
<w lemma="bloody" type="AJ0"> <seg function="mrw" type="met"
vici:morph="n">bloody </seg> </w>
<w lemma="rabbit" type="NN2">rabbits </w>
<w lemma="come" type="VVB">come </w>
<w lemma="and" type="CJC">and </w>
<w lemma="eat" type="VVB">eat </w>
<w lemma="i" type="DPS">my </w>
<w lemma="lawn" type="NN2">lawns</w>
<c type="PUN">?</c>
```

Figure 24.1 POS-tagged, lemmatised, and metaphor-tagged data

restricted, making this corpus appropriate for sociolinguistic study but not for more general forms of language description, such as lexicography.

Specialised corpora need not be so large. It is a relatively easy matter for a researcher to compile a corpus for their own research, teaching or translation purposes, since 'a corpus' – once planned and the texts selected and located – is one or more files saved in .txt format. The crucial point is that the texts must be selected for a clear purpose so that they can be said to be a representative sample of whatever type of language the researcher wishes to examine. It is also possible to call the complete works of an author, or all extant texts of a period, a corpus.

Although some researchers prefer to compile their own corpus, many corpora are available, often free of charge for academic use (see Xiao 2008). These are usually enhanced with metadata, i.e. data about the data, including date, source, and author of each text. Very often they are annotated, or 'tagged', meaning that information is inserted for each word, e.g. to specify its part of speech (POS), or to indicate the lemma (the base form, or root, which all derived forms can be traced back to, e.g. BE is the lemma for *be, being, been, am, are, is, was,* and *were*). Tagging can additionally be used to manage variant spellings (ibid.), which is particularly relevant when dealing with Middle and Early Modern English texts, or social media texts where abbreviations, creative spellings and typos are common. Semantic tagging also exists, but this is far more complex than POS-tagging or lemmatisation, because the number of possible semantic categories is non-finite (Rayson et al. 2004; see also Rayson 2009). Some researchers tag their data manually, often to highlight language functions. For example, Semino and Short (2004) tagged speech and thought presentation in a range of different genres; and a portion of the British National Corpus (BNC) has been tagged for metaphor (Steen et al. 2010). Figure 24.1 illustrates the sentence 'Why can't bloody rabbits come and eat my lawns?' (BNC data) that has been lemmatised, POS (part-of-speech)-tagged, and metaphor-tagged. In the example, it can be seen that each word is coded separately, e.g. 'lawn' is the lemma (w lemma='lawn') to which 'lawns', a plural common noun (type='NN2') belongs.

Combining a word and a tag in a corpus search makes it possible to carry out sophisticated searches: for example, a search for 'minute', which can be either a noun ('mɪnɪt) or an adjective (maɪ'nju:t), can be limited to just the adjective. If the data has been lemmatised, a search for the lemma BE will simultaneously retrieve all inflected forms of the verb, thus circumventing the need to carry out separate searches for each one. It is also possible to search by tag, thereby retrieving all instances of a tagged category, e.g. metaphors in the metaphor-tagged portion of the BNC data (Steen et al. 2010).

Concordancing software: main functions

The increasing availability of electronic text over the past two decades has made corpus compilation simple and accessible. However, the corpus is just one part of 'doing corpus linguistics' (Hunston 2013: 619), which involves combining a basic tool-box (the corpus data and specific software) with methodological know-how. Despite some claims to the contrary (e.g. McEnery and Hardie 2012) all corpus linguistics also makes use of theoretical frameworks, whether using traditional semantic and grammatical labels to describe the form and function of language items, or by referring to other branches of linguistics in order to interpret the data, e.g. by incorporating insights from cognitive linguistics, sociolinguistics, and so on.

Once the corpus data has been prepared, it is accessed using concordancing software designed to make the language data accessible via a range of on-screen viewing options. At its most basic, it allows the user to extract the searched-for word (node) together with a limited amount of surrounding context (co-text), displaying the output as a KWIC (key word in context) concordance such as that shown in Figure 24.2, which shows a KWIC concordance of 'minute' in a corpus compiled from three collections of *Sherlock Holmes* short stories (Conan Doyle 2007, 2008, 2011) hosted at Project Gutenberg www.gutenberg.org/. The user scans the output in a search for repetitions and regularities occurring to the right and left of the node, mainly reading vertically (from top to bottom) rather than horizontally (from left to right).

Although a corpus linguistics approach can be taken to texts in any language, English benefits particularly since it has a very simple morphology: even the most highly-inflected lemmas (e.g. BE) only have a handful of possible inflected forms. The corollary of this is that in English, words (more specifically, word forms) rarely have just one meaning. Working from the premise that meanings are associated with words in combination rather than in isolation, corpus linguistics allows researchers to find meanings by identifying the word patternings that characterise them. Even from the small amount of data shown in Figure 24.2, there are two distinct meanings of 'minute' in the data – the time period noun, and the size adjective. Looking more closely at the noun, in this data, 'minute' is not a precise measurement but instead means 'moment' ('a minute later', 'for a minute or so'); while the adjective 'minute' overwhelmingly refers to abstract nouns ('attention', 'examination') rather than physical objects, and can be paraphrased as 'extremely detailed', i.e. an indication of manner rather than size. While neither

```
1       in bed. Then they will not lose a minute, for the sooner they do their work the
2    Pall Mall, and then, leaving me for a minute, he came back with a companion whom I
3         after me. At first it was only a minute' s chat, but soon his visits lengthened,
4        to me." We waited in silence for a minute -one of those minutes which one can
5    the table, and began to study it with minute attention. My indignation at this calm
6       his losses or winnings at cards. A minute examination of the circumstances served
7    some 30 pounds, to say nothing of the minute knowledge which you have gained on every
8      there rose a thin spray of smoke. A minute later a carriage and engine could be
9        was leaning through the window. A minute later, however, when Hunter rushed out
10    There had been a ring at the bell. A minute later we heard steps upon the stairs,
11       wasting your time, sir, and every minute now is of importance,' cried the
12   his anger and resumed his seat. For a minute or more we all sat in silence. Then the
13    when your master left?" "Only for a minute or so. Then I locked the door and went
14    live. I sat frozen with horror for a minute or two. Then I seized the poker and went
15         had happened then? I stood for a minute or two to collect myself, for I was
16   had deduced from signs so subtle and minute that, even when he had pointed them out
17   room! Perhaps you will kindly wait a minute until I have examined the floor. No, I
```

Figure 24.2 KWIC concordance of 'minute' in *Sherlock Holmes*

of these meanings of ‘minute’ is unusual, they are sub-senses, not main senses of their respective noun and adjective forms, and the context allows us to identify them as such.

The interaction of words: collocations, wordlists, key words, clusters

Words tend to co-occur, or collocate, with a limited range of other words, and collocation makes it possible to distinguish between different meanings. Identifying collocations by their perceived frequency of occurrence in the language has always been possible (see especially Palmer 1933 and Firth 1957), but it does not follow that frequent collocations are also significant collocations. In corpus linguistics, collocation is tied to statistical measures of significance: a collocation, to be recognised as such, must occur at least twice in the corpus, and its statistical significance is determined using tests of standard deviation, e.g. *t-score*, or of observed/expected occurrence, e.g. *Mutual Information* (Church and Hanks 1990). Statistical tests offer validity and perspective, demonstrating the degree to which the co-occurrence of words in a collocation deviates from a hypothetically random distribution of words in the language (see Evert 2009). Computational retrieval and statistical calculation can also take account of collocates found not only in the immediate proximity of the node (contiguous collocations) but also, typically, up to five words before or after. Many concordancing software packages allow users to view the distribution of collocates, listing the number of times they occur in each position (Figure 24.3a) or by presenting their distribution in each position in descending frequency (Figure 24.3b).

Concordance patterns like the one in Figure 24.3b represent a first step in seeing recurrent phrasal chunks or multi-word expressions, but the researcher has to piece them together mentally. However, the identification of recurrent strings can also be computed in most software packages. Figure 24.4 shows the output for three-word clusters that incorporate the word ‘minute’ in the same *Sherlock Holmes* data. Three recurrent clusters are retrieved: ‘for a minute’ (9 occurrences), ‘a minute later’ (8) ‘a minute or’ (8), and the program used (WordSmith Tools v.7, Scott 2017) also offers suggestions as to how these relate to some longer clusters, e.g. ‘for a minute or two’.

The type of collocation seen in Figure 24.4, consisting of an uninterrupted string of at least three words, is a multi-word sequence. Corpus linguistics recognises three distinct types of multi-word sequence: clusters, n-grams, and lexical bundles. Clusters incorporate the search word, as in Figure 24.4, while n-grams contain no specified word but are all repeated strings present in the data. Both clusters and n-grams are identified on the basis of their frequency, i.e. they are effectively multi-word word-lists. Lexical bundles are a specific class of clusters

Word	*Texts*	*Total*	*Total left*	*Total right*	*L5*	*L4*	*L3*	*L2*	*L2*	*centre*	*R1*	*R2*	*R3*	*R4*	*R5*
MINUTE	3	34								34					
A	3	31	26	5					26			2	1	1	1
THE	3	15	7	8	1	1	3		2			2	2	1	3
FOR	3	11	10	1			1	9			1				
LATER	3	8	0	8							8				
OR	3	9	1	8	1						8		1		
AND	3	8	3	5	1		1	1			2			2	1
WE	3	7	2	5	1							3	2		
OF	3	7	4	3		1	1	2				2	1		

Figure 24.3a Detailed collocate list for ‘minute’ in *Sherlock Holmes*

L5	*L4*	*L3*	*L2*	*L2*	*centre*	*R1*	*R2*	*R3*	*R4*	*R5*
TO	WILL	THE	FOR	THE	MINUTE	LATER	TWO	WE	ON	THE
YOU	TO		IN	EVERY		OR	WE	WERE	AND	WHICH
OVER			OF			AND	MORE	WHEN	ALL	
THEN						HE	THE	THE		
							OF	THEN		
							SO	TO		

Figure 24.3b Concordance pattern list for 'minute' in *Sherlock Holmes*

Cluster	*Freq.*	*Length*	*Related*
FOR A MINUTE	9	3	FOR A MINUTE OR (7), FOR A MINUTE OR TWO (3), FOR A MINUTE OR MORE (3)
A MINUTE LATER	8	3	A MINUTE LATER WE (3)
A MINUTE OR	8	3	FOR A MINUTE OR (7), FOR A MINUTE OR TWO (3), A MINUTE OR MORE (3), FOR A MINUTE OR MORE (3)

Figure 24.4 Three-word clusters involving 'minute' in *Sherlock Holmes*

or n-grams which occur *with statistically-significant frequency in particular registers or genres* (Biber et al. 1999: 989, emphasis added). In other words, they occur significantly more often than other clusters/n-grams do in the register or genre being studied.

The computation of collocates relies on calculating the probability of two words occurring together on the basis of their frequency in the data. In order to do this, the software initially compiles a word list, i.e. a list of all word forms (types) in the data and the number of times they occur (tokens). Word lists offer an initial entry point into corpus data by showing the words that are present and their actual frequencies. Some words are more frequent than others; the top of a frequency-determined word list of any English language corpus will always feature closed-class items – articles and determiners, prepositions, and pronouns. The middle cut is lexically rich, featuring recurrent content words, especially basic lexis, while the lowest-frequency words are hyponyms, specialised terminology and other infrequently used words such as proper nouns, foreign words, and non-standard spellings. Words occurring only once in a corpus normally account for well over half the total number of tokens. Viewed on a graph, a frequency-based word list ought to take the form of a sharply-dropping curve with a very long 'tail' comprising the non-repeated forms. Word lists can be applied to studies of authorship attribution, historical change, and regional varieties (see contributions in Archer 2009). However, they cannot reveal significant, communicatively-meaningful frequency: to ascertain whether a frequent word is also a statistically significant (key) word, the word list for the data (the *focus corpus*, Kilgarriff 2009) is compared with another word list, prepared from a reference corpus (ibid.), to generate a key word list.

Key words reveal what a text is about, although precisely how they do so depends on the choice of reference corpus: the key words change when the reference corpus changes. By way of illustration, Figure 24.5 shows two different key word lists for the same *Sherlock Holmes* short story, 'A Scandal in Bohemia', calculated against the BNC and against the small – but focused – *Sherlock Holmes* corpus already described in this chapter. The most obvious difference between the lists is their length: the comparison with the focused corpus yields very few key words. All of those key words are also found on the list generated with reference to the BNC, but they occupy different ranks and their keyness score is very different. Of the top ten key words in the BNC comparison, *Holmes* and the pronouns 'I', 'my', 'his' and 'you' tell us about the *Sherlock Holmes* stories in general (Watson's first-person narrative, direct speech, predominance of male characters) rather than 'A Scandal in Bohemia' in particular. Less predictable to those who already know the stories are 'cried' and 'street' (ranks 19 and 21 respectively in the BNC comparison) and 'she', which is the only personal pronoun to appear in the comparison with the other *Sherlock Holmes* stories: these are items that a researcher might want to investigate in order to understand why they are key words.

Generating key words by comparing like with like (a specific story with the corpus of stories featuring the same protagonists, in the same genre, by the same author) allows us to identify the 'aboutness' (Phillips 1989) of the short story: the protagonists (King of Bohemia, Irene Adler) and significant objects and places (photograph, Briony Lodge) where the action takes place. Both of the comparisons shown in Figure 24.5 are valid, depending on what the researcher intends to us the key words for; but the differences in the results reminds us that keyness is not an absolute measure, and highlights how important it is to choose a reference corpus with care.

Although collocations, word lists, clusters and key words have been dealt with separately here, it is normal in corpus linguistics research to make use of all of these tools in combination, i.e. to navigate between key words, collocates, clusters, and KWIC concordances. In this way the abstracted, decontextualised view of the data presented in the various data lists

	A Scandal in Bohemia vs BNC			*A Scandal in Bohemia* vs *Sherlock Holmes*		
Rank	*Key word*	*Frequency*	*Keyness*	*Key word*	*Frequency*	*Keyness*
1	HOLMES	48	526.28	PHOTOGRAPH	21	71.99
2	I	261	364.58	MAJESTY	16	71.83
3	BRIONY	11	182.71	KING	17	61.83
4	ADLER	13	161.60	ADLER	13	54.68
5	MY	78	158.53	IRENE	13	54.68
6	MAJESTY	16	156.00	BRIONY	11	49.38
7	PHOTOGRAPH	21	150.65	SHE	71	42.50
8	IRENE	13	122.81	LODGE	11	33.82
9	SHERLOCK	11	120.08	NORTON	7	31.42
10	HIS	105	95.27	BOHEMIA	8	31.39
11	YOU	129	91.05			
12	UPON	25	82.38			
13	BOHEMIA	8	81.67			
14	LODGE	11	77.20			
15	AM	23	66.82			
16	KING	17	62.41			
17	ME	46	62.09			
18	IT	154	60.40			
19	CRIED	10	56.62			
20	NORTON	7	54.54			
21	STREET	18	54.37			
22	HE	109	54.15			
23	SERPENTINE	5	53.23			
24	SHE	71	49.54			
25	REMARKED	8	49.41			

Figure 24.5 Top 25 key words for *A Scandal in Bohemia* calculated against the BNC and *Sherlock Holmes*

is brought back into relation with the original (co)-text. How researchers do this is covered in the next section.

Corpus linguistics and the study of English: current issues

Corpus-driven, *corpus*-based, *or corpus*-assisted?

Although all corpus linguistics makes use of corpora, three distinct strands of research currently coexist: corpus-driven (Tognini-Bonelli 2001), corpus-based (ibid.), and corpus-assisted (Partington 2006). Corpus-driven research aims to cut through the heterogeneity and richness of natural language in order to uncover underlying regularities. Its central tenet is to 'trust the text' (Sinclair 2004), and so it is the patterns attested in the corpus data that determine the direction of the research. This is essentially an exploratory approach, in which word use is mapped out on the basis of co-occurrence features – collocation, colligation, semantic preference, and semantic prosody (Sinclair 1996). All frequently-occurring patterns are be treated on an equal footing, irrespective of their perceived salience. One of the major beneficiaries of the corpus-driven approach has been lexicography, particularly dictionaries for learners of English as a foreign language, where the documentation of non-salient but common uses of language is a high priority.

The corpus-based approach treats the corpus as a source of data on which the researcher can draw 'in order to explore a theory or hypothesis, typically one established in the current literature, in order to validate it, refute it or refine it' (McEnery and Hardie 2012: 6). More specifically, 'corpus-based' is used to describe research which makes use of corpora for purposes that go beyond the description of the data held in the corpus, and is typically used in conjunction with discourse analysis, stylistics, text linguistics, or other methods. The corpora used may be general reference corpora (to check general norms), and/or specialised corpora (to verify norms in a particular genre, register, or discourse); where their use differs from the corpus-driven approach is that only the central, most typical features are typically taken into consideration, leaving aside peripheral uses.

Corpus-assisted research combines the above approaches. It uses corpora to verify researchers' intuitions and thus lend validity to their interpretation, but very often it is to compare norms in the corpus with an 'oddity' in a text. As Partington explains, 'if texts are not compared to other bodies or corpora of texts it is not possible to know or to prove what is normal and only against a known background of what is normal and expected can we detect the unusual and meaningful' (2006: 6-7).

Corpora and language documentation

As mentioned already, the corpus-driven approach is closely associated with lexicography. Foremost in this area is COBUILD, a project which resulted in the publishing of a range of language reference books and the first ever dictionary to be compiled from a corpus, using the data to identify word senses, syntactic preferences, and frequency information. The early years of the project are documented in a collection of papers edited by Sinclair (1987), in which the enthusiasm and excitement of the research team leap off the pages. It was anticipated that corpus data would require language descriptions to be refined, but not that new ways of describing language would be necessary. The most important discovery, now taken for granted within corpus linguistics but still largely overlooked in theoretical linguistics, is that lexis and grammar tend not to operate on separate planes but are instead intertwined. Natural language is largely idiomatic (in the broad sense of the term), and meaning emerges from words in combination. Collocation is just one of the phrasal types to have been documented in detail. Others include collocational frameworks, lexicogrammatical frames, and semi-prepackaged phrases (see Philip 2011: 35–58).

Although corpora are now deemed essential in lexicography, their direct use in language teaching is rare. Data-driven learning (DDL, see Johns 1991) and other pedagogical applications of corpora are mainly restricted to researcher-teachers working in higher education (Leńko-Szymańska and Boulton 2015), and although learner corpora such as the International Corpus of Learner English (Granger et al. 2002) have shed light on various features of learner English, very little learner corpus research has filtered down directly into mainstream language pedagogy. The indirect use of corpora in English language teaching has, however, been widespread and is particularly evident in the intensified focus on collocation in general English as a Foreign Language textbooks, and the use of large amounts of authentic, albeit usually adapted, text (Meunier and Gouverneur 2009). Collocation is now viewed as an essential part of vocabulary building, necessary for the production of proficient, fluent speech and writing, and few language teaching textbooks fail to treat it systematically. Authentic text lies at the base use of increasingly text-heavy teaching materials: even though such texts are almost always adapted rather than reproduced wholesale (see Clavel-Arroitia and Fuster-Márquez 2014), they support the inductive approach to language learning and increase learners' exposure to phraseology (Meunier and Gouverneur 2007). Exposing learners to authentic texts mirrors, to some extent, the factors that contribute to mother-tongue acquisition, and has favourable repercussions on the acquisition of collocations, lexical bundles, and other native-like features (De Bot et al. 2005).

Two further areas of corpus-driven research have been influential in (academic) English language study. One is the compilation of the Academic Word List (Coxhead 2000), a list of around 3000 words found in general academic English, as attested in a 3.5 million-word corpus of academic texts. The list is widely available on the Internet, and many print and web-based teaching materials have been developed around it. Less well-known outside corpus linguistics is the lexico-grammatical approach to genre research. Biber's (1988) seminal study into spoken and written varieties of English demonstrated how registers can be differentiated by comparing the distribution of phraseological features across a range of dimensions. Such dimensions include, for example 'narrative versus nonnarrative discourse'; here, it is reasonable to expect narrative to feature e.g. more past tense forms, more verbs for speech and thought representation, fewer text-organising features and fewer instances of hedging strategies (amongst other variables) compared to non-narrative discourse. Later work (Biber 2006) demonstrated that related registers can be further differentiated on the basis of lexical bundle distribution. What is important to note is the contribution of corpus-driven analysis: intuitively characterised by lexical choices and the presence (or absence) of particular grammatical structures, Biber and other scholars have highlighted the phraseological nature of genre using frequency and co-occurrence measures that can only be revealed via the processing of large amounts of data.

While the use of corpora for lexicographical purposes is almost exclusively corpus-driven, this does not mean that corpora must always be used within such large-scale projects. Individual scholars routinely conduct small-scale studies into lexis, grammar, and phraseology using the same approach. Additionally, it must be stressed that it is not only the standard version of the language that is investigated: there is a vast body of research into all kinds of non-standard Englishes based on corpora of historical, geographical, age-specific and emerging varieties of the language. All these contribute to its documentation – for native speakers, for learners, and for philologists and scholars of the literature of past ages. However, corpus data is not only useful for lexicology; it is also used to analyse the communicative functions and effects of texts, as outlined in the next two sections.

Corpora and text analysis

In discourse analysis, the purpose of the research is not simply to document linguistic features, but to connect them with how language is used to construct meaning and a vision of the world. The use of corpora in this context allows comparisons to be drawn between forms located in the chosen text with general features of the discourse (or of the language) as a whole. In this area of research, specialised corpora are often compiled using texts that characterise the discourse being studied. One such specialised corpus, used to investigate discourses of migration (Gabrielatos and Baker 2008; Baker et al. 2008) was described in the section 'What is a corpus?' above. Using a specialised, discourse- or topic-specific corpus allows researchers to move from the micro-analysis of a single text to an intermediate level focusing on corpora of specialised discourse, to the macro-analysis of large amounts of data, so that generic features can be described (Bednarek 2009). It may also be informative to 'downsample' one or more texts from a corpus so that detailed examination can be carried out on a small component of the larger data set, using corpus methods or other linguistic approaches. Baker et al. (2008) do precisely this: they downsampled a selection of texts belonging to a precise time frame with the intention of subjecting them to a CDA (critical discourse analysis), after a quantitative analysis of the corpus suggested this time frame would be worth investigating in more detail.

Since corpus linguistics is centrally concerned with word use, in text and discourse analysis the researcher's focus alternates between the word, the text, and the corpus. If the research is corpus-driven, the ideal procedure would be to start with the corpus data as a whole, extract keywords, collocations and recurrent clusters, and use this information to formulate the initial research questions (e.g. 'Why does 'group(s)' collocate with 'ethnic' and with 'tribal', but not with 'racial'?', cf. Krishnamurthy 1996). In a corpus-based perspective, researchers select in advance which data to focus on, using corpus-external criteria, e.g. the desire to focus on a selection of near-synonyms, to uncover their similarities and differences in a given discourse. For example, Baker et al.'s (2008) study focused on 'refugee(s)', 'asylum seeker(s)', 'immigrant(s)' and 'migrant(s)', in a 140 million-word corpus of news articles dealing with the topic. Their research not only studies these terms: they were used as 'seed terms' for the initial corpus compilation (Gabrielatos and Baker 2008: 9; see 'What is a corpus?' above) to ensure that their corpus would be centrally relevant to the topic, rather than just a generic corpus of newspaper texts. Another way into the data is to perform a close reading of a sample of the corpus in order to identify words, semantic fields or structures of potential interest, and then to search for them in the full corpus. This approach is favoured by many metaphor scholars and is outlined in detail in Charteris-Black (2004).

A different use of corpus data is found in corpus-assisted (Partington et al. 2013) or corpus-informed (O'Halloran 2007) studies, in which the text being studied is generally not part of the larger corpus nor is it studied on the basis of findings derived from the corpus. Instead, corpus data is used to check how words in the text are typically used in the language as a whole. This allows researchers to verify their intuitions, and can support hypotheses regarding how readers are likely to interpret meanings (ibid.). Bolstering one's claims with corpus data ensures that the treatment of the text does indeed amount to analysis rather than interpretation, and, at the same time, counteracts any tendency to overinterpretation (O'Halloran and Coffin 2004).

At its most detailed, research fusing corpus linguistics and discourse analysis is capable of revealing not only the main topics of a discourse, but also lexicogrammatical patterns that communicate stance, positive/negative evaluation, and connotation, all of which operate above the level of word meaning. Of particular relevance in this context is semantic prosody (Louw 1993), the attitudinal, evaluative and pragmatic force that is encoded in the 'extended unit of meaning' (Sinclair 1996; see also Philip 2011: 38–82). In other words, a type of meaning usually considered intangible can actually be pinned down to specific patterns and structures in the language. Semantic prosody is subtly revealing and elusive in equal measure. Not identifiable in a single instance of language, and not inherent in word-level semantics, it is in the KWIC concordance that it surfaces.

Finding and defining semantic prosody requires careful analysis. In Louw (1993), KWIC concordances reveal how 'bent on' collocates with negative (destructive, disruptive) activities, including 'destroying', 'harrying', 'mayhem'. The expectation is, therefore, that this expression will normally be used to convey annoyance (the semantic prosody) in relation to individuals who are *bent on* such activities. Louw argues that intentional deviation from this expectation results in irony (1993: 171). Unintentional deviation, on the other hand, reveals insincerity (ibid). By way of example, Philip (2017) discusses an unfortunate slip of the tongue in an informal statement made on TV news by the former UK Prime Minister, David Cameron, who described the influx of refugees from war-torn Syria as 'a swarm of immigrants'. Corpus data confirms that 'swarm' is typically used to refer to large quantities of insects, particularly those that bite or sting, and as a result its semantic prosody conveys annoyance that such insignificant creatures should be so bothersome. To find 'immigrants' in the syntactic slot normally occupied by insects transfers this prosody onto the people arriving. Contemporary news reports confirmed the public reception of the phrase as being negative, dehumanising, and – importantly – revealing the speaker's private sentiments; statements to the press attest that Cameron had not used the expression deliberately (ibid.). O'Halloran's (2007) analysis of metaphorically-used words such as 'erupt' and 'simmer' offers a reminder of the subtlety of semantic prosody: different inflected forms (present participle, past simple) appear to harbour distinct evaluative meanings; and these may additionally be associated with particular registers, e.g. journalism.

Corpora and stylistics

Corpus stylistics is normally defined as the analysis of literary texts using corpus linguistic techniques, although some argue that its scope is wider, involving 'the application of theories, models and frameworks from stylistics in corpus analysis' (McIntyre 2015: 60–61). However, it is on literary texts than most corpus stylistic research currently concentrates. Using corpora changes the reading paradigm from the chronological, horizontal unfolding of the text, to a synchronic, vertical reading (Tognini-Bonelli 2001). While this can be said of all corpus analysis, this change in viewpoint is particularly marked in the study of narrative prose and drama: the narrative progression is fragmented, attention is drawn away from the gradual development of plot and character. Concentrated into the space of an on-screen concordance, subtle aspects of characterisation, plot, and style that are distributed throughout the text come to the fore.

Corpus-driven stylistics is illustrated in Toolan's (2009) work on narrative progression in short stories. He argues that if a form or feature is prominent enough to be noticed by the reader, it must also be identifiable formally, via corpus analytic techniques. Toolan identifies eight textual features in short stories that are central to prospection (clues that allow the reader to anticipate what is to befall the characters), all eight of which can be identified using corpus linguistics tools, including searching for particular word forms or classes (e.g. reporting verbs, modal verbs), extracting key words and their collocates, and investigating clustering of repetition. Toolan does not limit himself to studying key word lists nor the clusters of which they form a part; instead, he argues that the sentences in which a character key word appears can be extracted and recompiled to provide a potted version of the story. He also observes that key words have a tendency to cluster at particular points of the narrative, and suggests that such clustering indicates plot intensification. Since corpus linguistics analyses work best with repeated word forms, the only phenomenon that Toolan finds problematic is 'para-repetition' (ibid: 103), i.e. repetition of meaning which does not involve the reiteration of the same lexis: corpus software is primarily designed to retrieve recurrent word forms, not recurrent meanings.

Toolan's approach is original within corpus stylistics, where it is more common to use key words to identify the main topic, participants, and stylistic features of a text. For example, Culpeper (2009) uses them to investigate the links between style markers and keyness in Shakespeare's *Romeo and Juliet*, while Scott (2006) is interested in how they collocate with one another, thus revealing how characters, places, events and language interact. Fischer-Starcke (2010) proposes an analysis of Austen novels, starting with key words and then analysing the (four-word) clusters associated with them. Mahlberg (2013), investigates longer (five-word) clusters in Dickens' novels, in an attempt to identify general phraseological features of this author's style, particularly his 'authorial habit' (ibid. 60) of using repeated clusters both within one work and across different texts. Mahlberg has also focused on recurrent clusters within suspensions – the narrator comments that interrupt direct speech – using a purpose-built corpus tool, CLiC (Mahlberg et al. 2016). Mahlberg's (2013) analysis of body-part lexis in suspension clusters demonstrates how body language contributes to the depiction of characters' personalities, appearance, and typical behaviour.

In his early investigations of semantic prosody, Louw (1993) also discusses ways of interpreting poetry by comparing collocations with those found in a general reference corpus. He argues that the 'inescapable feeling of melancholia' (p. 162) experienced by readers of Larkin's 'Days' can be explained by referring to the habitual patterns found in the corpus. Larkin writes 'Days are where we live', which appears to be a neutral statement; yet an examination of 'days are . . . ' in the corpus reveals that it carries a semantic prosody of regret for time past which cannot be relived, not for present time and the actions carried out therein. In a similar vein, Semino (2010) makes use of corpora to validate conventional use of words and their collocates, this time within a metaphor-related study of Elizabeth Jennings' 'Answers'. Another way in which a literary text can be compared to language norms is illustrated by McIntyre (2015). He compares the relative frequencies of direct speech, indirect speech and narrator comment in Mark Haddon's (2005) *The Curious Incident of the Dog in the Night-time* with those found in a corpus of contemporary fiction, in order to confirm his hypothesis that the novel uses a disproportionately large amount of direct speech. McIntyre also compares the dialogues of the TV series *Deadwood* with a contemporary (19th-century) corpus of American English, to investigate the perceived authenticity of the characters' discourse (ibid.), finding both similarities and divergences in the use of anachronisms such as 'an honor and a pleasure'.

Key areas of dispute and debate

How is corpus linguistics to be done?

The most persistent area of dispute and debate within corpus linguistics is that of corpus-driven vs. corpus-based analysis (Tognini-Bonelli 2001). The debate is often polarised: at one extreme is an absolutist empirical stance, whereby the corpus data is reified, requiring the analyst to investigate all (and only) the language it contains; at the other extreme, the corpus is considered as nothing more than a convenient repository of examples which can be 'cherry-picked' at will. An alternative view of the same debate is to argue whether corpus linguistics is a theory or a method (McEnery and Hardie 2012; Viana et al. 2011). What emerges clearly from Viana et al.'s interviews with notable corpus linguists is that is it both theory *and* method, albeit in varying proportions depending on one's academic background and research interests, and on the scope and slant of each individual study. Corpus linguistics has made considerable contributions to linguistic theory, refining existing models and also proposing new ones. Corpus linguistics is also a method; it is one of many tools that any linguist can make use of, without necessarily embracing (or rejecting) existing theoretical stances, corpus-derived or otherwise. If two broad approaches are to be identified, therefore, it would be more accurate to speak of a lexicologically-oriented stance in which the data serves to make generalisations about the structures and functions of language, and a discourse-oriented stance in which the data is used to enhance the interpretation of texts.

The lexicologically-oriented stance can be seen in studies which focus on a limited set of words, rarely (if ever) examining the context that lies beyond the boundary of the KWIC concordance on-screen. This local focus allows for detailed examination of language items in their immediate textual environment and extrapolates to the corpus as a whole, making it possible to explain how meanings arise in context. Notable advances in linguistic theory have been made using this approach, particularly the idiom principle (Sinclair 1991), linear unit grammar (Sinclair and Mauranen 2006) and the theory of norms and exploitations (Hanks 2013). The idiom principle proposes that spoken and written text is normally composed of intersecting or superimposed phrasal fragments, rather than by alternating starkly between grammatical and lexical choices. Corpus data supports this notion: on-screen KWIC concordances as well as lists of collocates and n-grams demonstrate repeatedly that words co-occur in recurring patterns, that they 'prefer' to be used as part of a limited set of collocates, phrasal structures, syntactic positions, and so on. Linear unit grammar extends this observation, focusing on the way in which each consecutive word in an utterance or text reduces the potential for other words to appear. This theory of language can be seen in predictive text applications and Internet search engines, where the user is frequently prompted for ways of completing phrases after entering just one or two words. Linear unit grammar does not stop at three- or four-word sequences, however, but suggests that *in extremis*, entire texts may be built up by a process of prediction and exclusion based on the words that have already appeared. The theory of norms and exploitations is also a phraseological theory of language, but it aims to explain creative or unusual word combinations in relation to formulaic language including the collocations and n-grams that typify the idiom principle. Each of these theories may be described independently, but they share two principles: first, a rejection of the traditional opposition between grammar and lexis, and second, a view of language that is based on habit and familiarity rather than on a constant renewal and re-composition of word combinations. These theoretical notions are still viewed with scepticism outside corpus linguistics, where traditional views of grammar, syntax and semantics still hold sway.

Within the discourse-oriented stance, the analysis is primarily text-oriented rather than word- or language-oriented. In other words, the analysis of the lexical items is not an end unto itself (lexicological) nor is it intended to be automatically extrapolated to the language (or language variety under study) as a whole, but rather aims to contribute a quantitative aspect to the (predominantly qualitative) interpretation of texts. Ideally, several levels of interpretation should be included: 'macro- (large-scale quantitative analysis), meso- (small-scale quantitative analysis), and micro- (individual text analysis) levels' (Bednarek 2009), in the spirit of mixed-methods research (ibid.). The study by Baker et al. (2008), discussed in 'Corpora and text analysis' above, is an example of this approach: a large specialised corpus was compiled from a list of pre-selected terms which were then examined in the large corpus; successively, a smaller section of the corpus was isolated; finally, individual texts appearing in that sub-corpus were subjected to qualitative analysis using a CDA approach.

The two broad approaches just outlined tend not to overlap: individual corpus linguists favour one or the other, depending on where their initial training was conducted and the type of language research that interests them. Each will invariably claim that their preferred approach is 'better' than the other, but in truth there is no 'best' way of doing corpus linguistics research. Instead, researchers need to use the approach that is best suited to addressing their research objectives, combining as many features as necessary in order to reach this aim.

Integrating corpora with other linguistic analyses

Corpora introduce a degree of quantitative analysis in areas of language study that are predominantly qualitative, particularly discourse analysis, literary text analysis, and stylistics. Using corpus tools, the researcher can focus on isolated forms in a way that close (and chronological) reading of texts does not allow, picking out details that might otherwise go unnoticed. However, caution may be advised. McIntyre (2015: 60) remarks that some corpus linguists overstate their case by implying that text analysis carried out without corpus tools somehow lacks rigour (ibid.). Corpus linguistics provides a level of quantitative analysis and replicability that is difficult to attain without the aid of computers, but literary scholarship conducted along traditional lines is by no means inferior if it fails to include statistical scores, collocates listings and the like: it is, after all, primarily qualitative. Corpus methods can enhance such research by adding a rigorous quantitative dimension, but they cannot replace it entirely. Another potential pitfall awaiting corpus linguists working with literary text is to overlook the importance of the existing scholarship in the field, comprising both the detailed textual analyses just mentioned, and important insights into the context of production and reception of the texts under examination. Meaningful, insightful interpretation does not come about only as a result of empirical analysis: even the most impeccable analysis can appear naïve if not supported by adequate and appropriate background knowledge.

Criticisms of corpus linguistics, notably from (critical) discourse analysis and systemic functional linguistics, take issue with the validity of focusing on words in a restricted context. Although corpus linguistics techniques offer new insights, they cannot be seen as substituting the analysis of complete texts (Hunston 2013). Indeed, the close attention to words that is typical of corpus approaches can distort the interpretation of a text as a whole, in that it overlooks the ways in which the specific lexical items contribute to text-level meanings, including cohesion, coherence and linguistic function. For this reason – as in literary stylistics – corpus linguistics is often used to add a quantitative dimension to text linguistics, but it is predominantly viewed as an additional, complementary means of analysis, subordinate to existing qualitative methods. It offers one of several computer-based ways of 'reading' texts which allow scholars to enhance their analyses: it is indeed one of the earliest manifestations of what is now referred to as digital humanities.

Future directions

The increasing availability of electronic text has not only increased the scope for corpus linguistics studies: the appeal of corpus linguistics methods is extending beyond the language sciences and into the humanities at large. Corpus linguistics has much to offer the many areas of study which make use of language data, since the tools and analytical techniques developed for linguistic description are equally suited to the analysis of text-based source materials in history, geography, sociology, and elsewhere. While the primary purpose of digitisation is often simply to make precious documents available without exposing them to unnecessary deterioration, one important corollary is that a gold mine of previously under-documented language varieties is opened up for linguistic research. Not only are corpus linguists exploiting the greater availability of text data to linguistic ends; they are increasingly participating in cross-disciplinary research too, contributing their expertise in the processing and analysis of text data to other fields of study. Corpus linguistics, once seen as a niche area, is therefore poised to take on a pivotal role within digital humanities research.

Within corpus linguistics, the digitisation of library holdings has had a major impact on diachronic language study in particular. Although English corpus linguistics has encompassed historical varieties from the outset, the quantity and range of data available has always been limited in comparison with contemporary varieties. Drawing on data that is now available on digital format, thanks to the systematic digitisation of library holdings, historical corpus linguistics is now able to refine existing studies of grammar and lexis and is also able to address other linguistic phenomena within a historical perspective, such as pragmatics, which was previously beyond its reach (Kytö 2011).

Over the past decade the widespread use of social media has led to new ways of using language, and there is much to be investigated in the emerging varieties of English that ensue (see Spilioti, this volume). A hybrid genre is evolving that is part-spoken, part-written (Knight et al. 2014). 'Conversations' with others are increasingly asynchronous, characterised by short turns, non-standard spellings, and alternation between text, emoticons and images. Conversation threads may in fact comprise several interlaced conversations – as well as irrelevant intrusions (e.g. trolling) – meaning that the very notion of what 'a text' is needs to be refined or indeed redefined.

Corpus analysis tools continue to be developed in response to the specific needs of researchers, and researchers working with English have a distinct advantage since it is the best-resourced language both in terms of data availability (corpora, electronic text) and software. It is usually the test bed for new applications, with the result that innovations in English corpus linguistics tend to precede those in other languages. Data visualisation is currently a growth area. Once limited to the kind of output visible in Figures 24.2–24.5, there is a growing interest in graphic interfaces such as word clouds and dynamic models of word use. Word cloud technology is widespread and easily accessible, but output is normally static. Recent tools allow users to navigate between the word cloud and the texts from which it has been generated, e.g. *WordWanderer* (Dörk and Knight 2015). Word relationships are made visible in *GraphColl* (Brezina et al. 2015), which shows each word as a node, and draws lines of differing lengths to connect closer (significant) and more distant (less significant) collocates; the output is dynamic and can be manipulated on-screen using the mouse. These developments represent a growing trend for more flexible, interactive and meaningful forms of data visualisation, appealing to those outside the corpus linguistics community.

Corpus linguistics software can process and display data in such detail that some might be tempted to believe that the software is carrying out the linguistic analysis. However, the problem of repeated meanings which do not manifest in repeated word forms remains, as does the question of how to capture nuances of meaning which analysis of frequent collocations does not capture. Semantic tagging is not consistently reliable and improving automatic semantic-class assignation is a challenge: when dealing with hundreds of semantic classes, the error rate inevitably rises; and determining which class fits the word, given the context in which it occurs, introduces yet more complexity. Unlike grammatical classes, which are unequivocal, a word can belong to several semantic fields at the same time, meaning that even output which is 'correct' may not be 'complete'. Connected to the matter of semantic tagging is what is sometimes called 'long tail' semantics, in reference to the tailing off of repeated word forms in a corpus when viewed on a typical distribution curve (see 'Concordancing software: main functions' above). Corpus linguistics allows researchers to investigate frequent forms, but has yet to offer reliable means of retrieving frequent meanings, often realised as low-frequency or non-repeated forms in the long tail, and often clustering in single texts within the corpus (Serrano et al. 2009). Research into this area is only just beginning, and is driven by market concerns rather than purely academic interest: Internet search engines need to incorporate lesser-used lexicalisations of popular search-strings into their algorithms, so that the sites retrieved satisfy users' requirements. This technology will inevitably be made available within corpus linguistics, thus refining current semantic tagging systems and allowing users to search for meanings, not just words.

Further reading

Baker, P. and J. Egbert (eds) (2016) *Triangulating Methodological Approaches in Corpus Linguistic Research*. London: Routledge. In this volume, ten scholars tackle the same research question using the same 400,000-word corpus, each from their preferred methodological-analytical angle.

McEnery, T. and A. Hardie (2012) *Corpus Linguistics. Method, Theory and Practice*. Cambridge: Cambridge University Press. A good, all-round introduction to (English) corpus linguistics, with tasks and study questions.

Scott, M. (2017) *WordSmith Tools Version 7*. Stroud: Lexical Analysis Software. One of the most widely-used and functionally complete concordancing packages available; the demo version is free.

Sinclair, J. M. (2004) *Trust the Text*. London: Routledge. A collection of Sinclair's major writings on corpus linguistics, focusing particularly on analytical procedures, descriptive techniques, and theoretical implications.

Viana, V., S. Zyngier and G. Barnbrook (2011) *Perspectives on Corpus Linguistics*. Amsterdam: John Benjamins. Fourteen well-known corpus linguists give their answers to a set of general questions about the discipline, plus others that are specific to their field of expertise.

Related topics

- Stylistics: studying literary and everyday style in English
- Sociolinguistics: studying English and its social relations
- Discourse analysis: studying and critiquing language in use.

References

Archer, D. (ed.) (2009) *What's in a Word-List?* Farnham: Ashgate.

Baker, P., C. Gabrielatos, M. Khosravinik, M. Krzyżanowski, T. McEnery and R. Wodak (2008) 'A useful methodological synergy? Combining critical discourse analysis and corpus linguistics to examine discourses of refugees and asylum seekers in the UK press', *Discourse & Society* 19 (3): 273–306.

Bednarek, M. (2009) 'Corpora and discourse: A three-pronged approach to analyzing linguistic data', in M. Haugh (ed.), *Selected Proceedings of the 2008 HCSNet Workshop on Designing the Australian National Corpus*. Somerville, MA: Cascadilla Proceedings Project, 19–24.

Biber, D. (1988) *Variation across Speech and Writing*. Cambridge: Cambridge University Press.

Biber, D. (2006) *University Language: A Corpus-Based Study of Spoken and Written Registers*. Amsterdam: John Benjamins.

Biber, D., S. Johansson, G. Leech, S. Conrad and E. Finegan (1999) *Longman Grammar of Spoken and Written English*. London: Longman.

Brezina, V., T. McEnery and S. Watten (2015) 'Collocations in context: A new perspective on collocation networks', *International Journal of Corpus Linguistics* 20 (2): 139–173.
Charteris-Black, J. (2004) *Corpus Approaches to Critical Metaphor Analysis*. Basingstoke: Palgrave Macmillan.
Church, K. and P. Hanks (1990) 'Word association norms: Mutual information and lexicography', *Computational Linguistics* 16 (1): 22–29.
Clavel-Arroitia, B. and M. Fuster-Márquez (2014) 'The authenticity of real texts in advanced English language textbooks', *ELT Journal* 68 (2): 124–134.
Conan Doyle, A. (2011) *The Adventures of Sherlock Holmes*. Urbana, Illinois: Project Gutenberg. Retrieved June 13, 2017, from www.gutenberg.org/ebooks/1661
Conan Doyle, A. (2008) *Memoirs of Sherlock Holmes*. Urbana, Illinois: Project Gutenberg. Retrieved June 13, 2017, from www.gutenberg.org/ebooks/834
Conan Doyle, A. (2007) *The Return of Sherlock Holmes*. Urbana, Illinois: Project Gutenberg. Retrieved June 13, 2017, from www.gutenberg.org/ebooks/108
Coxhead, A. (2000) 'A new academic word list', *TESOL Quarterly* 34 (2): 213–238.
Culpeper, J. (2009) 'Keyness: Words, parts-of-speech and semantic categories in the character-talk of Shakespeare's Romeo and Juliet', *International Journal of Corpus Linguistics* 14 (1): 29–59.
De Bot, K., W. Lowie and M. Verspoor (2005) *Second Language Acquisition. An Advanced Resource Book*. London: Routledge.
Dörk, M. and D. Knight (2015) 'WordWanderer: A navigational approach to text visualisation', *Corpora* 10 (1): 83–94.
Evert, S. (2009) 'Corpora and collocations', in A. Lüdeling and M. Kytö (eds), *Corpus Linguistics: An International Handbook*. Vol. 2. Berlin: Mouton De Gruyter, 1212–1248.
Firth, J. R. (1957) *Papers in Linguistics 1934–1951*. London: Oxford University Press.
Fischer-Starcke, B. (2010) *Corpus Linguistics and the Study of Literature*. London: Continuum.
Gabrielatos, C. and P. Baker (2008) 'Fleeing, sneaking, flooding: A corpus analysis of discursive constructions of refugees and asylum seekers in the UK press, 1996–2005', *Journal of English Linguistics* 36 (1): 5–38.
Granger, S., E. Dagneaux and F. Meunier (eds) (2002) *The International Corpus of Learner English*. Louvain-la-Neuve: Presses universitaires de Louvain.
Hanks, P. (2013) *Lexical Analysis: Norms and Exploitations*. Cambridge, MA: MIT Press.
Hunston, S. (2013) 'Systemic functional linguistics, corpus linguistics, and the ideology of science', *Text & Talk* 33 (4–5): 617–640.
Johns, T. (1991) 'Should you be persuaded – two examples of data-driven learning materials', *English Language Research Journal* 4: 1–16.
Kilgarriff, A. (2009) 'Simple maths for keywords', in M. Mahlberg, V. González-Díaz and C. Smith (eds), *Proceedings of Corpus Linguistics CL2009*. Liverpool: University of Liverpool. Available at www.ucrel.lancs.ac.uk/publications/cl2009/171_FullPaper.doc
Knight, D., S. Adolphs and R. Carter (2014) 'CANELC: Constructing an e-language corpus', *Corpora* 9 (1): 29–56.
Krishnamurthy, R. (1996) 'Ethnic, racial and tribal: The language of racism?', in C. R. Caldas-Coulthard and M. Coulthard (eds), *Texts and Practices: Readings in Critical Discourse Analysis*. London: Routledge, 129–149.
Kytö, M. (2011) 'Corpora and historical linguistics', *Belo Horizonte* 11 (2): 417–457.
Leńko-Szymańska, A. and A. Boulton (eds) (2015) *Multiple Affordances of Language Corpora for Data-Driven Learning*. Amsterdam: John Benjamins.
Louw, W. E. (1993) 'Irony in the text or insincerity in the writer?: The diagnostic potential of semantic prosodies', in M. Baker, G. Francis and E. Tognini Bonelli (eds), *Text and Technology: In Honour of John Sinclair*. Amsterdam: John Benjamins, 157–176.
Mahlberg, M. (2013) *Corpus Stylistics and Dickens's Fiction*. London: Routledge.
Mahlberg, M., P. Stockwell, J. de Joode, C. Smith and M. O'Donnell (2016) 'CLiC Dickens: Novel uses of concordances for the integration of corpus stylistics and cognitive poetics,' *Corpora* 11 (3): 433–463.
McEnery, T. and A. Hardie (2012) *Corpus Linguistics. Method, Theory and Practice*. Cambridge: Cambridge University Press.
McIntyre, D. (2015) Towards an integrated corpus stylistics. *Topics in Linguistics* 16: 59–68.

Meunier, F. and C. Gouverneur (2007) 'The treatment of phraseology in ELT Textbooks', in E. Hidalgo, L. Querada and J. Santana (eds), *Corpora in the Foreign Language Classroom*. Amsterdam: Rodopi, 119–139.

Meunier, F. and C. Gouverneur (2009) 'New types of corpora for new educational challenges Collecting, annotating and exploiting a corpus of textbook material', in K. Aijmer (ed.), *Corpora and Language Teaching*. Amsterdam: John Benjamins, 180–201.

O'Halloran, K. (2007) 'Critical discourse analysis and the corpus-informed interpretation of metaphor at the register level', *Applied Linguistics* 28 (1): 1–24.

O'Halloran, K. and C. Coffin (2004) 'Checking overinterpretation and underinterpretation: Help from corpora in critical linguistics', in C. Coffin, A. Hewings and K. O'Halloran (eds), *Applying English Grammar: Functional and Corpus Approaches*. London: Hodder Arnold.

Palmer, H. E. (1933) *Second Interim Report on English Collocations*. Tokyo: Kaitakusha.

Partington, A. (2006) *The Linguistics of Laughter*. London: Routledge.

Partington, A., A. Duguid and C. Taylor (2013) *Patterns and Meanings in Discourse*. Amsterdam: John Benjamins.

Philip, G. (2011) *Colouring Meaning*. Amsterdam: John Benjamins.

Philip, G. (2017) 'Conventional and novel metaphors in language', in E. Semino and Z. Demjén (eds), *Routledge Handbook of Metaphor and Language*. London: Routledge, 219–232.

Phillips, M. (1989) *Lexical Structure of Text*. Birmingham: Birmingham ELR.

Rayson, P. (2009) *Wmatrix Corpus Analysis and Comparison Tool*. Computing Department, Lancaster University. Available at www.ucrel.lancs.ac.uk/wmatrix

Rayson, P., D. Archer, S. L. Piao and T. McEnery (2004) 'The UCREL Semantic Analysis System', *LREC 2004 Proceedings* 7–12.

Scott, M. (2006) 'Key words of individual texts: Aboutness and style', in M. Scott and C. Tribble (eds), *Textual Patterns: Key words and Corpus Analysis in Language Education*. Amsterdam: John Benjamins, 55–72.

Scott, M. (2017) *WordSmith Tools* (version 7). [computer software]. Stroud: Lexical Analysis Software.

Semino, E. (2010) *Metaphor in Discourse*. Cambridge: Cambridge University Press.

Semino, E. and M. Short (2004) *Corpus Stylistics*. London: Routledge.

Serrano, M. Á., A. Flammini and F. Menczer (2009) 'Modeling statistical properties of written text', *PLoS ONE* 4 (4): e5372. DOI 10.1371/journal.pone.0005372.

Sinclair, J. M. (ed.) (1987) *Looking Up*. Glasgow: Collins ELT.

Sinclair, J. M. (1991) *Corpus, Concordance, Collocation*. Oxford: Oxford University Press.

Sinclair, J. M. (1996) 'The search for units of meaning', *Textus* 9 (1): 75–106.

Sinclair, J. M. (2003) *Reading Concordances*. London: Longman.

Sinclair, J. M. (2004) *Trust the Text*. London: Routledge.

Sinclair, J. M. and A. Mauranen (2006) *Linear Unit Grammar*. Amsterdam: John Benjamins.

Steen, G., A. Dorst, B. Herrmann, A. Kaal, T. Krennmayr and T. Pasma (2010) *A Method for Linguistic Metaphor Identification: From MIP to MIPVU*. Amsterdam: John Benjamins.

Tognini-Bonelli, E. (2001) *Corpus Linguistics at Work*. Amsterdam: John Benjamins.

Toolan, M. (2009) *Narrative Progression in the Short Story*. Amsterdam: John Benjamins.

Viana, V., S. Zyngier and G. Barnbrook (2011) *Perspectives on Corpus Linguistics*. Amsterdam: John Benjamins.

Xiao, R. (2008) 'Well-known and influential corpora', in A. Lüdeling and M. Kytö (eds), *Corpus Linguistics. An International Handbook*. Vol. 1. Berlin: Mouton De Gruyter, 383–457.

25

Discourse analysis

Studying and critiquing language in use

Stephen Pihlaja

Introduction

'Discourse' is one of the most contested terms in linguistics and the social sciences. Consequently, 'discourse analysis' has come to cover a range of different techniques and approaches for the study of language in interaction and how this sheds light on larger issues of social structure. Discourse analysis focuses on how language is used and for what purposes. As an umbrella term, it describes a variety of analytic approaches with different understandings of what 'language above the sentence' means (Cameron 2001). While linguists might be able to talk about individual elements of language and linguistic features apart from the context in which they are used, discourse analysis is always tied to context. Context can include a range of factors that influence how discourse is produced, including the identity of speakers, their physical location, whether the interaction is synchronous, and so on. Historically, grammar and structure have been the key focus for linguists in understanding language as a system. However, with the ability to inexpensively record naturally occurring conversation, researchers were increasingly able to focus on interaction as it unfolded in real time. To understand how and why discourse develops as it does, analysts have created tools to analyse both empirical elements (like particular words belonging to a particular register) and non-empirical elements (like goals or intentions) of interaction. While studies of syntax, lexis, and phonology might focus on empirical investigations of structure and arrangement of phonemes and morphemes, i.e. elements of language that are observable, the focus in discourse analysis can be much more varied and depend on the goals of particular analysts. This chapter will look at the ways in which discourse analysis has been employed from a variety of different perspectives, starting with a description of several influential methods and theories and the important role each approach plays in the field of English Language Studies more generally.

Theories and methods

Discourse analysis focuses on interaction among people and looks beyond individual words, sentences, or utterances to describe the development of interaction and how it ultimately creates and sustains the social world. Conversation analysis (CA), as pioneered by

Sacks et al. (1974) remains, in many ways, the most systematic, recognised form of discourse analysis in this regard. CA is grounded in the field of ethnomethodology (Garfinkel 1967), which focused on the production of social order in everyday interaction in English-speaking contexts. Garfinkel argued that seemingly mundane, everyday interaction actually offered an important window into how norms and values in society were maintained. Growing out of this approach to understanding interaction, conversation analysts attend to regularities in both everyday and institutional talk, illuminating how social order is enacted in day-to-day interaction. CA employs detailed transcripts and close analysis of turn-taking and moment-to-moment interaction, allowing the analyst to see where small pauses or hesitations are meaningful in the development of a particular interaction. Sacks (1992), for example, analysed talk from calls to a suicide prevention line and showed that structures could be observed in interaction between the caller and the hotline worker. While Sacks' own work looked at regularities in conversation and how speakers accounted for their actions, CA was then developed for the description of regularities in conversations more generally. This includes different elements of interaction including turn-taking, repair, and how overlapping talk is resolved. By focusing on regularities and patterns, CA has shown that interaction is ordered and that the order in conversation is emergent.

CA is particularly useful in describing and analysing 'sequence' in interaction, showing that individual utterances follow directly from what has preceded the utterance in the conversation. This analysis can show not only how everyday discourse is ordered in terms of its structure, but how this order can offer insights into how speakers account for particular actions and create 'common sense' understandings of the world. The relationship between English language production and 'common sense' is particularly important for showing the role interaction plays in social life. Stokoe's (2010) analysis of talk in police interrogations about violence towards women provides an exemplar case of how CA can produce larger descriptions of how speakers make moral judgments. Stokoe shows that denial of specific crimes of violence by men often included some categorical denial of violence towards women. Rather than simply denying the act of violence, they would deny that violence towards women is the sort of thing that men do. The denial of violence was more than a rejection of a specific accusation of violence, and instead included an appeal to 'their character, disposition and identity memberships' (79). In her analysis, Stokoe shows larger 'common sense' understandings of how men should and should not act. The focus on the minutia of interaction and the moment-by-moment reasoning of speakers provides a window into deeper understandings of social contexts. In this case, *what* an individual says is as important as *how* they say it.

An emphasis on regularities and patterns can also be seen in narrative analysis, which developed around the same time as CA. Labov's (1972) work on storytelling and English language variation in the inner city of New York looked at structures above turns in conversations and provided descriptions of patterns of storytelling. This analysis also focused on the role stories played within the presentation of self and the development of community, with speakers using stories to establish their own experience of the world and accomplish 'sense-making' in interaction (Labov and Waletzky 1997: 335). Bamberg (1997) and Harré and van Langenhove (1998) and others (Bamberg and Georgakopoulou 2008; Deppermann 2013) have developed notions of 'positioning' within interaction to further describe the social action that takes place in both storytelling and interaction. How individuals position themselves and others can reveal larger 'story-lines' (Harré and van Langenhove's term) that give meaning to actions as well as provide reasoning for moral judgements. The positioning of self and others is also important for the allocation of rights and responsibilities, and in the structuring of hierarchical relationships where speakers exercise power and control. Sabat (2003) has shown how talk by caregivers about people with Alzheimer's disease can include 'malignant positioning'. This positioning deletes the rights of the person or people being spoken about, including the right to be heard. By describing someone with Alzheimer's disease as 'not knowing anything anymore' (p. 87), the caregivers position the person as being unable to speak for themselves. Others were then encouraged to discount and ignore what was being said by the patient. The ways patients were spoken about and how they and their actions were positioned also reveals beliefs about them and had the consequence of reducing the individual patient's rights by limiting their agency. The telling of a narrative or the positioning of another person creates a social world in which the person who is positioned is come to be seen in a particular way. Stories and narratives are then important ways for speakers to construct social contexts in which their own and others' actions are understandable. They show how a person views the social world while they are acting in it.

The connection between English language and culture is central to many methods of discourse analysis from a sociolinguistic perspective. Interactional sociolinguistics has its roots in linguistic anthropology and the work of Gumperz and Hymes (1972). Together, they developed forms of data analysis both from naturally occurring conversation and from interviews of speakers about their own communication practices. This model of analysis, like CA, focuses not only on what speakers are saying, but how meaning emerges in interaction. From an interactional sociolinguistic perspective, the analyst is looking at how speakers come to understand the meaning of others, and the connection between larger cultural phenomena and each individual's own identity (see Asprey and Lawson, this volume). While CA attends more exclusively to the regularities and patterns within conversation, interactional sociolinguists analyse larger societal contexts from a more recursive approach, one that does not limit the analysis to the discourse event. They can therefore begin to make larger claims about the role of different relevant issues in English Language Studies like multilingualism (see Garcia and Lim, this volume), as both linguistic and cultural phenomena.

Situated discourse analysis that foregrounds social and cultural production is also a feature of linguistic ethnography (Creese 2008; Rampton et al. 2004). Following a recursive methodology in the same way as ethnography from an anthropological perspective, linguistic ethnographers are open to research questions and methods developing as their investigation progresses. Linguistic ethnography highlights the role of the researcher as participant-observer and recognises the importance of taking into account their assumptions and biases (Tusting and Maybin 2007). Research questions and contexts are negotiated in the analyst's lived experience, allowing for a broad picture of language in context to emerge. Rampton (1995), for example, traced the relationships between ethnicity and English language use through close longitudinal observation in school settings (see also Madsen, this volume). These methods are particularly useful in projects where the researcher is initially unsure about the focus of analysis, allowing for adaptation.

Ethnography and ethnomethodology contrast with more structured approaches to English language analysis. Motivated by Halliday's (1973) functional grammar, different models of discourse analysis of clause structures to understand how speakers *do* things with language. Sinclair and Coulthard's (1975) model, for example, labels individual turns in conversation building on categories like 'transaction', 'exchange', 'move', and 'act'. They then analyse the ways in which utterances are organised around specific functions in discourse. Looking at discourse 'moves' in a classroom, analysts can then categorise interaction using further categories like 'opening', 'answering', and 'follow-up' and can describe how students and teachers interact with one another. This approach is particularly useful when describing discourse where there is a clear cultural expectation for how speakers should interact. For example, classroom roles of teachers and pupils are comparatively fixed and the potential for deviation from fixed ways of speaking, asking questions, and responding is minimal. The models, however, begin with relatively fixed concepts of what discourse constitutes and can be less useful in complex contexts with more fluid roles in interaction.

In English Language Studies, inductive, empirical analysis of naturally occurring data is the norm, but Foucauldian notions of discourse as larger social systems of ordering knowledge and power (Foucault 1981) do influence some forms of analysis. This can be seen most explicitly in critical discourse analysis (CDA), which investigates the ways in which ideology (see Spencer-Bennett, this volume) is replicated in interaction and discourse practices. In the contemporary context where English-speaking countries remain in dominant positions, studying the role of English in maintaining power relationships in language is particularly relevant. CDA, first conceived by Fairclough (1995), works at uncovering the ways in which ideology and dominant thinking in society affect the production of discourse, arguing that one cannot understand what is happening in interaction without understanding the larger power structures behind it. CDA focuses on connecting analysis of language in use to ideology, looking specifically at how power is maintained and perpetuated through particular language structures. CDA accepts that any form of discourse analysis starts from a particular value position, and holds that power structures in society perpetuate themselves, resulting in inequality. Finally, it addresses social and political problems (Wodak and Meyer 2002). CDA is also explicitly 'political', and concentrates on power structures that are in some way considered unbalanced or unjust. Because of this, CDA has been used most notably in analysis of political discourse, with the goal of highlighting the ways in which political structures favour powerful people and institutions. While Fairclough's (1995) original description of CDA was based on Halliday's functional grammar, CDA has come to encompass a much broader range of methods, analysing a variety of different linguistic features and structures, and makes an explicit link between the use of language and the influence of ideology. Musolff (2010), for example, has shown how metaphors of the 'body politic' were used in anti-Semitic discourse around the Holocaust to describe the German nation as a body that had been 'infected' by a foreign poison. Musolff shows how ideologies were developed through metaphoric language and had practical implications for how people thought and acted when conceiving of and talking about Jews as a disease to be eradicated.

Discourse analysis methods often work within a tension among different scales of language use, be they single utterances or conversations or long stretches of interaction. To look at much larger datasets, analysts can employ tools such as corpus linguistics (McEnery and Wilson 2001). While corpus linguistics has historically been used to look at patterns of lexis and grammar in the English language, in discourse analysis it can be used to connect different scales of language use. Baker (2006) has shown how corpus linguistics methods can be applied to smaller datasets, by investigating how patterns in specialised corpora differ from language use more generally. Key word analysis, for example, might show what topics and themes are particularly salient in smaller datasets compared to a reference corpus. By identifying patterns in relatively short stretches of discourse, analysts can also investigate the extent to which the trends they have observed emerge as discourse practices in a larger body of similar texts (see Philip, this volume). For example, Hardaker and McGlashan's (2016) analysis of Twitter looked at rape threats made towards feminist campaigner Caroline Criado-Perez. The analysis used a corpus of tweets to investigate frequency, collocation, and key words and built macro-descriptions of how sexual aggression was enacted, before looking at how particular hashtags fit into larger patterns. The mix of analysis from more than one scale offered an in-depth understanding of specific tweets as well as broader descriptions of aggression towards women on Twitter.

The approaches we have so far reviewed foreground interaction between speakers without looking specifically at individual cognitive contexts. By contrast, a discursive psychological perspective (Potter and Wetherell 1987) includes an increased focus on psychological states and the motives and intentions of the individual. It then uses this information to help describe and analyse interaction. Other methods for discourse analysis may, of course, take these issues into consideration. However, approaches to conversation from, for example, a CA perspective are less likely to discuss how speakers' utterances are motivated by their own feelings and thoughts. A discursive psychological approach, by contrast, makes use of psychological theory as part of the explanatory work of analysis. By considering what people want to accomplish in interactions, this approach examines the consequences of particular utterances on how users think and act. Edwards (2000), for example, has shown how talk in relationship counselling is 'action-oriented' and the way problems are formulated has the effect of constructing particular ways of both talking and thinking about the social world, and what each individual speaker wants to accomplish in that world.

Multimodal discourse analysis frameworks (Kress and van Leeuwen 2001; Jewitt 2009) have also grown as technology for video recording of interaction has developed in recent years. Although paralinguistic and other non-audio factors have long been understood to affect interaction, ability to capture the needed data to do analysis of these factors was limited. Cheap and readily available means of video recording has offered analysts the ability to consider another set of modes when analysing interaction. Like the insights afforded by the first close analyses of audio tape recordings, video recordings of naturally occurring conversations and interaction have provided new insights into the role of different modes in interaction. This can be seen in the development of gesture studies (Cienki and Müller 2008), which draws a connection among speech, thought, and gesture. New models for analysis have begun to stretch what is considered discourse, suggesting that researchers need to consider not only what speakers are saying, but what their bodies are doing when they are interacting with others (see Ravelli, this volume).

The Internet and the use of computers and mobile technologies has required adaptation of traditional ways of understanding the English language, particularly as digital communication can include creative use of code-switching and language choice (Androutsopoulos 2014). Differences in how language is produced in computer-mediated and online contexts has also required adaptation of analysis methods. Traditionally, spoken and written interaction have been clearly demarcated. However, the Internet has allowed for a variety of different modes of interaction on a variety of different scales, making previous categories difficult to apply. Analysts have taken different approaches to discourse in online contexts, from applying methods for offline interaction like CA (Paulus et al. 2016) to creating new methods, like Herring's computer-mediated discourse analysis (Herring 2004a). Herring argues that different tools need to be adapted to look at the 'four domains' of language online: structure, meaning, interaction, and social behaviour. By focusing on these different domains, discourse analysts can describe how online contexts produced particular ways of interacting and adapt discourse analytic tools to cope with the unique features.

Androutsopoulos' (2008) 'discourse-centred online ethnography' also adapts methods for analysis developed in offline spaces. In this model, discourse analysis occurs within the context of longitudinal observation and contact with users in online environments. To understand interaction within a massively multiplayer online game like World of Warcraft, for example, the researcher must be able to understand both the interaction within the game and the offline context where users play the game. Like ethnographic perspectives in offline contexts, discourse-centred online ethnography highlights that discourse practices which are salient in a specific context are not always obvious to an observer. By placing themselves 'in the field', the analyst can collect data that engages discourse data in a comprehensive way. Without the prerequisite background, understanding interaction on the site is likely to miss key features and come to conclusions that are limited. For analysts, it is not simply a question of keeping up with these technologies, but being able to place technologies in larger social contexts and doing reliable, valid discourse analysis that engages the both the physical environment of the user and the mediated context.

Technology continues to have consequences for the ways in which social interaction, cultural practices, and the English language develop, particularly as mobile technology and the Internet have grown ubiquitous. Language use in the presentation of oneself online has long been a key area of research for discourse analysts (Seargeant and Tagg 2014). While the conflation of different audiences and friend groups in social media spaces was initially described as 'context collapse' (Marwick and Boyd 2011), researchers have been increasingly interested in 'context design' (Tagg et al. 2017b) and the ways user language choice can be a resource for presentation of self to different audiences in the same online spaces (Androutsopoulos 2014). In these online contexts, understanding how and why discourse develops in the way that it does, particularly when the object of analysis like how users understand offensive behaviour (Tagg et al. 2017b), requires understanding a broader context for online social and discourse practices.

The interconnected nature of discourse is not a new concept. English language is a complex phenomenon (see Introduction of this volume) and its analysis requires taking into account the factors that influence it and its development. Larsen-Freeman and Cameron (2008) argue that the interconnected nature of discourse and the importance of a myriad of different factors in interaction can be described using principles of complex systems theory. As a complex dynamic system, one in which different elements and agents interact, discourse has some features of regularity and predictability, and the potential for dynamic changes at the same time. Complex dynamic systems are, importantly, non-linear, meaning that there is not always a clear cause-effect relationship and no clear beginnings and endings (Cameron 2015). The discourse dynamics approach looks at five levels of interaction:

- [Point Zero] is the initial conditions of an interaction, the state of the system immediately before the event being modelled or investigated . . .
- Level 1 represents activity on a timescale of milliseconds, such as automatic responses to another person or experience . . .
- Level 2 represents the level of minute-by-minute engagement and more controlled responses, for example, in conversation or language learning activity.
- Level 3 is the level of a single discourse event [be it a conversation, a novel, a YouTube video, etc] . . .
- Level 4 encompasses accumulated level 3 patterns that stabilise as attractors in the system, for example as learnt vocabulary items, empathic understandings, idioms, discourse genres, or ethical codes. These operate on a longer timescale beyond an immediate event, and may, as social change, spread across communities, groups or nations, as with the signing of a peace agreement.

(Cameron 2015: 44–45)

Cameron's research shows the way in which the different scales of discourse interact, and consideration of all levels is necessary to understand, describe, and analyse interaction among speakers. For example, Cameron (2012) has shown how the dynamic use of metaphor works in reconciliation discourse between a former member of the Irish Republican Army and the daughter of a British Member of Parliament who was killed by a bomb he placed. Metaphorical language like 'building a bridge' and 'going on a journey' emerge at specific points, but become important patterns for describing the experience of reconciliation more broadly among the speakers. The speakers repeat and expand the metaphor, both within particular and subsequent conversations, as the metaphorical language become salient and useful. By connecting discourse across levels, the researcher can use different tools at different moments to see how specific utterances come about from previous interaction and pre-existing conditions, as well as looking forward, to see how salient patterns develop.

While the forms of discourse analysis covered above represent a range of different approaches, they share several important similarities that are key for analysis in English Language Studies. First, they treat discourse as language in use and employ analysis of discourse to understand how meaning and social life are ordered. The approaches also see society as produced and developed in the everyday, day-to-day interaction of people. While institutional, governmental, religious, and media discourse are frequently the object of analysis, they are constituent parts of social interaction, not determinative. Understanding social life requires explicit attention to 'ordinary' interaction. Second, they all employ empirical data. Discourse analysis presupposes that 'discourse' is the object of study, and not reports of experiences or model sentences and discourses. Reports of experiences and model language use can be the object of analysis, but they are treated as situated discourse themselves, subject to the same analytic frameworks as everyday talk. Third, they are largely inductive, rather than deductive. The use of empirical data to drive theory is fundamentally different from approaches to discourse analysis which understand discourses as ways of framing knowledge (Foucault 1981). In the approaches, the role of the analyst is to identify patterns of language use as they occur, with the goal of showing how the patterns can be used to understand and describe the social world more broadly.

Key debates

Because of the variety of approaches to discourse analysis in English Language Studies, positions about what elements of interaction should be the object of study does create friction among scholars. Moreover, because discourse as a social phenomenon occurs in a vast variety of different contexts, with diverse speakers with diverse goals, any individual analytic framework or method is unlikely to account for every potential discourse event. Given the different scales of interaction, scholars have to make choices about where to begin analysis and what to focus on. This consequently leads to debates around what should be the object of analysis and the methods used to collect data. This section will focus on two debates around these issues.

What should or should not be considered as 'data' when doing discourse analysis is illustrated well in criticism of analysis of language using 'culture' to frame research. Ethnomethodological enquiry has long appreciated the need to consider the influence of cultural and physical contexts on interaction when doing discourse analysis. More recently, a similar attendance to language in cultural contexts has appeared as linguistic ethnography (Creese 2008). At the same time, this approach focuses less on the individual psychology of each speaker. By contrast, proponents of discursive social psychological approaches that argue individual psychological states must be taken into account in analysis are again the object of focus (Wetherell 2007). Wetherall writes: 'The study of language and culture are not sufficient in themselves. Psychological assumptions and presuppositions are unavoidable when language production is studied in its contexts of use.' (p. 661) The question of 'sufficiency' is a key one and applies to every form of discourse analysis, as researchers must be confident that the tools they have chosen to do their analysis will actually account for the phenomenon they are investigating. While proponents of particular forms of analysis might strongly argue for their own supremacy, 'sufficiency' of methods must always include analysts considering the aims, focus, and research questions of their particular projects and the form and quality of data they intend to analyse.

The identity of the analyst has also remained an important debate in discourse analysis, particularly their role in collecting data. Analysis of open-ended interviews highlights these issues, particularly their use in attempts to deduce 'intention' and 'motives' behind individual actions and the intended meanings of their utterances. While there has long been scepticism of interviews in the analysis of interaction, interviews have persisted as an important object of research in discourse analysis, particularly in methods that attempt to provide a participant perspective. Potter and Hepburn (2005) argue that the researcher must view interviews as interactional settings, where the interviewer plays an influential role in the production of discourse activity. The interview context is always oriented towards the questions chosen by the interviewer. Even in so-called 'open-ended' interviews, the interviewer plays the key role driving the topic of conversation. The context can, of course, become the object of research, as is the case in Stokoe's (2010) work on police interviews about domestic violence. How and why interviewees respond in the way they do in that particular context becomes part of the analysis. Regardless of the focus and aim, researchers make decisions about the discourse they choose to collect and analyse, and the decision-making processes determine the possible outcomes of any given project.

Decisions about how to proceed with analysis are, of course, not without biases and pre-existing beliefs that shape what should be analysed and why. In CDA, the 'critical' aim of the research is explicit at the outset, with researchers explicitly and unapologetically engaging 'political' analysis (Van Dijk 1997). This is not, however, without its own problems, particularly when attempting to develop empirical, inductive descriptions of discourse and the power structures embedded in English language use. With CDA's Foucauldian influence and a focus on exposing 'hidden' messages within discourse, CDA has been criticised for serving a particular, homogenous ideology itself, while lacking systematicity and rigour (Widdowson 2005). If the starting point is an attempt to affect positive change, than the validity of the research might be affected by these attempts. The same criticism might be used against linguistic ethnography, which also places importance on the individual analyst above concerns about systematicity. There is a need to both recognise subjective elements of discourse analysis and work within frameworks to understand and address this subjectivity, with the goal of producing analyses that are both reliable and replicable.

While there is a multitude of different ways of looking at discourse and doing discourse analysis from an English Language Studies perspective, scholars must recognise where common ground exists and benefit from areas where methods and approaches to discourse can be mixed. This is particularly important when considering how to approach new forms of data and contexts for analysis. While significant theoretical differences result in incompatibility between approaches, there is an increasing willingness to talk across methodological and theoretical differences to address research questions in creative and novel ways. This can be seen particularly in the development of corpus analysis throughout the 2000s, with the expansion of corpus linguistics tools into discourse analysis (Baker 2006; Partington et al. 2013). By adopting corpus linguistic approaches and adapting them for use in discourse analysis, researchers have increasingly been able to develop methods for answering complex questions about how and why particular patterns emerge in discourse, and make meaningful links between micro and macro levels.

Future directions

The Internet and mobile technologies emerging around its proliferation are likely to continue to create new spaces for discourse analysis, and will require serious considerations around the ways written and spoken communication are being done in new spaces, and the extent to which genuinely new ways of communicating are developing. While face-to-face interaction with others who are physically present remains a large part of most individuals' experience, increasingly interaction occurs on digital platforms or through digital devices. As we have seen, analysts have applied methods developed for offline contexts including both CA (Rendle-Short 2015) and narrative analysis (Page 2013). Because of the novelty and the relative impermanence of these technologies, particularly when compared with more stable technologies like the telephone, what technologies and platforms will remain most stable over time is difficult to know and what methods will prove to have the most staying power over time has yet to be seen. That said, interaction through mobile devices will continue to feature heavily in analysis, be it texting (Tagg 2012), the creation and consumption of online video (Pihlaja 2018), or storytelling (Page 2013). For researchers looking at interaction, technology offers two distinct affordances for research: first, in creating novel forms of discourse through communication technology, and second, in creating new and better representations of interaction being analysed as data. Herring (2004b) pointed out early in the history of research in computer-mediated communication that the extent to which 'new' technologies created 'new' practices and whether practices around these technologies continue when the technologies move on was an open question. This remains in many ways an open question, particularly as technologies improve quickly and genres are picked up and then dropped. Interest, for example, in 'blogging' as a genre type was a significant area of research in the 2000s, but has diminished as the popularity of blogging has decreased. The challenge for researchers is how to understand 'new' practices on popular platforms in light of technologies that have come before. For example, while MySpace is no longer a popular site for interaction with friends online, understanding how practices on that site developed is important for understanding Facebook or whatever social sites that follow. Because technologies do not emerge in vacuums, discourse analysts must work to understand the preconditions of discourse on both a local and global level.

The extent to which discourse analysis will continue to focus on spoken and written English language (and indeed, what will count as 'English') rather than visual representation will be a significant debate going forward. Multimodality as an object of research is unlikely to disappear as an issue, particularly considering interaction in online contexts among speakers from a variety of different contexts using English. In online discourse, there is now a spread of different text types and multimodal elements that cannot be easily categorised or analysed using traditional approaches to written and spoken texts. 'Memes' provide a good example of the difficulties of separating analysis of texts from their multimodal elements (for example, Gal et al. 2015; Ross and Rivers 2017). In a 'meme', an iconic image is overlaid with text that often has certain fixed lexico-grammatical elements, and elements that are determined by the creator of the meme to meet the needs of a particular context. The meme contains both the content of the message and the words that the creator has produced, but also a shared knowledge about the discourse practices when using specific images. This knowledge is much more difficult to substantiate and describe empirically than the lexico-grammatical features of a given meme. With the ability to publish images in the comments sections of Facebook pages, for example, discourse analysts looking at the comments cannot simply ignore images, particularly when they play an important role in the communicative practices of people online. The same issues apply to emojis, photos, stickers, and gifs, which have developed into key resources for online engagement (Zappavigna and Zhao 2017; Lim 2015; Sakai 2013). Where boundaries of English Language Studies can and should be drawn will continue to be of significant debate among discourse analysts, particularly as it relates to the earlier question of sufficiency in models of analysis.

With the spread of mobile technology, drawing clear lines between 'online' and 'offline' interaction has been and will continue to be more difficult. Researchers will increasingly need to collect data that engage a variety of discourse contexts, and use a variety of tools to bring together analysis of the discourse from disparate contexts in a meaningful way. Work by Rørbeck Nørreby and Spindler Møller (2015) shows the ways, for example, that Facebook interaction requires understanding of how social media pervades the lives of young people, without clear distinctions between what happens online and offline. Similarly, projects like the 'Translation and Translanguaging: Investigating Linguistic and Cultural Transformations in Superdiverse Wards in Four UK Cities' (Tagg et al. 2017a) have looked at the ways in which mobile technology is used in interaction among in superdiverse communities, developing important links between digital and traditional ethnography. This analysis shows that technological 'presence' through mobile technology means that interaction occurs in real time with people all across the world. For Chinese immigrants in Birmingham in the United Kingdom, connection to family in China is now possible in real time, with effects on English language, code-switching, and understanding of 'context' more generally. The issues addressed in the Translation and Translanguaging project are only likely to grow as digital communication expands and global mobility provides increasing affordances for interaction among superdiverse communities.

Finally, artificial intelligence (AI) will offer new opportunities for discourse analysts to contribute to building and researching technology that attempts to create 'natural' human interaction. Computer software has played a key role in corpus linguistics (see Philip, this volume), particularly as computers have improved their search capacity and ability to, for example, add semantic tags to words (Rayson 2008). Technology is likely to lead to new paths of research analysing how machines understand and produce language, for example, in relation to improved speech recognition (Xiong et al. 2016) and the effect of machine translation in interaction (Patil and Davies 2014). Neurologists are also likely to further understand language in the brain, with potential implications for how we understand the development of interaction and how the factors involved in communication interact to produce discourse. The ability of computer systems to identify patterns in speech and interaction has the potential to produce new tools for researchers by automating processes, such as transcription and semantic analysis. The better AI becomes at recognising speech, the more potential researchers will have to compare spoken language with large databases of spoken discourse and develop corpus linguistic tools that move beyond the written word to spoken discourse, gesture, and thought.

Conclusion

This chapter has offered a sample of a range of different approaches to discourse analysis, showing how scholars have used close, empirical analysis of interaction to describe how people make meaning in social contexts. In making decisions about the appropriateness of any given method for a specific project, researchers must consider the aims, focus, and research questions, before making a judgment about which method to choose. Ultimately, there must be a clear match between the goals of the research, data, and methods that have been chosen, allowing the researcher to make valid and reliable claims about the social world they are investigating. This includes awareness of the ways in which the researcher's own context and biases shape decisions about research. Regardless of the methodological approach, analysts must consider their own position in data collection and analysis, and how the choices they have made affect the results and their presentation.

Further reading

Cameron, D. (2001) *Working with Spoken Discourse*. London: Sage. Focusing on spoken discourse, this book provides a good starting point for research into analysis of a variety of perspectives, but looking at approaches to discourse analysis from a conversation analytic perspective.

Wetherell, M., S. Taylor and S. J. Yates (2001) *Discourse as Data: A Guide for Analysis*. London: Sage. This text provides a very good description of the practice of discourse analysis, from collecting data to various methods.

Wetherell, M., S. Taylor and S. J. Yates (2001) *Discourse Theory and Practice: A Reader*. London: Sage. A companion text to *Discourse as Data,* this text provides a comprehensive background for different theories of discourse analysis from a variety of different scholars.

Gee, J. P. and M. Handford (2013) *The Routledge Handbook of Discourse Analysis*. London: Routledge. An extended and comprehensive handbook covering many forms of discourse analysis in depth.

Jones, R. H., A. Chik and C. A. Hafner (2015) *Discourse and Digital Practices: Doing Discourse Analysis in the Digital Age*. London: Routledge. This collection provides case studies for doing analysis of online texts, discussing key issues and challenges.

Related topics

- English and social identity
- The language of social media
- Corpus linguistics: studying language as part of the digital humanities
- Multimodal English.

References

Androutsopoulos, J. (2008) 'Potentials and limitations of discourse-centred online ethnography', *Language@Internet* 5, accessed 6 June 2014.

Androutsopoulos, J. (2014) 'Languaging when contexts collapse: Audience design in social networking', *Discourse, Context & Media* 4–5: 62–73.

Baker, P. (2006) *Using Corpora in Discourse Analysis*. London: Bloomsbury.

Bamberg, M. (1997) 'Positioning between structure and performance', *Journal of Narrative and Life History* 7: 335–342.

Bamberg, M. and A. Georgakopoulou (2008) 'Small stories as a new perspective in narrative and identity analysis', *Text & Talk* 28(3): 377–396.

Cameron, D. (2001) *Working with Spoken Discourse*. London: Sage.

Cameron, L. (2012) *Metaphor and Reconciliation: The Discourse Dynamics of Empathy in Post-Conflict Conversations*. London: Routledge.

Cameron, L. (2015) 'Embracing connectedness and change: A complex dynamic systems perspective for applied linguistic research', *AILA Review* 28: 28–48.

Cienki, A. J. and C. Müller (2008) *Metaphor and Gesture*. Amsterdam: John Benjamins.

Creese, A. (2008) 'Linguistic ethnography', *Encyclopedia of Language and Education* 2: 229–241.

Deppermann, A. (2013) 'Editorial: Positioning in narrative interaction', *Narrative Inquiry* 23: 1–15.

Edwards, D. (2000) 'Discourse and Cognition', *Journal of Community and Applied Social Psychology* 10: 79–83.

Fairclough, N. (1995) *Critical Discourse Analysis: The Critical Study of Language*. London: Pearson.

Foucault, M. (1981) 'The orders of discourse', in R. Young (ed.), *Untying the Text: A Post-Structuralist Reader*. London: Routledge.
Gal, N., L. Shifman and Z. Kampf (2015) '"It Gets Better": Internet memes and the construction of collective identity', *New Media & Society* 18(8), 1698–1714.
Garfinkel, H. (1967) *Studies in Ethnomethodology*. Englewood Cliffs: Prentice Hall.
Gumperz, J. and D. Hymes (1972) *Directions in Sociolinguistics: The Ethnography of Communication*. New York: Wiley-Blackwell.
Halliday, M. A. K. (1973) *Explorations in the Functions of Language*. London: Edward Arnold.
Hardaker, C. and M. McGlashan (2016) '"Real men don't hate women": Twitter rape threats and group identity', *Journal of Pragmatics* 91: 80–93.
Harré, R. and L. van Langenhove (1998) *Positioning Theory: Moral Contexts of Intentional Action*. London: Blackwell Publishers.
Herring, S. (2004a) 'Computer-mediated discourse analysis: An approach to researching online behavior', in S. A. Barab, R. Kling and J. H. Gray (eds), *Designing for Virtual Communities in the Service of Learning*. Cambridge: Cambridge University Press, 338–376.
Herring, S. (2004b) 'Slouching toward the ordinary: Current trends in computer-mediated communication', *New Media and Society* 6: 26–36.
Jewitt, C. (2009) *The Routledge Handbook of Multimodal Analysis*. London: Routledge.
Kress, G. and T. van Leeuwen. (2001) *Multimodal Discourse: The Modes and Media of Contemporary Communication*. London: Bloomsbury Academic.
Labov, W. (1972) *Language in the Inner City*. Philadelphia: University of Pennsylvania Press.
Labov, W. and Waletzky, J. (1997) 'Narrative analysis: Oral versions of personal experience', *Journal of Narrative and Life History* 7: 3–38.
Larsen-Freeman, D. and L. Cameron (2008) *Complex Systems and Applied Linguistics*. Oxford: Oxford University Press.
Lim, S. S. (2015) 'On stickers and communicative fluidity in social media', *Social Media + Society* 1: 2056305115578137.
Marwick, A. and D. Boyd (2011) 'I tweet honestly, I tweet passionately: Twitter users, context collapse, and the imagined audience', *New Media & Society* 13: 114–133.
McEnery, T. and A. Wilson (2001) *Corpus Linguistics: An Introduction*. Edinburgh: Edinburgh University Press.
Musolff, A. (2010) *Metaphor, Nation and the Holocaust: The Concept of the Body Politic*. London: Routledge.
Page, R. (2013) *Stories and Social Media: Identities and Interaction*. London: Routledge.
Partington, A., Duguid, A. and Taylor, C. (2013) *Patterns and Meanings in Discourse: Theory and Practice in Corpus-Assisted Discourse Studies (CADS)*. Amsterdam: John Benjamins Publishing.
Patil, S. and P. Davies (2014) 'Use of google translate in medical communication: Evaluation of accuracy', *BMJ: British Medical Journal* 349. DOI: 10.1136/bmj.g7392.
Paulus, T., A. Warren and J. N. Lester (2016) 'Applying conversation analysis methods to online talk: A literature review', *Discourse, Context & Media* 12: 1–10.
Pihlaja, S. (2018) *Religious Talk Online: The Online Evangelical Language of Muslims, Christians, and Atheists*. Cambridge: Cambridge University Press.
Potter, J. and A. Hepburn (2005) Qualitative Interviews in Psychology: Problems and Possibilities. *Qualitative research in psychology* 2: 281–307.
Potter, J. and Wetherell, M. (1987) *Discourse and Social Psychology: Beyond Attitudes and Behaviour*. London: Sage.
Rampton, B. (1995) *Crossing: Language and Ethnicity Among Adolescents*. Harlow: Longman Pub Group.
Rampton, B., K. Tusting, J. Maybin, et al. (2004) '*UK Linguistic Ethnography: A Discussion Paper*', accessed 14 August 2012.
Rayson, P. (2008) 'From key words to key semantic domains', *International Journal of Corpus Linguistics* 13: 519–549.
Rendle-Short, J. (2015) 'Dispreferred responses when texting: Delaying that "no" response', *Discourse & Communication* 9: 643–661.
Rørbeck Nørreby, T. and J. Spindler Møller (2015) 'Ethnicity and social categorization in on- and offline interaction among Copenhagen adolescents', *Discourse, Context & Media* 8: 46–54.

Ross, A. S. and D. J. Rivers (2017) 'Digital cultures of political participation: Internet memes and the discursive delegitimization of the 2016 U.S Presidential candidates', *Discourse, Context & Media* 16: 1–11.

Sabat, S. (2003) 'Malignant positioning and the predicament of people with Alzheimer's disease', in R. Harré and F. M. Moghaddam (eds), *The Self and Others Positioning Individuals and Groups in Personal, Political, and Cultural Contexts*. Westport: Praeger.

Sacks, H. (1992) *Lectures on Conversation*. Oxford: Blackwell.

Sacks, H., E. A. Schegloff, and G. Jefferson (1974) 'A simplest systematics for the organization of turn-taking for conversation', *Language* 50: 696–735.

Sakai, N. (2013) 'The role of sentence closing as an emotional marker: A case of Japanese mobile phone e-mail', *Discourse, Context & Media* 2: 149–155.

Seargeant, P. and C. Tagg (2014) *The Language of Social Media: Identity and Community on the Internet*. Basingstoke: Palgrave Macmillan.

Sinclair, J. and M. Coulthard (1975) *Towards an Analysis of Discourse: The Language of Teachers and Pupils*. Oxford: Oxford University Press.

Stokoe, E. (2010) '"I'm not gonna hit a lady": Conversation analysis, membership categorization and men's denials of violence towards women', *Discourse & Society* 21: 59–82.

Tagg, C. (2012) *Discourse of Text Messaging: Analysis of SMS Communication*. London: Continuum/ Bloomsbury.

Tagg, C., A. Lyons, R. Hu, *et al.* (2017a) The ethics of digital ethnography in a team project. *Applied Linguistics Review* 271. 271–292.

Tagg, C., Seargeant, P. and Brown, A. A. (2017b) *Taking Offence on Social Media: Conviviality and Communication on Facebook*. London: Springer.

Tusting, K. and J. Maybin (2007) 'Linguistic ethnography and interdisciplinarity: Opening the discussion', *Journal of Sociolinguistics* 11: 575–583.

Van Dijk, T. A. (1997) 'What is political discourse analysis?', *Belgian Journal of Linguistics* 11: 11–52.

Wetherell, M. (2007) 'A step too far: Discursive psychology, linguistic ethnography and questions of identity', *Journal of Sociolinguistics* 11: 661–681.

Widdowson, H. G. (2005) *Text, Context, Pretext: Critical Issues in Discourse Analysis*. Oxford: Blackwell.

Wodak, R. and M. Meyer (2002) *Methods for Critical Discourse Analysis*. London: Sage.

Xiong, W., J. Droppo, X. Huang, et al. (2016) 'Achieving human parity in conversational speech recognition', *arXiv preprint arXiv:1610.05256*.

Zappavigna, M. and S. Zhao (2017) 'Selfies in "mommyblogging": An emerging visual genre', *Discourse, Context & Media* 20: 239–247.

26

Linguistic ethnography

Studying English language, cultures and practices

Lian Malai Madsen

Introduction

The understanding of languages as bounded, enumerable codes closely tied to distinct national and ethnic cultures has been questioned from a range of perspectives for the past three or four decades. Alternative ways of seeing and studying language have been contributed in particular by the vast research focusing on language as situated practice, such as linguistic anthropology (Hymes 1974; Silverstein 1985; Bauman and Briggs 2003; Agha 2007), interactional sociolinguistics (Gumperz 1982; Rampton 1995), and, more recently, research affiliated with the strand that has become known as *linguistic ethnography* which builds on these traditions (overviews in Copland and Creese 2015; Snell et al. 2015). This approach combines ethnographic methodology (observations, interviews etc.) with micro-analysis of recorded interactions (employing tools from conversation analysis and linguistics), and it sees social and linguistic categories and structures as being produced and reproduced through practices in everyday life. This line of research has also had an impact on studies of English language, since questioning the conceptualisation of language as an object in general inevitably throws into relief the idea of English as a distinct linguistic object as well (Pennycook 2007).

The ideological consequences and limitations of the established close association of (national) culture and language is put on display particularly in spaces of linguistic and cultural contact. Therefore it is not surprising that there has been a renewed concern with the theorisation of language and its relation to culture within linguistic ethnographic research in such contact zones that have developed as a result of globalisation. While much of this research has focused predominantly on unpredictability, hybridity, agency and creativity, recently scholars within the field have called for more attention to be paid to larger-scale social stratification and structuring (e.g. Rampton 2006; Collins 2009; Block 2014; Jaspers 2014; Madsen 2015). Within such research on language and globalisation English has held a central position, whether it has been seen as the productive linguistic accompanist of globalisation, the less pretty face of linguistic imperialism or the ludic, contextualised practices of global Englishes used by particular groups or individuals under particular circumstances (Pennycook 2007: chapter 2; cf. Blommaert 2010).

This chapter presents the foundation for these debates and discusses their relevance to the study of English language. Through examples of situated use of forms of English from research conducted among youth in heterogeneous urban contexts in Denmark, it unfolds the theoretical and empirical directions suggested by the linguistic ethnographic approach. Through this lens, the chapter illustrates the potential of starting with the lived local realities of language users and linking these to larger-scale socio-cultural processes through an ethnographic perspective and a close investigation of contexts.

Languages, languaging and communicative cultures

Linguistic ethnography, through a focus on lived local experiences, contributes to the challenging of traditional concepts of language. In this it connects to a longer and wider development in language research where the discontent with the traditional concept of language has been raised in different shapes, with different aims and within different scholarly traditions, but the critical voices share an emphasis on language use in *interaction*, a concern with *contextualisation* and attention to *social (re)-construction*. Linell (1998) characterises the shift away from viewing language as a bounded structural entity by contrasting what he refers to as a 'dialogic' view of language with the 'monologic' view characterising the traditional code understanding. A dialogic approach sees cognition, language and communication as inherently interdependent. Communication is not seen as the use of codes existing in readymade form before communication occurs; rather communicative acts are constructed through the practice of using language, that is through *languaging*, which is defined by (Jørgensen 2008: 169) as 'language users employ[ing] whatever linguistic features are at their disposal with the intention of achieving their communicative aims' (see also García and Wei 2014; Madsen et al. 2016 for discussions of the term), and communicative and linguistic meaning is focused in dialogue with various kinds of contexts and interlocutors (Linell 1998: 35). Communicative acts respond to and anticipate other acts, and although such acts are always situation-specific they also always 'make manifest aspects of culturally constituted routines and ways of seeing the world' (Linell 1998: 48). Language is seen as a socio-cultural artefact and as mediating cognition and communication. From such a practice-focused and constructionist understanding, language as a bounded entity becomes a highly problematic construct. Integrationists for example have called this concept a 'myth' (Harris 1998) and have taken linguists for 'language-makers' (Harris 1980), while linguistic anthropologists Bauman and Briggs (2003) have closely traced how the common idea today of a language has been constructed through consistent representations of languages as associated with particular national communities.

Linguistic re-conceptualisations

More recently within linguistic ethnographic research, and fuelled by empirical observations of linguistic hybridity in culturally diverse communicative contexts (e.g. in urban settings and internet communication), a range of different labels have been introduced. The new terms are meant to signal a reconceptualisation of the practices the authors observe. These include, among others, 'polylanguaging' (Jørgensen et al. 2016), 'metrolingualism' (Pennycook and Otsuji 2015) or 'translanguaging' (García and Wei 2014). These notions are in themselves not interchangeable and they are tied to specific places and projects, but the relative abundance of this type of terminology betrays a common, growing, twofold dissatisfaction. Empirically and theoretically the inventors of these labels are unhappy with 1) the explanatory adequacy of the traditional language concept; it is not precise enough or even distorts descriptions of the phenomena we can observe; and 2) the ideological and political implications of the concept of separate, bounded languages may be undesirable; the idea of language as a bounded code is tied to a specific language political history in which plurilingual behaviour and pluri- or transcultural affiliations are seen as problematic, and this can lead to disadvantages for particular language users (see discussion in Jaspers and Madsen 2016).

At the same time as voicing such discontent with the bounded code-model of language, this linguistic ethnographic research is also occupied with the significance of the bounded code understanding. There is a great interest in how language users associate linguistic resources with different languages on a normative and ideological level, and how these constructions are based in well-established (national-romantic) ideologies. Yet, while language*s* may be understood as bounded and even seemingly natural categories, it is emphasised that these categories are socio-cultural and socio-historical constructions not descriptive facts (Madsen et al. 2016). It has been thoroughly documented how speakers use multilayered combinations of linguistic forms, and how single linguistic forms do not necessarily carry clear distinct connections to specific codes or languages, and it is argued that when individuals refrain from drawing on parts of their entire linguistic repertoire, complex and heterogeneous as it will be, it also has a social motivation (Jørgensen et al. 2016). Emphasising that languages are ideological constructions also entails that widely used notions such as monolingualism, bilingualism and multilingualism are inadequate as descriptive tools. Instead they can be described as norms of behaviour that are built on the ideological presuppositions that a) languages may be separated and counted, and b) it is possible to establish when speakers possess languages (Jørgensen et al. 2016; Madsen et al. 2016).

Global Englishes

Within the field of English language studies and research on globalisation such recent discussions of the relationship between language, nation and culture have targeted both what Pennycook (2007: 19) refers to as a homogenic 'linguistic imperialism' and a heterogenic 'world Englishes' position. As Pennycook (2007: 20) states, the *homogeny position* suggests that the worldwide spread of English leads to homogenisation, while the *heterogeny position* focuses on how English is pluricentric. However, Pennycook argues that the pluralisation of English within the world Englishes approach is no less founded in close associations of nation and language than the imperialistic position and that it does not take us far enough in the direction of an adequate conceptualisation of English in the globalised world, because it remains exclusionary in its vision of English (e.g. it does not include creoles). As he claims, 'The irony here is that while resembling a pluralist, localised version of English, this paradigm reinforces both centrist views on language and dangerous myths about English' (Pennycook 2007: 22). Instead Pennycook advocates a critical approach to language (as explained above) as well as to globalisation. Rather than giving pre-eminence to economic relations, the cultural, social and political aspects of globalisation need to be taken into account with an approach considering both the historical dimensions and the culturally specific, linguistic articulations of worldliness. Pennycook urges that we ask 'what kinds of desires and mobilizations are at stake when English is invoked' (Pennycook 2007: 30) in specific encounters and communities.

The methodology of linguistic ethnography

Globalisation results in increasingly complex relationships between language and culture, not merely because intensified mobility and migration lead to the make-up of popultions becoming increasingly diverse, but also because individuals' possible linguistic expressions of identity and affiliations with socio-cultural values become more complex and less predictable. Since language and linguistic styles through repeated use come to be associated with particular people, places and purposes, language use is a prime heuristic for tracing the desires and mobilisations Pennycook refers to above, as well as the experience and construction of personal and social identities, cultural interpretations, social differentiation and alignments. Since such meanings are often communicated indirectly and linked to activities and background understanding we need appropriate research methods and tools for capturing this.

Linguistic ethnography is well tuned to attend to such unpredictability, to get beyond established categories and connections and to engage with the complexities of situated social identification and language use with its key principle that the contexts for communication should be investigated rather than assumed (Rampton et al. 2007; Copland and Creese 2015; Snell et al. 2015). The approach has developed among applied linguists in the UK with strong inspiration from North American linguistic anthropology as well as interactional sociolinguistics and discourse analysis (Snell et al. 2015: 2). It is an interdisciplinary research strand which comprises a range of data types such as field diaries, interviews, various documents and recordings of interactions in the pursuit of combining an ethnographic focus on insider-knowledge, rich contextualisation and participant reflexivity with the analytical refinement of linguistics and micro-analysis of interaction. It thereby allows us to analyse the details of communicative activities and their relation and sensitivity to the social contexts in which they are produced. This is done by combining analytical perspectives addressing different levels of context to investigate the links between semiotic practices in the here-and-now situations as well as the historical and socio-cultural embeddedness of the resources used. Linguistic ethnographic work which includes interactional data, as I will demonstrate in the examples below, typically takes into account how turns-at-talk relate to one another in a stretch of conversation. What do the individual turns do? What are the displayed reactions and alignments in the following turns by other participants? But also, how are the utterances composed with respect to accent, grammar and word choice, and how does the form relate to their function? In addition, it considers the types of activities relevant to the interaction. What are the participants engaged in during the conversation? Where does the interaction take place? Who are present? And what type of conversation is it? The linguistic ethnographic analysis will also involve the social relationship between the participants, and their former interactional history (accessed across a dataset also including the ethnographic observations). Finally, it addresses institutional, moral or ideological codes, values and identities possibly made relevant, reproduced or negotiated during particular and across a range of interactional encounters.

Linguistic ethnography shares theoretical underpinnings with linguistic anthropology. This US-based tradition also combines ethnographic and linguistic methodology, but tends to take culture as its principal point of analytic entry were linguistic ethnography which has developed within UK applied linguistics, typically takes language as the starting point. Both approaches, however, account for the consideration of the local, socio-cultural meanings given to particular semiotic resources and their relation to wider cultural models through the notion of indexicality (Silverstein, 2003). Indexicality refers to the associations between forms and (typical) usage, contexts of use and stereotypes of users that are (re-) created in communicative encounters through linguistic and other signs. An example of indexicality could be how forms of African American Vernacular English have become associated with hip hop (Cutler 2007). Indexical associations are metapragmatic which means that they characterise signs' links to pragmatically usable systems of signs and activities on various social levels. These levels range from widely circulating stereotypes to local speaker practices and contribute to enregisterment (Agha 2007); that is, the processes and practices whereby performable signs become recognised as belonging to distinct semiotic registers.

Thus a linguistic ethnographic approach to English language in the contemporary globalised world can grasp how forms of English become enregistered as part of recognisable semiotic models in particular cultural communities without relying on the language myths criticised by recent sociolinguists and integrationists. As I will argue below based on examples from research conducted in Copenhagen, such an approach can capture the complexity and heteroglossic character of local situated language use, but also pay attention to its wider socio-cultural embeddedness and thereby respond to recent calls that we do not lose sight of the stratifying forces and unequal relations in contemporary sociolinguistic orders.

Complexity, agency and stratification

Due to the concern within applied- and sociolinguistics with deconstructing the traditional language concept and highlighting its descriptive inadequacy, there has been a tendency to emphasise linguistic creativity, agency, unpredictability and hybridity. In line with post-structuralist thinking more generally (the so-called 'cultural turn' in social and political theory) the focus has shifted away from larger societal structures, socio-economic inequality and class relations. Class, in particular, has been problematised and considered of less relevance; it has been proposed that there is a decline in class awareness in particular among young people (Bradley 1996: 77), and that it is after all less clear what social class refers to in contemporary, rapidly changing societies. Instead ethnic culture and gender have been the dominating interpretive frameworks invoked (see discussions in Rampton 2006; Block 2014). Recently, however, several scholars have argued that we need to reintroduce social stratification, inequality and class in our ethnographic and linguistic analyses (Rampton 2006; Collins 2009; Madsen 2013; Block 2014). Based on a line of work within British sociology incorporating a view of class as a tacit sensibility Rampton suggests that

> In class societies, people carry class hierarchy around inside themselves, acting it out in the fine grain of ordinary life, and if we look closely enough, we may be able to pick it out in the conduct of just a few individuals.
>
> (Rampton 2010: 4)

Although class societies may be more difficult to depict in an area of globalisation, Coupland (2003: 470) writes:

> It would be naïve to assume that [. . .] globalised societies will be less unequal. We can be sure they will be more complex, and therefore that the critical capacity of sociolinguistics will be increasingly tested. But we can only critique what we can theorise, only theorise what we understand, only understand what we see, and only see what we look at.

As it has been demonstrated, for instance in Blommaert's (2010) work on African communities, English is centrally placed in the dynamics of inequality of globalised linguascapes, coexisting as an idealised (often inaccessible) ticket to economic and professional status and success and as a local pragmatic register of daily communication (Blommaert 2010: chapter 3). In addition, Englishes are closely connected to youth- and popular cultural flows (Pennycook 2007). I will now turn to look at the indexical values and the potential dynamics of inequality related to the use of English among adolescents in Copenhagen, while basing my interpretation of the complexity of situated language practices firmly in ethnographically based accounts of the context in which it occurs.

Indexicalities of English registers among Copenhagen adolescents

I will discuss two examples from two different linguistic ethnographic research projects conducted in Copenhagen because they illustrate well how different forms of English are used by Danish youth and how the local meaning of these ways of speaking can be grasped with a linguistic ethnographic approach. The first is from a linguistic ethnographic study of 16 children and adolescents (between 10 and 15 years old) in a martial arts club, where, from 2004 to 2005, I carried out observations and collected audio-recorded self-recordings from the participants as well as video-recorded group-conversations and audio-recorded semi-structured qualitative interviews (see description in Madsen 2015). The second is from a larger collaborative collection among students from two secondary school classes at the age of 13–16 (conducted 2009-2011) of similar ethnographic and linguistic data types (observations, recorded interactions in different settings and interviews, see Madsen 2013; Madsen et al. 2016). Both examples involve teenage boys (with a linguistic and ethnic minority background in the Danish context) and their use of English in entertaining performances, but they illustrate different ways of invoking indexical values and socio-cultural stereotypes through English features that are not easily captured without the ethnographic insights into the local community within which they are produced.

In excerpt 1, the two boys Murat and Ilias (14 and 15 years old) who participated in the martial arts study recorded themselves on their way back to Copenhagen on the train, after a regional talent team practice for young elite taekwondo fighters. Murat carried the mp3 recorder. Salim, another young male talent team member (but not a participant in my study otherwise), was present as well. Before Murat's first utterance, the boys had been engaged in playful teasing of Salim (in a stylised stereotyped immigrant speech style). Murat in this sequence then initiates a switch into English and seems to further contribute to the teasing frame. Note that English is used in a large part of the original speech (this is marked by italics in the translation; for transcription key see the Appendix at the end of this chapter).

Excerpt 1: Speak English

1	Murat:	you' re so desperate	*you're so desperate*
2		that you sleep with goats	*that you sleep with goats*
3		(0.3)	(0.3)
		[maybe]	[*maybe*]
4	Salim:	[who ?]	[*who* ?]
5	Murat:	you could have choose do:gs	*you could have choose do:gs*
6		or ca:ts	*or ca:ts*
7		or even ↑him	*or even ↑him*
		(1.1)	(1.1)
8		but you choose ↑goats hhh ((amerikanske accent-træk intonation/vokaler))	*but you choose ↑goats hhh* ((American accent features intonation/vowels))
		(1.0)	(1.0)

9	Salim:	no goats is better than him.	*no goats is better than him.*
10	Murat:	åh ha hhh ((griner))	oh ha hhh ((laughs))
11	Ilias:	i lige måde din nar.	you too you fool.
12 13 14	Murat:	jeg kan ikke tale engelsk det hedder i lige måde eggår hhh ((stiliseret jysk))	I can' t speak English it' s called you too right hhh ((stylised Jutlandic))
		(1.8)	(1.8)
15 16 17 18 19 20	Murat:	don' t try to change the subje subject you' ve got a exam in what in (.) one week and you start speaking Danish speak English you piece of shit ((amerikanske træk))	*don't try to change the subje* *subject* *you've got a exam* *in what in (.) one week* *and you start speaking Danish* *speak English you* *piece of shit* ((American features))
		(0.2)	(0.2)
21 22	Salim:	hhh hhh °piece of shit° hhh hhh((hvisker grinende))	hhh hhh °*piece of shit*° hhh hhh((whispers laughing))
		(1.7)	(1.7)
23	Murat:	I love you. ((forvrænget stemme))	*I love you.* ((distorted voice))
		(3.4)	(3.4)
24	Ilias:	°nå hvad så°	°well what' s up°
25	Murat:	SPEAK ENGLISH.	*SPEAK ENGLISH.*
26	Ilias:	næ ((Murat griner))	no ((Murat laughs))
		(2.9)	(2.9)
27	Salim:	you have an English exam.	*you have an English exam.*
28	Ilias:	↑*hold din kæft.* ((intonation karakteristisk for nutidig storbystil))	↑shut up. ((intonation characteristic of contemporary urban speech))
		(1.6)	(1.6)
29	Salim:	speak English	*speak English*
30	Ilias:	↑*hold din kæft.* ((samme intonation som ovenfor))	↑shut up. ((same intonation as above))

Murat's first utterance (lines 1–3 and 5–8) is an insult which builds on several taboos. It involves shortcomings with respect to sexuality and uncontrollable (or unsatisfied) sexual desires, and it evokes norm transgressions related to bestiality and homosexuality. At the same time it involves cues pointing to a playful frame: Murat laughs while he speaks, and the utterance is marked as a performance by a shift into American-accented English (mainly signalled by the stress pattern and the length of the vowels). The employed accent indexically points to urban American hip hop culture (e.g. Cutler 2007), which can also be associated with the activity of ritual insult. Salim's clarifying question in overlap with Murat's turn: 'who?'(line 4) and his reaction with a counter-insult 'goats is better than him' (line 10), indicates that Salim understands himself as the target of the insult and the appropriate responder. The fact that Salim's response to Murat includes reference to a third person, 'him', suggest that he understands Murat's 'or even him' (line 7) to refer to someone different from himself and this is likely to be Ilias, who is the only other person participating in this encounter. Thereby Ilias and Salim are both the targets of Murat's tease. The laughs accompanying the turns and the sequential order corresponding to that of ritual insult, with insult, counter-insult (line 10) and appreciation (line 11) further suggest that this is not a serious fight. Salim's reaction to Murat's insult is not a direct counter-insult, but rather a deflection developed from Murat's previous turn. Salim also employs English. Thereby he confirms the code choice of Murat, although Salim's contributions in English are pronounced with a rather Danish-sounding accent (this could be a matter of linguistic competence). Murat's response of surprised laughter shows alignment with Salim's contribution to the activity. The excerpt continues with several demands on Ilias to speak English, referring to school achievements because of an upcoming exam (line 25, 27, 29). Ilias does not seem willing to participate in this activity. He is playfully challenged, not only because of the content of the insults, but also because he does not treat the insults as laughable, as he is supposed to within this activity type, and because he does not follow the others' language choice.

The practice of ritual insult in this example does not only serve as a demonstration of the skills of causing offence for the entertainment of the interlocutors, but also of English skills. English skills are explicitly oriented to by the reference to the upcoming exam, but from the wider ethnographic accounts it is furthermore clear that these boys have discussed achievements in foreign language tests in school and linguistic competence several times both before and after this particular episode. In fact it is characteristic of their local community and communicative culture that they orient strongly to positive school results, while they also orient to global youth and popular culture, sports and school-related competition, toughness and street-credibility, and the way English is used here seems to invoke all of these aspects at once. In this case Ilias fails (or refuses) to demonstrate linguistic skills while Murat has success doing so. Salim appears to act more as a tag-along, echoing Murat's contributions. So Murat locally achieves a positioning as competent (youth culturally appropriate) English speaker as well as a skilled teasing performer. More generally, the excerpt illustrates how among these boys an English register not usually associated with school success (with its slang features, tabooed expressions and non-standard pronunciations), but rather with American popular culture, such as hip hop (and the image of tough masculinities related to this) can locally function as an index of positive school orientation as well.

Excerpt 2 illustrates a different type of situated linguistic performance in English which also relates to educational success, but in a different way. The sequence is a recording during a school break among class mates (13–14 years old). The girl Kurima and the boy Shahid had been discussing their results in a recent reading test. Shahid achieved a mid-level mark, but just before this excerpt he claimed that next time he would achieve top marks. Bashaar, who was another boy present in the school yard, joined the conversation at this point (again English in the original is marked by italics in the translation).

Excerpt 2: Heart of gold

1	Sha:	åh jeg er bedre end	Oh I' m better than
2		jer alle sammen mand	all of you man
3	Kur:	[na] ha:j	[no:]
4	Bas:	[you] (.) my friend you' ve	*[you] (.) my friend you've*
5		got a very beautiful	*got a very beautiful*
6		future in front of you	*future in front of you*
7		you' re gonna travel	*you're gonna travel*
8		to Lon↑don (.) and stu↑dy	*to Lon↑don (.) and stu↑dy*
9	Sha:	hey lad nu være (hvorfor	hey don' t (why should I)
10		skulle jeg) lad nu være	just stop doing that
11		med at gøre det herovre	that here (gu:) you shall
12		(gu:) du skal BARE IK gøre	just NOT do it over here
13		det herovre KORAN jeg	CORAN I shall not touch
14		skal ikke røre det der	that kind of
15		vand	water
16	Bas:	you' re gonna study in	*you're gonna study in*
17		Bol↑ton I think it' s	*Bol↑ton I think it's*
18		gonna be a very good eh	*gonna be a very good eh*
19		eh lesson for ↑you	*eh lesson for ↑you*
20		because you are are are	*because you are are are*
21		a man with a heart of	*a man with a heart of*
22		gold	*gold*
23	Sha:	thank you thank you	*thank you thank you*
24	Bas:	and and and and you have	*and and and and you have*
25		a good[brain]	*a good [brain]*
		((girls approach Bashaar	((girls approach Bashaar
		and interrupt))	and interrupt))

After Kurima has protested against Shahid's claim of being better than everyone, Bashaar begins a performance in English marked by a range of pronunciation features. Apart from the switch to English, the marked features include unrounded and fronted /u/ in *London* and *study*, rolled /r/ in *front* and *brain*, monophtong instead of diphtong in *brain*, aspirated final /d/ in *friend* and r-sound instead of /t/ in *beautiful*, as well as stress and pitch rise on the final syllables in certain words (London and Bolton). The pronunciation features leave the impression of a stereotypical index of an adult English learner (or a non-Anglo accent). In addition, the content, intonation and pauses index a performance of a public speech. After this sequence, some girls interrupt Bashaar and address Shahid. Bashaar reacts with the utterance: 'let me finish let me finish my speech with my boy with my son' and the girls after this react with a 'stop that Lebanese'. Thus, as a reaction to a friend's academic boasting, Bashaar performs the voice of a supportive fatherly persona praising the heart and the mind of his son and hoping for a bright future. In contrast to this evocation of high academic aspirations, the voice of this figure is performed with features associated with adult-learner English. This combination indexes a naivety on the part of the father figure, highlighting the unrealistically high ambitions in relation to the relatively poor academic value of the linguistic resources demonstrated here. Thereby Bashaar's performance seems to function locally as a playful sanctioning of a friend's boasting and evokes a stereotype of (unrealistic) parental expectations for a successful future.

The accented English performed by Bashaar here resembles what Jaspers (2011) identifies as the practice of 'talking illegal' among adolescents in Antwerp. Jaspers describes how the practice of stylising accented or 'incorrect learner speech' locally serves the purpose of critically engaging with and at the same time co-constructing dominant structures of societal and institutional inequalities. Thus, stereotypic ethnically-marked voices are used to highlight a general marginal social positioning associated with linguistic incompetence, rather than specific ethnic differences. From the wider ethnographic study we know that these adolescent boys, similarly to the boys in the martial arts club, orient positively to school achievements and we know from the participants' metapragmatic and linguistically reflexive accounts that speech practices stereotypically associated with ethnic minority communities are sociolinguistically placed in a contrasting position to standard, academic registers associated with high social status (see details in Madsen 2013). Thus there are several indications that within this community, relations of ethnic minority and majority are mapped onto relations of inequality related to social stratification and status. These insights thus supports the interpretation that the kind of employment of recognisable ethnically-coloured pronunciation or non-standard learner styles that Jaspers describes also seems to be at play in excerpt 2. The non-academic and incompetent associations stereotypically related to adult and newcomer-accented speech are here locally exploited playfully to put a friend in his place after he has explicitly claimed a perhaps too-ambitious academic and linguistic status.

These two examples of English speech by young Copenhageners exhibit the situated use of different registers. Murat performs an urban, hip hop-inspired tough character through the use of American accent features, slang and taboo expressions, within the frame of playful insulting; while Bashaar parodies a fatherly adult figure speaking in learner-accented English projecting high academic aspirations for his son within the frame of a public speech genre. Both examples are certainly creative and complex and they illustrate the speakers' agentive and reflexive linguistic practices in response to the immediate communicative concerns of entertaining and having fun with peers. Both examples, however, also throw into relief wider cultural stereotypes and relations of social status and inequality. English as idealised means of academic (and professional) success in a globalised world is invoked in both examples. But to get at how this indexical potential is relevant in the two case studies it is necessary to include the ethnographic contexts. Among the taekwondo practitioners this aspect of English is made relevant through their investment in English as school-related capital as well as resources associated with popular cultural practices. Among the adolescents in the school yard, this idealised image of English is in fact explicitly put on display in Bashaar's parodying performance and mocked through the accented speech of the character articulating the image. In both cases established stereotypical assumptions of what usually belongs together can be said to be disturbed; non-standard slang-infused English is integrated with displays of academic skills, and signs of particular ethno-cultural stigmatisation intersects with educational and socio-economic status relationships. Thereby these studies of the situated speech practices of youth in Copenhagen support Rampton's call for more attention to 'high' and 'low' status differences in contemporary sociolinguistics (Rampton 2010), and they show that although current rapidly changing societies may complicate the study of inequality in sociolinguistics it does not mean that socio-economic hierarchies, power and status lose significance. In this way the interactional activities of the young people observed in these studies complicate the picture drawn by influential stereotypic ideas circulating in society more widely, about the links between particular linguistic forms and social values, and a central principle of linguistic ethnographic research is, in fact, that such complications constructively add to our knowledge of language, categories and cultures (see also Blommaert and Dong 2010).

As another of the guiding principles of a sociolinguistics sensitive to contemporary complexity, Blommaert and Rampton (2015) point to the importance of remaining aware of what Silverstein (1985) refers to as 'the total linguistic fact'. Silverstein notes that the object of study of a science of language should be 'sign forms contextualised to situations of interested human use and mediated by the fact of cultural ideology' (1985: 220). This of course means that micro-analysis of contextualised human use should not only inform studies of sign forms, but the study of situated use needs to consider the elements of wider ranging ideology and patterns of available resources as well. With the discussion of these two episodes I have demonstrated how this can be done from a linguistic ethnographic perspective.

Future directions

As I have described at the beginning of this chapter, it is well documented in recent research on linguistic and cultural diversity that speakers in practice draw on their collective linguistic repertoires of resources to achieve their communicative aims in a given situation (within the restrictions of their abilities and with concern for the abilities of their interlocutors), and this complicates the very notion of a language. Linguistic ethnographic studies in diverse contexts have led to re-examinations of the traditional conceptions of a language or a variety as bounded and separable sets of linguistic features, and it has become clear that speakers' language use is often not limited by common associations of certain linguistic resources belonging to certain varieties or languages. We will continue in the future to observe how everyday communication is characterised by a mix of linguistic resources usually associated with different named languages or varieties and how they use multilayered combinations of linguistic forms not necessarily ascribable to any recognisable language. The idea of *languaging* rather than the use of languages and the point that the idea of separate linguistic codes needs to be seen as a socio-cultural and ideological construction rather than an unquestioned linguistic fact aptly captures linguistic practices as they occur. Agha's theory of enregisterment (2007) moreover appeals to and is fruitfully combined with this kind of approach to language with attention to how linguistic signs over time become associated with wider cultural formations and how these wider formations interact with everyday communication, and it has been widely employed and discussed within the past few years of sociolinguistic research.

As a theoretical conception, enregisterment concerns how we display and enact social functions of language by talking about and employing linguistic resources in particular ways, and it points out how the situated semiotic activities of language users over time shape the broader socio-historical development of language as social practice. Ways of speaking come to point to, or index, ways of being and acting, because they are repeatedly used in certain types of situations by certain types of speakers or talked about or parodied in certain ways (Agha 2007; Silverstein 2003). From an enregisterment perspective, speakers' interactional use of different linguistic forms (re)creates the stereotypic indexical values of the used forms. Hence, in interactional use of resources associated with different registers, the stereotypic indexical values of the registers can be said to be brought into play and used for situational purposes, such as to comment on a classmate's conduct. At the same time, the employment of linguistic resources continuously contributes to their enregisterment through ratified usage, and in this sense the indexical values of the linguistic features used are also (re)created. Thereby the concept of enregisterment can fill the gap left when the notion of language has been deemed insufficient and undesirable.

Seeing language as embedded in and depending on processes of enregisterment makes it possible to relate linguistic practice to interactional positioning and wider cultural alignments, and to talk about different styles or registers. This kind of analysis can then include the broader tendencies and historical pattern of usage of linguistic resources, and it is still useful for us to be able to recognise features as belonging to registers, because the speakers we study do draw on the understanding that certain linguistic resources belong to larger systems of resources in their interactional practices even if linguists consider language a myth. What is interesting is to investigate how a language, e.g. English, is constructed as a myth in particular contexts and how it relates to patterns of differences, social positions and patterns of inequality on different social scales.

It is certainly true that the relationship between material conditions, social affiliation, culture and linguistic conduct is not straightforward in contemporary globalised societies (Blommaert and Rampton 2015), and there is no reason to believe this will become less complicated. However, this is also the case for e.g. the relationship between ethnic inheritance, national alignments and language practice. If social stratification and class relationships are abandoned as interpretive frameworks in relation to language use on these grounds, the way ethnic differences link up with social stratification and inequality in contemporary sociolinguistic economies may be overlooked. The challenge is, of course, how we uncover these links, but the combination of detailed linguistic analysis, ethnographic investigation of contexts and consideration of enregisterment and indexicality appears a promising option.

Finally, studies of communication, cultural communities, linguistic practices and, not least, English, which are all in tune with the current focus on globalisation and the polycentric communicative conditions it entails (Blommaert and Rampton 2015; Blommaert 2010), pay increasing attention to computer-mediated communication (CMC) as a significant research site. Since online communication sites are by now common vehicles for self-expression, content sharing and engagement in both worldwide and local interest communities social media has, more recently, become an important field site also for linguistic ethnographic research (Varis and Wang 2011; Stæhr and Madsen 2015). The status of an ethnographic account in such research may not be simple, but as Varis and Wang (2011: 75) phrase it, such work clearly shows that 'Global cultures, codes and flows [. . .] are not swallowed without chewing' (see also Pennycook 2007; Stæhr and Madsen 2015). Appropriation of global cultural flows, often involving forms of English, are regulated by local norms and meaning-making. This is certainly the situation in the cases I have discussed above, e.g. when it comes to the way hip hop culture is understood within the local frame of educational activities, and in the case of the school-based study this involves CMC to a large extent (Stæhr and Madsen 2015). Hence there is a case to be made for linguistic ethnography in relation to sociolinguistic studies of CMC. Such a methodological framework and epistemological perspective can help uncover how wider cultural flows and practices are 'chewed' in specific context without losing sight of the relations to wider patterns of differences and stratification.

Coupland (2003) argues that what we can see depends on what we look at, and the argument of this chapter is that what we see also depends on *how* we look at it. Looking at English through the looking-glass of linguistic ethnography makes it possible to uncover how it is used and metapragmatically commented on in playful performances. In this way I have argued that the ecological descriptions provided by this approach helps uncover structuring principles of wider societal currency in low-key, that is, situated in the everyday, linguistic and interactional practices.

Appendix

Transcription key:

[overlap]	overlapping speech
LOUD	louder volume than surrounding utterances
xxx	unintelligible speech
(questionable)	parts I am uncertain about
((comment))	my comments
:	prolongation of preceding sound
↑	local pitch raise
(.)	short pause
(0.6)	timed pause
stress	stress
hhh	laughter breathe

Further reading

Copland, F. and A. Creese (2015) *Linguistic Ethnography: Collecting, Analysing and Presenting Data*. London: Sage. To read more about the methodology of linguistic ethnography.

Madsen, L. M. (2015) *Fighters, Girls and Other Identities: Sociolinguistics in a Martial Arts Club*. Bristol: Multilingual Matters. For an example of a linguistic ethnographic study of a leisure community discussing aspects of cultural and linguistic diversity.

Pennycook, A. (2007) *Global Englishes and Transcultural Flows*. New York: Routledge. To read more about Englishes and globalisation including discussions of language as a concept.

Rampton, B. (2006). *Language in Late Modernity. Interaction in an Urban School*. Cambridge: Cambridge University Press. For a comprehensive account of the significance of social class relations from a linguistic ethnographic approach.

Snell, J., S. Shaw and F. Copland (2015) *Linguistic Ethnography: Interdisciplinary Explorations*. London: Palgrave. For an interdisciplinary collection of contemporary studies employing linguistic ethnography.

Related topics

- English and colonialism
- World Englishes: disciplinary debates and future directions
- English and multilingualism: a contested history
- English and social identity
- The politics of English
- Sociolinguistics: studying English and its social relations.

References

Agha, A. (2007) *Language and Social Relations*. Cambridge: Cambridge University Press.

Bauman, R. and C. L. Briggs (2003) *Voices of Modernity: Language Ideologies and the Politics of Inequality*. Cambridge: Cambridge University Press.

Block, D. (2014) *Social Class in Applied Linguistics*. London and New York: Routledge.

Blommaert, J. (2010) *The Sociolinguistics of Globalization*. Cambridge: Cambridge University Press.

Blommaert, J. and J. Dong (2010) *Ethnographic Fieldwork: A Beginner's Guide*. Bristol: Multilingual Matters.

Blommaert, J. and B. Rampton (2015) 'Language and superdiversity', in K. Arnaut, J. Blommaert, B. Rampton and M. Spotti (eds), *Language and Superdiversity*. New York: Routledge, 21–48.
Bradley, H. (1996) *Fractured Identities: Changing Patterns of Inequality*. London: Polity Press.
Collins, J. (2009). 'Social reproduction in classrooms and schools', *Annual Review of Anthropology* 38: 33–48.
Copland, F. and A. Creese (2015) *Linguistic Ethnography: Collecting, Analysing and Presenting Data*. London: Sage.
Coupland, N. (2003) 'Introduction: Sociolinguistics and globalisation', *Journal of Sociolinguistics* 7 (4): 465–472.
Cutler, C. (2007) 'Hip-hop language in sociolinguistics and beyond', *Language and Linguistics Compass* 1 (5): 519–538.
García, O. and L. Wei (2014). *Translanguaging. Language, Bilingualism and Education*. Basingstoke: Palgrave Macmillan.
Gumperz, J. (1982) *Discourse Strategies*. Cambridge: Cambridge University Press.
Harris, R. (1980) *The Language Makers*. London: Duckworth.
Harris, R. (1998) *Introduction to Integrational Linguistics*. Oxford: Pergamon.
Hymes, D. (1974) *Foundations in Sociolinguistics: An Ethnographic Approach*. Philadelphia: University of Pennsylvania Press.
Jaspers, J. (2011) 'Talking like a Zerolingual. Ambiguous linguistic caricatures at an urban secondary school', *Journal of Pragmatics* 43: 1264–1287.
Jaspers, J. (2014) 'Stylizations as teacher practice', *Language in Society* 43 (4): 371–393, Matters.
Jaspers, J. and L. M. Madsen (2016) 'Special issue: Sociolinguistics in a languagised world: Introduction', *Applied Linguistics Review* 7 (3), 235–258.
Jørgensen, J. N. (2008) Poly-lingual languaging around and among children and adolescents. *International Journal of Multilingualism* 5 (3), 161–176.
Jørgensen, J. N., M. S. Karrebæk, L. M. Madsen and J. S. Møller (2016) 'Polylanguaging in superdiversity', in K. Arnaut, J. Blommaert, B. Rampton and M. Spotti (eds), *Language and Superdiversity*. New York and London: Routledge, 137–154.
Linell, P. (1998) *Approaching Dialogue: Talk, Interaction and Contexts in Dialogical Perspectives*. Amsterdam: John Benjamins.
Madsen, L. M. (2013) '"High" and "Low" in urban Danish speech styles', *Language in Society* 42 (2): 115–138.
Madsen, L. M. (2015) *Fighters, Girls and Other Identities: Sociolinguistics in a Martial Arts Club*. Bristol: Multilingual Matters.
Madsen, L. M., M. S. Karrebæk and J. S. Møller (eds) (2016) *Everyday Languaging: Collaborative Research on the Language Use of Children and Youth*. Amsterdam: Mouton De Gruyter.
Pennycook, A. (2007) *Global Englishes and Transcultural Flows*. New York: Routledge.
Pennycook, A. and E. Otsuji (2015) *Metrolingualism: Language in the City*. New York: Routledge.
Rampton, B. (1995) *Crossing. Language and Ethnicity Among Adolescents*. London: Longman.
Rampton, B. (2006) *Language in Late Modernity. Interaction in an Urban School*. Cambridge: Cambridge University Press.
Rampton, B. (2010) 'Social class and sociolinguistics', *Applied Linguistics Review* 1: 1–22.
Rampton, B., J. Maybin and K. Tusting (eds) (2007) 'Special issue: Linguistic ethnography', *Journal of Sociolinguistics* 11 (5): 575–583.
Silverstein, M. (1985) 'Language and the culture of gender', in E. Mertz and R. Parmentier (eds), *Semiotic Mediation*. New York: Academic Press, 219–259.
Silverstein, M. (2003) 'Indexical order and the dialectics of sociolinguistic life', *Language and Communication* 23: 193–229.
Snell, J., S. Shaw and F. Copland (eds) (2015) *Linguistic Ethnography: Interdisciplinary Explorations*. London: Palgrave.
Stæhr, A. and L. M. Madsen (2015) Standard language in urban rap – Social media, linguistic practice and ethnographic context. *Language & Communication* 40, 67–81.
Varis, P. and X. Wang (2011) Superdiversity on the Internet: A case from China. *Diversities* 13 (2), 71–83.

27
The psycholinguistics of English

Christopher J. Hall

Introduction

Psycholinguistic studies have revealed a great deal about the nature of the English language, even though the primary objective of the field has been to explain the neuropsychological structures and mechanisms which support the general human capacity for language. Psycholinguistics is concerned with three main issues. The first is the nature of mental representation of language: the organisation and storage of a person's language resources in memory, and how they are related to mentally represented conceptual knowledge, experience, and other cognitive capacities. The second is processing, concerning the mechanisms through which such resources are deployed in production and comprehension, through the modalities of speech, writing, and sign, and how these processes engage with individuals' non-linguistic knowledge, assumptions, and intentions. The third area, development, addresses the acquisition, ongoing modification (and possible attrition) of linguistic resources and processing mechanisms, as the result of innate capacities and social experience.

Psycholinguistics harnesses data from several sources to gain an understanding of these issues. In investigating processing, it has traditionally relied on behavioural data from controlled experiments, for example measuring the effects of prior exposure to semantically related words on target word recognition times ('priming') to investigate the organisation of the mental lexicon. To explore language development, experimental studies are complemented by observational data, where researchers have, for example, documented longitudinal changes in mean length of utterance in naturalistic settings. Increasingly, psycholinguistics is drawing on data from three sources which complement traditional methods. One source is the linguistic behaviour of people with language impairments, where psycholinguistics overlaps with speech-language pathology. Another source, related to impairment, is the measurement of brain activity, which has come to occupy a central role in recent years due to developments in neuroimaging technology and other measures of neural responses to stimuli. A third source of evidence is computational modelling, particularly associated with connectionist theories of language development and use (see below).

Modern psycholinguistics has its roots in the 'Chomskyan revolution' of the 1960s, when for the first time language was conceived theoretically as an innately determined cognitive capacity rather than as behavioural 'habits' or as a structural system divorced from the mental life of individuals. In the early stages of psycholinguistic research there was an almost exclusive focus on the competence and performance of monolingual speakers of standard varieties of English. Indeed, in the words of Norris et al. (2001: 652), '[p]sycholinguistics has a long and embarrassing tradition of claims for language-universality based on data from English alone'. Subsequently, in the latter decades of the last century, cross-linguistic work began to be conducted, using data from languages which are typologically distinct from English. Psycholinguistics has also emancipated itself from a strict adherence to innatist 'formal' theories of language, exploring alternative functional models which revisit some behaviourist concepts, as subsequent sections illustrate.

The psycholinguistics of English can be viewed from several perspectives. One can, for example, focus on particular structures at different levels of linguistic organisation and examine how they are acquired, the nature of their mental representation, and the manner in which they are processed and selectively impaired. English has many properties in common with other languages, especially those with which it shares historical roots. However, at the same time it is unique in many respects, particularly in the way it has been moulded by sustained contact with other languages, and as a consequence has diverged significantly from the diachronic trajectories of its continental cousins. From this perspective, psycholinguistic data can shed light on the distinctive nature of English itself, as it is stored in, and deployed by, the minds of its users. Alternatively, one can separate the acquisition of English from the ways it is represented and processed once acquired, and the ways in which it may be impaired. This is the way psycholinguistics as an academic field tends to be organised and pursued in scientific practice (i.e. in conferences and journals), with distinct (but increasingly overlapping) communities of scholars studying child development, second language acquisition (SLA), adult processing, and impairment. A third option is to approach the psycholinguistics of English from within particular theoretical orientations, and in what follows I indicate how English data have driven epistemological and ontological debate in the discipline.

Here, the focus will be on what research on mental representation, processing, and development reveal about English structure and usage, rather than, for instance, surveying milestones in the history of psycholinguistics which have been reached on the basis of English data. The focus is hard to maintain, however, given the primary goals of the discipline and its disproportionate reliance on English to test theory. Nevertheless, I have organised the chapter around psycholinguistic approaches to a selection of English structure and usage domains, giving a flavour of the methods used and how results have been used to support theory. The chapter begins with some observations about psycholinguistic perspectives on English, before exploring in more detail the development, representation, and processing of a selection of English lexical and grammatical phenomena, in users and learners of different varieties of the language. Some current approaches to the ongoing debate about the psychological validity of rules are then outlined, followed by a brief discussion of future directions. The chapter ends with some general conclusions about the contribution of psycholinguistics to the field of English Studies.

Critical issues and topics

In this section I describe psycholinguistic work on a selection of English lexical and grammatical features which are distinctive to the language (e.g. the lack of transparency in the writing system) or have been subjected to intense scrutiny because of the light they shed on broader theoretical issues (e.g. the past tense *–ed* suffix). The section then moves on to address psycholinguistic processes in the Englishes of different populations of users, from speakers of regional dialects to adult second language learners.

Words

The development of vocabulary and the processing (production and recognition) of words have been extensively studied in English (cf., Aitchison, 2012). This section describes psycholinguistic work on (a) written and (b) morphologically complex words, drawing on data from first language development, word recognition and production, and language impairment. Studies of these two lexical-level domains of English have contributed significantly to theoretical debate in the discipline.

English is notorious among languages with alphabetic writing systems for its lack of consistent mapping between phonemes and letters, as reflected in educational debates about the use of phonics to teach children to read and spell conventionally, so processing the written word presents users of English with problems that are not as acute in other languages. A comparison of primary school children learning the orthography of 13 different European languages (Seymour et al. 2003) found that the participants learning English were over twice as slow as those acquiring more transparent systems like Finnish. Some psycholinguists have proposed that readers of English use two different routes to read a word: either by matching the whole word with its entry in the mental lexicon (the 'direct route') or by using rules which match individual letters and letter groups (graphemes) with phonemes (the 'indirect route') (Rastle 2007). For skilled readers, the direct route is the default and explains our ability to read opaque letter combinations (such as *island*) and those which are exceptions to rules (such as *have* compared with *cave, Dave, gave, nave, pave, rave, save, wave*). The indirect route is, of course, important for reading words we have not encountered before and is therefore key to children's reading development. Proponents of 'dual-route' models such as this propose that in normal reading, both routes are followed and factors like word frequency determine which route is faster.

Claims that the indirect route is psychologically real (i.e. not just a theoretical construct) are made in part based on evidence from the phenomenon of phonological dyslexia. People with this impairment cannot read letter sequences they do not know, often modelled experimentally using so-called *non-words*: potential but non-occurring words in the language, like *tave*. They have no problem, however, reading words they know, whether they have regular or irregular/unpredictable spelling (e.g. *save*, *have*, *island*). According to the dual-route account, phonological dyslexics have an impairment of the indirect route, but the direct route is preserved. Conversely, people with a condition called surface dyslexia have trouble pronouncing written words that have irregular spelling (reading *island* as ['aislənd], for example) and are therefore argued to have an impaired direct route. Surface dyslexia is not attested in languages like Spanish or Serbian, which have a closer one-to-one mapping between graphemes and phonemes (cf., Harley 2014: 226).

Other psycholinguists argue that the indirect route, although important for reading development, is unlikely to be involved in normal (unimpaired) reading. Moreover, they contend that other sound-letter mappings beyond grapheme-phoneme correspondences can be detected and used by readers. For example, children learning how to spell may, on repeated exposure to printed words, detect analogically that *ave* is frequently pronounced [ev] across multiple words, and furthermore that the letter <a> in words like *save*, *hate*, and *came* consistently has the value /e/ when the letter <e> occurs after the postvocalic consonant. This has been simulated in computational psycholinguistics by connectionist models, which constitute complex networks of interconnected simple processing elements, like the neurons and synaptic connections of the brain. Such models, when 'trained' with words of different frequencies, can 'learn' how they are pronounced as a statistical learning problem, without any recourse to the kinds of grapheme-phoneme correspondence rules posited by the dual-route model (cf., Seidenberg 2007). English sound and spelling thus provide a laboratory for broader debate about the psychological nature of human language.

Another structural domain of English words which has been studied in detail by psycholinguists and has fuelled intense debate about the psychology of language (and, indeed, about cognitive systems more generally) is inflectional morphology, particularly the past tense. Like the debate on how reading skills are developed and deployed, the central issue revolves around regularity, and again a dual-route mechanism is pitched against a single connectionist model (Ambridge and Lieven 2011). The default past tense form of an English verb is the stem plus the *–ed* suffix. However, there are around 180 verbs for which the past tense involves an alternation of the vowel (e.g. *throw/threw*), more substantial changes (e.g. *bring/brought*), or no change at all (e.g. *hit/hit*). Children develop their knowledge of English past tense forms following a U-shaped pattern. They first appear to learn both regular and irregular forms as wholes, one by one. Then, typically from their third year, they start to produce forms like *throwed*, even if they have correctly produced *threw* previously, suggesting they have constructed a rule (add *–ed*) which they tend to overgeneralise. Finally, from around six or so, their overgeneralisations cease and they settle on the adult system.

A second set of psycholinguistic data involving English past tense forms comes from people with language impairments (e.g. Ullman et al. 2005). As with dyslexia, there is evidence of a 'double dissociation' between those who have trouble producing verbs with the regular past tense (e.g. in Broca's aphasia, an impairment of language production) and those with impaired access to irregular forms (e.g. in anomia, a word-finding deficit). Based on such evidence, some psycholinguists (notably Pinker 1999) have argued for a dual-route model of English inflection, whereby direct access to inflected forms (e.g. *glided* and *threw*) exists alongside a rule system (add *–ed* for past tense). The rule system will be invoked in language production for regular verbs (*glided*) and newly-coined or newly-encountered verbs (e.g. *googled*), but not for irregular forms. For the production of very frequent regular forms, it is likely that the direct route will result in access to the whole form before the rule can assemble the stem and suffix. People with Broca's aphasia are assumed to have an impaired rule system, whereas those with anomia are assumed to have impaired direct access to irregular forms in the lexicon.

Proponents of connectionism, on the other hand, have argued that the regular/irregular dichotomy emerges from lower-level regularities in the data to which English speakers are exposed (cf. Joanisse and McClelland 2015). According to this position, children detect phonological and semantic patterns, often obtaining locally in a small numbers of verbs, with rule-like behaviour emerging only as an artefact of the statistical properties of the input. For example, the verb *throw* is much more likely to be over-regularised to *throwed* than *hit* is to *hitted*, because *throw* has several regularly-behaving phonological neighbours (e.g. *showed, flowed, rowed, sowed*) whereas *hit* has none. Neuropsychological evidence has been offered to counter the single-route model, showing that the processing of regular and irregular past tense forms is associated with distinct neuro-anatomical regions (cf. Marslen-Wilson 2007). The debate continues, however, with Westermann and Ruh (2012), for example, presenting a connectionist model which seeks to integrate findings from both the dual- and single-route paradigms.

Finally, English derivational morphology (the production of new words through, for example, affixation) presents similar mental challenges to those of spelling and inflectional morphology. There are large areas of phonological and semantic transparency, reflected in high productivity, coupled with considerable opacity. For processing, this yet again suggests the possibility of direct vs indirect routes in both production and comprehension: transparent morphologically complex words (e.g. *brave/bravely*) might be assembled online in production and parsed in comprehension, whereas opaque combinations (e.g. *broad/breadth*) might be produced and recognised as single units. Data from psycholinguistic experiments suggest that although derivational structure is detected and exploited during processing, the morphemes are not stored independently, except when transparent and productive (Marslen-Wilson 2007). Recently, neuropsychological data have been reported which suggest that English derivational forms are processed in the brain bilaterally (i.e. engaging both cerebral hemispheres), unlike regular inflection which depends on left hemisphere regions involved in broader grammatical processing (Bozic at al. 2013). There are, of course, competing connectionist accounts of English derivational morphology (e.g. Seidenberg and Gonnerman 2000), which stress the graded nature of this part of the language system.

Grammar

Compared with other languages, English has relatively fixed word order and little inflectional nominal morphology (only number). Processing sentences to find out 'who did what to whom' depends to a large extent on global rather than local cues, for example how the nouns are ordered with respect to the verb (argument structure), rather than case marking (e.g. nominal inflections for subject or object). In production, speakers and writers must formulate a sequential plan to indicate the thematic roles of the arguments of the main verb of a clause (agent, patient, etc.). Due to the absence of rich inflection in English, and the optionality of grammatical items such as complementisers like *that*, potential ambiguity is rife. One of the most famous English sentences in psycholinguistics illustrates this: *The horse raced past the barn fell* is very hard to process, even though it is grammatically well formed (cf. *The chocolate left in the sun melted*). English speakers expect the first noun to be the subject of the verb following it, whereas in these sentences it is the object, and the verb next to it is part of a passive relative clause (the main verb comes right at the end). In other languages, the role of *horse* and *barn* might be disambiguated with inflections, the past participle *raced* might have a different inflection from the simple past *raced*, and an overt complementiser might be required (*The horse <u>that was</u> raced past the barn fell*).

Children acquiring English are exposed early on to many tokens of subject-verb-object constructions, in which the subject and object frequently correspond to agent-patient thematic roles (e.g. *Billy chased the dog*). This then becomes the 'canonical' (default, most expected) order for the child. It has long been claimed that children are delayed in their grasp of the English passive construction, often until the sixth year, because it reverses the canonical order (e.g. *The dog was chased by Billy*). Psycholinguists differ, however, on whether the difficulty is uniquely grammatical. Maratsos et al. (1985) offered evidence that it is only 'non-actional' passives that are difficult for children (e.g. *Billy was <u>scared</u> by the dog* should be harder than *Billy was <u>bitten</u> by the dog*), and that furthermore, short passives (without the *by*-phrase, e.g. *Billy was scared*) are easier than the full version. Two types of explanations have been offered, the first semantic, involving the degree of transitivity of the verbs involved, and the second syntactic, claiming that young children do not yet have access to complex grammatical principles for assigning thematic roles to noun phrases (NPs). But using syntactic priming, which involves measuring the extent to which individuals produce structures that they have just been exposed to, Messenger et al. (2012) showed that children as young as three do appear to have adult-like syntactic representations of the passive structure, independently of thematic role.

There are cases where English speakers prefer to produce passives rather than actives. The clearest cases are those where the object is animate. For example, speakers prefer to say *The man was hit by a truck* than *The truck hit the man*. This is in line with a general principle which favours earlier placement of animate over inanimate concepts in production (e.g. *I gave Kim a book* is preferred over *I gave a book to Kim*). Where both subject and object are animate, as in so-called reversible passives, processing is more taxing for adults, because the first noun in a sentence is more often an agent than a patient, and the sentence will make sense under this reading (i.e. *The girl was pushed by the boy* makes as much sense as *The girl pushed the boy*). People with impaired grammatical ability, such as those with Broca's aphasia, interpret reversible passives correctly at only chance level, compared with much higher levels of accuracy with non-reversibles. This may be due to their insensitivity to grammatical items with little inherent semantic content, such as English passive *be* V-*ed* (e.g. Ingram 2007: 251–253).

Another group that perform poorly with reversible passives are children with Specific Language Impairment (SLI) (Leonard 2014: 78). This neurological disorder affects language but is not attributable to brain damage, hearing loss, or intellectual disability. Since it appears to run in families, there has been much speculation (and many news stories) about a possible genetic cause. One English-speaking family of three generations, in which around half the family members exhibited symptoms of SLI, has been studied in depth, with initial reports stressing the specificity of the impairment and later ones questioning it (Gopnik, 1990; Vargha-Khadem et al. 1995). A gene called FOXP2 (the so-called 'grammar gene') emerged as a major factor in the development and transmission of the disorder. People with SLI do have disordered grammar, including past tense *–ed*, which they appear able to formulate a rule for, yet apply very inconsistently.

Unstandardised Englishes

It is a regrettable fact that the stimuli used in psycholinguistic experiments and language tests almost always assume the norms of 'Standard English', with the presence of unstandardised varieties generally ignored. An area of applied psycholinguistics that does focus on such varieties is literacy development, given that for speakers of regional and social accents, phoneme-grapheme correspondences are even less transparent than for users of standardised varieties (from which written norms originally developed). Many educationalists assume that this contributes to poorer literacy skills among speakers of unstandardised dialects. Yet recent psycholinguistic research (e.g. Terry 2014) presents evidence from experimental tasks suggesting that for African American English (AAE) speakers, it is their degree of phonological awareness, rather than the simple presence of dialect features, which accounts for their performance on tests of standard American English. Related to this, speech language therapists have often pointed out that speakers of unstandardised dialects are at risk of being diagnosed with language impairments, given their enhanced likelihood of scoring poorly on tests of metalinguistic knowledge of standardised forms. One study compared white and African American children who were either language-impaired or typically developing, using tests of metalinguistic knowledge vs tests of processing ability (Rodekohr and Haynes 2001). They found that both kinds of test distinguished impaired from typically developing children, but that on the knowledge test the AAE speakers performed significantly closer to the impaired children. They conclude that the use of processing tests can reduce bias against unstandardised dialect users in language screening.

Many monolingual children grow up with multidialectal input, for example when each parent speaks a different variety of English. Some psycholinguists have argued that such children develop in ways similar to early bilinguals, who have been demonstrated to construct less specific initial mental representations for word forms than their monolingual peers do. Durrant et al. (2015) tested this using a task in which infants of around 20 months heard words which matched one of a pair of images (e.g. they hear *cup* and see images of a cup and a clock), and their gaze direction and fixation were measured. In some trials the target was mispronounced (e.g. [gʌp] or [kɛp] instead of [kʌp]). The monodialectal children (both of whose parents spoke British Southwest English dialect) did not gaze at the target image after a mispronunciation, whereas children with parents who spoke two different dialects did. This suggests that children exposed to two dialects have less specific representations for word forms in their mental lexicons, such that divergences in pronunciation can be accommodated.

How (more commonly, how well) individuals can acquire a second dialect after their first is another topic which has seen expanding interest in recent years. Like SLA, work in this area examines the processes involved in naturalistic and educational contexts (the latter concentrating on the development of standardised varieties), but tends to focus on accent at the expense of other linguistic features. Siegel (2010) provides a survey of eight studies of naturalistic English second dialect acquisition, in which most of the features studied were phonological. There are very few cases in which individuals reached above 90% of target feature usage, and these are among the youngest learners studied. Finally, there are several studies of speech intelligibility within and across dialects, which often appear to show that some dialects are inherently more intelligible than others. McCloy et al. (2015), however, using more stringent controls than previous studies, conducted a perception task in which speakers of two different northern US dialects listened to tokens of each dialect in different levels of background noise. The results reveal the difficulty of teasing apart the effects of dialect features from idiolectal (individual) variation – a factor we return to subsequently.

English as a second language

There are now many more learners and non-native users of English than native speakers (NSs). Second language (L2) Englishes and how they develop is therefore a major area of interest for psycholinguists. The modern discipline of SLA can be traced to a dramatic shift in interest from practical issues of teaching to cognitive theories of learning, following the Chomskyan revolution. Although much research in the discipline now has a social, and indeed often an overtly *anti*-cognitive, orientation, cognitive issues are still central to SLA theory. As in other areas of psycholinguistics, English has been the dominant language studied, for the most part as a goal of adult learning in instructional contexts. But because English speakers can be L2 learners too, researchers have also collected substantial amounts of data on the development of other languages (notably Spanish in the USA and French in the UK and Canada). Indeed, two of the most psycholinguistically-oriented theories in SLA are the result of research on languages other than English. Processability Theory (cf. Pienemann and Lenzing 2015), originally developed on the basis of studies of learners of German, claims that the course of language development is constrained by what the learner can process at any given stage in their learning trajectory. For example, learners of English will only be ready to acquire the subject-auxiliary inversion construction for questions after they have learnt that questions are formed with an initial *wh-* word. Before then, they will produce utterances like *Where he has been?* Similarly, Input Processing (IP) theory (cf. VanPatten 2015), based originally on data from English-speaking learners of Spanish, aims to explain how principles of form-meaning mapping in comprehension can influence the emerging L2 system. One IP principle states that grammatical forms with more information content will be processed earlier than more redundant forms, e.g. English *–ing*, which marks progressive, over third person *–s* (one of the hardest forms for learners of L2 English to master).

A major focus of study on L2 Englishes in SLA and psycholinguistics more generally has been the ways in which the first language of learners influences the second. Studies of transfer, or more precisely cross-linguistic influence (CLI), have been conducted at all levels of language knowledge, from pronunciation to pragmatics. At the pronunciation level, 'foreign accent' is the norm for L2 English users, characterised by the use of phonemes like /d/ and /z/ for /ð/ and their unvoiced versions (e.g. *dese tings* or *zese sings* for *these things*). However, English is no different from other languages in being susceptible to CLI at this level, given that phonology is the earliest established component of linguistic knowledge in infancy and is particularly hard to displace. At the lexical level, CLI will vary according to the degree of overlap between learners' L1 and English. Adult learners whose L1 has inherited word forms from a common Germanic ancestor (such as Dutch) or has contributed word forms to English following conquest and cultural influence (such as Latin and its descendants), will find English vocabulary easier than L1 speakers of unrelated languages like Mandarin Chinese or Arabic. There is a great deal of evidence to suggest that cognate forms are automatically activated in the processing of L2 words, often leading to an assumption of translation equivalence (cf. Hall 2002). This happens even when it is not warranted, as in the case of so-called 'false friends' like Spanish *tuna* ('prickly pear') being taken as the translation equivalent of English *tuna*.

Research on the mental lexicons of bilingual speakers and learners of English has convincingly shown that the two vocabularies are stored in a single interconnected network, even at high levels of proficiency. A similar consensus has emerged more recently about grammatical resources and processing, and evidence is accumulating for co-activation of both languages in performance irrespective of the typological relatedness of the other language or the direction of CLI (L1→L2 or L2→L1). In a review article, Kroll et al. (2012) refer to evidence that bilinguals whose other language is completely unrelated to English (even American Sign Language) still activate it when reading English, and that bilingual Spanish NSs who live in English-dominant environments are influenced by English relative clause processing strategies when reading Spanish. Some grammatical constructions in English appear to cause problems for L2 learners because they do not exist in the L1, so no CLI is possible, either positive or negative. An example is the article system, typified by the distinction between indefinite *a* and definite *the*, used to determine NP reference. Chinese lacks articles, and Chinese-speaking learners of English often use them inconsistently in production. But a study using eye-tracking (Trenkic et al. 2014) reveals that in comprehension, intermediate proficiency learners, like NSs, used the information in articles as well as contextual information to disambiguate NP reference (albeit not as fast as the NSs). This evidence converges with the results of an increasing number of studies which suggest that L2 learners/users can process grammatical structures essentially the same way as NSs, using the same areas of the brain (e.g. Abutalebi and Della Rosa, 2012).

Key areas of dispute and debate

We have inevitably already touched on the central debate in psycholinguistics, namely whether the Chomskyan notion of rules operating on symbols is psychologically valid, or whether connectionism provides a more plausible explanatory framework. In this section, we explore three different ways in which this debate has been taken forward.

Usage-based approaches

Frequency is a key variable in psycholinguistics at the lexical level. There is robust evidence, for example, that infrequent words like *milt* (occurring twice per million) take longer to recognise than more frequent but otherwise similar words like *milk* (occurring 49 times per million). Yet up until relatively recently psycholinguists have not wanted to assign frequency a broader role in the psychology of language, because it evokes the idea of 'habit formation' associated with the behaviourist paradigm discredited by Chomsky. According to the Chomskyan position, language is an innate cognitive faculty constrained by a Universal Grammar (UG) of rules governing well-formed strings of symbols. It is UG that allows children to extract patterns from the input, which is seen to be inherently inadequate on its own. An alternative view in which input frequency is key has been gaining strength over the past decade or so in a family of theoretical approaches called Usage-based Linguistics (UBL). According to UBL, language is a cognitive resource constructed and continuously developing on the basis of individual users' analyses of the frequency and distribution of form-meaning pairings in the input experienced during usage events (Tomasello 2003). Instead of UG, learners use general-purpose procedures like analogy. Take the English passive, for example. Ambridge and Lieven (2011: 279) observe that 'children begin with lexically specific [. . .] frames (e.g. *it's broken*) that become increasingly abstract (e.g. → *it got VERBed by it* → *NP BE/GET VERB by NP*)'. The approach has also been extended to processing. MacDonald (2013) provides a particularly compelling usage-based framework for explaining processing phenomena as well as numerous facts about English grammar by showing how processing demands in production have helped determine the frequency and distribution of constructions like the passive and relative clauses, which in turn mould comprehension strategies.

The UBL approach has been applied to L2 Englishes also. Wolter and Gyllstad (2013), for example, show that Swedish learners of English are sensitive to the frequencies of collocations in English. But they also point out that CLI still plays a major role. This is confirmed also by Hall et al. (2017), who investigated the ways in which input interacts with other learning factors to shape lexico-grammatical features in the idiolect of a single expert user of L2 English. The UBL approach is likely to have particularly dramatic effects on SLA theory and our understanding of L2 Englishes in coming years, perhaps overturning several long-held assumptions. One emerging possibility is that many of the purported differences between native and non-native speakers are essentially the same as those observed *between natives*. Kaan (2014), for example, highlights the role of input frequency, the amount of competing forms, and the variable quality/consistency of lexical knowledge, as common factors which predict the degree to which both native and non-native users make predictions of upcoming material in online comprehension. Her position is completely consistent with UBL approaches to language development.

Individual differences

Although there are several (and some very well-known) case studies of first and second language development and impairment (e.g. Brown 1973), most studies in psycholinguistics are based on behavioural or neural activity data measured across groups, with results averaged out and taken as characterisations of whole populations (such as English NSs). Consistent with this approach, computational models simulate 'prototypical' development and processing. However, a growing interest in differences between individuals is now evident, often related to social experience, especially educational level. Street and Dąbrowska (2014), for example, report data which they interpret as showing that English-speaking individuals with lower academic attainment have greater problems in comprehending the passive that those with higher education. They explain this by appealing to UBL principles:

> Passive sentences are considerably more frequent in written texts [. . .] than in speech; because more educated participants tend to read more, their passive constructions are better entrenched, and hence accessed more reliably, which results in faster and more accurate performance.
>
> (p. 113)

Similarly, a study by Yap et al. (2012) using word recognition data from over 1,200 participants in the English Lexicon Project (see below), revealed marked stability within individual performance but substantial variability between individuals, correlated significantly with vocabulary size. Finally, Paradis (2011) examined the role of individual variables in a study of over 160 child acquirers of L2 English. He found that internal factors such as short-term memory capacity were better predictors of vocabulary size and accuracy with verbal morphology than external factors such as the richness of the input environment. Like Hall et al. (2017), he concludes that his findings are consistent with UBL, but that input is not the whole story. All the evidence so far suggests that, contrary to the UG position, the development of English (and by extension other languages) is not fully constrained by universal principles.

The phonics debate

Psycholinguists have not normally used their findings to influence applied linguistic practice, although their research has significant impact on applied issues like speech-language pathology and TESOL (Teaching English to Speakers of Other Languages). One arena in which they have advocated specific public policy measures is in the teaching of reading. Traditionally, the learning of letter names and their associated sounds was emphasised in teaching ('A is for *apple*, B is for *book*'; 'D-O-G spells *dog*'; etc.). In the 1960s there was a shift to 'whole-word' teaching, which de-emphasised the alphabetic principle, justified largely on the basis of the irregularity of English spelling, and later 'whole-language' teaching, which emphasised the top-down processing of text meaning over the bottom-up processing of word forms. Educationalists referred extensively to Goodman's (1967) suggestion that reading was a 'psycholinguistic guessing game' in which strategies for extracting meaning (from context, including pictures) were as important as rule-based processing of letter combinations. A couple of decades later, many psycholinguists (especially in the USA) started to voice their concern with 'whole-word' and 'whole-language' methods, vigorously supporting calls for a return to the teaching of grapheme-phoneme correspondence rules in the approach known as 'phonics'. According to Rayner et al. (2001: 56), 'The main rationale behind a phonics approach is that it explicitly teaches children both the alphabetic principle and the specific letter-phoneme correspondences that generalize across many English words.' They claim that phonics is consistent with both dual-route and connectionist models. But the pendulum continues to swing, with numerous psycholinguists now questioning phonics instruction and the assessment regimes that come with it. In the UK context, for instance, Gibson and England (2015) argue that the use of non-words in statutory phonics testing for primary school pupils is problematic. They express concerns about: (a) the validity of the test items themselves and teachers' ability to discriminate all plausible responses to them;

(b) the assumption that non-word reading performance involves the same mental processes as normal reading; and (c) the evidence that orthographically opaque languages like English lead to significant delays in reading development in the first place.

Future directions

Psycholinguistic studies of English will continue to benefit from new developments in neuropsychology, which should allow more fine-grained analyses of cognitive representation and processing for language. Two areas of future growth in the discipline which are rather more specific to English are: (a) the use of large computerised databases of language in authentic usage and of norms for specific words or constructions from psycholinguistic studies (e.g. average word recognition times); and (b) the recognition that English is now most typically processed and mentally represented as part of a multilingual repertoire, often by NNSs.

So-called 'megastudies' (cf. Keuleers and Balota 2015), originally developed for research on visual word recognition, use databases recording behavioural measures on several psycholinguistic variables, such as word frequency or spelling consistency, drawn from very large collections of words and individuals. They complement the traditional experimental approach that typically involves the comparison of participant behaviour on a small set of stimuli representing usually two variables to be correlated, selected by the experimenter. Megastudy data have been used to investigate several variables, including those just mentioned, as well as age of acquisition and imageability (how easily a word is associated with a visual image). The biggest megastudy database is the English Lexicon Project (freely available at http://elexicon.wustl.edu) which includes millions of measurements on over 40,000 words from several hundred participants. Crowdsourcing is also being increasingly used to obtain psycholinguistically relevant data on English. We have seen that word frequency is an important variable in processing; however, another significant measure is *word prevalence*, i.e. how many English speakers know the word, which can be measured through crowd-based experiments.

Work in applied linguistics on non-native speaker Englishes has recently begun to have an impact on mainstream linguistics and the ways in which linguists have tended to conceive of named languages as 'monolithic' entities, identified with monolingual speakers of standardised varieties. Although there is a great deal of psycholinguistic work on bi- and multilingual users of English, much of it deals with child or adult learners, rather than non-native *users*. With increased global movement of people and emphasis on English competence in national education policies, this group of English users is set to grow massively. Increasingly, their usage of English will be in lingua franca contexts, i.e. as a bridge language with people who have a different first language. In such contexts, shared group norms will inevitably be attenuated, so the manner in which they process English, and the ways in which their mental lexicons and grammars develop as a result of such post-instruction usage, are of considerable psycholinguistic interest (cf. Hall 2018).

Conclusion

Psycholinguistics has been informed by English data from the earliest days of its establishment as a discipline, with features of the language providing test cases for the development of theoretical models of language cognition. Yet psycholinguistics has also informed English Studies, especially in recent decades, by revealing how the language presents cognitive challenges which differ from those faced by users of other languages. Current approaches to psycholinguistics are less exclusively reliant on the precepts of theoretical linguistics than they were in the heyday of the Chomskyan revolution, with the result that the discipline has even greater potential to contribute to broader interdisciplinary enterprises like English Studies. When combined with corpus linguistics, for example, psycholinguistics can contribute to our understanding of variation and change in the language (e.g. Gries 2013). A psycholinguistic perspective therefore complements other approaches to English by revealing how, in addition to being a linguistic system, a community resource, and a potent marker of identity, it is also a cognitive resource which is developed, stored, and processed in individual minds.

Further reading

Bialystok, E., F. I. Craik and G. Luk (2012) 'Bilingualism: Consequences for mind and brain', *Trends in Cognitive Sciences* 16 (4): 240–250. This is a comprehensive review of issues in the psycholinguistics of bilingualism, using many examples from bilingual users of English and stressing the cognitive advantages of being bilingual.

Harley, T. (2014) *The Psychology of Language*. 4th edn. London: Psychology Press. This textbook is an impressive compendium of empirical findings and theoretical models in psycholinguistics, drawing mostly on English data.

Ingram, J. C. (2007) *Neurolinguistics: An Introduction to Spoken Language Processing and Its Disorders*. Cambridge: Cambridge University Press. A more narrowly neurolinguistic view of processing and impairment, also based mostly on English data.

Sparks, J. R. and D. N. Rapp (2010) 'Discourse processing—Examining our everyday language experiences', *Wiley Interdisciplinary Reviews: Cognitive Science* 1 (3): 371–381. An overview of issues in discourse processing, again using mostly English examples.

Vitevitch, M. S., K. Y. Chan and R. Goldstein (2014). 'Using English as a 'model language' to understand language processing', in N. Miller and A. Lowit (eds), *Motor Speech Disorders: A Cross-Language Perspective*. Bristol: Multilingual Matters, 58–73. An overview of phonological processing phenomena which are distinctive in English, in both normal and impaired language users.

Related topics

- The phonology of English
- The grammars of English
- Literacy in English: literacies in Englishes
- English and translation.

References

Abutalebi, J. and P. A. Della Rosa (2012) 'How the brain acquires, processes, and controls a second language', in M. Faust (ed.), *The Handbook of the Neuropsychology of Language*. Oxford: Blackwell, 516–538.

Aitchison, J. (2012) *Words in the Mind: An Introduction to the Mental Lexicon*. 4th edn. Chichester: Wiley-Blackwell.

Ambridge, B. and E. V. Lieven (2011) *Child Language Acquisition: Contrasting Theoretical Approaches*. Cambridge: Cambridge University Press.

Bozic, M., L. K. Tyler, L. Su, C. Wingfield and W. D. Marslen-Wilson (2013) 'Neurobiological systems for lexical representation and analysis in English', *Journal of Cognitive Neuroscience*, 25 (10): 1678–1691.

Brown, R. (1973) *A First Language*. Cambridge: Harvard University Press.

Durrant, S., C. Delle Luche, A. Cattani and C. Floccia (2015) 'Monodialectal and multidialectal infants' representation of familiar words', *Journal of Child Language* 42 (02): 447–465.

Gibson, H. and J. England (2015) 'The inclusion of pseudowords within the year one phonics "Screening Check" in English primary schools', *Cambridge Journal of Education* 46 (4): 1–17.

Goodman, K. S. (1967) 'Reading: A psycholinguistic guessing game', *Literacy Research and Instruction* 6 (4): 126–135.

Gopnik, M. (1990) 'Feature-blind grammar and dysphasia', *Nature* 344 (6268): 715.

Gries, S. T. (2013). 'Sources of variability relevant to the cognitive sociolinguist, and corpus- as well as psycholinguistic methods and notions to handle them', *Journal of Pragmatics* 52: 5–16.

Hall, C. J. (2002). 'The automatic cognate form assumption: Evidence for the Parasitic Model of vocabulary development', *International Review of Applied Linguistics* 40: 69–87.

Hall, C. J. (2018) 'Cognitive perspectives on English as a Lingua Franca', in J. Jenkins, W. Baker and M. Dewey (eds), *Routledge Handbook of English as a Lingua Franca*. London: Routledge, 74–84.

Hall, C. J., J. Joyce and C. Robson (2017) 'Investigating the lexico-grammatical resources of a non-native user of English: the case of *can* and *could* in email requests', *Applied Linguistics Review* 8 (1): 35–59.

Harley, T. (2014) *The Psychology of Language*. 4th edn. London: Psychology Press.

Ingram, J. C. (2007) *Neurolinguistics: An Introduction to Spoken Language Processing and Its Disorders*. Cambridge: Cambridge University Press.

Joanisse, M. F. and J. L. McClelland (2015) 'Connectionist perspectives on language learning, representation and processing', *Wiley Interdisciplinary Reviews: Cognitive Science* 6 (3): 235–247.

Kaan, E. (2014) 'Predictive sentence processing in L2 and L1. What is different?', *Linguistic Approaches to Bilingualism* 4 (2): 257–282.

Kroll, J. F., P. E. Dussias, C. A. Bogulski and J. R. Valdes Kroff (2012) 'Juggling two languages in one mind: what bilinguals tell us about language processing and its consequences for cognition', *Psychology of Learning and Motivation* 56: 229–262.

Keuleers, E. and D. A. Balota (2015) 'Megastudies, crowdsourcing, and large datasets in psycholinguistics: An overview of recent developments', *The Quarterly Journal of Experimental Psychology* 68 (8): 1457–1468.

Leonard, L. B. (2014) *Children with Specific Language Impairment*. Cambridge: MIT press.

MacDonald, M. C. (2013) 'How language production shapes language form and comprehension', *Frontiers in Psychology* 4 (226): 1–16.

Maratsos, M., D. Fox, J. Becker and M. Chalkley (1985) 'Semantic restrictions on children's passives', *Cognition* 19: 167–191.

Marslen-Wilson, W. D. (2007) 'Morphological processes in language comprehension', in G. Gaskell (ed.), *The Oxford Handbook of Psycholinguistics*. Oxford: Oxford University Press, 175–193.

McCloy, D. R., R. A. Wright and P. E. Souza (2015). 'Talker versus dialect effects on speech intelligibility: A symmetrical study', *Language and Speech* 58 (3): 371–386.

Messenger, K., H. P. Branigan, J. F. McLean and A. Sorace (2012) 'Is young children's passive syntax semantically constrained? Evidence from syntactic priming', *Journal of Memory and Language* 66 (4): 568–587.

Norris, D., J. M. McQueen, A. Cutler, S. Butterfield and R. Kearns (2001) 'Language-universal constraints on speech segmentation', *Language and Cognitive Processes* 16 (5/6): 637–660.

Paradis, J. (2011) 'Individual differences in child English second language acquisition: Comparing child-internal and child-external factors', *Linguistic Approaches to Bilingualism* 1 (3): 213–237.

Pienemann, M. and A. Lenzing (2015) 'Processability theory', in B. VanPatten and J. Williams (eds), *Theories in Second Language Acquisition: An introduction*. 2nd edn. London: Routledge, 159–179.

Pinker, S. (1999) *Words and Rules. The Ingredients of Language*. New York: Basic Books.

Rastle, K. (2007) 'Visual word recognition', in G. Gaskell (ed.), *The Oxford Handbook of Psycholinguistics*. Oxford: Oxford University Press, 71–87.

Rayner, K., B. R. Foorman, C. A. Perfetti, D. Pesetsky and M. S. Seidenberg (2001) 'How psychological science informs the teaching of reading', *Psychological Science in the Public Interest* 2 (2): 31–74.

Rodekohr, R. K. and W. O. Haynes (2001) 'Differentiating dialect from disorder: A comparison of two processing tasks and a standardized language test', *Journal of Communication Disorders* 34 (3): 255–272.

Seidenberg, M. S. (2007) 'Connectionist models of reading', in G. Gaskell (ed.), *The Oxford Handbook of Psycholinguistics*. Oxford: Oxford University Press, 235–250.

Seidenberg, M. S. and L. M. Gonnerman (2000) 'Explaining derivational morphology as the convergence of codes', *Trends in Cognitive Sciences* 4 (9): 353–361.

Seymour, P. H., M. Aro and J. M. Erskine (2003) 'Foundation literacy acquisition in European orthographies', *British Journal of Psychology* 94 (2): 143–174.

Siegel, J. (2010) *Second Dialect Acquisition*. Cambridge: Cambridge University Press.

Street, J. A. and E. Dąbrowska (2014) 'Lexically specific knowledge and individual differences in adult native speakers' processing of the English passive', *Applied Psycholinguistics* 35 (01): 97–118.

Terry, N. P. (2014) 'Dialect variation and phonological knowledge: Phonological representations and metalinguistic awareness among beginning readers who speak nonmainstream American English', *Applied Psycholinguistics* 35: 155–176.

Tomasello, M. (2003) *Constructing a Language. A Usage-Based Theory of Language Acquisition*. Cambridge, MA: Harvard University Press.

Trenkic, D., J. Mirkovic and G. Altmann (2014) 'Real-time grammar processing by native and non-native speakers: Constructions unique to the second language', *Bilingualism: Language and Cognition* 17 (2): 237–257.

Ullman, M. T., R. Pancheva, T. Love, E. Yee, D. Swinney and G. Hickok (2005) 'Neural correlates of lexicon and grammar: Evidence from the production, reading, and judgment of inflection in aphasia', *Brain and Language* 93 (2): 185–238.

VanPatten, B. (2015) 'Input processing in adult SLA', in B. VanPatten and J. Williams (eds), *Theories in Second Language Acquisition: An introduction*. 2nd edn. London: Routledge, 113–134.

Vargha-Khadem, F., K. Watkins, K. Alcock, P. Fletcher and R. Passingham (1995) 'Praxic and non-verbal cognitive deficits in a large family with a genetically transmitted speech and language disorder', *Proceedings of the National Academy of Sciences* 92 (3): 930–933.

Westermann, G. and N. Ruh (2012) 'A neuroconstructivist model of past tense development and processing', *Psychological Review* 119 (3): 649–667.

Wolter, B., & H. Gyllstad (2013) 'Frequency of input and L2 collocational processing', *Studies in Second Language Acquisition* 35 (03): 451–482.

Yap, M. J., D. A. Balota, D. E. Sibley and R. Ratcliff (2012) 'Individual differences in visual word recognition: Insights from the English Lexicon Project', *Journal of Experimental Psychology: Human Perception and Performance* 38 (1): 53.

28

Metaphor studies and English

Zsófia Demjén

Introduction

'Metaphors are necessary and not just nice', claimed Andrew Ortony as far back as 1975 (p. 45). Despite this claim, and many similar ones since, metaphor has arguably been a somewhat marginal topic in English language studies. This chapter puts it front and centre, highlighting some of the key contributions it can make to the field.

As a linguistic phenomenon, metaphor sits at the semantic level of language alongside lexis, though some also consider it a matter of thought. It has been the focus of scholarship for centuries in fields as diverse as rhetoric, philosophy, ethics, politics, philology, linguistics, literary and cultural criticism, psychology, and cognitive science. Its popular appeal was boosted in the 1980s with the publication of Lakoff and Johnson's *Metaphors We Live By* (1980) – a title testament to the centrality of the phenomenon – which continues to inspire especially cognitively-oriented research. Whatever their field, metaphor scholars generally agree that it is fundamental to understanding how language systems develop, and to how we organise and expand our knowledge about ourselves, our relationships, and our world (Cameron and Low 1999: xii). In this vein, the linguistic view of metaphor, which is the subject of this chapter, does not treat it as simply decorative, aesthetic, special, or indeed 'nice'.

Consider the following excerpt from *The Unabridged Journals of Sylvia Plath* (Kukil 2000: 185), where Plath, addressing herself as 'you', describes her feelings after having decided not to attend Harvard Summer School in order to have time to think, find out about herself and write:

> *you are paralyzed, shocked, thrown into a nausea, a stasis. You are plunged so deep in your own very private little whirlpool of negativism that you can't do more than force yourself into a rote*
>
> (July 6, 1953) (underlining added)

The everyday view of metaphor might recognise some of the underlined words, e.g. 'thrown', 'plunged', 'whirlpool', perhaps 'paralyzed', as metaphors and might describe them in evaluative terms as (un)creative, revealing, apt, or stale. From a linguistic perspective, however, all underlined words in this excerpt are instances of metaphor: they represent ways of talking, and potentially thinking, about one thing as if it was something else, where a similarity can be perceived between the two entities (Semino 2008). Metaphor is seen as a pervasive and ordinary part of all language use, and while specific instances can be decorative, aesthetic, and special, they are studied less for the purposes of evaluation or appreciation, and more for developing our understanding of what meanings they convey, how they do so, why they are used, and what the consequences of their use might be for different discourse participants. There are a number of valuable insights into language that can be gained from such a view of metaphor and I will illustrate some of these with reference to the excerpt above. (For a fuller discussion of the excerpt itself see Demjén 2015.)

First, the underlined words in the excerpt illustrate that subjective, personal, intangible, or abstract experiences, such as emotions, are often described using metaphors, frequently with several in combination. Metaphors convey meanings vividly and concisely and have been described as bridging the gap between the fluidity and continuity of life, and the discreteness of language as a set of symbols used to represent it (Ortony 1975). As a result, metaphors are often used as explanatory tools, in education for example. A second and related insight is that metaphors evaluate and frame the topics they describe in particular ways, highlighting some aspects, while backgrounding others (e.g. Semino et al. 2016). The metaphors in the excerpt above, for example, highlight the negativity and uncontrollability of certain emotions, while backgrounding their potentially fleeting and changeable nature. Attitudes towards and reasoning about the topic described are affected by such framings (Thibodeau and Boroditsky 2011) and for this reason, metaphor is frequently used as a persuasive tool in public and political communications, among others.

A third insight is related to the idea that some metaphors 'feel' more metaphorical than others. 'Thrown' and 'plunged' are easily identified as talking about the experiencing of emotions as if it was the physical, involuntary, and potentially violent movement of one's body from one place to another. A similarity can be perceived between these two in the sense that they are both unpleasant and not within one's control. Metaphoricity is arguably less obvious in the case of the underlined prepositions, with expressions like 'force' and 'shocked' sitting somewhere in between the two extremes. On the one hand, this illustrates that there is a cline of metaphoricity, ranging from non-metaphorical, through conventional, to novel expressions. On the other hand, this range is also to a certain extent indicative of a process of semantic change in the English language, where new expressions enter the lexicon as metaphors, become conventionalised and eventually lose their metaphoricity (Sweetser 1990). 'Rote' in the excerpt above could be seen as an example of a word that has lost its metaphoricity in current English usage (though its origins are uncertain according to the *Oxford English Dictionary* [*OED*]).

Metaphor studies involves a range of theoretical and methodological approaches, as well as applications in contexts as diverse as second language learning, advertising, politics, psychiatry, and neuroscience. A single handbook chapter cannot aim to do justice to all of these, so the majority of this chapter will be devoted to the aforementioned insights, which are particularly relevant to English language studies. The next section begins with a more detailed discussion of the concept of metaphor as a feature of language and thought. I then outline one well-established method for the systematic identification of metaphor in language before moving on to a discussion of why metaphor is worth considering in the context of English language studies. I focus specifically on the insights it can contribute to our understanding of language change, the success or failure of explanations in education, and the role of framing (including persuasion) in public health and political communications. Finally, I highlight key debates relevant to these areas and offer reflections on the future directions of metaphor studies.

Metaphor in language and thought

Broadly speaking, there are two main approaches to the study of metaphor in linguistics: those that focus on metaphor as primarily a matter of language (discourse-based approaches) and those that see it primarily as a matter of thought (cognitive approaches). The former has a long-standing tradition, starting with Aristotle's Poetics and Rhetoric (although Aristotle's work does not limit itself to language; see Mahon 1999), continuing with that of Locke, Vico, and Kant (see Jäkel 1999), and more recently seen in the work of scholars such as Kittay (1987) Reisigl (2006) and Ricoeur (2003 [1975]). Discourse approaches see metaphor as consisting of a figuratively-used word or expression (vehicle), which describes a concept or idea (topic) in terms of similarity. For example, 'whirlpool' in the excerpt above can be seen as the vehicle describing negative emotion (topic) as something that is difficult to get out of. In this way, metaphor helps to construct, represent and transform reality (Reisigl 2006). It is understood that metaphor is not rare – even Aristotle, although this is often ignored or misrepresented, noted the ubiquity of metaphor in conversation and writing (Mahon 1999) – and that it is one of a number of tropes that 'leap' from one semantic sphere to another (Reisigl 2006), allowing us to better understand previously obscure topics. This makes it particularly useful as a tool of explanation and persuasion, especially in education (Cameron 2003) and politics (Musolff 2006; Reisigl 2006).

This focus on language became sidelined, to some extent, in the 1980s with the publication of Ortony's edited collection *Metaphor and Thought* (Ortony 1979, 2nd edition in 1993) and Lakoff and Johnson's *Metaphors We Live By* (Lakoff and Johnson 1980, 2nd edition 2003). These volumes were instrumental in the paradigm shift that turned from viewing metaphor as a tool of language to a tool of thought, epitomised by the influential Conceptual Metaphor Theory (CMT) (Lakoff and Johnson 1980). The central tenet of CMT is that human thought and understanding relies on systematic sets of correspondences between so-called 'source' and 'target' domains (areas of meaning, or 'semantic sphere'). Source domains are usually concrete or physical and, so the theory goes, permit us to understand the more abstract target domain that they are used to describe. CMT goes so far as to say that only a few basic concrete concepts, such as physical location, motion in space or spatial orientation, are understood in a literal way (Grady 1997). We understand these literally, because we learn about them through the sensorimotor experiences of our bodies ('embodiment') (Lakoff and Johnson 1980; Lakoff and Turner 1989). Other, more abstract concepts can only be understood in terms of these basic literal categories. For example, 'life' is abstract, so in order to be able to make sense of it, we have to think about it in terms of something more concrete. Progress in life is understood as motion forwards in space, or even more specifically as 'a journey': *I've reached a crossroads in my life; she overcame huge obstacles on her road to success.* Within CMT, these two examples are seen as linguistic realisations of the conventional conceptual metaphor (denoted by small capitals) LIFE IS A JOURNEY, which we think by.

CMT had, and still has, intuitive appeal, but it has also been criticised, often for being less than specific about methodology. Despite relying on linguistic examples as evidence for conceptual metaphors, it did not make it clear how exactly metaphor was identified in language, nor how many linguistic examples were required to claim the existence of a conceptual metaphor (see for example Deignan 2005). In addition, early CMT scholars did not investigate or consider important variation in the form and discourse function of metaphor, depending on medium, register, or genre, and treated the English language not only as a homogeneous whole, but as representative (at least initially) of other languages.

Partly as a result of these shortcomings, there has been a resurgence of interest in metaphor in language and discourse. This does not mean that scholarship has turned away from the idea of metaphor as a characteristic of thought, but that a substantial proportion of recent work has 'taken discourse data seriously' (Zinken and Musolff 2009) and been more careful with asserting the existence of specific conceptual metaphors and the evidence used to support these (e.g. Cameron et al. 2010; Deignan 2005). This refocusing has enabled the investigation of underlying attitudes and ideologies embedded in metaphorical communication and the consequences this might have. It has led to new insights into language change and second/foreign language learning. It has illuminated some of the ways and circumstances in which metaphors can be helpful or harmful, including ways in which it contributes to or hinders our understanding of new ideas. Finally, the renewed focus on metaphor in language has also led to the development of some reliable methods of metaphor identification, and it is to one of these that I now turn.

Finding metaphor

For a claim such as 'all underlined words in the excerpt above are metaphors' to stand, it needs to be underpinned by a reliable and explicit method for metaphor identification, especially when it comes to the less clear-cut examples such as 'into' and 'force'. To respond to this need, a group of ten international metaphor scholars, from different disciplines, got together in the early 2000s and over several years developed an explicit, reliable, and flexible method for identifying metaphorically used words in language. This method is now known as the Metaphor Identification Procedure (MIP) (Pragglejaz Group 2007), more recently expanded into MIPVU ('VU' stands for 'Vrije Universiteit', where the group was based) (Steen et al. 2010). MIP goes as follows (adapted from Pragglejaz Group 2007: 3):

1 Read the entire text/discourse to establish a general understanding of its meaning.
2 Decide on what will count as a lexical unit in the text/discourse (i.e. will it always be the word, or will there be exceptions such as phrasal verbs and compound nouns?).
3
   a For each lexical unit in the text, establish its meaning in context (i.e. how does it apply to an entity, relation, or attribute in the situation evoked by the text?).
   b For each lexical unit, determine (with reference to a reliable, preferably corpus-based, dictionary) if it has a more basic contemporary/current meaning. Basic meanings tend to be more concrete; related to bodily action; more precise (as opposed to vague); historically older.
   c If the lexical unit has a more basic current/contemporary meaning, decide whether the contextual meaning contrasts with the basic meaning but can be understood in comparison with it.
4 If yes, mark the lexical unit as metaphorical.

Taking 'thrown' from the initial excerpt, the procedure would go as follows:

1 reading the extended co-text of the example to understand what is actually being talked about (e.g. feelings about having a lot of time to think).
2 parsing the text to determine whether 'thrown' is one lexical unit and not part of a phrasal verb, for example.
3
   a establishing that in context the lexical unit refers to something like 'experiencing an emotion suddenly and unexpectedly'

  b establishing that there is a more basic meaning; one that is more physical: 'to use force to move someone or something' or 'to send an object through the air' (Macmillan Dictionary 2009–2016)
  c deciding that 3a and 3b contrast, but can be understood in comparison to each other

4 marking 'thrown' as metaphorical.

This same procedure can also capture similes (or what Steen et al. (2010) describe as 'direct metaphor'), which are different only in that they signal comparison explicitly through 'like', 'as', 'as if', etc.

Aside from making metaphor analysis more systematic, a key contribution of MIP is its insistence on making any methodological decisions explicit. One has to state what counts as a lexical unit, which dictionary is used to establish basic meanings, and what if anything is to be excluded from consideration. For example, scholars sometimes decide to exclude closed-class (grammatical) words, such as the preposition 'into' in the initial excerpt, and/or highly delexicalised verbs (Hopper and Traugott 2003) such as *have*, *do*, *give*, *take*, *make*, *get*, *put*, and *like*, because basic meanings can be particularly difficult to establish when semantics have been diluted.

Once individual metaphors have been identified, the next step is to examine how metaphors pattern in texts, as robust interpretations of metaphor use rely on systematic patterns rather than individual examples. Depending on one's interests, this might involve looking at metaphor patterns or frequencies in source and target domains (or vehicles and topics), in parts of speech (Krennmayr 2014), within and across texts or genres (Deignan et al. 2013; Dorst 2015), and in patterns of novelty/creativity versus conventionality (Lakoff and Turner 1989; Semino 2008), among others. The reliable and replicable method of identification also enables scholars who wish to hypothesise about metaphor in thought to do so in a grounded manner, for example by referring to 'systematic metaphors' instead (Cameron et al. 2010). These denote persistent patterns of vehicles and topics in a particular discourse without claiming they have cognitive reality. Instead, a systematic metaphor simply indicates that there may be a cognitive basis for the patterns.

At this point some might wonder whether so much effort will actually pay off in terms of new insights gained. In the next section, I discuss findings of relevance to English language studies demonstrating why, I would argue, the answer is yes.

Current critical issues and topics of relevance for English language studies

Changes in meanings

As indicated previously, metaphor contributes to our understanding of the changes and developments in the meanings of words. Along with 'broadening' and 'narrowing', metaphor is one of the most commonly recognised types of lexical semantic change mechanisms (Urban 2014) and one that often helps us make sense of polysemy. It explains how different co-existing meanings of words might be related, and how old meanings of words are related to new ones (Sweetser 1990). Some have even suggested that metaphor accounts for around half of all meaning extensions in the lexical development of a language (Dirven 1985).

A simple example of polysemy through 'metaphorisation' (Traugott 2006) is the adjective *sunny*. Based on citations in the *OED*, which provides the dates for the first recorded examples of individual meanings, Anderson (2017) shows that the word initially meant 'characterized by or full of sunshine'. This meaning was recorded as early as 1300 and is still current today. An equally current meaning (which is why 'sunny' is polysemous), is 'bright, cheerful, joyous', which was first recorded in 1616. As this is a metaphorical sense, it is argued that metaphorisation has led to a change in meaning, resulting in polysemy. A similar process can be observed in some instances of semantic shift, i.e. when an old meaning disappears from usage and is replaced by a new meaning.

In addition, 'sunny' is arguably just one example of a broader pattern of metaphorisation, or metaphorical extension. Looking at the metaphorical meaning of sunny as 'bright, cheerful, joyous' again, it becomes clear that within that definition 'bright' is another polysemous word with a very similar trajectory. Its first sense in the *OED* is 'Shining; emitting, reflecting, or pervaded by much light' first recorded around 1000. Its figurative meaning 'lit up with happiness, gladness, or hope. Also, hopeful, encouraging, cheering' dates from 1751. The literal senses of 'sunny' and 'bright' are related, as are their metaphorical senses; they seem to have developed in the same way. And these are not the only two examples: 'beam', 'sparkling', and 'light up' have all developed new meanings via the same metaphorical extension (Anderson 2017). With recourse to CMT, this pattern can be explained as being motivated by the conceptual metaphor – a metaphorical way of thinking – HAPPINESS IS LIGHT (ibid.). We think about the abstract concept of happiness (target domain) in terms of the more concrete, physical experience of light. This results in multiple lexical items related to the semantic category of light (source domain), becoming used to metaphorically describe happiness, cheerfulness, excitement, and the like. The metaphoric extension from visual light to happiness can be seen as related to the broader pattern of understanding internal mental-affective processes in terms of external physical processes (e.g. the verb 'feel' denoting both haptic perception and emotion; the verbs 'see' and 'grasp' to mean 'understand') (Sweetser 1990).

A recent relevant study is the 'Mapping Metaphor with the *Historical Thesaurus*' project at Glasgow University (http://mappingmetaphor.arts.gla.ac.uk/), which is developing an overview of metaphorical connections made by speakers and writers of English over the entire history of the language. By studying records in the Historical Thesaurus, the team are able to track how words, from the domain of light for example, are used over time to describe other domains such as intelligence, knowledge, or indeed happiness. In this way, they can begin to see – literally, as the project is developing visualisations of its results – innovations in language motivated by metaphorical thinking at particular points in history in relation to different areas of experience. (For more, see Anderson et al. 2016.)

Language learning and education

Another broad area where investigating metaphor can provide insights is education. There are two main strands of research here: studies of how metaphor helps or hinders explanations of new ideas in education generally and studies related to how metaphor might be involved or used in the learning/teaching of a language such as English. (Low's (1988) seminal paper is a useful starting point on the latter.)

In the first strand, studies have investigated the role metaphor plays in first language or monolingual educational contexts (see for example Cameron (2003) and scholars in Aubusson et al. (2006)). Broadly speaking, in these contexts metaphor is often used to develop or 'constitute' new theories and ideas, fill terminological gaps, and to explain complex notions in understandable ways. These functions are, of course, related to the characteristics of metaphor outlined in the introduction to this chapter, and are also deployed in public communication – effectively public education – about complex, often scientific subjects such as climate change (e.g. Nerlich and Jaspal 2013). Metaphorical nouns (e.g. 'pump' for the human heart) can be particularly productive for constitutive or explanatory purposes (Cameron 2003), but metaphors can also be used to manage and mediate the activity of the classroom and the learning of the students (e.g. via instructions to 'go' or 'skip over' something), including the mitigation of face threats in feedback (Cameron 2003). An important finding to emerge from this body of research is that, while metaphors tend to be deployed for the purposes of explanation and elucidation, the specific ways in which this is done can sometimes have the opposite effect. For example, when Cameron (2003) explored 9-11 year-old students' understandings of the metaphors their teachers and textbooks used, she found that metaphorically used verbs combined with anaphoric reference could lead to misunderstandings. In 'The Earth is kept warm by the Sun's heat, and the atmosphere traps some of this heat so that it doesn't escape into space' the underlined anaphoric reference 'it' was mistaken as referring to 'the atmosphere' rather than 'heat', resulting in the misunderstanding of the topic of the metaphor 'escape'. In this case, Cameron (2003) argues, knowledge about the topic that the metaphor was meant to elucidate was required to correctly interpret the metaphor in the first place. Confusion as a result of metaphorical explanations in English is not just a feature of primary and secondary education, but also of higher education, where it can disproportionately affect international audiences. Littlemore (2001, 2003) and Littlemore et al. (2011), for example, found that international students sometime lacked the 'shared' linguistic and cultural knowledge to interpret lecturers' metaphors correctly.

The second strand of metaphor and education research, focusing on language teaching and learning, has also shown that particular metaphorical uses of English words can cause difficulties. For example, difficulties with comprehension can be related to the form of a metaphor. Picken (2005) found that 'invisible' metaphors, i.e. ones that were not signalled (e.g. by mentioning the topic alongside the vehicle; see also 'key debates' section below), were considerably more likely to be misinterpreted by Japanese learners of English than 'explicit' metaphors. This suggests that more subtle, unsignalled metaphors could require extra attention in the classroom. Metaphorically used words that are polysemous through metaphorical extension can also be problematic, especially if the various meanings of the equivalent word in the learner's first language are not the same as in the target language. This is because language learners rely on knowledge of patterns in their first language to work out meanings in the target language (MacArthur and Littlemore 2008). MacArthur (2017) gives the example of the verb 'strike': in its literal sense, this verb is roughly equivalent to the verb *golpear* in Spanish. However, its metaphorical use in English describing a sudden onset of an idea or a condition ('Louise was struck down with leukaemia' or 'another possibility that strikes me'), does not exist for the Spanish *golpear*. This means that in addition to learning the literal sense of 'strike', Spanish-speaking learners of English will have to be taught its possibilities for metaphorical extension, including any indirect evaluative meaning associated with it.

A further insight relevant to language teaching is evidence suggesting that if learners of English are provided with an explanation of how such figurative meanings of words are motivated by underlying conceptual metaphors, they are able to then generalise this information to new lexical items motivated in the same way (Boers 2000; Kövecses and Szabó 1996). This was shown specifically for phrasal verbs such as 'show up' and verbs of motion such as 'plunge'. At least in the short run, explanations of metaphorical motivation also facilitate recall by making these meanings more memorable. As metaphorical competence can contribute to grammatical, textual, illocutionary, sociolinguistic, and strategic competence (Littlemore and Low 2006) these effects are important for language teachers to consider.

Framing and persuasion

The final body of work relates not to what metaphor can contribute to our understanding of language and learning, but to what it can contribute to our understanding of language use and its relationship with reasoning and persuasion. I will focus on two contexts in particular: healthcare and political communication. There are several functions of metaphor at play here and they can be gathered under the umbrella function of 'framing'. As outlined in the introduction, metaphors frame or position topics in particular ways, highlighting some aspects while backgrounding others. This generates expectations and inferences in communication and subsequent action (Entman 1993).

A much discussed example in this context is the use of 'battle' or 'violence' metaphors in the context of cancer. Sontag (1979) was among the first to critique the use of metaphor which manifests in expressions such as 'he finally lost his brave battle with cancer' or 'my doctor recognised I was a born fighter', and the topic has been the subject of intense debate since (Semino et al. 2017). The argument goes that the battle metaphor expressed in these examples implies a particular relationship between the person and the disease (adversarial), and therefore reflects and reinforces a way of conceiving of and experiencing the illness, which can have a negative impact on the individual's sense of self. For example, patients might see themselves as losers if they do not get better, or as cowards if they refuse further treatment. The evaluative potential of metaphor (Deignan 2010) and its ability to connect with emotions is linked with this ability to frame topics (Ritchie 2013). This in itself is already an important insight. Because metaphor can be seen as not just a feature of language, but also of thought, even single instances of a metaphor can influence how we reason about and react to particular topics and issues. This has very tangible consequences in the context of politics.

In an experimental study, Thibodeau and Boroditsky (2011), for example, found that metaphor can have a powerful influence over how people think social problems like crime should be solved. They presented two groups of university students with different versions of a media crime report. In one case, crime was described in terms of a virus and in the other, in terms of a beast:

> Crime is a {wild beast preying on/virus infecting} the city of Addison. The crime rate in the once peaceful city has steadily increased over the past three years. In fact, these days it seems that crime is {lurking in/plaguing} every neighborhood. In 2004, 46,177 crimes were reported compared to more than 55,000 reported in 2007. The rise in violent crime is particularly alarming. In 2004, there were 330 murders in the city, in 2007, there were over 500.
>
> (Thibodeau and Boroditsky 2011: 3)

When increase in crime was described as the effect of a 'virus', participants tended to react and reason within the same biological or organic framing and to propose 'investigating the root causes'. On the other hand, when increased crime was described in terms of a 'beast', they preferred capturing and jailing criminals. Importantly, this effect on reasoning was covert: the research participants did not recognise metaphors as influential in their decisions and argued instead that they had reached their conclusions based on other (often numerical) information. Similar effects of metaphor have been studied in the context of discussions of immigration (Musolff 2015) and the role of the European Union (Musolff 2006). The strategic choice of metaphor can therefore be seen as a crucial tool of persuasion, able to create changes in people's reasoning – undetected.

So far, this discussion has focused on the more cognitive arguments around framing. Returning now to the topic of cancer, there is also additional insight to be gained from taking a discourse approach to the framing potential of metaphor. While it is certainly the case that violence-related metaphors can frame the experience of cancer in a way that is detrimental to people with the illness, Semino et al. (2017) also noted the opposite effect depending on the specific lexical manifestation of the metaphor, who was using it and when (see also Musolff (2015) for a similar line of argument in relation to metaphors of immigration). The metaphorical expression 'fighter' for instance, as used by cancer patients (e.g. 'my doctor recognised I was a born fighter' above), was exclusively used in 'empowering' ways. It implied a sense of control over the disease, and that the patient derived a positive sense of self from this positioning. It is therefore important that framing be considered as an effect of metaphor at both the conceptual and discourse linguistic levels (Semino et al. 2016).

Key debates

Despite the fact that metaphor studies as a field is not new and despite the numerous insights it can contribute to our understanding of language, ongoing debates and unresolved issues remain. One debate I have already hinted at above is around the good or harm that specific metaphors and metaphorical framings can do in different contexts. Here I restrict myself to two others: the status of metaphor versus other tropes and problems with delineating semantic fields.

While the definition of metaphor as 'talking, and potentially thinking, about one thing as if it was something else' is widely used, some would argue that it is not unique to metaphor but can capture other tropes as well. Simile, hyperbole, analogy, allegory, metonymy, synecdoche, etc. are all terms used to describe some form of meaning transfer: some are within semantic domains, some across; some can be in the form of single words, some cannot; some are more likely to be creative than others. Different traditions find different distinctions more or less important. Here I briefly consider simile and metonymy.

Similes are generally seen as 'an explicit statement of comparison between two different things, conveyed through expressions such as 'like', 'as if' and so on' (Semino 2008: 16), while metaphor is more of an implicit comparison. Steen et al. (2010) go so far as to call similes 'direct metaphors'. Yet the distinction can matter. There is evidence to suggest that when a figurative comparison is novel, it might be understood more quickly in the form of a simile than metaphor (Gentner and Bowdle 2008), except when the comparison is particularly apt (Haught 2013). This topic has also been debated via the concept of 'signalling' (e.g. Krennmayr et al. 2014). Differences in metaphor form, in terms of the presence or absence of signalling devices, can have an impact on the recall of particular metaphorical framing. Krennmayr et al. (2014) found that explicitly signalled figurative expressions, such as similes, which signal their metaphoricity via 'like', 'as if', etc., are more likely to be recalled. This result has bearings on metaphor's role in influencing reasoning, discussed in the previous section.

The distinction between metaphor and metonymy can also be important. Metonymy is similar to metaphor, but the meaning transfer remains within a semantic domain; in metonymy, the relationship between a vehicle and its target is one of association rather than similarity (Littlemore 2015). For example, a car could be described metonymically as a 'set of wheels', because wheels are associated with cars. But the distinction between metaphor and metonymy is difficult to maintain: just as there is a cline of metaphoricity ranging from non-metaphorical to novel metaphor, there seems to be a cline between metonymy and metaphor (Barnden 2010). Deignan (2005), for example, suggests that many metaphors which have the human body as their basis are based in metonymy. 'To get back on one's feet', when used to denote recovery from illness, describes recovery in terms of a physical manifestation of itself. Ill or infirm people are often weak and have to lie down, but once they regain their strength, they can stand on their feet again. Despite this continuum, the differences can have consequences. Littlemore (2015), for example, suggests that metonymy actually provides more subtle ways of communicating nuance and evaluation than metaphor – a distinction that can be important when the goal is to persuade 'gently'.

Another reason that the line between metaphor and metonymy can be difficult to draw, and this is, in fact, a broader issue in metaphor research, is that the definitions rely on being able to identify the boundaries of semantic fields or domains. Yet the boundaries between semantic domains are not fixed or clear-cut, but rather fuzzy at best (Barnden 2010). For example, it is difficult to say exactly where the boundary is between the semantic domain of 'sports' and that of 'warfare' (they also arguably share a lot of content). This has the potential to create, to date unresolved, problems. Even the MIP (Pragglejaz Group 2007) above relies to some extent on being able to identify semantic boundaries. Claiming that the contextual meaning of a lexical item is different enough from the basic meaning to amount to metaphor requires the assumption of dividing lines between areas of meaning. This becomes even more problematic when dealing with diachronic data to investigate language change. Semantic domain boundaries are not only difficult to draw at a particular point in time; diachronic studies additionally need to take into account the fact that they are likely to shift over time (Anderson 2017).

Future directions

Perhaps some of these debates will be resolved or become irrelevant with future research. There are a number of promising studies ongoing from various theoretical positions. The resurgence of discourse-based approaches, often drawing on evidence from large corpora, is likely to continue contributing practical as well as theoretical insights into metaphor and its role in language and communication. The recognition of the need for robust definitions and methods in metaphor research will likely do the same. However, perhaps the answers will arise not in the context of individual paradigms, methods or theoretical orientations, but from a perspective that has the potential to combine and reconcile insights from many. In this vein, one of the most exciting recent and ongoing developments is the application of dynamic systems theory to the study of communication generally and to the study of metaphor more specifically. Dynamic systems theory developed in the physical sciences (e.g. Holland 1995) to describe how complicated, multivariable systems coordinate and self-organise into coherent, functioning entities. In relation to metaphor, the idea of a dynamic system is evoked when trying to understand and account for the complexity of variation, patterns and relationships in the ways in which metaphor use develops and adapts in communication (e.g. Cameron and Maslen 2010; Gibbs and Cameron 2008). Gibbs and Cameron (2008) argue that metaphor 'performance' in interaction is influenced by a multitude of variables, including:

- Enduring metaphorical concepts, including conventional conceptual metaphors;
- Previously understood metaphorical utterances, i.e. what has been said or written before;
- Body movements and gesture;
- Gender and occupation – which may be generalisable to 'who we are in the world';
- The negotiation of intimacy and social distance between interlocutors;
- Conventional talk in specific socio-cultural groups (cf. Deignan et al.'s 2013 'discourse communities');
- Specific language and culture.

But the objective of this approach in metaphor studies, at least for now, is to recognise and begin to take account of the fact that metaphor use is always and continually shaped by a potentially infinite number of factors, rather than to list all the possible factors that influence metaphor use. More importantly, because it was designed to cope with the idea of an indefinite number of variables, the dynamic systems approach is able to integrate into a coherent whole multiple theoretical views of metaphor, including cognitive approaches with discourse-based approaches (Gibbs 2011, 2017). In fact, this approach might also finally be able to fully integrate insights gained from studies of multimodal metaphor, such as visual images (Forceville and Urios-Aparisi 2009) and gesture (Cienki and Müller 2008).

Concluding remarks

In this chapter, I have outlined some of the key insights that a study of metaphor can contribute to the field of English language studies. I focused on its role in explaining polysemy and language change, in helping or hindering the learning of language and the understanding of new concepts, and on its potential to frame topics in particular ways, thereby influencing reasoning. I also provided an overview of an established method of metaphor identification which provides studies with the systematicity and reliability needed to ensure that metaphor is understood as 'necessary and not just nice'.

Further reading

Dancygier, B. and E. Sweetser (2014) *Figurative Language*. New York: Cambridge University Press. An up-to-date, accessible, yet thorough introduction to figurative language in general, and metaphor specifically. The authors cover various discourse and cognitive approaches.

Semino, E. (2008) *Metaphor in Discourse*. Cambridge: Cambridge University Press. A detailed discussion of metaphor use in different contexts. It covers pattering, variation and functions of metaphor in literature, politics, science, education, and other genres.

Cameron, L. and R. Maslen (eds) (2010) *Metaphor Analysis: Research Practice in Applied Linguistics, Social Sciences and the Humanities*. London: Equinox. A collection of chapters dedicated to the methods of analysis in studying metaphor. It includes discussions of metaphor identification, categorisation, and labelling, as well as the use of computer-assisted methods.

Semino, E. and Z. Demjén (eds) (2017) *The Routledge Handbook of Metaphor and Language*. Abingdon: Routledge. A comprehensive collection of chapters covering formal and functional variation in metaphor across genres and contexts, metaphor in cognitive development and impairment, and applications and interventions using metaphor in various contexts, in addition to methodologies and theoretical underpinnings.

Related topics

- The historical study of English
- Persuasive language.

References

Anderson, W. (2017) 'Metaphor and diachronic variation', in E. Semino and Z. Demjén (eds), *The Routledge Handbook of Metaphor and Language*. Abingdon: Routledge, 233–246.

Anderson, W., E. Bramwell and C. Hough (eds) (2016) *Mapping English Metaphor through Time*. Oxford: Oxford University Press.

Aubusson, P. J., A. G. Harrison and S. M. Ritchie (eds) (2006) *Metaphor and Analogy in Science Education*. Dordrecht, Netherlands: Springer.

Barnden, J. A. (2010) 'Metaphor and metonymy: Making their connections more slippery', *Cognitive Linguistics* 21 (1): 1–34. doi: 10.1515/cogl.2010.001
Boers, F. (2000) 'Metaphor awareness and vocabulary retention', *Applied Linguistics* 21 (4): 553–571.
Cameron, L. (2003) *Metaphor in Educational Discourse*. London: Continuum.
Cameron, L. and G. Low (1999) *Researching and Applying Metaphor*. Cambridge: Cambridge University Press.
Cameron, L. and R. Maslen (2010) *Metaphor Analysis: Research Practice in Applied Linguistics, Social Sciences and the Humanities*. London: Equinox.
Cameron, L., R. Maslen and G. Low (2010) 'Finding systematicity in metaphor use', in L. Cameron and R. Maslen (eds), *Metaphor Analysis*. London: Equinox, 116–146.
Cienki, A. and C. Müller (2008) *Metaphor and Gesture*. Amsterdam, Philadelphia: John Benjamins.
Deignan, A. (2005) *Metaphor and Corpus Linguistics*. Amsterdam: John Benjamins.
Deignan, A. (2010) 'The evaluative properties of metaphors', in Z. Todd, A. Deignan and L. Cameron (eds), *Researching and Applying Metaphor in Use*. Amsterdam, Philadelphia: John Benjamins, 357–373.
Deignan, A., J. Littlemore and E. Semino (2013) *Figurative Language, Genre and Register*. Cambridge: Cambridge University Press.
Demjén, Z. (2015) *Sylvia Plath and the Language of Affective States: Written Discourse and the Experience of Depression*. London: Bloomsbury Academic.
Dirven, R. (1985) 'Metaphor as a basic means for extending the lexicon', in W. Paprotté and R. Dirven (eds), *The Ubiquity of Metaphor*. Amsterdam/Philadelphia: John Benjamins, 85–119.
Dorst, A. G. (2015) 'More or different metaphors in fiction? A quantitative cross-register comparison', *Language and Literature* 24 (1): 3–22.
Entman, R. M. (1993) 'Framing: Towards clarifiation of a fractured paradigm', *Journal of Communication* 43 (4): 51–58.
Forceville, C. and E. Urios-Aparisi (2009) *Multimodal Metaphor*. Berlin, New York: Mouton de Gruyter.
Gentner, D. and B. Bowdle (2008) 'Metaphor as structure-mapping', in R. W. Gibbs Jr (ed.), *The Cambridge Handbook of Metaphor and Thought*. New York: Cambridge University Press, 109–128.
Gibbs, R. W. (2011) 'Evaluating conceptual metaphor theory', *Discourse Processes* 48 (8): 529–562. doi: 10.1080/0163853X.2011.606103
Gibbs, R. W. (2017) 'Metaphor, language and dynamical systems', in E. Semino and Z. Demjén (eds), *The Routledge Handbook of Metaphor and Language*. Abingdon: Routledge.
Gibbs, R. W. and L. Cameron (2008) 'The social-cognitive dynamics of metaphor performance', *Cognitive Systems Research* 9 (1–2): 64–75. doi: 10.1016/j.cogsys.2007.06.008
Grady, J. (1997) *Foundations of Meaning: Primary Metaphors and Primary Scenes* (PhD Dissertation, University of California, Berkeley).
Haught, C. (2013) 'A tale of two tropes: How metaphor and simile differ', *Metaphor & Symbol* 28 (4): 254–274.
Holland, J. H. (1995) *Hidden Order: How Adaptation Builds Complexity*. Reading, MA, Wokingham, England: Addison-Wesley.
Hopper, P. J. and E. Traugott (2003) *Grammaticalization*. Cambridge: Cambridge University Press.
Jäkel, O. (1999) 'Kant, Blumenberg, Weinrich: Some forgotten contributions to the cognitive theory of metaphor', in R. W. Gibbs Jr and G. Steen (eds), *Metaphor in Cognitive Linguistics*. Amsterdam: John Benjamins, 9–27.
Kittay, E. F. (1987) *Metaphor: Its Cognitive Force and Linguistic Structure*. Oxford: Clarendon.
Kövecses, Z. and P. Szabó (1996) 'Idioms: A view from cognitive semantics', *Applied Linguistics* 17 (3): 326–355.
Krennmayr, T. (2014) 'What corpus linguistics can tell us about metaphor use in newspaper texts', *Journalism Studies* 16 (4): 1–17.
Krennmayr, T., B. Bowdle, G. Mulder and G. Steen (2014) 'Building metaphorical schemas when reading text', *Metaphor and the Social World* 4 (1): 65–89.
Kukil, K. (ed.) (2000) *The Unabridged Journals of Sylvia Plath*. New York: Anchor Books.
Lakoff, G. and M. Johnson (1980) *Metaphors We Live By*. Chicago: University of Chicago Press.
Lakoff, G. and M. Johnson (2003) *Metaphors We Live By*. 2nd edn. Chicago: University of Chicago Press.

Lakoff, G. and M. Turner (1989) *More Than Cool Reason: A Field Guide to Poetic Metaphor*. Chicago: University of Chicago Press.
Littlemore, J. (2001) 'The use of metaphor in university lectures and the problems that it causes for overseas students', *Teaching in Higher Education* 6: 333–351.
Littlemore, J. (2003) 'The effect of cultural background on metaphor interpretation', *Metaphor & Symbol* 18 (4): 273–288. doi: 10.1207/S15327868MS1804_4
Littlemore, J. (2015) *Metonymy: Hidden Shortcuts in Language, Thought and Communication*. Cambridge: Cambridge University Press.
Littlemore, J., P. Chen, A. Koester and J. A. Barnden (2011) 'Difficulties in metaphor comprehension faced by international students whose first language is not English', *Applied Linguistics* 32 (4): 408–429.
Littlemore, J. and G. D. Low (2006) 'Metaphoric competence and communicative language ability', *Applied Linguistics* 27 (2): 268–294.
Low, G. (1988) 'On teaching metaphor', *Applied Linguistics* 9: 125–147.
MacArthur, F. (2017) 'Using metaphor in the teaching of second/foreign languages', in E. Semino and Z. Demjén (eds), *The Routledge Handbook of Metaphor and Language*. Abingdon: Routledge, 413–425.
MacArthur, F. and J. Littlemore (2008) 'A discovery approach using corpora in the foreign language classroom', in F. Boers and S. Lindstromberg (eds), *Cognitive Linguistic Approaches to Teaching Vocabulary and Phraseology*. Amsterdam: Mouton de Gruyter, 159–188.
Macmillan Dictionary (2009–2016). Available at www.macmillandictionary.com/. Macmillan Publishers Limited.
Mahon, J. E. (1999) 'Getting your sources right: What Aristotle *didn't* say', in L. Cameron and G. Low (eds), *Researching and Applying Metaphor*. Cambridge: Cambridge University Press, 69–80.
Musolff, A. (2006) 'Metaphor scenarios in public discourse', *Metaphor & Symbol* 21 (1): 23–38.
Musolff, A. (2015) 'Dehumanizing metaphors in UK immigrant debates in press and online media', *Journal of Language Aggression and Conflict* 3 (1): 41–56.
Nerlich, B. and R. Jaspal (2013) 'UK media representations of carbon capture and storage: Actors, frames and metaphors', *Metaphor and the Social World* 3 (1): 35–53.
Ortony, A. (1975) 'Why metaphors are necessary and not just nice', *Educational Theory* 25 (1): 45–53.
Ortony, A. (ed.) (1979) *Metaphor and Thought*. New York: Cambridge University Press.
Ortony, A. (ed.) (1993) *Metaphor and Thought*. 2nd edn. New York: Cambridge University Press.
Picken, J. D. (2005) 'Helping foreign language learners to make sense of literature with metaphor awareness-raising', *Language Awareness* 14: 142–152.
Pragglejaz Group (2007) 'MIP: A method for identifying metaphorically used words in discourse', *Metaphor and Symbol* 22 (1): 1–39.
Reisigl, M. (2006) 'Rhetorical tropes in political discourse', in K. Brown (ed.), *The Encyclopedia of Language and Linguistics*. 2nd edn, Vol. 10. Oxford: Elsevier, 596–605.
Ricoeur, P. (2003 [1975]) *The Rule of Metaphor [La métaphore vive]* [The Rule of Metaphor] (R. Czerny, K. McLaughlin and J. Costello, Trans.). Abingdon: Routledge.
Ritchie, L. D. (2013) *Metaphor*. Cambridge, New York: Cambridge University Press.
Semino, E. (2008) *Metaphor in Discourse*. Cambridge: Cambridge University Press.
Semino, E., Z. Demjén and J. Demmen (2016) 'Metaphor and framing in talking about cancer: Cognition, discourse and practice', *Applied Linguistics*. doi: 10.1093/applin/amw028
Semino, E., Z. Demjén, J. Demmen, V. Koller, S. A. Payne, A. Hardie and P. Rayson (2017) 'The online use of 'Violence' and 'Journey' metaphors by cancer patients, as compared with health professionals: A mixed methods study', *BMJ Palliative & Supportive Care* 7: 60–66. doi: 10.1136/bmjspcare-2014-000785
Sontag, S. (1979) *Illness as Metaphor*. London: Allen Lane.
Steen, G., A. G. Dorst, J. B. Herrmann, A. Kaal, T. Krennmayr and T. Pasma (2010) *A Method for Linguistic Metaphor Identification: From MIP to MIPVU*. Amsterdam, Philadelphia: John Benjamins Publishing Company.
Sweetser, E. (1990) *From Etymology to Pragmatics: Metaphorical and Cultural Aspects of Semantic Structure*. Cambrdige: Cambridge University Press.

Thibodeau, P. H. and L. Boroditsky (2011) 'Metaphors we think with: The role of metaphor in reasoning', *PLoS ONE* 6 (2): 1–11. doi: 10.1371/journal.pone.0016782
Traugott, E. (2006) 'Semantic change: Bleaching, strengthening, narrowing, extension', in K. Brown (ed.), *Encyclopedia of Language and Linguistics*. 2nd edn, Vol. 11. Amsterdam: Elsevier, 124–131.
Urban, M. (2014) 'Lexical semantic change and semantic reconstruction', in C. Bowern and B. Evans (eds), *The Routledge Handbook of Historical Linguistics*. Abingdon: Routledge, 374–392.
Zinken, J. and A. Musolff (2009) 'A discourse-centred perspective on metaphorical meaning and understanding', in A. Musolff and J. Zinken (eds), *Metaphor and Discourse*. Basingstoke: Palgrave Macmillan, 1–8.

29
Multimodal English

Louise J. Ravelli

Introduction

Multimodal texts are a ubiquitous feature of today's communication landscape, and thus multimodal English should be a matter of central concern for English Language Studies. The issues of understanding, analysing and evaluating multimodal English have the potential to require dramatic revisions of most, if not all, areas of English Language Studies. Multimodal English is not just about looking at language in the context of a particular medium, such as 'the language of films' or 'the language of magazines' and so on. Rather, it is about communication through multimodal texts of which language is one part. How such texts work intersemiotically, and how that interaction impacts our fundamental understandings of what 'language' is, are central questions to the understanding of contemporary communication, particularly where digital technologies make such complex forms of texts readily available.

It is hard to imagine any form of communication in which English is *not* multimodal. Indeed, the perception that there is truly any monomodal communication is somewhat of a fiction. If language is written, it has a visual presence – whether it is handwritten, printed by a machine, or appearing on-screen in the form of pixels; whether it is produced in a small, neat font or something large and exuberant; whether it is black ink on a white page or multicoloured inks against a photographic image . . . all these add further layers of meaning to what is 'written'. If the communication is spoken, it may be loud or soft, it may be in a familiar accent or one which is strange, it may be accompanied by wild gestures or perhaps heard without any visual presence, there may be relative silence in the background or a cacophony of noise – all of which also add further layers of meaning to the communication taking place.

But it is important to recognize that there is a continuum from these inherent forms of multimodality – that is, the visual presence of written language, and the physical presence of spoken language – to the related phenomenon of explicit co-configuration of multiple modes. This might occur in a webpage which makes use of images, language, on-screen layout, and sound; or in a school textbook which combines language with pictures, diagrams, and page layout to make meaning; or in social media where language, images, sound, and hyperlinks can combine. Thus for this chapter, 'Multimodal English' includes the inherent sense of multimodality, as such an understanding challenges the primacy and exclusivity often accorded to language. But the stronger emphasis will be on the more explicit sense of co-configuration of multiple modes. In our contemporary world, the ubiquitous presence of explicitly co-configured multimodal texts dramatically changes the landscape of communication, and the study of such texts must be of central concern to English Language Studies – and of course, to *all* language studies. As (Kress and van Leeuwen (2001: 110) write,

> a past (and still existent) common sense [belief] to the effect that meaning resides in language alone – or, in other versions of this, that language is the central means of representing and communicating ... – is simply no longer tenable ... it never really was, and certainly is not now.

Historical perspectives

Multimodality as a communicative phenomenon is not new, but it 'is new as a *term*, a *conceptual terrain*' (Trimbur and Press 2015: 21; original emphasis). Within this terrain, there are multiple perspectives on the phenomenon. Van Leeuwen (2011: 668) defines it as 'a field of study investigating the common as well as the distinct properties of the different modes in the multimodal mix and the way they integrate in multimodal texts and communicative events' (see also Unsworth 2008: 8). It is closely related to terms such as 'multimedia' and 'new media', that is, digitally-enabled communicative forms which integrate multiple communicative resources (Hartley 2002), though it is not confined to digital texts. Thus a printed book with no pictures is still multimodal, as the font, paper, ink colour, layout, and binding all contribute to socially and culturally understood meanings. The multimodality is more obvious if the printed book contains illustrations: here, the two modes of language and image are being explicitly combined.

Interest in multimodality as a field of study is due in large part to the foundational work of Gunther Kress and van Leeuwen (2001, 2006). They outline common semiotic principles which underlie all multimodal texts, as well as an approach to the analysis of images which culminates in a 'grammar' – systems for relating visual resources to their social meanings. Their overall approach is one of social semiotics, that is, an understanding of meaning-making deeply embedded within an understanding of the social, which combines an exploration of semiotic resources with an understanding of the communicative practices in which these are based, including their histories, questions of individual agency, and the environment in which communication takes place. The work is heavily influenced by systemic functional linguistics (SFL, e.g. Halliday and Matthiessen 2004; Halliday 1978), including that all communication is socially and culturally situated and needs to be understood and explained in relation to those contexts, that meaning arises from systemically-available options, and that meaning is multifunctional. To use the terms of Kress and van Leeuwen (2006), any mode realizes representational (material), interpersonal (social), and compositional (semiotic) reality simultaneously.

Related social-semiotic approaches to multimodal communication include the work of O'Toole (2011) and O'Halloran (2004, 2008), who use a similar systemic functional base, while placing greater emphasis on other aspects of Halliday's grammatical model, such as the principle of rank. Complementary approaches include multimodal interaction analysis (Norris 2004), a branch of mediated discourse analysis (e.g. Scollon 1998; Scollon and Scollon 2003) which links a micro-analysis of everyday social interaction to broader social and political contexts. (See Jewitt 2009 and Norris and Maier 2014 for comprehensive overviews of these and related approaches).

Educational foci

The range of multimodal studies, despite its relative recency, is vast. Kress and van Leeuwen's and O'Toole's early work on images already included studies of children's drawings, classical art, popular media texts such as magazines and newspapers, school textbooks, and even sculptures. Since then, the range has expanded further to include such diverse texts as children's toys (e.g. Caldas-Coulthard and van Leeuwen 2001; Machin and van Leeuwen 2008), hairstyles (McMurtrie 2010), and the built environment (e.g. Ravelli and McMurtrie 2016). There are a wide range of relevant monographs, edited volumes, journal articles, and handbooks which manifest this diversity (see Further Reading, below). But in this chapter for multimodal English, I focus on those studies which emphasize questions of literacy and education, where language works together with other communicative resources in new ways. A strong educational focus was first advocated by the 'New London Group', a group of ten scholars from across the UK, the US, and Australia (New London Group 1996; Cope and Kalantzis 2000). In the context of emerging technological change and processes of globalization, they drew attention to the need to understand and provide a pedagogy for what they termed 'multiliteracies'. They argued that multiliteracies should be understood as going beyond basic senses of competency as a basis for literacy, to one in which 'language and other modes of meaning are dynamic representational resources, constantly being remade by their users as they work to achieve their various cultural purposes' (New London Group 1996: 64). This can be achieved by incorporating the key concept of *design*, 'in which we are both inheritors of patterns and conventions of meaning and at the same time active designers of meaning' (New London Group 1996: 65). Thus, users both make use of available patterns – grammars of relevant semiotic systems – and transform these through use.

These foundational ideas were explored via a number of different pathways. Studies of children's developing literacy, both prior to and at school (Kress 1997, 2003), highlighted just how semiotic was the work done by all modalities; that is, learning to communicate, to participate in society and culture, is not just a matter of learning language. Kress (2000: 338–339) shows that a seemingly 'trivial' child's drawing is as much a process of acculturation as learning to speak, and also that 'There is a semantic trade among speech, image, and writing (and other modes, and via other senses – taste, touch and feel)', that is, that each mode has its own affordances; modes are 'distinct in what they permit'. Succession in time, for example, is more easily afforded by language ('First, ... then... next') and spatial relations are more easily afforded by images (e.g. how parts fit together into a whole). It is not that one can't be done by the other, but each has its own logic, a 'functional specialization', and in this specialization, 'language is no longer the carrier of all meaning' (Kress 2000: 339). Thus, teachers need to attend to all the modalities, and recognize their students' agency in the process of text creation. The emphasis on pedagogy extends to the analysis of the multimodal resources that students access, such as computer games (Jewitt 2006), identifying how these can both support and challenge students' learning, and to the analysis of classrooms as important sites of multimodal integration, including how the placement of chairs and the positioning of the teacher instantiate a specific pedagogical style (Kress et al. 2005).

A similar interest in education and literacy in the context of multimodality has been pursued particularly vigorously from an SFL perspective, sometimes referred to as systemic functional-multimodal discourse analysis (SF-MDA, O'Halloran 2008), and strongly influenced by systemic functional approaches to genre-based literacy (Martin and Rose 2008).[1] The strong link to SFL in a pedagogical context affords the effective sharing of an explicit metalanguage which can connect language with other semiotic systems (Unsworth 2001, 2009), thus providing a coherent basis for understanding and critiquing complex multimodal texts. This work has explored the particularities of specific modes, such as the visual communication of children's picture books (Painter et al. 2013), as well as the multimodal texts and literacy demands distinctive to academic subject areas (Derewianka and Coffin 2008; O'Halloran 2005; Unsworth 2001, 2004). Research is now being extended to consider digital-specific resources (Unsworth and Thomas 2014), as well as the role of gesture in teaching (Hood 2011) and the contribution of other sensory modes to questions of literacy (Mills 2016).

These approaches have not only informed research into multimodal texts, but have also been integrated into school curricula, such as the new national Australian Curriculum for schools. For senior English (the last two years of school), the syllabus specifies that students be adept in creating, transforming, and adapting 'oral, written and multimodal texts in a range of mediums and styles' (Australian Curriculum, Senior Secondary English (n.d.)). While English Language Studies are not confined to (literary) subject English, it is here in particular where language skills are emphasized most strongly, and where the subject content is, at least in part, the textual products themselves, and that now necessarily includes multimodal texts. Importantly, however, such intentions need effective teacher education, appropriate resources, and meaningful assessment practices, in order to succeed. And the knowledge base needs to be underpinned by strong frameworks or grammars which enable the systematic analysis and interpretation of multimodal resources (Unsworth 2014).

Throughout the work of the New London Group and SFL-based approaches, questions of literacy are paramount. Multimodal English places yet further demands on literacy practices, as multimodal texts are 'sites for the integrative deployment of visual, verbal and acoustic semiotic resources' (Unsworth 2001: 279). That is, they are more than just language. Within these approaches, particular emphasis is placed on issues of critical literacy, and this means moving beyond basic recognition and reproduction literacies, towards literacy which enables reflection, that is, 'an understanding that all social practices, and hence all literacies, are socially constructed' and the ability to read the practices of 'inclusion and exclusion' which are necessarily entailed in such social construction (Unsworth 2001: 15). Critical perspectives are particularly foregrounded in the work of Multimodal Critical Discourse Studies (Machin 2013), developing from earlier Critical Discourse Analysis (CDA) work (Fairclough 2010).

The term 'critical' means 'denaturalizing', bringing to light understandings – especially in relation to manifestations of power – which are otherwise hidden. Hence, all these approaches – overlapping and intersecting as they do – target and investigate the social and cultural implications of multimodality, both generally, and particularly for its impact on an understanding of language.

Current critical issues and topics

Rethinking English Language Studies in the context of multimodality requires some fundamental shifts in perspective. In the first instance, the multimodal resources themselves must be understood: if it is now the case (if ever it was not) that English is essentially and fundamentally multimodal, what are these 'other' modalities and what do they contribute to communication? Language has long been studied to understand its component parts, its grammar, the nuances of its meanings, its discourse patterns. Attention now also needs to be given elsewhere. Kress and van Leeuwen's (2006) grammar of visual images shows that images with people in them can be positioned to create direct eye contact with the viewer (or not); be positioned above or below the viewer's eyeline; or to look close or far away. Such choices create different interpersonal positions with and for the viewer – including meanings of intimacy or formality, power or equality. At the same time, the arrangement of multiple visual elements as part of a larger composition (a page with words and pictures, for example, or multiple pictures) can prioritize some parts of the composition over others, for example by using the size of the elements or lighting effects to create salience; it can use resources such as framing to show separation or unity among the parts; and a reading/viewing sequence can be constructed by the placement of elements or by the inclusion of vectors (visible and invisible diagonal lines, such as arrows, or the direction of a gaze). This means that not all parts of a visual composition have equal value, and such resources can position readers/viewers to view the elements as having different information values and specific interrelationships. Further, the components of an image may include dynamic vectors, indicating action, or may simply present elements, creating stasis. Representation can thereby show what things 'do' and/or what they 'are'. Understanding these different kinds of meanings requires some appreciation of the grammar of images: that gaze is a resource that can be used for interpersonal effect, for example; or that placement creates organization and reading paths; and that vectors can create a sense of action taking place.

Callow (2013) shows how a seemingly simple children's picture book uses images to expand on the nature of the characters relayed in the story. He analyses a two-page spread from a book called *Fox* (Wild and Brooks 2000), where a drawing of a large and scary fox is placed higher than and almost surrounding a little bird; the fox's words are positive and friendly, but his stance and gaze, directed at the bird, suggest something else. For a child, learning 'to read' this kind of text means a lot more than understanding the words. The picture is just as much a part of the story, and it is the tension between the two which gives excitement and suspense to the tale. Literacy, here, includes 'reading' the image, and reading the relationship between the image and the words.

The power of explicit knowledge of visual resources is being added to that of explicit grammatical knowledge of language in primary and secondary schools, as with Painter et al. (2013), who extend the description of visual resources found in children's picture books. They reveal how images can be used to encourage the reader to share the point of view of a depicted character, for example, by showing a part of a character's body *as if* it were extended from the reader's body, or by looking from behind a character, *as if* the reader is seeing what the character sees. Such extensions to the visual grammar reveal how young readers are apprenticed into ways of appreciating, attending to, and understanding stories, through the clever deployment of visual strategies. As Kress and van Leeuwen (2006) underscore, images are neither transparent nor simple; their complex meanings require a carefully considered grammar as a basis for developing explicit pedagogical resources and interventions.

Such concerns apply not only to issues of literacy for children, but to critical literacy issues for the adult world also. For example, the complexity of messages created through the intersection of visual and verbal meanings, and their power in construing ideological understandings, has been demonstrated in relation to such domains as news discourse (Bednarek and Caple 2012), and the presentation of war in video games (van Leeuwen and Machin 2005). And while visual resources are perhaps the most pervasive and accessible 'other' communicative mode, all communicative resources create challenges for understanding multimodal English. Ongoing research into other communicative resources includes the role of sound (e.g. van Leeuwen 1999), of animated text (da Costa Lima Carneiro Leão 2013), and of specific media such as PowerPoint (Djonov and van Leeuwen 2012) and websites (Zhang and O'Halloran 2012).

In addition, as all texts are socially and culturally situated, specific cultural literacies also need to be accommodated. Something as obvious as left-right reading practices in western cultures, which affect the 'reading' of an image, as much as the reading of written text alone (Kress and van Leeuwen 2006) need to be considered as potentially impinging on a user's understanding of that text. Kress (2000) underscores the importance of accounting for multimodal texts in TESOL contexts, demonstrating that the substance of a science lesson is as likely to be carried by images as by written language, and in ways that are functionally specialized – that is, the one resource does not simply replicate what can be said/shown in the other, but they each contribute unique meanings.

While understanding the individual modes which contribute to multimodality is a necessary step in achieving a fuller understanding of multimodal English, an additional critical issue is the 'multi' side of this communication revolution: what is the impact on language and communication when multiple resources work together to create a unified text? The New London Group identified that multimodality is, after all, about *multiple* modalities, that it hinges on the 'patterns of interconnection' among modes (New London Group 1996: 78), and Unsworth adds that 'we need to understand how these different modalities separately and interactively construct different dimensions of meaning' (Unsworth 2001: 9).

One example of the fundamental change that this interaction brings relates to the nature of reading patterns. In cultures which have writing that goes left to right, top to bottom, a linear reading pattern predominates, also moving from left to right, top to bottom, verso (left) page before recto (right).[2] But if the 'page' is, say, a two-page spread in a school textbook, with various images and paragraphs scattered around it, a linear reading path may well be quite unsuitable, and indeed the resource of layout takes on new significance in terms of understanding how the parts of the text relate to the whole (Kress 2010: 141–145, see also Matthiessen 2007). Exley and Cottrell (2012) note that 'seemingly simple and short multimodal texts make exceedingly complex reading demands of their [young] readers' (p. 97). Layout and design may effectively support a reader's capacity to identify important information – or it may not – and such understandings must be part of teaching and understanding relevant literacy practices (Unsworth 2014). Many would be familiar with a primary school child's first attempts at creating a PowerPoint presentation: every effect of colour, transition, animation, and sound will be deployed, not necessarily enhancing the communicative outcomes! Or, on the other hand, many would also be familiar with a dull and monotonous presentation, presenting written work on-screen, and not using the affordances of the technology; equally unsuccessful.

The reimagining of 'English language' as 'multimodal English' requires the reevaluation of other core notions, including genre (Bateman 2008; Bowcher and Yameng Liang 2016). News reports, for example, occur now less and less frequently in printed forms, and the shift to online environments is not just a shift in the mode of production, but is leading to changes in the genres that are used to convey the news. These are moving away from extended hard-news reports, structured around a nucleus (headline and lead) and satellites (subsequent developments of the nucleus) (White 1997; Feez et al. 2010), towards such genres as the newsbite: brief items, usually with a thumbnail picture, a hyperlink to a more extended version, and a brief textual description. These are more than simple alerts to what is to come, but serve important roles in their own right, functioning to accommodate the continuous time scale of digital news and indicate the relative salience of multiple items competing for attention (Knox 2007). Other emerging news genres include the image-nuclear text (Caple 2013), where large images are paired with brief verbal descriptions, inevitably requiring a pun between the image and text, and thus requiring the reader to actively move between the two to understand the whole. Bednarek and Caple (2012: 182) give the example of an arresting photo of a drought-ridden landscape, with the caption 'Dry hard with a vengeance', creating a pun between the 1995 Hollywood movie, 'Die Hard: With a Vengeance' and the severity of the drought as depicted in the image. 'Reading' the news, then, includes recognizing the role of these deceptively simple genres in shaping and guiding attention and reading patterns, and in creating meaning.

And because of the shift to digital communication, even what we understand to be 'language' is changing. Mills and Unsworth (2015) draw attention to the new affordances of digital texts, which challenge traditional reading skills. More than just displaying a page on a screen instead of printing it onto paper, new resources such as hyperlinking necessitate different skills of information searching and aggregation on the part of the reader. They note that

> The online environment can be a challenging landscape for readers, who must make use of self-regulation and persistence to avoid the cognitive overload and disorientation experienced by an endless sea of hyperlinked reading pathways. They must engage in active decision-making processes, engaging in predication of partially obscured web content that is hidden behind navigational links. Online reading requires careful planning, monitoring, predicting, and questioning, and involves moving speedily and efficiently by skimming and summarizing valid findings.
>
> (Mills and Unsworth 2015: 10)

Similarly, Zappavigna (2012) shows that the medium itself can change the message. In investigating the language used in Twitter and other social media, she demonstrates that social media resources such as the hashtag (#) and the character address (@) create 'searchable talk' and allow for affiliation around shared interests and values. That is, community can be created through these online resources; hashtags such as #jesuischarlie being a notable recent example. Part of the literacy of using these media is understanding such potential.

Diversity of approaches

Areas of diversity within multimodal studies include variations in theoretical approach and methods, issues of stabilizing terminology in an emerging and evolving field, and concretizing evidence for claims around multimodality. These are all framed here as sites of productivity and potential, rather than as problems; knowledge is, after all, like an ecosystem, and diversity is necessary to its health and longevity.

In terms of theoretical antecedents, the various frameworks described above such as the New London Group, SF-MDA, and CDA all share a socially-oriented basis of some sort, as well as long-standing interests in issues of education and literacy. Differences arise both between these groups (in so far as any can be said to have distinct boundaries) and within, in focus and in method. For example, SF-MDA will foreground system networks as a way of explaining meaning potential; multimodal interaction analysis (Norris 2012) foregrounds social action and the role of psychological tools and material objects in mediating this. Distinctly different approaches include cognitive perspectives on multimodality (Mayer 2005), although as Pelletier observes (Pelletier 2008: 81), social and cognitive approaches do not often meet in the middle, and it will be evident that this chapter concentrates on the social.

The diversity of available approaches has led to innovations in methods for capturing, transcribing and analysing multimodal texts. Close, qualitative work, often based on just a few or sometimes even just one text, is very evident in multimodal research, and has an important role to play in terms of explaining nuances and complexities of meaning, particularly where it can be used to explicate an underlying system (Hasan 1989). But other methods are being developed for larger-scale studies, including developments of corpus-based work which accommodates multimodal texts (e.g. Baldry and Thibault 2005; Lim Fei et al. 2015), and specific software to facilitate transcription and analysis (e.g. O'Halloran et al. 2012).

A particular challenge for studies of Multimodal English can be the boundaries between and overlaps among new terms. One such instance includes the overlaps and confusions between terms such as 'mode', 'modality', and 'medium'. While sometimes used interchangeably, Kress and van Leeuwen make an important distinction between 'mode' and 'modality'. 'Mode' has an explicit theoretical value: 'it is an organizing and shaping meaning-resource, it is at the same level as *discourse* and *genre*' (Kress 2010: 114), and this theoretical positioning means that 'mode' is in fact *separate from* 'a particular material means of expression' (van Leeuwen 2011: 674). A mode occurs where society seeks to 'control and maintain' media for purposes of developing 'more abstract, more explicit, and more systematic forms of knowledge' (Kress and van Leeuwen 2001:79). So the sound of a mechanical door closing on a train might simply be a by-product of the mechanical action – it exists as a material construct. Or the mechanics may be adjusted to produce a sound which is more soothing – it is now a mode, enmeshed in complex processes of judgements about what is soothing, what is stressful, who should control this, and why (Kress and van Leeuwen 2001). So the two terms are not, in fact, interchangeable. One additional source of confusion is that 'mode' is related to, but also distinct from, the systemic functional sense of 'mode' as a key component of register (Halliday 1978). Additionally, 'modality' has further meanings elsewhere, for example, related to issues of truth-value in Kress and van Leeuwen's (2006) grammar of images.

Similarly, there is little clarity on how to account for the 'multi' side of multimodality. The New London Group proposed 'multiliteracies' as a way of capturing the centrality of multiple modes in an understanding of literacy (that is, that literacy could no longer be thought of in terms of language alone). But they also emphasized not just the co-presence of multiple modes, but the 'integration of significant modes of meaning-making, where the textual is also related to the visual, the audio, the spatial, the behavioral' (New London Group 1996: 64). This has sometimes been accounted for as 'intersemiosis', or 'the *interaction* of the different semiotic modes constitutive of [a text] ... a coordination of semiosis across different sign systems' (Ravelli 2000: 508; original emphasis). 'Intersemiotic complementarity' has also been proposed (Royce 2007) to explain how, in the case of visual-verbal relations, 'the intersemiotic semantic relationship *between* the visual and verbal modes' can be used 'to explain just what features make multimodal text visually-verbally coherent' (p. 63; original emphasis). That is, how do the parts make up the whole? Painter et al. (2013) argue that the phenomenon to be accounted for is not so much that of 'multimodality', but of 'intermodal' complementarity, that is, where the individual modes, such as the visual and verbal working together in children's picture books, each retain their own distinctive affordances (see also Bateman 2014 for an extended discussion of how visual–verbal relations can be theorized). Here, the slight differences in terms point to important distinctions in theory, which is to be expected in a domain which has only recently begun to receive theoretical attention. Such contestations are, indeed, a site of productivity, a way to make scholars reflect on the issues at stake. While Kress cautions that 'Careful theoretical work needs precise instruments' (Kress 2010: 105), it also needs to be remembered that sometimes, the terminology used just needs to be 'good enough' for the task at hand (Macken-Horarik et al. 2011; Exley and Cottrell 2012).

Perhaps a more serious issue of dispute is the status of claims made around multimodality. There can be a tendency to circularity in claims based on hand-picked examples (Thomas 2014), where examples are chosen to illustrate a particular point, such as the Given-New information value (realized by left-right placement of elements within the image) proposed by Kress and van Leeuwen (2006), and then those examples are taken as proving the existence of the phenomenon. There is no doubt that the close, qualitative analysis of individual examples is an essential tool in both exploring and explicating multimodal texts, but at the same time it raises questions about the nature of the evidence, counterposed in part by attempts to validate claims through larger corpus-based studies (Bateman 2008). Studies of multimodality grapple with the complex interplay of phenomena and require a thorough rethinking of long-held assumptions based on a study of language alone, as well as rethinking of the theories of communication used to address multimodality, which have themselves of course also been based on language. It is therefore not surprising that new theoretical formulations need to explicitly account for even such basic concepts as the sign, as well as for the impact on terms and concepts derived from specific theoretical frameworks, such as rank or metaredundancy, from the perspective of SFL (Martin 2011).

Future directions

More than two decades ago, the New London Group were sufficiently prescient to identify the centrality of multimodality to an understanding of communication. The tasks they identified then have been vigorously pursued, but remain incomplete. There is an ongoing challenge to continue to explore and explain individual modes: what are these 'other' resources, and how do they work? For those modes which have already been examined in some detail, such as the visual, much still remains to be done, not least of which is substantiating claims, accounting for social histories and impact, and extending the work to new genres. For those modes which have received less attention, the task is even greater. Beyond individual modes, it is of course the 'multi' side of multimodality which demands further exploration, not only finding satisfactory theoretical models, but also using this knowledge to understand the complex forms of communication which impinge on everyday life. How does a reader make sense of a whole text with many different component parts? How can language, image, layout, and sound be integrated to create a coherent text? How do such resources work together – in harmony or in counterpoint – to persuade and influence?

Most importantly, the significance of all this research for social understandings needs to continue to be pursued. In particular, the role of multimodality in critical literacy must not be underestimated: the communicative world has changed, is changing, and will keep on changing, and research needs to change with it. Pedagogy and curricula need to change, too: being literate includes understanding how to read a film, recognizing that children's picture books influence as much by image as by word, and that being able to communicate requires more than the spoken or written word alone.

Importantly, however, such intentions need effective teacher education, appropriate resources, and meaningful assessment practices, all underpinned by strong grammars of multimodal resources, in order to succeed.

Language remains an intrinsic feature of communication, which needs to be understood in and of itself. But at the same time, language has lost its position as the centre of the communication process, and it certainly does not achieve communication in isolation from other communicative resources. The interaction of language with, as well as the specificities of, other modes of communication, must be accounted for. For anyone with an interest in English Language Studies, this is a future which must be embraced.

Notes

1 These approaches are especially strong in Australia, and the genre-based approach is sometimes referred to as 'the Sydney School', but neither are confined to either Australia or Sydney.
2 Ignoring the capacity to scan ahead, back-track, etc.

Further reading

de Silva Joyce, H. and J. Gaudin (2007) *Interpreting the Visual: A Resource Book for Teachers*. Putney: Phoenix Education. Along with Callow (2013), this provides excellent exemplification of how to apply visual analysis in the classroom.

de Silva Joyce, H. and J. Gaudin (2011) *Words and Pictures: A Multimodal Approach to Picture Books*. Australia: Phoenix Education. This provides an accessible introduction to visual-verbal interaction in children's picturebooks.

Goodman, S. (2007) 'Visual English', in S. Goodman, D. Graddol and T. Lillis (eds), *Redesigning English*. New York: Routledge & The Open University, 113–160. This provides an accessible and comprehensive overview of reconsidering English language as a visual phenomenon.

Kress, G. (2003) *Literacy in the New Media Age*. London: Routledge. This is a foundational text examining the impact of technological change on society and culture.

Jewitt, C. (ed.) (2009) *The Routledge Handbook of Multimodal Analysis*. London: Routledge. This provides a comprehensive overview of approaches to, domains of, and techniques for, multimodal analysis.

O'Halloran, K. (Series Ed.) (n.d.) *Routledge Studies in Multimodality*. This series of monographs explores a variety of multimodal resources.

Related topics

- The relevance of English language studies in higher education
- Literacy in English: literacies in Englishes
- Media, power and representation
- The language of social media
- Discourse analysis: studying and critiquing language in use.

References

Australian Curriculum, Senior Secondary English (n.d.) Available at www.australiancurriculum.edu.au/seniorsecondary/english/english/curriculum/seniorsecondary#page=3, accessed May 2016.

Baldry, A. and P. Thibault (2005) *Multimodal Transcription and Text Analysis*. Oakville: Equinox.

Bateman, J. (2008) *Multimodality and Genre: A Foundation for the Systematic Analysis of Multimodal Documents*. Basingstoke: Palgrave MacMillan.

Bateman, J. (2014) *Text and Image: A Critical Introduction to the Visual/Verbal Divide*. London: Routledge.

Bednarek, M. and H. Caple (2012) *News Discourse*. London: Continuum.

Bowcher, W. and J. Yameng Liang (2016) 'GSP and multimodal Texts', in W. Bowcher and J. Liang (eds), *Society in Language, Language in Society: Essays in Honour of Ruqaiya Hasan*. New York: Palgrave MacMillan, 251–274.

Caldas-Coulthard, C. R. and T. van Leeuwen (2001) 'Baby's first toys and the discursive construction of babyhood', *Folio Linguistica* 35 (1–2): 157–183

Callow, J. (2013) *The Shape of Text to Come: How Image and Text Work*. Newtown: PETAA (Primary English Teaching Association Australia).

Caple, H. (2013) *Photojournalism: A Social-Semiotic Approach*. London: Palgrave MacMillan.

Cope, B. and M. Kalantzis (eds) (2000) *Multiliteracies: Literacy Learning and the Design of Social Futures*. London: Routledge.

da Costa Lima Carneiro Leão, G. (2013) *A Systemic Functional Approach to the Analysis of Animation in Film Opening Titles* (Unpublished PhD Thesis, University of Technology, Sydney).

Derewianka, B. and C. Coffin (2008) 'Time visuals in history textbooks: Some pedagogic issues', in L. Unsworth (ed.), *Multimodal Semiotics: Functional Analysis in Contexts of Education*. London: Continuum, 187–200.
Djonov, E. and T. van Leeuwen (2012) 'Normativity and software: A multimodal social semiotic approach', in S. Norris (ed.), *Multimodality in Practice—Investigating Theory-in-Practice-Through-Methodology*. London: Routledge, 119–138.
Exley, B. and A. Cottrell (2012) 'Reading in the Australian Curriculum English: Describing the effects of structure and organisation on multimodal texts', *English in Australia* 47 (2): 91–98.
Fairclough, N. (2010) *Critical Discourse Analysis: The Critical Study of Language*. Harlow: Longman.
Feez, S., R. Iedema and P. White (2010) *Media Literacy*. Sydney: NSW Adult Migrant Education Services.
Halliday, M. A. K. (1978) *Language as Social Semiotic*. London: Arnold.
Halliday, M. A. K. and C. Matthiessen (2004) *An Introduction to Functional Grammar*. 3rd edn. London: Arnold.
Hartley, J. (2002) *Communication, Cultural and Media Studies: The Key Concepts*. London: Routledge.
Hasan, R. (1989) *Linguistics, Language and Verbal Art*. Oxford: Oxford University Press.
Hood, S. (2011) 'Body language in face-to-face teaching: A focus on textual and interpersonal meaning', in S. Dreyfus, S. Hood and M. Stenglin (eds), *Semiotic Margins: Meanings in Multimodalities*. London: Routledge, 31–52.
Jewitt, C. (2006) *Technology, Literacy and Learning: A Multimodal Approach*. London: Routledge.
Jewitt, C. (ed.), (2009) *The Routledge Handbook of Multimodal Analysis*. London: Routledge.
Knox, J. (2007) 'Visual-verbal communication on online newspaper home pages', *Visual Communication* 6 (1): 19–53.
Kress, G. (1997) *Before Writing: Rethinking the Paths to Literacy*. London: Routledge.
Kress, G. (2000) 'Multimodality: Challenges to thinking about language', *TESOL Quarterly* 34 (2): 337–340.
Kress, G. (2003) *Literacy in the New Media Age*. London: Routledge.
Kress, G. (2010) *Multimodality: A Social Semiotic Approach to Contemporary Communication*. London: Routledge.
Kress, G., C. Jewitt, J. Bourne, A. Franks, J. Hardcastle, K. Jones and E. Reid (2005) *English in Urban Classrooms: A Multimodal Perspective on Teaching and Learning*. London: Routledge.
Kress, G. and T. van Leeuwen (2001) *Multimodal Discourse: The Modes and Media of Contemporary Communication*. London: Arnold.
Kress, G. and T. van Leeuwen (2006) *Reading Images: The Grammar of Visual Design*. 2nd edn. London: Routledge.
Lim Fei, V., K. O'Halloran, S. Tan and K. Marissa (2015) 'Teaching visual texts with the multimodal analysis software', *Educational Technology Research and Development* 63 (6): 915–935.
Machin, D. (2013) 'What is multimodal critical discourse studies?' *Critical Discourse Studies* 10 (4): 347–355.
Machin, D. and T. van Leeuwen (2008) 'Toys as discourse: Children's war toys and the war on terror', *Critical Discourse Studies* 6 (1): 51–65.
Macken-Horarik, M., K. Love and L. Unsworth (2011) 'A grammatics 'good enough' for school English in the 21st century: Four challenges in realizing the potential', *Australian Journal of Language and Literacy* 34 (1): 9–23.
Martin, J. R. (2011) 'Multimodal semiotics: Theoretical challenges', in S. Dreyfus, S. Hood and M. Stenglin (eds), *Semiotic Margins: Meanings in Multimodalities*. London: Continuum, 243–270.
Martin, J. R. and D. Rose (2008) *Genre Relations: Mapping Culture*. London: Equinox.
Matthiessen, C. M. I. M. (2007) 'The multimodal page: A systemic functional exploration', in T. Royce and W. Bowcher (eds), *New Directions in the Analysis of Multimodal Discourse*. New Jersey: Lawrence Earlbaum, 1–62.
Mayer, R. (ed.) (2005) *The Cambridge Handbook of Multimedia Learning*. Cambridge: Cambridge University Press.
McMurtrie, R. (2010) 'Bobbing for power: An exploration into the modality of hair', *Visual Communication* 9 (4): 399–424.
Mills, K. (2016) *Literacy Theories for the Digital Age: Social, Critical, Multimodal, Spatial, Material and Sensory Lenses*. Bristol: Multilingual Matters.

Mills, K. A. and L. Unsworth (2015) 'The literacy curriculum: A critical review', in D. Wyse, L. Hayward and J. Pandya (eds), *The Sage Handbook of Curriculum, Pedagogy and Assessment*. Thousand Oaks: SAGE.

New London Group (1996) 'A pedagogy of multiliteracies: Designing social futures', *Harvard Educational Review* 66 (1): 60–92.

Norris, S. (2004) 'Multimodal discourse analysis: A conceptual framework', in P. Levine and R. Scollon (eds), *Discourse and Technology: Multimodal Discourse Analysis*. Washington, DC: Georgetown University Press, 101–115.

Norris, S. (ed.) (2012) *Multimodality in Practice: Investigating Theory-in-Practice-Through-Methodology*. Routledge, New York.

Norris, S. and C. D. Maier (eds) (2014) *Interactions, Images and Texts: A Reader in Multimodality*. Boston: De Gruyter Mouton.

O'Halloran, K. (ed.) (2004) *Multimodal Discourse Analysis: Systemic Functional Perspectives*. London: Continuum.

O'Halloran, K. (2005) *Mathematical Discourse: Language, Symbolism and Visual Images*. London and New York: Continuum.

O'Halloran, K. (2008) 'Systemic functional-multimodal discourse analysis (SF-MDA): Constructing ideational meaning using language and visual imagery', *Visual Communication* 7 (4): 443–475.

O'Halloran, K., A. Podlasov, A. Chua and E. Marissa (2012) 'Interactive software for multimodal analysis, in J. Holsanova (ed.), Special issue: Methodologies for multimodal research', *Visual Communication* 11 (3): 352–370.

O'Toole, M. (2011) *The Language of Displayed Art*. 2nd edn. London: Leicester University Press.

Painter, C., R. Martin and L. Unsworth (2013) *Reading Visual Narratives: Image Analysis of Children's Picture Books*. Sheffield: Equinox.

Pelletier, C. (2008) 'The Cambridge handbook of multimedia learning: Review', *Information Design Journal* 16 (1): 81–83.

Ravelli, L. (2000) 'Beyond shopping: Constructing the Sydney Olympics in three-dimensional text', *Text* 20 (4): 489–515.

Ravelli, L. and R. J. McMurtrie (2016) *Multimodality in the Built Environment: Spatial Discourse Analysis*. London: Routledge.

Royce, T. (2007) 'Intersemiotic complementarity: A framework for multimodal discourse analysis', in T. Royce and W. Bowcher (eds), *New Directions in the Analysis of Multimodal Discourse*. New York: Lawrence Erlbaum & Assoc., 63–110.

Scollon, R. (1998) *Mediated Discourse as Social Interaction*. London: Longman.

Scollon, R. and S. Scollon (2003) *Discourses in Place: Language in the Material World*. London: Routledge.

Thomas, M. (2014) 'Evidence and circularity in multimodal discourse analysis', *Visual Communication* 13 (2): 163–189.

Trimbur, J. and K. Press (2015) 'When was multimodality? Modality and the rhetoric of transparency', in A. Archer and E. Breuer (eds), *Multimodality in Writing: The State of the Art in Theory, Methodology and Pedagogy*. Leiden: Brill, 19–42.

Unsworth, L. (2001) *Teaching Multiliteracies Across the Curriculum: Changing Contexts of Text and Image in Classroom Practice*. Buckingham: Open University Press.

Unsworth, L. (2004) 'Comparing school science explanations in books and computer-based formats: The role of images, image/text relations and hyperlinks', *International Journal of Instructional Media* 31 (3): 283–301.

Unsworth, L. (ed.) (2008) *Multimodal Semiotics: Functional Analysis in Contexts of Education*. London: Continuum.

Unsworth, L. (ed.) (2009) *New Literacies and the English Curriculum: Multimodal Perspectives*. London: Continuum.

Unsworth, L. (2014) 'Multimodal reading comprehension: Curriculum expectations and large-scale literacy testing', *Pedagogies: An International Journal* 9 (1): 26–44.

Unsworth, L. and A. Thomas (eds) (2014) *English Teaching and New Literacies Pedagogy: Interpreting and Authoring Digital Multimedia Narratives*. New York: Peter Lang.

van Leeuwen, T. (1999) *Speech, Music, Sound*. London: Macmillan.

van Leeuwen, T. (2011) 'Multimodality', in J. Simpson (ed.), *The Routledge Handbook of Applied Linguistics*. London: Routledge, 668–682.

van Leeuwen, T. and D. Machin (2005) 'Computer games as political discourse: The case of Black Hawk Down', *Journal of Language and Politics* 4 (1): 119–141.

White, P. R. (1997) 'Death, disruption and the moral order: The narrative impulse in mass-media hard news reporting', in F. Christie and J. R. Martin (eds), *Genres and Institutions: Social Processes in the Workplace and School.* London: Cassell, 101–133.

Wild, M. and R. Brooks (2000) *Fox.* Crows Nest, NSW: Allen and Unwin.

Zappavigna, M. (2012) *Discourse of Twitter and Social Media: How We Use Language to Create Affiliation on the Web.* London: Continuum.

Zhang, Y. and K. O'Halloran (2012) 'The gate of the gateway: A hypermodal approach to university homepages', *Semiotica* 190: 87–109.

30
English and translation

Sara Laviosa

Introduction

In the era of globalization, English is the most coveted and most translated language in the world, and plays a dominant role as the pre-eminent international lingua franca. A concomitant linguistic and cultural phenomenon is the increasing use of several languages in various domains of social and institutional life, which in turn generates growing demand for translation and interpreting services on a global scale. In such supranational organizations as the European Union, for example, the policy of communicating in 24 official languages generated a translation output of 1.9 million pages in 2015, according to figures from the European Commission's Directorate-General for Translation. These interrelated transnational and transcultural developments are reorienting the interdisciplinary field of applied linguistics in terms of a 'multilingual turn', a trend which foregrounds 'multilingualism, rather than monolingualism, as the new norm of applied linguistic and sociolinguistic analysis' (May 2014: 1).

Within this perspective, the present chapter assesses the world status of English in terms of its central role in the international translation system. It gives an overview of the discipline of translation studies, and expounds upon the ways that the theory and praxis of translation can be beneficial to English language studies with reference to five areas of research. The first of these is the transmission of English-language cultural values across the globe. The second is the study of in-text translation in 21st-century prize-winning novels by transnational writers. The third is the influence of English on other languages through Anglicisms. The fourth is the role of ELF, and the fifth is the adoption of pedagogies that integrate translation and translanguaging practices for TESOL. The chapter concludes by summarizing the main issues addressed and provides some pointers for the future.

Current critical issues and topics

The results of survey studies of linguistic preferences in various sociocultural contexts, along with the findings emerging from the analysis of statistical data on published translations, indicate the high-level status currently occupied by the English language, as well as its cultural prominence compared with other global languages. A 2011 study carried out by

Ginsburg and Weber (2011, in Pandey 2016), for example, shows that the language most European citizens consider useful is English (67%, not counting native speakers). This study also reports a significant shift in linguistic attitudes in the younger generation. Fifty-seven per cent of those aged 15 to 29 claim to know English, versus only 26 per cent of those aged 60 and older. As they observe, this constitutes a doubling of numbers within one generation, while in contrast there is almost no change for other European languages.

As regards linguistic trends in such supranational organizations as the United Nations (UN), a survey by the same authors reveals that the vast majority of UN officials prefer to receive their emails in English. And, in their analysis of Eurovision Song contests, they record that most songs are performed in English. Also, the data recorded by the Nobel Foundation reveal that the highest number of prizes in literature from 1901 to date has been awarded to authors writing in English (Pandey 2016). Similar to Ginsburg and Weber's study of Europe, Graddol observes a shift towards a preference for English among younger-generation Indians. The figures he reports indicate that, while enrolment in English-medium schools is rising, that in Marathi-medium schools is falling (2010, in Pandey 2016: 33). Furthermore, in 2009, South Korea was reported to have allocated 40 per cent of its national educational budget to English education (Ricento 2015, in Pandey 2016). Moreover, Phillipson, writing in 2009, predicted that enrolments of foreign students in Britain were expected to expand at a rate of 8 per cent per annum till 2020 (2009, in Pandey 2016: 26).

Consonant with these trends are the strategies adopted by the publishing industry as regards the choice of books to be translated. In Britain and North America, works in translation make up a smaller proportion of those in comparison with many parts of the world (Hale 2009; Büchler and Trentacosti 2015). In the United Kingdom and Ireland, for example, the percentage of all translations published from 1990 to 2012 is around 3 per cent of all published books compared with 12.28 per cent in Germany, 15.90 per cent in France, 33.19 per cent in Poland and 19.7 per cent in Italy (Büchler and Trentacosti 2015).

English is also very much the world's leading language of origin of translations (i.e. source language). In 2008, according to UNESCO statistics (from the Index Translationum database), 47,258 books were translated from English, followed by 6,899 from German, 6,570 from French, 2,922 from Italian, 2,551 from Spanish and 1,534 from Russian. However, with 5,347 English-language translations published in 2008, English is only the fourth translating language (i.e. target language) after Spanish (8,214), French (10,289) and German (11,064).

Not only is the number of books translated into German, French and Spanish much higher compared with English-language translations, but the majority of those translations are also from English (7,362 into German, 6,446 into French and 4,788 into Spanish). In sharp contrast, languages such as Arabic and Chinese have a very small share (less than 1%) in the total number of translated books worldwide (Cook 2012, in Pandey 2016: 23). A similar asymmetry is found in statistical data on Indian literary production. Narayanan (2012, in Pandey 2016: 23) observes that in 2008 only five works of fiction and poetry originally written in Indian languages were published in the United States, while popular English titles, including such comics as *Superman* and *Spiderman*, are readily translated for the populous Indian market.

In summary, then, English is by far the most translated language in the world, but far less is translated into it. This trend indicates a trade imbalance. British and American publishers sell translation rights for many English-language books, but buy fewer rights to publish English-language translations of foreign books (Venuti 2008). Such an uneven flow of translations characterizes the hyper-central role of English in the hierarchical structure of the world-system of translation (Heilbron 1999), and has important cultural consequences. As Venuti argues, by translating large numbers of the most varied English-authored books, foreign publishers sustain the international expansion of British and American cultures. In turn, British and American publishers produce

> cultures in the United Kingdom and the United States that are aggressively monolingual, unreceptive to foreign literatures, accustomed to fluent translations that invisibly inscribe foreign texts with British and American values and provide readers with the narcissistic experience of recognizing their own culture in a cultural other.
>
> (Venuti 2008: 16)

In a similar vein, Pandey contends that the inverse relationship between the number of translations from English into other languages and the number of English translations provides evidence 'for a continued unidirectional, rather than bidirectional, flow of culture and linguistic capital in the "seemingly" deterritorialized' world of today (2016: 25). She claims that cultural industries such as publishing sustain the high value of English over other languages. As she explains, 'It is the massive visibility, particularly in and through publishing – linguistic creation of sorts – which has transformed English to the culturally "coveted' language of global currency today' (2016: 34). The investigation of the textual translation procedures that perpetuate this alleged one-way flow of culture, by effacing the cultural values of other languages in English translations and encoding English cultural values in texts translated into other languages, is one of the main concerns of translation studies that is relevant to the study of English, and is thus an issue we shall move to in the following section.

Key areas of dispute and debate

In order to discuss the relationship between English language studies and translation with reference to the five areas of enquiry earmarked earlier in the introduction, it is appropriate to give an overview of the current state of translation studies. Assessing the state of the art of the discipline will provide the foundation for addressing, in the final section, the more general question concerning the importance of integrating the study of the theory and praxis of translation in the broad curriculum area of English language studies.

Since 1972, when Holmes presented the paper 'The Name and Nature of Translation Studies' at the Third International Congress of Applied Linguistics, the title Translation Studies has been used in the English-speaking world to refer to an international and interdisciplinary academic field concerned with the description, theory and praxis of translation and interpreting. The following outline of Holmes's framework is based on his paper initially published in the posthumous collection edited by van den Broeck in 1988 (2nd edn., Holmes 1988/1994) and reprinted in the second edition of *The Translation Studies Reader* (Venuti 2004).

Holmes sets two main goals for the discipline. The first is to describe the phenomena of translating and translation(s); this activity is the concern of descriptive translation studies (or translation description). The second is to establish general principles that explain and predict these phenomena; this activity is the concern of theoretical translation studies (or translation theory). Translation description and translation theory constitute the two branches of pure research. The third branch, applied translation studies, concerns itself with translator training, translation aids, translation policy and translation criticism. Holmes also briefly outlines the historical and methodological dimensions of the discipline. The former deals with the history of translation theory, translation description and applied translation studies. The latter discusses issues concerning the object of study for the discipline together with the methodologies that are most appropriate for research carried out in the different subdivisions of the field.

Holmes shared his vision of the emerging discipline in the wake of the elaboration of linguistic-oriented approaches to translation study and the development of the practice-oriented North American workshop approach to literary translation which had been taking place in American universities since 1963. Translated modern literature was growing in popularity at this time, and continued as a trend throughout the 1960s and 1970s (Gentzler 2001). Meanwhile in Britain at this time, the first specialized university postgraduate courses in translation and interpreting were being established (Munday 2001:6). Since the early 1970s, translation studies has grown rapidly, particularly in the last two decades, as evidenced by the rising number of undergraduate and graduate translation programmes worldwide: from 250 in 1994 (Caminade and Pym 1998: 283) to an estimate of over 600 today (Kim 2013: 102). Translation studies has also visibly established itself academically through dedicated journals, book series, encyclopedias, dictionaries, readers and abstracting services. Moreover, from a transdisciplinary perspective, the study of translation has attracted scholars in fields as varied as linguistics, pragmatics, history, critical discourse analysis, philosophy, literary theory, journalism, multilingualism, languages education, anthropology, sociology and film studies (cf. Baker 2010).

The transmission of English-language cultural values

As was pointed out earlier, the cultural hegemony of English is reflected in and maintained by global publishing strategies involving both the choice of books to be translated from English into other languages and the use of textual translation procedures that are dependent on domestic cultural values when the translating language is English. An example of the former strategy is the global best-selling phenomenon of J. K. Rowling's series of books featuring the schoolboy wizard Harry Potter, which has been translated into more than 70 languages. As Abravanel observes, J. K. Rowling's novels portray a nostalgic vision of Englishness through a literary strategy that 'rests upon narratives of heritage, history and little England much like those that began most clearly to be told in the early 20th century. Hogwarts, with its echoes of both Oxbridge and Eton, is itself a little England' (2012, in Pandey 2016: 24). So, Rowling's children's books represent British culture and symbolize the nation's past greatness.

An example of an English literary translation that inscribes the foreign text with domestic values is *Declares Pereira*, Patrick Creagh's 1995 version of Antonio Tabucchi's Italian political thriller *Sostiene Pereira* (1994). As Venuti (2004: 485–487) explains, the novel is set under the Portuguese Salazar's regime in 1938. It was published in the year that a centre-right coalition led by Silvio Berlusconi's Forza Italia party gained power in Italy. It resonated with those who perceived the narrative not merely as an allusion to Benito Mussolini's dictatorship, but as an allegory of current political events. It was seen as a symbol of resistance by those who opposed the new political situation and became a bestseller within a year of publication. Tabucchi's book belongs to an Italian narrative tradition of resistance novels during and after the Second World War.

Here are a few examples of the lexical shifts adopted by Creagh with the intent to render some expressions, as he himself affirms (Creagh 1998, in Venuti 2004: 485), more colloquial in English than in Italian (in brackets are alternative renderings provided by Venuti to show the inventiveness of Creagh's translations): 'taceva' ('silent') is translated as 'gagged'; 'quattro uomini dall'aria sinistra' ('four men with a sinister air') as 'four shady-looking characters'; 'stare con gli occhi aperti' ('stay with your eyes open') as 'keep your eyes peeled'; 'un personaggio del regime' ('a figure in the regime') as 'bigwig'; 'senza pigiama' ('without pyjamas') as 'in his birthday-suit' and 'va a dormire' ('go to sleep') as 'beddy-byes' (Tabucchi 1994; Creagh 1995, in Venuti 2004: 485).

As Venuti maintains, Creagh's lexical shifts from the current standard dialect of spoken Italian to various colloquial dialects in British and American English have the literary effect of establishing a relation to the English genre of political thrillers such as Graham Greene's *The Confidential Agent* (1939), which is set during the Spanish Civil War, like Tabucchi's novel. The linguistic resemblances between Creagh's translation and Greene's novel, which portrays a more cautious liberalism compared with Tabucchi's leftwing resistance to fascism, at once inscribe an English-language cultural history in the Italian text and displace the original historical dimension (Venuti 2004: 486–487).

In-text translation in 21st-century prize-winning transnational fiction

In a linguistic study that draws on cultural and globalization studies, stylistics, translation studies, semiotics and postcolonial studies, Pandey (2016) examines the multilingual strategies employed by 21st-century prize-winning transnational authors over the decade between 2003 and 2014, focusing particularly on Aravind Adiga, Monica Ali, Jhumpa Lahiri, Neel Mukherjee and Salman Rushdie. Pandey contends that, unlike their counterpart 20th-century literary works that aimed at creating an alienating effect on readers, thus foregrounding linguistic and cultural heterogeneity, current uses of multilingualism 'enhance semiotic transparency; encourage linguistic equivalency; and ultimately, aim at rendering a mediatory effect on the reader' (2016: 101). She names this use of multilingual textuality 'shallow multilingualism' and argues that its aim is to create a familiarizing effect that aims at 'making the Other similar to the self' (Cavagnoli 2014, in Pandey 2016: 102).

Pandey analyses various different translation strategies. In *Brick Lane* (2003), for example, Monica Ali uses linguistic tagging to tell, rather than show, the Anglophone reader of any code switches into or out of Bengali or other languages at salient points in the novel. In so doing, she signals the occurrence of self-translations into English and renders the source language invisible. An example of how Ali reminds the reader that a literary action occurs in Bengali and not in English is in the following excerpt from a dialogue between Nazneen and her husband Chanu (Ali 2003, in Pandey 2016: 183):

> 'What is this called?' said Nazneen.
> Chanu glanced at the screen. 'Ice skating,' he said, in English.
> 'Ice e-skating,' said Nazneen.
> 'Ice skating,' said Chanu.
> 'Ice e-skating.'
> 'No, no. No e. Ice skating. Try it again.'
> Nanzeen hesitated.
> 'Go on!'
> 'Ice es-kating,' she said, with deliberation.
>
> Chanu smiled. 'Don't worry about it. It's a common problem for Bengalis. Two consonants together causes a difficulty. I have conquered this issue for a long time. But you are unlikely to need these words in any case.'

Then there is this example of self-translation combined with an appositive parallel translation of an italicized Bengali sentence (which is rendered in a transliterated and anglicized form), in a dialogue between Nanzeen (whose words are rendered in English while they are actually uttered in Bengali) and her lover Karim (Ali 2003, in Pandey 2016: 180):

> 'Why do you like me?' she asked one day, hoping that the words came naturally, as if she had just thought of them.
>
> He was in a playful mood. '*Keno tumake amar bhalo lage*?' Who says that I like you? His fingers touched the hollow of her throat.

In providing these translations 'Ali', observes Pandey, 'takes no chances in alienating her readers. They are indeed in 'familiar' territory' (Pandey 2016: 180).

An example of translation via parallel juxtaposition occurs in a scene of exorcism (Ali 2003, in Pandey 2016: 177–178):

> Then the exorcism began. As a warm-up exercise the fakir and his two helpers in circles around the servant boy, half singing and half-speaking verses, words which locked into each other as tightly as bones in a hand [. . .]
>
> *Ke Katha koyre, dekha deyna*
> *Ke Katha koyre, dekha deyna*
> *Node chode, hater kache*
> Faster and faster went the chanters, faster and faster flew the words
>
> [. . .]
>
> *Ke Katha koyre, dekha deyna*
> Who talks, not showing up
> Who talks, not showing up
> Moves about, near at hand.

Through the multilingual strategies illustrated above, Ali, like Jhumpa Lahiri in *Unaccustomed Earth* (2008), enables the Anglophone reader to understand Bengali in and through English, thus simultaneously minimizing the linguistic hardship of decoding real bilingual encounters and foregrounding English. As Pandey argues, 'For Anglophone readers, this strategy renders in both formal and thematicized terms a visibilization of English, with a concurrent invisibilization of Bengali' (2016: 179). In a similar fashion, in *The Lives of Others* (2014) Neel Mukherjee provides an extensive paratextual glossary at the end of his novel to enable readers to understand the meaning of unitalicized multilingual words and phrases used throughout the narrative, including the original Indian names of tropical shrubs and trees (Pandey 2016: 122–123).

In Salman Rushdie's *The Enchantress of Florence* (2008) Urdu, Arabic, Turkish and Chaghatai italicized lexicalizations are translated meticulously via parenthetical explanation, as here in the words for *doli* and *arthi* (Rushdie 2008, in Pandey 2016: 261):

> She was a *doli-arthi* prostitute of the Hatyapul, meaning that the terms of her employment stated that she was literally married to the job and would only leave on her *arthi* or funeral bier. She had to go through a parody of a wedding ceremony, arriving, to the mirth of the street rabble, on a donkey-cart instead of the usual *doli* or palanquin.

Other types of in-text translations used by Rushdie are parenthetical translation, as in: '*Sulh-i-kul*, complete peace', and contextual translation, by means of which the meaning of the foreign word can be inferred from contextual clues, as in the following excerpt: 'He had gone to the Akhsi fortress near Andizhan – ah, where the delicious *mirtimurti* melons grew!' (Rushdie 2008, in Pandey 2016: 261–262).

The influence of English on other languages

Another area of translation studies enquiry tied to the world status of English is the investigation of its influence on other languages. The analysis of Anglicisms at a lexical, morphosyntactic and textual level has recently attracted considerable scholarly interest, particularly in Europe, in view of the need to harmonize a national with a transnational identity as well as promote multilingualism, cultural diversity, mutual intelligibility and cultural unity (Furiassi et al. 2012). The assumption underpinning this growing body of research is that, in the wake of globalization, translation is a mediator of language change induced by English source texts as a result of the operation of the law of interference posited by Toury (2012). The law of interference states that 'in translation, phenomena pertaining to the make up of the source text tend to force themselves on the translators and be transferred to the target text' (p. 310), particularly when translating from a highly prestigious language/culture to a less prestigious one. Yet, the empirical evidence is far from consistent, since there is considerable variation across target languages, domain-specific discourses, text types and types of Anglicisms. It is therefore still debatable whether translation plays a significant role in the process of the Anglicization of European languages.

An example of a piece of research that produced ambiguous results as regards the hypothesis of a direct influence of English textual norms through translation is the Covert Translation project, carried out at the German Science Foundation's Research Centre on Multilingualism at the University of Hamburg from 1999 to 2011 (House 2011, 2013). The study involved the analysis of a one-million word diachronic parallel corpus made up of English original texts and their German translations and a diachronic corpus made up of comparable original German texts published during the same timespan. The two corpora constitute a representative sample of three genres: computer instructions, popular science texts and business communication, published from 1978 to 1982 and from 1999 to 2002 (2006 for economic texts). Based on the findings of cross-linguistic studies, the analysis was premised on the assumption that, whereas in English there is a preference for an implicit, indirect and addressee-focused style, in German there is a preference for an explicit, direct and content-focused style. The findings did not support unequivocally the hypothesis that there is a direct influence of English on German texts through translation. Three explanatory hypotheses are suggested in order to make sense of these fuzzy results:

- Translation as a mediator of the English take-over: the translation process effects change.
- Universal impact of globalization: translation as reflector of change and not instigator thereof.
- Translation as cultural conservation: the translational process resists change (House 2011: 205).

It can reasonably be argued that, as one of many forms of language contact in today's globalized world, translation can be considered just one of the means of transferring Anglo-American norms into receiving languages. Indeed, as Anna Mauranen (2008) contends,

> Languages are in a constant state of change on account of internal as well as external developments even without translational influence. Thus, although in many ways it is an apt description to call translations hybrid texts, [. . .] it is clear that they constitute a natural and substantial part of any language that exists in the written mode.
>
> (2008: 45)

English as a Lingua Franca (ELF)

Translation studies scholars have recently begun to explore the role of English as a global language (Campbell 2005; House 2009, 2012, 2013; Mauranen and Ranta 2009; Taviano 2013a, 2013b), that is 'as a dynamic and hybrid language whose complexity cannot be fully grasped without taking into account its interaction with other languages and cultures' (Taviano 2013a: 156). This view is gaining ground in translation studies, where it is proposed as a theoretical framework underpinning the teaching of ELF in translator training programmes. In a special issue of *The Interpreter and Translator Trainer*, guest edited by Taviano (2013b) and entitled 'English as a Lingua Franca and Translation: Implications for Translator and Interpreter Education', translation educators from different European countries put forward a student-centred and critical pedagogical approach. The bedrock of their envisioned pedagogy is to raise awareness among trainee translators about the theoretical implications of the spread of ELF, such as its impact on other languages and the role played by translations in this process, while equipping them with the varied skills required by the globalized language industry, such as editing specialized texts written in ELF and translating into and out of it.

Within this broad perspective, Bennett (2013) exposes two aspects of the dominant role of ELF in academic writing that are particularly relevant to translator training. The first is the tendency to adhere to the rhetorical norms of English Academic Discourse (EAD) when translating research articles into English. The second is the tendency to transfer the rhetorical patterns of EAD when translating research articles from English into less prestigious languages such as Portuguese. This poses a dilemma for translators. If they defy dominant stylistic conventions they may be criticized for being incompetent by editors and peer-reviewers. If they conform to the norms established by international academic publishing, they may contribute to the loss of language variety in the construction and dissemination of knowledge.

Bennett (2013: 184) argues that '[a]s cultural mediators *par excellence* [. . .] translators are uniquely positioned to help raise awareness of these issues amongst the various parties involved' and, to this end, they should develop not only inter-linguistic skills, but also critical, negotiation and consultancy abilities so as to bring about long term changes to the system as a whole.

Consistent with this claim, Bennett expounds three broad strategies that she adopted during her teaching, namely critical analysis, writing skills, and mediation and negotiation (p. 184). Students undertook critical discourse analysis of excerpts from English and Portuguese academic writing so as to unveil the cultural differences encoded in the two types of discourse. They then analysed examples of conventional and non-conventional translations and explained the different strategies adopted in terms of the author's status and the epistemology prevailing in the receiving culture at the time. Another exercise aimed at developing analytical abilities involved the examination of different translations of the same original text, of which only one was accepted by the publishers. Next, starting from the premise that students need to internalize conventions before being able to resist them in a conscious way, Bennett employed monolingual and bilingual activities to hone writing skills in English and Portuguese (2013: 186). The former involved editing texts written by non-native English speakers that contain examples of discourse transfer. The latter involved dividing students into groups and translating a piece according to a different brief, e.g. publishing in an international journal or in the faculty's journal. Finally, the ability to negotiate and mediate between authors and receivers such as editors and conference organizers was developed through role play and the writing of short reports designed to explain and legitimate a particular translation strategy. An essential characteristic of Bennet's pedagogy is the integration of translanguaging, in the form of critical analysis of comparable and parallel texts, and translation for developing writing skills in ELF.

Teaching English to Speakers of Other Languages (TESOL)

Language and translation educators share similar concerns about the dominance of the Anglo-American model of academic writing and the threat it may pose to linguistic and cultural diversity. They are both acutely aware of the tension between the demands of international publishing and the ecological importance of pluralizing language use through translingual and transcultural strategies that preserve local identities and the different ways in which knowledge is construed and exchanged. The translation of texts produced in the academic fields of humanities and social sciences can play a role, alongside original writing, in resisting the uniformity of standard forms of international writing. The starting point for achieving such a goal is the development of a critical pedagogy that empowers multilingual language learners and translator trainees, so that norms can be accepted or challenged in a conscious way.

The aim of such an ecologically-oriented pedagogy is to form students as multilingual individuals who are 'sensitive to linguistic, cultural and, above all, semiotic diversity, and willing to engage with difference, that is, to grapple with differences in social, cultural, political, and religious worldviews' (Kramsch 2014: 305). It is a holistic, critical and self-reflexive pedagogy that integrates bi/multilingual practices such as translation (Laviosa 2014a, 2014b, 2015, forthcoming) and translanguaging (García and Li Wei 2014) in order to raise cross-lingual and cross-cultural awareness and sensitivity as well as foster social values and develop learning strategies.

Such a pedagogy is framed within the multilingual paradigm in applied linguistics, which in turn reflects 'the complexities of contemporary individual experiences in multi-layered communities' and is sparking a serious interest in 'the language entitlement and education of all learners as social actors and global citizens in a complex world' (Conteh and Meier 2014: 1). Within this broad perspective, ecological approaches to educational linguistics posit that the process of language learning is both cognitive and social as well as historical, cultural, emotional, kinaesthetic, interpersonal and moral (van Lier 2000, 2004; Kramsch 2009). At the core of an ecological understanding of language for pedagogic purposes is the tenet that language is a semiotic ecosystem. As van Lier (2004: 53) explains, 'Language is always a meaning-making activity that takes place in a complex network of complex systems that are interwoven amongst themselves as well as with all aspects of physical, social, and symbolic worlds.' So, ecological linguistics focuses on the study of 'language as relations (of thought, action, power), rather than as objects (words, sentences, rules). It also relates verbal utterances to other aspects of meaning making, such as gestures, drawings, artefacts, etc.' (p. 251).

A case study described by García and Kano (2014) uses various translanguaging activities to examine the bilingual strategies used by ten Japanese American students of middle-school and high-school age attending a course on academic essay writing for the Scholastic Achievement Test (SAT), which is required for admission into US universities. The course was taught privately by Kano in the home of one of the students over a six-month period. The syllabus design followed three steps (2014: 263):

- Students read bilingual texts on the topic about which they were assigned to write. These bilingual texts were presented side by side, or there was an English text coupled with a parallel translation in Japanese, or a set of English and Japanese texts about the same subject, but not parallel translations.
- Students discussed the bilingual readings mostly in Japanese.
- Students wrote an essay in English on the topic of the bilingual reading and the discussion in Japanese about the readings.

A 'stimulated recall technique' was used to elicit the students' perceptions of translanguaging as pedagogy and as a learning strategy. This technique involved videotaping portions of translanguaging-enriched instruction and then interviewing the students in Japanese about what they were thinking and doing during the task that was videotaped. The analyses of the interviews show that translanguaging enabled students to move back and forth between their entire linguistic and discursive repertoire, which played an important role in the development of metalinguistic and metacognitive awareness. While the emergent bilinguals used translanguaging 'as *support*, and sometimes to *expand* their understandings' (García and Kano 2014: 265, original emphasis), the experienced bilinguals consciously used translanguaging 'for their own *enhancement*' (2014: 265, original emphasis). More specifically, they translanguaged to bolster and enrich their bilingual abilities, demonstrating their greater autonomy and ability to self-regulate the development of either language (2014: 272). The authors suggest that classroom translanguaging would also be effective with monolingual students who are learning an additional language.

Within the same ecologically-oriented pedagogical framework, holistic cultural translation into and out of ESOL is advocated for the multilingual language classroom (Laviosa 2014a, 2015, forthcoming). A holistic approach to translating culture involves considering the cultural elements represented in the source text that need to be negotiated because they may present difficulties for the target audience, so as to enable 'greater cultural interchange and more effective cultural assertion in translation' (Tymoczko 2007: 233). Tymoczko suggests some cultural elements that might be regarded as a guide for interpreting the source text and for determining the overall representations of culture in the target text. These are the signature concepts of a culture (e.g. words pertaining to heroism in early medieval Irish texts such as *honour*, *shame*, *taboo*), key words (they point to the cultural elements chosen by the writer or speaker to structure a text), conceptual metaphors, discourses, cultural practices, cultural paradigms (e.g. humour, argumentation or the use of tropes), overcodings (e.g. dialects, heteroglossia, intertextuality, quotation or literary allusion) and symbols (e.g. flower symbolism) (Tymoczko 2007: 238–244).

This methodology was integrated into the syllabus design of a three-credit module taught as part of a professional development course for secondary school ESOL teachers (Laviosa 2015). Working collaboratively in groups, the teacher trainees (half of them native English speakers) analysed and translated salient scenes from Gianni Amelio's bilingual drama *La stella che non c'è*/*The Missing Star* (2006). The pedagogic unit was organized into four phases. The previewing phase involved introducing the ecological approach to language learning and the concept of holistic cultural translation, which presupposes that translation is a form of representation (a translation stands in place of the original text), transfer (of meaning, function or form across languages) and transculturation (transmission and uptake of borrowed cultural forms in the receiving language). After giving a brief summary of the story narrated in the film, the students viewed the film without subtitles as part of their homework. The post-viewing activities involved the textual and multimodal analysis of five selected scenes. The analysis was guided by a brief introduction to the contents of each scene and by a series of open questions that invited students to reflect on the themes addressed in the film. This phase was followed by the production of pedagogic subtitles from Italian to English. Finally, students compared and contrasted their individual analyses and translations in class and reported on the results by means of an oral presentation. At the end of the module they critically reflected on their learning experience:

> The experience of analyzing film dialogues and engaging in pedagogic subtitling through collaborative learning has enabled us to pay close attention to form as well as meaning, text as well as context. This type of analysis has enhanced our understanding of the nature and symbolic power of language as well as the interrelationship between language and culture in a translingual and transcultural environment such as the one represented in the film and the one that we ourselves created and experienced in class. Working in groups of L1 Italian and L1 English speakers enabled us to refine our interpretation of the source text so as to relay its linguistic and cultural meanings in the target language as accurately and fluently as we could possibly do.
>
> (Laviosa 2015: 85)

As shown by these real-life examples of TESOL practices (see also earlier section on the influence of English on other languages), translanguaging and cultural translation complement each other in pursuing a common goal, i.e. forming self-reflexive and responsible meaning-makers who are sensitive to the relativity of norms and capable of asserting the right to language and cultural variety as language users and translators alike.

Future directions

As indicated by the title of the 8th European Society for Translation Studies Congress in 2016, *Translation Studies: Moving Boundaries*, the academic field of translation studies is opening up and reaching out, more than ever before, to neighbouring disciplines that share certain of its key concerns and areas of enquiry. English language studies is one such discipline. This chapter has surveyed five research areas which are linked together by a running theme that is also germane to the study of the English language, i.e. the role that translation plays in our globalized world where English takes centre stage.

Translation studies scholars are investigating this multifaceted linguistic and sociocultural phenomenon from a theoretical, empirical and applied stance consonant with the multilingual orientation that is making inroads in 21st-century applied linguistics. The insights gained from this growing body of interdisciplinary research are making a significant contribution to our understanding of English and Englishes. At the same time, they are enriching current conceptualizations of translation as well as language and translation pedagogies and professional practices.

We have come a long way from the simple notion of translation as the process of transferring a text from a source language to a target language and the product, or target text, which results from this process. This concept, framed within an instrumental paradigm, is now considered too narrow for a global discipline such as translation studies. From a cross-cultural and hermeneutic perspective, translation is regarded as an interpretive act. Congruent with this model is the view that, as a result of the process of mediating between the source language and culture and the receiving language and culture, the translator inscribes the source text with an interpretation that transforms its form, meaning and effect according to the intelligibilities and interests of the translating culture. The process of interpreting involves the application of interpretants. These may be formal, such as a notion of equivalence, a concept of style, genre-specific lexis and syntax, or thematic such as given values, beliefs, representations, discourses. Both formal and thematic interpretants originate primarily in the receiving culture (see earlier section on the transmission of English-language cultural values and Venuti 2017a). While the instrumental model upholds the concept of translation as the transfer of an invariant contained in the source text and renders the translation invisible, the hermeneutic model raises awareness about the agency of translators and empowers them just like the notion of 'holistic cultural translation' does (see earlier section on TESOL).

Consistent with this general view of what translation is and entails, research into literary multilingualism has highlighted the process of translation that is involved in writing and reading hybrid literary texts characterized by creative forms of code switching, parenthetical explanations, self-translations or paratextual glosses (see earlier section on in-text translation in 21st-century prize-winning novels by transnational writers). These kinds of in-text translations, that are also a distinctive feature of literacy autobiographies produced by non-native learners of English (see Canagarajah 2013), question the traditional monolingual concept of translation as a form of transfer from one national language to another and from a source text to a target text. Hence, as Meylaerts (2013: 528) says, the 'concept of "translation" itself, complemented with the epithet "cultural", seeks to broaden its signification, until now restricted to an intertextual and interlingual scope'.

We have concurrently progressed from a traditional, transmissionist and teacher-centred approach to translation learning and teaching to socioconstructivist pedagogies that emphasize student-centred, collaborative, project-based and process-oriented teaching methods (see earlier section on the influence of English on other languages; see also earlier section on TESOL). These developments are having a beneficial impact on higher education, particularly in Europe, Canada and the United States, where the study of translation and interpreting into and out of English is offered on the undergraduate and graduate levels in departments of Applied Linguistics, Languages, Languages and Cultural Studies and Comparative Literature. These courses attract students not only from humanities disciplines such as English, film and television production, world literature, modern languages, but also from engineering, law, medicine and science (cf. Venuti 2017b). These innovative courses give equal emphasis to translation theory, research and praxis. Their goal is not only to develop translator and interpreting skills to be employed in the expanding multilingual and multicultural language industries, but also to give students a university education that enhances their knowledge of the fields and disciplines in which they plan to specialize. It is with such a desirable goal in mind that translation and English language studies might derive mutual benefit from being integrated in a broad interdisciplinary curriculum designed within a critical and self-reflective pedagogical paradigm.

Further reading

Munday, J. (2017). *Introducing Translation Studies: Theories and Applications*. Abingdon: Routledge. This book provides a comprehensive, user-friendly introduction to the theories and concepts that have been developed in the academic field of translation studies from its inception in the early 1970s to the present day.

Olohan, M. (2004). *Introducing Corpora in Translation Studies*. London: Routledge. This volume introduces the use of computer corpora both as a tool for translators and a methodology for analysing the process of translation.

Millán, C. and F. Bartrina (eds) (2013) *The Routledge Handbook of Translation Studies*. Abingdon: Routledge. This collected volume provides an overview of the discipline of translation studies. It is divided into five parts: Translation Studies as an academic discipline; Defining the object of research in translation studies; Theoretical frameworks and research methodologies; Specialized practices; and Future challenges.

Venuti, L. (ed.) (2012) *The Translation Studies Reader*. 3rd edn. Abingdon: Routledge. The third edition of this classic reader gives emphasis to 20th-century developments in translation theory and research. The readings in the final section focus on the new topics of translation and world literature and translation and the internet.

Related topics

- World Englishes: disciplinary debates and future directions
- TESOL
- Corpus linguistics: studying language as part of the digital humanities.

References

Baker, M. (ed.) (2010) *Critical Readings in Translation Studies*. London: Routledge.

Bennett, K. (2013) 'English as a Lingua Franca in academia: Combating Epistemicide through translator training', *The Interpreter and Translator Trainer* 7 (2): 169–193.

Büchler, A. and G. Trentacosti (2015) Publishing Translated Literature in the United Kingdom and Ireland 1990–2012, *Statistical Report*, May 2015, Available at www.lit-across-frontiers.org/wp-content/uploads/2013/03/Translation-Statistics-Study_Update_May2015.pdf.

Campbell, S. (2005) 'English translation and linguistic hegemony in the global era', in G. Anderman and M. Rogers (eds), *In and Out of English, For Better, For Worse?* Clevedon: Multilingual Matters, 27–38.

Caminade, M. and A. Pym (1998) 'Translator-training institutions', in M. Baker (ed.), *Routledge Encyclopedia of Translation Studies*. London and New York: Routledge, 280–285.

Canagarajah, S. (2013) *Translingual Practice: Global Englishes and Cosmopolitan Relations*. London and New York: Routledge.

Conteh, J. and G. Meier (2014) 'Introduction', in J. Conteh and G. Meier (eds), *The Multilingual Turn in Languages Education: Opportunities and Challenges*. Bristol: Multilingual Matters, 1–14.

Cook, G. (2012) 'ELF and translation and interpreting: Common ground, common interest, common cause', *Journal of English as a Lingua Franca* 1 (2): 241–262.

Creagh, P. (trans.) (1995) *Declares Pereira: A Testimony*. London: Harvill.

Furiassi, C., V. Pulcini and F. Rodríguez González (eds) (2012) *The Anglicization of European Lexis*. Amsterdam and Philadelphia: John Benjamins.

García, O. and N. Kano (2014) 'Translanguaging as process and pedagogy: Developing the English writing of Japanese students in the US', in J. Conteh and G. Meier (eds), *The Multilingual Turn in Languages Education: Opportunities and Challenges*. Bristol and New York: Multilingual Matters, 258–277.

García, O. and Li Wei (2014) *Translanguaging: Language, Bilingualism and Education*. Houndmills, Basingstoke and New York: Palgrave Macmillan.

Gentzler, E. (2001) *Contemporary Translation Theories: Second Revised Edition*. Clevedon: Multilingual Matters.

Heilbron, J. (1999) 'Towards a sociology of translation: Book translations as a cultural world-system', *European Journal of Social Theory* 429–444.

Hale, T. (2009) 'Publishing strategies', in M. Baker and G. Saldanha (eds), *Routledge Encyclopedia of Translation Studies*. 2nd edn. London and New York: Routledge, 217–221.

Holmes, J. S. (1988/1994) 'The name and nature of translation studies', in R. van den Broeck (ed.), *Translated! Papers in Literary Translation and Translation Studies*. Amsterdam: Rodopi, 67–80.

House, J. (2009) 'Subjectivity in English as Lingua Franca discourse: The case of *you know*', *Intercultural Pragmatics* 6 (2): 171–193.

House, J. (2011) 'Using translation and parallel text corpora to investigate the influence of global English on textual norms in other languages', in A. Kruger, K. Wallmach and J. Munday (eds), *Corpus-Based Translation Studies: Research and Applications*. London: Bloomsbury, 187–208.

House, J. (2012) 'English as a global Lingua Franca: A threat to multilingual communication and translation?', *Language Teaching* 47 (3): 1–14.
House, J. (2013) 'English as a Lingua Franca and translation', *The Interpreter and Translator Trainer* 7 (2): 279–298.
Kim, M. (2013) 'Research in translator and interpreter education', in C. Millán and F. Bartrina (eds), *The Routledge Handbook of Translation Studies*. London and New York: Routledge, 102–116.
Kramsch, C. (2009) *The Multilingual Subject: What Foreign Language Learners Say About Their Experience and Why it Matters*. Oxford: Oxford University Press.
Kramsch, C. (2014) 'Teaching foreign languages in an era of globalization: Introduction', *The Modern Language Journal* 98 (1): 296–311.
La stella che non c'è/The Missing Star. Dir. Gianni Amelio. Perf. Sergio Castellitto, Ling Tai, Angelo Costabile. Rome: 01 Distribution S.R.L., 2006. DVD.
Laviosa, S. (2014a) *Translation and Language Education: Pedagogic Approaches Explored*. London and New York: Routledge.
Laviosa, S. (ed.) (2014b) *Translation in the Language Classroom: Theory, Research and Practice*. Special Issue of *The Interpreter and Translator Trainer* 8:1.
Laviosa, S. (2015) 'Developing translingual and transcultural competence through pedagogic subtitling', *Linguaculture* 6 (1): 73–89.
Laviosa, S. (forthcoming) 'Cultural translation in language teaching', in S.-A. Harding and O. Carbonell i Cortés (eds), *The Routledge Handbook of Translation and Culture*. London and New York: Routledge.
Mauranen, A. (2008) 'Universal tendencies in translation', in G. Anderman and M. Rogers (eds), *Incorporating Corpora: The Linguist and the Translator*. Clevedon: Multilingual Matters, 32–48.
Mauranen, A. and E. Ranta (eds) (2009) *English as a Lingua Franca: Studies and Findings*. Newcastle upon Tyne: Cambridge Scholars Publishing.
May, S. (2014) 'Introducing the 'multilingual turn', in S. May (ed.), *The Multilingual Turn: Implications for SLA, TESOL and Bilingual Education*. London and New York: Routledge, 1–6.
Meylaerts, R. (2013) 'Multilingualism as a challenge for translation studies', in C. Millán and F. Bartrina (eds), *The Routledge Handbook of Translation Studies*. London and New York: Routledge, 519–533.
Munday, J. (2001) *Introducing Translation Studies: Theories and Applications*. London and New York: Routledge.
Pandey, A. (2016) *Monolingualism and Linguistic Exhibitionism in Fiction*. London: Palgrave Macmillan.
Tabucchi, A. (1994) *Sostiene Pereira: Una testimonianza*. Milan: Feltrinelli.
Taviano, S. (2013a) 'English as a Lingua Franca and translation', *The Interpreter and Translator Trainer* 7 (2): 155–167.
Taviano, S. (ed.) (2013b) *English as a Lingua Franca and Translation: Implications for Translator and Interpreter Education*. Special Issue of *The Interpreter and Translator Trainer* 7(2).
Toury, G. (2012) *Descriptive Translation Studies – and Beyond*. Revised edn. Amsterdam and Philadelphia: John Benjamins.
Tymoczko, M. (2007) *Enlarging Translation, Empowering Translators*. Manchester: St. Jerome.
van Lier, L. (2000) 'From input to affordance', in J. P. Lantolf (ed.), *Sociocultural Theory and Second Language Learning*. Oxford: Oxford University Press, 245–260.
van Lier, L. (2004) *The Ecology and Semiotics of Language Learning. A Sociocultural Perspective*. Boston: Kluwer Academic Publishers.
Venuti, L. (2004) 'Translation, community, Utopia', in L. Venuti (ed.), *The Translation Studies Reader*. 2nd edn. London and New York: Routledge, 482–502.
Venuti, L. (2008) *The Translator's Invisibility: A History of Translation*. 2nd edn. London and New York: Routledge.
Venuti, L. (2017a) 'Introduction: Translation, interpretation, and the humanities', in L. Venuti (ed.), *Teaching Translation: Programs, Courses, Pedagogies*. London and New York: Routledge, 1–14.
Venuti, L. (ed.) (2017b) *Teaching Translation: Programs, Courses, Pedagogies*. London and New York: Routledge.

Index

Page numbers in italics refer to figures; page numbers in bold refer to tables.